WORKS IN POLITICAL PHILOSOPHY

ORESTES A. BROWNSON:
WORKS IN POLITICAL PHILOSOPHY

SERIES EDITOR: *Gregory S. Butler*

VOLUME I

The American Republic:

Its Constitution, Tendencies and Destiny

VOLUME II

Works in Political Philosophy

1828–1841

Works in Political Philosophy

Volume II

1828–1841

ORESTES A. BROWNSON

with an introduction by
Gregory S. Butler, series editor

ISI Books

2007

Copyright © 2007 ISI Books, the imprint of the Intercollegiate Studies Institute

All rights reserved. No part of this publication may be reproduced or transmitted in any form or by any means, electronic or mechanical, including photocopy, or any information storage and retrieval system now known or to be invented, without permission in writing from the publisher, except by a reviewer who wishes to quote brief passages in connection with a review written for inclusion in a magazine, newspaper or broadcast.

Brownson, Orestes Augustus, 1803-1876.
    The early writings / Orestes A. Brownson ; with an introduction by Gregory S. Butler. — Wilmington, DE : ISI Books, c2007.

        p. ; cm.
        (Orestes A. Brownson, works in political philosophy ; v. 2)

        ISBN-13: 978-1-933859-06-4
        ISBN-10: 1-933859-06-7
        Selections from 1828-1841.

        1. United States—Politics and government—1815-1861—Philosophy. 2. Constitutional history—United States. 3. Political science—Philosophy. I. Butler, Gregory S. II. Title. III. Series.

JK216 .B76 2006   2006929186
320.473—dc22   0701

Book design by Beer Editorial and Design

ISI Books
Intercollegiate Studies Institute
3901 Centerville Road
Wilmington, Delaware 19807
www.isibooks.org

*T*o Emily
As you set out upon the world, know that we are ever with you.

—GSB

Contents

Editor's Introduction
by Gregory S. Butler IX

An Essay on the Progress of Truth 1
NOVEMBER 1827–MARCH 1828

The Essayist 35
JULY–SEPTEMBER 1828

Free Inquiry 49
AUGUST 1828

Free Enquirers 53
MARCH 1829

Church and State I 57
MAY–SEPTEMBER 1829

Equality 85
SEPTEMBER 1829

Church and State II 89
NOVEMBER 1831

Social Evils and Their Remedy I 93
MAY 1834

Memoir of Saint-Simon 101
JUNE 1834

Independence Day Address at Dedham, Massachusetts 111
JULY 1834

Progress of Society 125
   JULY 1835

New Views of Christianity, Society, and the Church 149
   1836

Democracy 203
   JANUARY 1838

Slavery–Abolitionism 237
   APRIL 1838

Tendency of Modern Civilization 255
   APRIL 1838

Religion and Politics 287
   JULY 1838

The American Democrat 305
   JULY 1838

Abolition Proceedings 321
   OCTOBER 1838

Specimens of Foreign Literature 345
   OCTOBER 1838

Democracy and Reform 355
   OCTOBER 1839

Observations and Hints on Education 387
   APRIL 1840

The Laboring Classes 411
   JULY 1840

Progress Our Law—A Discourse 441
   OCTOBER 1840

Conversations with a Radical—By a Conservative 451
   JANUARY–APRIL 1841

Social Evils and Their Remedy II 529
   JULY 1841

Notes 551

Index 557

Editor's Introduction

The essays selected for this volume represent the earliest phase of Orestes Brownson's literary career. They span more than a decade of work, from his early philosophical and theological reflections of the late 1820s, through the Transcendentalism of the 1830s, and into the critical and highly creative output of the early 1840s. While upon his conversion to Catholicism in 1844 Brownson rejected many of the philosophical and theological premises contained in this volume, they continue to be of interest to the serious student of American history and political thought. They are the product of a very active, inquisitive, and naturally gifted literary mind, and they touch upon a wide range of subjects in the areas of philosophy, politics, religion, and culture. As such, they may be regarded as an iconic representation of the larger nineteenth-century literary movement known as the American Renaissance—in spite of the fact that Brownson is one of that movement's most neglected figures. Moreover, the very fact that Brownson later rejected his own conclusions should pique our interest. What exactly was he saying in his early career that might be ultimately incompatible with a traditional Christian view of politics and society? And what was in those early arguments themselves which might have contributed to his conversion? It is my hope that the present volume will facilitate scholarly investigation into such questions.

From the outset the reader should be aware of a characteristic feature of Brownson's early writings that is routinely emphasized by his commentators: it is highly unsystematic and rather mercurial. Octavius Brooks Frothingham's classic study *Transcendentalism in New England: A History* contains one of the earliest references to Brownson's peculiar literary temperament:

> Mr. Brownson was a remarkable man, remarkable for intellectual force, and equally for intellectual wilfulness. His mind was restless, audacious, swift; his self assertion was immense; his thoughts came in floods; his literary style was admirable for freshness, terseness and vigor. Of rational stability of principle he had nothing, but was completely at the mercy of every novelty in speculation. That others thought as he did, was enough to make him think otherwise; that he thought as he had six months before was a signal that it was time for him to strike his tent and move on. An experimenter in systems, a taster of speculations, he passed rapidly from one phase to another. . . .[1]

There is certainly an element of truth to such observations, as the early Brownson publicly embraced at one time or another varieties of New England Protestantism, Unitarian-Universalism, Transcendentalism, and European-style socialism. However, it is my view that much of the secondary literature has overplayed the mercurial side of Brownson, to the point that the most significant aspects of his life and career have been eclipsed. As I have written elsewhere, I believe that there is an underlying unity to the early Brownsonian corpus that too often escapes the casual reader.[2] His frequent changes of heart were not inexplicably random, nor were they necessarily indicative of a lesser mind mired in contradiction and confusion. Brownson himself was aware of the tendency among his critics to draw such conclusions, to which he responded in the autobiographical work *The Convert* (1857). His philosophic self-understanding was quite classical, in the Socratic sense; he thought of his early career as a long, dialectical process of discovering what it means to be human and how such an understanding might relate to the political dimension of existence. We ought, in the absence of any countervailing evidence concerning his sincerity, to take him at his word. I would therefore suggest that it is the classical experience of *zetesis* that connects the disparate elements in his work and ultimately makes his ideas not only intelligible as political philosophy, but relevant for a contemporary audience that, like Brownson, is also situated in a cultural environment awash in a sea of spiritual and intellectual uncertainty. The materials in the current volume are therefore arranged chronologically by publication date. It is my hope that the reader might profit not only from the content and argument of the individual essays, but also from the larger story they tell about Orestes Brownson's unique historical journey across the New England intellectual landscape.

I do not intend in the following pages to comment on the content of these essays, at least in any comprehensive way. I prefer that the student encounter them fresh, as it were, with an awareness of their general historical context and main themes as a guide. With that in mind, let us here situate the early Brownson within the larger picture of early-nineteenth-century European and American political thought.

Orestes Brownson came of age during the 1820s, a time in which the complex of ideas and symbols that I will call "high modernity" were making their way over from the Continent. I use this expression in much the same way that political theorist Eric Voegelin used it in his various works on the history of Western political ideas, including the well-known *New Science of Politics*.[3] Under the impact of Voegelin and others, our contemporary understanding of modernity has undergone significant modification. This change has occurred through a body of critical scholarship that challenges the widely held notion that the modern world is characterized primarily by the triumph of secular rationalism and the steadily declining influence of religion. Voegelin's work represents (among many other things) an extended analysis of the various revolutionary movements that have captivated the attention of the West since the Renaissance. His general thesis is that the self-understanding of modern man, as revealed through the leading revolutionary ideologists, has been shaped by an intense desire to resupply postmedieval Western culture with a profound sense of high civilizational purpose, a purpose that can only be fully understood as an expression of *ersatz* religious aspiration. Many of the characteristic movements and thinkers of modernity, in other words, had distinct spiritual aspirations that prove valuable to understanding their rise to power throughout the Western world. This thesis has greatly aided our understanding of the lines of continuity that stretch from Renaissance humanism to the Protestant Reformation to the great age of revolutionary ideologies, an age that reached its high-water mark in the mid-nineteenth century.

Brownson's early thought was shaped in important ways by modernist symbols, particularly as they were translated by the New England Transcendentalists and imbued with certain millenarian eschatological expectations of Reformation origin. The Renaissance symbols of individualistic regeneration and social transformation had a marked impact upon both the German and French romantics, and it was through these sources that they exerted considerable influence on the New England literati. One can trace the origins of this movement to the political thought of Jean-Jacques Rousseau, a figure who is particularly representative of the modern romantic *ethos* and who exerted a considerable (if rather indirect) influence on Brownson. For Rousseau, human beings are essentially fulfilled by living according to the "simple impulse of nature," the inner prompting of the heart that constitutes the ground of all morality.[4] The emotional and spiritual power of this perfect abstraction is augmented by its sharp contrast with the corruption of the surrounding society. Rousseau therefore believes in the possibility of man's "perfectibility,"[5] to be achieved by the universal liberation of the individual from all custom, tradition, and law.

The Transcendentalists owed a debt to Rousseau through the ethical idealism of Johann Fichte and Immanuel Kant, who were widely read across New England in the early nineteenth century.[6] Under the direct influence of Rousseau, Kant elevated simple obedience to duty above rationalistic philosophizing, and he understood obedience to self-imposed law as the *sine qua non* of genuine enlightenment.[7] A follower of Kant,[8] Fichte abandoned his own rationalistic tendencies in favor of a sort of romantic heroism, one driven by his conception of the human soul as divine. For Fichte, the fact of consciousness "stands and testifies for itself"; God is "a reflection of the soul in its own atmosphere" and "is one of the soul's creations."[9] The supernatural resides within the conscience, where all truth and conviction find their origin: "what contradicts [the] authority [of the conscience], or makes us unwilling or incapable of rendering obedience to it, is most certainly false, even should I be unable to discover the fallacies through which it is reached...."[10]

For Rousseau, Kant and Fichte, the political finds its logic in such notions. It therefore takes on a peculiarly millenarian flavor. Indeed, the political thought of all three would eventually influence some of the more dramatic and violent forms of European political messianism. For Kant, the development of human enlightenment becomes a historical task for the species as a whole; he expected the advent of an international community of the regenerate wherein, according to Voegelin, "the meaning of individual existence is to participate instrumentally in the collective progress."[11] Fichte, Voegelin continues, is possessed of the same spirit of political re-divinization but confines his "apocalyptics" to the German nation.[12] Fichte advocated for Germany the consolidation of a despotic socialist state (the totalitarian *Geschlossene Handelsstaat*),[13] for he saw an excessive preoccupation with material enterprise as a particularly significant obstacle to the development of the personal moral will. The romantic political thought of Rousseau was, of course, highly influential among the theorists of the French Revolution. It was also a clear forerunner of the utopian Marxist symbol of "the withering away of the state." Rousseau anticipates the advent of a realm of perfect freedom associated with the absolute triumph of the "General Will," understood as the innermost longing of all humanity for the innocence and purity of our pristine, primordial condition. The task of the Great Legislator's "moral law" is to illuminate the absolute truth of the General Will to the point where it is consciously recognized by all individuals; according to Rousseau, this is necessary because "we always want what is good for us, but we do not always see what it is." The Legislator "should feel that he is, so to speak, in a position to change human nature, to transform each individual . . . into a part of a larger whole from which this individual receives, in a sense, his life and his being. . . ."[14] Once performed, this task takes society to the "highest point of perfection," a point that becomes luminous as the perfectly free "association" in which each individual "obeys only himself"[15] as a re-creation of the state of nature. The political will then virtually disappear, for "a state thus governed needs very few laws."[16]

The collective consciousness of the American Transcendentalists was animated by a similar attachment to the romanticist existential imperative, if not its totalitarian political end point. This can be seen in their production of an impressive body of literature aimed at the education of the individual, particularly with respect to his spiritual capacities. In Rousseau-like fashion, Emerson remarked that "the highest end of government is the culture of men; and . . . if men can be educated, the institutions will share their improvement and the moral sentiment will write the law of the land."[17] In similar fashion, Brownson, as a Christian Rousseauist of sorts, holds up the ideal of the "self-taught man," to be assisted only in the "instinctive development of the young mind" in the "direction of nature."[18] All are equally capable of enlightenment, Brownson teaches, if they are taught to follow "the simple dictates of reason, the plain injunctions of morality."[19] The mission of education ought to be to break habits of "servile dependence on the thoughts of others, the reverence for the past, [and] the acquiescence in authority."[20] This achievement is the essential precondition for social and political progress, the "last epoch" of which will be marked by the absence of "command authority" and the universal "reign of benevolence."[21]

Such views led the early Brownson to have little faith in majoritarian democracy as an agent of reform. In the current state of societal imperfection, he writes, political power of any type is bound to threaten the liberty of the enlightened, which are as yet a small minority.[22] The majority, to put it plainly, "mistake their own interests," for at present their "standard of morality is too low."[23] This position is similar to that of Rousseau, who similarly rejected majoritarian democracy, "the will of all," as a poor substitute for the infallible General Will.[24] In Brownson, what passes for the General Will is the revelatory education of the species as a whole.[25] "The grand lever of reform, the mighty power that is to carry society forward to its perfection, is Christian morality."[26] Genuine democracy—i.e., the rule of absolute justice and equality—will emerge only through "a new and a higher view of Christian morality,"[27] brought about by "fervent prayer for more faith in God, in truth, in justice, in humanity."[28] In the meantime, argues Brownson, we ought to play the role of the political *conservative*, respecting American institutions as they are. In his 1838 essay "Democracy," he says that "the whole that can be done may be summed up in the words, let reformers do all in their power to *educate the people, and through the people the generation to come.*"[29]

The passion for spiritual renewal through individual enlightenment thereby flowed into intense humanitarian expectations for social transformation. These expectations run throughout the social and political commentary of such literary organs as the *Dial*, the *Christian Examiner*, the *Western Messenger*, and Brownson's own *Boston Quarterly Review*. Transcendentalist literature looked forward to the progressive elimination of a wide assortment of social evils: drunkenness, vile prison and sanitarium conditions, capital punishment, worker exploitation, poverty, war, ignorance, slavery, undemocratic political institutions, gender discrimination, prostitution, crime, and the like. In this way, European-style romanticism coincided with the early-nineteenth-century rebirth of American Puritan consciousness in the form of the so-called "Second Great Awakening." The jeremiads of Timothy Dwight, Asahel Nettleton, Francis Wayland, and Lyman Beecher sounded the call for spiritual renewal, yes, but they also sought to reawaken in the popular mind the familiar millennialist idea that the American republic was to be the primary redemptive agent in history, chosen by God to perfect itself and the world. Brownson's earliest essays in the *Gospel Advocate* are imbued with an evangelical, revivalist spirit, and like many of the preachers of New England he mixed that revivalism seamlessly with expectations of social and political progress. While Brownson took pains to dissociate himself from the Calvinist and more theocratic political elements of the Second Awakening, including the voluntary association movement,[30] it is clear nonetheless that he shared their vision of a coming Christian commonwealth, a vision rendered unique by its Rousseauistic elements. Under the influence of both an indwelling Holy Spirit and the promptings of natural sentiment, mankind will at last constitute the Kingdom of God on earth, as "temptations to vice will be removed; crimes will become less and less frequent till they finally disappear, and our jails and penitentiaries [will] be thrown open, or converted to abodes of virtue and happiness."[31] Moreover, Brownson and his neo-Puritan allies shared the conviction that the United States was destined by divine providence to be the social and political arena for the commencement of their millennial vision.

This intriguing merger of American and European modernism reaches its most mature form in Brownson's small book titled *New Views of Society, Christianity, and the Church* (1836). This work was heavily influenced by both radical spiritualist Christianity and French romantic political thought, especially that of Saint-Simon and his followers. The progressivist ideology of history presented in *New Views* expressed Brownson's conviction that a new form of political, social, and religious organization loomed on the horizon for the modern world, a new ordering of civilization that would destroy all antagonism and secure the universal reign of peace. It represented his vision of the humanitarian "church of the future," destined to become the third and final manifestation of the divine within time, replacing both the primitive Catholic and incomplete Protestant manifestations. The high point of Brownson's early thought thereby appears remarkably similar to both the Saint-Simonian and Comtean versions of the Religion of Humanity. It must be understood as a peculiarly American form of the neo-Gnostic speculation that has become widely recognized, by Voegelin and others, as characteristic of modern revolutionary ideologies. Brownson's fascination with the possibility of marrying revolutionary modernist symbols to progressivist humanitarian Christianity is a rather consistent thread of meaning running throughout his early writings, in spite of the various and conflicting public doctrinal confessions he was prone to make.

The essays Brownson wrote in the five years following the publication of *New Views* are grounded in this point of view, even if it is occasionally obscured by Brownson's institutional conservatism. His fondness for the *form* of the American constitutional order, particularly its decentralism, should not mislead us into supposing that his political thought was in keeping with the *substance* of that order. From the impressive series of political essays of 1838 through the famous "Laboring Classes" tract and the brilliant "Conversations" dialogue, we see Brownson expressing in various ways his fervent hope and expectation that America is soon to witness the inevitable, progressive unfolding of social perfection—in fact, the earthly reign of divine justice. Throughout this period, however, he rejects the notion that this outcome must involve the centralization of power. Indeed, he sees the abandonment of the American federal principle, including the idea of states' rights, as ultimately *inimical* to the interests of humanity and progress. This position certainly makes Brownson unique among the early-nineteenth-century reformers. And while it does not necessarily indicate a fatal inconsistency in his thought, this political conservatism does perhaps betray Brownson's lack of sufficient familiarity with the substantive philosophical underpinnings of American constitutionalism, a theoretical foundation that, in the end, must give pause to any humanitarian reformer wishing to operate within the institutional form of the republic. The form of American constituionalism is grounded largely on a premodern understanding of the possibilities and limits of human nature. This understanding, in turn, is not isolated from the form of the state but rather constitutes its *substance* and supposes that the order of civil society ought to be structured accordingly. The choice is clear: maintain a revolutionary, perhaps millenarian understanding of progress, and abandon the American constitutional order; or, reject humanitarian progressivism and explore further one's instinctive attachment to the federalist political genius by investigating its substantive philosophical claims. Indeed, beginning in 1841, Brownson begins to take notice of the rough outlines of this dilemma and sets out to resolve the matter over the coming months. The result was a significant turning point in the political philosophy of Orestes Brownson, as we shall see in volume 3 of this series.

 This book could not have been produced without the generous assistance I have received from several individuals and institutions. I owe the greatest debt to my wife Lauren and daughters Emily and Anna, whose extraordinary patience, support, and encouragement I do not fully deserve. I am also grateful for the dedicated work of four exceptional research assistants—Christine Boerner, Rebecca Wiggins, Sarah Fillmore, and Sarah Gontijo—in gathering and editing the material gathererd here. The preparation of the manuscript was made possible in part by a generous grant from the New Mexico State University College of Arts and Sciences, which enabled me to visit the Brownson archives at the University of Notre Dame. I would also like to express my appreciation to the Department of Government faculty; it is a joy to work among such dedicated and professional colleagues. Finally, I wish to thank the Intercollegiate Studies Institute for recognizing the value of Orestes Brownson and his impressive contribution to American letters.

GREGORY S. BUTLER
NEW MEXICO STATE UNIVERSITY

An Essay on the Progress of Truth

NOVEMBER 1827–MARCH 1828

Essay No. I

I this week commence a series of numbers on the progress of moral reform throughout the world. I shall continue them if I have leisure and health, until I either exhaust my subject or my knowledge. The importance and interesting nature of this subject, as well as my own method of treating it, will be unfolded as I proceed, hence need not be labored in an exordium.—As a motto to my inquiry I select Isaiah, chap xxxv. 1.

"The wilderness and the solitary place shall be glad for them; and the desert shall rejoice and blossom like the rose."

The final emancipation of the human race from sin, misery and death, is a source of pleasing contemplation, and may justly employ the attention of those, who despair of ever finding consolation from the prospective improvement of man while an inhabitant of this sublunary state. At a convenient time, we should not hesitate to wing imagination through regions of ether, and survey a beautified universe bending around the throne of Light, bursting amid the rays of Jehovah's love; but the present requires us to consider what amelioration the progress of Truth will make in the condition of human society below.

Whatever bliss there may be in store for us in that unseen world to which we are all hastening, the present is all we can call our own. We are now inhabitants of the earth, and our chief inquiry should be—how can we render it a pleasing and desirable habitation? I am a believer in life and immortality beyond the grave; but I am not ambitious of being one of that number who forget earth for heaven—who, to ensure the joys of that invisible kingdom; forego the rational pleasures of this.

The present generation owes a duty to all succeeding ones. The course we take will have a greater or less effect upon the morals or happiness of our latest posterity. We live not for ourselves alone; we are connected with all nations, all generations of men. Let us not, then, because we expect soon to remove to some distant clime, demolish or suffer to decay, the institutions necessary to give peace and felicity to our successors. There are those, who think, if our future welfare or happiness after death be secured, there is no necessity of troubling ourselves about our condition here; and if this generation was the last of the human race, there would be some force in the consideration. But "one generation passeth and another cometh, but the earth abideth forever." The parent finds sufficient inducement to labor, that he may secure his child a competent support; the philanthropist looks through futurity to ages yet unborn, and, while his bosom swells with the prospect, he invokes the genius of improvement to transmit them such institutions as shall preserve external peace and internal tranquility—to transmit them such a fund of knowledge, that the evils with which we and our forefathers have been afflicted, may never reach them.

Is this no inducement to labor? Look back then upon past ages; what deplorable ignorance has debased the human mind! Man has been the slave of both civil and ecclesiastical tyrants. The dignity of his nature has been forgotten amid the bigotry and superstition with which he has been governed. At one time, he is seen rushing with ruthless fury against his brother; at another bowing and cringing before a God of his own manufacture—the property of a fellow lordling, who supports the luxury of his table with the produce of his blood—the dupe of designing hypocrites, who made him sick, that they may be paid for curing him—filled with a zeal for God, fired with enthusiasm for his law, he is seen dealing forth death upon all whose zeal and enthusiasm are different from his own.—Robbed by the political despot of the right of pursuing happiness and enjoying the fruit of his labor—divested by the priest of the liberty of conscience and all the felicity of mental independence, he rises in gaudy ignorance or splendid poverty, in the most abject servitude and the most degrading superstition. A prey to all the evils of his physical constitution and the calamities incident to life, rendered thrice double severe by his own folly and the exorbitant exactions of his brethren; war sweeps off its millions, carries mourning to as many cottages, and childlessness to as many mothers. Theological wrangling, intestine divisions and domestick discord, destroys what little repose might otherwise have been received!—Say ye friends of the human race! do you wish those evils to go down to posterity? Have you no anxiety to remove these evils, that the wrongs and outrages which you have suffered may not be entailed upon your offspring?

But if these considerations have no weight with the philanthropist of the day, it only shows the degradation of their minds, the narrowness of their conceptions, and the feeble claim they have to the name they assume; and no stronger argument is required to show the importance of a reformation throughout the world. Those, however, who can join in the prospective improvement of our race while here, reasons sufficient to call forth their exertions will contemplate with delight the improvement itself, and huger with inexpressible gratitude to God, on the certainty it will in due time be effected.

The improvement of which we speak, or the reformation which we desire, is one that will recognize the original equality of the human family—secure to them all the rights which nature has given them, whether as individuals or members of society. The government of the country recognizes many of our original rights and in a good degree secures them. The reformation we seek, will base all institutions whether civil or ecclesiastical, upon this original equality, and will call forth all the energies of statesman, moralists or divines to preserve it. Government will then aim at the good of the governed; political, and other rulers will be the servants, not the masters of the people—will be chosen for the good of the whole, not of a few, and be supported from a conviction of their utility, not because they have been born to hereditary advantages, or been forced upon us by circumstances over which our partiality for ancient usages would give us no control.

Men will then be free in their persons, free to pursue happiness, and free to enjoy the good of their labors. Amid this freedom, industry will awake and all will be enabled to find a competent support. Temptations to vice will be removed; crimes will become less and less frequent till they finally disappear, and our jails and penitentiaries be thrown open, or converted to abodes of virtue and happiness.

The mind will then have recovered its independence; conscience will not then be bound by the fetters of priestcraft; but it will become the monitor to virtue, the friend of mankind—will entwine around each heart the cords of fraternal affection, and no more break a brother on the wheel or burn him at the stake. Reason will have regained her long lost dominions; her mild and gentle laws will extend peace through all her empire, and preserve the quietness and felicity of every bosom. The happy children of men will form the cheerful circle around the evening fire; give free exercise to all the kind and benevolent feelings of the heart, with no gloomy personage to destroy their heaven born harmony, with his furious declamations and horrid denunciations! Implicit faith in unintelligible dogmas will find no adherents. Each will claim the right of examination; whatever is not congenial with facts, corroborated by universal experience, will be laid aside as a remnant of ancient superstition.

Religion will then rest on its support on a knowledge of human nature, not on the assertions of ignorant or interested men. It will not be a fruitful source of unhappy contention, will not tend to alienate the affections of brethren, nor drive them to the commission of the foulest crimes that ever blackened the page of history; but it will encourage all those good actions, cherish all those kind feeling, render all that mutual assistance which our dependant situation requires.

Such is the improvement we seek, such is the reformation that will be accomplished when men shall have recovered mental independence, and shall dare reason on the nature and propriety of existing institutions; when they shall acknowledge no law but *reason*, no religion but *justice*, no morality but *humanity* in all its forms.

Essay No. II

The opposition to the emancipation of the human race from the bondage of their numerous masters, will be long and obstinate. There are so many notions abroad; so many vague and inconsistent theories are proclaimed by the learned, and enforced by those who claim the direction of the public mind, upheld by those in authority, and eagerly embraced by the multitude; the simple dictates of reason—the plain injunctions of morality, are so readily consigned to forgetfulness, that he who comes forward with a plain and rational scheme, is in danger of being doomed to suffer the contempt of the ignorant, and the persecution of the designing.

The experiment has been fairly tried: to the advocates of a blind and unnatural religion, and to the adherents of a cruel and despotic policy, every indulgence has been granted; we have listened with the most profound attention; we have believed with the most yielding credulity, and obeyed with the most persevering enthusiasm. The popular instructors, from their first existence, have contended earnestly for "the faith"—extolled the purity of their principles, and the wonderful efficacy of their instructions in making society virtuous and man universally happy. Alas! Discord has marked their proceedings, confusion their preaching; and notwithstanding man was totally depraved at first, he has been growing worse ever since!

The circumstances of the age call aloud for reform. There has been so much tinsel; so many pretenses have been made; so much noise about religion and divine communications has been heard; that men, whose minds have been enlightened by science—whose hearts are warmed by philanthropy, and whose bosoms bleed with compassion for the human race, have turned with disgust from every thing bearing such a recommendation, and sought in nature alone, a remedy for infatuated man. They may have gone too far; but every truly enlightened mind will reject with disdain every notion that contradicts the great principles of universal existence, or supersedes the necessity of studying them. I am no enemy to religion; but I would listen with attention, and examine with the most diligent caution;—whatever is not conducive to our happiness while here, I reject is unworthy [of] our attention. Happy would be for all men, if they would come to this conclusion. But the obstacles to be surrounded in coming to this are many. They rise like mountains, and we tremble as we survey the broadness of their base and the sublimity of their tops. The heirs of antiquity are so numerous and so tenaciously embraced, that no wonder timorous souls are despondent. No improvement can be affected while men retain their veneration for institutions merely because they are ancient; for until many, who now labor with the most preserving assiduity to perpetuate such veneration, shall cease from their pernicious task, and turn their attention to ascertain what is beneficial to man in his social and individual capacity. But the struggle to accomplish this, will be long and arduous. Princes who hold their power on the precarious tenure of artificial distinctions in the human family, will be unwilling to enlighten their subjects. Truth is dreaded by them, for they well know the right, by which they govern, has no existence in the nature of things. Should people learn, the God of the Universe made all men originally equal, privileged classes would lose their prerogatives, and he reduced to a level with the rest of mankind. Kings would then depend on the suffrages of their subjects for election.—This, the crowned heads of the Earth well know. Hence it was, they saw with consternation the independence of this country, and armed their united forces against Republican France. It is the apprehension that truth may enter the dark recesses of their deluded, degraded subjects, that binds together the "Holy Alliance" of Europe and it is this that drives them to extinguish every ray of liberty that might for a moment illume the darkness of despotism!

Kings and potentates will, from a regard to their own interest, oppose any innovation upon the old order of things. Their power is founded in ignorance, supported by arbitrary and unnecessary distinctions, and has no recommendation but hoary age. Consequently they have nothing so much to fear as a spirit of inquiry, and close investigation.—Such a spirit would undermine the thrones on which they are seated, and trample in the dust every vestige of their tyranny! They will, it must be expected, use every exertion in their power to prevent any alteration in the condition of their people.

Our religious education, and the nature of our ecclesiastical institutions, are much more powerful obstacles in the march of improvements. These form an impediment much more difficult to remove, because supported by more stubborn, more numerous, and more complicated prejudices. It is here to, where reformation is most needed. Whoever has turned over the historic page and traced man through his *religious* career, has wandered in the midst of crime, through scenes the most foul and horrible that a fancy can paint. Man, though doomed to suffer from the physical circumstances of his condition—though he is a child of sickness and distress—a prey to every calamity—affected by every change in this ever changing state, may forget the whole, in the magnitude and numberless variety of the evils he has heaped upon him by his pretended *spiritual assistants*.

From time immemorial, men have formed themselves into religious association; and under the pretense of superior sanctity, of more successfully promoting their own and their brethren's welfare, have presumed to dictate to the world what it must believe, and what ceremonies it must observe. To over awe the mind and make it submissive to what all the better feelings of the heart oppose, inspiration has been pretended, and the voice of the Almighty has been made to sanction errors too absurd to be believed on less authority. The venders of this inspiration have usurped an undue ascendancy over the lives and consciences of men, as degrading to those who obey as it is profitable to those who rule.

Particular churches have been established, and the priest has promised heaven to all who unite, and denounced the most horrid doom upon all who refuse. A creed was drawn up for the church; the more unintelligible the better, because the aid of the priest in its explication becomes thus the more necessary; a system of external duties is enjoined, the more absurd, or the farther removed from common utility the better, for its observance thus most clearly draws the line of distinction between those who belong to the church, and those denominated the world. All that is required to maintain the purity of one's character, is to believe this unintelligible creed, and damn all who doubt it; to perform external duties enjoined, which usually consist in assembling together, making a few grimaces, and genuflections, repeating over, parrot like, a few unmeaning words, in doing penance, supporting the church, and treating with infinite contempt or extreme cruelty all who pay less reverence to such pious *indispensables*. This maintains one's claim to holiness, opens to him the doors of the church here, and of heaven hereafter—gives him a passport to regions of glory, and entitles him to endless beatitude in the mansions of felicity.

A class of men have been produced—fanatics, who have labored with a zeal and perseverance worthy a better cause, which, had they been properly directed, would have done honour to themselves, and been of the highest utility to man. But alas! Their zeal was not according to knowledge. They have been deceived by an unreal form—they have contended for a phantom—overlooked the great duties of justice and humanity—encouraged a blind worship, for they knew not what—tolerated a bigoted, superstitious religion equally derogatory from God, and unprofitable to man.

Antiquity is replete with instruction. So many valuable lessons are taught by her examples that we should frequently recur to her sacred archives. The farther our retrospection runs, the more have we to deplore—more prevalent and more absurd is the superstition. Implicit reliance on the priest, augur, soothsayer, sybil, or whatever name designated their character, comprised nearly the whole of man's moral and religious duties. The priests were mere tools of state; whatever they taught was designed to promote the interest of their masters, or to advance their own ambitious prospects. Thus it was with the priests of Greece, of Rome, and man of the oriental nations. Their religion was upheld for the express purpose of exacting that submission, and that support, which they despaired of otherwise obtaining. And the whole machinery was as much regulated by the state government, as any other department of state police. The philosophers, indeed, discarded the silly and absurd tales of which their religion was composed; they would have labored to enlighten the minds and lead men to the practice of moral virtue, but the infatuated multitude, ever true to the hand that oppresses them, were the first to condemn any effort made for their amelioration.

The Jewish theocracy, however useful it might have been in its first establishment, soon became no better than that of other nations. The priests usurped nearly all the power, and seemed to regard little else than the receiving of their tithes and other offerings. They uttered, to be sure, the most horrid denunciations if the people thought for themselves, or became weary of their hierarchy. If the people worshipped Baal, notwithstanding they themselves had made the worship of the true God too grievous to be borne, they usually succeeded in overwhelming the nation with calamity, and when led away captive by their enemies, told them it was the just resentment of the Almighty for their apostacy. But all this was apparently not because they cared more for one religion than another, only to support that one which best supported them.

Essay No. III

Jesus Christ, about 18 centuries ago, appeared. He digested the crude notions of religion, then prevalent—selected from the systems already known, what was universally obligatory, to which he made some new accessions, and finally gave us a religion of reason and common sense, as pure, doubtless, as the circumstances of our condition require. His tragic death and the subsequent preaching of his disciples gave his doctrine a rapid and wide extension; but it had no sooner gained ascendancy over the ancient religion, than those in authority sought to make it subservient to state policy, dependant on courts and levees.

Christianity was diverted from its natural course, and instead of ameliorating the condition of man, making him more happy by making him virtuous, it uncapped the bottomless pit and permitted monsters of cruelty and blood to fill the earth with rapine and war.—The sickly wretch substituted for the fair daughter of heaven, never softened the heart, never called into action the virtuous principles of our nature, but allowed the appetites all their force, and the passions to rage uncontrolled.

Be sound in the faith, tell a religious experience, and support the church, was a passport through the society of the holy here, and to the regions of the glorified hereafter! This maintained the sanctity of one's character, regardless of moral goodness, and this being all that was required, little more was sought. Justice and mercy fell into disrepute, humanity was unknown, and common sympathy consigned to the land of forgetfulness. Zeal for the Church usurped the place of every other virtue. Then were seen swarms of mendicants pillaging the scanty pittance of the villagers, for which they gave indeed a few *holy relics*, such as "sanctified rice."

— "Tears which saints had wept,
A thousand years in vials kept."

Then were seen hordes of monks who cloaked every species of iniquity under the sacred garb of piety, constantly laboring to increase the wealth and independence of the church. Then, too, holy enthusiasm raged. Mothers, without a complaint, could see their sons and wives their husbands, turn from their warm embrace, confined in the dungeon of the Inquisition, brought before the *Ghostly Father*, or burned on the *Auto de Fe!*

Different in forms, but the same in spirit, are the religionists of the present day. Men, professedly holy, do not hesitate to declare from the desk, the supposed guardian of virtue, that the abandoned profligate is *less dangerous* in society, and more likely to be *saved*, than the honest upright citizen, renowned for his benevolence and general humanity. Faith is raised over morality, and those who style themselves sound in *that*, arrogate to themselves all that is correct in theory, or virtuous in practice, and denounce the most horrid doom upon all who do not bear the same character.

They indeed have an ardent love for God, manifest great anxiety to maintain the glory of his power and the honour of his character. They are ever ready to let him save, from endless woe, souls which his veracity stands pledged to make eternally miserable. But alas! They have so much to do to assist Omnipotence, they are unable to regard the wants of a neighbor. Or, if they have time to bestow a casual glance upon the necessities of a brother, their benevolence evaporates in prayer for his never dying soul, while the body is left to starve!

Men frequently change the name of their sect while they retain the spirit of their former opinions. The primitive Christians, with few exceptions, retained all the distinctive features of the several systems of faith from which they had been converted. A Jewish Christian was in general still a Jew, except in name and the observance of some few ceremonies. Papal Rome was Pagan Rome, under a new appellation. Images of gods were replaced by pictures of Christ and his Apostles, deified heroes by canonized saints, and the Pantheon became as much crowded with the one as it had been with the other.

The beads, crucifixes and holy trinkets, had in so much reverence by thousands of *nominal* Christians, are good evidence, that the Gospel of Christ, in the manner it was preached, has not much elevated their conceptions of things, or given them any very exalted ideas of God or his service. The superstitious members of the Roman and Greek churches who regard these trifles, are no more worshippers of the true God, than were the blind votaries of Bacchus, Hercules or Apollo; nor indeed Protestants who place their highest sanctity in the observance of certain days or ceremonies—they are as much idolators as were the deluded adorers of Wodin or Thor.

Most European nations, together with the civilized part of America, embrace unanimously the Christian religion; but it is not unfrequently, we find the *spirit* of that blessed doctrine exhibited in much greater perfection by the untutored natives or our forests. The *meek and humble* disciple of Christ, may blush for his own want of goodness when he marks the native generosity of the savage.—Little research is necessary to show the rational man, that the boasted religions of the day bear strong marks of consanguinity to the long since obsolete superstitions of ages we hope may never return.

The religions of Greece and Rome are contemned, and justly. No man of common sense, but discards the Deistical notions of the Orientals, and the arrogant pretensions of the Pharisees of Palestine; but the most popular sentiments of our time are only a gross compound of them all, in which each ingredient retains all its peculiarities. The man that should draw a parallel of ancient faith, particularly of the Pharisees, with the most approved modern notions would be pronounced a severe satirist on the faith, and if he was in the synagogue would soon be cast out.

The directors of our opinions have discovered this identity, and to prevent any evil which might fall upon themselves, have very discreetly forbid the comparison, and prohibited investigation and the exercise of our own understanding. The reformer wishes to convince the people, the notions they imbibe are supported neither by reason nor revelation; he is commanded to lay reason aside, and is told the priest, *who cannot lie*, has declared these notions to be inspired. He refers them back to their origin, explains the causes which gave them birth, the reasons which first gained them notoriety, and the circumstances which have perpetuated their existence to the present time: the vengeance of the clerical despot here, and the threatened wrath of Omnipotence hereafter, is the reward he receives for his benevolent intentions.

The Reformer expostulates:—"God has made man a rational being; can he be displeased with the exercise of the noblest faculty he has given us? The notions you imbibe, O people! are unreasonable and contradictory; they are dishonourable to God and injurious to man. The consequences of such sentiments are seen in that spirit of contention which pervades every department of society—in the readiness with which parents, for the love of God, can discountenance their children, and children their parents for the same cause—in the alienated affections of brethren—the hostility, the animosity with which brother attacks brother, and sister rails against sister. O peace! Heaven born word! There is musick in thy name, but alas! Theological wrangling has driven thee from our bosoms, and banished thee from our dwellings! The domestic circle is invaded, and tranquility forsakes the fireside! Malice and rage are the priest—Fanaticism the multitude! Ignorance and cupidity urge them on, and tho' *Religion* may flourish, *Happiness* is gone.— Where is the man that dare assert the independence of the mind? Where the society not torn by contending factions? Where the community not distracted by intestine broils and the heart-withering conduct of professed religionists? O whither has wandered the genius of Christianity! Whither has fled the native benevolence and forbearance of the human heart? God of Love! Restore to man the exercise of his reason, that in contending for religion, he may not destroy every thing worthy the name!"

> O the lover may
> Distrust that look which steals his soul away:
> The babe may cease to think that it can play
> With heaven's rainbow; alchymists may doubt
> The shining gold their crucible gives out:
> But Faith—fanatic *Faith*—once wedded fast
> To some dear falsehood, hugs it to the last.

The appeal to facts—to the benevolent feelings of the heart, but enrages the deluded votaries of a blind and unnatural religion, and calls down upon him who makes it the curses and indignation of the ignorant, the superstitious, the bigoted and the designing. "Licentious innovator!" "Infidel!" "Blasphemer of God and Reviler of the Saints!" are the honourable epithets he receives and the manes by which posterity shall learn the extent of his philanthropy.

Men have so long been taught to distrust their own reason—so long heard enforced, as the only means of their eternal salvation, receive implicitly what the priest shall dictate, that the great body of the people have forgotten that all were originally equal, and endowed with the same right to judge for themselves. They consider the various notions transmitted them by circumstances of which they never think, are absolutely necessary to maintain proper reverence for the God of heaven; they consider them sacred as the light of Jehovah's throne, and they would sooner part with life itself that renounce them. They believe their eternal all is at stake, if they do not swallow all the ancient whims however absurd or pernicious—all, all is gone! A place of eternal, inconceivable torture remains as their inevitable doom!

Essay No. IV

The least reflection, one would suppose, might convince the most sceptical that this excessive veneration—this implicit reliance, is the result of the craft of a class of man, who wish to revel in luxury without sharing the common burden. That man must be grossly infatuated who imagines the All Wise Parent of nature has suspended the eternal weal of his children upon the contingency of their believing certain religious dogmas. The religious opinions of the age may, indeed, have been transmitted to us from remote antiquity; they may be consecrated by the blood of martyrs, and endeared by the memory of our fathers who believed them; but the man, who disclaims all authority but reason, and all creeds but truth, will consider all these external ornaments of little importance, and every argument founded upon them, he will ever treat with contempt.

The grand secret is disclosed. No man is against reason, until reason is against him. People that reason cannot be duped. In order to maintain their authority over our minds, priests have told us it is offensive to God, that we exercise this noble faculty. Should men reason, the injustice of their practices would be discovered and the solidity of their claims be called in question.

Many of those sentiments which have been outstripped by the improvements in natural and moral science were, no doubt, in their first establishment useful. The first preachers of them considered them true, and very likely proclaimed them with the benevolent intention of ameliorating the condition of man. It was probably by the same desire, that they were induced to represent them as coming from God; and with the wish of insuring them a cordial reception; they were also led to make it criminal to doubt their truth. But ambitious men converted the precautions, those philanthropists had to preserve their sentiments, to a source of individual aggrandizement, assuming to themselves the prerogatives of the Most High—pretending to be under the immediate influence of his spirit, they declared to the people, "whatever we do, however absurd or pernicious in its tendency, is suggested by the Holy Ghost, and you will be torn by demons if you do not believe it."

A traffic in human souls the most deleterious in its consequences, was carried on by these spiritual merchandisers; but the people, however much oppressed and borne down by the heavy burdens they had to bear, must not complain, because their complainings would be against Heaven, whose vengeance would flash instant death upon them if they dared murmur against his will.

They brought forward their sacred books, written in a style and language wholly unintelligible to the great body of the people. These books they said were from God, and no one must expect salvation that has the audacity to doubt them. To the complaint from the people that they could not understand these books, they answered, "true, many things in them are hard to be understood, which many wrest to their own destruction, but God has conferred on his servants, *the priests*, the privilege of understanding them; believe what we say, give us of your substance to support us, and our children and we will guide you to heaven."

If the people complained the doctrines preached were unreasonable or contradictory; they were answered, what is contradictory to *us*, may be perfectly consistent to God—with him doubtless black and white are the same. What to shortsighted man appears unreasonable may be perfectly reasonable with God;—with him it may be perfectly reasonable to say, infinite goodness may produce infinite evil, and still retain the character of infinite goodness.

Thus wearied with undue usurpations, the mind lost its elasticity, and finally yielded itself an abject slave to its spiritual master, placed unbounded confidence in what he taught, and obeyed with the most persevering enthusiasm what he commanded. The evil effects of such a state of things have come down to us. The cloven-footed monster which preyed upon our ancestors has come hither to embitter our felicity, and to render us gloomy vassals to clerical dominion.

Adventurous spirits from the old world have felled our forests, converted the wilderness into a fruitful field—erected on the fastnesses of wild beasts, cities which bid fair to rival the numbers, wealth, commerce and refinement of any which Europe can boast. Liberty has given additional splendor to our noon day sun; freedom has brightened the fires of our evening skies, and mental independence has given verdure to our fields and beauty to our landscapes. Here the care worn son of despotic climes has found a home; oppressed virtue an asylum; and bleeding humanity, driven from the courts of tyrants, a retreat.

The enemies of the human race have cut their way to our peaceful shores, have entered our paradise, coiled themselves around the tree of knowledge, and are now presenting us the "death-distilling fruit." The claims, which the inhabitants of the old world are already beginning to spurn, are brought hither to bind the sons of those fathers, who taught the world by their example to discard every species of tyranny.

My country! More is thy peril, greater is thy danger, than when the gigantic power of a transatlantic prince sent its minions to ravage thy courts and destroy thy women and children. A direful doom awaits thee; the chains of a more dreadful slavery are even now clanking in thy ears;—

repose not too much confidence in the virtue of thy sons—the mode of attack is secret and the movements of the enemy silent.

A clerical hierarchy is threatened us, and the utmost vigilance is requisite to avert the impending danger. The leaders of the grand enterprise are as crafty as they are ambitious. The missionary cause, like the Crusades against the Infidels, was thrown out to engage the great body of the people, that the engine might move unobserved. The sympathies of the people were enlisted by many a pathetic description of poor heathens dropping into hell; the purse was opened money was at the disposal of the reverend dignitaries who had shown so much compassion upon the wretched pagans.

They sought, as the next step, the superintendance of literature—they have obtained the management of nearly all the seminaries of learning; and, to make their triumph complete, they established their Sabbath schools, introduced their tracts and other books fraught with their own peculiarities, and thus they could begin with the infant and attend him through all the stages of his education. Immense power has thus been thrown into their hands; and they hold in their hands, to use their own exaggerated expression, "the lever that moves the moral world." In this department their plan has succeeded.

One thing remains to be accomplished—this done, and their plan has succeeded in every part. This thing, is to get the supreme control of our political institutions. This, indeed, *remains* to be done; but there is some fear it may be nearer affected than any philanthropist is willing to believe. The proposal that none but *Christians* should be elected to any office—the attempt to persuade the freemen of these states to vote for no man unless he belong to some church, if it succeeds, will pave the way to designate the *particular* church; and when such a measure has succeeded, a majority of the favored church will compose the grand council of the nation. Woe be to thee, O Columbia, when that shall be the case.

Essay No. V

The preceding numbers may seem rather an essay on the progress of error, but the exposition they contained was deemed necessary to point out the nature of the evils to be removed, and to exhibit some of the obstacles which ever have had and probably ever will have a tendency to impede the march of truth. The task was by no means pleasing. To trace the mind in its downward course is an ungrateful employment calculated to arouse the angry feelings and call forth the resentment of those whose lives and errors may be discovered and exposed, without receiving the commiseration of even those who wish to see mankind more virtuous, consequently more happy.

The benevolent heart weeps in sorrow over the follies, the aberrations and inconsistencies of the children of men; it deeply deplores their misery and wretchedness, the severity with which they oppress each other; anxious for their amelioration it raises its inquiries—"Indulgent God! Is man eternally ordained to be the dupe and slave of man? Shall he never regain his independence, and be free to exert his mental powers in the acquisition of knowledge; be free to study the works of his Creator, and while his bosom glows with gratitude to his Heavenly Father, be free to repose with confidence on the paternal affection of the Sovereign of nature?" The opposition to this has been already stated. It is aided by all the powers of darkness, but it is hoped the remainder of this essay will evince the "omnipotence of truth," and bring to weary and disconsolate man, the joyful intelligence that it shall prevail to the annihilation of error, and to the eternal banishment of evils which have so long afflicted the human race.

Nature gave to man the law of liberty, and entwined a desire for independence around every fiber of his heart. Amid all the usurpations of tyrants, under all the oppressions so liberally heaped upon him, some secret thought recurs to his native dignity; he rises enraged at the shackles of his slavery, indignant spurns the thought and demands his rank in the scale of being. He may be misled, he may mistake the road to the land of Freedom, he may deceive himself in the choice of means, to promote his felicity, but he will never relinquish the attempt. His errors shall serve to correct him, and his follies shall teach him wisdom.

A cursory view of the past may be profitable, towards enabling us duly to appreciate the present and to form rational conjectures respecting what may hereafter prevail.

The origin of the world is involved in impenetrable darkness; and notwithstanding some may assert, it had its birth only the other day, the man who "knows how little can be known" will be convinced that the period is so remote that it is useless to expect any *minute* details of its infantile history. Whether man lived alone or in society in that early stage of existence, what language they spoke, or what opinions they formed are alike hidden from the sharpest ken of those who live at this lapse of time. What passed before the flood, together with a number of years since, may be delivered over to lawless poets and the lovers of fiction to be peopled with such inhabitants as their prolific imaginations may choose to create. Those also who are dissatisfied with the present, and despair of finding any thing better in the unexplored regions of futurity, may paint to themselves a golden scene in those days long since forgotten. Then perhaps the earth yielded her fruit without labor; then perhaps the heavens wore perpetual sunshine and the fields were clothed with continual verdure, uniting at all times the hopes of spring with the enjoyments of autumn; then the air may have been pure and man a stranger to disease may have reclined in the ambrosial abode or basked amid beds of flowers, free from want or satiety, pain of body or remorse of mind; then too the morning may have been vocal with his hymns of praise, and the evening may have repeated his devotions to his God; but alas! Very different is the picture since history has usurped the province of fable, and too faithfully recorded the follies, the crimes and sufferings of mankind.

The earliest records in our possession represent the inhabitants of the earth as divided into petty hordes, continually making war upon each other; subsisting by the chase, pasturage, some rude agriculture and plunder. They united under a chief, in whose abilities they could place confidence, who led them forth to battle, but returned them to an equality with the rest when the object was attained or when the war was over. In time of peace the father governed his family without submitting to the authority of a higher tribunal; in cases, however, where the interests of the tribe or nation were involved, the whole were summoned and the deliberations of the most experienced were listened to with profound reverence and their advice followed with little deviation.

Religion was then but little more than that respect due to a superior, or that reverence due from a child to its father, together with gratitude to those who were considered benefactors of the community. Under the patriarchal from of government every father was the priest in his own family, as may easily be seen in the history of Abraham. Religion being then free from the doubt and mysticism in which it has since been involved, was easily learned and easily practiced, hence the necessity of a person to devote himself wholly to explaining and enforcing it, was unfelt.

The relations given of Osis, Bacchus and Jupiter show plainly enough, what was the early situation of men and also what was the character of the Gods they worshipped. Men must indeed be ignorant when it becomes necessary to have a God to teach them agriculture; but it was said of Osiris a principal deity among the Egyptians, that while king of that country, he had taken unwearied pains, to civilize his subjects and to teach them to cultivate their lands. Hence he was represented by the *Apis* or Ox, because that animal being the most useful one in tilling the ground was the most proper emblem to perpetuate the memory of him who had taught the art.

The *Oak* was sacred to Jupiter because he first taught men to live upon acorns. Men could not have advanced far in the knowledge of things, when they deified a man for showing them acorns were good to eat, nor could this simple act become a proof of his divinity.

Many became Gods because they had *killed* some monster, such as the Minotaur the Hydra, &c. It is not however to be supposed that the most ignorant considered these as creatures of the world; they only served them as benefactors of the country to which they belonged, or for which they had done them signal services. It is true they were worshipped, but probably at first, the worship was nothing more than a decent respect paid to their memories by those who felt themselves under obligations to them for the utility of their lives. But the poets and orators who celebrated their achievements and enumerated their virtues, in their exaggerated strain, represented them as a superior order of beings, inhabitants of the stars or the celestial regions, who had submitted to privation and distress on earth for the benefit of its inhabitants, but had now departed, returned to their former place of residence and were looking for sacrifice and offering, as due for the benefits they had conferred. Hence perhaps, the first ideas entertained of a superior being: hence originated the fables and absurdities of the heathen Mythology.

It is admitted the poets and philosophers, speaking of Osiris Bacchus or Jupiter address him as "the *greatest* and *best* of beings, the *father of Gods and men*" but this must be understood rather as complimentary than as conveying their real sentiments, for the accounts which the same persons give of their god in other places are utterly inconsistent with such declarations. The words of De la Motte in reply to Madame Davier may be properly introduced in this place: "What! Could Homer seriously believe Jupiter to be the Creator of gods and men? Could he think him the father of his own father Saturn, whom he drove out of heaven, or of Juno his sister and his wife, of Neptune and Pluto his brothers or of the nymphs who had charge of him in his childhood, or of the giants who made war upon him and would have dethroned him if they had been then arrived at the age of manhood? How well his actions justify the Latin epithets, *Optimus Maximus*, so often given him, all the world knows."

The idea of one supreme Being, Creator of all things seems not to have made any part of the religious creeds of antiquity. The ancients deified men and paid them religious worship. They erected temples to the sun moon and the hosts of heaven, they dedicated altars to the hidden virtue of mere astrological conceits, and sacrificed to the elements of nature; but the worship of the true God was unknown.

Abraham during the early part of his life was an idolater, and his views of God for a long time were extremely defective. The supposition that God required him to offer up in sacrifice his beloved son Isaac, argues great ignorance of the perfections of the Deity, for which he was justly reproved by the voice that called to him just as he was about to stretch forth the sacrificial knife. Abraham no doubt showed in this act his willingness to obey God, and notwithstanding he erred in respect to the nature of his duty the readiness he had to discharge it, was accounted to him for righteousness.

However exalted were the conceptions which Moses had of the attributes of Jehovah, if he be the author of the book of Genesis he certainly was far from having found him out to perfection. He frequently represents him as moving from place to place, also as being disappointed, grieving and repenting for what he had done; all which when applied to the Deity must be grossly improper; for if he move from one place to another he cannot be Omniscient, and if he be disappointed his wisdom must be finite, and if he repent, he cannot be immutable. This is not urged as an argument against the Divine authenticity of the book, for the state of the human mind at that time necessarily required an imperfect system, for one that was perfect would have exceeded its powers of comprehension.

Essay No. VI

The most extraordinary increase of divine light which the records of antiquity have preserved, is to be found in the system of religion and politics established by Moses, the great Prophet and Lawgiver of the Jews. To us it is a matter of perfect indifference, by what means he received the knowledge of that system, whether by inspiration or philosophical research—whether his ideas of God were wholly original with himself, or collected from the opinions of different theologians—whether the ritual he instituted, the sacrifices and offerings he enjoined upon his followers, were invented by him, or modified from the existing practices of other nations or sects with which he had become acquainted; since it is only at the institution itself we look, and for its correctness and real utility in producing the happiness of mankind we inquire.

Many of the ideas Moses entertained of Jehovah, are such as the most enlightened theologians of all subsequent ages even to the present, have held in the highest estimation, and are such as the most sceptical respecting the divine authority of the Bible, must pronounce to be in accordance with eternal truth. He called Him an Almighty Being, the Creator of all worlds and all beings, the Father of the spirits of all flesh. He considered Him one and indivisible, without any particular form or likeness by which he could be represented. Thus far Moses and the Christian philosopher agree. The physical character and essence (if the terms mean any thing) of God, were as clearly understood, and as fully made known by him as by any of his successors; for indeed, no one that knows his own weakness will ever expect to have any clear conceptions upon a subject so far exceeding the sublimest flight of human thought. With regard to the moral character of God, the same cannot be said. There runs through the whole of the Mosaic economy, traces of partiality in the Being it professes to adore, and it cannot be denied, his character is drawn rather from the suggestions of man's dark understanding than according to the light which the beauty, order and utility of nature every where sheds with divine effulgence upon our eyes. The right for one nation to extirpate another, not sparing even the women and children, and to possess their land, is not now admitted by those who can pretend to have any correct views of justice; and the prince who should profess to have received from God a commission to such effect, would be looked upon by all judicious persons either as a gross impostor, designing to turn the religious prejudices of the people to the channel of his own ambition, or as a mad man more fit to be the inmate of an insane hospital, than to hold the reigns of government. The case of the Canaanites rests on the same ground for a justification, and it is presumed no Christian believes the moral perfection of *his* God, would allow him to issue such a commission at this time, however proper it might have been in the days of Moses and Joshua.

The declaration contained in the second precept of the decalogue, that Jehovah is "a jealous God visiting the iniquities of the fathers upon the children to the third and fourth generations," if it be understood as teaching that God punishes the children for the crimes of their parents, is certainly opposed to every principle of moral equity, if we, at this period can be supposed to have any correct idea of the term.

Moses seems to have been too contracted in his views of the providence of God. His regard for all *His* children. He seems to convey the idea, (and it is certain his followers obtained it,) that Jehovah held all the world in abhorrence but themselves, and that the children of Israel were the only nation on earth on which he had the least compassion. Perhaps this may be justified. All the world were idolators, and it accordingly became necessary for Moses, who abhorred idolatry, to place the strongest guards possible around his people to prevent them from adopting the odious practice. Hence it might have been necessary to impress his followers with the idea that God hated idolators. The guard, strong as it was, however, did not prevent them from embracing the idolatry of the nations which surrounded them.

Moses made no distinction between moral and ceremonial duties. The want of this distinction, though probably unfelt at the time his system was established, soon became the occasion of great neglect of the substantial virtues, and very useful in enabling those who had the desire, to make the observance of the *form* pass for the *power* of godliness. The externals of religion as they are usually called, are nothing of themselves, and are to be valued only according to their power of leading men "to do justly, to love mercy, and to walk humbly with their God."

Moses erred in establishing so many rites and ceremonies. His numerous sacrifices and offerings, whether considered as gifts, designed to express the devotion of those who made them, or as expiatory, intended to atone for the commission of moral evil, and to placate the Deity, evince clearly enough, his want of proper notions of the Divinity, and due attention to that kind of worship which a God of absolute perfection must demand of his intelligent creatures. But in this he may be excused, as in the case of divorcement, they were permitted on account of the hardness of heart or gross conceptions of the people. Still it may be urged, the effect of so many rites and ceremonies was to draw off the attention of the worshipper from the substance, and lead him to depend only on the shadow. The writers of the 50th Psalm, the 1st chapter of Isa. and the 6th of Micah, have adopted a more rational, and it is presumed a more correct sentiment on this subject, and may be adduced as a strong argument to prove that the ideas of religion among the Jewish prophets, had improved, or approximated the truth, during the lapse of days from Moses to Micah.

The ideas of punishment found in the laws contained in the system under examination, seem to have too much of the nature of revenge. The penal code seems calculated to nourish a vindictive spirit, rather than that mild lenient, and which experience, as well as the Gospel, has proved to be most conducive to the felicity of society, and consequently most pleasing to God.

An "eye for an eye," was their proverb among themselves; and their most approved method for redressing a wrong, was to inflict the same degree of injury upon the offender, which had this singular advantage, it doubled the amount of suffering my making two evils where was but one before. The same as would be the case, a man burns down my house, I burn down his so that both our families may be left destitute. The most unreasonable exactions was their demand from those in their power; hence, one reason why they were so much detested by the nations by which they were surrounded. Supposing God hated all the world but themselves, and believing he had designed to heap upon all nations except their own, the most severe judgements, they arrogated to themselves the province of interpreters of his will, and presumed to measure out his justice according to their own ideas of the desert of *their*, and by consequence, his enemies.

The admission of slavery was another imperfection in the Mosaic system. This, however, seems to have been the besetting evil of all the political systems of antiquity; and it must be said, in palliation of the Jewish Lawgiver, that he made many wise and benevolent regulations to alleviate the condition of the slaves he permitted his followers to hold.

Another defect was in blending his civil and ecclesiastical affairs. This had a tendency to encourage encroachment upon the rights of the people by the priests, and to produce a servile or superstitious disposition on the part of the governed. This was actually the case. No priests ever encroached more upon the prerogatives of the people than the Jewish, and no people were ever more blindly devoted to their priests than the Jews.

Essay No. VII

It is not intended by pointing out some of the defects of the Mosaic system, to lesson the real value of that institution; but merely the to evince the fact that the most perfect of the numerous systems of religion transmitted us from remote ages, does not contain that clear and consistent view of the moral perfections of the Almighty, nor that comprehensive, correct and satisfactory detail of the various duties belonging to our individual and social relations which the general diffusion of knowledge at this time would lead us to expect from a system formed under the immediate direction of the Most High.

If Christians are in the habit of admitting the divine authenticity of the Jewish scriptures, they should also recollect that the Institution itself was abolished by the introduction of Christianity. If the Institution had been perfect, it should have remained; but inasmuch as a system of religion given by God, has superseded this, we are at perfect liberty to consider it defective, and to examine the correctness of the several parts or the beauty and utility of the whole, in the same manner we would, had it been of human origin.

Christ did not hesitate to pronounce some of its maxims incorrect, and to give new ones in their place: "Ye have heard that it hath been said, 'an eye for an eye, a tooth for a tooth;' but I say unto you, resist not the injurious." See Matthew v. 38, 39. His decision in the case of divorcement was very different from Moses, and may serve to explain the reason of many other of the laws found in his code. See Matthew xix. 7, 8. The disposition of the Jews was so intractable, and the state of improvement was such, that different laws would have been either useless or pernicious.

But he who loves truth and desires to follow her sacred injunctions, will not ask for scriptural authority, to convince him, that that is wrong which comes in contact with enlightened understanding, or to give him liberty to express his honest convictions, when from the best information he can obtain, the cause of religion and humanity, require it. To conceal fraud is to be an accomplice of imposition, and to be silent when we have discovered it, is to declare our friendship for the original perpetrators. If we have ascertained that the creeds of our brethren contain error mixed with truth, we ought to invite and assist them to make a separation, that they may reject that which is bad, but hold fast that which is good.

There is no intention in the writer of this article, by telling the world there are imperfections in the Mosaic system, to weaken their faith in the Christian religion; but he would, by exciting them to an examination of the subject, induce those who wish to know the truth, to study the Christian, instead of the Jewish scriptures. For the Jewish being given to man in a state less improved and less refined, admits many things which would be improper under the Christian dispensation.

People have generally imagined the Jewish scriptures did not contain all the truth; yet all they did contain was truth. A greater error need not be imbibed. This was the very case with the Jews; and, to convince them of this mistake, the Apostles labored long and hard. No fact is or can be clearer, than that the new dispensation contains things in opposition to the old. Hence, as Christians, we should form our sentiments from the new. If we wish to be Jews we may study the old.

Divines know these things, but they continue to practice on the maxim, "It is no harm to deceive a man to his benefit." The experiment has been tried; but all deception is found to be against the best interests both of the deceiver and the deceived; and though a partial good may sometimes be practiced, yet seldom, if ever, is it sufficient to overbalance the evil. Priests suppose, that because we have hitherto been taught that the Bible was, every word of it, dictated by the Spirit of God, if they should now disclose the truth, that some of it does not contain sentiments proper for us to believe, we would reject the whole. Hence, to make people believe the truth, we must preach a certain mixture of falsehood, and we must become dishonest for the benefit of mankind. This language is too degrading—it is more than the independent spirit of man can bear. It says to a fellow being, "You are incapable of managing you own concerns—your ears are such you must not hear the truth but you must have some one to oversee your affairs and preach to you falsehood." Can any thing be more insulting? Can there be any thing more destructive to every thing valuable in the human bosom, or virtuous in human society? And who is the being that presumes to read this language in our ears—is it a God? No, it is a frail mortal, like ourselves, as ignorant and equally liable to err. Let, then, the lesson return to himself, and let him say, how he should be pleased to have such language pronounced in his own ears. Honesty is the best policy; and he who has not sufficient independence to speak what he believes to be truth, is not fit to be a teacher, or to have the least concern with instructing mankind.

From an examination of the Mosaic system it is learned that the best system antiquity could boast, would not be called perfect now. Other systems there were, but they were inferior to this, and may therefore be permitted to rest in the tombs where for ages they have been inurned. The Mosaic was a great advance from the idolatry which preceded it. The prophets made many improvements in the religion left by Moses; but it was still imperfect.

Essay No. VIII

On commencing the inquiry into ancient opinions, I intended to run over the various systems of religion which had, at different times, occupied the attention of mankind, and to have marked the gradual improvement of each, that encouragement might be afforded to the almost despairing philanthropist that truth was progressive; and it may confidently be expected that the revolutions of the future will accelerate its march, as well as those of the past; but I found myself laboring to prove what few will deny; and also exhibiting that kind of proof which but few would appreciate. The question—*"Cui bono?"*—also occurred: What benefit will it be to mankind, to call from the tombs, where for ages they have been inurned, the ashes of those errors which employed the cogitation, of the speculative and contemplative—which fired the zeal of the enthusiastic, or promoted the designs of the ambitions for enslaving mankind, and trampling on the ruins of all that is noble or endearing in the human bosom? All that we can say with certainty, is, that man acquires his knowledge by observation and experience. Time enlarges experience, and continual researches extend our observations; hence, every generation may leave its successor an increasing fund of knowledge, which may be transmitted, still enlarged, to later posterity.

In conformity to this maxim, we find antiquity, or the remotest period of which we can obtain any record, was extremely ignorant. The true character of God was unknown; man's moral and religious obligations but vaguely perceived and improperly enforced; physical and intellectual science had no name; the true principles of philosophizing, or the rules to be observed in our search after truth, were undiscovered; hence little can be found to satisfy the mind of the inquirer—he returns in disgust, and seeks relief in contemplating the present, or expatiating in the boundless expanse of futurity. But as you come down you find an improvement. As men acquire leisure for study, they detect old errors, but generally substitute new ones in their place, which again, in their turn, give way to others more lately invented.

Formerly men pretended to a great deal more knowledge than they do now; but since we have abated some in our pretensions, I am inclined to believe we are, in reality, more knowing; for there is more truth than poetry in Pope's definition of wisdom—"to know how little can be known." Most of the moral, religious, and philosophical systems which we have received from our ancestors, are merely hypothetical. They elicit genius, but it is often of an unchastened kind. Their authours had mental greatness, perhaps superior to ours, but they were deficient in science or a true knowledge of nature.

Time was when the priests were in possession of all the knowledge, as well as the religion, of the community; and experience has shown us very clearly how willing this class of people are to enlighten the great mass of mankind. Now they do indeed labor to diffuse knowledge, but they did not do it until the laity came in possession of it by other means. Had priests pursued the course which the policy of that body suggested as the most proper, we might perhaps, at this time, been bowing down to Egypt's "dok ox," as the fit object of our religious veneration; or, perhaps, fashioning with Aaron the golden calf, as the emblem of the God of nature. But they have been driven from their policy and have been compelled to resign the keys of science, and to relinquish their exclusive claims to the chair of literature. The keys of heaven and hell they are indeed permitted to retain, but the great body of the people believe they have neither power to open the one or shut the other.

The ancients may be excused in some degree for the absurdity of their religious systems, for they depended wholly upon their priests; and as priests always delight to amuse the credulous by marvelous stories and astonishing miracles, we may suppose they revealed them in all the wild luxuriance of mysticism, and dealt out to the gaping multitude without measure, the pious absurdities of their midnight dreams, and the holy raptures of their unlicensed, yet unreproved imaginations.— Their dreams and raptures may now supply matter for an evening tale, and may excite our risibility or raise our indignation at their impositions upon their brethren; but they will not gain a moment's credence, or create the least regret that they are never to return. With these remarks we bid adieu to those airy castles and fantastic fabrics which once employed the imaginations, and excited the hopes and fears of mankind; for though God may have spoken to them face to face, they were subject to the same law that governs us. The tree of knowledge must wait the nourishment of slow experience before it can expand its branches, afford shade or beauty, yield fragrance or fruit.

Christianity has done much for mankind. But alas! The best system is of no avail to minds still slumbering in the cells of ignorance. Though its rays beam with power, they cannot pierce at once the mighty deep of superstition; nor can their warmth penetrate in a moment the icy heart of the bigot and melt it to philanthropy. It has done much and much is now doing; but it would have done more if men had known at its first exhibition, what bitter experience has since taught, that, though science is not religion, she is the handmaid of religion. There may be science without religion, but religion cannot claim much purity nor usefulness without science. But science has flourished under the fostering sun of Christianity, and its reciprocal influence has brightened that sun, expanded his rays, and given him a more agreeable and a more permanent warmth.

One circumstance which now exists, promises to be of vast utility in enlarging the boundaries of our knowledge. Philosophers now build on experiment. The fondness for hypotheses and love of theorizing, which so long checked the growth of knowledge, are now, in some measure laid aside for matters of fact, and it is now ascertained to be folly to build on conjecture, or to pretend to know that which we have never seen, or investigated with any of our senses. True philosophy now attempts to analyze nature, exhibit her various phenomena, but not to explain them. The composition of bodies is ascertained, and the changes to which they are liable, are, in many instances, predicted. The mind also is subjected to the same analysis; its susceptibilities developed, and the various classes of its changes, as they are affected by its relation to matter or to itself, are defined. The same rule, the same method is finding its way into religion, and the most beneficial results may be anticipated.

Essay No. IX

Science has shed her "lucid rays" over many nations and the most abject slaves of ignorance have caught a glimpse—faint indeed, but sufficiently powerful to make them dissatisfied with their condition, and to enable them to mediate some amelioration. The invention of the art of printing, has furnished the philanthropist with successful weapons, to combat the foes of the human race and vindicate the cause of wisdom and virtue. Armed by this invention, he has already shaken thrones, filled the hearts of tyrants with dismay and the courts of despotism with consternation! The mighty fabric of bigotry and superstition, which cost the labor of ages to erect and which were cemented by the blood of millions, already trembled to their foundations before his successful attacks. Several nations have been compelled to throw off the burden of political servitude and others have been obliged to abate the rigor of their institutions and the severity of their laws.

The enlightened benefactors of mankind, a few years since in this country, lighted the beacon of universal emancipation and Europe saw the illumination; France assembled in its rays, increased its effulgence.—Did she fall? She reflected splendor as she "kissed the dust." From her temporary defeat we are enabled to learn the rules of our future exertions to avoid the rock on which she split and the whirlpool in which she was tossed. The march of liberty may be more slow hereafter than was anticipated but what is lost in severity will be gained in permanency. But France shall rise. The republican principles of her revolution, though now apparently dormant shall yet spring up and yield a plenteous harvest. Her martyred patriots still live in her bleeding memory, and sooner shall the enemies of the human race arrest the sun in his progress or roll back the wheels of nature, than prevent the resuscitation of the cause for which they bled and its complete triumph over the tyrannical principles which have for a time obscured its glory!

The overgrown power of the Pope of Rome, has become little more than nominal. The splendid dome of Popery, erected from the spoils of almost every heathen temple and ornamented with the paintings of almost every heathen artist, is nearly demolished. The "bulls" of the Vatican are now regarded as harmless things, and their thunderings cease to terrify mankind. The church which was not improperly styled the "mother of harlots" has begun her reformation and bids fair to outstrip her daughters in this laudable work. Calvinism has had its day. There have been converts that could gravely declare, that man a heretic who did not believe "God has not created all men to like estate but to some has fore-appointed life and to others death and as they were created to the one or the other or they were elected to eternal life or reprobated to misery inconceivable, and themselves thus elected or reprobated were eternally and unchangeably designed and so definite that one cannot be added or diminished, and all this for the manifestation of his sovereign mercy and his vindictive justice. But where is the man that will now boldly advocate in all its native deformity, this consummation of absurdity and cruelty, this focus in which all the objectionable parts of the most objectionable theories ever dreamed of by man have concentrated their power?

We have Calvinists in name, but they are most of them ashamed of the peculiar tenets of the successful champions of malevolence, whose name they bear. Every sober minded man among them is much more solicitous to conceal these doctrines or to give them a more inviting dress than he is to exhibit them as believed by our ancestors. Edwards and Hopkins in our country, men possessing by no means small abilities have endeavoured to reconcile the *decretum horrible* of Calvinism with the universal benevolence of God, and notwithstanding they have concluded it is best upon the whole, to compel a part to weep eternally in hell that the righteous in heaven may have their bliss consummated, they have borne testimony strong as was in their power to the fact that God is a being of universal benevolence—a truth when once admitted by the mind puts in the back ground all these imaginary fears and burning hells which Calvin placed in the front.

The Church of England, though originally Calvinistic or nearly so, now pays very little attention to the doctrine of election and reprobation—except it be to discountenance it. She indeed retains her thirty-nine articles but they have not much control over the sentiments of the clergy in general.

The Methodists sprang up in the last century and although in point of doctrine they have done little more than to declaim against the horrid tenets of the Reformer of Geneva[1] they have by their unwearied exertions done much to benefit in many places the lower classes of mankind—these unfortunate persons whom the clergy of more popular churches have generally treated with neglect.

These are indeed trifling considerations when our minds take in the vast family of man, but as they show that the most enlightened religious institutions are purifying themselves, we catch the hope that they will soon be prepared to instruct the more ignorant and to shed the rays of truth upon the benighted parts of our earth. They show, the spirit of investigation is abroad, and however powerful or obstinate the enemies it has to encounter, it will never return till wreathed with laurels of victory. These apparently minute consequences show us there is a redeeming principle in human society and however slow may be its operations it will finally produce a glorious renovation.

The last century has done much, and should the same exertions be made and be attended by the same success for one hundred years to come the world will appear almost entirely different from what it was one hundred years back. The work is begun, and the first obstacles are surmounted. The path now before us is plain, and as the wheel of improvement acquires celerity from its own motion the remaining part of the road will be run with more quickness, ease and safety than that already traversed.

The labors of our predecessors though apparently feeble produce astonishing results and instead of wondering why we are no further advanced we should rather wonder why we have progressed so far. A few centuries back the world was in darkness and "gross darkness covered the people," a senseless jargon disturbed the schools, a philosophy was taught which had little effect but to render more imperious the gloom of ignorance which brooded over the nations. War in its grossest forms and in its most malignant aspect was multiplied to an extent which threatened the world with depopulation. This "horrid monster" is now made to wear a milder garb, and much is done to render his march tolerable. That philosophy is discarded and a new one commenced which rests on experiment not conjecture for its authority. That jargon is not longer heard and our seminaries have learned it is their province to teach their subjects *things* rather than words.

Improvements in navigation have brought all nations within the vicinity of each other. Commerce has made us acquainted with all. The art of printing will convey to all, almost instantaneously the discoveries of each. Hence what we gain cannot be lost. Our discoveries and improvements are embodied in so many books and read in so many different languages that nothing less than a universal conflagration can destroy the whole.

True many nations are yet ignorant, barbarous and savage, and exhibit a faithful picture of what all once were, but missionaries are flying with the wind to each; and though what they carry is of no great consequence they will open with a communication, make us acquainted with their language, manners and customs and enable us to transfuse through their ignorant mass those truths which at once correct the head and amend the heart. It is thus the arts of the enemy shall operate to his own ruin, and the efforts made to extend the dominions of priestcraft be the means of its final overthrow. One, however, would naturally suppose there was a shorter and more direct road to the desired object. But all men are not philosophers, but few reflect seriously on the propriety or impropriety of the measures they adopt. The majority of mankind are borne along the tide of things as passion or belief gives the impulse, without attempting to correct their progress or even to inquire where they are likely to land. Men are governed more by their prejudices than by their reason and these are generally so obstinate that nothing short of miscarriage can subdue their power. Experience is surely a dear school but we have a great many who will learn in no other way and some not even in this. Hence the march of truth has sometimes been by a circuitous route. The obstacles which impeded her footsteps were not always to be surmounted at once. She has many times apparently slackened her progress and permitted the fables of men to pave for her a way to certain victory. Such is the Missionary scheme contemplated either as to the motives of its founders or the measures adopted to carry it into execution. Contemptible indeed is the motive. It is no other than to spread those unintelligible doctrines, sometimes strangely called the "doctrines of grace" among the Heathen—those doctrines which must excite the ridicule or disquiet of every man's mind that is freed from the leading strings of his mother. Contemptible and worse are the measures adopted to prosecute this scheme. But I will not mention them for may posterity never learn how grossly depraved were the most popular religionists of the 19th century. The selling of Joseph into Egypt was not commendable in itself considered but the consequences were good, and the same perhaps may hereafter be said of the Missionary scheme. The same perhaps too of the petty institutions of Sabbath schools. When the first lessons taught are veneration for the church which adopt them. These and all similar measures will finally produce a reaction. Woe then to the pride of their abettors, for it shall receive a deadly wound!

Truth is the pebble in the lake and however small at first are the circles, or however, slow they may succeed each other, they will continue till they have spread over the whole surface. Truth has already disclosed to the once despised inhabitants of the southern half of our Continent the balm of personal liberty and national independence, she armed them against the tyrants that oppressed, she led them to victory and though her triumph be not yet complete she will finally spread a richer wealth over the sand then the silver of Potosi or the gold of Mexico could purchase. The wrongs of Montezuma shall be avenged and science flourish over all the territory beheld by the disgraceful conqueror of the Inca of Peru.

Greece shall emerge from the gloom of Turkish vassalage; science and literature revisit the land of Plato; liberty triumph again on the plains of Marathon, and be maintained by the justice of Aristides. Nor here shall end the march of Truth. India shall behold her effulgence—cast aside her idol gods—recognize the original equality of the human family—treat them all as brethren, and worship with gratitude the common Father of all. The Minstrel of Zion shall retake his harp from the willow, and heavenly music shall reecho from the mountains of Jerusalem. Nor ye sable sons of Africa shall truth forget to light the darker features of your doom. Distant, yes ye degraded men, distant is the day, but come it shall, to restore to you the rights to which nature and nature's God entitle you, and give your long abused country its place among the nations of the earth. Ye wanderers of Arabia's desert, and ye tribes that roam the forest, a glorious sun shall shed his enlightening beams upon your desolations. Showers shall distill their genial influence upon your land, and the desert shall be glad with the rest, and the wilderness and the solitary place rejoice and blossom as the rose. The Genius of Emancipation is hurrying over the world—he bears on his wings the long wished for relief, and fast as the wheel of improvement can move, it shall be borne to you.

Such are the suggestions of hope—such are the conclusions warranted by a review of the past and the contemplation of the present. Philanthropists, awake! Your exertions shall be crowned with success. Regard not the proscriptions of the ignorant and the designing. Disapprobation from those who are incapable of perceiving the value of your labors, and from those who have no desire to witness the renovation you wish to produce, you must expect, but be not discouraged. Posterity will reap the fruit of your toil, and the unbounded felicity which you may transmit to future generations will fully compensate you for any sacrifices you may be compelled to make. Let your voices be heard! Ye friends of Truth, of Science, of Liberty and Religion in its purity, break your long silence, let the echo of your voices ring back from every quarter—man shall be free! Tyranny, whether civil or ecclesiastical, shall be annihilated—wars will cease—contentions end. Peace and unbroken harmony shall reign wherever the voice of man is heard, or wherever the sun emits his golden beams.

The Essayist

JULY–SEPTEMBER 1828

Essay No. 7

All mankind desire to be happy—all labor continually to gratify this desire. Whence, then the cause of failure, for fail mankind do? Misery rears her horrid front, and scatters her noxious effluvia through every atmosphere. All countries, all ages, all ranks, all conditions, bear the impress of her footsteps and exhibit the insignia of her triumphs. Why is this monster permitted to prey upon us? Why are we the subjects of her lamentably permanent reign? "Man is born to suffer—he must submit to the dominion of Misery," say the desponding and faint hearted. "He must be miserable here that he may be happy hereafter," say our divines and all those who know more of heaven than they do of earth, and are better acquainted with Jehovah than with men. "God, as a kind and beneficent father, has, in his wisdom, deemed it proper to inflict terrible evils on his children, that they may know how to appreciate enjoyments," it is said, and from time immemorial this stupid doctrine has been preached, to justify tyrants in their usurpations and priests in the maintenance of their craft. Did a people suffer from a despotic government, they were dissuaded from choosing a milder form, for it was better they should suffer; they would feel so much the more happy when they were relieved. Did the priest make us miserable, (reader, pardon the supposition,) did he make us sick with the silly tales he told—miserable by the dreams he made us believe, and wretched by robbing us of the bread we wanted for our children. Why, all was well; we should be so much the more happy *when* we become happy.

If God makes me miserable today, what surety have I that he will not make me the same tomorrow? If God makes his children miserable, who shall make them happy? Poor consolation indeed, to be told that our sufferings come from God. From him we had hoped to receive good. To him we had hoped to fly as a place of refuge, as a shelter from the storms of affliction which beat upon us. But if he send afflictions, if he hurl the bolts of adversity, what is there left? What hope? What tower of defense? "O, the misery we suffer will do us good, and make us happier; it is only a blessing in disguise." So forsooth, we reason, ingenious to perpetuate our sufferings. Grant that good sometimes follows evil, does not evil sometimes follow good? And why not say—that our enjoyments are evils in disguise?—Whatever produces agreeable sensations, we call good; and we call ourselves happy in proportion as these sensations are predominant.—Evil and misery are the reverse. To say evil may be good and misery may be happiness, is to confound all distinctions, to destroy all knowledge, to deny the superior desirableness of any object, of any pursuit or of any act. Pain is not pleasure. No sophistry can make it so. Pain is an evil; no matter whether the pain proceed from real or imaginary objects, whether it be unavoidable or removeable, temporal or eternal, it is an evil, an absolute evil, proportioned to the intensity of the sensation. It is the opposite of all I call good, the destruction of which my experience teaches me is for my happiness. Hence, to me it is an evil. I do not know what it may be to other beings, or what I may receive from it in some other world; but here, while it lasts it is an evil.

"Whatever is, is right," says Pope, but Pope had a much better faculty at making rhymes than ethics. There is an evil in the world. Every body suffers more or less. Every body desires to be happy, yea, labors to be. Why, it is asked again, are they not? It is because we are doomed to be miserable? Who doomed us? Or who has stamped us with such a curse? Jehovah? Breathe it not—think it not. It is a foul slander upon his character. The Bible declares "Jehovah is good," and who does not know that goodness cannot produce evil, nor subject its offspring to its dominion? If God be good he is not the cause of our sufferings, and to charge them upon him must betray our want of respect for his character.

"But our sufferings are punishments from God," some will say. But for what does *he* punish? For our vices? Why so? What is vice? It is a wrong action; but what is a wrong action? One which brings misery. Why does it bring misery? Because it is wrong?—No; but it is wrong because it brings misery. To punish one, then, because he has done wrong, is only because he has brought *some* misery upon himself to make him *more* miserable.—That is, if a man burn down his barn, he must have his house burned; or if he cut off one hand, he must lose the use of the other; or if he break another man's head, he must have his own broken! O, fine principle! This would multiply suffering as fast as any one could wish. But why does God punish? Could he not prevent crime? Or does he choose to permit, or allow, or, as others say, compel its commission, that *he* may have the inexpressible pleasure of punishing it, and *we* the favor of feeling a great deal better when we get over it?

Why then do we suffer? The cause is in ourselves. Deity has made us as he saw fit—it is not ours to find fault. He made the world as he liked; that is none of our business. He has established a certain fixed order, which I call the order of nature, or certain laws which may be called the laws of nature. Why he established these laws I know not, I ask not. But this much experience has taught me, when we obey these laws we are happy; when we disobey we are miserable. The cause of our suffering is not in the bosom of Jehovah; but in our deviating from the order, the laws which he has established. The cause of our deviation is ignorance. Every man pursues that course he believes will lead to enjoyment. He fails only because he took a wrong course. Show him the right and he will pursue with a zeal and perseverance proportioned to his desire for happiness.

The reason, then, why we are not happy, is because we are ignorant of the means of bettering our condition. We have been studying nursery tales, when we should have been learning the best means of procuring food, clothing and shelter; have been poring over musty volumes of legendary lore, when we should have been examining things contiguous to us, or objects connected with our welfare—endeavoring to propitiate the gods, when we should have been conciliating the affections of men—and disputing about angels and demons, when we ought to have been studying ourselves. All we want is instruction. Let nature be our instructor, her lessons our delight, and we shall be happy. Let men study to be honest, industrious in some useful calling, benevolent to their fellow creatures. This will be more profitable than obsolete creeds, silly tracts, foolish catechisms, or stupid folios of polemical theology, with the whole list of *et ceteras*. Yes, let us pursue this course and all will be well and happiness become the birthright of our children.

Essay No. 8

What shall be *done?* not, what shall be *believed,* is the question which now presses upon us, and imperiously demands a serious answer. What shall be done? Not to purchase *heaven,* or bribe the favor of the Almighty; but *what shall be done to produce and perpetuate the rational enjoyment of the human race?* Something *must* be done! The circumstances with which we are surrounded forbid us to be idle or inactive.

Ignorance is collecting her forces—cupidity is calling her armies into the field—a terrible conflict is just ready to take place,—not between rival religious dogmas—not between the votaries of different systems of faith, but between truth and error, between folly and common sense; between the friends of civil and religious liberty, and the advocates of ecclesiastical domination and clerical vassalage. The clergy, and their minions, and their dupes, are determined to perpetuate the gloom of the dark ages, where it exists, and reproduce it where it has been dispelled.

Americans have boasted their love of liberty, the freedom of their civil and ecclesiastical institutions; they have said to the old world, *"Mark our example and follow it."* But ah me! This boasting must soon be dismissed, this invitation to other countries to compare their governments with ours must not be indulged, unless we call forth our sleeping energies and drive from our hitherto happy land the clerical monster which now threatens us with his ghastly reign.

The noble emotion, the conscious dignity we once felt at the mention of our country's name, and at the recital of the toils, sufferings and achievements of our fathers, will give place to shame for our supineness, or deep regret that we cherished a viper to destroy us. There is, there can be no want of proof, *that our liberties are endangered,* that we, like Spain, are to be devoured by monks, priests, and the *pretended lovers of God,* unless we combine to prevent a doom so horrible.

What shall be done? Shall we, who bid defiance to kings, and made thrones tremble to their base—shall we, who first set the world an example of a free government, founded on the inalienable rights of man, now submit to the disgrace, the degradation of a spiritual hierarchy? Shall we, who half a century ago, were so jealous of our rights that we would rather involve our country in all the evils of war, than pay a trifling tax, lest we should countenance a doctrine which might encourage tyrants to oppress us, now contribute immense sums to the ignoble leaders of a barbarous superstition, to enable them to overturn our political edifice, and trample the rights of conscience in the dust?

My religious sentiments are sufficiently known. Whether I am orthodox or heterodox, dissenter or conformist, is no man's business, nor do I care what religious creed my countrymen adopt. All that can be desired on this subject is, is, that every denomination have the privilege of expressing their own opinions and the liberty to support them by such arguments as they possess. Let every one tell his own belief or keep it to himself just as he please; but let no mortal presume to censure another for the opinions he may adopt. Let truth and error both rest on their own resources, and there will be no danger of truth's losing the victory. Truth needs no protection to be able to cope with error, hence laws in her favor are unnecessary. If any doctrine needs the aid of government to maintain its standing, it may be fairly presumed that it has not truth in its favor, consequently to grant it protection is the same as to nourish falsehood, we want no law in favor of any particular sentiment. Truth spurns such aid, and to grant it to falsehood would be highly pernicious. Hence we want no law religion, or which is the same thing, neither the cause of truth or human felicity requires any such establishment.

But there are many in this enlightened country—yea, some from the desk have dared pretend it is necessary we have a religion established by law. Such pretenses are mere mockery. Do we want the scenes of persecution, of blood, of death in its most appalling form which the old world has beheld, *brought* hither to convert our paradise into a hell filled with impious monks and hypocritical priests? If not, let us cease from supporting any of the misnamed benevolent societies of our country. Let every liberal, every enlightened, and philanthropic minded man take a decided stand against the highhanded measures with which this country is replete. The courts and splendid establishments are beginning to have too much influence over our people, and we think because England, or some other country subject to an arbitrary government, has a religious establishment, we must; and so we can be like other nations. Let this influence be pointed out and discouraged. Let the superiority of plain republican institutions be faithfully shown; let the value of freedom be felt—the arts of the hypocrite and the wretched conduct of hireling priests be held up to public contempt, and the danger with which we are threatened will be averted.

To accomplish this it becomes necessary that there be exertions used. The press must be active. Truth must be told and the unsuspecting awakened to a sense of their danger. Let minor differences among liberal Christians be forgotten, and let them cordially unite to preserve mental independence, free inquiry, and rational liberty both civil and ecclesiastical. The call for union is imperious; the object is sufficiently important and the interest is the same. Let these men of liberal feelings and wishes combine to overthrow Dr. Ely's *Christian party in politics*, by discountenancing every criterion of decision which does not refer solely to a man's *moral* worth. By doing this, something will be done, and this something can and must be immediately done, or all is lost.

Essay No. 10

As faith, by the majority of mankind, is deemed to be more important than philosophy, this number will be devoted to its consideration. I speak of religious faith. The objects of this faith are, the existence of God, his providence, the accountability of man to him, and a future state of happiness or misery. To discuss these subjects or to inquire their truth or falsity, is not my present aim; nor indeed do I know that I possess any *infallible* criterion by which I can *positively* pronounce any thing concerning them. Each of them lies beyond the boundaries of *my* knowledge, though I do not wish it to be understood that I consider there are no reasons which can justify our belief of them, but that we can never positively know them. They are therefore matters of faith and rest for the most part on that kind of evidence which we are but ill prepared to collate in this mode of existence.

Such being the character of the principal articles of religious belief, or such the foundation on which they rest, we seriously inquire their importance? What is their utility? How far shall we make them the principles of our actions, or the rules by which our actions should be governed? To give a clear and satisfactory answer to these questions, is neither easy nor safe, in the present state of society. But fear is something with which the writer of this essay is unacquainted, and to be told the subject is difficult is only giving him an additional motive to attempt the removal of its embarrassments.

What is the importance of religious faith?—Mankind have ever since the age of history embraced all the articles I have enumerated, experience informs us what *has* been its importance, and the tale it unfolds is too mournful to repeat. But two classes of benefits can be expected from adopting a religious faith; one is happiness in the other world, and the other greater felicity here. With regard to the first class I can only say it has reference to a world I have never explored, and to a mode of existence of which I am totally ignorant. Whether the opinions I adopt in this world will have any effect on my condition in the next or not, is something which I cannot know till I "shuffle off this mortal coil." I believe this thing or that, but it will make no difference in the truth respecting it.

The second, "to produce greater felicity here," demands our attention, for we cannot, consistently, be indifferent to any thing which is advantageous to us, poor mortals while traveling through this world. This class of benefits may be numerous. It should be closely examined, not with a prejudiced, but with an impartial eye. We want the truth, but have no anxiety to deceive or be deceived. Is a belief in the articles we have enumerated essential to the happiness of mankind here, is the question. How shall it be answered?—Shall we appeal to experience? Shall we ask what effect this belief has had on the nations which now sleep beneath our feet? What can that tell more than they were miserable? We may speak of wars, of outrages, and sufferings, which it makes us weep to recollect, but tho' a religious faith was the *apparent* cause, we may be answered, they were occasioned by the abuse of faith, and we have no means of disproving the assertion. Mankind have been miserable without it. They are miserable now, they are quarreling about faith; but they might quarrel about something else, if they had no faith.

Another consideration is important. How many articles shall we adopt? All above enumerated? But why stop here? Why not do as mankind always have done, add a thousand more? Or who shall present the world from doing the same hereafter? Mankind never have agreed. Christians, though they nominally admit all I have stated, explain these articles so as to mean things diametrically opposite, and each tells the other he will be damned if he does not believe as he does. How shall this evil be prevented? We all appeal to the Bible, but the Bible either gives us no information on the subject or may be, and actually is so interpreted, as to give about equal support to contradictory systems. For instance, one believes the Bible proves a devil, another believes it does not—one believes the Bible proves all but a few favorites will be eternally damned, another believes it proves all will be eternally happy—one is confident the Bible declares God is angry every day, and another one is equally confident that the Bible declares God is love and that anger rests in the bosom of fools. Hence our difficulties multiply.—For if we agree what shall be the common source of our faith—we each claim the privilege of interpreting the books according to our own understandings, of turning the streams which flow from the common fountain into the channel of our own particular opinions. If we agree on the number and names of the articles we are to believe, we can easily find means by our exposition of these articles to damn each other for the glory of God and the good of souls. What shall we say? Shall we give up all faith? By no means. Why not? What is its utility? Its utility is the comfort or consolation a belief in a God and a future state may afford the suffering son of humanity. But does every system of faith do this? No: if such was the case one system would not be preferable to another. But no system but one which represents God as boundless in his goodness, and promises an eternal state of ceaseless bliss can do this. Such then is the system we will patronize.

But shall we make this system a rule of our conduct? Yes, if we understand it. But as we are liable to mistakes, it will be the more safe to act only as experience has determined to be most for our felicity. To attempt to convert every body to our belief is not very wise. It immediately produces a sectarian spirit, which, if we know any thing, we know cannot be beneficial to ourselves or others. One important consideration is necessary in reference to our contending for faith; what we believe may be true or it may not, and our anxiety to circulate it should never exceed the ratio of good it will produce.

But it may be asked, is not faith necessary to please God? I know nothing about that;—the only way I know of pleasing God (if he can be pleased) or which it appears the most rational to believe will be pleasing to him, is that we do good, i.e. do justly, love mercy, and endeavor to make our brethren of the human family happy.

So far as reason goes in this matter, it informs us religious faith is a subject between the individual and his God, that is, it is an individual concern with which society has nothing to do. "But should not preachers endeavor to inoculate their own views or to establish their own religious faith?" The preacher's office is to point out to us what we should *do*, and persuade us to its performance. But what he believes has nothing to do with this. Faith in religious dogmas is no part of man's *duty*, and should be considered rather as indifferent, yet may be proposed to an audience for their adoption or rejection. The reasons by which it is supported may be presented, the advantages supposed to flow from it clearly stated; but here the preacher must stop—another step carries him beyond his province.

My opinion is nothing, but my conviction is that faith is less important than philosophy;—that if we would be happy we must pay less attention to the examination of religious dogmas than heretofore, and devote more to the investigation of those subjects which are within the limits of our means of observation.

Essay No. 11

The language of reason has been so long neglected that mankind dare not hear it; and nothing is more startling to a vast portion of our unfortunate brethren, than to be told the paths they are required to walk is plain, smooth, impeded by no remarkable obstacles, and leading through a pleasant champaign, adorned with flowers and variegated foliage, but broken with no enchanted mountains, and inhabited by no mysterious beings who challenge the combat. My two last numbers were designed to correct the pernicious influence of former education, by informing the inquirer after truth, that all he has to do, is, to make use of his senses, to exercise his eyes, his ears, his power of discovering objects as they are; not to exert his imagination to find out what certain assumed premises ought to be. They were also designed to call the attention from those things which we cannot know in this slate of existence and to place it upon those things which are within the sphere of our observation and are immediately connected with our happiness or misery in this world.

I am a professed Christian. I consider the morals, enjoined by Jesus Christ, to be excellent; the doctrines he taught, to wit, the character he gave of our heavenly Father and the hope he gave his followers of a future state of happiness, are certainly very pleasing to every one who is depressed by adversity or suffering under the numerous casualties of life. But whether these doctrines are true or not I cannot *absolutely* know. I may believe, but my belief is not knowledge. The whole economy of nature evinces very clearly, that what is most necessary to our preservation and felicity is within our reach, unencumbered by the numerous difficulties which surround those which are less important. Philosophy, or as I have explained it a knowledge of things as they are, being within our power, to a certain extent, at least so far as we can examine, is more important than a religious theory which consists of opinions respecting certain beings and words which may or may not be, that is, so far as we can at present by the aid of our senses know.

I am no enemy to religion. I value my religious faith, and would use all means in my power to convince others it is true. But my religion consists more in doing than believing. For I *believe* it is more acceptable to the Lord for us to do justly and be merciful, than to offer sacrifice, however sweet may be the incense or rich the perfume. If I am deceived in this conclusion I have one advantage, the actions my belief enjoins, experience proves to be useful to man while here; and if I do not serve God by this conduct, I have the satisfaction of contributing to the happiness of his children, and if I do not secure a heaven in the invisible world I at least enjoy one here—Hence to me reason says "give up no certainty for an uncertain good. You know not whether your conduct will have any influence on another world, but you do know it has an influence upon your enjoyments in this. And since you cannot be certain, whether you can make yourself happy hereafter, neglect no opportunity to prolong your existence and increase your felicity in the world where you find yourself."

This precept obeyed, the whole of man's attention would be turned to the answering of two important queries: First, how can I preserve my existence to the latest possible date? Second, how can I make this existence a source of the highest happiness of which my constitution is, or can be made susceptible? The preservation of life being the first object, we should be led to inquire, not what religious creed shall we adopt, but what things shall we avoid as injurious to life, and what shall we seek to gain as beneficial? Here opens a field of inquiry. Nature must be examined. The qualities of the articles fit for food must be ascertained and the best kind determined, and the quantity which will have the best effect fixed. We must become acquainted with the medicinal properties of every thing, that we may know how to cure the diseases which might at times attack the human body or mind. And this would also require an acquaintance not only with the diseases themselves but with the causes producing them; whether they be in our diet, our climate, our mode of life, the nature of our pursuits, in our action or indolence, &c. This inquiry, would in fact, lead us to study every thing which can be known; and when we had ascertained this, we should be prepared to answer the second, how can I make my life a source of the highest felicity which I am capable of receiving.

The answer to the first, is the answer to the second. For it will be found, that nothing, which has a tendency to shorten our life, can be productive of our happiness. The first inquiry, must necessarily ascertain the influence which any body of matter can exert over us, or rather the relation of the human body to every object which does or can affect it, and also the nature and tendency of every pursuit and of every action about which man can be employed. In these inquiries, experience is our only guide.

Religion will not be forgotten. But from holding the first it may be reduced to a subordinate rank. What this rank is, it is not my intention now to discuss; but I wish mankind to know that religion demands our attention only as it is subservient either to the preservation of our existence or the enlargement of our felicity. Jehovah has revealed to us all that we can suppose he designed we should know, and this is all comprised in the golden maxim, "do by others as you wish them to do by you."—That is, we should always be just and merciful, for we always wish others to be so to us. God himself is unknown; he dwells in thick darkness, surrounded by the deep counsels of the Divinity, which no man can approach, much less penetrate. To attempt to scan him is utterly vain. Our optics cannot reach him; we have no sense by which we can detect him and no power by which we can fathom his wisdom or ascertain the depth of his designs.—Had it been necessary we should have known more of him, it is rational to suppose he would have more fully disclosed himself. But as he has not chosen to do this, we must be content with the study of those objects which are within our reach.

The Bible is a valuable book. It contains many glorious truths, which it is important we should become acquainted with. But these truths are but few in comparison of the whole number it is important to learn. The Bible tells us what we ought to believe respecting another world, what will be our condition there, and what relation we shall hold to the Father of spirits. This disclosure may be of use to us. But the only use yet discovered, is that when we become weary of this world, and sickened with its scenes, we can please ourselves with anticipation a new and better world. This anticipation is, no doubt, frequently the source of joyfully sublime emotions, and very often makes ample amends for the scorn and injustice of the world. To destroy or to wish to destroy in any man's mind this anticipation, this hope of bliss to be, is not, cannot be a proof of kindness or a mark of any thing but a desire to sport with the feelings of the unfortunate by gratifying our own vanity.

Perhaps the remark is not exactly correct, that the only use of religion is the hope, the consolation it affords the unfortunate, or rather some may apprehend it is not. It is supposed by most who have written on this subject, that religion is the foundation of every virtue. This I do not believe, because I do not believe that virtue is what religionists generally define it to be. According to the opinions of those, who honour themselves with the title of orthodox, virtue is, not merely a good action, but a strong desire to obey the will of God. An action, according to these persons, doctors perhaps they ought to be called, an action is not good because it produces pleasurable emotions, but because Deity has commanded it. Hence murder, suicide or any act however destructive to others or to ourselves, might be called good, providing God has commanded it. I shall not stop to inquire whether this be correct or not, but simply observe that it is not in the power of Deity to make evil good, and as we can never have positive knowledge of what Deity commands, it will be best to consider, that a virtuous act which experience shows us has a tendency to produce happiness; and that it is good, not because Deity has commended it, but because it is beneficial. Placing virtue on this footing, my remark respecting the use of religion will be found to be correct, so far as this world is concerned.

This number closes the Essayist. When I commenced this series of articles, I intended they should contain a regular dissertation on natural religion; but ill health prevented, accordingly they consist of only detached articles, on subjects which I hope have not been wholly uninteresting. If they shall remove any encumbrances to free inquiry, give new confidence to the aspirant after truth, or afford some hints which will serve to guide him in his progress, the object for which they were written will have been obtained.

Free Inquiry

August 1828

The present is emphatically an age of inquiry and close investigation. No veil of antiquity, no character, however sacred, protects sentiments from the test of strict examination. This augurs well. For I am fully confident that truth is able to bear its way, and will finally prevail. Ignorance has long feared to present her opinions to the eye of reason, or to submit to the deductions of wisdom and enlightened philosophy. The spirit of the age may give her uneasiness, deprive her of sleep or give her unpleasant dreams; but this is no cause of alarm. I rather rejoice at it; for if I have embraced sentiments which will not bear the test of the closest scrutiny, if I know my own heart, I have no wish to retain them. But, Mr. Editor, I remark a number of sentiments, advanced by some liberal publications, conducted by men, for whose boldness and independence of mind I cannot but have the most profound respect, which, to my understanding, seem poorly calculated to benefit the present state of society, or to comfort and console mankind under the pressure of calamities which have hitherto been found inseparable from this mode of existence.

I am not ambitious to be one of that number who sit down under every unfortunate occurrence, say it is unavoidable, and console themselves with imagining a happy world in some other state of being, where bliss shall be unbounded, enhanced, no doubt, by the remembrance of pain endured here. No, Sir, I would examine carefully, and whatever unpleasant circumstances I could remove should be done. But the condition of mankind is various. Some have little time for reflection. The immediate wants of nature demand all their attention. The man sees a wife, a child, whom he tenderly loves, looking to him with anxious eyes for a subsistence which he scarcely knows how to procure, and which the least contingency may render impossible. This class is by no means small. And though it is generally overlooked and too often neglected in our estimate of what is good for mankind, yet this is the class most deserving the attention of philanthropists. Can we calculate how much relief religion, the hope of future life affords these our unfortunate brethren? It often converts the lowly cottage into a palace of bliss, gives a smile of content to the little circle when partaking of the last scanty pittance spread upon the board; it smoothes the haggard brow of poverty, and disarms affliction of its power to render us unhappy. Take away this hope, tell the poor man, beaten by the tempest of adversity, scorned by the wealthy, the proud and the vain, that he must trudge along a few days more, then sink to the grave unhonored and forgotten—that his body shall molder to dust, his sympathies, his affections, the warm emotions of his bosom shall sleep the cold unending sleep of nonentity—tell him this, O sceptic! And can you think the tidings will be welcome, that he will hail you as his benefactor? Pause, O sceptic! Weigh well the matter before you snatch from the poor, the neglected part of community, the only solace they have in their journey through life.

But this is not the only class that needs the aid, the consolations of religion, the balm infused through the soul by the hope of future life. The great, the learned, the philosophical must at times resort to the same fountain, however much they may affect to despise its streams. No man is always great. Everyone, notwithstanding all his boasted superiority, must descend from his elevation to the littleness of man. The student will at times become weary of his books, the learned of their researches, the philosopher of his examinations and logical deductions. Notwithstanding the whole of ancient and modern literature may have been accumulated, the whole arena of nature may be exposed to view, there are, and we know not but there ever will be, moments when the mind will sicken at the sight and spurn even the weight of thought.

'Tis in these moments we wish rather to *feel* than to *reason*—to indulge a silent communion with the God of nature rather than to pursue the track of demonstration. It is then we feel the full value of religion. It relieves us from weariness and fills up a vacuum which would often be felt in the best informed minds. There is something sublime, something peculiarly adapted to our condition, to our habits, if not to our nature, in feeling ourselves in the kind embrace of an affectionate Father who knows all our wants, and is ever ready to relieve them—in prostrating ourselves before him and pouring into his paternal bosom, the various sensations which swell our souls—in adoring him for his kindness and his benefactions. It may be folly; but I must confess myself so far a fool as to attribute to such folly most of the happy sensations which have made me willing to encounter the reproach of men, and devote myself to the melioration of my brethren. Under its influence, if it be *folly*, I have felt my heart expand with benevolence to the human family—have felt anxious to soothe the afflicted, to protect the friendless, and reform the vicious. It may be *folly*, but I know not as society could long exist without such folly. It may not be philosophy; but philosophy, cold, stern and forbidding as she may sometimes seem, never discountenances any thing which has a tendency to soften the rigors of our condition, or to make us happier or better. I have been a votary of philosophy—I have sought her influence, and basked amid the rays of her sun. I love her still, and would ever solicit her to direct me; but I cannot, at present, abjure my God, or relinquish my hope of future existence.

But setting these considerations aside—allowing the sentiments which some publications advance, have not the cold, chilling aspect sometimes ascribed to them; that they do not deprive us of some of the strongest motives to virtue, and of some of the sublimest sensations of which we are susceptible, I am to be convinced that there is no evidence in nature, even setting aside revelation, of a future state of existence.

Nature with one voice proclaims the existence of a Supreme Power and Intelligence, to whom are ascribable all the phenomena of the Universe. True, he is in a great measure hidden from conception; but from the little we can perceive of him, it seems fair to infer, that he is a wise, great and good being. Hence it seems equally fair to infer, that his actions are directed to some end; and as we are unable to conceive of a power which can thwart his intentions, we think it is just to conclude that the end he has in view will be attained. We do not know what this end is; but if we propose an end, it should correspond to the greatness and goodness which we believe God to posses. To force beings into existence for a day, afflict them with excruciating pains, and take their life at evening, is not, cannot, in our estimation of things, be a proof of goodness. If God be good, I think we may reasonably infer a future state of being.

The condition of man, his capability of improvement, the structure of the mind which seems capable of almost infinite expansion, the pleasure derived from the acquisition of knowledge, and the adaptation of the various objects of creation to increase this pleasure, and aid the pursuit of knowledge, our love for life, our ardent desire for its prolongation, the hope which seems to be almost universal as to time or country for such an existence, the analogies of nature, what we discover in some of the minor grades of being; though they are not, I admit, positive proof of such a state, yet they do, I think, render it probable. To assert that there can be no such existence, is more than any one should presume to do. I know as well that there will be such a life, as any one does that there will not. The case is, we neither of us *know* any thing about it. But the considerations I have mentioned, to me, appear to render such conclusion; to say the least, probable.

It is not my intention to discuss this subject, but I submit these remarks with the hope that every argument brought against the utility of a future state of existence, may be listened to with extreme caution, and not be admitted without the most careful, and the most close examination. The publications to which I allude, are, no doubt, disseminating much useful knowledge, they are doing much to break the chains of bigotry and superstition. This is well. They will undoubtedly expose many of the abuses of religion; this is wanting, and I hope all the abuses of religion may be laid open, and all the secret machinations of priests be exposed to public contempt; but Mr. Editor, I also hope, that every philanthropist will be cautious not to pass indiscriminate censure, or involve religion itself in the ruins of superstition.

Free Enquirers

MARCH 1829

Those who call themselves Orthodox may be sure of our respectful attention, long as we are able to write; but they will pardon us if we leave our examinations of the validity of their claims to pay our compliments to another class who are making some noise in our little world. This class is composed of deists, skeptics, Free Enquirers, and materialists. By the by, a friend, more timorous than discerning, whispered in our ear the other day that somebody thought the editor of the *Gospel Advocate* had a strong claim to admission into this honorable corps. Be this as it may, our sentiments are neither the better nor the worse for any supposed coincidence between them and those advocated by the classes we have mentioned. We, however, wish our friends to look at our statements and if what we allege for facts be true, they must not censure us, for we cannot make truth bend to their wishes nor to our own. Each one must bend himself to the truth or else he will always find cause for dissatisfaction. But our readers need not be alarmed. For, before we conclude to dispense with the Gospel, to abjure our Savior, and relinquish our hope in a future state of existence, we shall change the name of our paper, our friends shall have timely warning.

But it was the Free Enquirers we proposed to notice. How numerous this class may be we cannot say nor is it of much consequence. The organs of the party in this country are the *Free Enquirer*, lately published at New Harmony, but now transferred to New York; *The Corre-*

spondent published also at New York, and one or two more publications, we believe, though we have no knowledge of any except these two.

The Free Enquirer is edited by Miss Frances Wright, Robert Dale Owen, and R. L. Jennings. Miss Wright is a lady of talents and of no small philosophical acquisition. Did we believe in the transmigration of souls, we might think old Epicurus had reappeared in the person of Miss Wright, different from what he appeared in the garden, only in the acquisition of a few feminine graces and perhaps a few visionary notions common to both sexes. We mean this as no reproach for we consider Epicurus best deserving the name of philosopher of anyone antiquity can boast. We were agreeably surprised to find Dr. Good, in his Book of Nature, has not been ashamed to rescue the name of the philosopher from the reproach which has so long deceived the world.

Miss Wright's avowed object is to improve the condition of the human race. This is a good object. We can wish her success in this; for anyone who can feel, knows there is need enough. We have seen two of her lectures on knowledge. We approve them and indeed we have advanced the same principles both in our sermons and in our essays. There is nothing in the lectures which should alarm the honest enquirer after truth.

It will, however, be remarked, these lectures are only abstract principles. Perhaps we should differ in our deduction from these principles and in our application of them to the improvement of the human race. We believe, however, Miss Wright would in carrying her first principles out in detail leave man destitute of all religious notions and deprive him of the benefit of all written laws. Man must have religion. He has always had some kind, and to us there appears nothing better calculated to elevate his conceptions and ennoble his nature than the religion of Jesus. Written laws, and indeed all government would be unnecessary, if mankind were just; but whether all can be made so is very doubtful to us. Man is a bundle of appetites and passions, irregular and violent in their operations. Some government will be necessary until his nature is changed, which we think will require more power than the Free Enquirer can exert. And whether the change would make the man better is a matter of doubt. Some things are beautiful in theory, but are the reverse in practice. Miss Wright has *a beau ideal*, perhaps good, but most probably like all ideal beings better suited to some other world than to this.

Her coeditors, Mr. Owen and Mr. Jennings, we presume, are of the same sentiments with herself. They are men of no mean abilities. Mr. Owen has been the principal acting editor of the *Enquirer* for some time past. We have read his productions with pleasure. He is a good natured man. Cares little about any man's God or creed; and, what we like him for, he always keeps his temper and manifests a truly catholic spirit. But we should think him blest or curst with too much philosophical indifference to work any extensive revolution. Men are successful in proportion to their zeal, not to their knowledge. Of Mr. Jennings we know little; some few of his articles we have seen, which elicit some talent.

The *Correspondent* is edited by George Houston and is very different in character from the *Free Enquirer*. The *Enquirer* may certainly claim the praise of liberality; but the *Correspondent*, in the rancor of sectarianism, may contest the palm with the most staunch, thoroughgoing orthodox publications of the day. Mr. Houston will pardon our freedom, but we think if he cannot exhibit as powerful arguments as religionists, he can match them in virulence. And if he does not believe the orthodox creed, he seems not much deficient in its spirit.

Fools and knaves, dupes and impostors, are the charitable epithets he heaps upon us poor creatures who are so old fashioned as to believe the Bible. Alas for the believer in the Bible! He can expect no mercy at the hands of the relentless editor. We have sometimes thought if the spirit which breathes in his paper should become predominant that we foolish creatures who cling to the religion of Jesus would be put to death merely that the land might be purged of the enemies to his beautiful theory. Though upon second thought we conclude it would be like the spirit of all sects when in power, treat kindly all who submit. Mr. Houston has suffered imprisonment for his sentiments. He, no doubt, feels acutely. We would make all allowances necessary. But we do think one precept from that book he despises would be comfortable to his feelings. It is the precept which requires us to forgive our enemies.

The sentiments of this paper are such as are held by modern deists, or, perhaps materialists; we have not read the paper attentively. The value of such sentiments have been pretty well tested. We are not very sure they will be useful to the world. We do not, however, deny the editors of these papers the right to circulate their sentiments. They have the same right we have to circulate ours. But still we do not perceive their peculiar worth.

Both these papers attack religion. If they hurled their blows at superstition only, it would be well. It may be the result of education, it may be folly; but we have found religion very comfortable to our feelings. When we were overwhelmed with adversity (and we have been), it was not a little consoling to reflect the world is under the control of a wise, powerful and good Being who will cause all things to work together for good, and that our light affliction here will work for us a far more exceeding weight of glory.

We are opposed to superstition, to bigotry, and to false systems of religion. But we have not yet become so *enlightened* as to be pleased with universal skepticism, or with the cold unfeeling dreams of the deist, or the colder speculations of the materialist. Creation loses its beauty, the world its charms, when we consider it the fortuitous production of chance or of blind necessity. And then, to think we live, toil a few days, sink into the grave and are no more, is not well calculated to prompt exertion, or keep up our spirits amid the numerous incidents of life.

But if these editors convince us (and we are willing to be convinced) that their course is calculated to regenerate the world and make man universally happy, they may then have our good wishes and our cooperation. They go too fast for us. We condemn them not, but would say, the progress of truth is always slow, and they, in our opinion, far outstrip her in the race.

Church and State I

May–September 1829

May 2, 1829

At this time when the agitation of the public mind on the subject named in the caption of this article menaces some mighty convulsion, the patriot and the friend to equal rights should stand firm and watchful, ready to repel every invasion on the rich inheritance left us by our fathers. The writer of this disclaims the character of an alarmist. He is not ambitious to be thought one of that number whose idle fears brood over imagined dangers, and conjure up monsters or giants at every step, armed for the destruction of our rights. No, he has confidence in the virtue, in the intelligence and the firm and determined adherence to liberty which characterizes the great body of the citizens of these United States. He would disclaim his country and banish himself to some desolate region if he thought the lessons of antiquity were forgotten, or if the memory of our struggle for independence were not embalmed in almost every heart.

The citizens of our country are attached to liberty; they almost idolize their government and there are but few comparatively speaking of our whole population that would not sacrifice their lives to preserve the freedom of our institutions. But paradoxical as it may seem there appears to us serious cause for alarm. Men are creatures of circumstance. Parties are the same. A party starting on the best principles and having the best object to accomplish may, nay often do, in the pursuit of their favorite object involve the most serious and even the most injurious consequences in their exertions.

We will not indulge in invective, nor will we waste our time in blaming those who now threaten us with the destruction of all for which we wish to live. The motives of men, the secret springs of their actions, are not exposed to our view and we shall not assume the prerogative of the Almighty to look into their hearts. Their actions, their measures, are open to inspection and we shall exercise our right to animadvert when we think them wrong.

It is said religionists are endeavoring to *unite* church and state. I do not believe this to be the wish of those who manifest the most unfriendly disposition to our government. The Presbyterians are accused of wishing to unite church and state. I do not believe the accusation to be correct. They would reject with scorn any interference of the government with their religious affairs, except to give them money if the government pleased. No, their ambition, if they have any, is of a higher kind. They want no *union* but they might not refuse to *control* the state, to make the state subservient to their own views.

I see no plan on foot, which to me appears designed to effect a union between church and state, but the measures which have alarmed me seem calculated to keep the church separate from the state, to raise up an ecclesiastical government which shall control the civil. The Presbyterian clergy, and I fear others as well as they, have a number of projects, for what purpose they were started I know not and care not. They were ostensibly started for the purpose of evangelizing the world. Thousands gave their support and thousands still give their support from this conviction. The object is ostensibly good. Men engaged to accomplish it with the best motives and by exercising the best feelings of the heart. But there is not the less danger on that account. We have not less dread from the mistakes of conscience than from the violence of depravity. A man, conscious of rectitude of intention, fully convinced the object of his wishes is good, will hear no reason, yield to no argument or persuasion which might show him the danger of his course.

But where is the danger? Men love power; parties are actuated by the same passion. Our religious people have engaged in mighty plans. They have enlisted a great army who are all engrossed in the benevolent enterprise. Difficulties occur, obstacles to the completion of their designs are presented, they therefore will naturally labor to acquire power.

To become able to control the civil government, to make that bow to their dictation will throw an immense disposable force into their hands, and enable them if that be their wish to establish their creed or to gratify their ambition by the exercise of power if that be their object. The natural progress leads to this result and though thousands may be engaged who never dream of such a conclusion, yet their strong desire to do good by giving influence to their party directly leads to it or will if circumstances are favorable. This is their reasoning. "Our object is most glorious. It is to advance the cause of the Redeemer, and to benefit mankind. We have the good of mankind at heart, but alas! We have not the power to do the good we wish, we must therefore increase our power." Thus selfishness seems excluded and the conviction that they are increasing their influence for the benefit of the world sanctifies, in their own view, all their measures.

But there is a danger. Men ambitious of personal aggrandizement, and such men are never wanting, will join this party; mold its ruling passion to their own interest, and by making a skillful use of time and circumstance, they will not only defeat the good intended but effect much injury. Here is the danger. The orthodox seem now ripe for some ambitious clerico-demagogue to execute his plans. By concealing his designs, adopting the watchword, and making free use of the cant phrases of the party, and paying hypocritically the necessary homage to popular institutions, he may accomplish his nefarious projects ere many apprehend danger. This is what I fear.

Did the great body of our citizens believe there were any serious plan adopted to render the church independent of the state, to raise up an ecclesiastical hierarchy to overwhelm our civil institutions, they would rise in their majesty and consign it to nonentity. But the majority believe the thing is impracticable and hence those who are suspected of the design defend themselves upon the apparent impossibility of its being accomplished. Our danger is in our security. Were we awake, were we watchful on this subject, there could be no danger. But we slumber; and those who would enslave us are constantly administering soporifics that they may be left to act unobserved.

I have been called to this subject by a letter which I have just read from Dr. Ezra Stiles Ely to a Mr. Montgomery in Virginia, in which the Dr. disclaims all intention or wish to give his creed a legal establishment, and also disclaims the same not only on his part, but on the part of the Presbyterian clergy generally. It little avails one accused of stealing to declare he is no thief or for one accused of injustice to say he is honest. Dr. Ely, however honest or upright may be his intentions, however firm his attachment may be to our civil institutions, has lost the confidence of the public; and however much he may be esteemed by his party, his name will never until he performs some extraordinary lustration be free from reproach. As a man I know him not, as an individual I attach to him no consequence, as the mouthpiece of a party he should be severely rebuked; and his projects should be treated with indignation. To spare him is treason to liberty. In his language is concentrated the violence of sectarism, the rancor of exclusive orthodoxy, and the impudence of benighted bigotry. He brands as *Deists* and *rejecters of Christianity* those who advocate equal right, carries the reproach to the government, which he thinks will favor *Deism* sooner than any class of Christians. I shall bestow on him some attention and promise my readers that the suspected union of church and state or as I should term it, the usurpation of the church over the state, with what facts I can collect on the subject, shall be laid before them and fully discussed. The times require watchfulness and we dare not join with those who cry "peace, peace," when there is no peace. The public mind must be fully aroused or we fear the gloom of monkism will spread over the land.

July 25, 1829

Some time since we published an article, under the above head, and promised to remark still further upon the subject, as we should find leisure. We have been prevented from continuing our remarks for the want of room, but we will assure our readers and our orthodox friends generally that we have not and probably shall not abandon the subject.

We have already stated that we did not think a *union* of church and state, the particular object of clerical ambition, that they aimed at a higher object, designing to make the state *bow* to the church and statesmen obey the dictation of priests. The Presbyterian would revolt at the idea of being a Presbyterian if the law compelled him to be one; and should this government ever make the requisition, he would exhibit all the turbulence of John Knox, and for aught we know, the unconquerable rebellion of his Cameronean ancestors. But the Presbyterian, while free to embrace what religion he pleases for himself, has never shown himself unwilling to *force* his religion upon others. He doubtless would have no objection that government should give him the means to render contemptible all who do not choose to adopt his faith.

The measures which have been adopted are of a dangerous character. Measures, which if not soon overthrown, will one day doom our much loved country to experience the sad reverses which have blackened the history of all others. Of all crafts priestcraft is the most subtle in its designs, the most successful in its measures, and the most dreadful in its influence.

The history of the past should warn the present. Saul, the first and best of the Kings of Israel, was opposed, was branded with reproach, lost his kingdom and his life merely because he did not choose to be a tool of the priests of his nation. David, a king unprincipled and pusillanimous, an adulterer and a murderer, was raised to his throne and supported on it, pronounced a man after God's own heart, for no other known virtue than devotion to the priest. The whole history of the kingdoms of Israel and Judah clearly demonstrate the danger of an overgrown and ambitious priesthood. They oppressed the people, plotted with the enemies of the nations, and were seldom unable to have the nation conquered by some petty neighbor. They screened themselves from indignation by saying God was angry because they went after idols and therefore *sold* them into the power of their enemies to be punished. There is no doubt they were *sold*, and just as little that the priests took care to secure the *price*.

The Christian Church started without any patronage of state. At first, weak, it depended on divine protection and the force of persuasion. But not contented with this, they soon organized themselves into a separate government, formed a sort of republic, governed by their bishops. Organizing their body more artfully, cementing it more firmly, and concentrating its power, they were at length enabled to place at their head the Emperor of Rome, and to have their religion established as the religion of the Empire. Under Constantine the church triumphed, but the triumph of the church was the downfall of the empire. The emperors turned bishops, invaded with impunity the few rights left the people, and neglected the welfare of their subjects to settle the question either by the arguments of reason or the sword whether Christ was of the *same* or a *like* substance with the Father? With bishops for their ministers and ecclesiastics for counselors they hastened the Dark Ages which hung with horrid night over the world.

What are we doing now? Our clergy are at work. They have a government *separate* from the state. They have disciplined or are disciplining their followers, amassing vast funds, which they hold independent of the state; they are preparing a powerful army, under skillful leaders, and for what? Yes for what?

We think one government enough for one people. "No man can serve two masters." No man can serve the priest and be true to the civil government, at least, to a civil government like ours. The clergy, who have organized the government to which we allude and which must be termed an ecclesiastical government, have few feelings in common with the spirit of republicanism. Look at the plan of this government. It consists first of individual churches, governed by certain individuals termed elders. These elders with the church which they govern are accountable to the Presbytery, which is composed of ministers and ruling elders from the individual churches. This Presbytery is accountable for its measures to the Synod, which is composed of delegates from the several Presbyteries. The Synod in its turn to the General Assembly, which is composed, if we mistake not, of delegates from all the Synods in the United States.

From this rapid sketch it may easily be seen the Presbyterians have a very well organized government, a government which exerts a more powerful control over the true believer or is deemed more binding by him than our national and state governments. Ask the conscientious Presbyterian which of the two governments he ought to obey in case they should happen to clash, and he will readily say, the "ecclesiastical," for he is bound to obey God rather than man. Should then this ecclesiastical government have views different from those entertained by our civil government, it may easily be told on which side will be found the adherents or the members of the ecclesiastical establishment.

Now it should be borne in mind the "General Assembly" is in fact the supreme government of the Presbyterian Church. From it there is no appeal and it is difficult to conceive even that the people can overrule its measures, unless they rise en masse and say "we will not hear the clergymen of which it is composed preach." But then the clergy need only threaten the rebels with excommunication and with the fire of hell to recall them to obedience. This "Assembly" consists of individuals from all parts of the country; they can meet in secret conclave, adopt such measures as they choose. By private circulars they can fix the duty of every clergyman of their denomination, and they will never want for means to excommunicate and destroy anyone who has the boldness to disobey or to refuse to support their measures.

If a church rebels that can be excommunicated, so of a Presbytery or of a Synod. When we consider the terror there is in excommunication from the church of God to every sincere Presbyterian, we may form some idea of the control this assembly has over the church. We ought also to take into our account the habitual deference to the clergy, reverence for their persons and conviction of their importance, in saving the soul, which inspire the breast of every true believer and faithful member, then we may without much difficulty perceive it no hard matter for this Assembly to bring nearly the whole body of their church into their measures; and when the measures are to aggrandize the church we shall find none to dissent among the whole body.

No one will deny such a government as this, though professing obedience to the powers that be, is not dangerous, only when their leaders will adopt no dangerous measures or have power to effect. We may see then on what a brittle thread is suspended our liberty. Give this church the exquisite kind of leaders and sufficient power and they may dictate every measure of government, blast the reputation of every political man who refuses to bow to them. We propose to show in our future numbers that the leaders of the church mentioned have the disposition and are fast acquiring the power to control our civil government.

August 8, 1829

In our last we gave a promise that in our future numbers we would show the leaders of the orthodox party have the disposition and are fast acquiring the power to control our civil government. We are duly sensible of the high character the clergy sustain; we know full well the measure of their revenge upon the audacious spirits who presume to question the sincerity of their professions, and we would not prefer the charge we have without sufficient evidence to support it. We are hostile to no one. We should despise our self if we could descend to the meanness of fixing the odium of the measure upon any class, for the sinister purpose of gaining credit for our particular tenets. We have foresworn the spirit of sectarianism, and we despise it as much, and would oppose it as quick, in a Universalist as in a Calvinist. This we think may easily be supported from the course we have pursued and from the liberal censures we have received from many who possess the name though not the spirit of Universalism.

We respect no man merely for his profession, or indeed if any, it should be the hitherto humble but always important professions of the agriculturalist and of the mechanic. On the pursuits of these depend the very existence of society; and if we must have a privileged class, these shall have our vote to be its members. The clergy have indeed long made one of the privileged class, but it has long been the misfortune of the world to value things in an inverse ratio to their real worth. A clergyman should be respected as a man, but not as a clergyman, and he should be valued according to his real utility to the world. To us it is a matter of indifference how the world be benefited if the benefit be actually conferred, whether it be in preaching, in singing or in praying. The clergy have an interest in common with the rest of mankind. When they do not imagine they have a *separate* interest, we shall never be found opposing them; when they do, we shall deem it our duty to admonish them and bid the people "beware!"

If we turn to the history of the clergy and learn what has been their character in times past, we may also learn that to *suspect* the clergy as ambitious of obtaining an undue proportion of power is no crime and to find it really so would not contradict their established character.

With the history of the priesthood we have made our self somewhat familiar. This indeed was our duty since the world will have it, we are a priest our self, though we think not a very worthy member of the ancient and honorable fraternity. But our familiarity with their history has not increased our respect for the institution nor for its members; and certainly we have seen no cogent reason why we should wish to be under the immediate control of the clergy. We pass over the many gross impositions they have palmed upon us, the pious frauds they have committed and the thousand silly stories they have made us believe. The people in these respects have little reason to blame any but themselves; they should never have resigned their own understandings.

If we may credit anything in history we may pronounce the *accumulation of* POWER, the leading object of the clergy in all ages and in all countries of the world. We will not pretend to say the accumulation of power has been always for the purpose of their own aggrandizement, we should hope to find the majority actuated by nobler motives, but whether so or not, they have always converted the power when acquired to exalt the dignity and to secure the independence of their own order. They may have deemed that they needed power to be useful and that the greater their influence, the more beneficial they might be to the world. This indeed might be true and might have been a laudable ambition had they always been infallible and not subject to the same imperfections as the rest of mankind. But if one is killed, we do not know that it helps the matter to have lost his life from a benevolent or from a murderous intention in the one who killed him. Though this consideration may lessen the guilt it does not remove the injury; and though we may not *blame* the clergy, we have suffered and it is little matter of importance to the sufferers, to be told it was done by persons desiring to benefit them or by those wishing only to benefit themselves.

There can be no doubt many of the clerical profession have been honest men, but even the honest have not been much less injurious than the dishonest. They have given a sanctity to the institution, which has preserved it and thus prevented the abolition of the order and with it its numerous train of evils. But honest or dishonest, benevolent or malevolent, they always seem anxious to have their hand in everything which is doing, they have claimed the honor of every important discovery, of the introduction of every useful measure; and when they were unable to support the claim, or when it was notorious the measure or discovery was independent of them, they have branded it impious and persecuted the author. We might mention a Galileo, a Tycho Brahe and a host of others who have spread a halo of glory around the human race, men to whose bold and persevering efforts, the present philosopher is so deeply indebted; but they felt the weight of clerical wrath and Galileo was incarcerated for teaching, and obliged to recant, to renounce as false a doctrine which every schoolboy is now instructed to believe true.

We said the priesthood have always aimed at the accumulation of power. They have; and they have never given sleep to their eyes nor slumber to their eyelid when they had it not or until they had set some machine to work to procure it. Masters of the human heart, they have laughed when the people talked of liberty; and when the people by positive laws abolished their powers they recovered it by enforcing the law of superstition. An empire has never been enslaved but the priests have upheld the masters, produced for the tyrants aid sacred texts and pious expositions. They have contributed their share in fomenting most wars whether foreign or civil. They seldom refuse their prayers or deny the benefit of their holy rites to the king or to the officer who hearkens to their lessons, nor have they ever been sparing in their anathemas to the one who contemns God by refusing to consult them.

They preach the divine right of kings, advocate legitimacy and maintain the inviolability of the throne whenever they can thus secure a splendid establishment for themselves; and they proclaim the sovereignty of the people and justify innovation when they have anything to hope for themselves by a change. They cry down education, or seem to encourage it, just as it is deemed necessary to maintain, or to increase their influence over the human mind. Their policy has always been the same, though the measures adopted vary as circumstances require. In an age of ignorance and wonder, they performed miracles, maintained their power by confounding the reason and rendering the judgement useless. When the people became too enlightened to pay implicit confidence to all their marvelous works and marvelous stories, they anathematized knowledge and extolled ignorance as the mother of devotion. They stamped a celestial curse upon the exercise of the mental powers and offered heaven to those who would believe without reason.

When the keys of knowledge were finally wrested from them by the hands of the profane laity; when science began to blaze forth in powerful contrast to the rays of darkness shed by them, and when they could no longer lull the active mind asleep, they became learned, seemed to advocate knowledge. They placed themselves at the head of all the seminaries of learning, became tutors in the families of the opulent, and penetrating into courts they became the instructors of kings and princes. Thus they managed to control what they could not prevent nor destroy, and to turn into the channel of their own ambition the stream which might have watered the whole earth.

Nor did they encourage knowledge though they fostered education. They called the mind from the contemplation of nature, from acquiring a knowledge of things, to ponder over their venerated lore; and they wasted on the obscurity of a long since fulfilled prediction, or in acquiring a dead language of dead people who left in their history neither greatness to imitate nor wisdom to admire, the time and the powers which under more favorable circumstances would have made us acquainted with the means of improving our condition of relishing the beauties of nature and of adoring the beneficent Father of all. They taught words without ideas, made their pupils learned without knowledge and substituted praise for science in the room of science itself, and self-conceit in the place of love of true wisdom.

Wherever the priesthood has been predominant the people have been enslaven; the mind has been deprived of its vigor, bound in the shackles of a senseless superstition, it has been incapable of exertion. Vice has been encouraged. Donations to the church for the benefit of the clergy has supplied the place of virtue, and atoned for a life of crime. Zeal in defending the absurdities and immoralities of the predominant religion has been deemed sufficient to open the gates of heaven and give a claim to the joys of the blest. Proffering peace they have given us the sword; professing to beat the sword into the ploughshare and the spear into the pruning hook, they have converted the implements of husbandry into the instruments of war; promising a heaven hereafter they have given us a hell on earth; and claiming to be the ambassadors of God and the messengers of love, they have stirred up the demon discord, alienated the affections of kindred, invaded the sacred apartments of domestic life, destroyed conjugal, filial and fraternal affection; trampled upon the rights of conscience and cursed, in the name of God, all who have not pronounced them a blessing to the human race and given them tithes of all they possess.

Arrogant in their pretensions, claiming exemption from the common frailties of humanity, and familiar intercourse with the invisible God, they have demanded implicit obedience and heaped the whole mountain of their vengeance upon the inquisitive spirit who presumed to enquire the warrant of their authority or the propriety of their conduct. Long as they could, they smothered the desire for knowledge and that Christendom is now enlightened they say is owing to them; though the most careless reader of history must know they persecuted with a relentless spirit the philosophers and reformers to whom we are indebted for modern improvements. Such has been the character of the clergy and such the evils they have heaped upon the human family; such their general features, wherever found or whatever name they bear, Pagans, Jews or Christians, Mussulmans or Brahmans, followers of Zoroaster or worshiper of the Lama, and if there be any difference if one class be worse than another, the palm of the greatest *evil is fairly due the Christian*.

Such is their character. We are at loss to reconcile the discrepancies we find between their professions and their practice. With the best profession on earth or to be found even in heaven, their practice has even disgraced his majesty of hell by being charged to him. Had they come to us as men and acknowledged themselves of like passions with the rest of us, having the same imperfections and liable to the same errors, we could have passed over their inconsistencies, by supposing they had mistaken the best means to make the world virtuous; but when they come as chosen servants of God we are confounded. To call them honest but ignorant, would be to accuse Jehovah of having made an unwise choice, and to pronounce them knowing but dishonest, seems not much better, and yet we know of no other alternative.

Such having uniformly been the character of the clergy, such having been their constant aim and practice, and such the abuses they have tolerated, that we ask, did we wrong to suspect? Did we wrong to bid our readers watch! But we have more than suspicion, we have more than *cause* for suspicion, we have evidence to our mind clear and satisfactory. The orthodox clergy have engaged in a vast enterprise; a mighty project is conceived and all the energies of the order are in requisition to bring it forth. Whatever it may turn out to be, we have seen enough to convince us it was unholy in its conception and if executed will be ungodly in its influence.

Our readers will perceive this portrait is designed to show what power the clergy have heretofore aimed at and the evils they have inflicted. They will from this view admit it is *possible* for the clergy now to aim at similar power, and if they obtain it, what surety have we that they will not bring similar evils in their train? We have not yet dismissed this subject. Facts are to be laid before our readers and facts which will make them enquire, "where is the spirit which achieved our independence?" shall be laid before them.

August 22, 1829

But few facts are required to establish what has been asserted respecting the disposition of the clergy; if they are suspected of aiming at the supreme control of all matters, whether of church or state, a slight view of their profession will render it impossible to separate this disposition from their own views and feelings in reference to their duty.

The clerical office is different in kind from all others. The clergyman does not receive his appointment from man; he bows to no human tribunal; he acknowledges no human laws as equal to those he is entrusted to enforce; pleading the appointment of the Almighty as the warrant of his authority; he holds, as he imagines, the laws of God, laws which all earth and all heaven are bound to obey. He stands commissioned from the court of heaven, a court to which all earthly courts must bow. Placed thus high above all human authority, all civil governments must be the ministers of his will; and all kings, rulers and magistrates, must be his waiting boys.

The clergyman fancies himself the ambassador of God; clothed with divine authority, he comes wrapped in the dignity of heaven; he claims all the submission due to the majesty of his master, and all the attention and deference due to the sacredness and the high importance of his mission. He comes not to negotiate peace between contending rivals, but, as the minister of the lawful sovereign who has regained his throne to proclaim terms to defeated rebels; not to persuade, but to command them to ground the weapons of their rebellion and to return to their duty; to submit themselves to their rightful sovereign against whom they had rebelled.

He considers all men in a state of rebellion and that they must support the church of God before they can be treated as lawful subjects. His message is, "Children of men! Hear the words of the Almighty King. You have rebelled against your sovereign, you have leagued with his enemies, you have attempted to wrest from his hand the scepter of command, you have labored to dethrone him, and you have trampled his laws under your feet. In this state of rebellion you are entitled to no mercy, are deserving no compassion. But the King, your legitimate sovereign, is no tyrant. He has declared your death, but he will spare you if you will submit; if you accept the offers he makes, you are reprieved, you are pardoned. Throw down your arms; trust yourself to his mercy; support the church which he has planted as a rallying point for all who will return to their duty, and all shall be well; flock to this standard, the standard of the rightful Lord and of the true God, and your rebellion shall be forgotten, your sins blotted out."

From this message, which every clergyman feels himself commissioned to deliver, it is evident that to support the church is the duty of all, as the only sure test of their obedience to God. From this we learn that the church is deemed superior to the state, and certainly its officers superior to the officers of civil government. All are bound to obey God, rulers as well as people; to obey God, we must support the church; and as the clergy are the officers of the church, as they are the ministers of God, the interpreters of his will, the ones he makes use of in his intercourse with the human family, therefore, by a slight change of terms, the whole comes to this conclusion, to obey God is to support the church; to obey, or to support the church, is to consult the will of the clergy, and to yield implicitly obedience to their commands.

Such is the dignity and high authority with which the clergyman fancies himself clothed that it is impossible he should deem it proper for him to sanction the measures adopted by a rebel government, and in his estimation every government is rebellious that does not support what he believes the cause of God. With these feelings, can he deem it wrong to advise those rebel governors or rulers of their duty? Or *compel* them to perform it when they will not be persuaded? Certainly not. He is appointed God's vice-regent on earth; it is his duty to be faithful to his master and he would feel self-condemned should he neglect to make governments as well as people obey the will of heaven.

And why should it be considered strange that clergymen should have the disposition with which they are charged, when the very warrant they plead, when the charter of their order imperiously requires them to exercise it? It would be strange, indeed, if the confidants of the Almighty, persons acquainted even with his *secret* will—individuals whom he has called and qualified with the effusion of his spirit to lead men to heaven, and to be the instruments of their eternal salvation it would be strange, indeed, that they should have no desire to direct us in our duty here, and instruct us in what relates to this world as well as what relates to another; and it might seem strange we should distrust those who enjoy the confidence of the Omniscient God, or that we should obey them less in reference to time than to eternity.

The message of the clergyman has been stated; let it be more particularly examined. According to all his preaching, the first duty of the people is to "seek the kingdom of God." This, by a liberal translation, is the "church militant." The people must take little thought for this world, they must fix their thoughts on eternity, remember this is not their abiding place, that there is in eternity a blessed city and that it should be their principal object to enquire by what means they can receive in that happy place a mansion of felicity for themselves. Towards this object as the magnet of the soul it is said every desire should point; and to gain it, no sacrifice should be deemed too great—no, not the loss of a right eye, a right hand, or even of life itself.

As the means to gain this, everybody knows, the church must be supported. This being the temple of God, whatever gift made to it, whatever obedience is paid to its mandates, God accepts as if done to himself, and will amply reward us for it in the eternal world. It is therefore we are commanded to support the church. It is the visible glory of God; by supporting it we glorify God. Hence it is, we are to give to the church and to give as we shall wish we had given when we come to die. Hence the frequency with which the clergy dwell on this theme; and hence, too, the liberality which the pious and the devout and the sinner about to die, anxious to atone for a misspent life, manifest in their donations. For the whole of man's duty maybe summed up in a word, "support the church."

But this duty is binding on men in their collective as well as in their individual capacity; on rulers as well as upon the ruled; upon all in authority, as well as upon those who must obey; and all authority is from God, and as all rulers hold their power as a trust from him, they are bound to exercise it according to his will, to use all for his glory. Now, as the clergy are the appointed interpreters of the divine will, and as they claim to be sole directors in all matters relating to his glory, the whole resolves itself into this conclusion, "All rulers are bound to obey what the clergy tell them is the will of God, and to do what *they* declare will be for his glory."

Hence it is easy to perceive that the profession of the clergy naturally generates the disposition with which they are charged; and it requires no peculiar intellectual acuteness to discover that when a clergyman has a selfish or ambitious spirit, he may hide under the duties of his profession the worst and the most dangerous designs. It has already been shown that the clergy have never been wanting in the disposition to make the sanctity of their profession subservient to individual aggrandizement; and it seems proper they should exhibit strong proofs of a reformation before they can make the judicious believe they will not conduct in the same manner again. If honest in his profession, the priest must have the disposition with which he is charged; he cannot think it wrong for him to control civil government for he is above it, and the glory of God requires him to do it; if dishonest, nothing better can be expected, and none who have any discernment will consider themselves more safe.

Such are the clergy, such their profession; let their conduct now pass in review. The last 25 years have been a busy time with the priesthood, years of great activity; of great mental agitation, years replete with danger, and it is hoped they will not prove barren of instruction. Every engine seems to have been put in motion; every machine which clerical ingenuity could construct has been put in operation; and every method which could reinstate the clergy in their lost possessions, and reestablish an odious hierarchy, degrading to the name of religion, and disgraceful to the people who will bear it has been adopted and with no small success.

It will be unnecessary to run over all their arts and machinations. As one proof of their wishes, and strongly presumptive of their designs, our readers are referred to a CIRCULAR which the orthodox handed round among those of their own stamp. It is three or four years since it found its way into the public journals and we are satisfied its authenticity is beyond a doubt and its genuineness no subject of dispute. The orthodox are charged with it and they have never, to our knowledge, denied it. A few extracts will show its spirit and its object.

After touching lightly upon the apparent union which then existed among several denominations of Christians, upon the *brotherly love*, upon the awakened zeal and extended religious impressions occasioned by Theological Seminaries, Bible, Missionary, and Tract Societies, and the probable blessings which were to flow from the establishment of the National Tract Society at New York under the united care and superintendence of the most distinguished clergy of various denominations, it proceeds:

"From this view of sentiment and feeling, students of different persuasions can meet and read the same religious authors, in the same Institutions, under the same Professors for the acquisition of Theological knowledge. Thus, while errors and corruptions are detected and exposed, will correct and orthodox religious sentiments be promulgated and defended by learned Students employed in the same holy and divine calling, for one common purpose. It is by these means, we see so many of our first men becoming converts, more and more to the Christian faith, and devoted to the interests of Bible, Missionary, and Tract Societies. At the seat of the General Government, we see Congress electing Chaplains in rotation to offer up prayers for the success of their deliberations. While we witness such concert among the higher orders of society, as to religious worship, with a favorable disposition to the distribution of Religious Tracts, properly composed, we have a good right to conclude it will *issue in a wise National Creed*, and that the most pious and enlightened men in our country will see the impropriety of sending out Missionaries and Divines to preach the Word of Life with discordant and conflicting views."

"This pious unanimity and zeal will be apt to produce its own temporal reward. See the want of it in the late war, when the influence of many disaffected Clergymen was powerfully and successfully exerted to paralyze the energy and operations of government. They were not then allowed to feel and enjoy the benefits which their religious labors might confer on their country Since, their station has become more respected; the most respectable layman feels himself honored to join the Presbyterian and Baptist, the Episcopalian and Methodist, assembled together to deliberate on the best means which their joint councils may suggest for the extension of religious knowledge. The Clerical robe is becoming less the theme of scoffers, and more and more a proud and honorable badge to him, who, for his Theological attainments is entitled to it."

"By enlisting moral and religious, and consequently numerical force, in the cause of Religion, all the opposition of infidelity will be borne down and overpowered. Until those collisions and conflicts of opinion, growing out of the same Christian belief, shall be annihilated or greatly abated, our country in times of distress and danger may be divided and distracted by religious feuds and quarrels. The business of Government ought, as much as possible, and may be practicable, to produce unanimity and concord, both in our civil and religious institutions."

"As sure as the force of circumstances produces order and system in the world, and as sure as there is a tendency and gravitation in natural and physical bodies towards each other, so sure, in the moral and religious world, will the lesser bodies or sects be attracted to the largest. Among refractory and apostate spirits, opposition may be expected, *but it will be made to yield to the power and influence of evangelical truth.*"

"A reference to the state of Christianity in England, furnishes an ample solution to this position. A great majority of the people there are reconciled to the established order, and unite in giving their support to the State. I do not say this because I am an Episcopalian, for I am not; but to enforce the necessity of unanimity in the prevailing religion of the State; or, of making it *National in its form, tendency, and operation;* since that may be considered orthodox, which has the most adherents, who are made so by birth, education, or accident; as each sect pretends, from Scripture, to derive proof to its system. It is the force of circumstances we have been speaking of, which has produced the established religion of England, the choice of its people, and which is necessary to its peace, the security of the Government, and the strength of the nation."

"What a beneficial influence would it have on public sentiment and feeling, if the index of its character should be distinguished by a more *national costume*, which would be solemn and imposing, and such as would secure to the sacerdotal character that reverence which is due to it. The emblems of worship, properly prepared and arranged, and approved of by a majority of the nation, might be made to correspond with it in other respects. Will it be believed, that thus qualified, any of the leading sects of this country would repel the *sanction of the government* if offered to them? Are the professors of worship in England to be, and would those in this country, preferring a different mode, be consigned to perdition for differing from each other?"

"From what has been said we may rationally conclude, that a zealous cooperation among the most respectable religious sects in our country is tending to a consolidation, in the principles, doctrines, and forms of worship, so desirable to every true Christian, and which may eventually bring about a Conventional arrangement as to a settled form. These anticipations may be further realized, in securing from Congress an appropriation of a portion of the public lands, to a limited, and yet sufficient number of the Clergy, and for a well defined course of Education. This is prospective, and those who are fastidious about it, may gradually sacrifice their prejudices and scruples, which will be likely to be dissipated by the light of religious knowledge, on the altar of harmony and concord."

September 5, 1829

But few remarks are here required to place the extracts made in our last in their true light. The authors of the circular seem confident the various measures which they mention, and which the orthodox clergy advocated with characteristic zeal at that time, and which they cherish with all of maternal fondness at this time—the authors seem confident these measures will result "in a wise national creed." This seems to have been at the date of the circular the object of their wishes, and we shall soon proceed to show their disposition has not changed.

By forming this combination, or by bringing about this consolidation of the principal religious denominations, and thus enlisting "numerical force" on their side, "all the opposition from infidelity will be borne down and overpowered." Now this term "infidelity" is a word of vague import, very different in its meaning at Rome than at Constantinople. It means, however, in religious parlance, whatever opposes the orthodox, or predominant religion in the country in which it is used. It is the chief weapon of the orthodox, the principal argument used by the clergy to silence those who are doubtful about the propriety of their measures. It is thrown as a mark and the person to whom it is applied is designated to destruction, or as deserving the abhorrence of those who love the clergy. Still, to an enlightened mind, the application of the term is a badge of honor; as in fact the word infidel denotes a person who prefers honesty to hypocrisy, and liberty and mental freedom with the few to slavery with the many. The clergy would overpower all infidels, stop their voices, and prevent them from enjoying those rights for which our fathers fought, bled and died.

This topic must not be so soon dismissed. There is a large class of our population, aye, and the very bone and marrow if you please of our population, who study rather the ordinary concerns of life than theology; who, having the interest of their country at heart, have not found leisure to attend to all the nice distinctions, invisible to all but theological eyes, in which religion is made to consist. These persons, marking the contending factions of religionists, the general uncertainty of all their speculations, adopt a moral practice for themselves; or, at least, treat the great topics of dispute among zealots with indifference, and sometimes, perhaps, with silent contempt. These men, heretofore, have been our public spirited citizens; they have been our warm hearted patriots; the defenders of our country, the framers of our constitution; our magistrates, representatives, and presidents. Under this description is ranked a Franklin, a Jefferson, a Madison, and by far the larger number who are conspicuous in our history, a large share of those whose virtues have rendered our republic illustrious, who have pointed out to her the path of glory.

But these persons, by the orthodox, would be accounted infidels because they professed but little and practiced much. These persons, by the religionists, are held up as mournful proof of the depravity of human nature, as men with superb talents, but destitute of grace; and who, with all their excellencies, with all their virtues, with all the utility of their lives, are now probably suffering the gnawings of that worm which never dies. Instead of teaching the youth to imitate their virtues and their usefulness, the clergy tell them to avoid their practices, and to look with horror upon their want of zeal for the church.

But these persons are persons of this description, who have filled the public offices in the gift of a free people with so much dignity, with so much usefulness and glory to their country; are to be "borne down and overpowered," compelled to become sectarians before they can hold any public office, hypocrites before they can be trusted with the public good. Such a course would soon stamp our republican government with infamy; would, to the no small joy of all crowned heads, overthrow our free institutions, and rear a detested monarchy on the ruins of liberty. It were indecent to express our abhorrence of this plan, or the indignation it must excite in every enlightened, in every patriotic bosom. But such, fellow citizens, is the avowed object of our idolized priests, to effect which they declare themselves at work. We would invoke the shades of the martyrs of our revolution to frown indignant upon such measures, and upon the shameless avowal of them. We may not be endangered, but alas, we may feel too secure. There is something rotten, there is something wrong, when a class of men, so numerous and so powerful as the orthodox clergy, dare avow such sentiments, or when they can even embrace them.

The clergy seem anxious to be distinguished by a "national costume," which, *"solemn and imposing,"* will secure the "sacerdotal character" its dignity. Not willing to trust to the naked beauty of religion, and rest their dignity on the utility of their lives, on the benevolence of their characters, they are ambitious of a *dress* which shall extort unmerited respect, and give them undue influence which they despair of obtaining by the simplicity of their doctrines, or from the beneficence of their practice.

"These anticipations," they think, "will be realized in securing an appropriation of a portion of public lands, to a limited and yet a sufficient number of clergy, and to a well defined course of education." There is no difficulty in comprehending this sentence. If the clergy were always equally intelligible, the world would not be disgraced by religious contentions, nor the church deformed with incomprehensible dogmas. Congress has the care of large tracts of public lands, some very valuable, and almost indescribably excellent. These lands would make a fine patrimony for the church.

Reader, how do you think the clergy expect to grasp these lands? Such men as Col. Johnson would not be too ready to bestow such valuable presents upon a class of men who have abused him and all other patriots, who have disturbed the ashes of the dead and branded with reproach those who gained our independence. But think ye of no feasible plan? Let none be members of Congress but those who are devoted to the clergy, none but those who depend on the orthodox for their votes; let none but these have charge of our public lands and how long would it require to obtain a law appropriating a part or all of these lands to the service of the church? If the orthodox could govern the polls, these men would fear no public censure, they would be supported in their unhallowed measures.

Have not the orthodox a plan adopted; have they not avowed it their intention to support no man for office, unless he is sound in the faith? Whether so or not, what we have alleged shows very clearly the orthodox are determined to receive some state patronage; that they are laboring to gain for themselves an establishment that will interfere with the rights of our citizens; that they are laboring to accomplish an object which menaces with death every spark of genuine liberty. True, we are told the people of these United States are too well enlightened to ever submit to this. It may be so. We pray God the result may prove it so. But of one thing we feel confident, that if we remain inactive, boasting how well we are enlightened, we may regret that we had not deemed ourselves more ignorant.

The disposition which we charged to the clergy appears from what has been said evidently theirs. But we have more facts to offer; language which speaks, or should speak, in a voice of thunder to every freeman. We shall present our readers with the part of a famous sermon of Doct. E. S. Ely, of Philadelphia, preached on the anniversary of our independence, deemed an appropriate discourse for our nation's jubilee. The extracts we shall make have been already before our readers, but they should be repeated till every one gets them by heart; till every manly principle of his bosom burns with honest indignation at the unhallowed spirit which dictated them. They form a link in our chain of evidences and ought not to be left out. Had the author of the sermon a conscience and did he believe in the awful day of judgment about which he preaches, he would tremble lest this sermon should rise up against him and condemn him to that hell to which he so liberally dooms the infidel and the heretical. But God is merciful and we rejoice to think that even Ezra Stiles Ely will yet become holy and happy.

It is only necessary to remark, Dr. Ely is one of the leading members of the Presbyterian church, being standing clerk of their general assembly, and the one often pitched upon to write and publish their reports. No censure has been passed upon him for this publication by the church to which he belongs, though that church has not been sparing in its denunciations upon those who have condemned his sentiments. From the high standing of the man and the general approbation of his party, together with many other circumstances not necessary to mention now, we consider the sermon official, as authorized, at least, bearing the implied sanction of the whole Presbyterian order in the United States. We would not be uncharitable nor would we degrade charity to mere blindness and credulity; but here follow the extracts, they may speak for themselves.

"Let it be distinctly stated and fearlessly maintained in the first place, that every member of this Christian nation, from the highest to the lowest, ought to serve the Lord with fear, and yield his sincere homage to the Son of God. Every ruler *should* be an avowed, and a sincere friend of Christianity He should know and believe the doctrines of our holy religion, and act in conformity with its precepts. This he *ought to* do; because as a man he is required to serve the Lord; and as a public ruler, he is called upon by divine authority 'to kiss the Son.'"

"Our rulers, like any other members of the community who are under law to God as rational being, and under law to Christ, since they have the light of divine revelation, ought to search the Scriptures, assent to the truth, profess faith in Christ, keep the Sabbath holy to God, pray in private, and in the domestic circle, attend on the public ministry of the word, be baptized, and celebrate the Lord's Supper. None of our rulers have the consent of their Maker that they should be pagans, Socinians, Mussulmans, deists, the opponents of Christianity."

"In other words, our Presidents, Secretaries of the Government, Senators, and other Representatives in Congress, Governors of States, Judges, State Legislators, Justices of the Peace, and city Magistrates, are just as much bound as any other persons in the United States, to be *orthodox* in their faith, and virtuous, and religious in their whole deportment. They may no more lawfully be bad husbands, wicked parents, men of *heretical opinions,* or men of dissolute lives, than the obscure individual who would be sent to Bridewell for his blasphemy and debauchery."

"God, my hearers, requires a Christian faith, a *Christian profession,* and a Christian practice of all our public men; and we as Christian citizens ought, by the publication of our opinions to require the same."

"Secondly—Since it is the duty of all our rulers to serve the Lord and kiss the Son of God, it must be most manifestly the duty of all our Christian fellow citizens to honor the Lord Jesus Christ and promote Christianity by electing and supporting as public officers the friends of our blessed Savior. If all the truly religious men of our nation would be punctual and persevering in their endeavors to have good men chosen to fill all our national and state offices of honor, power and trust, their weight would be soon felt by politicians; and those who care little for the religion of the Bible, would for their own interest, consult the reasonable wishes of the great mass of Christians throughout our land.

"I propose, fellow citizens, a new sort of union, or, if you please, *a Christian party in politics,* which I am exceedingly desirous all good men in our country should join; not *by subscribing a constitution* and the formation of a new society, but by adopting, avowing, and determining to act upon truly religious principles in all civil matters."

"If three or four of the most numerous denominations of Christians in the United States, the Presbyterians, the Baptists, the Methodists and Congregationalists for instance, should act upon this principle, our country would never be dishonored with an *avowed Infidel* in her national cabinet or capitol. The *Presbyterians* alone could bring *half a million of electors* into the field, in opposition to any known advocate of deism, Socinianism, or any other species of avowed hostility to the truth of Christianity. If to the denominations above named we add the members of the Protestant Episcopal Church in our country, the electors of these five classes of true Christians, united in the sole requisition of *apparent* friendship to Christianity in every candidate for office whom they will support, *could govern every public election* in our country, without infringing in the least upon the charter of our civil liberties."

"It will be objected that my plan of a truly Christian party in politics will make hypocrites. We are not answerable for their hypocrisy if it does."

"It will be objected, moreover, that my scheme of voting on political elections according to certain fixed religious principles, will create jealousies among the different denominations of Christians. But why should it? Our rulers which we have elected are of some, or of no religious sect. If they are of no religious denomination, they belong to the party of Infidels. If they are of any of the denominations of true Christians, it is better, in the judgment of all true Christians, that they should be of that one company than in the company of Infidels."

"I am free to avow, that other things being equal, I would prefer for my chief magistrate, and judge, and ruler, a sound Presbyterian; and every candid religionist will make the same declaration concerning his own persuasion; but I would prefer a religious and moral man, of any one of the truly Christian sects, to any man destitute of religious principle and morality."

"Let us all be Christian politicians, and govern ourselves by supreme love to our blessed Master, whether we unite in prayers or in the election of our civil rulers. Let us be as conscientiously religious at the polls as in the pulpit, or house of worship."

"Let us never support by our votes any immoral man, or any known condemner of any of the fundamental doctrines of Christ for any office; and least of all for the Presidency of these United States. Let us elect men who dare to acknowledge the Lord Jesus Christ for their Lord in their public documents. Which of our Presidents have ever done this? It would pick no infidel's pocket, and break no Jew's neck if our President should be so singular as to let it be known that he is a *Christian* by his Messages, and an advocate for the Deity of Christ by his personal preference of a Christian temple to a Socinian conventicle. It would be no violation of our national constitution, if our members of Congress should quit reading of newspapers and writing letters on the Lord's day, at least during public worship, in the Hall of Representatives."

"We are a Christian nation; we have a right to demand that all our rulers in their conduct shall conform to Christian morality; and if they do not, it is the duty and privilege of Christian freemen to make a new and a better election."

September 19, 1829

The sentiments contained in the extracts from Dr. Ely, inserted in our last, have obtained no small notoriety. When compared with the object stated in the "Circular," we have noticed, little doubt is left as to the real object of the Orthodox. Their intentions become obvious and their plans are exhibited in bold relief. They proposed an amalgamation of the principal religious denominations from which it is hoped will result a "wise national creed." And to maintain this creed, they express themselves desirous of procuring "a portion of the public lands" for the benefit of the clergy. That is in plain English, our orthodox friends wish to fix the support of the clergy upon a solid basis to obtain for them sufficient state patronage to have them paid from the national treasury.

Our government, instead of being a civil institution must become the pillar of the church and employ its influence and resources in the maintenance of ecclesiastical discipline. The government, indeed, is not required to say what religion it will support, but it is to bow to the most numerous and the most influential party. This is evident from the whole tenor of the orthodox logic. They complained of the committee in Senate, because they did not grant the prayer of the petitioners respecting the Sabbath Mail. They blamed the committees, on the ground that the petitioners had the majority of the Republic on their side. Hence on their ground, when the majority of the people ask government to aid their religion, government must do it.

We ask not, say the people, government to decide what religion we shall have, but to protect the religion which we have. Protect the religion of the minority? No. But the religion which the majority have said they will have. Hence it is plain to what class of the clergy, the public funds must be appropriated: not to all, but to a limited, yet sufficient number of the orthodox, and that sect may be considered orthodox who have the greatest numerical force. On this ground, the authors of the

"Circular" would have religion established and by so doing "all opposition from *infidelity* would be borne down and overpowered."

No doubt such an object may seem very desirable for some, but to those who may chance to be of the minority, it may not seem worthy of all praise. But how is it to be accomplished? Our Government, say those religionists, is bound to obey the will of its constitution for that is the will of the majority. Governments like ours can be molded with perfect ease when the people are rightly instructed and are properly marshaled to the work. The majority of the people may say "we will have such a religion," no one can prohibit them. They may say they will have a certain sum paid to the preachers of that religion, and the national treasury must pay it; the people are sovereigns. Only one thing is wanting, that is to have those who manage the government prepare to adopt the measures. Now for Dr. Ely's plan.

"I propose fellow citizens a new party in politics—a Christian party." What is this for? Reader canst thou not perceive? Know then the orthodox want the government to aid them, to patronize their plans and to give them the public lands. Infidels would not do this. It is therefore necessary to have none but *Christians* elected to any office, yea more, none but orthodox Christians, who are ready to aid the orthodox clergy in the support of their party. We will have a Christian party in politics, we will elect none but of a certain faith, and those we elect must understand we elect them for the promotion of our religion. They must know their duty is to aid our plans as a sort of compromise for their election.

Such is the plan. Americans, when you submit to this, when you ask a religious *profession* of your representatives, your legislators, judges and other officers, you may expect Salem witchcraft to return and the period of hanging Quakers and banishing Baptists will again come round. You may think this day is far distant. Be it so. But God in mercy avert it from our children and grant the Beast, which preyed upon our ancestors, may not live to devour our children.

While on this subject, the memory of the past rises, crowded with mournful images, pictures appalling to less sensitive hearts than ours strike the vision; a warning voice from other days comes on each breeze. Sad as the funeral dirge sighing through the cypress grove, it bids us "beware." The hallowed name of religion may become the password to death and the zeal, which the profession of piety consecrates, may be fed with unholy fires and burn to the lowest hell. Cold is the heart that does not love the great Author of nature, unfeeling and unrefined is the sensibility that does not receive its highest bliss at the altar of the Most High; but colder still and more dead to feeling the one which can even contemplate, without "trembling alive all o'er," the return of priestly ignorance and clerical misrule. The clergy have reigned. They have, seated upon the thrones of the Caesars, made their power felt far beyond the farthest limits of the Roman name. And then "darkness was visible" relieved only by the fires which lit the victims to their tomb, Is that period to return? Is that gloom to be spread over our sun lighted land? It may be so.

But why declaim? Why call up the melancholy picture of other times? Why weep over the woes endured by generations gone? Whoever knew priestcraft softened with tears or mellowed by visions of sorrow? Priestcraft! Offspring of hell! Relentless as death, all devouring as the grave, with an imagined warrant from God stalks forth with the spirit of the devil and spares neither age, sex nor condition; neither vice nor virtue, nor aught good or bad, dear to the heart or indifferent, that may grapple with its plans of universal dominion. If defeated, it sits like Marius on the ruins of Carthage, smiling in scorn, writhing its lips with revenge and planning new scenes of murder and devastation. If successful, it breathes with the withering siroc and fattens on the sighs, tears and woes of its enslaved victims. A heartless monster! Hoping to reach heaven by filling up mountains of wretchedness, or if doomed to hell, anxious to involve a universe in its ruin. But enough. It was in honor of this monster Dr. Ely preached his sermon, and it is for this, their God, the orthodox clergy are laboring, and at his shrine they pay their morning and evening devotions. Deluded wretches, let them worship on, but God forbid any more should be seduced to join in their unholy worship!

We need look no further. Dr. Ely has exhibited the plan. He has told us for whom we must vote and he has declared it his anxious desire to form a party, which shall obey the directions he has given. That party is forming; his principles are being reduced to practice, and who can tell the results? Do they lack power? Our future numbers will consider this enquiry. Sabbath schools must pass in review and we shall glance at the Mammoth Bible Society, and other misnamed benevolent institutions and ask, how large are their funds? How fast are they increasing? Who has the control of these funds? And what warrant have we that these funds will be judiciously managed and properly expended? Reader, turn not idly from this subject, man may "steal the livery of the Court of Heaven to serve the Devil in."

Equality

September 1829

  The man who is capable of looking on human society with the eye of a philosopher, who can compare causes and effects, trace the secret springs of actions, and determine the influence of prevailing institutions, will readily perceive the cause of the crime and misery now prevalent is chiefly owing to the inequality which exists among us and which almost every institution tends to perpetuate and increase.

  Perhaps it is not possible to bring all to the same standard while individual enterprise is allowed, and allowed it must be unless we would destroy society; it is hardly to be expected that all will be of the same size, that all will be equally successful. But it were a mournful truth, a depressive thought, to say nothing can be done, that we cannot lessen the distance between the parts or classes as they now exist. It were thinking meanly of man, meanly of his social powers, to say he is susceptible of no better state of society than the present. It were indeed paying little attention to past experience, as well as turning blindly from what may be seen in almost every exertion of which we are capable.

  There is no natural difference between the members of society. The child of the poor is not, when born, more ignorant or more helpless that the child of the rich. In acquiring knowledge, the children of the opulent and powerful are not more apt, nor do they learn with greater ease or distinguish with greater accuracy than those of an opposite description. The ornament of science has often been the child of poverty, and the lower classes of society have yielded as great geniuses as the world can boast. There is not then, in the physical or intellectual powers of mankind, any reason why one class should be oppressed, why one should be called the higher and the other the lower. Nor, indeed, is there anything in their moral natures which should continue the inequality which now exists. The reason why we should despair of a reform, if despair we must, is found somewhere else.

The reason is not abstruse; it is on the surface, and the stupefied may understand and the blind almost see it. No matter how society became thus divided. It is divided, and we may see what perpetuates this division.

We have a privileged class which sprung up during ignorant ages. Time has confirmed their power and long habit has made us conclude we cannot live without them. We have the clergy, a nonproductive class, who, in this country, consume annually twenty millions of dollars. These are employed to do what every man could do a great deal better for himself. They watch the interests of religion. But religion is a thing between the individual and his God; and it is much better for the individual to go directly to the throne of grace and pray for himself than it is to hire a priest to do it for him. For whatever we would have well done, we should do ourselves and not employ a hireling. But this class obtain a livelihood from their calling; consequently they will do all they can to flatter themselves and those who support them; their order is necessary.

Another class, an unproductive class, in many respects a privileged class, live upon the earnings of others, and trample upon those who support them, the lawyers. These men are but a moth to us. They professionally pretend to aid individuals in obtaining justice; but by the uncertainty they introduce into the laws, by the ambiguous manner in which laws themselves are framed, the aid becomes doubtful, for it is no sign a man has the right because he succeeds, or that he is wrong because he failed. Laws are always an evil, the less we have of them the better. We send men to our legislature, we pay them high wages; they frame or enact at every session a large number of laws, drawn up with that peculiar ambiguity that, without a seven years study, the most talented cannot hope to understand them. Instead of taking common sense and natural justice for our guide, we attempt to shape our actions according to these unintelligible laws, get into a dispute and spend our whole fortune to pay the law to help us out.

Now if this class were all employed in cultivating the earth and the legislators were compelled to *fast* till they had transacted their business, or until they learned old laws should be just before they made new ones, that old duties should be defined before additional ones are imposed, we might hope for something valuable. The best law is a high moral feeling and the best lawyer is he who can best draw forth the moral and intellectual faculties of the youth. Law never made a man honest, but it has made many a man bankrupt not only in wealth but in integrity and in respectability. Let laws be simplified, be reduced in number and always founded on natural justice; let legislators follow the plough and lawyers obtain their fee by pursuing the employment of the agriculturalist or the mechanic, and we should soon see crime diminishing and equality prevailing. But the lawyer will oppose this innovation.

Perhaps the inequality which reigns between the rich and the poor is the most destructive to peace and virtue. One man has a capital, he may employ it in agriculture; he finds the poor, sets them to work; if their number be great and nobody else to employ them, he reduces their wages so low that though they may live they can never hope to be otherwise than poor. These laborers have families and thus the number which must depend on the rich for employment and on the wages he may please to give for a support is constantly increasing, and the wages will diminish in proportion to the number of the laborers. Hence it is the laboring class of community are soon reduced to the lowest state of wretchedness.

A man has some hundred thousand dollars. He erects a large manufacturing establishment. The market is empty. The tariff or something else excludes foreign competition; demand is high; he employs a large number of laborers, men, women and children; gives decent wages and still finds it profitable. Others have also a capital; other establishments are erected; the market is soon supplied; thence follows a reduction of wages. The laborer must work more hours, produce more to obtain the same support. But this greater production gluts the market, a surplus is produced, and this reduces the wages still lower; and, it will be found, the more the laborer produces the poorer he grows. This seems a hard case, that plenty should increase poverty a surplus should produce want. Yet so it is. The inequality which exists tends to perpetuate and increase itself.

But, there is a greater evil not yet mentioned. While one class labors and the other enjoys, the laboring class will always be considered the lowest. A new scale of worth will be introduced, the reverse of what it should be. A man will be respected in proportion to his idleness. Hence, the laborer learns to loathe his labor, he is impatient of his employment, he is anxious to be rich that he may be idle and be respected. Now spring the temptations to crime. The struggle to be rich commences; all ties are forgotten; all principles of honor and morality are abandoned. Fair means or foul, the intention is to be rich. Some perhaps are stimulated by want to relieve themselves, others anxious to place themselves on a level with those who consider themselves above them. Crime becomes frequent, jails and gibbets are in requisition, &c.

This theme need not be pursued. The remarks made elicit the inequality which exists, they show the evil which flows from it and also that it is for the apparent interest of the higher classes to promote it. Something ought to be done. Political doctors manage this subject very poorly and religious doctors still worse. Religious teachers tell the poor to be content for if poor here they shall be rich hereafter. Political teachers devise means to increase the surplus produce, blindly imagining abundance will remove the evil when in fact we already produce more than enough. We may prohibit the manufactures of other nations and this may afford temporary relief, but it is only an opiate that may calm but cannot remove the disease.

Equality must be introduced. Every man should produce for himself or everyone should be engaged in some branch of productive industry. This would secure to each one a competence. In those branches which the individual cannot master, the principle of cooperation may be introduced. But there should be no such thing as a laboring class and consuming class, one separate from the other. Secure to every man the products of his own labor and the evil will disappear. These are only a few hints thrown out on which we intend to enlarge as we have leisure, particularly to point out how the proposed plan may be carried into effect.

Church and State II

November 1831

"Church and State." Start not, gentle reader, at these appalling words. We are not now about to make a set attack on the orthodox. We have heretofore given an exposé of what we deemed the dangerous movements of a certain class of divines and some of their adherents; we now propose to make some observations, which may be worthy the consideration of those who profess to be the advocates of liberal sentiments.

There is need of caution in our charges upon any class of people. Charges of the appalling nature of those which are made against the orthodox should not be thoughtlessly uttered, nor repeated on slight evidence. We gain nothing when we accuse our neighbor of that of which he is not guilty; we gain nothing when we charge him with crimes which cannot be proved; we gain nothing by vague declamation and continual accusation. This is, in some measure, a matter-of-fact age; and we should be careful that we make no charge that is not substantiated by clear and specific proofs.

This is an age of great fermentation; men's minds are too much agitated, and it does not behoove the philanthropist to increase the fearful excitement. Although the age requires facts rather than abstract principles, it yet has a tendency to association—to act by combination, and to approve, or condemn, on mere party grounds. In politics we no longer ask "is he capable? Is he honest?" But, is the proposed candidate for office a firm adherent of our party? In religious and ecclesiastical matters we seldom ask, "is the measure just? Is it likely to be attended by beneficial results?" But, "is it orthodox? Is it the measure of *our* party? Will it advance *our* sect?" This is a bad state of things; but let the professedly liberal, ask, if they are not doing something, as well as the orthodox all, to perpetuate it?

If the orthodox propose a measure, no matter how good, how desirable, and how feasible, it is enough to ensure it opposition from one portion of community, that it has an orthodox origin. Should the liberal party propose a measure of like character, equally just and desirable, it will be decried, by the orthodox as an infidel measure. This is wrong. We should recollect the orthodox are our fellow beings, our fellow citizens, and many of them our fathers, our sons, and our brothers. They are not without good qualities; they have warm hearts and not infrequently clear heads. They deserve from us, at least, respectful treatment; and their measures should be viewed as the measures of brothers: if good, opposed; if bad, lamented; and if of dangerous tendency, approved. We are never to forget they have the same rights that we have, and that it is possible they may suggest some good things as well as we all.

But it may be said "the orthodox oppose us, encroach on our rights and are aiming at a control of all that is dear to us." Be it so. Because the orthodox abuse us, that is no reason why we should abuse them. Their conduct is not the measure of our duty. And if we do by them as they do by us, wherein are we better than they? And why have we any right to call ourselves the liberals? We must treat them justly though they treat us unjustly; we must be kindly affectioned towards them though they misuse, misrepresent and persecute us. It is no reason that we should do wrong because they do. Let us be just, though the world be wrong; and say with the Sage of Monticello, "that it is better to set the world an example of a good action, than to imitate a bad one."

It is to be feared that many who oppose the orthodox, do not enquire carefully enough, what spirit dictates their opposition. We may oppose a bad thing in a wrong spirit, and thus be as blameworthy as though we had opposed a good one. It should be the wish of the liberals to build up what is right, rather than to put down what is wrong. It is no reason why we should oppose the benevolent, or ostensibly benevolent, institutions of the day, because they are supported by the orthodox. If an orthodox man does good, let us be glad; if a heterodox man does good, let us be equally glad.

We have opposed the missionary operations, because we have thought they were doing little, or nothing, for the heathen, and because the missionary society is amassing immense funds, that we fear will give to the party possessing them, an undue influence. So we oppose all those great plans on which we have before commented, not because they are supported by the orthodox; but because, by presenting some grand objects which equally enlist the feelings of all denominations, they will amass immense wealth from them all, which is likely to pass under the control of *one* sect, and thus that one obtain an undue ascendancy. This we apprehend is the only ground of opposition which a good Christian can assume.

We oppose the "Sunday School Union," though not Sunday schools. We are perfectly willing the Presbyterians should have them; we only object to their abuse. We object to any one sect's soliciting scholars on the ground no sectarianism is introduced into the schools, and then making it the great object to indoctrinate them into the peculiar notions of the party. Let it be done openly and we have nothing to say. Let each sect stand on its own ground, and boldly acknowledge the object of the Sunday schools is to train up adherents to itself, and then we know where to meet them.

With regard to church and state, it is trusted the writer of this need make no allusion to his own opinions. They have been too often stated to require repeating. We would remark, the constant cry of "Church and State," will do harm to the liberal party. The cry will ere long cease to alarm; and then, if there be a party in favor of a union of church and state, they may move on unmolested, at least, regardless of all our solemn warnings, and strong appeals to the public. We but betray our folly, or our love of fault-finding, when we keep eternally harping upon "the dangerous movements of the orthodox." Where there is error let it be exposed, with charity, but with firmness; where there is an attempt made on our liberties, there let it be met by a bold and manful resistance—meet it with determination, but in good temper. There is no need that liberal papers should be all the time filled with articles on this subject; still less, that every man who can scribble a paragraph, and who calls himself a liberal because he hates the orthodox, should be all the time venting his spleen. If there be a measure of dangerous tendency, let it be faithfully exposed, and then let the matter rest, till something new transpires.

We make these remarks because we deem them called for; and because they define the course we shall for ourselves pursue. It should be the object of those who conduct liberal papers, to liberalize the minds of their readers; to enlighten the understanding; and to promote an elevated tone of moral and religious feeling. It should be their object to discover what is true, rather than to detect what is false; to establish what is useful, rather than to pull down what may be hurtful; and to "unite all hearts, if they cannot reconcile all opinions." Christ prayed for his disciples that "they might all be one," and if there be one thing more desirable than another in this world, it is that we cultivate unity of heart, and be animated by a fellow feeling. Let us who are arranged with the liberals, strike out some truly liberal ground—let us take our stand, on high and holy ground, above the petty disputes of the day where every sincere lover of true religion, where the wise and the good of all denominations may unite, and labor for the spread of the Redeemer's kingdom and the melioration of the human race.

We do not mean that we are never to enter on debatable ground, but, that whenever we do it is to be done with that elevation of mind, and that liberal tone of feeling, that will ensure the respect of the enlightened portion of community who may differ from us, and retain their friendship though they remain unconvinced. We are all liable to err, and this consideration should teach us mutual forbearance, and admonish us to contend for our peculiar opinions modestly, though we do it firmly. By observing this course controversy may be disarmed of its evils, different opinions may be safely compared, and a good hope indulged that truth will be elicited.

Social Evils and Their Remedy I

MAY 1834

A Review of Charles B. Taylor, *Social Evils and Their Remedy* (New York: Harper Bros., 1834)

That the Messrs. Harper should give to the public an American edition of this work is nothing strange; but that a clergyman should be its author is more than we can account for, without a supposition which we are unwilling to make. The clergyman who really understands and is prepared to fill his mission is the workingman's true friend. The Gospel is emphatically the workingman's religion. They were "the common people who heard Jesus gladly"; and it was because "the poor had the Gospel preached unto them" that John was instructed to infer that the Messiah had come. By "preaching the Gospel to the poor," we are not to suppose was merely meant proclaiming to them its great truths, but that the Gospel which contemplated the moral and social elevation of the poor, of the lower classes, was there proclaimed. This the Gospel did contemplate and insured it when it proclaimed the fraternity of the human race; and it is this which makes it a religion for the many, peculiarly good news to the millions.

The author of the book before us gives us no evidence that he has ever suspected this. He seems not to be aware that by virtue of his office he is bound to be the poor man's friend and the unshrinking advocate of the equal rights of all men. He sees a broad line of distinction between the higher and the lower classes of society, but he sees no evil in it. He sees evil only in the uneasiness of the lower class, in its efforts to equal or to exchange places with the higher. This book, coming as it does from a clergyman, would, if anything could, justify infidelity and render indifference to religion a virtue. It breathes a spirit that would crush every effort of the people to meliorate their social condition. Its sentiments are worthy [of] none but an antediluvian politician, such as none but a slave can embrace or a tyrant wish to propagate. Its language is, "Vulgar Mechanics, to your places. Stand ready bitted and saddled for your masters' pleasure. Be brutes, as you are, and dream not that you are human beings." Such is the lesson with which it would cure social evils and such the lesson its publishers would read to the liberty-loving workingmen of America!

With these remarks we dismiss this little production but not the subject it professes to discuss. That subject is one not to be lightly dismissed by him who is conscious that there are duties which he owes to his fellow-beings. We fear, however, that too many do lightly dismiss it. We fear there are those who would brand such as believe that there are great and grievous social evils which demand redress, as agitators, demagogues, Jacobins, or persons of desperate fortunes, who have nothing to lose but everything to gain by a change. We fear there are those and even clergymen too who, with their faces turned to the past, have no inward visions of a greater good for the human race, who dream not that as the professed disciples of Jesus they are bound to desire a progress and to labor to set their fellow-beings forward in knowledge and virtue. We fear there are those who, because they find this world "a vale of tears" to the many, confounding the actual with the possible, infer that it always must be so, that God decreed it, and that it is impious not to be resigned to it. We fear; God grant that we fear without reason! We wish not to complain. But we would to God that all, and especially every clergyman, felt that the Gospel was given to effect a great moral and social reform in man's earthly condition, that Jesus was a reformer, that the apostles were reformers, that he and they suffered martyrdom as reformers, and that whoever would be a true disciple of Jesus must love all men, even the most abandoned, well enough, if need be, to die as he did, upon the cross for their salvation; that everyone felt that he owes a vast debt to the community—a debt which cannot be paid so long as a single human being is deprived of his rights, a single vice remains to be corrected, a single new truth to be promulgated, or the least additional good to be obtained for any portion of our fellow-beings. We should feel this. It should sink deep into our hearts and forbid us to desist from an earnest inquiry after a remedy for all social evils of whatever name or magnitude.

We say *remedy*. For we are not of that number who believe the evils of the social state are irremediable. We are not of that number who believe the earth is smitten with the malediction of heaven and that groans and tears are man's inevitable lot. We have seen suffering, we have heard complaints, we have seen and shared in man's miseries; but we never dared believe their cause was lodged in the bosom of the Divinity. We have seen the hand of God at work in the affairs of men; but we have seen it at work only for good. We have seen it pouring "oil and wine" into the wounded heart, binding up the broken spirit, and making the sufferer whole; but we have not seen it pushing man forward in a career of madness and compelling him to be "the greatest plague and tormentor of his kind." We have seen the factitious distinctions of society, and the tremendous evils they involve, but we have seen in them no marks of the wisdom and goodness of God; we have seen in them only the foolishness and wickedness of man. "The foolishness of man perverteth his *way*, and his heart fretteth against the Lord." If these evils are the work of man they are not imperishable, if man has made them, man can unmake them. At least, it can be no disrespect to the Deity to labor to remove them.

But what is the remedy for our social evils? Who is able to answer? Not he who, condemning first principles and what he calls abstract science, applauds himself for being only a *practical* man; not he who denies all disinterestedness, and judging from his own heart, pronounces selfishness the governing principle of everyone's life; not he who is unconscious of the great duties involved in the spiritual brotherhood of the human race; not he who has to learn that his nature is allied to the Divinity and is susceptible of indefinite perfectibility; nor he who sees in the Gospel no great social principle, which in its progressive development must not only modify but recast society and place it upon an entirely new base. The remedy is in Christianity—in Christianity, not as a dogma, not as a system of belief, but as a grand, all-comprehending principle of moral and social action. It can be found only by carrying out into all the details of social and private life those great moral maxims which Jesus disclosed in his teaching and exemplified in his life. But how is this to be done? Not by saying, as it is said on either hand, it cannot be done; but by a full confidence that it can and *must* be done, and by engaging in earnest to do it. The pulpit alone cannot do it. *That* has spoken. Its voice, we trust, has alarmed many a one's conscience, arrested many a sinner in his mad career, called back many of the erring, and often consoled and confirmed the good; but alone it is too weak to check and roll back the full tide of depravity. It must be aided by education.

EDUCATION! He who pronounces that word pronounces the remedy for the evils of man's social condition. But not he who speaks only of intellectual education. Many know their duty, but do it not. Many a man's understanding is right whose feelings are wrong. Man's *whole* nature must be educated. *Educated*, we say; by which we mean the right exercise, training, or disciplining of man's whole physical, intellectual, and moral nature. The body must be so educated as to insure it health, active and vigorous limbs; the feelings should be so disciplined that those which furnish the energy for useful and virtuous action may always be predominant; and the intellect should be so developed that the right and the best means of obtaining it shall always be obvious.

Education should have a religious foundation. Those who propose a system of education which excludes religion propose nothing really practicable or desirable. Aside from that part of man's nature which finds its sphere of activity only in what pertains to religion, man is but an animal, or a mere creature of barren logic. In either case he ceases to be a human being who adds to his animal propensities and his reasoning powers those moral instincts which are the distinguishing characteristics and which constitute the real glory of human nature. All that is generous, touching, or sublime in our nature is intimately allied to the religious sentiment, and withers and disappears whenever that is struck with death. We would have all our systems of education recognize this truth. The great object of all our schools should be to reveal the mind to itself, to make the soul conscious of its lofty and deathless energies, and of its power to grow by an ever-enlarging virtue into the likeness of the Divinity. But in making religion the base of education, we should detach it from its various forms, disengage it from all its sectarian connections, and present it simply as a sentiment of the heart, a law of the soul, as the great principle which is forever urging man forward towards higher and more advanced states of living. In school we would consider it as the principle of perfectibility and occupy the young mind only with its spirit and results.

We know there are those who would exclude religion from our schools; but we believe it is only because they identify it with dogmas, and its instruction with sectarian strife and animosity. Did they view it as we do, they could not object to it. It does seem to us that no one not in love with depravity, no one who ever stops to gaze on an opening flower, to inhale its sweet perfume, or to catch the wild note of a forest songster, no one who feels the least emotion on beholding the distant mountains with harmonious outlines, the ocean where its "waves sleep on its bosom," or when the storm lashes them into fury, the deep blue vault of heaven lighted up with its thousands of evening fires, a generous sentiment, an act of heroism or of disinterested affection, can object to religion, which, as we view it, and as we would have it introduced into schools, is but the right exercise of our highest and most glorious faculties—neither more nor less than the perception of the beautiful and true, sympathy with the pure and spiritual, veneration for the holy, love for the good, gratitude for the munificent and the kind, and an eternal up-shooting of the soul towards perfection.

But however thorough, however religious, education may be made, the education of a few will not be enough. Egypt was the cradle of learning, of arts and sciences; but she has fallen. Greece was once the academy of the civilized world. Her philosophers sounded the depths of the human mind. Her poets and orators stand unrivaled. Her artists seized upon the idea of the beautiful, detached it, reembodied it, in forms which remain and will remain models through all coming time. But Greece has fallen. Rome, once the haughty mistress of the world, was rich in statesmen, heroes, learned men, poets, and orators. But she has fallen, and comparative solitude reigns upon the "seven hills" of her greatness. Why have all these fallen and veiled their glory in the dust? Not for the want of the educated few, but of the *many—for the want of an educated, enlightened population.* The lights which shot from the educated few were but flashes soon lost in the profound darkness which enveloped the mass of the people. The education of a few is not enough. The millions must be sent to school—not merely sent to school for two or three months in a year for half dozen years, but must be educated in the fullest, broadest sense of the term. The whole population of a country and eventually of the world must be educated. This is the remedy for social evils, education, moral, intellectual, and physical, based on religion, and universally diffused, and this, too, is a remedy which can be applied.

Can be applied. The stationary philosophers may contradict us. They may allege such a thing never has been, therefore never can be; that children are born with unequal capacities and that it is folly to dream of making all equal; but they will not move us. We admit that children are born with different capacities, that education can never make all equal, but it does not follow from this that all cannot be educated. Education cannot create; we admit it can *only* unfold and aid the growth of the germs which nature originally wishes, but all except idiots have the genius and are susceptible of a spiritual as well as a physical growth. That all can reach the same size we do not pretend; but that all with proper culture can grow, will grow, is a truth we presume no one will controvert. Let this culture be given to all, let all have the means of attaining the largest growth of which they are susceptible; we ask no more.

To infer that all cannot be educated because all have not been is a species of logic long since superannuated. It is too late in the day to measure the future by the past. He who should wish to do it would have sided with the judges that condemned Socrates to drink the hemlock, would have joined the cry of the multitude in reference to Jesus, "Crucify him, Crucify him"; he would have recommended the burning of Huss and Jerome and Bruno, and the incarceration of Galileo; ridiculed Columbus for his new geographical notions, laughed at Franklin and his kite, and made sport of Fulton and his steamboat. Had this spirit prevailed, all those mighty discoveries and inventions which have given man his empire over nature would never have been made or would have been stifled in their birth. The melioration of laws for which humanity now justly applauds herself, the improvements in the science of government which in our case have taken a rapid stride towards perfection, would never have been effected, and instead of having the spectacle of a free people to contemplate, we should have had only masters and slaves. No. The past does not, cannot, in the sense in which the stationary philosopher alleges it, measure the future. There has been through all the past a progress, and this bids us look for still greater hereafter. If from the past it be allowable to predict the future, let it be from past improvements that we infer future ones.

We cannot dismiss this article without referring to the duty which one generation owes to another. The child must be "trained up in the way he should go," but he cannot train himself. The education, at least its rudiments, must be *given*. Parents, guardians, or legislators must provide for it. The existing generation must bestow it on the rising. The rank the generation to come after us will hold, the advances in civilization which it will make, depend almost entirely on the education we give it. How, then, does our duty to educate *all* the children of our country rise in importance! How do almost all other considerations dwindle into insignificance compared with this! Who does not in this recognize an immense responsibility which rests upon him? Who would shrink from it and not do his duty?

For ourselves we are glad that the duty of educating one generation is given to another. It prevents us from feeling that we stand alone. It is an arrangement which connects us with all the past and with the whole future. We are an epitome of the vices and follies, the virtues and intelligence of all past ages; and our action, good or bad, upon the generation to follow us, will be felt by the remotest posterity. We occupy a commanding position. No action can be without its result. No word can drop idly to the ground. A word, little heeded when spoken, may kindle up a virtuous energy in some bosom, which shall pass from that to another, from that to still another, till there be collected a moral force sufficient to shake the empire of evil and then to create an entire new order of things. Every man may, in consequence of this law of our social development, be contributing something to the knowledge and virtue and happiness of the most distant generations. No one is too low, no one is too obscure, to be able to aid forward the glorious work of moral and social improvement. No matter how few or how apparently isolated from the world may be the friends of humanity, their exertions can never be lost. Their most private acts may prove to be the highest public benefits; their most secret devotions may be nourishing principles, cherishing a force of character which will one day pass from them to some beyond their circle, to increase in power and activity till the whole world feel and own their influence.

This is the grand secret of all human improvement, the action of man upon man and of generation upon generation. This is the principle by which Jesus accomplishes the grand reform he commenced. It was by the action of man upon man, of generation upon generation, that the germ of moral and social perfection which he deposited in the earth was to be nurtured into life. The nation in which he appeared has passed away. The conquerors of his countrymen have been conquered, and their conquerors in their turn have passed under the yoke, but that germ remains. It has sprung up, received fresh beauty and verdure from every storm which has passed over it, and it has now risen to afford shade and shelter to nearly half the earth; but that it has survived the revolutions of ages and reached its present growth has been the result of no other principle. Man has imparted something to man, and one individual has kindled up the soul of another. One generation has accumulated something that its predecessor had not, which it has imparted to its successor to be still enlarged.

Let us not overlook this grand principle of reform, and so long as we have it in our power thus to aid in setting the human race forward in the march of improvement let us not be discouraged. We have in our hands the lever which moves the moral world. Let us learn to use it with effect. Let us feel the sublime power with which it invests every individual of the human family. This lever is education; and when we see the mighty power it holds what importance does it not receive! What attention does it not demand! Let all our thoughts be turned towards the means of making it thorough, religious, universal, and with the least possible delay. We are called to do this by every consideration which can arrest the understanding or touch the heart. We are called to it by all our love of human happiness, by all our aversion to pain, by all our desire to share in great and glorious actions. Whoever we are, whatever our party, sect, creed, or mode of worship, here is a field broad enough for us all, and in which we may all labor in peace. Fathers and mothers! Religionists and politicians! Clergymen and legislators! Patriots, philanthropists, and reformers! Here is the object equal to your gentlest affections and to your loftiest ambition. Lend it the concentrated powers of all your minds and hearts, of your whole souls. God grant ye may!

Memoir of Saint-Simon

JUNE 1834

A Review of works by the followers of Claude Henri de Rouvroy, Comte de Saint-Simon, including the Paris lecture series (organized by Barthélemy Prosper Enfantin and Saint-Amand Bazard) known as *L'Exposition de la doctrine de Saint-Simon,* 1829–1830.

Everybody has heard of the Saint-Simonians, a new sect of philosophers, politicians, and religionists which a few years ago appeared in France. They made much noise and attracted no little attention for a time by the novelty of some of their notions and by the enthusiasm with which they supported them. It is said, how truly we know not, that they have latterly run into many wild and mischievous extravagancies, and that the day of their glory is past. However this may be, they have left indelible traces of their new system on the philosophical and religious opinions of France; and since they are now making their appearance in England, and since we have seen it stated that they intend visiting this country, we have thought it not too late to be both interesting and profitable to give a more detailed account of their doctrines than is within the reach of our readers generally. In this article, however, we can do little more than furnish some notices of Saint-Simon himself, the prophet of the sect, which we collect almost entirely from the works before us.

Claude Henri Saint-Simon, son of the Duc de Saint-Simon, the author of the "Memoirs," was born April 17, 1760, of one of the noble families of France, which traces its descent, through the Counts of Vermandois, from Charlemagne. He had early a presentiment of his destined greatness, and from the age of seventeen he caused himself to be awakened in the morning with the words, "GET UP, COUNT YOU HAVE GREAT THINGS TO DO." His heated imagination presented before him the royal founder of his family, who foretold to him that to the glory of having produced a great monarch should be added through him that of producing a great philosopher.

He entered the military service at seventeen, and the year after came into this country, where he made five campaigns with distinction, under the orders of Bouillié and Washington. He became acquainted with Franklin and studied the political organization of our United States; for while here he busied himself much more with political science than with military tactics, for which he had no great fondness. It is from this period that he dates his philosophic tendency. "The war," he says, "in itself did not interest me; but its object interested me very much, and this enabled me to support its labors without repugnance. 'I will the end,' I often said, 'I should then will the means.' But my disgust for the trade of arms was complete, so soon as I saw peace approach. From that moment I saw clearly what was to be my future career. My vocation was not to be a soldier. I was carried to a very different and, I may say, an opposite kind of activity. To study the development of the human mind, and afterwards to labor to perfect civilization, such was the object I proposed to myself, and to which I devoted myself without repose, consecrating to it my whole life. This new kind of activity began then to engross all my powers. The remainder of my stay in America was employed in meditating on the great events I had witnessed, in seeking to discover their causes and to foresee their results. I saw then that the American Revolution must signalize a new political era, necessarily determine an important progress in general civilization, and cause great changes in the social order then existing in Europe."

Scarcely had he returned to Europe when he was called upon to witness the breaking out of the French Revolution. This spectacle, at once magnificent and terrible, could not fail to affect him deeply; but looking beyond the vulgar horizon, into the future as well as into the past, he was able to distinguish its causes and to appreciate its results.

He saw in this grand event the practical application of the theories founded by the reformers in the fifteenth and sixteenth centuries, and popularized by the philosophers in the eighteenth century, the legitimate destruction of a moral and social order which no longer responded to the interests and the sentiments of society; and at the same time he saw that this crisis, called to prepare the soil for the seed, contained in itself no germ of reorganization and that it could be definitively terminated only by the production of a new principle of social classification. To discover this principle, bring it out, and establish it, was what he considered his mission. He viewed the French Revolution as having only a destructive mission, necessary, important, but incomplete for humanity; and therefore, instead of being carried away by its current, as were nearly all whose sympathies were like his, he applied himself to the accumulation of the materials required for the erection, on the ruins of the old, of a new social edifice, to remain, to improve in beauty, grandeur, strength and symmetry forever.

His first care was to procure the pecuniary resources necessary for his work. To this end he engaged in some immense financial speculations, which were crowned with great success. "I desired fortune," he said, "only as the means of organizing a grand industrial establishment, to found a school to perfect science, in a word, to contribute to the progress of light, and to the melioration of the fate of humanity." The grand establishment was organized, but it failed; and his partner, who did not share his philanthropic, or, as some may say visionary views, separated from him, much to Saint-Simon's disadvantage, whose ability to manage pecuniary matters alone does not seem to have been of the highest order.

However, faithful to the plan he had traced, he employed the feeble remains of his fortune saved from the ruin of the establishment, the attempted industrial and scientific school, to perfect his own scientific education. His object was to introduce into the French school a grand scientific theory which should embrace all the sciences and all the facts of science. But this required preliminary labors. It was necessary to know the actual condition of science and the history of its discoveries. Seven years were devoted to these preliminary labors. He did not confine himself to libraries. He sat down opposite the Polytechnic School; he contracted a friendship with several of its professors and employed three years with their aid in making himself master of the current knowledge respecting inorganic bodies. Good cheer, good wine, much attention to the professors, to whom his purse was open, seem to have made them communicative, and to have procured him all the facilities he could desire. "I had, however," he says, "great difficulties to surmount. My brain had lost its malleability; I was no longer young. But I enjoyed some advantages, extended travels, the intercourse of able men which I sought and obtained, an early education by d'Alembert, an education which had woven me a metaphysical net so compact that no important fact could pass through it."

After three years, in 1801, he left the Polytechnic School and seated himself near that of medicine. Here he formed a connection with the physiologists and did not leave them till he had obtained a full knowledge of their general ideas on organic bodies. He then visited England, Switzerland, and a part of Germany. "My object," he says, "in going to England was to inform myself whether the English had discovered any new general ideas. I returned, assured that they had upon their stocks no new capital idea." His opinion of Germany was little more favorable. "I brought from Germany the conviction that general science was yet in its infancy in that country since it was there founded on mysticism; but I conceived a hope of its ultimate progress on seeing the whole of that great nation passionately engaged in a scientific direction."

Saint-Simon did not content himself with studying the sciences and the learned; he wished to know artists and their inspirations, and to compare their genius with that of scientific speculators. His house, thus, for a year, became the resort of the most distinguished men in Paris of both classes. Seven years had now been employed in forming an acquaintance with the various branches of human knowledge and he felt himself able to draw up an inventory of the scientific wealth of Europe.

But now commenced his severest trials, his greatest labors. His fortune, shaken by the failure of the "grand establishment," was wholly dissipated by his pursuit after knowledge. His friends deserted him. From this time he must live in want, in suffering, in humiliation. He must remain *alone with the consciousness of what he is*, and for a longtime this consciousness proved itself able to sustain his courage. His first occupation was to recast philosophy. Napoleon had said to the Institute, "Give me an account of the progress of science since 1789. Tell me what is the actual state of science, and what are the means necessary to make it advance." The Institute replied to this magnificent question merely by a series of partial, historical reports, which being tied together by no general view could give to science no real impulse. Saint-Simon undertook to remedy this defect. He conceived and executed his *Introduction aux Travaux Scientifiques du XIX Siècle*, in two volumes quarto, a great work, in which he deposited the germ of most of the ideas he afterwards developed. In this work he demonstrates for the human race what Bacon had for the individual, that intellectual activity has two general, alternate modes of operation, *analysis* and *synthesis*, the mode *a priori*, and the mode *a posteriori*; he makes it appear that science, considered in the assemblage of all the men who cultivate it passes successively, but at distant intervals of time, from *analysis* to *synthesis*, from the search after facts to the construction of theories; that the greatest step which the human mind can be made to take in the direction of the sciences is to determine the proper time to pass from one mode to the other; he takes it upon him to prove that the learned of Europe, for a century engaged in the paths of analysis, have sufficiently explored them, and that they ought to abandon them for a general or synthetic point of view. In a word, he required the learned to return to the point of view of Descartes, which they had entirely forgotten for that of Newton. "Descartes," he says to them, "had monarchized science. Newton republicanized it, he *anarchized it*. You are only learned anarchists, you deny the existence, the supremacy of a general theory." He afterwards enumerated the principal conceptions of the learned during the 17th and 18th centuries; particularly that of Condorcet on the progressive development of the human race. He furnished the means for the study of this development, a study elevated by him to the rank of a positive science. The learned did not regard him, but the future will comprehend him.

But it was chiefly in reference to a social and political end that he sought to stimulate the zeal of the learned. The destructive wars which followed the French Revolution made him feel every day more vividly the necessity of reorganizing a general doctrine and a central European power. Preoccupied, as he was at this epoch, with the importance of the sciences, it was to the scientific that he addressed himself to realize his project. He wished to elevate them to the height of such a mission. "From the 15th century up to this day," he says to them, "the institution which united the European nations, and curbed the ambition of people and of kings, has been successively enfeebled. It is now completely destroyed. A general war, a fearful war, a war which threatens to devour the whole European population, has already existed for twenty years and harvested many millions of men. You alone can reorganize European society. Time presses—blood flows—hasten to declare yourselves." But he spoke in vain. The learned were as little moved by the anarchy of Europe as by the anarchy of science. Saint-Simon did not know, at this moment, that it was from HIMSELF ALONE must proceed the doctrine and the men capable of reestablishing unity, order, harmony.

The year eighteen hundred and fourteen arrives. Always ardent to pursue under the most suitable form the object from which he never in any circumstances allowed himself to be diverted, he abandons the direction essentially speculative, which till now he has followed, to engage in political labors. He soon perceives the new character, which the development of industry must impart to society and to the forms of government. He speaks no longer, as before, to the learned. He turns to the industrious classes and devotes then years to the work of making them comprehend the new social rank they are destined to hold. He writes and publishes successively several works but they produced no great sensation. He who labors for the industrious classes does nobly but he must not expect to be very readily comprehended nor very cordially thanked. But let no one on this account desert them. They curse the hand that would unloose their fetters only because they fear its design is to rivet them firmer. At this period of his life Saint-Simon presents himself in a touching attitude. He lived in poverty, in want, in neglect. He labored incessantly in his own opinion for the good of his fellow beings; yet no one thanked him; no one aided him; no one cheered him onward; but all united in loading him with obloquy and abuse. "These fifteen days," he writes, "I have lived on bread and water. I have labored without fire. I have sold everything, even to my wearing apparel, to defray the expense of some copies of my work. It is the passion for science and public happiness, it is the desire to find the means for terminating, in a gentle manner, the fearful crisis in which all European society is engaged, that has plunged me into this distress. It is therefore without a blush that I avow my wants, and solicit the assistance needed to put me in a condition to continue my work."

One day, one single day, in this terrible situation, scorned and abandoned by the very men for whom his life was a perpetual sacrifice, his courage fails him. He doubts his mission; he is in despair; he asks, he wills, he seeks to die. His hand is armed against himself; the ball grazes his forehead. "But his hour is not yet come." His work must not be left incomplete. He has created a philosophy of the sciences, a philosophy of industry; he must live long enough to find the religion destined to unite the two creations. He must now be the prophet of the law of love. "God," say his disciples, in apostrophizing him, "God has left thee to fall only to prepare thee for a still grander initiation; and see, from the bottom of the abyss he raises thee, exalts thee even to himself. He sheds over thee the religious inspiration which vivifies, sanctifies, renews thy whole being. Henceforth it is no longer the learned man, no longer the workingman, that speaks. A hymn of love escapes from his mutilated body. THE DIVINE MAN IS MANIFEST. 'New Christianity' is given to the world! Moses *promised* to mankind universal brotherhood; Jesus Christ *prepared* it; Saint-Simon *realizes* it. The church *really* universal is about to be born. The reign of Caesar ends; a pacific takes the place of a military society; and the universal church governs the temporal as well as the spiritual, in the outer as well as in the inner court. Science is holy, industry is holy, for they seem to improve the condition of the poorest classes and to bring them near to God. Priests, the learned, the industrious, these are the whole society; chiefs of the priests, chiefs of the learned, chiefs of the industrious, these are the whole government. And all *good* is the *good* of the church, and every profession is a religious function, a grade in the social hierarchy. To each one according to this capacity, to each capacity according to its works. The reign of God is at hand. All prophecies are fulfilled. Saint-Simon, now thou mayest die, for THOU HAST DONE GREAT THINGS."

Saint-Simon closed his career with his religious work called *New Christianity*. He died the 19th of May, 1825, in obscurity, in want, attended by his only disciple, who received his last revelations and who became the chief of the sect. If we may believe his disciples, Saint-Simon was a man of exalted worth. His only passion, according to them, was the public good. Liberty, industry, philosophy in all that it has of the sublime were the constant themes of his meditations. He had an almost unequaled nobleness of soul and of sentiment. His conversation was clear, lively, brilliant, able in a few hours to make perceptible and palpable, ideas which it would require volumes fully to develop. He never talked of himself. He discarded all the factitious distinctions of society, and shone by himself alone, by the man that was in him. His genius was great but his heart was greater. All his ideas passed through his heart.

He was never known to complain of a single human being, although he had made many ingrates. He had an inconceivable simplicity of manner, always seized the tone and placed himself within the reach of the one who enjoyed his conversation; and such was his flexibility of mind that while the wisest carried away the hope of returning to profit by his conversation, the ignorant left him with the idea that they had instructed him. He was lavish of his thoughts, cared not who profited by them, provided they were diffused. It was his delight to collect around him young men, the men of the future, and to procure them the means of opening to themselves an honorable career by their labors or their writings. No selfishness was discovered to sully the beauty of his character. He knew how to acquire wealth, had acquired it more than once, but his regard for the interests of others and little care for his own made him diffuse it faster than he could obtain it. "If there were not generosity in the heart," said he, "it would always be a good calculation."

His enemies, indeed, allege many things against him. The most important is that he was a very troublesome beggar. His disciples do not deny the charge; they allege that it was his desire to do mankind good that reduced him to beggary. They, however, do not pretend that lie was perfect. They consider him not as the type of perfection but of an eternal progress towards perfection. They see in him an advance prophetic of the advance of humanity. They think he ascended high the ladder whose steps, through the infinite, lead up to God. He leaped an immense chasm and now lends a helping hand to his disciples to leap the same and to place themselves by his side. He ended a thousand times greater than he began; and death does not interrupt his eternal progress. "Great God!" say his disciples, "he is and always will be before thy face; he is and always will be *with us, in us*. It will always be by him that we shall develop ourselves and make our way to thee. The being of Saint-Simon, growing more and more perfect, is at each moment made up of all that we can conceive of love, of wisdom, and beauty under a human form. It is to the being composed of these that our worship, our admiration, and our souls are devoted. Old religions, wholly *stationary*, have the type of what they reverence in the past; our religion, *wholly progressive*, places it in the future; and one of the finest results of our progress is that we every day become able to represent our type to ourselves under a more attracting and a more perfect form."

This may be a little mystical to those of our readers who have long had thinking made easy to them. It is not the *man* they worship. It is not the man Saint-Simon they reverence. They pay their homage to the progress he manifested, to the truths he disclosed, and to the passionate love of humanity which controlled him. They revere him as a model for them to imitate only in his progress and in the object towards which he directed his labors. They do not look at him as he was in the past, to see what they should be; they look at him where his continued progress has elevated him and thus gather strength to press onward and upward after him.

With the Saint-Simonians everything is progress, everything changes to man's conception as he advances. God enlarges, becomes pure, wise, and beautiful, in proportion as the mind that contemplates him enlarges, becomes pure, clothed with wisdom, and adorned with beauty. This idea is undoubtedly just. The God of the ignorant is not the God of the enlightened. Every man has a God of his own, exactly proportioned to his degree of mental and moral progress. That which a man worships is always the highest worth of which he can form any conception. The Negro ascribes to his ill-shapen *fétiche* the highest excellence he can conceive, and you must enlarge his mental and moral capacity before he can worship a God of higher and more moral attributes. You change not the object of man's worship by changing the name of his God. The Jew, who ascribed to his Jehovah no higher qualities than the Greeks did to Jupiter, was no more a worshiper of the true God than they. The same is true of the Christian. If mankind worship the true God now any more than formerly, it is because there has been an advance, because the human mind has grown and become able to take in the idea of a purer, sublimer, and more beautiful Divinity.

We delight to apply this thought to Christianity somewhat as the Saint-Simonians apply it to their prophet. Christianity is to every Christian the type of moral and religious perfection; but that type varies in different ages, in different individuals, and even in the same individual at different epochs of his life. Christianity, in the minds of those who embraced it in the early centuries, was a low thing to what it is now. No matter what it was in the mind of its Author; where it was embraced it was measured not by his mind, but by the minds of those who embraced it. It can never in any mind mean a greater degree of moral and religious perfection than that mind is capable of receiving, understanding, appreciating. There must be almost an infinite difference between Milton's Christianity and that of the Abbeé Paris. Still, one was a Christian as well as the other. One age, one sect is Christian, as well as another, when compared with itself. Each is modeled after the same type, each takes in the highest worth of which it can form any conception. But the type stands an amount exactly proportioned to the progress which has been made. Christianity then, can never be outgrown. We may pursue an eternal career of progress and at each step will the term Christianity enlarge its meaning, and the word Christ designate purer, lovelier, sublimer worth!

But to return. Saint-Simon, viewed as he may be, was undoubtedly no ordinary man. His views are those of no ordinary mind. They bear the stamp of originality of a mind in pursuit of variety, in love with the beautiful, and, in its own estimation, wedded to humanity, and longing to redeem, exalt, and make it happy and forever more happy. We have dwelt long upon his career, perhaps too long for the patience of our readers; but we delight to trace such a character, we find instruction in its very extravagancies. We shall take up his system as developed by his disciples, as we find time and room.

Independence Day Address at Dedham, Massachusetts
JULY 1834

*F*riends and Fellow Citizens,

We must have cold hearts if they do not beat with warm emotions on the return of this day; we must have dull spirits if they be not stirred by the proud recollections of the anniversary we have met to celebrate.

No party victory, no triumph of ephemeral interests, calls us together on this day. We have met to commemorate an event dear to humanity—an event in which man throughout the world has a deep and lasting interest, in which he may find matter for sympathy, gratulation and hope. We have come together to celebrate Freedom's Birthday. Not the Birthday of Freedom merely for this country, but for the world, for man universally.

There was a deeper meaning in that Declaration of the Congress of '76 to which we have just listened than that of the political independence of this country. That independence was indeed declared, that independence has indeed been won and defended by deeds of heroism and self-sacrifice, unsurpassed in the world's history, but it enters for only a small affair into what should occupy our thoughts on this day. The struggle between the then feeble colonies and the mother country deserves all the eulogies it has received, but we are not here merely to recall it. A higher and a holier triumph than that of arms, or even that of the political independence of any country, excites the warm emotions of our hearts and calls forth our sympathy. We celebrate the triumph of humanity. No limited horizon confines us today. A boundless heaven spreads out over us and the whole human race comes within the scope of our vision.

I pray you, fellow citizens, not to take a narrow view of the American Revolution. There was more in that Revolution than the American and British armies. The past and the future were there. The spirit of immobility and the spirit of progress met there in terrible conflict; humanity all entire, was there, and ours was but the battleground where it conquered the power to take another step forward in its eternal career of improvement. In that Revolution there were debated not merely the interests of a few colonists and their descendants, but man's whole future was debated and decided. We should then look beyond the battleground, beyond the contending armies, to the cause then in question, to the principle which came out from the battle triumphant. To that cause, to that principle, sacred be this day. Sacred be this day, not merely to military triumph, not merely to deeds of heroism, nor of patriotism, but to the progress of the human race, to the political redemption and social installation of humanity.

The cause in question fifty-eight years ago this day was that of the human race, the principle then declared was the equality of mankind. "All men are created equal," is the noble sentence that embodies the doctrine contended for by the Congress of '76, maintained and triumphantly established by the revolutionary army. I will not say that at that epoch, the assertion "all men are created equal," was suspected of the deep and full meaning we now assign it. I am not certain that the signers of the Declaration of Independence intended to assert by it anything more than the political equality of different communities, and the right of each community to choose its own form of government. But Providence makes men the unwitting instruments of advancing his designs, and often puts into their mouths, words big with a meaning they little suspect, and sometimes with a meaning they are little able to appreciate. The time had come for the great principle of equality for which Christianity during so many ages had been paving the way, to be ushered in and set to work in the affairs of the world; and Providence so overruled it, that our fathers in asserting the rights of communities, asserted those of individuals, and in declaring one community's rights equal to those of another, uttered that soul-kindling truth, man equals man, man measures man, the world over.

I know of no topic more appropriate to this day than this great truth of man's equality to man. I therefore ask your indulgence to some desultory, perhaps commonplace, comments upon it, which I am desirous to bring before you and which I should be glad to bring before the whole American people.

In speaking of equality, I pray you not to misinterpret me. There is a sense in which it is not true that "All are created equal." It is not true that all men are born with the same capacities. There are original differences, intellectual, moral and physical, which no education that ever has been and which I venture to predict, none that ever will be devised can overcome. One child is born weak and sickly, another strong and healthy; one is quick and another is slow to learn; one can take in only isolated facts, dwell only on the minuteness of detail, another rises to causes and delights to trace first principles; one has no perception of the beautiful, sees nothing in nature to admire, and never rises to contemplate anything higher than food, clothing and shelter; another seizes upon the ideal of the beautiful, detaches it, reembodies it, in forms before which all real beauty grows pale; one from the earliest moment is sweet tempered, another is sour tempered; one from a very early period is deeply affected by religious considerations, draws all his delight from meditating on God, the human soul, heaven and eternity, another cannot be made to think seriously of anything which goes above or beyond this present life. In these and a thousand other instances men are not, and we do not believe they ever will be, equal. We infer this from all experience, and from all acquaintance with human organization, and with the reciprocal action of mind and matter. And I by no means mean to assert that in these respects and in others of a like kind, "All men are created equal."

When I contend for equality, that all men are created equal, I mean that all have a common nature, are brothers of the same family, heirs of the same inheritance, having the same general faculties, the same general wants, and the same general elements of knowledge and virtue. I mean that all have equal rights, that in all our social intercourse and relations, in all our governmental and educational provisions, man should be considered as measuring man. In a word, I mean that one man has no rights over another which that other has not over him, and that no one should have the power to derive any benefit from another without giving to that other a full, an exact equivalent.

I here mean something more than that specious kind of equality which English and French statesmen and some even in our own country would give us, that is, simply equality before the laws. There are too many at home and abroad who have no higher notions of equality, or at least who contend that no other equality is practicable or consistent with social order. I am not able to express the abhorrence I feel for this doctrine. It is plausible, but it has no soundness. Its terms are popular, but its spirit is consistent with a very gross system of privilege. It is by doctrines like this that the enemies of the people contrive to mislead and enslave them.

There may be a great and most mischievous inequality, even in those countries where no man is above the laws. Laws may be framed so as to be very unequal in their influence upon different classes of society, and that too, without bearing on their face the marks of the least inequality. One class of community may have no temptations to steal, but very great temptations to defraud, to overreach, to oppress the poor; another class may be strongly and almost exclusively, tempted to steal; a law then punishing fraud, overreaching, or oppression, with a simple fine, while it punished stealing with death or imprisonment, would be anything but equal in its practical effect. And in fact, even in those countries where equality before the laws is recognized, the laws are generally framed so as to fall with the most tremendous weight upon offenses to which the poor are almost exclusively exposed.

Imprisonment for debt is a case in point. The rich, the poor, the honest and the dishonest are before this law, so far as its face is concerned, equal. But the rich man cannot be imprisoned for debt unless it be his choice; the dishonest have generally address enough to escape, and consequently to all practical purposes, it is a law exclusively against the honest poor man. Is there not here, and in cases like these, a distinction, and a most odious distinction tolerated by government? Yet in these and a thousand other cases that might be mentioned, all are equal before the laws. He who transgresses the law incurs its penalty. And what boots it that it is so, if the laws are made so as to strike only one part of community, and that too, the part it ought especially to protect?

I mean then by equality, if not that all men have equal capacities, at least something more than equality before the laws. I not only ask for equality before the laws, but for equal laws for laws which shall not only speak the same language to all, but which shall have the same meaning for all, the same practical effect upon all. All have the same rights, and I ask that these rights be in no instance invaded, that all be in a situation to demand them, to defend them if attacked, and to enjoy them freely and fully.

Those of our orators who have no higher ambition than to flatter the people, inflate national vanity, and show themselves off in rounded periods, tell us that equality, even in this broad sense, is already gained in this country. But no such thing. We have equality in scarcely any sense worth naming. Will you pretend that we are equal as long as a large portion of our community lies at the mercy of any political demagogue who knows how to veil his liberticide designs under a pretended love of the *dear* people? Will you say that we are equal while all our higher seminaries of learning are virtually closed to all except the rich? Equal while we have those who are born with the right to live in luxury and idleness, while there are others who are born with only the right to starve if they do not work? Equal, while one part of community can and do lay under contribution the labor of the other, make it the means of their wealth and power, and the means too of riveting the firmer the chains of those who perform it? I allude not here to Negro slavery. I allude to that marked distinction which exists all over the world and which is every day becoming more glaring in our own country between the workingmen and the idlers, between those who produce and are poor and those who produce not and are rich; between those who perform all the productive labor and those who are crafty enough, *enterprising* enough, to obtain all its fruits. I allude here to what may seem to you no evil, but to me it is an evil, an evil of immense magnitude, one which lies at the bottom of nearly all the social evils which exist amongst us. And as long as this evil exists we are not free. There is a worm gnawing into the very heart of that tree of liberty which our fathers have planted.

Is my language severe? Be it so. I am not here to flatter. I stand not here to boast what a free, enlightened and virtuous people we are. I would not utter a note of discord to mar the harmony which the recollections of this day should always produce; but I cannot avoid saying that we are not that free, enlightened and virtuous people our Fourth of July orators and our political demagogues have made us believe we are. We have boasted too much. We must become more modest. Our freedom is written on paper, our equality is registered in our Constitutions, but of what avail is that, if it be not written in our hearts and registered in our souls?

We have a constantly besetting sin. We compare ourselves not with our own future, but with the people and institutions of the old world. Because in some respects we are really less wicked than they, we infer that we are as good as we can or ought to be; because our institutions are really better than theirs we conclude they are the best we ought to desire. We flatter ourselves that because we have taken one step, that we have run the whole career of improvement; that because we have begun well, that we have nothing further to do but to applaud ourselves for what we have done. Here is our besetting sin. Here is the rock on which we are liable to split. We look backward, not forward; to what we have done rather than to what we should do, and compare ourselves with what others are instead of comparing ourselves with what we may and ought to be.

God, in his providence, has assigned to the American people an important mission. He has given it us in charge to prove what man is, to develop his whole nature, and show of what he is capable. As the first step towards the completion of this mission, we are to bring out and carry into practice that grand, comprehensive principle, "All men are created equal." This we have not yet done. Our mission is only begun. We have only started in the race, and let us not sit down and fold our hands as if we had reached the goal and won the race. But let us be aware that we have done nothing, if we stop where we are. Our motto must be "Onward, onward, till the work be done."

And do not, I entreat you hastily conclude, that all is done that can be done. Beware how you infer, because there never has been a greater degree of equality in any country than already exists in ours, that none greater is desirable or attainable. Beware, how you set bounds to human improvement. Providence, nature, nor grace has ever yet said to man in his progressive career, "Hitherto shalt thou come, but no further." We are in but the infancy of the world, in but the first, faint dawnings of civilization. Time and the progress of events have it in charge to unfold and nourish in that creature man, now so weak, so contemned, a moral and social growth not yet dreamed of by the firmest of the believers in his indefinite perfectibility. There are wrapped up in the bottom of his soul, the germs of lofty and deathless energies, which go beyond, immeasurably beyond and above the strongest, the sublimest, he has as yet been able to exhibit. Far, far is he from having attained his full height. Let thought stretch its pinions and soar to the highest point it can reach and man in his upward flight shall yet rise above it.

Let not this be doubted. There is in the belief of this a kindling power, a something which gives us a lofty enthusiasm and creates within us the energy to realize it. Let no one forget that one law of our nature, one which distinguishes us from the brute, is IMPROVEMENT. The beaver of today builds not his house with more skill, makes it not more convenient than did the beaver of four thousand years ago. He has not surpassed the first of his race. He knows no progress. But man has outstripped his ancestors. Generation improves upon generation, and the schoolboy of today is above the wisest of the Greeks. Let us not overlook nor underrate man's power of progress. Let us not, when a noble object is proposed, one for which all the better part of our nature cries out, let us not be deterred from pursuing it by the objection, "It never has been, therefore it cannot be." This is the cowardly sluggard's objection. What! Has there been no progress? Has there never been gained at one epoch nothing which did not exist before that epoch? What! Have I only dreamed of the creations of science, of industry, and genius? Is it a dream, that mariner's compass which opens a pathway in the deep and brings together the most distant corners of the earth? Is it a dream, that ART OF PRINTING, an art that electrifies the mass of mind, creates a universe of thought and opens a medium of intercourse between all nations and all ages? Is it a dream, that bold navigator who discovered this new world and led the way to this mighty republic and to all the civilized life on this western hemisphere? Is it a dream, those proud triumphs of science which have subdued nature, disclosed to us new worlds embedded in what were once counted simple elements, which have snatched the lightning from the clouds and guided the harmless fire? Is it a dream, the discovery and application of the wonders of steam which makes the ships walk the sea regardless of wind or tide? Is it a dream, this free government, this splendid creation of human wisdom, which we so loudly and so justly boast, whose origin we this day commemorate? And yet all these are modern things. None of the ancients knew them. They have come out from Christianity, and some of them have come up into life within our own memories. Either these are dreams, the flitting visions of a distempered fancy, or things may take place at one epoch, which had no existence before it. In other words, there has been, there is, there may be, a progress. Man even in his infancy has done wonders, what will he not do in his manhood?

Let us then bid adieu to the arguments of those who have eyes only for the past, and who exert themselves only to keep the human race from marching to its end. Let us bid adieu to the spirit of immobility and imbibe the spirit of movement, the spirit whose look is upward and whose motion is onward. The equality I have designated is not impracticable. It is a truth which we must bring out of the abstract and clothe with life and activity. God never made one portion of mankind to live in idleness, in uselessness, and in luxury, and another part to live in toil and want; he never made some to be masters and some to be slaves, some to live and grow rich by skillfully, not to say dishonestly, availing themselves of the labors of others the many to be "hewers of wood and drawers of water" to the few. God has never done this. He created all men with equal rights and made one capable of measuring another. He created all of "one blood," made them to be brothers, fellow beings, to aid, not to worry and devour each other. This is a truth taught us from heaven. It is a distinguishing doctrine, as it is one of the brightest signatures of the divine origin of Christianity. Christianity teaches it by declaring him alone the greatest who best serves the human race. He who would be greatest among you, let him become your servant . And dare we say that here is a truth taught us, a duty enjoined upon us by religion itself, that is impracticable? And what is it that makes it impracticable, if it be so? It is nothing but our conviction that it is impracticable, nothing but the continual cry that it is impossible. It is this that unmans us and keeps us back in a condition we should have long since outgrown. To him that believeth all things are possible. If ye had faith as a grain of mustard seed, ye might remove mountains. It is the want of faith, the want of full conviction in its practicability that renders it impracticable. Take hold of the work with both hands, let your minds, your hearts, your very souls be in it, and no matter how difficult it is, you will accomplish it; mountains will give way before you, and your path will become smooth and easy. Men can, ay, men must, men will realize the equality for which I am contending. I see them pursuing it, I hear them crying out for it, and heaven and earth shall pass away sooner than they shall not obtain it.

But they will gain it not by a miracle. It must, as must all improvements in man's moral and social condition, be obtained by natural means, by the exertion of those powers which God has given us. Our present work is to realize this equality. How shall it be done? Important question have I asked—one on the right answer to which much depends for our country's future and for the future of humanity. How shall we realize, not in our professions and in our paper constitutions, but in our social condition, intercourse and relations, that equality is recognized I will say taught, enjoined, in Christianity, and adopted as the basis of our political institutions? We have not yet done it. There is a striking discrepancy between our practice and the theory we avow. We have borne witness to a degree of equality which we have not yet created. How shall we do it?

Not by government alone. We cannot legislate our citizens into the equality we desire. Government, in fact, is much more limited in the sphere of its operations than is commonly imagined. In its best state, its mission is mostly negative. It is charged merely to prevent one man from invading the rights of another; to maintain an "open field and fair play" to individual genius and enterprise. In countries overrun with despotism, a free government may seem to be the greatest good to be desired, the greatest that God can bestow; but our own experience may teach us that it does not embosom and necessarily bring along with it every good. We have a free government. Here all offices are open to merit alone, and the whole body of the people are free to elect whom they will to be their servants or the agents of their power. But look at the men who sometimes fill high stations. Can you believe they are, one half of them, the choice of the people? I know the people may be deceived, but never so as to prefer some men who have filled some of the highest offices in their gift. We all know that party management, the intrigues of party leaders render the right of suffrage in perhaps a majority of cases where it is worth having a nullity. A few individuals of one party get together and make a nomination, a few individuals of another party make another nomination and my boasted right of suffrage is dwindled down to a choice between these two nominations. I may dislike them both but unless I choose not to vote at all or throw my vote away I must vote for one or the other.

But pass over this, let all party management and party sins sleep in forgetfulness, suppose the people select the men they really prefer, always elect the very best men in the state or nation, and very little is gained. No matter how good laws are, they will remain on your statute books a dead letter unless demanded by the public; and the public if ignorant or immoral, or but feebly moral, will not be very likely to demand any very good laws. A community in which privilege obtains, in which inequality prevails, will not often be very unanimous, in demanding or in obeying laws which have an equalizing tendency, which seek the good of the poorest and most numerous class instead of that of the richest, smallest and most highly favored class.

I value a free government, a popular government, ay, if you will, a democratic government, for I have not a feeling about me that is not democratic. But a free government is powerless without a free people. No matter how much freedom you incorporate into your paper constitutions, you can never have any more practiced than is written in the hearts and on the characters of the people. I therefore expect little from government, I ask little, but to be let alone. Its nature is never to lead, but to follow. The people must precede it, opinion must go before it. If the people go right government cannot go wrong. If the people love right character, liberty and equality will be maintained, let what will be the character of the government, and whoever may be the men entrusted with its management. We sometimes express fears for our government, we sometimes fear that our free institutions may become a prey to some aspiring demagogue who will succeed in erecting a throne of despotism on the ruins of our temple of liberty. It may be so. But it will not be so because that demagogue is wicked, is talented and powerful; but because the people will have become corrupt, because liberty will no longer be written in their hearts and because they will have ceased to have any freedom in their souls. It is, then, of comparatively little consequence, that fierce contention we witness among politicians. I view with almost perfect indifference the contests between the great leading parties which now distract our country. They are only struggles between those who *have* and those who *want* office. The country, humanity, moral and social progress are not in those struggles. We must leave them and to a certain degree, legislative enactments, take our stand upon higher and holier ground, and speak directly to the people as moral, intelligent, religious and social beings. We must dare look on truth and dare hold it up, that by its light there may be formed just such characters as we need to support our free institutions.

I know of but one means of introducing the equality and of effecting that moral and social reform in our country and throughout the world, which every good man sighs and yearns for, and that means is education. I do not mean ability to read and write, and cipher, with a smattering of geography and grammar, and the catechism in addition. I mean EDUCATION, the *formation* of *character*, the moral, religious, intellectual, and physical training, disciplining, of our whole community. Our common schools do not do this. They are better than nothing, but they do not educate us. Our higher seminaries may do something towards educating us, but little towards fitting us for our mission. They educate us to be fond of distinctions, to be fond of popularity and to look with contempt on the people. And glad am I that no more of our community are able to give their children *such* an education.

We want a republican education, an education which shall accustom the child from the first to see things valued according to their worth—not in the market—but in themselves; an education which shall raise our children above the factitious distinctions of society, which now pervert our judgments, and which shall teach them to value every man according to his intrinsic worth, without any regard to his position in society and even without any reference to the length of his purse or to the fineness of his coat. In a word we want an education that shall breathe into the child that very spirit which dictated the assertion, "God has created all men equal"; that very spirit which filled the hearts, nerved the souls of our fathers and made them stake life, property and honor, in defiance of a transatlantic tyrant and in defense of the rights of man—which shall breathe into the child the very spirit of that Gospel which is glad tidings to the poor, which declares, "Blessed are the poor for theirs is the kingdom of heaven" that we all have one Father, and that we all are members of the same vast brotherhood of humanity—an education which shall make us feel that man wherever seen is our brother, woman wherever found is our sister, and he who injures a human being commits an offense against us, he who wrongs a man wrongs us, the arrow that wounds another's heart has sped deep into our own—an education that shall make us good Christians, give us firm and manly characters consistent with truth and full of love to mankind.

We have now no such education. We have indeed little support for liberty or morality. We have established a free government, but we have done comparatively nothing to preserve it. We have declared ourselves in favor of freedom and left that freedom to take care of itself. There is no such thing amongst us as educating our children *in reference* to their moral and social destination, in reference to those duties which devolve upon them as citizens of this republic—of this republic which God in his providence has appointed to be the school whence are to go out the doctrines and the men destined to regenerate the world.

The education we now patronize, teaches us no doctrines of equality, none of philanthropy. Our first lesson is to make a good bargain, our second to get rich, our third to look out for ourselves, and our fourth and last is that if some are unhappy, if our wealth has been the occasion of others' poverty, if unholy distinctions prevail, we must thank God we are not among the wretched, and the wretched must believe for their consolation, that the distinctions in society of which they complain, are, as a writer in a popular periodical has it, "the express appointment of God."

Long as such an education is the best we have, we cannot accomplish our mission, we cannot perform that grand and beneficent work which Deity has assigned us. The fact is, we forget the millions; we fix our eyes and the eyes of our children on the few. We covet and teach them to covet their wealth and their distinctions. We legislate for the few, not for the many. Our legislators seem not aware that there are such creatures as workingmen in existence, except in the penal part of their legislation. They legislate for capitalists, landholders, stockholders, corporations, master mechanics, and those generally who make use of the labors of others, but very seldom for the journeyman mechanic, the laborers in your factories, and those generally who perform the physical labor of community, unless indeed they have some law with a severe penalty to enact; then, indeed, the workingman is by no means neglected. But in this I blame not our legislators. They seldom know any better. They do not know that such a thing as the people exists, or if they do, they know that they were raised to their dignity of legislators by deserting the people and that they must continue to desert or neglect them or lose it. This is an evil, and one that cannot be removed unless our children are taught that the people are the human race, and that he alone has any moral worth who devotes himself without reserve to their greatest good; unless we give to our children that republican education I have pointed out, and form them, not to despise the people, not to be masters of the people, but servants of the people, to raise themselves and to carry the people up with them.

And not only a few children must be educated in this way, but all the children of our whole community. All need it, all have a right to it, all may demand it. Society is bound to give it, and if it does not it forfeits its right to punish the offender. And not one sex alone must be educated, but the children of both sexes. Woman's is the more important sex, and if but one half of our race can be educated, let it be woman, instead of man. Woman forms our character. She is with us through life. She nurses us in infancy, she watches by us in sickness, soothes in distress, supports us in adversity and cheers us in the melancholy of old age. The rank determines that of the race. If she be high minded and virtuous with a soul thirsting for that which is lofty, true and disinterested, so is it with the race. If she be light and vain, with her heart set only on trifles, fond alone of pleasure—alas! For the community where she is so, it is ruined! Let all then, all the children of both sexes, have this republican education for which I contend. And all the coming generations may have it. We have only to will it. There is nothing we cannot do if we but will to do it. We talk much about education. We speak of its vast importance, of its absolute necessity, but seem to imagine that talking is enough. But we must will it. We must act. We must take hold of the work, take hold of it in earnest, put forth all our energies, and rest not till it be done.

Let there be once established a system of equal, republican education, of an education for all the children of our land, whether rich or poor, male or female, an education which shall be such as our position in the moral, political, religious and philosophical world demands, and the equality on which I have dwelt will be obtained, our government will be firmly established, our free institutions will begin to unfold their beauty, man will prove that he is capable of self-government, humanity will disclose its mighty power of progress, and we shall have accomplished our mission. The light of our example will then reach the darkest corners of the earth, all nations will then turn towards us with admiration and for guidance. Freedom will be vindicated, liberty will become universal, all the world will be free, all will be peace, love, and progress towards perfection. Noble result! By the eye of faith I see the auspicious day when it shall be so, dawn on the world. I see the moment draw near when man shall no longer see an enemy in man, when wars shall end, tyrannies be abolished, and oppression cease, and "every man sit under his own vine and fig tree with none to molest or make afraid."

Young men! Ye who are full of the future, whose souls are full of energy, and whose hearts burn to do grand and glorious deeds, 'tis yours to hasten that day. Your fathers have done nobly. They have begun a magnificent work, but it is yours to finish it. The mission of your fathers is ended. They have departed. Gone are they who so nobly dared, so bravely struggled, to gain you a country and liberty for the world! Gone are they who signed that immortal paper which has this day been read in our hearing. Gone are they who stood firm, in those days which "tried men's souls." I see but here and there one lingering behind as if unwilling to quit the scene till they can bear some good tidings from you, their children, to those who have preceded them. And gone too is HE whose soul was full of chivalry, whose heart was full of the love of humanity, liberty's representative and champion in two worlds! He is gone! And you are left alone. Alone, young men, to your own energies and philanthropy. A grand and comprehensive work is bequeathed you. The men of the revolution have given it you in charge to regenerate the world. Prove yourselves equal to your mission. And ere long free principles and just practice will become universal; man will prove himself equal to his destiny, act worthy of his lofty nature and heavenly origin. Imbibe the spirit which animated the hearts and nerved the souls of your fathers fifty-eight years ago, and you will extend your influence from circle to circle till it spread over the whole of human society and the song of freedom, of peace and love resound from every corner of the earth and rise in swellings strains to mingle with the full chorus of angels and the blessed above.

Young men! Look forward with full faith to such a glorious consummation; fix your eyes upon it; march towards it, as steadily and as firmly as your fathers did to win the political liberty we now boast. Contemplate the inspiring vision; let it fill your souls with a noble enthusiasm, and believe nothing gained till you have realized it. Feel that you live only for man, and that your mission is to set him forward with more rapid strides towards that perfection after which his soul hungers and thirsts. Make this the end of all your exertions, and never tire in this work of philanthropy. Do this and you will preserve your country free; do this and you will regenerate the world. Do this and all posterity shall bless your memories, and God himself approve your conduct and welcome you to heaven.

Progress of Society

JULY 1835

A Review of *An Essay on the Moral Constitution and History of Man* (Edinburgh: W. Tait, 1834)

This is a valuable work on a very important subject. It is the production of no commonplace mind. Every page of it bears the proofs of strong, independent, and original thought. Whoever thinks at all on his own moral nature, or on the destiny of mankind, will read it with deep interest, and find much in it to prompt inquiry, to warm his heart, and guide his thoughts.

The object of this essay, as stated in the preface, is, "to show that mankind collectively, or society, was destined to grow from infancy to maturity in the same way as individuals are, and that the due consideration of this truth explains the origin of moral evil, the cause of its prevalence under varied forms and extent, and the means of its cure"; and also to consider "as connected with the actual progress of society, the means of its *education*, provided by Divine Providence, in the different revelations he has given to mankind. These were completed, doctrinally, by Christianity; but the world being incapable, at the first promulgation of the Christian religion, to comprehend, still more to practice its lessons, the time had not yet arrived for the actual success of the doctrine; nor has it yet arrived; but the era is approaching."

The author's point of departure is progress. Man does not come into the world full-grown. Individually and collectively, he is designed by Providence to pass from rude and feeble beginnings, to maturity, to the strength and perfection of which he is capable. Knowledge and virtue are to be acquired, by slow and toilsome effort, often at the expense of temporary suffering and evil.

The individual and the species are both subject to the same law of development. In attaining maturity, each passes successively under the dominion of different sets of faculties. In infancy the individual is a mere animal, affected chiefly by the appetites, instincts, and passions of animal life. These are all essentially selfish, having for their object the preservation, nutrition, and health of the individual. To these succeeds the imagination. Under the dominion of the imagination the individual has a great curiosity to learn the causes and the uses of everything; but he is credulous, particularly charmed with the wonderful, and becomes the easy dupe of every tale that is told him.

The intellectual powers come next in order, and assume, or try to assume, the mastery; but the remains of preceding influences and bits, together with the circumstances by which the man is surrounded and which tempt or compel him to fight his way through the world, prevent this mastery from being complete, often from being even predominant. Under the reign of the intellect the follies and prejudices of childhood and youth are surmounted, knowledge and strength are gained, but not wisdom and happiness. There remains another set of faculties to be developed, the moral sentiments. These are last in order; their predominance constitutes the maturity, the perfection of human nature, and gives moral wisdom, which is the proper attribute of age.

Society comes under each of these different sets of faculties in the same order. The infancy of society is the savage state, in which the animal passions predominate as in children. Savages are wholly occupied with the means of self-preservation and the gratification of their natural appetites and instincts. The next epoch in social progress is marked by the predominance of the imagination. This is the age of superstition. The imagination, usurping the prerogative of reason, attempts to account for all the phenomena of nature by its own conceits. Whatever is extraordinary it imputes to some mysterious influence; it peoples the world with imaginary beings—some above, some below men, some good, some bad—who are forever interfering with the affairs of mankind, and with the ordinary course or general laws of nature; and, when it has exhausted itself with these fanciful creations, it resorts to the supposed influence of occult qualities, of charms, and of magic. Under a more seductive form, it gives rise to the fables of the poets and to the sublime reveries of the Platonic and oriental philosophies.

Childhood and youth cannot comprehend the reason of their duties, they must therefore be commanded. They must be governed by *authority* and the rule of their duty is *obedience*. The social epochs, which correspond to childhood and youth in the individual, require, therefore, a different code from that which may be introduced at a more advanced stage of society. They find their moral expression in the code of authority, which appeals, not to conviction, nor to love, but to *fear*, and, in cases of obstinacy, resorts to *force*.

To the imagination succeeds the predominance of the intellect. This epoch begins by "chopping logic," attempting, by dint of syllogisms and hypotheses, to penetrate the secrets of nature, or to illustrate the teachings of divine revelation, and ends by hitting upon the true method of philosophizing, of which Bacon is the representative; but which can be successfully followed in this epoch, only in the department of physics. The intellect, being in advance of the imagination, requires a more perfect moral code. It demands the code of justice, which finds its expression in law, a rule of right between equals. This code, at first, like that of authority, appeals to fear, and resorts to force; but, after its precepts come to be established in the reason and the habits of men, they are voluntarily obeyed, and its appeal may be said to be to honor.

The fourth epoch—the golden age of the poets, which however, was not in the infancy of the world, but which shall be in the latter day—is to come. We are now in a state of *transition* from the age of matured intellect to that of mature wisdom or moral sentiment, with more of the former element as yet than of the latter, and more occupied with the laws of nature than with those of humanity, but ready to pass to the last stage, which is analogous to that of experienced age in the individual. In this last stage, however, the wisdom of society will rise superior to that of individuals. It will not be tarnished by any of the physical infirmities incidental to individual life. It will not be deteriorated by the personal bad habits of former years. All the evils of former generations may and will die with them, all the good may and will survive; because their posterity will have acquired the wisdom to reject the one and to cherish the other,—to profit by the experience, knowledge, and accumulations of their fathers.

This social epoch will have for its moral expression the code of benevolence. The precepts of this code may be easily distinguished from those of authority, or of justice. Authority commands, and the one commanded has no right to ask why he shall obey; justice says, do no wrong to others, submit to no wrong from them. But this cannot be the maxim of a definitive state of society. It is liable to perpetual misconstruction. We may think we are doing no wrong to others when we are doing them great wrong; and we may believe others are doing us a wrong which we should redress when they are not. It will always make a great difference in our estimate of any particular action whether it be done to us or by us to others. All efforts to obtain a perfect state of society by the rules of justice must prove ineffectual because the rules themselves are imperfect. Something higher and broader is demanded. This will be found in the code of benevolence, which says, do *more* than justice to others, submit to *less* than justice from them. This, on the one hand, requires us to *forgive* those who injure us, and, on the other, to inquire not what others may claim from us as a matter of right but what good we are able to do them.

This is the natural order of individual and social progress; but it is not effected by man's unaided powers. The child is set forward by the education it receives from the father; so is society by divine revelation, designed to educate not the individual merely but the species. Revelation, like education, does not seek to supersede the natural powers but to develop and strengthen them. Education must regard the age and capacities of its subject, at first give the most simple and easy, and gradually proceed to the more complex and difficult; so God does not communicate all truth at once, but gives it in different portions at different times as the wants and capacities of society demand or allow. His object in all his revelations is to prepare men for the reign of benevolence. To this end the whole series of revelations points from that made to our first parents in Eden to that made through Jesus Christ. The first revelation was of the simple elements of religion and natural science, and the last was of that sublime code of morals destined to govern the last epoch of society. Between these two, society had received all the great truths of natural religion and the precepts of justice; the object of Jesus, who closed the series of revelations, was not, therefore, to reveal any new religious doctrines or to give any new sanctions to the precepts of justice, but to introduce and establish the moral code of benevolence. The peculiarity of the Gospel, then, is in its morality, in the fact, that it bases morality, not on fear nor honor, not on authority nor justice, but on love. "Thou shalt love thy neighbor as thyself."

We have here given but a meager outline of this very interesting essay; but we cannot give a fuller analysis of it without exceeding our limits. We may add, however, that the development of the system we have sketched exhibits the marks of a master. The limitations which some of the general principles require, and which we have not room to notice are in most cases stated; and the objections which may occur are in general taken up and satisfactorily answered. We would mention especially that brought against the triumph of benevolence, from the supposed inherent depravity of human nature. It is admitted that man brings into the world with him the seeds of evil, but it is contended that he also brings with him the seeds of good. That he is subject in some degree to error and liable to sin is not denied; but he has also the capacity to feel and act liberally and may be brought under the dominion of benevolence. The position that its morality is the only peculiarity of the Gospel is supported with much earnestness and strength of argument, and the causes which have aided or retarded its progress are treated with great ability. Nearly two thirds of the essay are taken up with these, and evince a patience of research, a philosophical candor, and a Christian tenderness in discussing opinions which are deemed false and mischievous, that cannot be too much commended. That the author is always correct, that he gives to all opinions and events their true influences, or that he always assigns them their true origin is more than we are willing to assert. We have noticed, in the perusal of his work, a number of points, mostly subordinate matters, on which we should disagree with him; but when he errs, he, for the most part, sheds a light that will enable others to correct him.

But, however much we might object to some things in the work which we have introduced and which we commend to our readers, we are happy to agree entirely with its general theory. That society has a growth analogous to that of the individual; that Christianity, as well as all other revelations, was designed to aid that growth; that its morality is the only peculiarity of the Gospel; that its morality is based on benevolence, and forms a code under which the whole human race must ultimately pass is our fixed belief, and has long since been ranked by us with those truths which we make our governing principles of action.

In a former article we spoke of the progress which Christianity has effected. We advanced the doctrine of the essay before us that mankind collectively has a growth precisely analogous to that of the individual. This is a doctrine which enables us to recall the past without wrath or bitterness. All past social institutions have had and fulfilled their mission. They are not to be tried by the present but by that epoch in the progress of society to which they belonged. Tried by this standard, most of the institutions which we now condemn will be found to have been good in their day, and the evil which is charged against them belonged, not to their origin, but resulted from their lingering too long, from their outliving their time.

Judaism is almost infinitely below Christianity, viewed either as social or as a religious system; but who will contend that Judaism was a bad institution in its day? It was adapted to its age and country, and was better for that age and country than Christianity would have been. Christianity would have been too pure and spiritual to be comprehended. It could not have reached the consciences of the people upon whom Judaism was to act, and would have been to them only system of license. Despotism, justly abhorred by all free men, was in its origin a victory achieved by humanity. The condition of those who live under the severest despotism is preferable to that of those savage hordes who submit to no authority but that of an extemporary chief chosen to lead them to war or plunder. There is no society in the savage state; there is aggregation, but not society. The elements of society are indeed there, for they belong to human nature; but they are isolated, and for the most part inoperative. But under a despotism, there is society, rude, imperfect, we admit; still it is society with its look upward and its step, slow indeed, but onward.

Similar remarks might be made of all other systems of religion, of government, of legislation, and of philosophy which have reigned in the past. None of them, perhaps, would be good now because we are in advance of the respective epochs of their usefulness; but in the time and country when and where they were adopted, they were salutary reforms, important victories gained by the progress of society. Each of them, if compared with its predecessor, will be found to have been a forward step in the march of improvement. That they were all imperfect, nobody who comprehends them will deny; but they were as perfect as their respective stages of social progress would admit. It is impossible to give to the child the perfect notions of things which become the man; so is it impossible to give to the infancy of society those perfect social institutions which are suitable only to its full age; or, if we could, it would be like clothing the infant in the dress of a full-grown man.

But, if we acquit the past, we must not forget the duty of the present. We must neither feel nor act as if all progress was ended, and man had attained all the perfection of which he is capable. There is to be a progress through all the future, as there has been one through the past; but the future progress must always be elaborated in the present. The child prepares the youth, the youth prepares the man; and in like manner this generation must prepare its successor, and that must prepare the one to come after it. The duty of the present, then, is great; its position is one of great consequence; it can act on future time, and hasten or retard, in some degree, the progress of society through all coming generations. It will discharge its duty very much in proportion to its estimate of itself and its hopes for the future. If it be satisfied with itself or if it believe that nothing better is possible its exertions will be feeble, and its contributions to future progress will be hardly worth naming. For ourselves, we believe the present greatly superior to whatever has gone before it; but it does not satisfy us. We do not declaim against it, we attempt to comprehend it; we contemplate it with gratitude to God but it does not come up to our idea of good. There flit across our mental vision the shadows, at least, of something immeasurably better.

That all will agree with us in our estimate of the present or in our hopes for the future is more than we expect. Men's notions of society are much influenced by the position from which they view it. He who is at ease himself, rich, enjoying ample leisure, and associating only with the most favored individuals in the community, will call society as it is, very nearly, if not quite, perfect; he will be prone to forget, or not to suspect, the vast amount of suffering that lies beyond him; and, unless perchance he has learned something more of Christianity than its dogmas, he will be very liable to look upon the manual laborer, not as a fellow immortal, with rights, duties, interests, and feelings, sacred as his own, but as a mere instrument of his wealth or pleasure, made to be used for his service, and sufficiently provided for if fed and clothed and comfortably lodged. It will be difficult for him to comprehend any measures taken to benefit the workingmen as a class, and any interest shown in their behalf will seem to him to flow from a Jacobinical spirit or from an over-refined sentimentalism. But the poor man who trudges daily to his toil, feeling himself hardly more respected than an implement of husbandry, and able, with all his exertions, barely to keep his wife and children from starving, will believe society as it is, very imperfect; he will call this a bad world, and hard and bitter thoughts will pass through his mind, as he gazes on the palace of the rich or sees its lordly owner roll by him in his carriage.

We do not censure or approve either. The views of both are natural, if not inevitable, if we take into the account their respective positions. The guinea often slips between men's eyes and the truth; and, from not seeing the truth, it is very natural that they should come to deny it. For ourselves, we share fully the views of neither of the two individuals we have introduced as the representatives of the two extremes of society. It has been our lot to see society on more than one side. Indeed we have seen it on all sides. We know what it can give, and what it requires to be endured, and we say again, it does not satisfy us. We cannot avoid dreaming, if dreaming it prove to be, of something greatly its superior. We see endured by all classes a vast mount of evil, to which we cannot reconcile our love of humanity. We see noble energies misdirected, false modes at judging adopted, factitious distinctions to obtain and be defended. All over the world, even in its most favored portions, there is an inequality in wealth, in moral, intellectual, and social advantages, which we believe wholly inconsistent with the full exercise of Christian love. Everywhere one part of our fellow beings are wasting away in luxury, indolence, listlessness, and dissipation; and another part pining in want and neglect, devoured by discontent and envy; and when we see this, we can call it neither good nor necessary. We ask that it may be cured and we turn to the future with full faith that it will be.

But, in expressing ourselves thus decidedly against the present and in favor of the future, we would guard against being misinterpreted. We are not among those who believe society, as it is now organized, is radically wrong. Its roots are in human nature itself and a society radically different cannot be obtained till we procure another human nature. We would not destroy present society; we see in it the germs of all that we desire should be; but we would carry it forward to its perfection. The work, in which we would enlist the friends of humanity, is one of improvement, not of destruction.

In speaking against inequality, we do not propose that all the members of the community should be in precisely the same condition. This is not a world in which all things and all men can be reduced to one dead level. The Creator everywhere delights to put himself forth in variety and it is variety that makes up the charm of life. Life were a dull scene were we all in precisely the same condition, of precisely the same size, and of precisely the same way of thinking and feeling. Better, far better, were all the storms and tempests which rage from the greatest inequality than such a dead and deadening calm. Were such a state of uniformity, of monotony, once brought about, gone were all our enterprise, all motives to exertion, all hopes of further progress; society would be dead and would rot, as it is said the ocean does when the long calm has hushed the tide and the wave on its bosom.

There are different classes in the community and there always will be so long as there shall be a diversity in men's natural gifts or in the business of society. But diversity is not inequality. The shoemaker differs from the blacksmith; but he is not, because he is a shoemaker, necessarily inferior or superior to the blacksmith. A division of labor undoubtedly necessary to civilization and to the progress of society, but this says nothing in favor of inequality. The arguments usually adduced to prove that inequality is an essential element in civilization, merely prove the advantages of a diversity in men's talents and of a division of labor. We see a necessity for different classes, but none for a *subordination* of classes. We know not why the mechanic or even the common day-laborer should not so far as his trade or occupation is concerned claim equality with any member of the community; and certainly we cannot understand the justice of excluding him from any of the means of becoming so far as his native talents admit a great and a good man. There should be nothing in labor to degrade the laborer or to operate to his disadvantage. Whatever is necessary to be done should be counted not only honest but honorable. No man should be estimated by his employment or his social position, but by what he is in himself, independent of all adventitious circumstances whatever; and the means of moral and intellectual growth, so far as society can furnish them, should be within the reach of the humblest as well as the proudest member of the community.

But we are willing to admit, because we believe it true, that mankind are not and cannot be equal. Men are born with equal rights, but not with equal capacities. All have the elements of the same nature, but these elements are more developed in some than in others. Some will be leaders, others will only follow. Go into any family or school, when the external circumstances are as nearly equal as possible and you will find someone who is the leader, some two or three who arrange and control the play and the pleasures of all the rest. Nature has given us an aristocracy, though it has left its particular character, under a certain aspect, to accident. When war is deemed the business and the glory of society, the best warriors, heroes, constitute the aristocracy; when religion fills men's minds and hearts, the ministers of religion, priests, are the aristocrats, or, to borrow a Saint-Simonian expression, the chiefs of the people; when learning is the public passion, the aristocracy is based on literature, as it is said to be now in China; when wealth is counted the supreme good, and money-getting the chief end of man, the accumulators of wealth, businessmen, are the aristocrats, the leaders of mankind. In a word, the aristocracy is always based on the spirit of the age or country and composed of those who best represent that spirit.

But against this, which we consider the order of nature, the appointment of God, we have nothing to urge. It is a wise and beneficent appointment and would involve no evil if the aristocracy were based, as it one day will be, on the morality of the Gospel, and composed of those who best represent the spirit of Jesus. Some, even then, would be greater than the rest, but there would be no subordination of classes, no exclusive privileges, no monopoly of social advantages. All would have the same object, be in the same path, and engaged in the same work. If some received a higher reward than others, it would be only relatively higher; compared with his capacity, no one would receive more than another, and each would receive in proportion to his capacity to enjoy. It would be in that case an aristocracy of real virtue; an aristocracy taking the lead in true excellence. Give us such an aristocracy and we will fall contentedly into our rank; and, if there are many above us, we will adopt the sentiment of the old Grecian patriot, who, on losing an election, rejoiced that his country had three hundred better men than himself.

We admit then an original inequality in men's capacities; we believe that the Almighty has established an aristocracy; but this is something very different from admitting, that all the distinctions and their attendant evils, which now obtain in society, are of Divine appointment. They are the natural but not the necessary result of the original inequality in men's capacities. A man may sow tares in his field; if he does, they will grow there as naturally as wheat, and grow too by a law of God; but the law of God does not compel a man to sow tares instead of wheat. If the aristocracy be based on anything else than Christian morality, it will occasion more or less of evil; but this is because the aristocracy rests upon a wrong foundation, bears a wrong character. Now, unless we are prepared to say that God has ordained that the aristocracy shall rest upon that wrong foundation, bear that wrong character, and to say it would be virtually saying that he ordains all sin, we must abandon the notion that all the distinctions and the evils consequent upon them, which obtain in society; are of Divine appointment.

But, in charging them upon the aristocracy, we have not traced them to their origin. The aristocracy does not make the people but the people the aristocracy. Show us your people, and we will tell you who are your aristocrats. They are those who represent the spirit of their times and country the best of all their contemporaries. In censuring them we censure the predominant spirit of their epoch, a spirit which controls the lowest as well as the highest. The aristocracy then is not alone in fault. It but shares a common error. The whole people, individual exceptions of course, are wrong, and the evil complained of can be cured only by infusing a better spirit into the whole mass of society.

The aristocracy of our country is based on wealth. The accumulators of wealth are our leaders. But why are they so? These are leaders only by virtue of a spirit in those to be led, which responds to the spirit in those who would lead. Did we not all love wealth, bow to it, cringe to it, the poor even more than the rich, and estimate a man's worth by the length of his purse, wealth could create no aristocracy amongst us. Were the great mass of our population able to say with him, in the Revolution, to whom the British commissioners offered a large sum to desert the cause of his country, "Tell your master, I am poor, but the King of England is not rich enough to buy me," wealth would have no power over us. But so long as we make it the god, at whose shrine we pay our devotions, it will govern us, and our leaders will be those who engage in its accumulation with the greatest energy and success.

But we have extended these remarks, designed to prevent us from being misapprehended by our readers, too far. We return to the duty of the present in relation to the future. This duty is to labor for the future progress of society. We do not stop to prove that society may be carried forward to greater perfection than that to which it has now attained. There are few who cannot form to themselves an idea vastly superior to it. That ideal will be realized. God has not given us the capacity to form to ourselves loftier and yet loftier ideals, merely to mock us with our impotence. The power of execution may, indeed, fall short of the power of conception; but both can grow, and the growth of one always strengthens the other. Progress there will be. The loftiest ideals of the most gifted of men will be realized. Man is made for a higher destiny than he has yet attained. And he will attain it. That is written. But how? What are the principles by which he should be governed in his efforts to do it? This is the question to be answered; and to answering this question we shall devote the remainder of this article.

Our hope for the future progress of society is not exclusively, nor mainly, in government. This is the age of political economy; the point of view of most of those who would be reformers is political. And their hope is in the action of government upon the masses. The agency of government in the progress of society is not to be overlooked; but it belongs not to government to take the initiative. Government is the creature, not the creator, of any particular state of society; and its mission is to collect, concentrate, and facilitate the operation of the spirit of a people.

All social reforms must be the effect of individual reform. Any change in the public institutions of a country, not demanded by a corresponding change in the individual character of those whose opinions can influence government, will be injurious instead of salutary. Joseph the Second of Germany attempted some reforms in his empire, reforms which could have proceeded only from a sincere regard for the well-being of his subjects; but, being mistimed, they miscarried, and served merely to disturb the peace of his reign, to increase the prejudice against innovation, and to retard the cause he had so much at heart. Declare a race of ignorant, degraded slaves, free, and your declaration will not make them free; give them all the forms of a republican government, with all the guarantee of the most clearly defined constitutions, and they will not be less slaves, and slaves with the disadvantage of being in want of a master to keep them in order. Vain are all the forms of a free government, where freedom is not in the hearts and the habits of the people, as individuals.

A notion has prevailed to some extent, and, perhaps, is not yet wholly abandoned, that man is the creature of external circumstances, and that any given description of character may be produced by a proper modification of external circumstances. Government, as having the most control over external circumstances, has, therefore, been considered the great agent of reform. The whimsical, but philanthropic Owen has pushed this theory to its last results, and thus furnished the means of its refutation. It is a theory which springs from a sensual and superficial philosophy, a philosophy that overlooks the most important element of human nature, man's power to originate action of himself, by his own internal energy. Man acts upon circumstances, as well as they upon him; and it depends mainly on him, whether they control him, or he them. Were it not so, were he indeed a spinning-jenny, then we admit that the modification of external circumstances might make him a spinning-jenny of the most approved fashion.

It was thought at one time, that a free government could go alone, that it had some magic-working power by which it could at once convert the rudest materials into polished stones for its social edifice. Experience is correcting this error, as it will correct many others. We are beginning to perceive that it is not a free government that makes a free people, but a free people that makes a free government. No people will be more free, wise, or just, in its collective capacity, than it is in its individual capacity. What is called the collective wisdom of a nation, when it speaks through public institutions, is only a compromise between the most and the least advanced of the individuals of which it is composed. It is only an average of the wisdom of private individuals. If some fall below it, others rise above it. The wisest and best men of a nation are always in advance of the government. Government cannot come up to their ideal without losing sight of the many. The wise and the good must labor to bring the many up to their ideal, and in proportion, and only in proportion, as they do it, may government advance.

We admit, however, that government is a powerful agent in the progress of society. It has done much, and we trust it will do much more; but it is not omnipotent. It must bend to the spirit of the people. Could we get a legislature mad enough to enact a community of goods or an equal division of property, their enactment could not become a law. It is not the legislature, nor the court, nor the sheriff and his *posse*, that can give to a legislative act the power of law. It is the spirit of the people on whom it is to operate. Look at our people, with a strong sense of property, appreciating to its full extent the value of the *meum,* and do you believe they would submit to a community of goods, or to an equal division of property? Or suppose a statute limiting the amount of property which may be held, could it become a law? Every businessman in the community would trample it under foot; or if not, every species of fraud would be resorted to, for evading it and concealing the amount of property actually possessed. Where such a statute could become a law, it would not be needed, for there the love of wealth would not be too strong. That the love of wealth is too strong in our own country, as well as in many others, is true; that it is the source of many evils is also true; but the remedy is not in legislation, not in government, but in calling into exercise a higher and a purer principle of action.

This purer and higher principle must be sought in the Gospel of Jesus Christ. In our efforts to effect the future progress of society we must be guided solely by the principles of Christian morality. There is no way to carry society forward to its perfection but by making its individual members good Christians. We know that some will smile at this answer. No matter. It is possible that we have given as much of study, brought as great a love of humanity and as strong a desire for progress to the problem we have proposed as those who will smile in contempt at the solution we have offered.

We repeat it; the grand lever of reform, the mighty power that is to carry society forward to its perfection, is Christian morality. In making this assertion, we do not plunge into the arena of theological warfare, we touch not the field from which ascend the battle-shouts of conflicting sectarians; we rise to higher and broader ground, and plant our footsteps, not on the dogmas of the Gospel, but on its simple, sublime, and universal morality. We leave the dogmas about which theologians wrangle; they have their truth, have had their use, but they do not constitute the peculiarity of the Gospel. They are nowhere made by the author of the Gospel the direct object of his instructions. Even the doctrine of the Divine unity, great and glorious as we view it, although recognized by Jesus, is never recognized as one that he was sent to teach but as one already known and believed. The same remark is true of the doctrine of a future state of existence. Jesus alludes to it, but not as a doctrine of his own, whose revelation made a part of his mission; he assumes it, illustrates it, and makes use of it to enforce his morals, but does not make it an object of direct instruction. When questioned respecting it, he refers the interrogator to a previous revelation. It is the same with all the great doctrines of theology. We say not that they are not true, are not important, but they had been revealed previously to the coming of Christ, and needed not to be revealed again.

We assert without fear of denial from anyone who has made this a subject of distinct investigation, that all the great theological doctrines, properly so called, which are connected with Christianity and considered essential to it, were known and believed at the time of our Savior. The unity of God, it is well known, was a distinguishing doctrine of Judaism. We meet in the Old Testament, also, the doctrine of God's paternity, and distinct intimations of his sin-pardoning character. It is true, God's justice reigns in Judaism, but his mercy is also there. "Let the wicked forsake his way, and the unrighteous man his thoughts; and let him return unto the Lord, and he will have mercy upon him; and to our God, for he will abundantly pardon." There may be some question, whether the Jews, in the time of Moses, believed in a future state and a righteous retribution after death; but there can be none that they, or at least a portion of them, believed in both long before the birth of Jesus. Socrates and Plato certainly believed in a life to come; and indeed no people have ever yet been discovered, of whom it could be said with certainty, that they did not believe in some kind of a life beyond this life. The most savage tribes have their land of shadows, their world of spirits, where are their fathers, and where they hope to rejoin them when they die. How men came to the knowledge of these doctrines, whether naturally or supernaturally, by a deduction of reasoning, by the unfolding of a law of their own nature, or by a direct communication from God himself, we do not now inquire. It is sufficient for our present purpose that they were known before the coming of Christ. This we assert. They may all be found in religions existing before the Gospel was given, if not in precisely the Christian form, at least the same in their elements, in their foundation.

It is important that we do not forget this. We believe in the originality of the Gospel; but if the Gospel be asserted to be the revelation of a mere system of theology, its originality remains to be proved. Its originality, and its only peculiarity, in our opinion, is in its morality. We find its theology, at least "for substance of doctrine," elsewhere; but nowhere else its morality. We find in one place a morality based on selfishness; in another, one like the Jewish, "an eye for an eye, a tooth for a tooth," based on justice; but nowhere one on the broad, omnipotent, and indestructible principle of love. This is peculiar to the Gospel, this distinguishes it by broad lines from all other religions, and this, and this alone, is the direct object of its instructions. Nothing else is taught in that simple and sublime Sermon on the Mount; and, when Jesus alludes to the love of our heavenly Father for his children, it is to deduce from it motives for them to love one another. His leading object, whether taken from his own words or from the commentaries of his apostles, obviously was to establish the reign of love or benevolence. His first words were, "Repent for the kingdom of heaven is at hand." The "kingdom of heaven" and the "kingdom of God" mean precisely the same thing; and by the kingdom of God, we must understand the reign of God. God is love; the reign of God, then, is the reign of love. God reigns in that heart where love reigns. He dwells there. "He that dwelleth in love," says John, "dwelleth in God and God in him." Jesus expressly declares, that the new commandment he gave, or the addition he had come to make to the reigning code of morals, was that his disciples should love one another. "A new commandment give I unto you, that ye love one another; as I have loved you, that ye also love one another. By this shall all men know that ye are my disciples, if ye have love one towards another." Now that which should distinguish the disciples as the disciples of Christ, must be considered the peculiarity of what he taught. This was love one to another; and this, we think, fully authorizes our assertion, that the peculiarity of the Gospel was in basing its morality on love, or benevolence.

This "love one to another," which Jesus enjoined, was not a narrow love, to be shut up within the enclosure of his professed followers. It was the broad principle of universal philanthropy. "Ye have heard that it hath been said, Thou shalt love thy neighbor and hate thine enemy; but I say unto you, Love your enemies, bless them that curse you, do good to them that hate you, and pray for them that despitefully use you and persecute you, that ye may be the children of your Father who is in heaven; for he maketh his sun to rise on the evil and on the good, and sendeth rain on the just and the unjust." It is not then a meager system of morals that the Gospel enjoins. Its principles extend beyond the outward act, beyond the narrow circle of our friends or our own sect; they go deep into the heart, and quicken a love for universal man. They command us to love one another, to love even our enemies, as well as Christ loved us; that is, well enough, if need be, to die for our fellow beings as Christ died for us. Here lies our hope, in this grand principle of love to man, and we expect the progress of society only in proportion as men come to love one another better.

Existing social evils have their cause. What is that cause? Say, with our radical politicians, that it is in bad government, and the question is only removed one step, not answered. What is the cause of bad government? If it be in the depravity of rulers, whence that depravity? "They are chosen from the wrong class," say our working-men; "they should be chosen from our ranks, and then they would take care of our interests, and, if our interests were taken care of, all social evils would vanish." Perhaps so. We have great tenderness for the workingmen; we have mourned over their depressed condition, and we rejoice to see them making efforts to elevate themselves to the social rank to which they are entitled; but we have no great respect for their moral or political philosophy. Admit that all the officers of government were taken from the working classes, or from those who really and preeminently have their interests at heart; and does it necessarily follow that the interests of those classes would always be promoted? Do the workingmen never mistake their own interests in their private capacity? Who will assure us, then, that they may not mistake it, in acting in a public capacity? And is this the way to cure the evils of society; to have every man and every class pursue his or its own interest, regardless of that of any other, to support a system of universal competition? This is the very system now in operation; and we may answer the question, What is the cause of social evils? by saying, It is in the fact that each man, whether rich or poor, is pursuing his own interest, or what he believes his own interest, without regard to that of his fellow. And why does he do this? Because he is selfish, does not love his neighbor as himself. All the social evils of which anybody complains, may be traced to the predominance of the selfish propensities. The standard of morality is too low; men's notions of duty fall infinitely below the Christian standard.

Are we wrong? What is the morality of the world? In its best possible shape, it is "Look out for yourself; take care of *Number One*; but," it added in a lower tone, "do no wrong to others." This is all that is aimed at, and more than is accomplished in practice. In practice, the clause spoken in a low tone in theory is sunk, and the maxim runs, "Look out for yourself, keep what you have, and get all you can." In all the varieties of trade and business transactions, every man means to enrich himself, to make his own end of the bargain as much the best as he can; and, if he makes it a great deal the best, he boasts of it, however much the one with whom he trades may suffer. Such we say is the spirit of trade, the predominant spirit in all business transactions, and with a vast majority of the community, though there are no doubt many honorable individual exceptions.

Now what better is to be expected from this morality, than that which we already have? Here is the morality of self-interest; and, in the monstrous inequality in wealth, in learning, in moral and intellectual culture, which glares upon the stranger on entering this city, we see the best it can effect; and even better than it can effect, for benevolence has been here, and in no city on earth has it been more active. It is in vain to expect anything better without a higher standard of morality. If we make interest the governing motive, we must expect all individuals and all classes to be governed by their views of it. These views will always be partial and conflicting. The carpenter and the timber-merchant will contend, that all houses should be constructed of wood; the brick-maker and the brick-layer will prefer brick; the fur-cap manufacturers will encourage the wearing of fur caps; but the hatter will complain that in so doing, they injure his business and take, as it were, the bread out of his mouth. All the trades will be mutually opposed, and perpetual clashing must be the result. There is no such thing as reconciling all classes, all the divisions of labor, and making society harmonious without having men aim at something higher than the morality of selfishness.

Existing social evils, we have said, may be traced to the predominance of the selfish propensities; it is evident, then, that we must have recourse to the predominance of the benevolent affections for a cure. The predominance of these is what the Gospel contemplates, and what we mean by the morality of love. Now we love ourselves, if not exclusively, at least chiefly; but the Gospel commands us to love our neighbor as ourselves. Here is a higher principle than selfishness, a broader principle than justice. Selfishness is satisfied when self is provided for; justice contents himself with doing and receiving no wrong; love goes beyond both, and can be satisfied only by doing good, not by doing some good, but the greatest good in its power. It does not wrap itself up in itself, but it goes out of itself; with its hands filled with benefits, it goes out into the streets, the lanes, the by-paths, into the humble shed of poverty, and into the loathsome dungeon of the prisoner, to find objects to bless; and it returns not as long as it can find a single human being borne down by a burden too great for his strength, a single tear in a human eye to be dried, a single wounded heart into which it can pour the "oil and wine," or a single bruised spirit that it may bind up.

Such is love. Such is the principle that would reign were Christian morality predominant. All crimes would fail, all wrongs would cease. There would be no unmitigated poverty, no ostentatious display of wealth to increase the vanity of the possessor and the discontented envy of him that has it not. There would be no *exploitation de l'homme par l'homme*, as the Saint-Simonians happily express the reigning vice of the past; no encroaching; no turning of one's superior knowledge to one's own exclusive advantage, but to supplying the deficiencies of others; trade would become, what it should be, the mutual exchange of benefits; everywhere would reign peace, harmony, and joy; man would give his heart and his hand to his brother, and society would present a picture on which even God himself might look with approbation.

Such were society, were love once to become predominant, to run through all our actions, and to preside over all the intercourse of man with man. "*Were it* predominant, ay, were it," it is said; "but it is not, it *cannot* be. Men are selfish, each one for himself, no one for his brother, and it is folly to expect that all will come under the influence of the law of love." We have heard this objection to our hopes of future progress, at least in substance, in the humble shed of poverty, in the palaces of the rich, in the shop of the mechanic, in the fields of the agriculturist, behind the counter of the merchant, in the halls of legislation, from the bar, the bench, and the pulpit; but we dare not give utterance to the outraged feelings with which we have always heard it. We never hear it but with deep abhorrence. Let it never proceed from the lips of a professed disciple of Jesus. Whoever thou art, if thou hast no more faith in human virtue, no more faith in the power of human nature to come under the government of the pure and godlike principle of love, than this objection implies, blush to enter the pulpit, to speak in the name of one whose disciples are to be known only by having "love one towards another," in the name of one who commands all men to love even their enemies, and whose avowed object was to turn men from their iniquities, to bring them to God, and to make them perfect as their Father in heaven is perfect!

Do we use strong language? We know it, and we mean it. The interests of religion, of humanity, demand it; and he who does not bring out the great principle of the Gospel, and insist in strong terms on its being admitted, preached, and obeyed, seems to us to fail in his duty to God and to man. He is a poor missionary, who begins by saying to those to whom he addresses himself, "My brethren, the religion I bring you is an excellent thing. Its morality is of the purest and most elevated character. If obeyed it would have the most happy effect; but then you must not be so foolish as to suppose it generally practicable. A few gifted individuals alone can ever come under its influences; the great mass of mankind can never be governed by it." Suppose one of our missionaries to the Indians should thus address his heathen audience, and what would be the influence of his preaching? What the answer that would be returned him? "Go back to your own country; if your Gospel morality is impracticable, why come ye here to disturb our minds and the state of our society by proclaiming it?" Or, if he should not tell them that it is impracticable, if he should so feel, with what success would he preach? Would he be likely to speak in those earnest and thrilling tones, which go to the heart and the conscience, fasten conviction and lead to reformation? He who would go forth to convert the world should go in faith; he should believe what he preaches, and not only believe it true, but practicable.

The question between us and those who urge the objection we are considering is not, whether we are visionaries, dreaming of social perfection which can never be realized, but, whether the Gospel be or be not a practicable scheme of morals. We throw ourselves upon the Gospel. We have stated its morality, and what would be the social result, were it obeyed. Nobody, who reflects a moment, will accuse us of misstating that morality, or pretend that our inferences are illegitimate. There is, then, no escape for the objector but in arraigning the Gospel itself. The blow with which he would demolish us, he must reserve for our Master. Was Jesus a visionary, preaching a morality which only a few, if indeed any can practice; or did he proclaim a moral law adapted to universal human nature, and consequently one which all men have the power to obey? This is the question. To this question we wait a reply, leaving the objector to settle it with one who "needed not that any should testify of man, for he knew what was in man."

We are aware that we have presented the subject in a light in which it is not usually contemplated; but we are confident that we have presented it in its true light. We believe that one great reason why the Christian ministry has not been more efficient is that it has not had full faith in the practicability of the Gospel morality. It has, we own, labored with great diligence and fidelity in its calling; but it has often left the people where it found them—dead in a worldly policy, or consumed by a crackling fanaticism or an unmeasured zeal for dogmas of faith. It has had no just conception of the extent of the morality it was called to preach, and of course no belief in its practicability or in the state of society which it was destined to introduce. It has therefore been unable to speak as its Master spoke; its words have been powerless, and its tones lifeless. It could not go to the people in the fullness of faith, and consequently it could not adopt the tone and manner of reality, which alone can make a preacher successful.

We mean not to apply these remarks to the Christian ministry in its relation to religious dogmas. These have been believed, and at times so believed that the idea of proving them could not find admittance into the head of him who preached them. They have been to the preacher, not opinions, but realities; and when they have been so, he has spoken with power and fastened conviction. But it was not a moral conviction. No man has yet gone forth and preached the great law of love as the peculiarity of the Gospel, and preached it in full faith of its universal obligation and practicability; for it has not yet been so believed, except by here and there an individual. But those who do not so believe, are so far unbelievers in the Gospel, and in their influence in some respects the most fatal class of unbelievers. Here is the call for reform. Men must be brought to believe the Gospel; not its theology, for that the majority of the civilized world already believe, but its morality.

We do not make these remarks to condemn the past, nor to censure the present, but to point out what is our duty for the future. There is a time for all things. We know that men move slowly, and that the progress of ideas is like that of the apparent motion of the sun; we cannot see the sun move, but, after a while, we see that it has moved. We do not complain, because the great truth for which we contend has not been brought out distinctly before. It required time to wear out the old morality, to exhaust theological discussions, and to fix the basis of our ever progressing religious theory. That is now done, and the epoch has arrived for extending our views, and making the exclusively theological element, with which the religious world has been engaged for so many ages, give place to the moral element, which alone constitutes the peculiarity of the Gospel. The Christian world is now distracted, torn into contending sects, and exhibiting a spectacle saddening to the hearts of all the real friends of humanity. These sects must be brought together, these alienated hearts must be united, and these scattered and inoperative elements must be brought into one grand and complete whole. But this cannot be done by any system of theology whatever. It can be done only by striking a chord which shall vibrate alike through all moral nature. We can do it only by a new and a higher view of Christian morality. We have cleared away the rubbish of a false and mischievous theology; we have brought men back, at least in theory, to the simple doctrines inculcated in Scripture, to those which are based on everlasting truth, which are in perfect harmony with man's intellectual nature, those on which Jesus based his morality; and now we must bring out that morality, and hold it up to the admiration and love of all hearts.

The first step to this is to comprehend the extent of that morality, and to obtain the conviction of its practicability. We have said that it is the law of love, a law that requires us to love one another as Christ loved us, that is, well enough, if need be, to die for our fellow beings as Christ died for us. This is the principle of Christian morality. It is, we believe, practicable. Jesus preached it, commanded his disciples to preach it to "every creature," and that too without ever intimating that all men could not obey it. Let the preacher, when he reads the discourses of Jesus to his congregation, when he calls upon his hearers to love God with all the heart, mind, and strength, and their neighbors as themselves, catch the meaning of what he utters, and he will want no arguments to prove that men can "have that mind in them which was also in Christ Jesus"; and, when he comes once to believe that they can, he will speak with such firm persuasion of the truth of what he utters, that "his words will be with power." Let him comprehend his mission, and its grandeur will waken all the higher and better principles of his soul, kindle up a moral enthusiasm that will carry him through every difficulty, and make him mighty in the work of turning men's hearts to

God. This is what is implied by the ministerial office. It is a practical answer to the objection brought against our hopes; and, till men will admit, that the preacher is inducted into his office to preach an impracticable scheme of morals, we shall consider a further answer, at least to professed Christians, as unnecessary.

New Views of Christianity, Society, and the Church
1836

Preface

It must not be inferred from my calling this little work *New Views* that I profess to bring forward a new religion, or to have discovered a new Christianity. The religion of the Bible I believe to be given by the inspiration of God, and the Christianity of Christ satisfies my understanding and my heart. However widely I may dissent from the Christianity of the church, with that of Christ I am content to stand or fall, and I ask no higher glory than to live and die in it and for it.

I believe my views are somewhat original, but I am far from considering them the only or even the most important views which may be taken of the subjects on which I treat. Those subjects have a variety of aspects, and all their aspects are true and valuable. He who presents any one of them does a service to humanity; and he who presents one of them has no occasion to fall out with him who presents another, nor to claim superiority over him.

Although I consider the views contained in the following pages original, I believe the conclusions, to which I come at last, will be found very much in accordance with those generally adopted by the denomination of Christians, with whom it has been for some years my happiness to be associated. That denomination, however, must not be held responsible for any of the opinions I have advanced. I am not the organ of a sect. I do not speak by authority, nor under tutelage. I speak for myself and from my own convictions. And in this way, better than I could in any other, do I prove my sympathy with the body of which I am a member, and establish my right to be called a Unitarian.

In what I have written here as well as in all I have written elsewhere and on other occasions, I have aimed to set an example of free thought and free speech. I ask no thanks for this, for it was my duty and I dared not do otherwise. Besides, theology can never rise to the rank and certainty of a science till it be submitted to the free and independent action of the human mind.

It will at once be seen that I have given only a few rough sketches of the subjects I have introduced. Many statements appear without the qualifications with which they exist in my own mind, many parts are doubtless obscure for the want of fuller developments, and the whole probably needs to be historically verified. But I have done all I could without making a larger book, and a larger book I could hope that nobody would buy or read. I may hereafter fill up my sketches and complete my pictures; but it would have been useless in the present state of the public mind to attempt more than I have done.

For my literary sins I have a right to some indulgence. My early life was spent in far other pursuits than those of literature. I make no pretensions to scholarship. For all my other sins—except those of omission, for which I have given a valid excuse—I ask no indulgence. I hope I shall be rigidly criticized. He who helps me correct my errors is my friend.

Those who feel any interest in "The Society for Christian Union and Progress"—a society collected during the past summer, and of which I am the minister—may find in this volume the principles on which that society is founded, and the objects it contemplates. To the members of that society and to those who have listened to my preaching these views will not be new.

If any of my readers wish to pursue the subject touched upon in my Introduction, I would refer them to Benjamin Constant's great work *De la Religion considérée dans sa Source, ses Formes et ses Développements*; to *Religion and the Church*, a book by Dr. Follen, which he is now publishing in a series of numbers; and especially to Schleiermacher's work *Ueber die Religion: Reden an die Gebildeten unter ihren Verächtern*, a work which produced a powerful sensation in Germany when it first appeared, and one which cannot fail to exert a salutary influence on religious inquiry among ourselves. A friend, to whom I am proud to acknowledge myself under many obligations, has translated this work in the course of his own private studies and I cannot but hope that he may be induced ere long to publish it.

With these remarks I commit my little work to its fate. It contains results to which I have come only by years of painful experience; but I dismiss it from my mind with the full conviction, that He, who has watched over my life and preserved me amidst scenes through which I hope I may not be called to pass again, will take care that if what it contains be false it shall do no harm, and if it be true that it shall not die.

Boston, Nov. 8, 1836
Introduction

Religion is natural to man and he ceases to be man the moment he ceases to be religious.

This position is sustained by what we are conscious of in ourselves and by the universal history of mankind.

Man has a capacity for religion, faculties which are useless without it, and wants which God alone can satisfy. Accordingly wherever he is, in whatever age or country, he has—with a few individual exceptions easily accounted for—some sort of religious notions and some form of religious worship.

But it is only religion, as distinguished from religious institutions, that is natural to man. The religious sentiment is universal, permanent, and indestructible; religious institutions depend on transient causes, and vary in different countries and epochs.

As distinguished from religious institutions, religion is the conception, or sentiment, of the Holy, that which makes us think of something as reverend, and prompts us to revere it. It is that indefinable something within us which gives a meaning to the words venerable and awful, which makes us linger around the sacred and the time-hallowed, the graves of heroes or of nations,—which leads us to launch away upon the boundless expanse, or plunge into the mysterious depths of being, and which, from the very ground of our nature, like the Seraphim of the prophet, is forever crying out, "Holy, holy, holy, is the Lord of hosts; the whole earth is full of his glory."

Religious institutions are the forms with which man clothes his religious sentiment, the answer he gives to the question, What is the holy? Were he a stationary being, or could he take in the whole of truth at a single glance, the answer once given would be always satisfactory, the institution once adopted would be universal, unchangeable, and eternal. But neither is the fact. Man's starting-point is the low valley, but he is continually—with slow and toilsome effort it may be—ascending the sides of the mountain to more favorable positions, from which his eye may sweep a broader horizon of truth. He begins in ignorance, but he is ever growing in knowledge.

In our ignorance, when we have seen but little of truth, and seen that little but dimly, we identify the Holy with the merely terrible, the powerful, the inscrutable, the useful, or the beautiful; and we adopt as its symbols, the thunder and lightning, winds and rain, ocean and storm, majestic river or placid lake, shady grove or winding brook, the animal, the bow or spear by means of which we are fed, clothed, and protected; but as experience rolls back the darkness, which made all around us appear huge and spectral, purges and extends our vision, these become inadequate representatives of our religious ideas; they fail to shadow forth the holy to our understandings; and we leave them and rise to that which appears to be free from their limited and evanescent nature, to that which is unlimited, all-sufficient, and unfailing.

We are creatures of growth; it is, therefore, impossible that all our institutions should not be mutable and transitory. We are forever discovering new fields of truth, and every new discovery requires a new institution, or the modification of an old one. We might as well demand that the sciences of physiology, chemistry, and astronomy should wear eternally the same form, as that religious institutions should be unchangeable, and that those which satisfied our fathers should always satisfy us.

All things change their forms. Literature, art, science, governments change under the very eye of the spectator. Religious institutions are subject to the same universal law. Like the individuals of our race, they pass away and leave us to deck their tombs, or in our despair, to exclaim that we will lie down in the grave with them. But as the race itself does not die, as new generations crowd upon the departing to supply their places, so does the reproductive energy of religion survive all mutations of forms, and so do new institutions arise to gladden us with their youth and freshness, to carry us further onward in our progress, and upward nearer to that which "is the same yesterday, to-day, and forever."

Chapter I: Christianity

About two thousand years ago, mankind, having exhausted all their old religious institutions, received from their heavenly Father through the ministry of Jesus of Nazareth a new institution which was equal to their advanced position, and capable of aiding and directing their future progress.

But this institution must be spoken of as one which was, not as one which is. Notwithstanding the vast territories it acquired, the mighty influence it once exerted over the destinies of humanity, and its promises of immortality, it is now but the mere shadow of a sovereign, and its empire is falling in ruins. What remains of it is only the body after the spirit has left it. It is no longer animated by a living soul. The sentiment of the holy has deserted it, and it is a byword and a mockery.

Either then Jesus did not embrace in his mind the whole of truth, or else the church has at best only partially realized his conception.

No institution, so long as it is in harmony with the progress of the understanding, can fail to command obedience or kindle enthusiasm. The church now does neither. There is a wide disparity between it and the present state of intellectual development. We have discovered truths which it cannot claim as its own; we are conscious of instincts which it disavows, and which we cannot, or will not, suppress. Whose is the fault? Is it the fault of humanity, of Jesus, or of the church?

Humanity cannot be blamed, for humanity's law is to grow; it has an inherent right to seek for truth, and it is under no obligation to shut its eyes to the facts which unfold themselves to its observation. It is not the fault of Jesus, unless it can be proved that all he contemplated has been realized, that mankind have risen to as pure, and as happy a state as he proposed; have indeed fully comprehended him, taken in his entire thought, and reduced it to practice. Nobody will pretend this. The fault then must be borne by the church.

The church even in its best days was far below the conception of Jesus. It never comprehended him, and was always a very inadequate symbol of the holy as he understood it.

Christianity, as it existed in the mind of Jesus, was the type of the most perfect religious institution to which the human race will, probably, ever attain. It was the point where the sentiment and the institution, the idea and the symbol, the conception and its realization appear to meet and become one. But the contemporaries of Jesus were not equal to this profound thought. They could not comprehend the God-Man, the deep meaning of his assertion, "I and my Father are one." He spake as never man spake—uttered truths for all nations and for all times; but what he uttered was necessarily measured by the capacity of those who heard him, not by his own. The less never comprehends the greater. Their minds must have been equal to his in order to have been able to take in the full import of his words. They might—as they did—apprehend a great and glorious meaning in what he said; they might kindle at the truths he revealed to their understandings, and even glory in dying at the stake to defend them; but they would invariably and inevitably narrow them down to their own inferior intellects, and interpret them by their own previous modes of thinking and believing.

The disciples themselves, the familiar friends, the chosen apostles of Jesus, notwithstanding all the advantages of personal intercourse and personal explanations never fully *apprehended* him. They mistook him for the Jewish Messiah, and even after his resurrection and ascension, they supposed it to have been his mission to "restore the kingdom to Israel." Though commanded to preach the Gospel to "every creature," they never once imagined that they were to preach it to any people but the Jewish, till the circumstances, which preceded and followed Peter's visit to Cornelius the Roman centurion, took place to correct their error, it was not till then that any one of them could say, "Of a truth, I perceive that God is no respecter of persons; but in every nation he that feareth him and worketh righteousness is accepted with him." If this was true of the disciples, how much more true must it have been of those who received the words of Jesus at second or third hand, and without any of the personal explanations or commentaries necessary to unfold their meaning?

Could the age in which Jesus appeared have comprehended him it would have been superior to him, and consequently have had no need of him. We do not seek an instructor for our children in one who is not able to teach them. Moreover, if that age could have even rightly apprehended Jesus, we should be obliged to say his mission was intended to be confined to that age, or else to admit that the human race was never to go beyond the point then attained. Either Jesus did not regard the future of humanity, or he designed to interrupt its progress, and strike it with the curse of immobility; or else he was above his age and of course not to be understood by it. The world has not stood still since his coming; the church has always considered his kingdom as one of which there is to be no end; and we know that he was not comprehended, and that even we, with the advantage of nearly two thousand years of mental and moral progress, are far —very far—below him.

If the age in which Jesus appeared could not comprehend him, it is obvious that it could not fully embody him in its institutions. It could embody no more of him than it could receive, and as it could receive only a part of him, we must admit that the church has never been more than partially Christian. Never has it been the real body of Christ. Never has it reflected the God-Man perfectly. Never has it been a true mirror of the holy. Always has the holy in the sense of the church been a very inferior thing to what it was in the mind and heart and life of Jesus.

But we must use measured terms in our condemnation of the church. We must not ask the man in the child. The church did what it could. It did its best to "form Christ" within itself, "the hope of glory" and was up to the period of its downfall as truly Christian, as the progress made by the human race admitted. It aided the growth of the human mind; enabled us to take in more truth than it had itself received; furnished us the light by which we discovered its defects; and by no means should its memory be cursed. Nobly and perseveringly did it discharge its duty; useful was it in its day and generation; and now that it has given up the ghost, we should pay it the rites of honorable burial, plant flowers over its resting place, and sometimes repair thither to bedew them with our tears.

To comprehend Jesus, to seize the holy as it was in him, and consequently the true idea of Christianity, we must, from the heights to which we have risen by aid of the church, look back and down upon the age in which he came, ascertain what was the work which there was for him to perform, and from that obtain a key to what he proposed to accomplish.

Two systems then disputed the empire of the world; spiritualism[1] represented by the eastern world, the old world of Asia, and materialism represented by Greece and Rome. Spiritualism regards purity or holiness as predicable of Spirit alone, and matter as essentially impure, possessing and capable of receiving nothing of the holy,—the prison house of the soul, its only hindrance to a union with God, or absorption into his essence, the cause of all uncleanness, sin, and evil, consequently to be condemned, degraded, and as far as possible annihilated. Materialism takes the other extreme, does not recognize the claims of Spirit, disregards the soul, counts the body everything, earth all, heaven nothing, and condenses itself into the advice, "Eat and drink; for tomorrow we die."

This opposition between spiritualism and materialism presupposes a necessary and original antithesis between spirit and matter. When spirit and matter are given as antagonist principles, we are obliged to admit antagonism between all the terms into which they are respectively convertible. From spirit is deduced by natural generation, God, the priesthood, faith, heaven, eternity; from matter, man, the state, reason, the earth, and time; consequently, to place spirit and matter in opposition, is to make an antithesis between God and man, the priesthood and the state, faith and reason, heaven and earth, and time and eternity.

This antithesis generates perpetual and universal war. It is necessary then to remove it and harmonize, or unite the two terms. Now, if we conceive Jesus as standing between spirit and matter, the representative of both—God-Man—the point where both meet and lose their antithesis, laying a hand on each and saying, "Be one, as I and my Father are one," thus sanctifying both and marrying them in a mystic and holy union, we shall have his secret thought and the true idea of Christianity.

The Scriptures uniformly present Jesus to us as a mediator, the middle term between two extremes, and they call his work a mediation, a reconciliation—an atonement. The church has ever considered Jesus as making an atonement. It has held on to the term at all times as with the grasp of death. The first charge it has labored to fix upon heretics has been that of rejecting the atonement, and the one all dissenters from the predominant doctrines of the day have been most solicitous to repel is that of "denying the Lord who bought us." The whole Christian world, from the days of the apostles up to the moment in which I write, have identified Christianity with the atonement, and felt that in admitting the atonement they admitted Christ, and that in denying it they were rejecting him.

Jesus himself always spoke of his doctrine, the grand idea which lay at the bottom of all his teaching, under the term "Love." "A new commandment give I unto you, that ye love one another." "By this shall all men know that ye are my disciples, if ye have love one to another." John, who seems to have caught more of the peculiar spirit of Jesus than any of the disciples, sees nothing but love in the Gospel. Love penetrated his soul; it runs through all his writings, and tradition relates that it at length so completely absorbed him that all he could say in his public addresses was, "Little children, love one another." He uniformly dwells with unutterable delight on the love which the Father has for us and that which we may have for him, the intimate union of man with God, expressed by the strong language of dwelling in God and God dwelling in us. In his view there is no antagonism. All antithesis is destroyed. Love sheds its hallowed and hallowing light over both God and man, over spirit and matter, binding all beings and all being in one strict and everlasting union.

The nature of love is to destroy all antagonism. It brings together; it begetteth union and from union cometh peace. And what word so accurately expresses to the consciousness of Christendom, the intended result of the mission of Jesus, as that word peace? Every man who has read the New Testament feels that it was peace that Jesus came to effect, peace after which the soul has so often sighed and yearned in vain, and a peace not merely between two or three individuals for a day, but a universal and eternal peace between all conflicting elements, between God and man, between the soul and body, between this world and another, between the duties of time and the duties of eternity. How clearly is this expressed in that sublime chorus of the angels, sung over the manger-cradle,—"Glory to God in the highest, on earth peace and goodwill to men!"

Where there is but one term there is no union. There is no harmony with but one note. It is mockery to talk to us of peace where one of the two belligerent parties is annihilated. That were the peace of the grave. Jesus must then save both parties. The church has, therefore, with a truth it has never comprehended, called him *God-Man*. But if the two terms and their products be originally and essentially antagonist; if there be between them an innate hostility, their union, their reconciliation cannot be effected. Therefore in proposing the union, in attempting the atonement, Christianity declares as its great doctrine that there is no essential, no original antithesis between God and man; that neither spirit nor matter is unholy in its nature; that all things, spirit, matter, God, man, soul, body, heaven, earth, time, eternity, with all their duties and interests, are in themselves holy. All things proceed from the same holy Fountain, and no fountain sendeth forth both sweet waters and bitter. It therefore writes "HOLINESS TO THE LORD" upon everything, and sums up its sublime teaching in that grand synthesis, "Thou shalt love the Lord thy God with all thy heart and mind and soul and strength, and thy neighbor as thyself."

Chapter II: The Church

The aim of the church was to embody the holy as it existed in the mind of Jesus, and had it succeeded, it would have realized the atonement; that is, the reconciliation of spirit and matter and all their products.

But the time was not yet. The Paraclete was in expectation. The church could only give currency to the fact that it was the mission of Jesus to make an atonement. It from the first misapprehended the conditions on which it was to be effected. Instead of understanding Jesus to assert the holiness of both spirit and matter, it understood him to admit that matter was rightfully cursed, and to predicate holiness of spirit alone. In the sense of the church then he did not come to atone spirit and matter, but to redeem spirit from the consequences of its connection with matter. His name therefore was not the Atoner, the Reconciler, but the Redeemer, and his work not properly an atonement, but a redemption. This was the original sin of the church.

By this misapprehension the church rejected the mediator. The Christ ceases to be the middle term uniting spirit and matter, the *hilasterion*, the mercy-seat, or point where God and man meet and lose their antithesis, the Advocate with the Father for humanity, and becomes the avenger of spirit, the manifestation of God's righteous indignation against man. He dies to save mankind, it is true, but he dies to pay a penalty. God demands man's everlasting destruction; Jesus admits that God's demand is just, and dies to discharge it. Hence the symbol of the cross, signifying to the church an original and necessary antithesis between God and man which can be removed only by the sacrifice of justice to mercy. In this the church took its stand with spiritualism, and from a mediator became a partisan.

By taking its stand with spiritualism the church condemned itself to all the evils of being exclusive. It obliged itself to reject an important element of truth, and it became subject to all the miseries and vexatious of being intolerant. It became responsible for all the consequences which necessarily result from spiritualism. The first of these consequences was the denial that Jesus came in the flesh. If matter be essentially unholy, then Jesus, if he had a material body, must have been unholy; if unholy, sinful. Hence all the difficulties of the Gnostics—difficulties hardly adjusted by means of a Virgin Mother and the Immaculate Conception; for this mode of accommodation really denied the God-Man, the symbol of the great truth the church was to embody. It left the God indeed, but it destroyed the man, inasmuch as it separated the humanity of Jesus by its very origin from common humanity.

Man's inherent depravity, his corruption by nature followed as a matter of course. Man by his very nature partakes of matter, is material, then unholy, then sinful, corrupt, depraved. He is originally material, therefore originally a sinner. Hence original sin. Sometimes original sin is indeed traced to a primitive disobedience, to the Fall; but then the doctrine of the Fall itself is only one of the innumerable forms which is assumed by the doctrine of the essential impurity of matter.

From this original, inherent depravity of human nature necessarily results that antithesis between God and man which renders their union impossible and which imperiously demands the sacrifice of one or the other. "Die he or justice must." Man is sacrificed on the cross in the person of Jesus. Hence the vicarious atonement, the conversion of the atonement into an expiation. But, if man was sacrificed, if he died as he deserved in Jesus, his death was eternal. Symbolically then he cannot rise. The body of Jesus after his resurrection is not material in the opinion of the church. He does not rise God-Man, but God. Hence the absolute Deity of Christ, which under various disguises has always been the sense of the church.

From man's original and inherent depravity it results that he has no power to work out his own salvation. Hence the doctrine of human inability. By nature man is enslaved to matter; he is born in sin and shapen in iniquity. He is sold to sin, to the world, to the devil. He must be ransomed. Matter cannot ransom him; then spirit must—and "God the mighty Maker" dies to redeem his creature, to deliver the soul from the influence of matter.

But this can be only partially effected in this world. As long as we live, we must drag about with us this clog of earth—matter—and not till after death, when our vile bodies shall be changed into the likeness of Christ's glorious body, shall we be really saved. We are not then saved here; we only hope to be saved hereafter. Hence the doctrine which denies holiness to man in this world, which places the kingdom of God exclusively in the world to come, and which establishes a real antithesis between heaven and earth, and the means necessary to secure present well-being and those necessary to secure future blessedness.

God has indeed died to ransom sinners from the grave of the body, to redeem them from the flesh, to break the chains of the bound and to set the captive free; but the effects of the ransom must be secured; agents must be appointed to proclaim the glad tidings of salvation, to bid the prisoner hope, and the captive rejoice that the hour of release will come. Hence the church. Hence too the authority of the church to preach salvation—to save sinners. And the church is composed of all who have this authority and of none others, therefore the dogma, "Out of the church there is no salvation."

The church is commissioned; it is God's agent in saving sinners. It is then his representative. If the representative of God, then of spirit. In its representative character, that is, as a church, it is then spiritual, and if spiritual, holy; and if holy, infallible. Hence the infallibility of the church.

The holy should undoubtedly govern the unholy; Spirit then should govern matter. Spirit then is supreme; and the church as the representative of spirit must also be supreme. Hence the supremacy of the church.

The church is a vast body composed of many members. It needs a head. It should also be modeled after the church above. The church above has a supreme head, Jesus Christ; the church below should then have a head, who may be its center, its unity, the personification of its wisdom and its authority. Hence the pope, the supreme head of the church, vicar of Jesus, and representative of God.

The church is a spiritual body. Its supremacy then is a spiritual supremacy. A spiritual supremacy extends to thought and conscience. Hence on the one hand the confessional designed to solve cases of conscience, and on the other creeds, expurgatory indexes, inquisitions, pains and penalties against heretics.

The spiritual order in heaven is absolute; the church then as the representative of that order must also be absolute. As a representative it speaks not in its own name, but in the name of the power it represents. Since that power may command, the church may command; and as it may command in the name of an absolute sovereign, its commands must be implicitly obeyed. An absolute sovereign may command to any extent he pleases—what shall be believed as well as what shall be done.

Hence implicit faith, the authority which the church has alleged for the basis of belief. Hence too prohibitions against reason and reasoning which have marked the church under all its forms, in all its phases and divisions and subdivisions.

Reason too is human; then it is material; to set it up against faith were to set up the material against the spiritual; the human against the divine; man against God: for the church being God by proxy, by representation, it has of course the right to consider whatever is set up against the faith it enjoins as set up against God.

The civil order, if it be anything more than a function of the church, belongs to the category of matter. It is then inferior to the church. It is then bound to obey the church. Hence the claims of the church over civil institutions, its right to bestow the crowns of kings, to place kingdoms under ban, to absolve subjects from their allegiance, and all the wars and antagonism between church and state.

The spiritual order alone is holy. Its interests are then the only interests it is not sinful to labor to promote. In laboring to promote them, the church was under the necessity of laboring for itself. Hence its justification to itself of its selfishness, its rapacity, its untiring efforts to aggrandize itself at the expense of individuals and of states.

As the interests of the church alone were holy, it was of course sinful to be devoted to any others. All the interests of the material order, that is, all temporal interests, were sinful, and the church never ceased to call them so. Hence its perpetual denunciation of wealth, place and renown, and the obstacles it always placed in the way of all direct efforts for the promotion of well-being on earth. This is the reason why it has discouraged, indeed unchurched, anathematized, all efforts to gain civil and political liberty, and always regarded with an evil eye all industry not directly or indirectly in its own interests.

This same exclusive spiritualism borrowed from Asia, striking matter with the curse of being unclean in its nature, was the reason for enjoining celibacy upon the clergy. An idea of sanctity was attached to the ministerial office, which it was supposed any contact with the flesh would sully. It also led devotees, those who desired to lead lives strictly holy, to renounce the flesh, as well as the world and the devil, to take vows of perpetual celibacy and to shut themselves up in monasteries and nunneries. It is the origin of all those self-inflicted tortures, mortifications of the body, penances, fastings, and that neglect of this world for another, which fill so large a space in the history of the church during what are commonly called the "Dark Ages." The church in its theory looked always with horror upon all sensual indulgences. Marriage was sinful, till purified by holy church. The song and the dance, innocent amusements, and wholesome recreations, though sometimes conceded to the incessant importunities of matter, were of the devil. Even the gay dress and blithesome song of nature were offensive. A dark, silent, friar's frock was the only befitting garb for nature or for man. The *beau ideal* of a good Christian was one who renounced all his connections with the world, became deaf to the voice of kindred and of friends, insensible to the sweetest and holiest emotions of humanity, immured himself in a cave or cell, and did nothing the livelong day but count his beads and kiss the crucifix.

Exceptions there were; but this was the idea, the dominant tendency of the church. Thanks, however, to the stubbornness of matter, and to the superintending care of Providence, its dominant tendency always found powerful resistance, and its idea was never able fully to realize itself.

Chapter III: Protestantism

Everything must have its time. The church abused, degraded, vilified matter, but could not annihilate it. It existed in spite of the church. It increased in power, and at length rose against spiritualism and demanded the restoration of its rights. This rebellion of materialism, of the material order against the spiritual, is Protestantism.

Matter always exerted a great influence over the practice of the church. In the first three centuries it was very powerful. It condemned the Gnostics and Manicheans as heretics, and was on the point of rising to empire under the form of Arianism. But the oriental influence predominated, and the Arians became acknowledged heretics.

After the defeat of Arianism, that noble protest in its day of rationalism against mysticism, of matter against spirit, of European against Asiatic ideas, the church departed more and more from the atonement, and became more and more arrogant, arbitrary, spiritualistic, papistical. Still matter occasionally made itself heard. It could not prevent the celibacy of the clergy, but it did maintain the unity of the race and prevented the reestablishment of a sacerdotal caste, claiming by birth a superior sanctity. It broke out too in the form of Pelagianism, that doctrine which denies that man is clean gone in iniquity, and which makes the material order count for something. Pelagius was the able defender of humanity when it seemed to be deserted by all its friends, and his efforts were by no means unavailing.

Matter asserted its rights and avenged itself in a less unexceptionable form in the convents, the monasteries and nunneries, among the clergy of all ranks, in that gross licentiousness which led to the reformation attempted by Hildebrand; and finally it ascended—not avowedly, but in reality—the papal throne, in the person of Leo X.

The accession of Leo X to the papal throne is a remarkable event in the history of the church. It marks the predominance of material interests in the very bosom of the church itself. It is a proof that whatever might be the theory of the church, however different it claimed to be from all other powers, it was at this epoch in practice the same as the kingdoms of men. Poverty ceased in its eyes to be a virtue. The poor mendicant, the barefooted friar, could no longer hope to become one day the spiritual head of Christendom. Spiritual gifts and graces were not now enough. High birth and royal pretensions were required; and it was not as a priest, but as a member of the princely house of Medici that Leo became pope.

The object of the church had changed. It had ceased to regard the spiritual wants and welfare of mankind. It had become wealthy. It had acquired vast portions of this world's goods, and its great care was to preserve them. Its interests had become temporal interests, and therefore it needed, not a spiritual father, but a temporal prince. It is as a prince that Leo conducts himself. His legates to the imperial, English and French courts, entered into negotiations altogether as ambassadors of a temporal prince, not as the simple representatives of the church.

Leo himself is a sensualist, sunk in his sensual pleasures, and perhaps a great sufferer in consequence of his excesses. It is said he was an atheist, a thing more than probable. All his tastes were worldly. Instead of the sacred books of the church, the pious legends of saints and martyrs, he amused himself with the elegant but *profane* literature of Greece and Rome. His principal secretaries were not holy monks but eminent classical scholars. He revived and enlarged the university at Rome, encouraged human learning and the arts of civilization, completed St. Peter's, and his reign was graced by Michael Angelo and Raphael. He engaged in wars and diplomacy and in them both had respect only to the goods of the church, or to the interests of himself and family as temporal princes.

Now all this was in direct opposition to the theory of the church. Materialism was in the papal chair, but it was there as a usurper, as an illegitimate. It reigned in fact, but not in right. The church was divided against itself. In theory it was spiritualist, but in practice it was materialist. It could not long survive this inconsistency, and it needed not the attacks of Luther to hasten the day of its complete destruction.

But materialism must have become quite powerful to have been able to usurp the papal throne itself. It was indeed too powerful to bear patiently the name of usurper; at least to be contented to reign only indirectly. It would be acknowledged as sovereign, and proclaimed legitimate. This the church could not do. The church could do nothing but cling to its old pretensions. To expel materialism and return to Hildebrand was out of the question. To give up its claims, and own itself materialist, would have been to abandon all title to even its material possessions, since it was by virtue of its spiritual character that it held them. Materialism—as it could reign in the church only as it were by stealth—resolved to leave the church and to reign in spite of it, against it, and even on its ruins. It protested, since it had all the power, against being called hard names, and armed itself in the person of Luther to vindicate its rights and to make its claims acknowledged.

The dominant character of Protestantism is then the insurrection of materialism, and what we call the reformation is really a revolution in favor of the material order. Spiritualism had exhausted its energies; it had done all it could for humanity; the time had come for the material element of our nature, which spiritualism had neglected and grossly abused, to rise from its depressed condition and contribute its share to the general progress of mankind. It rose, and in rising it brought up the whole series of terms the church had disregarded. It brought up the state, civil liberty, human reason, philosophy, industry, all temporal interests.

In Protestantism, Greece and Rome revived and again carried their victorious arms into the East. The reformation connects us with classical antiquity, with the beautiful and graceful forms of Grecian art and literature, and with Roman eloquence and jurisprudence, as the church had connected us with Judea, Egypt and India.

Chapter IV: Protestantism

That Protestantism is the insurrection of matter against spirit, of the material against the spiritual order, is susceptible of very satisfactory historical verification.

One of the most immediate and efficient causes of Protestantism was the revival of Greek and Roman literature. Constantinople was taken by the Turks, and its scholars and the remains of classical learning which it had preserved were dispersed over western Europe. The classics took possession of the universities and the learned, were studied, commented on, appealed to as an authority paramount to that of the church and—Protestantism was born.

By means of the classics, the scholars of the fifteenth century were introduced to a world altogether unlike and much superior to that in which they lived—to an order of ideas wholly diverse from those avowed or tolerated by the church. They were enchanted. They had found the ideal of their dreams. They became disgusted with the present; they repelled the civilization effected by the church, looked with contempt on its fathers, saints, martyrs, schoolmen, troubadours, knights and minstrels, and sighed and yearned and labored to reproduce Athens or Rome.

And what was that Athens and that Rome which seemed to them to realize the very ideal of the perfect? We know very well today what they were. They were material; through the whole period of their historical existence, it is well known that the material or temporal order predominated over the spiritual. They are not that old spiritual world of the East which reigned in the church. In that old world—in India for instance—where spiritualism has its throne, man sinks before God, matter fades away before the presence of spirit, and time is swallowed up in eternity. Industry is in its incipient stages, and the state scarcely appears. There is no history, no chronology. All is dateless and unregistered. An inflexible and changeless tyranny weighs down the human race and paralyzes its energies. Ages on ages roll away and bring no melioration. Everything remains as it was, monotonous and immovable as the spirit it contemplates and adores.

In Athens and Rome all this is reversed. Human interests, the interests of mankind in time and space, predominate. Man is the most conspicuous figure in the group. He is everywhere, and his imprint is upon everything. Industry flourishes; commerce is encouraged; the state is constituted, and tends to democracy; citizens assemble to discuss their common interests; the orator harangues them; the aspirant courts them; the warrior and the statesman render them an account of their doings and await their award. The *People*—not the gods—will, decree, make, unmake, or modify the laws. Divinity does not become incarnate as in the Asiatic world, but men are deified. History is not theogony, but a record of human events and transactions. Poetry sings heroes, the great and renowned of earth, or chants at the festal board and the couch of voluptuousness. Art models its creations after human forms, for human pleasure or human convenience. They are human faces we see; human voices we hear; human dwellings in which we lodge and dream of human growth and human melioration.

There are gods and temples, and priests and oracles, and augurs and auguries, it is true; but they are not like those we meet where spiritualism reigns. The gods are all anthromorphous. Their forms are the perfection of the human. The allegorical beasts, the strange beasts, compounded of parts of many known and unknown beasts which meet us in Indian, Egyptian, and Persian mythology, as symbols of the gods are extinct. Priests are not a caste, as they are under spiritualism, springing from the head of Brahma and claiming superior sanctity and power as their birthright, but simple police officers. Religion is merely a function of the state. Socrates dies because he breaks the laws of Athens—not, as Jesus did—for blaspheming the gods. Numa introduces or organizes polytheism at Rome for the purpose of governing people by means of appeals to their sentiment of the holy; and the Roman Pontifex Maximus was never anything more than a master of police.

This in its generality is equally a description of Protestantism, as might indeed have been asserted beforehand. The epoch of the revival of classical literature must have been predisposed to materialism or else it could not have been pleased with the classics, and the influence of the classics must have been to increase that predisposition, and as Protestantism was a result of both, it could be nothing but materialism.

In classical antiquity religion is a function of the state. It is the same under Protestantism. Henry VIII of England declares himself supreme head of the church, not by virtue of his spiritual character, but by virtue of his character as a temporal prince. The Protestant princes of Germany are protectors of the church; and all over Europe, there is an implied contract between the state and the ecclesiastical authorities. The state pledges itself to support the church on condition that the church support the state. Ask the kings, nobility, or even church dignitaries, why they support religion, and they will answer with one voice, "Because the people cannot be preserved in order, cannot be made to submit to their rulers, and because civil society cannot exist without it." The same or a similar answer will be returned by almost every political man in this country; and truly may it be said that religion is valued by the Protestant world as a subsidiary to the state, as a mere matter of police.

Under the reign of spiritualism all questions are decided by authority. The church prohibited reasoning. It commanded, and men were to obey or be counted rebels against God. Materialism, by raising up man and the state, makes the reason of man, or the reason of the state, paramount to the commands of the church. Under Protestantism, the state in most cases, the individual reason in a few, imposes the creed upon the church. The king and Parliament in England determine the faith which the clergy must profess and maintain; the Protestant princes in Germany have the supreme control of the symbols of the church, the right to enact what creed they please.

Indeed the authority of the church in matters of belief was regarded by the reformers as one of the greatest evils, against which they had to contend. It was particularly against this authority that Luther protested. What he and his coadjutors demanded was the right to read and interpret the Bible for themselves. This was the right they wrested from the church. To have been consequent they should have retained it in their hands as individuals; it would then have been the right of private judgment and, if it meant anything, the right of reason to sit in judgment on all propositions to be believed. To this extent, however, they were not prepared to go. Between the absolute authority of the church, and the absolute authority of the individual reason, intervened the authority of the state. But as the state was material, the substitution of its authority for the authority of the church was still to substitute the material for the spiritual.

But the tendency, however arrested by the state, has been steadily toward the most unlimited freedom of thought and conscience. Our fathers rebelled against the authority of the state in religious matters as well as against the authority of the pope. In political and industrial speculations, the English and Americans give the fullest freedom to the individual reason; Germany has done it to the greatest extent in historical, literary and philosophical, and to a very great extent, in theological matters, and France does it in everything. All modern philosophy is built on the absolute freedom and independence of the individual reason; that is, the reason of humanity, in opposition to the reason of the church or the state. Descartes refused to believe in his own existence but upon the authority of his reason; Bacon allows no authority but observation and induction; Berkeley finds no ground for admitting an external world, and therefore denies it; and Hume finding no certain evidence of anything outward or inward, doubted—philosophically—of all things.

Philosophy is a human creation; it is the product of man, as the universe is of God. Under spiritualism, then, which—in theory—demolishes man, there can be no philosophy; yet as man, though denied, exists, there is a philosophical tendency. But this philosophical tendency is always either to skepticism, mysticism, or idealism. Skepticism, that philosophy which denies all certainty, made its first appearance in modern times in the church. The church declared reason unworthy of confidence, and in doing that gave birth to the whole skeptical philosophy. When the authority of the church was questioned and she was compelled to defend it, she did it on the ground that reason could not be trusted as a criterion of truth, and that there could be no certainty for man, if he did not admit an authority independent of his reason, not perceiving that if reason were struck with impotence there would be no means of substantiating the legitimacy of the authority.

On the other hand, the church having its point of view in spirit, consulted the soul before the body, became introspective, fixed on the inward to the exclusion of the outward. It overlooked the outward; and when that is overlooked it is hardly possible that it should not be denied. Hence idealism or mysticism.

Under the reign of materialism all this is changed. There is full confidence in the reason. The method of philosophizing is the experimental. But as the point of view is the outward—matter—spirit is overlooked; matter alone admitted. Hence philosophical materialism. And philosophical materialism, in germ or developed, has been commensurate with Protestantism. When the mind becomes fixed on the external world, inasmuch as we become acquainted with that world only by means of our senses, we naturally conclude that our senses are our only source of knowledge. Hence sensualism, the philosophy supported by Locke, Condillac, and even by Bacon, so far as it concerns his own application of his method. And from the hypothesis that our senses are our only inlets of knowledge, we are compelled to admit that nothing can be known which is not cognizable by some one or all of them. Our senses take cognizance only of matter; then we can know nothing but matter. We can know nothing of the spirit or soul. The body is all that we know of man. That dies and there ends man—at least all we know of him. Hence no immortality, no future state. If nothing can be known but by means of our senses, God, then, inasmuch as we do not see him, hear him, taste him, smell him, touch him, cannot be known; then he does not exist for us. Hence atheism. Hence modern infidelity, in all its forms, so prevalent in the last century, and so far from being extinct even in this.

The same tendency to exalt the terms depressed by the church is to be observed in the religious aspect of Protestantism. Properly speaking, Protestantism has no religious character. As Protestants, people are not religious, but coexisting with their Protestantism, they may indeed retain something of religion. Men often act from mixed motives. They bear in their bosoms sometimes two antagonist principles, now obeying the one, and now the other, without being aware that both are not one and the same principle. With Protestants, religion has existed; but as a reminiscence, a tradition. Sometimes, indeed, the remembrance has been very lively, and seemed very much like reality. The old soldier warms up with the recollections of his early feats, and lives over his life as he relates its events to his grandchild, —

"Shoulders his crutch and shows how fields are won."

If the religion of the Protestant world be a reminiscence, it must be the religion of the church. It is, in fact, only Catholicism continued. The same principle lies at the bottom of all Protestant churches, in so far as they are churches, which was at the bottom of the church of the Middle Ages. But materialism modifies their rites and dogmas. In the practice of all, there is an effort to make them appear reasonable. Hence commentaries, expositions, and defenses without number. Even where the authority of reason is denied, there is an instinctive sense of its authority and a desire to enlist it. In mere forms, pomp and splendor have gradually disappeared, and dry utility and even baldness have been consulted. In doctrines, those which exalt man and give him some share in the work of salvation have gained in credit and influence. Pelagianism, under some thin disguises or undisguised, has become almost universal. The doctrine of man's inherent total depravity, in the few cases in which it is asserted, is asserted more as a matter of duty than of conviction. Nobody, who can help it, preaches the old-fashioned doctrine of God's sovereignty, expressed in the dogma of unconditional election and reprobation. The vicarious Atonement has hardly a friend left. The Deity of Jesus is questioned, his simple humanity is asserted and is gaining credence. Orthodox is a term which implies as much reproach as commendation; people are beginning to laugh at the claims of councils and synods, and to be quite merry at the idea of excommunication.

In literature and art there is the same tendency. Poetry in the last century hardly existed, and was, so far as it did exist, mainly ethical or descriptive. It had no revelations of the Infinite. Prose writers under Protestantism have been historians, critics, essayists, or controversialists; they have aimed almost exclusively at the elevation or adornment of the material order, and in scarcely an instance has a widely popular writer exalted God at the expense of man, the church at the expense of the state, faith at the expense of reason, or eternity at the expense of time. Art is finite, and gives us busts and portraits, or copies of Greek and Roman models. The physical sciences take precedence of the metaphysical, and faith in railroads and steamboats is much stronger than in ideas.

In governments the tendency is the same. Nothing is more characteristic of Protestantism than its influence in promoting civil and political liberty. Under its reign all forms of governments verge towards the democratic. "The king and the church" are exchanged for the "constitution and the people." Liberty, not order, is the word that wakes the dead, and electrifies the masses. A social science is created, and the physical well-being of the humblest laborer is cared for, and made a subject of deliberation in the councils of nations.

Industry has received in Protestant countries its grandest developments. Since the time of Luther, it has been performing one continued series of miracles. Every corner of the globe is explored; the most distant and perilous seas are navigated; the most miserly soil is laid under contribution; manufactures, villages and cities spring up and increase as by enchantment; canals and rail-roads are crossing the country in every direction; the means of production, the comforts, conveniences and luxuries of life are multiplied to an extent hardly safe to relate.

Such, in its most general aspect, in its dominant tendency, is Protestantism. It is a new and much improved edition of the classics. Its civilization belongs to the same order as that of Greece and Rome. It is in advance, greatly in advance, of Greece and Rome, but it is the same in its groundwork. The material predominates over the spiritual. Men labor six days for this world and at most but one for the world to come. The great strife is for temporal goods, fame or pleasure. God, the soul, heaven and eternity are thrown into the background, and almost entirely disappear in the distance. Right yields to expediency, and duty is measured by utility. The real character of Protestantism, the result to which it must come, wherever it can have its full development, may be best seen in France, at the close of the last century. The church was converted into the pantheon, and made a resting place for the bodies of the great and renowned of earth; God was converted into a symbol of the human reason, and man into the man-machine; spiritualism fell, and the revolution marked the complete triumph of materialism.

Chapter V: Reaction of Spiritualism

What I have said of the Protestant world cannot be applied to the present century without some important qualifications. Properly speaking, Protestantism finished its work and expired in the French revolution at the close of the last century. Since then there has been a reaction in favor of spiritualism.

Men incline to exclusive spiritualism in proportion to their want of faith in the practicability of improving their earthly condition. This accounts for the predominance of spiritualism in the church. The church grew up and constituted itself amidst the crash of a falling world, when all it knew or could conceive of material well-being was crumbling in ruins around it. Greece and Rome were the prey of merciless barbarians. Society was apparently annihilated. Order there was none. Security for person, property, or life, seemed almost the extravagant vagary of some mad enthusiast. Lawless violence, brutal passion, besotting ignorance, tyrants and their victims, were the only spectacles presented to win men's regard for the earth, or to inspire them with faith and hope to labor for its improvement. To the generation of that day, when the North disgorged itself upon the South, the earth must have appeared forsaken by its Maker, and abandoned to the devil and his ministers. It was a wretched land; it could yield no supply; and the only solace for the soul was to turn away from it to another and better world, to the world of spirit; to that world where tyrants do not enter, where wrongs and oppression, sufferings and grief, find no admission; where mutations and insecurity are unknown, and where the poor earth-wanderer, the time-worn pilgrim, may at length find that repose, that fullness of joy which he craved, which he sought but found not below. This view was natural, it was inevitable; and it could lead only to exclusive spiritualism—mysticism.

But when the external world has been somewhat meliorated, and men find that they have some security for their persons and property, that they may count with some degree of certainty on tomorrow, faith in the material order is produced and confirmed. One improvement prepares another. Success inspires confidence in future efforts. And this was the case at the epoch of the reformation. Men had already made great progress in the material order, in their temporal weal. Their faith in it kept pace with their progress, or more properly, outran it. It continued to extend till it became almost entire and universal. The eighteenth century will be marked in the annals of the world for its strong faith in the material order. Meliorations on the broadest scale were contemplated and viewed as already realized. Our republic sprang into being, and the world leaped with joy that "a man child was born." Social progress and the perfection of governments became the religious creed of the day; the weal of man on earth, the spring and aim of all hopes and labors. A new paradise was imaged forth for man, inaccessible to the serpent, more delightful than that which Adam lost, and more attractive than that which the pious Christian hopes to gain. We of this generation can form only a faint conception of the strong faith our fathers had in the progress of society, the high hopes of human improvement they indulged, and the joy too big for utterance, with which they heard France in loud and kindling tones proclaim *Liberty* and *Equality*. France for a moment became the center of the world. All eyes were fixed on her movements. The pulse stood still when she and her enemies met, and loud cheers burst from the universal heart of humanity when her tricolored flag was seen to wave in triumph over the battlefield. There was then no stray thought for God and eternity. Man and the world filled the soul.

They were too big for it. But while the voice of hope was yet ringing, and *Te Deum* shaking the arches of the old cathedrals,—the convention, the Reign of Terror, the exile of patriots, the massacre of the gifted, the beautiful, and the good, Napoleon and the military despotism came, and humanity uttered a piercing shriek, and fell prostrate on the grave of her hopes!

The reaction produced by the catastrophe of this memorable drama was tremendous. There are still lingering among us those who have not forgotten the recoil they experienced when they saw the republic swallowed up, or preparing to be swallowed up, in the empire. Men never feel what they felt but once. The pang which darts through their souls changes them into stone. From that moment enthusiasm died, hope in social melioration ceased to be indulged, and those who had been the most sanguine in anticipations, hung down their heads and said nothing; the warmest friends of humanity apologized for their dreams of liberty and equality; democracy became an accusation, and faith in the perfectibility of mankind a proof of disordered intellect.

In consequence of this reaction, men again despaired of the earth; and when they despair of the earth, they always take refuge in heaven; when man fails them, they always fly to God. They had trusted materialism too far—they would now not trust it at all. They had hoped too much—they would now hope nothing. The future, which had been to them so bright and promising, was now overspread with black clouds; the ocean on which they were anxious to embark was lashed into rage by the storm, and presented only images of dismasted or sinking ships and drowning crews. They turned back and sighed for the serene past, the quiet and order of old times, for the mystic land of India, where the soul may dissolve in ecstasy and dream of no change.

At the very moment when the sigh had just escaped, that mystic land reappeared. The English, through the East India Company, had brought to light its old literature and philosophy, so diverse from the literature and philosophy of modern Europe or of classical antiquity, and men were captivated by their novelty and bewildered by their strangeness. Sir William Jones gave currency to them by poetical paraphrases and imitations; and the Asiatic Society by its researches placed them within reach of the learned of Europe. The church rejoiced for it was like bringing back her long lost mother whose features she had remembered and was able at once to recognize. Germany, England, and even France became Oriental. Cicero, and Horace, and Virgil, Aeschylus, Euripides, and even Homer, with Jupiter, Apollo, and Minerva were forced to bow before Hindu bards and gods of uncouth forms and unutterable names.

The influence of the old Braminical or spiritual world, thus dug up from the grave of centuries, may be traced in all our philosophy, art and literature. It is remarkable in our poets. It molds the form in Byron, penetrates to the ground in Wordsworth, and entirely predominates in the Schlegels. It causes us to feel a new interest in those writers and those epochs which partake the most of spiritualism. Those old English writers who were somewhat inclined to mysticism are revived; Plato, who traveled in the East and brought back its lore which he modified by western genius and molded into Grecian forms, is re-edited, commented on, translated, and raised to the highest rank among philosophers. The Middle Ages are reexamined and found to contain a treasure of romance, acuteness, depth, and wisdom, and are deemed by some to be Dark Ages only because we have not light enough to read them.

Materialism in philosophy is extinct in Germany. It is only a reminiscence in France, and it produces no remarkable work in England or America. Phrenology, which some deem materialism, has itself struck materialism with death in Gall's work by showing that we are conscious of phenomena within us which no metaphysical alchemy can transmute into sensations.

Protestantism, since the commencement of the present century, in what it has peculiar to itself, has ceased to gain ground. Rationalism in Germany retreats before the Evangelical party; the Genevan Church makes few proselytes; English and American Unitarianism, on the plan of Priestley and Belsham, avowedly, material, and being, as it were, the jumping-off place from the church to absolute infidelity, is evidently on the decline. There is probably not a man in this country, however much and justly he may esteem Priestley and Belsham, as bold and untiring advocates of reason and of humanity, who would be willing to assume the defense of all their opinions. On the other hand Catholicism has revived, offered some able apologies for itself, made some eminent proselytes, and alarmed many Protestants, even among ourselves.

Indeed everywhere is seen a decided tendency to spiritualism. The age has become weary of uncertainty. It sighs for repose. Controversy is nearly ended and a sentiment is extensively prevailing that it is a matter of very little consequence what a man believes, or what formulas of worship he adopts, if he only have a right spirit. Men, who a few years ago were staunch rationalists, now talk of spiritual communion; and many, who could with difficulty be made to admit the inspiration of the Bible, are now ready to admit the inspiration of the sacred books of all nations; and instead of stumbling at the idea of God's speaking to a few individuals, they see no reason why he should not speak to everybody. Some are becoming so spiritual that they see no necessity of matter; others so refine matter that it can offer no resistance to the will, making it indeed move as the spirit listeth; others still believe that all wisdom was in the keeping of the priests of ancient India, Egypt, and Persia, and fancy the world has been deteriorating for four thousand years, instead of advancing. Men go out from our midst to Europe, and come back half Catholics, sighing to introduce the architecture, the superstition, the rites, and the sacred symbols of the Middle Ages.

A universal cry is raised against the frigid utilitarianism of the last century. Money-getting, desire for worldly wealth and renown, are spoken of with contempt, and men are evidently leaving the outward for the inward, and craving something more fervent, living, and soul-kindling. All this proves that we have changed from what we were; that, though materialism yet predominates and appears to have lost none of its influence, it is becoming a tradition; and that there is a new force collecting to expel it. Protestantism passes into the condition of a reminiscence. Protestant America cannot be aroused against the Catholics. A mob may burn a convent from momentary excitement, but the most Protestant of the Protestants among us will petition the legislature to indemnify the owners. Indeed, Protestantism died in the French revolution, and we are beginning to become disgusted with its dead body. The East has reappeared, and spiritualism revives; will it again become supreme? Impossible.

Chapter VI: Mission of the Present

We of the present century must either dispense with all religious instructions, reproduce spiritualism or materialism, or we must build a new church, organize a new institution free from the imperfections of those which have been.

The first is out of the question. Men cannot live in a perpetual anarchy. They must and will embody their ideas of the true, the beautiful, and the good,—the holy, in some institution. They must answer in some way the questions, "What is the holy? What is the true destination of man?"

To reproduce spiritualism or materialism, were an anomaly in the development of humanity. Humanity does not traverse an eternal circle; it advances; it does not come round to its starting point, but goes onward in one endless career of progress towards the Infinite, the Perfect.

Besides, it is impossible. Were it desirable, neither spiritualism nor materialism can to any considerable extent, or for any great length of time, become predominant. We cannot bring about that state of society which is the indispensable condition of the exclusive dominion of either.

Spiritualism just now revives; its friends may anticipate a victory; but they will be disappointed. Spiritualism, as an exclusive system, reigns only when men have no faith in material interests; and in order to have no faith in material interests, we must virtually destroy them; we must have absolute despotism, a sacerdotal caste, or we must have another decline and fall like that of the Roman empire, and a new irruption like that of the Goths, Vandals and Huns.

None of these things are possible. There are no more Goths, Vandals or Huns. The north of Europe is civilized. Northern and central Asia is in the process of civilization through the influence of Russia; England is mingling the arts and sciences of the West with the spiritualism of India; France and the colony of Liberia secure Africa; the Aborigines of this continent will in a few years have vanished before the continued advance of the European races; merchants and missionaries will do the rest. No external forces can then ever be collected to destroy civilization and compel the human race to commence its work anew.

Internally, modern civilization has nothing to fear. It contains no seeds of destruction. A real advance has been made. A vast fund of experience has been accumulated and is deposited in so many different languages, that we can hardly conceive it possible that it should be wholly lost or greatly diminished. The art of printing, unknown to Greek and Roman civilization, multiplies books to such an extent, that it is perfectly idle to dream of any catastrophe, unless it be the destruction of the world itself, which will reduce them to a few precious fragments like those left us of classical antiquity.

There is, too, a remarkable difference in the diffusion of knowledge. In the best days of classical antiquity, the number of the enlightened was but small. The masses were enveloped in thick darkness. Now the masses have been to school, and are going to school. The millions, who then were in darkness, now behold light springing up. The loss of one individual, however prominent he may be, is not felt. Another is immediately found to fill his place.

Liberty exists also to a much greater extent. The rights of man are better comprehended and secured. The individual man is a greater being than he was in Greece or Rome. He has a higher consciousness of his worth, and he is more respected, and his interests are felt to he more sacred.

Labor has become more honorable. In Greece and Rome labor was menial; it was performed by slaves, at least by the ignorant and brutish. Slavery is disappearing. It has only a small corner of the civilized world left to it. As slavery disappears, as labor comes to be performed by freemen, it will rise to the rank of a liberal profession, and men of character and influence will be laborers.

The improvements in the arts of production have become so extensive, and the means of creating and accumulating wealth are so distributed, and the amount of wealth has already become so great and is shared by so many, that it is impossible that there should ever come again a scene of general poverty and wretchedness to make men despair of the earth, and abandon themselves wholly to the dreams of a spirit-land. There must always remain something to hope from the material order, and consequently, whatever may be the influence of a sudden panic, or a momentary affright, always a check to the absolute dominion of spiritualism.

Nor can materialism become sovereign again. It contains the elements of its own defeat. The very discipline, which materialism demands to support itself, in the end neutralizes its dominion. As soon as men find themselves well off in a worldly point of view, they discover that they have wants which the world does not and cannot satisfy. The training demanded to ensure success in commerce, industrial enterprises, or politics, strengthens faculties which crave something superior to commerce, to mere industry, or to politics. The merchant would not be always estimating the hazards of speculation; he dreams of his retirement from business, his splendid mansion, his refined hospitality, a library, and studious ease; the mechanic looks forward to a time when he shall have leisure to care for something besides merely animal wants; and the politician to his release from the cares and perplexities of a public life, to a quiet retreat, to a dignified old age, spent in plans of benevolence, in aiding the cause of education, religion, or philosophy. This low business world, upon which the moralist and the divine look down with so much sorrow, is not quite so low after all, as they think it. It is doing a vast deal to develop the intellect. It is full of high and expanded brows.

It is true that money getting, mere physical utility has at this moment a wide influence, and may absorb the mind and heart quite too much. Still the evil is not unmixed. That man who tortures his brain, spends his days and nights to accumulate a fortune, is much superior to him who is content to rot in poverty, who has no courage, no energy to attempt to improve his condition. He is a better member of society, is worth more to humanity. It is a great day, even for spiritualism, when all the people of a country are carried away in an industrial direction. Speculation may be rife, frauds may be common; many may become rich by means they care not to make known; many may become discontented; there may be much striving this way and that, much effort to get up, keep up, to pull or to push down; but the many will sharpen their faculties, and gain the leisure and the means and the disposition to attend to the spiritual part of their being. It does my heart good to witness the industrial activity of my countrymen. I see very clearly the evils which attend it; but I also see every year the general level rising, and the moral and intellectual power increasing. So is it too with our political struggles. They quicken thought, give the people the use of language, a consciousness of their power, especially of the power of mind, and upon the whole they do much to elevate the general character. Those quiet times we look back upon and regret, either were not as quiet as we think them, or they were quiet because they had not enough of thought to move them. They were, as still, but too often as putrid, as the stagnant pool.

The science which is now introduced into commerce, into the mechanic arts and agricultural pursuits, and which is everyday receiving a greater extension and new applications, while it preserves the material order, also keeps alive the spiritual, and gives us a check against the absolute ascendancy of materialism.

We cannot then go back either to exclusive spiritualism, or to exclusive materialism. Both these systems have received so full a development, have acquired so much strength, that neither can be subdued. Both have their foundation in our nature, and both will exist and exert their influence. Shall they exist as antagonist principles? Shall the spirit forever lust against the flesh, and the flesh against the spirit? Is the bosom of humanity to be eternally torn by these two contending factions? No. It cannot be. The war must end. Peace must be made.

This discloses our Mission. We are to reconcile spirit and matter; that is, we must realize the atonement. Nothing else remains for us to do. Stand still we cannot. To go back is equally impossible. We must go forward, but we can take not a step forward, but on the condition of uniting these two hitherto hostile principles. Progress is our law and our first step is Union.

The union of spirit and matter was the result contemplated by the mission of Jesus. The church attempted it, but only partially succeeded, and has therefore died. The time had not come for the complete union. Jesus saw this. He knew that the age in which he lived would not be able to realize his conception. He therefore spoke of his Second Coming. The church has always had a vague presentiment of its own death, and the birth of a new era when Christ should really reign on earth. For a long time the hierophants have fixed upon ours as the epoch of the commencement of the new order of things. Some have gone even so far as to name this very year, 1836, as the beginning of what they call the millennium.

The particular shape which has been assigned to this new order, this latter day glory, the name by which it has been designated, amounts to nothing. That some have anticipated a personal appearance of Jesus, and a resurrection of the saints, should not induce us to treat with disrespect the almost unanimous belief of Christendom in a fuller manifestation of Christian truth, and in a more special reign of Christ in a future epoch of the world. All the presentiments of humanity are to be respected. Humanity has a prophetic power.—"Coming events cast their shadows before."

The "second coming" of Christ will be when the idea which he represents, that is, the idea of atonement, shall be fully realized. That idea will be realized by a combination, a union, of the two terms which have received thus far from the church only a separate development. This union the church has always had a presentiment of; it has looked forward to it, prayed for it; and we are still praying for it, for we still say, "Let thy kingdom come." Nobody believes that the Gospel has completed its work. The church universal and eternal is not yet erected. The cornerstone is laid; the materials are prepared. Let then the workmen come forth with joy, and bid the Temple rise. Let them embody the true idea of the God-Man, and Christ will then have come a second time; he will have come in power and great glory, and he will reign, and the whole earth will be glad.

Chapter VII: Christian Sects

This age must realize the atonement, the union of spirit and matter, the destruction of all antagonism and the production of universal peace.

God has appointed us to build the new church, the one which shall bring the whole family of man within its sacred enclosure, which shall be able to abide the ravages of time, and against which "the gates of hell shall not prevail."

But we can do this only by a general doctrine which enables us to recognize and accept all the elements of humanity. If we leave out any one element of our nature, we shall have antagonism. Our system will be incomplete and the element excluded will be forever rising up in rebellion against it and collecting forces to destroy its authority.

All sects overlook this important truth. None of them seem to imagine that human nature has or should have any hand in the construction of their theories. Instead of studying human nature, ascertaining its elements and it wants, and seeking to conform to them, every sect labors to conform human nature to its own creed. No one dreams of molding its dogmas to human nature, but everyone would mold human nature to its dogmas. Everyone is a bed of Procrustes. What is too short must be stretched, what is too long must be docked. No sect ever looks to human nature as the measure of truth; but all look to what they are pleased to call the truth, as the measure of human nature.

This were well enough if human nature had only been made of wax, or some other ductile material. But unfortunately it is very stubborn. It will not bend. It will not be mutilated. Its laws are permanent and universal; each one of them is eternal and indestructible. They war in vain who war against them. Be they good or be they bad, we must accept them, we must submit to them and do the best we can with them.

But human nature is well made, its laws are just and holy, its elements are true and divine. And this is the hidden sense of that symbol of the God-Man. That symbol teaches all who comprehend it, to find divinity in humanity, and humanity in divinity. By presenting us God and man united in one person, it shows us that both are holy. The Father and Son are one. Therefore we are commanded to honor the Son as we honor the Father, humanity as Divinity, man as well as God. But the church has never understood this. No sect now understands it. Hence the contempt with which all sects treat human nature, and their entire want of confidence in it as a criterion of truth. They must correct themselves. "The Word was made flesh and dwelt among us."

To reject human nature and declare it unworthy of confidence as the church did, and as all sects now do, is—whether we know it or not—to reject all grounds of certainty, and to declare that we have no means of distinguishing truth from falsehood. Truth itself is nothing else to us than that which our nature by some one or all of its faculties compels us to believe. The fact that God has made us a revelation does not in the least impair this assertion. God has revealed to us truths which we could not of ourselves have discovered. But how do we know this? What is it but the human mind that can determine whether God has or has not spoken to us? What but the human mind can ascertain and fix the meaning of what he may have communicated? If we may not trust the human mind, human nature, how can we ever be sure that a revelation has been made? Or how distinguish a real revelation from a pretended one? By miracles? But how determine that what are alleged to be miracles, really are miracles? Or the more difficult question still, that the miracles, admitting them to be genuine, do necessarily involve the truth of the doctrines they are wrought to prove? Shall we be told that we must believe the revelation is a true one, because made by an authorized teacher? Where is the warrant of his authority? What shall assure us that the warrant is not a forgery? Have we anything but our own nature with which to answer these and a hundred more questions like them and equally important?

If human nature has the ability and the right to answer these questions, where are the limits of its ability and its right? If we trust it when it assures us God has spoken to us, and when it interprets what he has spoken, where shall we not trust it? If it be no criterion of truth, why do we trust it here? And if it be, why do we disclaim it elsewhere? Why declare it worthy of confidence in one case and not in another? It is the same in all cases, in all its degrees; and whether it testifies to that which is little, or to that which is great, it is the same, and its testimony is of precisely the same validity.

If we admit that human nature is the measure of truth,—of truth for us, human beings—then we admit that it is the criterion by which all sects must be tested. It is then the touchstone of truth. Every sect must be approved or condemned according to its decision. No sect must blame humanity for not believing its doctrines. If after they have been fairly presented and fully comprehended they are rejected, they are proved to be false, or at least to be only partially true. It is no recommendation to advocate doctrines repugnant to human nature; nor is it any reproach to defend those which are pleasing to the natural heart. Humanity loves the truth and can be satisfied with nothing else. The sect, then, which ceases to make converts should abandon or enlarge its creed.

Sects in general are and will be slow to learn this truth. Each sect, because it has all the truth to be seen from its standpoint, takes it for granted that it has the whole truth. It does not even dream that there may be other standpoints, from which other truths may be seen, or the same truths under other aspects; and therefore it concludes when its doctrines are rejected, that they are rejected because human nature is perverse or impotent, because men cannot or will not see the truth, or because they naturally hate it. Let it change its position and it will soon learn that the horizon, which it took to be the boundary of truth, was in fact only the boundary of its own vision.

All sects, however, have their truth and are serviceable to humanity. Each one has a special doctrine which gives prominence to some one element of our nature, and is therefore satisfactory to all in whom that element predominates. But as that element, however important a one it may be, is not the whole of human nature, and as it can hardly be predominant alike in all men, no sect can satisfy entire humanity. Each sect does something to develop and satisfy the separate elements of humanity, but no one can develop and satisfy all the elements of humanity and satisfy them as a whole.

Spiritualism and materialism are the two most comprehensive sectarian doctrines which have ever been proclaimed. But neither of these is comprehensive enough. Either may satisfy a large class of wants, but each must leave a class equally as large unsatisfied. One has always been opposed by the other, and mutual opposition has finally destroyed them both. Humanity is still sighing for what it has not. It is seeking rest but finds none. And rest it will not find, till its untiring friends gain a standpoint, from which, as with one grand panoramic view, they may take in all elements in their relative proportions, and exact distances, in their diversity and in their unity, till they have gone up and down the earth and collected and brought together its disjointed members, which contending sects have torn asunder, and molded them into one complete and lovely form of truth and holiness.

Where is the Christian sect that is engaged in this work? Where is the one that deems it desirable or possible? All the sects of Christendom, so far as it concerns their dominant tendency, fall into the category of spiritualism, or into that of materialism. Catholicism is virtually the church of the Middle Ages. It is but a reminiscence. It has no life, at least no healthy existence. It belongs to spiritualism. Calvinism, bating some few modifications produced by Protestant influence, is only a continuation of Catholicism. It is decidedly spiritualistic. Its prayers, its hymns and homilies are deeply imprinted with spiritualism. It repels the material order, and exhorts us to crucify the flesh, to disregard the world and to think only of God, the soul and eternity.

In the opinion of the Calvinist, the world lies under the curse of the Almighty. It is a wretched land, a vale of tears, of disease and death. There is no happiness below. It is vain, almost impious, to wish it till death comes to release us from the infirmities of the flesh. As long as we live we sin; we must carry about a weary load, an overwhelming burden, a body of death. Man is a poor, depraved creature. He is smitten with a curse, and the curse spreads over his whole nature. There is nothing good within him. Of himself he can obtain, he can do nothing good. He is unclean in the sight of God. His sacrifices are an abomination, and his holiest prayers are sinful. His will is perverted; his affections are all on the side of evil; his reason is deprived of its light, it is blind and impotent, and will lead those who trust to its guidance down to hell.

By its doctrine of "foreordination," Calvinism annihilates man. It allows him no independent causality. It permits him to move only as a preordaining and irresistible will moves him. It makes him a thing, not a person, with properties but without faculties or rights. Whatever his destiny, however cruel, he has no right to complain. Spirit is absolute and has the right to receive him into blessedness or send him away into everlasting punishment, without any regard to his own wishes, merit or demerit. Hence Calvinists always give supremacy to the spiritual order. They fled from England to this then wilderness world, because they would not conform to a church established by the state; and when here they constituted the church superior to the state. In theory the Pilgrims made the state a mere function of the church. In order to be a citizen it was necessary that one should first be a church member. And for the last twenty years the great body of Calvinists throughout our whole country have been exerting all their skill and influence to raise the church to that eminence from which it may overlook the state, control its deliberations and decide its measures.

His doctrine of "hereditary total depravity" has always compelled the Calvinist to reject reason and to rely on authority—to seek faith, not conviction. Protestant influences prevent him in these days from submitting to an infallible pope, but he indemnifies himself by infallible creeds, councils, synods and assemblies. Or if these fail him, he can ascribe infallibility to the "written Word." Always does he prohibit himself the free exercise of his own understanding, and prescribe bounds beyond which reason and reasoning must not venture.

By the dogma of Christ's vicarious death, he takes his stand decidedly with spiritualism, denies the atonement, loses sight of the mediator, and rejects the God-Man. He cannot then build the new church, the church truly universal and eternal. It is in vain that we ask him to destroy all antagonism. He does not even wish to do it; before the foundations of the world, its origin and eternity were decreed. God and the devil, the saint and the sinner, in his estimation, are alike immortal.

Universalism would seem to a superficial observer to be what we need. Its friends call it the doctrine of universal reconciliation, and they group around the love of God that which constitutes the real harmony and unity of creation. But Universalists do not understand themselves. They have a vague sense of the truth, but not a clear perception of it. As soon as they begin to explain themselves, they file off either to the ranks of spiritualism, or of materialism.

The larger number of Universalists, among whom is, or was, the chief of the sect, contend that all sin originates in the flesh and must end with it. The flesh ends at death, when it is deposited in the tomb; therefore, "he that is dead is freed from sin." Sin is the cause of all suffering; when sin ends, suffering ends. Sin ends at death, and therefore after death no suffering, but universal happiness.

This doctrine is as decidedly spiritualism as oriental spiritualism itself. If the body be the cause of all sin, it certainly deserves no respect. It is a vile thing, and should be despised, mortified, punished, annihilated. Universalists do not draw this inference, but they avoid it only by really denying that there is any sin, or at least by considering the consequences of sin of too little importance to be dreaded.

The body, however, according to this doctrine is a curse. Man would be better off without it than he is with it. It deserves nothing on its own account. Wherefore then shall I labor to make it comfortable? I shall be released from it tomorrow, and enter into a world of unutterable joy. Let my lodging tonight be on the bare ground, in the open air, destitute of a few conveniences, what imports it? Can I not afford to forego a pleasant lodging for one night, since I am ever after to be filled and overflowing with blessedness? Universalism, then, according to this exposition of it must inevitably lead to neglect of the material order. Its legitimate result would be, not licentiousness, but a dreaming contemplative life, wasting itself away in idleness, watching the motion of the sun, and wishing it to move faster, so that we may be the sooner translated from this miserable world, where nothing is worth laboring for, to our Father's kingdom where is music and dancing, songs and feasting forever and ever.

Universalists have, however, existing side by side with this exclusive spiritualism, some strong tendencies to materialism. Spiritualism and materialism are nearly balanced in their minds, and constitute, not a union of spirit and matter, but a parallelism which has no tendency to union. But when the true doctrine of the atonement is proclaimed, Universalists will be among the first believers. None will rejoice more than they, to see the new church rise from the ruins of the old, and none will attend more readily or with more zeal at its consecration.

Unitarianism belongs to the material order. It is the last word of Protestantism, before Protestantism breaks entirely with the past. It is the point towards which all Protestant sects converge in proportion as they gain upon their reminiscences. Every consistent Protestant Christian must be a Unitarian. Unitarianism elevates man; it preaches morality; it vindicates the rights of the mind, accepts and uses the reason, contends for civil freedom, and is social, charitable and humane. It saves the Son of man, but sometimes loses the Son of God.

But it is from the Unitarians that must come out the doctrine of universal reconciliation; for they are the only denomination in Christendom that labors to rest religious faith on rational conviction; that seeks to substitute reason for authority, to harmonize religion and science, or that has the requisite union of piety and mental freedom, to elaborate the doctrine which is to realize the atonement. The orthodox, as they are called, are disturbed by their memory. Their faces are on the back side of their heads. They have zeal, energy, perseverance, but their ideas belong to the past. The Universalists can do nothing till someone arises to give them a philosophy. They must comprehend their instincts, before they can give to their doctrine of reconciliation that character which will adapt it to the wants of entire humanity.

But Unitarians are every day breaking away more and more from tradition, and every day making new progress in the creation of a philosophy which explains humanity, determines its wants and the means of supplying them. Mind at this moment is extremely active among them, and as it can act freely it will most certainly elaborate the great doctrine required. They began in rationalism. Their earlier doctrines were dry and cold. And this was necessary. They were called at first to a work of destruction. They were under the necessity of clearing away the rubbish of the old church, before they could obtain a site whereon to erect the new one. The Unitarian preacher was under the necessity of raising a stern and commanding voice in the wilderness, "Prepare ye the way of the Lord, make his paths straight." He raised that voice, and the chief priest and Pharisees in modern Judea heard and trembled and some have gone forth to be baptized. The Unitarian has baptized them with water unto repentance, but he has born witness that a mightier than he shall come after him, who shall baptize them with the Holy Ghost and with fire.

When the Unitarian appeared, there was on this whole earth no spot for the Temple of the living God, the temple of reason, love and peace. For such a spot he contended. He has obtained it. He has began the Temple; its foundations already appear, and although the workmen must yet work with their arms in one hand, he will see it completed, consecrated, and filled with the glory of the Lord.

Chapter VIII: Indications of the Atonement

The church was the result of three causes, the Asiatic conquests of the Romans, the Alexandrian school of philosophy, and the Christian movement of the people.

By the Asiatic conquests of the Romans, spiritualism and materialism were brought together upon the same theater and placed in the condition necessary to their union. Eastern and western ideas were mingled in strange confusion throughout the whole of the Roman empire during the first three centuries of our era, and the attempt to unite them, to combine them into a regular and harmonious system, could hardly fail to be made.

This attempt was made by the Alexandrian philosophers. These philosophers called themselves eclectics. Their avowed object was to unite the East and the West, European and Asiatic ideas, to reduce to a regular system the ideas of all the various schools of philosophy. They did it as perfectly as they could with the lights they had and the experiments they had made.

The Christian movement of the people was apparently very unlike that of the Alexandrian. The early Christians were the farthest in the world from being philosophers. They were inspired. They were moved by an impulse of which they asked, and could have given no account. God moved in them, and spoke through them; gave them lofty enthusiasm, a resistless energy of character, and prepared them to do, to dare, and to suffer anything and everything. At his command they went forth to conquer the world, and they did conquer it; not, as it has been well remarked, by killing, but by dying.

We understand today what it was that moved the early Christians. What was inspiration in them is philosophy in us. They had an instinctive sense of the synthesis of spirit and matter. Yet they thought nothing of spirit and matter. They disturbed themselves not in the least with spiritualism and materialism, with the East and the West, with Europe and Asia. They saw mankind sunk in sin and misery, weary and heavy laden, and they went forth strong in the Lord to raise them to virtue, to convert them to Christ and to give them rest. They did not speculate, they did not reason, they saw and felt and acted.

These and the Alexandrians met, and the church was the result. The share of the Alexandrians in the construction of the church has always been acknowledged to be very great. Perhaps it was greater than any have suspected. Certain it is that they furnished the Fathers their philosophy, and they may be pronounced without much hesitation, the real elaborators—not of Christianity, but of the dogmas of the church.

All men feel more or less the desire to account to themselves for what they are. For a time they may be carried away by a force not their own, and they may be so engrossed with varied and exciting action and events, that they have no time to think; but at the first moments of calmness and self-consciousness they will ask what has moved them, what was the power which carried them away and whither have they been borne. This was the case with the early Christians. The first excitement over, and the visits of inspiration having become less frequent, they desired to explain themselves to themselves, to give a name to the instincts they had obeyed, to the Divinity which had moved them, and to the destiny they had been fulfilling. The Alexandrians answered all their questions. They explained the Christians to themselves, and henceforth their explanations were counted Christianity.

These three causes of the old church, or analogous ones, reappear today for the first time since that epoch; and is not their reappearance an indication that a new church is about to be built?

The East and the West are again on the same theater. The British by means of the East India Company have reconquered the father-land of spiritualism, and brought up from the graves of ages its old literature and philosophy, and mingled them with those of the West, the fatherland of materialism. The church itself has introduced not a little spiritualism into Christian civilization, while Protestantism by encouraging the study of the classics has reproduced Greece and Rome. The two worlds, the two civilizations, the two systems to be atoned or united are now in very nearly the same relative condition as they were at the birth of the church. They are thrown together into the crucible.

Alexandria, too, is reproduced with the modifications and improvements which two thousand years could not fail to effect. Eclecticism is declared to be the philosophy of the nineteenth century. Not one of the exclusive systems, which obtained during the last century, has now any life. Materialism is a tradition even in France; idealism has exhausted itself in Germany, and England has no philosophy.

Schelling had at least a presentiment of eclecticism in his doctrine of identity; Hegel has greatly abridged the labors of its friends; Fries and his disciples observe its method, and Jacobi virtually embraced it. In our own country it has produced no great work, and perhaps will not; but it is avowed by many of the best minds among us, and is the only philosophy we have, that has not ceased to make proselytes.

In France, however, eclecticism has received its fullest developments. M. Cousin has all but perfected it. He has presented us the last results of the philosophical labors of his predecessors and contemporaries, and furnished us with a method by which we may construct a philosophy which may truly be called the science of the absolute, a philosophy which need not fear the mutations of time and space, and may be sure that its sovereignty will be complete and undisputed as fast and as far as it comes to be understood.

M. Cousin has not only given, us, as it were, a geometrical demonstration of the existence of nature and of God, but he has also demonstrated that humanity, nature and God have precisely the same laws, that what we find in nature and humanity we may also find in God, and that when we have once risen to God we may come back and find again in nature and humanity all that we had found in him. This at once destroys all antithesis between spirit and matter, between God and man, gives man a kindred nature with God, makes him an image or manifestation of God, and paves the way for universal reconciliation and peace. If God be holy, man, inasmuch as he has the very elements of the Divinity, is also holy. God and man may then unite in an everlasting and holy union, Justice and Mercy kiss each other, and—all antagonism is destroyed.

The third cause, the inspiration of the people, is no less remarkable now than it was in the first centuries of our era. When God would produce a great result, one which requires the cooperation of vast multitudes, he does not merely inspire one man; he does not speak plainly in distinct propositions to a few, and leave them to speak to the many; but he gives an impulse to the masses, and carries away all the world in the direction of the object to be gained. People seem to themselves to be acting from their own impulses, and to be obeying their own convictions; but they are borne along by an invisible and resistless power towards an end of which they have a vague presentiment, but no distinct vision.

This is the case now. The time has come for a new church, for a new synthesis of the elements of the life of humanity. The end to be attained is union. How would an inspiration designed to give the energy, the power to attain this end be most likely to manifest itself; in what way could it manifest itself but by giving the people an irresistible longing for union, and a tendency to unite, to associate on all occasions and for all purposes not inconsistent with union itself? And what is the most striking characteristic of this age? Is it not the tendency to association, a tendency so strong that it appears to the cool spectator like a monomania?

This tendency shows itself everywhere. All over Christendom, men seem mad for associations. They associate for almost everything, to promote science, literature, art and industry, to circulate the Bible, to distribute religious tracts, to diffuse useful knowledge, to improve and extend education, to meliorate governments and laws, to soften the rigors of the prison house, to aid the sick, to relieve the poor, to prevent pauperism, to free the slave, to send out missionaries, and to evangelize the world. And—what deserves to be remarked—all these associations, various as they are, really propose in every instance a great and glorious end. They all are formed for useful, moral, religious, philosophical, philanthropical or humane purposes. They may be badly managed, they may fail in accomplishing what they propose, but that which they propose deserves to be accomplished. Sectarians may control them; but in all cases their ends are broader than any sect, than all sects, and they alike commend themselves to the consciences and the prayers of mankind, in some of these associations, sects long and widely separated come together, and find to their mutual satisfaction that they have a common ground, and a ground which each one instinctively admits to be higher and holier than any merely sectarian ground.

This tendency too is triumphing over all obstacles. Sects, which opposed this or that association because principally under the control of this or that sect, have slowly and reluctantly ceased their opposition, and have finally acquiesced. Individuals, who for a time resorted to ridicule and abuse to check associations, are now silent and they stand amazed as did those who listened to the Apostles on the day of Pentecost. Those who apprehended great evils from them now seek to withstand them only by counter associations. To resist them is in fact out of the question. One might as well resist the whirlwind. There is a more than human power at the bottom of them. They come from God, from a divine inspiration given to the people to build the new church and realize the atonement, a universal and everlasting association.

This tendency or inspiration will, in a few days, meet the eclectic movement, if it have not already met it; and what shall prevent a result similar to that which followed the meeting of the early Christian inspiration and the Alexandrian eclecticism? This inspiration is, indeed, at this moment, apparently blind, but it and modern philosophy tend to the same end. They have then the same truth at bottom. They must then have a natural affinity with one another. They will then come together. The philosophy will explain and enlighten the inspiration. They who are now mad for associations will comprehend the power which has moved them, they will see the end towards which they have been tending without their knowing it, and they will give to the philosopher in return zeal, energy, enthusiasm, and there will then be both the light and the force needed to construct the new church.

And I think I see some indications that this meeting of inspiration and philosophy is already taking place. Something like it has occurred in Germany, in that movement commenced by Herder, but best represented by Schleiermacher, a man remarkable for warmth of feeling, and coolness of thought, a preacher and a philosopher, a theologian and a man of science, a student and a man of business. It was attempted in France, where it gave birth to "Nouveau Christianisme," but without much success, because it is not a new Christianity but a new church that is required.

But the plainest indications of it are at home. In this country more than in any other is the man of thought united in the same person with the man of action. The people here have a strong tendency to profound and philosophic thought, as well as to skillful, energetic and persevering action. The time is not far distant when our whole population will be philosophers, and all our philosophers will be practical men. This is written on almost every man's brow in characters so plain that he who runs may read. This characteristic of our population fits us above all other nations to bring out and realize great and important ideas. Here too is the freedom which other nations want, and the faith in ideas which can be found nowhere else. Philosophers in other countries may think and construct important theories, but they can realize them only to a very limited extent. But here every idea may be at once put to a practical test, and if true it will be realized. We have the field, the liberty, the disposition, and the faith to work with ideas. It is here, then, that must first be brought out and realized the true idea of the atonement. We already seem to have a consciousness of this, and it is therefore that we are not and cannot be surprised to find the union of popular inspiration with profound philosophical thought manifesting itself more clearly here than anywhere else.

The representative of this union here is a body of individuals rather than a single individual. The many with us are everything, the individual almost nothing. One man, however, stands out from this body, a more perfect type of the synthesis of eclecticism and inspiration than anyone else. I need not name him.[2] Philosophers consult him and the people hear his voice and follow him. His connection with a particular denomination may have exposed him to some unfriendly criticism, but he is in truth one of the most popular men of the age. His voice finds a response in the mind and in the heart of humanity.

His active career commenced with the new century, in that place where it should, and in the only place where it could,—in the place where a republic had been born and liberty had received her grandest developments and her surest safeguards. There he has continued, and there he has been foremost in laying the foundation of that new church which will soon rise to greet the morning ray, and in which a glad voice will chant the hymn of peace to the evening sun. Few men are so remarkable for their union of deep religious feeling with sound reflection, of sobriety with popular enthusiasm. He reveres God and he reverences man. When he speaks he convinces and kindles.

When rationalism was attacked he appeared in its defense and proclaimed, in a language which still rings in our ears, the imprescriptible rights of the mind. After the first shock of the war upon rationalism had been met, and a momentary truce tacitly declared, he brought out in an ordination sermon the great truth which destroys all antagonism and realizes the atonement. In that sermon—the most remarkable since the Sermon on the Mount—he distinctly recognizes and triumphantly vindicates the God-Man. "In ourselves are the elements of the Divinity. God, then, does not sustain a figurative resemblance to man. It is the resemblance of a parent to a child, *the likeness of a kindred nature."* In this sublime declaration, the Son of God is owned. Humanity, after so many years of vain search for a Father, finds itself here openly proclaimed the true child of God.

This declaration gives us the hidden sense of the symbol of the God-Man. By asserting the divinity of humanity, it teaches us that we should not view that symbol as the symbol of two natures in one person, but of kindred natures in two persons. The God-Man indicates not the antithesis of God and man; nor does it stand for a being alone of its kind; but it indicates the homogeneousness of the human and divine natures, and shows that they can dwell together in love and peace. The Son of Man and the Son of God are not two persons but one, a mystery which becomes clear the very moment that the human nature is discovered to have a sameness with the divine.

Chapter IX: The Atonement

The great doctrine, which is to realize the atonement and which the symbol of the God-Man now teaches us, is that all things are essentially holy, that everything is cleansed, and that we must call nothing common or unclean.

"And God saw everything that he had made, and behold it was very good." And what else could it have been? God is wise, powerful and good; and how can a wise, powerful and good being create evil? God is the great fountain from which flows everything that is; how then can there be anything but good in existence?

Neither spiritualism nor materialism was aware of this truth. Spiritualism saw good only in pure spirit. God was pure spirit and therefore good; but all which could be distinguished from him was evil, and only evil, and that continually. Our good consisted in resemblance to God, that is, in being as like pure spirit as possible. Our duty was to get rid of matter. All the interests of the material order were sinful. St. Augustine declared the flesh, that is the body, to be sin; perfection then could be obtained only by neglecting, and as far as possible annihilating it. Materialism, on the other hand, had no recognition of spirit. It considered all time and thought and labor bestowed on that which transcends this world as worse than thrown away. It had no conception of inward communion with God. It counted fears of punishment or hopes of reward in a world to come mere idle fancies, fit only to amuse or control the vulgar. It laughed at spiritual joys and griefs, and treated as serious affairs only the pleasures and pains of sense.

But the new doctrine of the atonement reconciles these two warring systems. This doctrine teaches us that spirit is real and holy, that matter is real and holy, that God is holy and that man is holy, that spiritual joys and griefs, and the pleasures and pains of sense, are alike real joys and griefs, real pleasures and pains, and in their places are alike sacred. Spirit and matter, then, are saved. One is not required to be sacrificed to the other; both may and should coexist as separate elements of the same grand and harmonious whole.

The influence of this doctrine cannot fail to be very great. It will correct our estimate of man, of the world, of religion and of God, and remodel all our institutions. It must in fact create a new civilization as much in advance of ours as ours is in advance of that which obtained in the Roman Empire in the time of Jesus.

Hitherto we have considered man as the antithesis of all good. We have loaded him with reproachful epithets and made it a sin in him even to be born. We have uniformly deemed it necessary to degrade him in order to exalt his Creator. But this will end. The slave will become a son. Man is hereafter to stand erect before God as a child before its father. Human nature, at which we have pointed our wit and vented our spleen, will be clothed with a high and commanding worth. It will be seen to be a lofty and deathless nature. It will be felt to be divine, and infinite will be found traced in living characters on all its faculties.

We shall not treat one another then as we do now. Man will be sacred in the eyes of man. To wrong him will be more than crime, it will be sin. To labor to degrade him will seem like laboring to degrade the Divinity. Man will reverence man.

Slavery will cease. Man will shudder at the bare idea of enslaving so noble a being as man. It will seem to him hardly less daring than to presume to task the motions of the Deity and to compel him to come and go at our bidding. When man learns the true value of man, the chains of the captive must be unloosed and the fetters of the slave fall off.

Wars will fail. The sword will be beaten into the ploughshare and the spear into the pruning hook. Man will not dare to mar and mangle the shrine of the Divinity. The God looking out from human eyes will disarm the soldier and make him kneel to him he had risen up to slay. The warhorse will cease to bathe his fetlocks in human gore. He will snuff the breeze in the wild freedom of his native plains, or quietly submit to be harnessed to the plough. The hero's occupation will be gone, and heroism will be found only in saving and blessing human life.

Education will destroy the empire of ignorance. The human mind, allied as it is to the divine, is too valuable to lie waste or to be left to breed only briars and thorns. Those children, ragged and incrusted with filth, which throng our streets, and for whom we must one day build prisons, forge bolts and bars, or erect gibbets, are not only our children, our brother's children, but they are children of God, they have in themselves the elements of the Divinity and powers which when put forth will raise them above what the tallest archangel now is. And when this is seen and felt, will those children be left to fester in ignorance or to grow up in vice and crime? The whole energy of man's being cries out against such folly, such gross injustice.

Civil freedom will become universal. It will be everywhere felt that one man has no right over another which that other has not over him. All will be seen to be brothers and equals in the sight of their common Father. All will love one another too much to desire to play the tyrant. Human nature will be reverenced too much not to be allowed to have free scope for the full and harmonious development of all its faculties. Governments will become sacred; and while on the one hand they are respected and obeyed, on the other it will be felt to be a religious right and a religious duty to labor to make them as perfect as they can be.

Religion will not stop with the command to obey the laws, but it will bid us make just laws, such laws as befit a being divinely endowed like man. The church will be on the side of progress, and spiritualism and materialism will combine to make man's earthly condition as near like the lost Eden of the eastern poets, as is compatible with the growth and perfection of his nature.

Industry will be holy. The cultivation of the earth will be the worship of God. Workingmen will be priests, and as priests they will be reverenced, and as priests they will reverence themselves and feel that they must maintain themselves undefiled. He that ministers at the altar must be pure, will be said of the mechanic, the agriculturist, the common laborer, as well as of him who is technically called a priest.

The earth itself and the animals which inhabit it will be counted sacred. We shall study in them the manifestation of God's goodness, wisdom, and power, and be careful that we make of them none but a holy use.

Man's body will be deemed holy. It will be called the temple of the living God. As a temple it must not be desecrated. Men will beware of defiling it by sin, by any excessive or improper indulgence, as they would of defiling the temple or the altar consecrated to the service of God. Man will reverence himself too much, he will see too much of the holy in his nature ever to pervert it from the right line of truth and duty.

"In that day shall there be on the bells of the horses, *holiness unto the lord*; and the pots in the Lord's house shall be as the bowls before the altar. Yea, every pot in Jerusalem and in Judah shall be Holiness unto the Lord of hosts." The words of the prophet will be fulfilled. All things proceed from God and are therefore holy. Every duty, every act necessary to be done, every implement of industry, or thing contributing to human use or convenience, will be treated as holy. We shall recall even the reverence of the Indian for his bow and arrow, and by enlightening it with a divine philosophy preserve it.

"Pure religion, and undefiled before God and the Father is this, to visit the fatherless and the widows in their affliction, and to keep one's self unspotted from the world." Religious worship will not be the mere service of the sanctuary. The universe will be God's temple, and its service will be the doing of good to mankind, relieving suffering and promoting joy, virtue and well-being. By this, religion and morality will be united, and the service of God and the service of man become the same. Our faith in God will show itself by our good works to man. Our love to the Father, whom we have not seen, will be evinced by our love for our brother whom we have seen.

Church and state will become one. The state will be holy, and the church will be holy. Both will aim at the same thing, and the existence of one as separate from the other will not be needed. The church will not be then an outward visible power, coexisting with the state, sometimes controlling it and at other times controlled by it; but it will be within, a true spiritual—not spiritualistic—church, regulating the heart, conscience and the life.

And when this all takes place the glory of the Lord will be manifested unto the ends of the earth, and all flesh will see it and rejoice together. The time is yet distant before this will be fully realized. We are now realizing it in our theory. We assert the holiness of all things. This assertion becomes an idea, and ideas, if they are true, are omnipotent. As soon as humanity fully possesses this idea, it will lose no time in reducing it to practice. Men will conform their practice to it. They will become personally holy. Holiness will be written on all their thoughts, emotions and actions, on their whole lives. And then will Christ really be formed within, the hope of glory. He will be truly incarnated in universal humanity, and God and man will be one.

Chapter X: Progress

The actual existence of evil, the effects of which are everywhere so visible, and apparently so deplorable, may seem to be a serious objection to the great doctrine of the atonement, that all things are essentially good and holy; but it will present little difficulty, if we consider that God designed us to be progressive beings, and that we can be progressive beings only on the condition that we be made less perfect than we may become, that we have our point of departure at a distance from our point of destination. We must begin in weakness and ignorance; and if we begin in weakness and ignorance we cannot fail to miss our way, or frequently to want strength to pursue it. To err in judgment or to come short in action will be our unavoidable lot, until we are instructed by experience and strengthened by exertion.

But this is no ground of complaint. We gain more than we lose by it. Had we without any agency of our own been made all that by a proper cultivation of our faculties we may become, we should have been much inferior to what we now are. We could have had no want, no desire, no good to seek, no end to gain, no destiny to achieve—no employment, and no motive to action. Our existence would have been aimless, silent and unvaried, given apparently for no purpose but to be dreamed away in an eternal and unbroken repose. Who could desire such an existence? Who would prefer it to the existence we now have, liable to error, sin and misery as it may be?

Constituted as we are, the way is more than the end, the acquisition more than the possession; but had we been made at once all that is promised us by our nature, these would have been nothing; we should indeed have had the end, the possession, but that would have been all. We should have been men without having first been children. Our earlier life, its trials and temptations, its failures and its successes, would never have existed. Would we willingly forego that earlier life? Dear to all men is the memory of childhood and youth; dear too is the recollection of their difficulties and dangers, their struggles with the world or with their own passions. We may regret, do regret, suffer remorse, that we did not put ourselves forth with more energy, that the enemy with which we had to contend was not more manfully met; but who of us is so craven to wish those difficulties and dangers had been less, or that the enemy's forces had been fewer and weaker?

God gave his richest gift when he gave the capacity for progress. This capacity is the chief glory of our nature, the brightest signature of its divine origin and the pledge of its immortality. The being which can make no further progress, which has finished its work, achieved its destiny, attained its end, must die. Why should it live? How could it live? What would be its life? But man never attains his end; he never achieves his destiny; he never finishes his work; he has always something to do, some new acquisition to make, some new height of excellence to ascend, and therefore is he immortal. He cannot die, for his hour never comes. He is never ready. Who would then be deprived of his capacity for progress?

This capacity, though it be the occasion of error and sin, is that which makes us moral beings. Without it we could not be virtuous. A being that does not make himself, his own character, but is made, and made all he is or can be, has no free will, no liberty. He is a thing, not a person, and as incapable of merit or demerit as the sun or moon, earthquakes or volcanoes. As much superior as is a moral to a fatal action, a perfection wrought out in and by one's self to a perfection merely received, as much superior as is a person to a thing, albeit a glorious thing, so much do we gain by being made for progress, by having a capacity for virtue, notwithstanding it be also a capacity for sin, so much superior are we to what we should have been had we been created full grown men, with all our faculties perfected.

But moral evil, by the superintending care of Providence and the free will of man, is often if not always a means of aiding progress itself. The sinner is not so far from God as the merely innocent. He who has failed is further onward than he who has not been tried. The consequences of error open our eyes to the truth; the consequences of transgression make us regret our departure from duty and try to return; the effort to return gives us the power to return. Thus does moral evil ever work its own destruction. Rightly viewed, it were seen to be no entity, no positive existence, but merely the absence of good, the void around and within us, and which by the enlargement of our being, we are continually filling up. It is not then a person, a thing, a being, and consequently can make nothing against the doctrine, which asserts the essential holiness of all things.

But men formerly supposed evil to be a substantial existence, as much of an entity as goodness. But then came the difficulty, whence could evil originate? It could not come from a good source, for good will not and cannot produce evil. But evil exists. Then all things do not come from the same source. One good and holy God has not made whatever is. There must be more gods than one. There must be an evil god to create evil, as well as a good God to create good. Hence the notion of two gods, or two classes of gods, one good and the other bad, which runs through all antiquity, and under the terms God and the devil, is reproduced even in the Christian church.

But this notion is easily shown to be unfounded. If one of the two gods depend on the other, then the other must be its cause, its creator. In this case, nothing would be gained. How could a good God create a bad one, or a bad god create a good one? If one does not depend on the other, then both are independent, each is sufficient for itself. A being that is sufficient for itself, that has the grounds of its existence within itself, must be absolute, almighty. There are then two absolutes, two almighties; but this is an absurdity, a contradiction in terms. This notion then must be abandoned. It was abandoned, and the evil was transferred to matter. But matter is either created or it is not. If it be created, then it is dependent, and that on which it is dependent is answerable for its properties. How could a good God have given it evil properties? If it be not created, then it is sufficient for itself; it has the grounds of its own existence within itself; it is then absolute, almighty, and the absurdity of two absolutes, of two almighties, is reproduced.

Still we need not wonder that men, who saw good and evil thickly strewn together up and down the earth, the tares everywhere choking the wheat, should have inferred the existence of two opposite and antagonistic principles, as the cause of what they saw. Nor is it at all strange that men, who felt themselves restrained, hemmed in, by the material world, who carried about with them a material body forever importuning them with its wants and subjecting them to a thousand ills, should have looked upon matter as the cause of all the evil they saw, felt and endured. As things presented themselves to their observation they judged rightly. We may, by the aid of a revelation, which shines further into the darkness and spreads a clearer light around us and over the universe than any they had received, be able to correct their errors, and to perceive that the antagonism, in which they believed, has no existence in the world of reality; but we must beware how we censure them for the views they took. They saw what they could see with their light and from their position, and we can do no more. Future generations will have more favorable positions and a stronger and clearer light than we have, and they will be to us what we are to the generations which went before us. As we would escape the condemnation of our children, so should we refrain from condemning our fathers. They did their duty, let us do ours,— serve our own generation without defaming that to which we owe our existence and all that we are. All things are holy, and all doctrines are sacred. All the productions of the ever-teeming brain of man, however fantastic or unsubstantial their forms, are but so many manifestations of humanity, and humanity is a manifestation of the Divinity. The Son of Man is the incarnate God. He who blasphemes the spirit with which he works and fulfills his mission in the flesh, blasphemes the Holy Ghost. Silent then be the tongue that would lisp, palsied the hand that would write the smallest censure upon humanity for any of the opinions it has expressed, however defective, however far from embracing the whole truth, future or more favored inquirers may find them. Humanity is holy, let the proudest kneel in reverence.

This doctrine of progress, not only accounts for the origin of evil and explains its difficulties, but it points out to us our duty. The duty of every being is to follow its destiny, to seek its end. Man's destiny is illimitable progress; his end is everlasting growth, enlargement of his being. Progress is the end for which he was made. To this end, then, it is his duty to direct all his inquiries, all his systems of religion and philosophy, all his institutions of politics and society, all the productions of genius and taste, in one word all the modes of his activity.

This is his duty. Hitherto he has performed it, but blindly, without knowing and without admitting it. Humanity has but today, as it were, risen to self-consciousness, to a perception of its own capacity, to a glimpse of its inconceivably grand and holy destiny. Heretofore it has failed to recognize clearly its duty. It has advanced, but not designedly, not with foresight; it has done it instinctively, by the aid of the invisible but safe-guiding hand of its Father. Without knowing what it did, it has condemned progress, while it was progressing. It has stoned the prophets and reformers, even while it was itself reforming and uttering glorious prophecies of its future condition. But the time has now come for humanity to understand itself, to accept the law imposed upon it for its own good, to foresee its end and march with intention steadily towards it. Its future religion is the religion of progress. The true priests are those who can quicken in mankind a desire for progress, and urge them forward in the direction of the true, the good, the perfect.

Conclusion

Here I must close. I have uttered the words UNION and PROGRESS as the authentic creed of the new church, as designating the whole duty of man. Would they had been spoken in a clearer, a louder and a sweeter voice, that a response might be heard from the universal heart of humanity. But I have spoken as I could, and from a motive which I shall not blush to own either to myself or to him to whom all must render an account of all their thoughts, words, and deeds. I once had no faith in him, and I was to myself "a child without a sire." I was alone in the world, my heart found no companionship, and my affections withered and died. But I have found him, and he is my father, and mankind are my brothers, and I can love and reverence.

Mankind are my brothers,—they are brothers to one another. l would see them no longer mutually estranged. I labor to bring them together, and to make them feel and own that they are all made of one blood. Let them feel and own this, and they will love one another; they will be kindly affectioned one to another, and "the groans of this nether world will cease;" the spectacle of wrongs and outrages oppress our sight no more; tears be wiped from all eyes, and humanity pass from death to life, to life immortal, to the life of God, for God is love.

And this result, for which the wise and the good everywhere yearn and labor, will be obtained. I do not misread the age. I have not looked upon the world only out from the window of my closet; I have mingled in its busy scenes; I have rejoiced and wept with it; I have hoped and feared, and believed and doubted with it, and I am but what it has made me. I cannot misread it. It craves union. The heart of man is crying out for the heart of man. One and the same spirit is abroad, uttering the same voice in all languages. From all parts of the world voice answers to voice, and man responds to man. There is a universal language already in use. Men are beginning to understand one another, and their mutual understanding will beget mutual sympathy, and mutual sympathy will bind them together and to God.

And for progress too the whole world is struggling. Old institutions are examined, old opinions criticized, even the old church is laid bare to its very foundations, and its holy vestments and sacred symbols are exposed to the gaze of the multitude; new systems are proclaimed, new institutions elaborated, new ideas are sent abroad, new experiments are made, and the whole world seems intent on the means by which it may accomplish its destiny. The individual is struggling to become a greater and a better being. Everywhere there are men laboring to perfect governments and laws. The poor man is admitted to be human, and millions of voices are demanding that he be treated as a brother. All eyes and hearts are turned to education. The cultivation of the child's moral and spiritual nature becomes the worship of God. The priest rises to the educator, and the schoolroom is the temple in which he is to minister. There is progress; there will he progress. Humanity must go forward. Encouraging is the future. He, who takes his position on the "high table land" of humanity, and beholds with a prophet's gaze his brothers, so long separated, coming together, and arm in arm marching onward and upward towards the perfect, towards God, may hear celestial voices chanting a sweeter strain than that which announced to Judea's shepherds the birth of the Redeemer, and his heart full and overflowing, he may exclaim with old Simeon, "Lord, now lettest thou thy servant depart in peace, for mine eyes have seen thy salvation."

Democracy

January 1838

We have introduced this Address, because it gives us an opportunity for expressing ourselves on the vexed and sometimes vexatious question of democracy. In common with the great body of our countrymen, we are sturdy democrats; and, do what we can to prevent it, democracy will more or less tincture all that we write. But in order to avoid all just occasion of offense to those—if such there be—in whose minds the word *Democrat* calls up unpleasant associations, and to save ourselves from being misapprehended or misinterpreted, we design, in this article, to give as clear and as satisfactory an exposition, as we can, of what we understand by democracy, and of the sense in which we consider ourselves and wish others to consider us democrats.

1. We may understand by democracy a form of government under which the people, either as a body or by their representatives, make and administer their own laws. This is the original and etymological sense of the word; and in this sense, a democrat is one who believes in, or contends for a popular form of government. All, or nearly all Americans are democrats in this sense of the word. We have established a democratic government, both for the confederacy and for the several states; and there are few among us, if any, who would exchange it for another. Some may have less faith than others in the utility or permanence of this form of government; here and there one, perhaps, may be found with an individual preference for a limited monarchy; but virtually the whole people are seriously and honestly bent on preserving the

institutions the wisdom of our fathers adopted. There may be those who question the propriety of this or that public measure, who object to this or that law, but none who object very strenuously to the form of the government itself. The American people are not revolutionists. They are conservatives, and to be a conservative in this country, is to be a democrat.

2. By the word *Democracy* we may designate the great body of the people, the unprivileged many, in opposition to the privileged few. In this sense of the word, a democrat is one who sympathizes with the masses, and who contends that all political and governmental action should have for its end and aim the protection of the rights and the promotion of the interests of the poorest and most numerous class. The whole, or nearly the whole American people are democrats also in this sense of the term. There may be differences of opinion, as to the means of promoting the good of the many, as to what constitutes their good, and as to the amount of good God has made them capable of receiving, obtaining, or enjoying, but none as to the principle that the government is bound to seek "the greatest good of the greatest number."

3. The term *Democracy* may also be applied, as it is applied in this country, to a certain political party. There is a political party in this country called the Democratic party. It sprang up on the adoption of the Federal Constitution, to which it was opposed, and which it refused to accept without some important amendments. It came into power with Mr. Jefferson, in 1801, and has had at least the nominal control of the general government ever since, though it has seldom had a majority in all the states. Its first party appellation was that of Anti-Federalist; in 1798 it was called the Republican party; since 1812, especially since 1825, it has assumed the name of the Democratic Republican or Democratic party. When we use the word *democracy* to designate this party, we call an adherent of this party a democrat. A democrat in this sense, however, does not imply so much the one who believes in the general doctrines of the Democratic party, and who countenances its principal measures, as the one who enters its ranks, puts on its livery, submits to its rules and usages, and feels himself bound by his duty to his party to vote for its candidates and to support its policy, whether he like them or not. He must be a good man and true, one on whom the party can count, and who will not disturb it by any obstinate adherence to the convic-

tions of his own understanding, or the dictates of his own conscience. In the sense of a member of this party, a considerable number of the American people are not democrats. Some are not democrats because they disapprove the doctrines and measures of the Democratic party; others, because they have a very great aversion to being swallowed up in a multitude that goes hither and thither, just as some irresponsible will directs.

We are of the latter class. We do not call ourselves democrats in a party sense, because we have a great dislike to party tyranny, and because, wherever we are, we must speak according to our own convictions, and act as seemeth to us good, without asking the leave of a party. In a party sense, we are nothing. There is no party that can count on our fidelity. In politics, as in morals, theology, and philosophy, we are eclectics, and hold ourselves free to seek, accept, and support truth and justice wherever we can find them. No party is always wrong; no one is always right. We agree with all parties where they agree with us; but where they do not agree with us, we cannot and will not surrender our own convictions for the sake of agreeing with them or with any one of them.

4. The word *Democracy*, in the last place, may be taken as the name of a great social and political doctrine, which is now gaining much in popularity, and of a powerful movement of the masses towards a better social condition than has heretofore existed. In this sense the word is used in England and on the continent of Europe, though not often in this country. A democrat, in this sense of the word, is rather a philosophical, than a party democrat. He takes the word, not in a party and historical sense, but in a broad, philosophical sense. He distinguishes between party democracy as it exists in this country, and philosophical democracy, or democracy as it should be. With the first we do not concern ourselves. In the second, we take a deep interest, both as a man and as a citizen; and this Review will ever be found its fearless and untiring advocate.

But, what is philosophical democracy? Or the social and political doctrine, which may be called, not in an historical and party sense, but in a philosophical sense, the democratic doctrine? This is not a question without significance. It is a question it behooves every American citizen to ask, and, as far as he can, to answer. It needs a deliberate answer, such an answer as it has never yet, to our knowledge, received. Not a few of those who call themselves democrats are entirely ignorant of what democracy is, and wholly unable to legitimate the doctrines or the measures they support. Notwithstanding the much that has been said and written about democracy, it is yet more of an instinct, an impulse, a sentiment, than an idea. The masses feel its power and yield to its direction, but they see not whither they are going, and they comprehend not wherefore they ought to suffer themselves to be borne along on its current. They go, perhaps, where they ought to go, but they go blindly, without legitimating or being able to legitimate their course. It will not be useless then to attempt to seize this vague sentiment, this democratic instinct, and to do something to present it in a form that shall enable men to perceive what it is, and what are the grounds on which it may be legitimated.

Democracy, in the sense we are now considering it, is sometimes asserted to be the sovereignty of the people. If this be a true account of it, it is indefensible. The sovereignty of the people is not a truth. Sovereignty is that which is highest, ultimate; which has not only the physical force to make itself obeyed, but the moral right to command whatever it pleases. The right to command involves the corresponding duty of obedience. What the sovereign may command, it is the duty of the subject to obey.

Are the people the highest? Are they ultimate? And are we bound in conscience to obey whatever it may be their good pleasure to ordain? If so, where is individual liberty? If so, the people, taken collectively, are the absolute master of every man taken individually. Every man, as a man, then, is an absolute slave. Whatever the people, in their collective capacity; may demand of him, he must feel himself bound in conscience to give. No matter how intolerable the burdens imposed, painful and needless the sacrifices required, he cannot refuse obedience without incurring the guilt of disloyalty; and he must submit in quiet, in silence, without even the moral right to feel that he is wronged.

Now this, in theory at least, is absolutism. Whether it be a democracy, or any other form of government, if it be absolute, there is and there can be no individual liberty. Under a monarchy, the monarch is the state. "*L'Etat, c'est Moi*," said Louis the Fourteenth, and he expressed the whole monarchical theory. The state being absolute, and the monarch being the state, the monarch has the right to command what he will, and exact obedience in the name of duty, loyalty. Hence absolutism, despotism.

Under an aristocracy, the nobility are the state, and consequently, as the state is absolute, the nobility are also absolute. Whatever they command is binding. If they require the many to be "hewers of wood and drawers of water" to them, then "hewers of wood and drawers of water" to them the many must feel it their duty to be. Here, for the many, is absolutism as much as under a monarchy. Everybody sees this.

Well, is it less so under a democracy, where the people, in their associated capacity, are held to be absolute? The people are the state, and the state is absolute; the people may therefore do whatever they please. Is not this freedom? Yes; for the state; but what is it for the individual? There are no kings, no nobilities, it is true; but the people may exercise all the power over the individual that kings or nobilities may; and consequently every man, taken singly, is, under a democracy, if the state be absolute, as much the slave of the state as under the most absolute monarchy or aristocracy.

But this is not the end of the chapter. Under a democratic form of government, all questions, which come up for the decision of authority, must be decided by a majority of voices. The sovereignty, which is asserted for the people, must, then, be transferred to the ruling majority. If the people are sovereign, then the majority are sovereign; and if sovereign, the majority have, as Miss Martineau lays it down, the absolute right to govern. If the majority have the absolute right to govern, it is the absolute duty of the minority to obey. We who chance to be in the minority are then completely disfranchised. We are wholly at the mercy of the majority. We hold our property, our wives and children, and our lives even, at its sovereign will and pleasure. It may do by us and ours as it pleases. If it take it into its head to make a new and arbitrary division of property, however unjust it may seem, we shall not only be impotent to resist, but we shall not even have the right of the wretched to complain. Conscience will be no shield. The authority of the absolute sovereign extends to spiritual matters as well as to temporal. The creed the majority is pleased to impose, the minority must in all meekness and submission receive; and the form of religious worship the majority is good enough to prescribe, the minority must make it a matter of conscience to observe. Whatever has been done under the most absolute monarchy or the most lawless aristocracy may be reenacted under a pure democracy, and what is worse, legitimately too, if it be once laid down in principle that the majority has the absolute right to govern.

The majority will always have the physical power to coerce the minority into submission; but this is a matter of no moment in comparison with the doctrine which gives them the right to do it. We have very little fear of the physical force of numbers, when we can oppose to it the moral force of right. The doctrine in question deprives us of this moral force. By giving absolute sovereignty to the majority, it declares whatever the majority does is right, that the majority can do no wrong. It legitimates every possible act, for which the sanction of a majority of voices can be obtained. Whatever the majority may exact, it is just to give. Truth, justice, wisdom, virtue can erect no barriers to stay its progress; for these are the creations of its will, and may be made or unmade by its breath. Justice is obedience to its decrees, and injustice is resistance to its commands. Resistance is not crime before the civil tribunal only, but also *in foro conscientiae*. Now this is what we protest against. It is not the physical force of the majority that we dread, but the doctrine that legitimates each and every act the majority may choose to perform; and therefore teaches it to look for no standard of right and wrong beyond its own will.

We do not believe majorities are exceedingly prone to encroach on the rights of minorities; but we would always erect a bulwark of justice around those rights and always have a moral power which we may oppose to every possible encroachment. The majority, we believe, always leave the minority in possession of the greater part of their rights, not however as rights, but as favors. It is to this we object. We cannot, and will not, consent to receive as a boon, what we may demand as a right. Our liberties belong to us as men; and we would always feel that we hold them as our personal property, of which he who despoils us is a thief and a robber.

The effects of this doctrine, so far as believed and acted on, cannot be too earnestly deprecated. It creates a multitude of demagogues, pretending a world of love for the *dear* people, lauding the people's virtues, magnifying their sovereignty, and with mock humility professing their readiness ever to bow to the will of the majority. It tends to make public men lax in their morals, hypocritical in their conduct; and it paves the way for gross bribery and corruption. It generates a habit of appealing, on nearly all occasions, from truth and justice, wisdom arid virtue, to the force of numbers, and virtually sinks the man in the brute. It destroys manliness of character, independence of thought and action, and makes one weak, vacillating—a timeserver and a coward. It perverts inquiry from its legitimate objects, and asks, when it concerns a candidate for office, not, who is the most honest, the most capable? But, who will command the most votes? And, when it concerns a measure of policy, not, what is just? What is for the public good? But, what can the majority be induced to support?

Now as men, as friends to good morals, we cannot assent to a doctrine which not only has this tendency, but which declares this tendency legitimate. That it does have this tendency needs not to be proved. Everybody knows it and not a few lament it. Not long since it was gravely argued by a leading politician, in a Fourth of July Oration, that Massachusetts ought to give Mr. Van Buren her votes for the presidency, because, if she did not, she would array herself against her sister states, and be compelled to stand alone, as the orator said with a sneer, "in solitary grandeur." In the access of his party fever, it did not occur to him that Massachusetts was in duty bound, whether her sister states were with her or against her, to oppose Mr. Van Buren, if she disliked him as a man, or distrusted his principles as a politician or a statesman. Many good reasons, doubtless, might have been alleged why Massachusetts ought to have voted for Mr. Van Buren, but the orator would have been puzzled to select one less conclusive, or more directly in the face and eyes of all sound morals, than the one he adduced. The man who deserves to be called a statesman never appeals to low or demoralizing motives, and he scorns to carry even a good measure by unworthy means. There is within every man, who can lay any claim to correct moral feeling, that which looks with contempt on the puny creature who makes the opinions of the majority his rule of action. He who wants the moral courage to stand up "in solitary grandeur," like Socrates in face of the Thirty Tyrants, and demand that right be respected, that justice be done, is unfit to be called a statesman, or even a man. A man has no business with what the majority think, will, say, do, or will approve; if he will be a man, and maintain the rights and dignity of manhood, his sole business is to inquire what truth and justice, wisdom and virtue demand at his hands, and to do it, whether the world be with him or against him, to do it, whether he stand alone "in solitary grandeur," or be huzzaed by the crowd, loaded with honors, held up as one whom the young must aspire to imitate, or be sneered at as singular, branded as a "seditious fellow," or crucified, as was Jesus, between two thieves. Away then with your demoralizing and debasing notion of appealing to a majority of voices! Dare be a man, dare be yourself, to speak and act according to your own solemn convictions, and in obedience to the voice of God calling out to you from the depths of your own being. Professions of freedom, of love of liberty, of devotion to her cause, are mere wind when there wants the power to live, and to die, in defense of what one's own heart tells him is just and true. A free government is a mockery, a solemn farce, where every man feels himself bound to consult and to conform to the opinions and will of an irresponsible majority. Free minds, free hearts, free souls are the materials, and the only materials, out of which free governments are constructed. And is he free in mind, heart, soul, body, or limb, he who feels himself bound to the triumphal car of the majority, to be dragged whither its drivers please? Is he the man to speak out the lessons of truth and wisdom when most they are needed, to stand by the right when all are gone out of the way, to plead for the wronged and downtrodden when all are dumb, he who owns the absolute right of the majority to govern?

Sovereignty is not in the will of the people, nor in the will of the majority. Every man feels that the people are not ultimate, are not the highest, that they do not make the right or the wrong, and that the people as a state, as well as the people as individuals, are under law, accountable to a higher authority than theirs. What is this higher than the people? The king? Not he whom men dignify with the royal title. Every man, by the fact that he is a man, is an accountable being. Every man feels that he owes allegiance to some authority above him. The man whom men call a king, is a man, and inasmuch as he is a man, he must be an accountable being, must himself be under law, and, therefore, cannot be the highest, the ultimate, and of course not the true sovereign. His will is not in itself law. Then he is not in himself a sovereign. Whatever authority he may possess is derived, and that from which he derives his authority, and not he, in the last analysis, is the true sovereign. If he derive it from the people, then the people, not he, is the sovereign; if from God, then God, not he, is the sovereign. Are the aristocracy the sovereign? If so, annihilate the aristocracy, and men will be loosed from all restraint, released from all obligation, and there will be for them neither right nor wrong. Nobody can admit that right and wrong owe their existence to the aristocracy. Moreover, the aristocracy are men, and as men, they are in the same predicament with all other men. They are themselves under law, accountable, and therefore not sovereign in their own right. If we say they are above the people, they are placed there by some power which is also above them, and that, not they, is the sovereign.

But if neither people nor kings nor aristocracy are sovereign, who or what is? What is the answer which every man, when he reflects as a moralist, gives to the question, Why ought I to do this or that particular thing? Does he say because the king commands it? The aristocracy enjoin it? The people ordain it? The majority wills it? No. He says, if he be true to his higher convictions, because it is right, because it is just. Every man feels that he has a right to do whatever is just and that it is his duty to do it. Whatever he feels to be just, he feels to be legitimate, to be law, to be morally obligatory. Whatever is unjust, he feels to be illegitimate, to be without obligation, and to be that which it is not disloyalty to resist. The absolutist, he who contends for unqualified submission on the part of the people to the monarch, thunders, therefore, in the ears of the absolute monarch himself, that he is bound to be just; and the aristocrat assures his order that its highest nobility is derived from its obedience to justice; and does not the democrat, too, even while he proclaims the sovereignty of the people, tell this same sovereign people to be just? In all this, witness is borne to an authority above the individual, above kings, nobilities, and people, and to the fact, too, that the absolute sovereign is justice. Justice is then the sovereign, the sovereign of sovereigns, the king of kings, lord of lords, the supreme law of the people, and of the individual.

This doctrine teaches that the people, as a state, are as much bound to be just, as is the individual. By bounding the state by justice, we declare it limited; we deny its absolute sovereignty; and, therefore, save the individual from absolute slavery. The individual may on this ground arrest the action of the state, by alleging that it is proceeding unjustly; and the minority has a moral force with which to oppose the physical force of the majority. By this there is laid in the state the foundation of liberty; liberty is acknowledged as a right, whether it be possessed as a fact or not.

A more formal refutation of the sovereignty of the people or vindication of the sovereignty of justice is not needed. In point of fact, there are none who mean to set up the sovereignty of the people above the sovereignty of justice. All, we believe, when the question is presented, as we have presented it, will and do admit that justice is supreme, though very few seem to have been aware of the consequences which result from such an admission. The sovereignty of justice, in all cases whatsoever, is what we understand by the doctrine of democracy. True democracy is nor merely the denial of the absolute sovereignty of the king, and that of the nobility, and the assertion of that of the people; but it is properly the denial of the absolute sovereignty of the state, whatever the form of government adopted as the agent of the state, and the assertion of the absolute sovereignty of justice. Still, we are not insensible to the fact, that the doctrine of the sovereignty of the people marks an immense progress in political science, and in the sense in which they, who assert it, mean to assert it, it is no doubt true.

Sovereignty may be taken either absolutely or relatively. When taken absolutely, as we have thus far taken it, and as it ought always to be taken, especially in a free government, it means, as we have defined it, the highest, that which is ultimate, which has the right to command what it will, and which to resist is crime. Thus defined it is certain that neither people, nor kings, nor aristocracies are sovereign for they are all under law and accountable to an authority which is not theirs, but which is above them, and independent of them.

When taken relatively, as it usually is by writers on government, it means the state, or the highest civil or political power of the state. The state, we have seen, is not absolute. It is not an independent sovereign. It is not, then, in strictness, a sovereign at all. Its enactments are not in and of themselves laws, and cannot be laws, unless they receive the signature of absolute justice. If that signature be withheld they are null and void from the beginning. Nevertheless social order, which is the indispensable condition of the very existence of the community, demands the creation of a government, and that the government should be clothed with the authority necessary for the maintenance cf order. That portion of sovereignty necessary for this end, and, if you please, for the promotion of the common weal, justice delegates to the state. This portion of delegated sovereignty is what is commonly meant by sovereignty. This sovereignty is necessarily limited to certain specific objects, and can be no greater than is needed for those objects. If the state stretch its authority beyond those objects, it becomes a usurper, and the individual is not bound to obey, but may lawfully resist it, as he may lawfully resist any species of injustice—taking care, however, that the manner of his resistance be neither unjust in itself, nor inconsistent with social order. For instance, the state assumes the authority to allow a man to be seized and held as property; the man may undoubtedly assert his liberty, his rights as a man, and endeavor to regain them; but he may not, in doing this, deny or infringe any of the just rights of him who may have deemed himself his master or owner. The Israelites had a right to free themselves from their bondage to the Egyptians, but they had not the right to rob the Egyptians of their jewelry.

Now this qualified, limited sovereignty, which in the last analysis, as we have said, is no sovereignty at all, is the sovereignty which has been asserted for the people, and to this sovereignty they are undoubtedly entitled. This sovereignty, which is the sovereignty of the state, may be vested in one man, and then the government is a monarchy; it may be vested in a few, and then the government is an aristocracy, or an oligarchy; it may be vested in the priesthood, and then the government is a hierarchy, or a theocracy, as it is more frequently called, because the priesthood never claim the sovereignty in their own name, but in the name of God, the priestly name for justice, the absolute sovereign; or, in fine, it may be vested in the people, and then it is a democracy, and a democracy, although the exercise of authority be in fact assigned to one man or to a few nobles, if the one man or the few nobles are held to derive their authority to govern from the people. France, in theory, was a democracy under Napoleon, although the exercise of authority was delegated to one man, and made hereditary in his family.

If the question come up, which of these various forms of government is the best, we answer unhesitatingly, that which vests sovereignty in the people. One thing may be affirmed of all forms of government. Wherever the supreme power of the state is lodged, they who are its depositaries always seek to wield it to their own exclusive benefit. Government is, whatever its form, invariably administered for the good of the governors. Theorists, indeed, tell us that government is instituted for the good of the governed; but that they are wrong is proved by the experience of six thousand years. Some have thought that governments were made for the good of the people; they who think the people were made for the good of governments, think more conformably to fact. They who have the power invariably seek to derive the greatest profit possible from it for themselves. Thus, in a monarchy, all things must be held subordinate and subservient to the interests and glory of the monarch; in a theocracy, all succumbs to the priesthood; in an aristocracy, the few must ride, though the many trudge on foot; in a democracy, the many are cared for, though the few be neglected. Without claiming any peculiar merit for the governing class in a democracy, we say, therefore, that a democracy is the best form of government for humanity—as much better as it is that the many shall be well off, though the few suffer, than it is that the few should be clothed in purple and fine linen, and fare sumptuously every day, while the many lie at their gates, covered over with the rags and bruises of poverty and abuse, begging to be fed with the few crumbs which may chance to fall from their tables. So far, then, as sovereignty is to be affirmed of the state, we say let it be affirmed of the people. If we be told that the people are incapable of using it to their own good, we say, let them use it to their own hurt then. They will have a hard time of it, even with a good share of infernal aid to boot, to govern themselves worse than kings, nobilities, and hierarchies have hitherto governed them.

We suppose all that any body really means by the sovereignty of the people is that the highest civil or political power in the state is the people; and that all officers of the government, whether bearing royal, patrician, or plebeian titles, are to be regarded, not as the governors or rulers of the people, but as the simple agents of the people, to whom they are directly accountable for their official conduct. This we hold to be a truth; and the fault we find with them who assert the sovereignty of the people is not with the doctrine they seem to themselves to be setting forth, but with their neglect of the obvious limitations of that sovereignty. The advocates of popular sovereignty have taken good care to limit the authority, to circumscribe and define the powers of the government, so as to keep it in due subordination to the people, from whom it derives its existence; but they have not taken as good care to guard the people, as individuals, against the people, as a body politic. They have limited the government, which is a creature of the body politic, but they have left the body politic itself in possession of unlimited sovereignty. In denying the sovereignty of the people, we mean to deny to the body politic unlimited authority, or the right to act at all, in any way, or by any agents whatever, on any except certain specific objects, indispensable to the maintenance of social order, and, if the phrase will be taken strictly, the common weal.

But the doctrine of the popular sovereignty, whatever its unsoundness or dangerous tendency, when asserted without any qualifications, has had an important mission to execute, and it has done no mean service to humanity. From the moment it was first asserted up to the present, it has been the rallying point of the friends of freedom and progress; and, as things have heretofore been, neither freedom nor progress were possible to be attained without it. It is not for nothing, then, that the friends of freedom and progress, in this and other countries, cling to the sovereignty of the people; and we are not to be astonished, if they now and then stretch it somewhat beyond its legitimate bounds, and continue to defend it, even after its mission is perfected. We do not willingly let go a doctrine which has stood us in good stead in our days of darkness and trial; nor is it an easy matter for us to determine with precision the exact amount of good it has done, or may yet do us. Moreover, we are slow to learn that in contending for the same form of words, we are not always contending for the same doctrine, and that in giving up an old form of words, we do not necessarily give up the old truth we had loved. Words ever change their import as change the circumstances amid which they are uttered. The form of words, which yesterday captained the doctrine of progress, today contains a doctrine which would carry us backward. The watchword of liberty under one set of circumstances becomes under another set of circumstances the watchword of tyranny. It is the part of the wise man to note these changes, and to seek out new watchwords as often as the old ones lose their primitive meaning.

So long as the sovereignty of the people was the denial of the sovereignty of kings, hierarchies, and nobilities, it was true, and was the doctrine of progress. The assertion of the sovereignty of the people was necessary to legitimate popular liberty. In every human heart, there is a more or less lively sense of legitimacy. Men revolt from one authority, not because it oppresses them, or restrains them in the free use of their persons or property, but because they regard it as illegitimate, as a usurper; they submit to another authority and uphold it, although it impose severe burdens, take the fruits of their labors to squander on its pleasures, their daughters for its debaucheries, and their sons for its battles, because they hold it to be legitimate, the rightful sovereign, which they are bound in conscience to obey. To uphold the first, or to resist the last, would in their estimation be alike disloyal. This sense of legitimacy meets us every where throughout the whole of modern history. It has made the people sustain a corrupt and demoralizing hierarchy, cling to old forms of government, and fight for old abuses, long after the reformer has appeared to demand meliorations from which they could not fail to profit. It is so deeply rooted in modern civilization—indeed, in human nature itself—that to eradicate it is impossible. In point of fact, we ought not to eradicate it even if we could, for at bottom, it is one of the noblest attributes, we may say the distinguishing attribute, of man himself, that, without which man would cease to be man. It is, in the last analysis, identical with the sense of right, the correlative of the sense of duty. Take it away and right and wrong would be empty names, man could acknowledge no sovereign, feel no obligation; and never be made to comprehend the fact that he has rights. The principle in itself is good and must be retained if man is to be preserved. But it depends almost entirely on circumstances, whether the sense of legitimacy shall be combined with a truth, or with a falsehood. If the individual be enlightened so as to discern the true sovereign, then this sense of legitimacy makes him invincible in the support or defense of the right, of freedom, of progress; but if he be darkened by ignorance or warped by prejudice, so as to mistake the true sovereign for the one who is no sovereign, then does it make him equally invincible in the support and defense of the wrong, the bitter and untiring foe of freedom and progress.

Now at that period of modern history when the popular movement began to manifest itself, legitimacy was almost exclusively attached to the hereditary monarch, and passive obedience was the order of the day. Opposition to the monarch was revolting to the general sense of right; and yet, the cause of the people could not advance without opposing him, and in some instances not without dethroning and even decapitating him. The monarch was held to be sacred and inviolable; but so long as he was so held, the cause of the people must sleep. The people must desist from their efforts to meliorate their condition, unless they could discover some means by which opposition to the hereditary monarch should become sacred and venerable in the eyes of conscience. To act against their sense of right, is what the people never do. A mob may be excited; and, in the intoxication of the moment, it may trample on justice and humanity; but the people are always serious, conscientious in what they do. Long ages will they endure the most grievous wrongs and the most grinding oppression; but to relieve themselves at the expense of what they conceive to be justice—that will they do never. Knowingly, intentionally, they never do wrong. When they have laid it down or found it laid down in their conscience that the hereditary monarch is the legitimate sovereign, they gather round each, the smallest even of his prerogatives, and defend it at the sacrifice of their lives.

Here, we perceive, was a serious difficulty to be removed. The physical power was on the side of the people; but physical power is as chaff before the wind whenever it has to encounter spiritual might. The people had numbers and the physical strength to gain their freedom but they dared not. Conscience disarmed them. They felt that they were bound to obey the monarch and they had no courage to resist him. The stoutest and bravest are children and cowards in a war against conscience. What could be done? How could opposition to the monarch be made to appear justifiable to those who had been taught and long accustomed to hold him sacred and inviolable? Assuredly, by denying his absolute sovereignty, that is, his legitimacy. But this alone was not enough. Sovereignty must be somewhere. There must be a sovereign; we feel that there is somewhere an authority we are bound to obey. Where is it? If the monarch be not sovereign, who or what is? Had this question been asked at Runnymede, it might have been answered that the nobles were sovereigns; but Louis XI in France and the Tudors in England had rendered such an answer invalid. The old feudal chiefs had succumbed to the lord paramount and ceased to be regarded as legitimate sovereigns by the people. If the question had been asked of Hildebrand, he might have said, that God is the legitimate sovereign; but this, at the time of which we speak, would only have been reasserting the supremacy of the church, which Protestantism had denied. The philosopher might have answered it, as we have answered it today, in favor of justice; but the people were not philosophers then, and to have told them to submit to justice would only have been to tell them to obey the laws, which again would only have been telling them to obey the monarch from whom the laws emanated.

Under these circumstances it is evident, that the legitimacy of the monarch could be denied only in favor of the people. The people was the only competitor of the king for the throne that it was possible to set up. The people, not the king, is the legitimate sovereign, was the only answer the question admitted. All government is for the good of the people and every government, which fails to effect the good of the people, is by that fact rendered illegitimate and may be lawfully opposed. Kings are crowned to protect the rights and promote the interests of the people, and are, therefore, answerable to the people for the use they make of the power given them. The people, in fine, are superior to kings and may judge them. The people then are the sovereign authority. "The people are sovereign"; what words, when first they were uttered! The moment they were uttered, the people sprang into being and were a power—a power clothed with legitimacy and capable of imparting sanctity and inviolability to its adherents. The people could now legitimate their opposition to the hereditary monarch. In opposing him, they were but calling its servant to an account of his stewardship. They were not contending against just authority, for license, for disorder, but for order, for liberty, for the legitimate sovereign against the usurper. They were able, therefore, to shelter the reformer, and to save him from those compunctions of conscience with which, otherwise, he would have been visited for opposing an authority he had been taught to reverence and long accustomed to obey. The doctrine of the sovereignty of the people made their cause a legitimate, a holy cause, and gave men the right and made it their duty to assert and maintain it.

In this way, the doctrine of the popular sovereignty has wrought out deliverance for the people. It has made the people kings and priests and declared it sacrilege to touch the least of their prerogatives. This is its victory for humanity. In the old world, where the masses are trodden down by the privileged orders, it may still have a mission. There it may not have ceased to be the doctrine of progress and may yet need its soldiers, battles, and martyrs. But here its mission is ended and its work done. Here it is the doctrine of yesterday and not of tomorrow. To assert it, is not to deny the sovereignty of kings, hierarchies, and nobilities; for kings, hierarchies, and nobilities, thank God! are not at home on American soil; and, if by some mischance they should be transplanted hither, they would not thrive, they would soon droop, die, and be consumed in the fires of freedom, everywhere burning. The assertion of the sovereignty of the people with us, can be only the assertion of the right of the majority to tyrannize at will over the minority, or the assertion that the people taken individually, are the absolute slaves of the people, taken as a whole. No; the sovereignty of the people, has achieved its work with us, and the friends of freedom and progress must anoint a new king. Democracy today changes its word and bids its sentinels require of those who would enter its camp, not "The sovereignty of the people," but "The sovereignty of justice."

Democracy, as we understand it, we have said, is, on the one hand, the denial of absolute sovereignty to the state, whatever the form of government adopted, and on the other hand, the assertion of the absolute sovereignty of justice. It therefore commands both the people and the individual to be just. It subjects both to one and the same law; and, while it commands the citizen to obey and serve the state with all fidelity, so long as it keeps within its legitimate province, it takes care not to forget to remind the state that it must leave the citizen, as a man, free to do or to enjoy whatever justice permits, commands, or does not forbid.

According to our definition of it, democracy reconciles conflicting theories and paves the way for the universal association of the human race. By enthroning justice it accepts and explains the leading ideas of theories apparently the most contradictory. Every theory, which obtains or ever has obtained currency, embraces some essential element of truth. He, who has yet to learn that the human mind never does, never can believe unmixed falsehood, has no reason to boast of his progress in philosophy. The monarchist has a truth. His truth is that sovereignty is necessarily absolute, one and indivisible. This truth the democrat accepts. In declaring justice the sovereign, he declares the sovereign to be absolute, one and indivisible. The authority of justice is unbounded, and there are not two or more justices, but one justice—one God. The error of the monarchist is in confounding the absolute sovereign, in practice at least, with the man whom men call a king. This error the democrat escapes.

The theocrat has a truth, a great truth. His truth is that the highest and best,—God, is the sovereign. The democrat asserts the same thing. Justice is the political phasis of God, it is identical with God, and in asserting its sovereignty, the democrat asserts precisely the same sovereignty as does the theocrat. The error of the theocrat is in making the priesthood the symbol of this sovereignty and the authoritative expounders of its decrees. This error the democrat escapes by adopting no symbol of sovereignty, but the universal reason which is ever shining in the human soul, and in making the people in a few instances, and the individual in all the rest, the only authoritative expounders of its decrees.

The truth of the aristocrat is that some men are greater and better than others, and that the greatest and best should govern; that is, that wisdom and virtue, not vice and folly should rule. This truth the democrat by no means rejects. He believes as strongly as any aristocrat that there are diversities and even inequalities of gifts, that in all communities there are a few men, God-patented nobles, who stand out from the rest, the prophets of what all are one day to be; and he contends that these are the natural chiefs of the people, and that they ought to govern. In asserting that justice is sovereign, he necessarily asserts that they in whom justice is most manifest, in whom God dwells in the greatest perfection, should have the most influence, the most power; but at the same time, he asserts as a necessary consequence of this, that their power should be moral, spiritual, not physical. The error of the aristocrat is in looking for these God-patented noblemen in a particular class, in an hereditary order, or in a special corporation; and in seeking to give them in addition to the superior power with which they are naturally endowed, the physical power of the state and the factitious authority of an established regime. This error the democrat avoids. He proclaims equal chances to equal merit, and leaves every man free to find the place and to wield the authority for which nature, God, has fitted him.

The old-fashioned democrat's truth is that there shall be no political authority in the state which does not emanate from the people, and which is not accountable to the people; that where there must be state action, it shall be the action of the whole people, not of one man, or of a few men, who may have an interest directly hostile to the interests of the great body of the people. His error is in the fact that he does not take sufficient care to mark the bounds of the people's authority and to preserve to the citizen his rights as a man. The democrat, in our sense of the word, accepts the truth, and avoids the error.

It may be seen from these few examples that democracy accepts and explains all. It is not monarchy, it is not aristocracy, it is not theocracy, in the sense in which the word has been appropriated, nor is it democracy as some would teach us to understand it, but it is a sort of chemical compound of them all. It is a higher and a broader truth than is contained in any one of these systems, one which comprehends and finally absorbs them all.

Democracy is the doctrine of true liberty. The highest conception of liberty is that which leaves every man free to do whatever it is just to do, and not free to do only what it is unjust to do. Freedom to do that which is unjust according to the laws of God or, which is the same thing, the law of nature, is license, not liberty, and is as much opposed to liberty as lust is to love. "A free government," say the Old English lawyers, "is a government of laws," and they say right, if law be taken absolutely and not merely as the enactment of the human legislature. Where there is an arbitrary will above the law, be it the will of the one, the few, or the many, there is, in theory at least, absolutism, and the room for pure despotism. A free government must be a government, not of the will of one man, nor of the will of any body of men, but a government of law; not of a law which a human authority may make or unmake, but of that which is law in the very nature, constitution, and being of this system of things to which we belong. Under a government of law in this sense, where authority may never do, command, or permit, only what the immutable law of justice ordains, men are free; they live under the "perfect law of liberty," and may attain to the full and harmonious development of all their faculties.

Governments have not yet been brought under this law. Hitherto, they have all been more or less arbitrary, and have sought to make the law, rather than to discover and publish it. They have, therefore, often declared that to be law which is not law, imposed burdens on the individual, for which nature, God, never designed him, and attempted to do what they have no capacity to do, what ought not to be done at all, or if done, to be done by the individual. Forgetful of their legitimate province, transcending the bounds which nature had marked out for them, they have created an artificial state of society, disturbed the natural relations between man and man, invaded the individual's rights in all directions, and cursed the human race with the unutterable woes of tyranny and oppression. The democrat enlightened by the study of past ages, and still more by the study of human nature as it unrolls itself to the observer, in the consciousness of the individual, comes forward today, and summoning all governments, whatever their forms, to the bar, tells them in the name of God and humanity that they have no lawmaking power, that they must limit their legislative functions to the discovery and promulgation of the law, that they must lay aside the robe and diadem, the scepter and the sword, and sit down at the feet of nature as simple disciples; that they must study to conform their enactments to the enactments of God, which are written in God's book, the universe, and especially in the universe in man; and that they must deem it their duty and their glory, to leave man and society free to achieve the destiny to which God hath appointed them. It will be long before this lesson will be heard or regarded. The mania for governing has become too universal to be speedily cured. But we need not despair. The world rolls on and becomes wiser with each revolution. Governments are meliorating themselves. The doctor of medicine begins to admit that, notwithstanding the efficacy of his drugs, nature is the best physician; and the time may not be so far distant as our fears would indicate, when the doctor of laws shall own that nature is the best and only lawgiver. That time must come. The human and divine laws must become identical, the Son must be one with the Father, and the God-Man be realized.

Democracy takes care not to lose the man in the citizen. In the free states or rather free cities of antiquity, there were rights of the citizen, but no rights of man. As a citizen, the individual might use his personal influence and exertions in making up the decision of the city; but when the decision was once made up, he was bound in conscience, as well as compelled by physical force, to yield it, whatever it might be, the most unqualified submission. He had no rights sacred and inviolable beyond the legitimate authority of the city. In a question between the city and himself, he could demand nothing as his right. The city was in no way responsible to him; but he owed it everything he had, even to his life. Athens condemns Socrates to death, and sends him to prison to await his execution. His friends provide the means, and urge him to escape. No; Socrates is a conscientious man. He knows his duty. Athens has condemned him to die, and he is bound, as a good citizen, to submit to her sentence. He drinks, therefore, the hemlock at the appointed time, of his own accord, and dies in discharge of his duty to the laws of the city of which he acknowledged himself a citizen. As a citizen of Athens, Socrates knew he could not save his life without incurring the guilt of disloyalty. He had no rights as a man that he might plead. He felt himself as much the slave of Athens as the Persian was of the "Great King." His rights as a man were sunk in those of the citizen and those of the citizen were sunk in those of the city.

Here was the great defect of ancient democracy. In Athens, in any of the ancient republics, there was no personal liberty. One individual might indeed call in the city to maintain his rights, in a dispute with another individual; but beyond this, he had no rights. There was municipal liberty, but no individual liberty. The city could bind or loose the individual at its will, declare him a citizen, or degrade him to a slave, just as she deemed it most expedient. The city differed in no respect from an absolute monarchy, save in the fact, that the absolute sovereignty, in the case of the city, was supposed to be vested in the majority of the citizens, instead of being vested in one man, as in the monarchy. But she was as absolute, and in case she could get a majority of voices, she might go as far and play the tyrant to as great an extent, as the king of Persia himself. Her democracy was then by no means liberty. It was liberty, if you will, for the city, but none for the individual man. The individual man was not recognized as an integer; he was, at best, only a fraction of the body politic. He was, in truth, merely a cipher; without inherent value, augmenting the value of the city, indeed, if placed at her right hand, but counting for nothing if placed at her left hand. But, thanks to the feudal system, and still more to Christianity, an element is introduced into the modern city, which was unknown in the ancient, the element of individuality, by virtue of which the individual man possesses an intrinsic value which he retains in all positions, and instead of a fraction, becomes a whole.

Modern democracy, therefore, goes beyond the ancient. Ancient democracy merely declared the people the state; the modern declares, in addition, that every man, by virtue of the fact that he is a man, is an equal member of the state—universal suffrage and eligibility, two things the ancients never dreamed of—and that the state is limited by justice, or, what is the same thing, the inalienable rights of man. These inalienable rights of man are something more than the rights of citizenship, or certain private rights, the rights of one man in relation to another, which the state is bound to protect; they stretch over nearly the whole domain of human activity, and are, in the strictest sense of the word, rights of the individual in relation to the state, rights of which the state may not, under any pretense whatever, deprive him, and to whose free-exercise it may, in no case whatever, interpose any obstruction. In the ancient democracies the individual, if a member of the ruling race, was a citizen with duties; in the modern, he adds, in theory, to the citizen with duties, the man with rights. Democracy, as we understand it, does not give all the rights to the state, and impose all the duties on the individual. It places the state under obligation to the citizen, in the same manner, and to the same extent, that it places the individual under obligation to the state.

This, if we mistake not, is a novelty. The old doctrine, and the one yet prevalent, recognizes in the state nothing but rights and in the individual nothing but duties. We bear not a little of the responsibility of citizens to the state. Patriotism, although not recognized in the Christian code, is made one of the cardinal virtues. Men must love their country, support its government, give it their time, their talents, their property, and, if need be, their lives. But what may they claim in return; that is, demand as their right? The privilege of paying taxes and—a grave. The responsibility of society to the individual sounds as a strange doctrine in our ears. Few admit it and fewer still comprehend it. The state, we deny not, owns that it is bound to act the part of judge, between man and man, and to vindicate him whose rights a brother invades; but it owns no obligation, in a question between itself and the individual man. It may take all he hath, and give him nothing in return, unless it please. If he trespass on its rights, it may send him to the treadmill, the galleys, the dungeon, the scaffold, or the gibbet; but he has no right to do aught in his own defense against its invasions. He has no rights which he may hold up, and in the name of God and of humanity, command it to respect. However rudely authority may treat him, grossly invade what in truth are his rights, however insupportable the burdens it may lay on his shoulders, he must not even protest. It can do no wrong. But happily this old doctrine is giving way. Governments are beginning to comprehend that they are not created merely for the purpose of laying and collecting taxes, that they are servants, or rather agents, and not masters, and that it is their mission merely to see that what eternal justice ordains, be respected and obeyed alike by themselves and the individual.

Democracy declares that the state as well as the individual has rights and duties. Where the rights and duties of the individual begin, there end those of the state; where those of the state begin, there end those of the individual. Where is this point? This is the great political problem of our epoch. The conciliation of individual with social and of social with individual rights, and the subordination of all social and individual action to the laws of justice, the law of nature, or the law of God, is the mission of the moralist and politician throughout humanity's whole future.

Something in reference to the first of these problems has been attempted in all countries, which have adopted constitutional governments. In this work, England claims precedence of all other nations. She has been the first, we believe, to establish a constitutional government. She has done more than any other nation for the extension of the practice of individual liberty, though, it must be admitted, she has done less than some others to enable the world to legitimate that liberty as a right. Her citizens have a large share of practical freedom; but, in theory, they hold it not as a right, but as a grant. And they defend it not by an appeal to the rights of man, but by an appeal to certain parchment rolls, carefully preserved in the archives of state. Magna Carta is not an enumeration of natural rights, but a grant—a forced grant, if you will—of certain specified privileges. Her bill of rights, drawn up in 1688, is the same. Her Parliament assembles by virtue of a writ from the king, not by virtue of the right of the people of England to be represented. Her liberty, in a word, is an admirable thing as a fact, but totally indefensible on the only ground on which liberty is defensible at all, that of natural right. Of this the Englishman has an instinctive sense at least, for he never calls his liberty by the broad name of the natural liberty of man, but English liberty; and the English nation, while it has everywhere contended for liberty as a grant, has spared neither money nor blood to suppress it, wherever it has been asserted as a right. English liberty rests solely on compact and is defended solely by an appeal to charters and precedents. Hence, the contempt with which all English statesmen speak of "abstract right," and their uniform practice of legitimating their measures, not by justice but by precedent. The minister of state entrenches himself behind a wall of precedents; the member of parliament asks for precedents; the lawyer alleges precedents in favor of his client; the judge decides according to the precedents; and no one thinks of inquiring what is right, but what are the precedents? This is all in perfect keeping. An Englishman has no business to inquire for justice; for his liberty is a precedent and not a right, founded on precedent not on justice; though it must be said in his favor that his precedents are often coincident with justice.

France, if we mistake not, has taken a step beyond England. We do not mean to say that France has more liberty than England, as a fact, but she has more as a right. The king has ceased to *octroyer* the charter;

he accepts it, and in theory, it emanates from the people. The French people are therefore the sovereign of the king. This is much; it is at least the entering wedge to freedom. The old monarchy of Louis XIV is abolished, the old feudal nobility is extinct, and the *Bourgeoisie*, or middle class, is now on the throne. This class is the one in every community the most praised; and it is always accounted the most virtuous. Perhaps it is so. It certainly has some very respectable virtues. It is composed of merchants, bankers, manufacturers, lawyers, large farmers, in a word of the stirring, business part of the community. It has no affection for hereditary nobility and none for the doctrine of equality. It has no objection to leveling down to itself those who are above it, but it has an invincible aversion to leveling up to itself those who are below it. It demands a laboring class to be *exploited*, but it loves order, peace, and quiet. These, however, it knows are incompatible with the existence in the community of an ignorant, vicious, and starving populace; it, therefore, will attend to the wants of the lower classes up to a certain point. It will build them, if need be, churches, and establish ministries for the especial purpose of teaching them to be quiet; it will furnish them with the rudiments of education, see that they are fed, clothed, maintained in a good working condition, and supplied with work. All this it will do for those below itself; and this, though not enough, is more than a little; and when this is done more will be undertaken. This is the first step; and when the first step is taken, the rest of the way is not difficult. The *prolétaires* soon disappear, and the *canaille* become men and citizens. We are, therefore, far from deprecating, with some of our friends, the "monarchy of the middle classes." We believe its reign in a certain stage of social progress, not only inevitable, but desirable. We believe no worse calamity could at this moment befall France, than the overthrow of the present dynasty of the *Bourgeoisie*. Its reign will and must be salutary, however far short it may come of satisfying the wishes, or the views of the ardent friends of liberty. It has a mission to execute and when it shall have executed its mission it will then give way to the monarchy, not of a class, not of an order, but of humanity, of justice. France appears to us to be on the route to freedom. May she obtain it! With her fine social qualities, and after all her toils, and struggles, and sacrifices, she deserves it.

But it is to our own country that we must look for constitutional government in the worthiest sense of the word. In the bills of rights which precede several of our constitutions, we have attempted to draw up an inventory of the natural rights of man, rights, which authority must ever hold sacred and which the people, in their associate capacity, can neither give nor take away, in no shape or manner, alter or abridge. In the Constitution of the United States, and in those of the several states, we have attempted to define the natural boundaries of the state, to fix its authority, and to determine the modes of its action. These constitutions and these bills of rights may be very imperfect; they may not enumerate all the rights of the individual, and they may not accurately define the powers of the people in their capacity as a state, but if so we may perfect them at our leisure. They recognize the great principle for which we contend, that the people are not absolute, that the individual has rights they cannot alter or abridge, and which it is the duty and the glory of authority to preserve untouched, and which it may neither invade nor suffer to be invaded. They teach us that if society has powers the individual must obey, the individual has rights society must respect; that if the people as a body politic may do some things, there are some things they may not do; and that if majorities may go to a certain length, there is a line they may not pass. They teach us then what we have denominated the great democratic doctrine and they prove that doctrine to be the doctrine of the American people, however far short they may fall of its perfect realization.

There may, indeed, be some among us, who, affected by their reminiscences of English Whiggism, regard our constitutions and bills of rights, not as attempts to enumerate the natural rights of man, and to define the natural powers of government, but as compacts between the people as individuals, and the people as a state, or, more properly, as declarations of what the people in convention assembled have willed to be the rights of individuals, and have ordained to be the powers of government. According to these persons, our liberties are not, in the strict sense of the word, rights, but grants. They are not grants from what is technically called the government, but from the people in convention assembled. They are not limitations of the supreme authority of the state, but favors which that authority is pleased to confer on its subjects. The people in convention assembled might have willed, had they chosen so to do, that the powers of government should be more or less than they now are, or that our rights should be different from what they are now declared to be. They were competent to draw the boundary line between the authority of the state and the rights of the individual where they pleased. By meeting again in convention, they may unmake all our present rights, and make such new ones as seems to them good.

But this view of our bills of rights and constitutions we are not prepared to admit. It implies the absolute sovereignty of the people, a doctrine we have denied and refuted. The people, neither in convention nor out of it, can make or unmake rights. If they can, if they may bind or unbind as they please, then are we, as we have already shown, absolute slaves as individuals to the will of the majority. If we allow that the people make the rights of the individual, we deny the validity of his rights, and deprive him of everything to oppose to the tyranny of the many. Bills of rights and constitutions can avail him nothing when it is a question, not between him and the ministers of state, but between him and the state itself. They limit the action of his majesty's ministers, but not of his majesty himself. But this is not the fact. If these bills of rights and constitutions enumerate on the one hand all our natural rights, and recognize nothing to be a right which is not a right by decree of justice; and if they on the other hand accurately define the powers of government, they are unalterable, and are as much binding on the people in convention, as they are on the people's ministers of state, or on the individual. In denying sovereignty to the people, we deny that the people can make or unmake rights, bind or unbind; we limit their functions to the discovery and promulgation of the law, as it is in justice, which is anterior and superior to all conventions. Consequently our rights, in truth, are the same before as after the sitting of the convention. If we had no rights before, we have none now.

It is true that, in the form of our bills of rights and constitutions, there are some things which would seem to authorize this English interpretation of them; and no doubt many statesmen and most lawyers, have so interpreted them, and done it very honestly too; but in reality our institutions are fundamentally distinct from the English, based on an entirely different idea; and instead of interpreting our bills of rights as grants, we ought to interpret them as an attempted inventory, more or less exact, of the natural rights of man; and our constitutions, instead of compacts, should be regarded as attempts to determine and fix the legitimate powers of government. They are shields interposed between the minority and the majority, between the individual and the people. The people say to the individual and the majority say to the minority, by these instruments, not merely that they *will* exercise their authority according to the rules herein specified, but that, errors excepted, they have no *right* to exercise it according to any other rules. Constitutions are not needed by majorities; they are needed merely as a moral force by the minority, who want the physical force to protect themselves against the aggressions of the majority. They are not needed, as some suppose, to constitute the people a body politic. The people are as much a body politic, before assembling in convention and adopting a constitution as afterwards. Bodies politic, rights of societies or of individuals, are not things to be created by a few arbitrary slopes, curves, and angles on parchment. Right and wrong, for governments, individuals, and societies, for cities and citizens, are eternal and immutable.

For ourselves, we have no patience with the notion that we hold our liberties as grants. We do not like to be sent to rummage in the dark and dusty cabinets of old state papers, and to decipher old worm-eaten parchments, in order to find out what our liberties are, and what is the authority by which we may legitimate them. The charter, by virtue of which we legitimate our rights, is no charter engrossed on parchment, but one which God Almighty has engrossed on the human heart. The Magna Carta, to which we appeal, is no grant forced from King John, King Edward, King Harry, King William, nor any other king, from no hierarchy, no aristocracy, from no democracy or conventions of the people, but that which God gave us, when he made us men, and by virtue of which we are men. We consult no constitution to learn what our rights and duties are, but the constitution of human nature itself. And all constitutions which do aught but faithfully transcribe that, we declare null and void from the beginning. We are free, not because the king wills, not because it is the good pleasure of the nobility, not because the priesthood grants permission, not because the people in convention ordain, but because we are men. It is not a privilege of American citizenship, but a right of universal humanity.

By assuming this position, democracy gains a vantage ground for humanity. If we hold our rights not by virtue of compacts, grants, or decrees of conventions, then we hold them by virtue of our human nature. Our rights and duties belong to us as men, as human beings. Then all who are men, human beings, have the same rights and duties. If all have the same rights and duties, then, in matter of right and duty, all men are equal. Hence, the grand, the thrilling, tyrant-killing doctrine of EQUALITY—THE DOCTRINE THAT MAN MEASURES MAN THE WORLD OVER. Men may be diverse in their tastes, dispositions, capacities, and acquirements; but so long as they all have the same rights and the same duties, so long it may be affirmed of them with truth that they are equal one to another, in all respects in which equality does not tend to lose itself in identity. This doctrine will not remain unfruitful.

If all men have equal rights and duties as individuals, then is society bound to treat them as equals. If she exalt one or depress another, confer a favor on this one and not on that, place one in a more favorable position for the enjoyment of his rights or the performance of his duties than another, then is she partial, and therefore unjust, therefore illegitimate; then does she disturb the original equality, which God established between man and man, and therefore does she become an usurper, to be driven back to her legitimate province. This rule is broad; it reaches far, but society will one day observe it.

No government or society has ever yet respected this equality. In the Grecian and Roman city, the individual, as we have seen, counted for nothing. There were municipal rights but no rights of man. The city might do what it pleased. The same remark may be made of all aristocratic and monarchical governments. All, like the English parliament, have called themselves omnipotent, have usurped all the rights of man, and claimed them, as their own property. Claiming, as their own property, all possible rights susceptible of being exercised by individuals, they have claimed, as a natural consequence of this, the right to parcel out the exercise of these rights to individuals or to corporations, as they pleased. Hence PRIVILEGE, a private law, by which authority confers a special favor, or grants to an individual or a corporation, the right to do what he or it had not the right to do before, or exempts him or it from a duty, which was previously obligatory. Authority, under the character of a privilege, confers on this man the exclusive right of baking all the bread for a given number of people, upon that one the right to distill corn into whiskey, upon this company the exclusive right to buy and sell slaves, and upon that one the right to traffic at a certain place in certain kinds of foreign productions, upon this one the right to wear a certain ribbon or garter, and of receiving the income of certain lands or offices. We need not be particular on this head. Society is and ever has been filled, and covered over, with privileges of every name and nature.

Our first emotion on contemplating this immense system of privilege, which has grown up through successive ages, is that of indignation. We go even so far as to rail at the privileged, and to charge the whole to their selfishness and rapacity. But after a while, after having penetrated more deeply into the matter, we calm ourselves, and suppress our wrath and indignation. The evil lies not at the door of the privileged alone. Few, at least not many, of the unprivileged would have refused to accept these privileges, had they been offered them. Of those who declaim against privilege now, not the smallest half do it somewhat on the principle that the fox declaimed against the grapes. The error is not in the privileged, the evil is not in the fact that one set of men rather than another enjoy the privileges; but in the fact that authority ever presumed to have any privileges to grant, any favors to confer. The evil lies not in the fact that privileges have been conferred, but in the fact that governments have been allowed to usurp, and hold as its own, all the rights of the people as individuals. Having usurped these rights, having robbed them from individuals, governments could, perhaps, do no better than to parcel them out under the name of privilege. It was only under this name, only by favor, that individuals could get back some portion of that of which authority had robbed them. Unequal as this must necessarily be in its bearing on the whole mass of individuals, it was nevertheless better to get back something in this way than to be left entirely destitute. He, who has been robbed of his all by the highwayman, can sometimes do no better than to accept back part of the contents of his purse as a present.

It is true that what was granted as a favor should, if granted at all, have been granted as a right; but every favor granted weakened, in the end, the government which granted it, and did something towards raising it up a successful rival. Every individual who became one of the privileged, became one who would not easily be reduced to slavery again. When the crisis came between him and authority he would claim his privilege as his right and defend it with his life. Paradoxical as it may seem, modern liberty is the natural, if not the legitimate, child of privilege. These special grants and monopolies, which are so abhorrent to democracy, have been the means, or one of the means, by which the mighty Demos has broken himself loose from the grasp of the monarch, and become strong enough and wise enough to demand, as his right, what he had formerly been proud and most thankful to receive as a boon. These special grants and monopolies have, in reality, been victories gained by the people over their masters, so many provinces wrested from the dominion of the usurper. The system of privilege, therefore, though founded on usurpation, and unjust and unequal in its bearing, has been the means or one of the means, under God, of carrying onward the progress of society and of restoring to individuals, in some measure, the exercise of rights of which authority had violently dispossessed them.

But while we admit all this, while we admit and even contend, that during the past under the circumstances which existed, privilege was one of the means by which individual freedom was to be obtained, we contend that democracy is right, today, and in this country, in asserting herself, as she does in the Address before us, as "equality against privilege." For a time privilege was to be resorted to, as we sometimes resort to one evil to cure another; but it needs no argument to prove that that time has gone by and that the doctrine of privilege has ceased to be the doctrine of progress. Humanity demands today her rights; she has ceased to solicit favors. She makes no war upon the privileged few; for, aside from their character as the privileged, they are her children and equally as dear to her heart as any of the other members of her vast family; but she proclaims in a voice which all must hear and shall respect, that all which anyone may, in obedience to justice, enjoy, he may demand as a right, and that he needs no patent from human authority to empower him to do whatever is right in the sight of God, and that all the patents in the world cannot make it just for him to do what in the sight of God it is wrong for him to do.

Democracy, we repeat it, does not declaim against men for having accepted privileges when it was admitted that governments had them to bestow; but it tells governments, and the people in this country, as the only government we acknowledge, that they have no privileges to grant, no favors to confer. They have nothing to deal out to individuals. If they have favors to bestow, will they be good enough to tell us where they got them. Did they take them from individuals? Then have they no right to them. What belongs to the individual can never become the rightful property of the government. If it was ever the property of individuals, it is now, and individuals may possess it without asking permission of the government. If the powers in question be not individual rights, the property of individuals, then has government no right to confer them and the individual no right to receive them. Governments can confer on individuals no powers which God has not given them; and, if individuals claim, by authority, that which is not theirs by Divine right, or do, under cover of manmade law, what is not authorized by God's law, they are guilty, and must be condemned, if not in the civil court, at least in the court of conscience. Governments have, therefore, no privileges to confer, and individuals have no right to ask or to receive them. The government can confer on one individual only what it has robbed from him or from another. Has it a right to rob one individual for the sake of enriching another? Or is it desirable that it should first rob a man of his rights, and then give them back to him in the form of a present or a privilege? Whenever governments forbid this man to do what he has a natural right to do, or authorize that man to do what he has not a natural right to do, it assumes the power to readjust the regulations of Infinite Wisdom, and to recast the handy work of God. We know of no governments that have the right to assume so much. We have a profound respect for the wisdom and governmental skill, manifested by those who are charged with the management of our state and national governments; but we very much distrust their capacity to enter the courts of heaven as cabinet ministers to the All-Wise. It is enough for even our enlightened governments, in this most enlightened country, to sit down at the feet of Great Nature, as humble disciples, content to learn and obey what God ordains.

The great error of government, in all ages of the world, has been that of counting itself the real owner and sovereign disposer of the individual—that of disfranchising all individuals and then pretending to redistribute individual rights according to its own caprice, interests, or necessities. To put an end to this system of privilege is now the great aim of democracy. Its object is to restrict governments, whether royal, aristocratical, or popular, to their legitimate province, and individuals to their natural rights and to teach both to perform those duties and those duties only, which everlasting and immutable justice imposes. To this it steadily makes its way; for this it struggles; and this it will ultimately achieve.

The reduction to practice of the theory we have now imperfectly, but we hope distinctly set forth, will demand great changes, and more changes, perhaps, than anyone can foresee; and changes, too, which can be introduced at once, in no country, without violence, and probably not without bloodshed and great suffering. He who pleads for justice will not be anxious to promote violence, bloodshed, or suffering. There may be times when the kingdom of heaven must be taken by violence, and when a people should rise up and demand its rights at whatever sacrifice it may be. But there is and there can be, in this country, no occasion for any but orderly and peaceful measures for the acquisition of all we have supposed. We must not dream of introducing it all at once. We must proceed leisurely. Let the men of thought speculate freely and speak boldly what comes to them as truth; but let the men of action, men who have more enthusiasm than reflection, greater hearts than minds, and stronger hands than heads guard against impatience. Practical men, men of action, are, after all, the men who play the most mischief with improvements. Our principle is, no revolution, no destruction, but progress. Progress is always slow, and slow let it be; the slower it is the more speed it makes. So long as we find the thinkers busy canvassing all great matters, discussing all topics of reform, and publishing freely to the world the result of their investigations, we have no fears for the individual, none for society. Truth is omnipotent. Let it be uttered; let it spread from mind to mind, from heart to heart, and in due season be assured that it will make to itself hands, erect itself a temple, and institute its worship. Set just ideas afloat in the community and feel no uneasiness about institutions. Bad institutions, before you are aware of it, will crumble away, and new ones and good ones supply their places.

We hold ourselves among the foremost of those who demand reform and who would live and die for progress; but we wish no haste, no violence in pulling down old institutions or in building up new ones. We would innovate boldly in our speculations; but in action we would cling to old usages and keep by old lines of policy till we were fairly forced by the onward pressure of opinion to abandon them. We would think with the radical, but often act with the conservative. When the time comes to abandon an old practice, when new circumstances have arisen to demand a new line of policy, then, we say, let no attachments to the past make us blind to our duty or impotent to perform it. All we say is, let nothing be done in a hurry and let no rage for experiments be encouraged.

We are far from being satisfied with things as they are. We have had, perhaps, our turn with many others, of mourning over the wide discrepancy there is between the American theory and the American practice, and days and nights have given to the question, how shall the evil be remedied? The only answer, we can give, is one, perhaps, that will show little more than how ineffectually we have inquired. All we can answer is simply, let each man keep at work freely and earnestly in his own way; let all labor together, to raise the standard of thought, to give a higher, freer, and fresher tone to American literature; more purity and rationality to our theology; more depth and soundness to our philosophical speculations; to embody less of expediency and more of Christ in our systems of morality; and withal, let there be fervent prayer for more faith in God, in truth, in justice, in humanity, and then, let things take pretty much their own course. The whole that can be done may be summed up in the words, let reformers do all in their power to EDUCATE THE PEOPLE, AND THROUGH THE PEOPLE THE GENERATION TO COME.

Slavery-Abolitionism

APRIL 1838

A Commentary on William E. Channing's *Slavery*, 4th edition, revised (Boston: James Munroe & Co., 1836)

We have not introduced this little volume of Dr. Channing's for the purpose of reviewing it. It has been too widely circulated and too generally read to permit such a purpose to be either necessary or proper. The public have long since made up their minds respecting its merits and are quietly giving it the high rank it deserves. In our opinion, though not wholly unexceptionable, it is the best book that the present discussion of slavery among us has called forth and the only one we have met that we can read with anything like general satisfaction. With its general estimate of slavery, its lofty moral tone, and its profound reverence for the rights of man, we sympathize with our whole soul; but some of its special views, and the traces of a doctrine tending somewhat to centralization, which we here and there discover, and of which we believe the author to be unconscious, we cannot entirely approve.

We place this work at the head of this article merely for the purpose of testifying in general terms our high appreciation of its merits, and because it gives us an occasion of expressing our own views at some length on the subject of slavery. The subject of slavery is fairly before the public and it must be met. However much we may regret its agitation at this time, when all thoughts should be turned to the settling of the financial affairs of the nation, we must suffer it to be discussed and take part in its discussion. We would merely add, let it be discussed calmly, without passion, and in a truly Christian spirit.

We say without any hesitation that we are wholly and totally opposed to slavery and that we do not consider it any question at all with the American people, whether it be a good or an evil. We believe that question is decided by the Declaration of Independence and forever put at rest. To attempt to prove that slavery is wrong, that it is not to be perpetuated, and that it ought to be abolished, as soon as it can be, is to insult every true American's mind and heart, and that too, whether he live north or south of Mason's and Dixon's line. We have much mistaken the character of our southern brethren, if there be one among them that will for one moment contend that slavery is the proper estate of a man.

That man has no absolute right to hold his brother man in slavery is but a necessary inference from the fact that slavery is wrong. It can never be right, no man can ever have the right, to do wrong. Every slaveholder, then, ought to do all he can do to rescue his fellow beings, whether black or white, from the servitude in which he finds them, or to which he may have reduced them. If slavery be wrong, his duty is plain. He must, if in his power, remove it. Here is no room for dispute, no need of argument.

Again, we hold that slavery must and will be abolished. The whole force of modern civilization is against it, and before the onward march of that civilization it must be swept away. To this result we do not believe that our southern brethren are opposed. Some of them may believe that slavery is fixed upon them forever, may believe that its abolition is impossible, and therefore may undertake to invent good reasons for its continuance; but secretly none of them love it and the immense majority of them would rejoice to be rid of it.

But while we contend that slavery is wrong, that it is wrong to hold slaves, and that the slaveholder ought to labor with all his power for its abolition, we do not agree with our friends the Abolitionists in denouncing slaveholders, and in declaring that no slaveholder can be a Christian. Reformers should war against systems not against men. Paul was always careful to have it understood, that he did not "wrestle against flesh and blood, but against principalities, against powers, against the rulers of the darkness of this world, against spiritual wickedness in high places."

For ourselves, we have learned that men may profit by institutions opposed to the best good of humanity without necessarily being bad men. Many practices, which, in one view of the case, strike us as altogether wrong, in another point of view, appear to us as excusable, if not even as justifiable. The older we grow, the more we see—we speak personally—the less and less are we disposed to be censorious. The world is *not* all wrong, everything is not out of place, and every man is not a devil. Thank God! We every day acquire fresh faith in human virtue; and while we bate nothing in our zeal or efforts for progress, we become able to look with more and more complacency on the world, and to feel that, of all God's prophets, we are not the only one that is left alive. There are more than we who have not bowed the knee to Baal.

If slaveholding were purely an individual act, we confess, we should doubt the possibility of the slaveholder's being a good man save at the expense of his intelligence. But slaveholding, in our southern states, for instance, is not an individual but a social act. Slavery is not an individual but a social institution, and society, not the individual conscience alone, is responsible for it. The question is not, Is slaveholding wrong? But, can a man who adheres to, and attempts to profit by a wrong social institution be a good Christian man? Must he necessarily be a sinner? This is the question and we wish our moralists and divines would answer it. It is an important case of conscience, and reaches, perhaps, further than we are ordinarily aware of. Society always has been and everywhere is imperfect. All its institutions are more or less imperfect, more or less in opposition to absolute justice. We may all of us be getting our living today by means of institutions, as unjust in themselves as abolitionists have shown slavery to be. If no man who adheres to, or profits by, a wrong social institution, can be a good man, that is, a Christian, what shall we do with the upholders of monarchy, hereditary nobility, corrupting hierarchies, with Mahometans, Brahmins, all who live in an imperfect social state and profit by unjust social institutions? Nay, what shall we do with ourselves; for who of us has anything which we can say positively has come into our possession without the aid of any wrong social institution? We should, it seems to us, view with suspicion all rules of judgment, which in their operation must overstock hell and leave heaven an unpeopled desert.

For ourselves, we ask no questions of the slaveholder that we do not of any other man. Is the slaveholder faithful to all his engagements, in the discharge of all the private virtues? Does he cultivate piety towards God and love to man? Does he make slavery as light a burden as he can; that is, does he treat his slaves with kindness and respect? Does he inquire into the character of his social institutions and do what he can to perfect them? If so, we must call him a good Christian. We know the abolitionists may say that it is his duty to free his slaves at once; and so should we, if it depended on his individual will whether he should free them or not. But this matter of freeing the slaves is a matter for the community rather than the individual slaveholder. As a member of the community, the individual should do all he can do to hasten the period when the community shall unfetter the slave and let him go free. Before that period he cannot free his slaves even if he would.

But we are told by the South, that this is their affair and not ours, and that we have no right to meddle with it. Is the South right? This brings us to the question, what rights have we at the North in regard to southern slavery? This after all is the real question before the American people, and unhappily this question has become so entangled with other questions, that it is difficult to give it a separate and distinct answer. Our own opinion on the matter we have hinted in a foregoing article, but we deem it necessary, in justice to ourselves and to the cause of liberty, to go more fully into it and to state more at large the grounds of our opinion. We do this the more readily because nobody can for one moment suspect us of any desire to palliate slavery or to prolong it. All who know us, know well that we are heartily opposed to every form of slavery, and that our whole life is devoted to the cause of universal liberty to universal man—a cause for which we have made some sacrifices and for which we are ready, if need be, to make more and greater sacrifices.

In all that concerns their internal regulations, institutions, and police, we regard the several states which compose the Union, as distinct, independent communities. We are to be regarded as one people, as one nation, only in the several respects specified in the Constitution of the United States. In all other respects we are not one nation, but twenty-six independent nations, and stand in relation to one another, precisely as the United States as one nation stands in relation to France, England, or Mexico. We of Massachusetts have no more concern with the internal policy and social institutions of South Carolina, for instance, than we have with the internal police of Russia, Austria, or Turkey. Slavery, then, in the states is not a national institution; that is, not an institution over which the people of the United States, in the sense in which they are one people, have any control. The right of the people of the non-slaveholding states, in relation to slavery in the southern states, is precisely what it is in relation to it in Constantinople, or in any foreign slaveholding state.

In one respect slavery may in this country be regarded as a national and not as a state institution. The Constitution of the United States allows slavery to form one of the bases of national representation. All the states have a legal right to concern themselves with this question. We of the North, if we choose, may undoubtedly use all just means to amend the Constitution so that slavery shall not be represented in Congress. Whether it is desirable so to amend the Constitution, is a question of policy, which we do not now undertake to decide. Slavery in the District of Columbia and in the territories belonging to the United States is a different matter from slavery in the states, and, for aught we can see, may constitutionally be acted upon by the Congress of the United States. Whether Congress should act upon it in the District and the territories is a question on which good men will differ. For our own part, we wish slavery, when abolished, to be abolished by a concert of all the slaveholding states, together with the Congress of the United States. We can see little utility in abolishing it at present in the District of Columbia and the territories. To petition Congress to do it is only to petition Congress to do indirectly what all parties agree it may not do directly, that is, abolish slavery in the states.

Here is the ground of the objection, which the South makes to the reception of antislavery petitions by Congress. These petitions literally touch the question of slavery only in the sections of the slaveholding country, over which Congress has exclusive jurisdiction, but really, and in the minds of those who get them up, they are petitions for the abolition of slavery in the states themselves. Does any body believe, that, if Congress should grant the prayer of the petitioners, slavery would stand a year in this country? Do not all the abolitionists believe that the abolition of slavery in the District of Columbia and the territories, by Congress, would necessarily involve its abolition in all the slaveholding states? Is not this also the belief of the South? What, then, is the true character of the petitions with which Congress is flooded in regard to slavery? Are they not in fact, though not in name, petitions for Congress to interfere with the internal police of the southern states? So the South regards them, and on this ground it opposes their reception. Is the South right in this? Have we a right to petition Congress to abolish slavery in South Carolina? Have we a right to petition Congress to violate the Constitution of the United States? A right to petition it to do indirectly, what it may not do directly, openly, avowedly? Yet we have unquestionably the right to petition Congress to abolish slavery in the District of Columbia and the territories, and the South have been unwise and impolitic, to say the least, in denying it. By denying it, they have mixed up with the question of abolition that of the right of petition, which has in reality no connection with it. The abolitionists have by this means been able to make themselves regarded as the defenders of the right of petition, a right dear to all New England men, from the memory of the struggle of their fathers of England in the seventeenth century with Charles Stuart. And yet, virtually, the South are, in this very controversy, truer defenders of constitutional rights than the abolitionists. The abolitionists are technically, literally right, and the South technically, literally wrong; and hence their efforts work altogether against them and recruit the ranks of abolitionists by thousands. Abolitionists never rejoiced more sincerely than they did at the passage of Mr. Patton's Resolution. Congress, we believe, ought to receive the petitions as the less of two evils and to treat them with all proper respect.

But to return to the question of the right of the people of the free states to interfere with slavery. What is this right? How far does it extend? The right of the people of the non-slaveholding states in relation to southern slavery is precisely their right in relation to any of the social institutions of France or England. They have the same right to labor for the abolition of monarchy or the House of Lords in England that they have for the abolition of slavery in any of the southern states. What is this right? How far does it extend? In our opinion simply to the free and full discussion of the question. As men, as citizens, in this respect, of independent communities, and therefore divested of none of our natural rights by any other community, we have the right to discuss freely, and give our views unreservedly, on all questions which concern humanity. We have, for instance, a perfect right to question the legitimacy of monarchy, to show, if we can, that it is a bad institution, that it is founded in usurpation, that it does great wrong to man, and that it ought to be abolished forthwith. We may also throw all the light in our power on the means of abolishing it, and offer what we believe to be sound and cogent reasons for abolishing it. So of slavery. We may examine it, publish all the facts we can collect respecting it, speak, print, publish, in the limits of our respective states, fully and freely, our honest convictions of its nature, tendency, justice, injustice, the necessity, the duty, the means of its preservation or removal. This we believe is the extent of our right of interference. A step further than this contravenes international law and encroaches upon the rights of the slaveholding states.

The right here stated and to this extent we claim for ourselves. We claim it on the ground that we are men and have therefore a right to interest ourselves in whatever concerns men as men. We claim it on the ground that we are citizens of a state which allows, which guarantees free discussion, freedom of speech and the press, and which no other state has any right to interfere with or seek to control. This right the South must not presume to deny us. While we respect her rights, she must respect ours. If we may not interfere with her legislation, she must not interfere with ours. Moreover, neither the North nor the South has any right to abridge or restrain freedom of discussion because freedom of discussion is one of the rights of man and therefore older than governments and raised above their legitimate reach. The South has erred in denying us this right. In doing this she has struck a blow at our independence, made the abolitionists, with no great consistency however, appear to be the champions of free discussion and induced not a few to join them under this character, that never would have joined them as simple abolitionists.

Still, we are inclined to believe, that the South has never intended to deny us the right to discuss in our own way the abstract question of slavery. All she has really intended to do is to assert her right to manage her internal police as she judges proper, and to deny, as a necessary inference from this, our right to interfere with it. The real question at issue between the abolitionists and the South is not whether slavery be good, bad, or indifferent, but whether one state has the right to avow the design of changing the institutions of another state, and of adopting a series of measures directed expressly to that end? This is the question. In all that concerns them as states, these United States are as independent on one another as are England and France. France has as much right to interfere in the internal police of England, as Massachusetts has in the internal police of South Carolina. Slavery is unquestionably a matter which falls within the powers of the states, as independent, sovereign states. In relation to this question, then, all the states stand to one another precisely as foreign nations. The question then comes up in this shape: have we the right to avow the design and to adopt measures to control the internal legislation of a foreign nation? The question needs no answer. Everybody knows that we have not, at least so long as we acknowledge the independence of that nation.

Nor does it alter the nature of the question, that the actual interference is by individual citizens and not by the state. What the state is prohibited from doing, it can never be lawful for the citizens to do. Interference in the affairs of foreigners is as unlawful on the part of individual citizens as of states. Who will pretend that La Fayette had any more right to interfere in the quarrel between this country and England, than France herself had? And who will pretend to justify La Fayette's interference by international law? France was at peace with England, and La Fayette, as a subject of France, was bound to keep that peace. We adduce not this case to censure La Fayette, whose chivalrous aid to the cause of American Independence we appreciate as highly as do any of our countrymen, but simply to show that the obligations of the state bind the citizen. Our Canadian neighbors are now in a quarrel. Has this nation a right to interfere in that quarrel? Certainly not under its existing treaty obligations to England. It may side with the Canadians, but not without involving itself in a war with England. Its duty, if it would preserve its peace relations with England, is to remain neutral. Is not the duty of the citizens the same? Can an American citizen take up for the Canadians, without losing his character of American citizen, and forfeiting the protection of American laws?

If the individual citizens may do in relation to an independent state, what the state may not do, the consequences are not difficult to be foreseen. If the citizens of this State may associate to do what the State itself may not do, all that is requisite to enlist the whole force of the State in that which it is unlawful for the State to do, is to waive the State, and band all the citizens together into what shall be called a voluntary association. If half a dozen citizens may unite in an abolition society, pledged to emancipate the slaves, all the citizens of the state may do it. And when all the citizens of the state have thus formed themselves into an association, what is that association but the state under a different name? The interference of such an association would be as efficient, to say the least, as that of the state itself. And if the citizens of a state may thus lawfully associate for changing the institutions of foreign nations, we ask, what security can one foreign nation ever have in relation to another? It is of the greatest importance to the peace and safety of nations that citizens or subjects observe with scrupulous fidelity the engagements of their respective governments. The abolitionists themselves were of this opinion in relation to the interference of our citizens in the affairs of Texas.

Nor, again, will it do to say that slavery is an institution of so peculiar a character that we may claim the right of interfering with it without claiming the right to interfere with the whole internal police of foreign nations. In the first place, it is not an institution peculiar in its kind. Something similar to it is found in every state in which the law makes any discrimination between individual citizens. The principle which legitimates southern slavery may be found incorporated, if we are not much mistaken, into the constitution and laws of every state in the Union. In every state in which restrictions are placed on eligibility, as in this state, or in which the law presumes to say who may and who may not exercise the right of suffrage, or in which there are monopolies or exclusive privileges recognized by law, there is the seminal principle of slavery. But waive this as not essential to our argument. In the next place, we say we have no right to make any inquiry concerning the institutions of foreign nations, for the purpose of ascertaining which of them we have or have not the right of undertaking to abolish. We cannot do this without denying the independence of the nation in question. Do we acknowledge South Carolina, for instance, to be a free and independent state? Do we acknowledge her sovereignty to be absolute so far as not limited by the Constitution of the United States? Then what right have we to take the revision of her doings? Can we do this without virtually denying her sovereignty? Can we deny her sovereignty without giving her just cause of offense? And when we admit her sovereignty, do we not acknowledge her right to establish such institutions as she pleases? If then she pleases to establish slavery, is it not her affair, and one of which we have debarred ourselves, by the acknowledgment of her sovereignty, from taking any cognizance?

But it may be said, that slavery is unjust, that no state has the right to establish an unjust institution; therefore, South Carolina has no right to establish slavery. Grant it. What then? Who has the right to determine the question, as to the justice or injustice of the institution, South Carolina or we? If she be an independent state, she has the right to be her own judge as to the rectitude of her decisions. She is not accountable to us, and we have no right to arraign her before our tribunal. If we believe her decision unjust we may undoubtedly tell her so; but so long as we admit her independence, we must speak to her as an equal, not as a culprit. We must concede her right to judge for herself; we must disavow the right and the intention of dictating to her; and we must confine ourselves to the simple statement of our reasons, as one man may state to another man his reasons for not agreeing with him in opinion. If, however, instead of doing this, we begin by formally declaring her in the wrong, by denouncing her as awfully wicked, by stirring up wrath and indignation against her, by solemnly pledging ourselves not to cease our exertions till we have compelled her to reverse her decision, and by adopting all the measures in our power which we believe conducive to that end, do we not then fail to treat her as an independent state, refuse to acknowledge her right to judge for herself, and are we not, to all intents and purposes, waging war against her?

It will be seen from what we have said that we do not question the proceedings of the abolitionists on constitutional grounds. We do not believe that we of the North have made a compact with the South, by which we are debarred from interfering with slavery. We find in the Constitution of the United States no such compact. None such in fact was needed. Slavery exists in the states by virtue of no constitutional guarantee, but solely by virtue of state sovereignty. The question in relation to it stands precisely as it did before the formation of the national government, and we have precisely the same rights, and only the same rights, of interference with it that we should have had, had no national government ever been formed. The states are older than the Union, and they retain in their own hands all the rights of sovereignty not, in so many words, conceded to the Union. Now as the disposition of slavery is not conceded to the Union, it belongs as a matter of course to the states. By belonging to them it stands precisely as it did before the Union was consummated. As the states before the Union were so many independent nations, the question of slavery in them is to be treated solely as a question between foreign nations. Interference with it in one state by the citizens of another state is to be regulated by international and not by constitutional law. Had the Union not been effected, everybody knows that efforts by the citizens of Massachusetts to free the slaves in South Carolina, efforts begun and carried on with express reference to that end, would have been a violation of international law, especially if accompanied with perpetual denunciation of South Carolina, and by their very character threatening to disturb her internal peace and tranquillity. Now this, which would have been true without the Union, we contend, is true under it. The South, we think, must therefore place her defense on the ground of state sovereignty. It is as striking against state sovereignty, as denying the independence of the several states, as claiming for the citizens of one state jurisdiction over the legislation of another, that we view the proceedings of abolition societies with suspicion and alarm. To say the least, they assert the justice of a species of propagandism, which, if admitted, must strike at all national independency, and which will not fail to disturb the peaceful intercourse of nations, embroil them in war, and deluge the earth in blood. He who comes forth as the champion of liberty must bear in mind that he is under no less obligation to defend the rights of communities than he is the rights of individuals. He who loves America and would live and die for American liberty should look well before he adopts a course which may embroil the several states in a civil war, or in the end change the relations which now subsist between the national government and that of the several states. Liberty is as much interested in maintaining inviolate the rights of the national government, on the one hand, and especially of the several states which compose the Union, on the other hand, as she is in freeing the slave. In the measures the abolitionists adopt there is a deeper question involved than that of Negro slavery. All who are accustomed to look below the surface of things may see that it is a question of no less magnitude than that of changing the whole structure of the government of this country, and possibly that of destroying the liberty of the whole American people. When hundreds and thousands of our citizens are banded together to trample on the rights of independent communities in the holy name of freedom herself, we confess we are not a little alarmed for the rights of the individual. One barrier leaped, another may be; and when communities can no longer make their rights respected, what can the individual do?

But we shall be told that all our fears are idle, all our reasonings groundless, for abolitionists do not propose to do anything more than we have conceded them the right to do; that is, to express freely their honest convictions on the question of slavery. We deny this. The abolition societies, as everybody knows, are not formed for the discussion of slavery but for its abolition. Their members are pledged to the "immediate emancipation of the slaves without expatriation." Lawyers may have been consulted and the wording of their constitutions may be technically within the letter of the law, but we know, and everybody knows, that the real end, the avowed end, of their formation is not merely to give utterance to certain opinions on the question of slavery, but to effect its abolition. They are not formed for deliberation, for discussion, but for action, and action, too, within the limits of states of which abolitionists are not citizens.

But we shall be told again that, admitting the abolition societies are formed for the abolition and not the discussion of slavery, they do not contravene international law because they adopt for the purpose of carrying their end only legal and constitutional means, such means as the laws of nations permit them to adopt. This undoubtedly is the real ground on which the abolitionists rest their defense. We object to it because we are not yet able to perceive that the legitimacy of the means, in themselves, can legitimate an unlawful end. It is admitted that the abolitionists have no legal right to emancipate the slaves. Yet the emancipation of the slaves is what they propose to do. They propose to do what the laws of nations prohibit them from doing. Are any means directed to that end lawful to be used?

The abolitionists, it will be said, do not propose to emancipate the slaves, except as the effect of the expression of their opinions and feelings on the subject of slavery. We question this statement; but admit it for a moment. The abolitionists—unless they choose to break with the slaveholding states, to refuse to sustain the relation of friends to them, and to come into open war with them—are bound by the laws of nations to refrain from all words and deeds which will disturb their peace and tranquillity, stir up insurrection in them, sully their reputation, or excite public indignation against them. Now we may undoubtedly discuss the question of slavery, but not so as to produce any of these results. Free discussion is itself subjected to this restriction. So long as we wish to be at peace and amity with foreign nations, we are bound to treat all their institutions, as their institutions, with respect. We have no more right to denounce them, to slander them, to speak to their prejudice, or to injure them in any way, because their institutions differ from ours, or from what we believe just, than we have an individual whose creed we happen to disbelieve. We may reason against such a man's creed, but we are bound to see that our reasoning against it do not result in any injury to him. If we should represent him as one with whom his neighbors should hold no intercourse, brand him as a sinner of the deepest dye, hire editors of papers to publish him to the world as such, and hold public meetings and pass public resolves to the effect that, if he do not change his creed instantly, he shall be placed out of the pale of humanity, we should most assuredly transcend our rights in regard to him, and give him just cause of complaint against us. Now the abolitionists pursue a course like this towards the slaveholding communities, and they do this for the express purpose of freeing the slave. They may in all this be only giving utterance to their honest convictions and feelings, but have they, under plea of free discussion, a right to titter themselves in this manner? Can they do this and be in a state of peace with those communities?

The abolitionists say they use only moral and rational means, merely arguments addressed to the reason and the conscience. Is it so? To what kind of a reason or a conscience is denunciation addressed? Is it so? What mean then these fifteen hundred affiliated societies, spread over the non-slaveholding states, pledged to the immediate emancipation of the slaves? Are these societies' arguments addressed to the individual reason and conscience of the slaveholder? What is the rationale of this argument? What is its legitimacy? Many hundreds of thousands of men, women, and children, all solemnly pledged to effect the immediate emancipation of the slaves, are banded together in some fifteen hundred societies; therefore slavery is a sin; therefore no slaveholder is a Christian; and therefore every slaveholder must immediately emancipate his slaves! We confess this is a species of logic that passes our comprehension. That these societies, by banding together the majority of our population, may so concentrate public opinion, and bring it to bear with such force on the institution of slavery, that the slaveholder shall feel himself unable to withstand it, and therefore compelled to free his slaves, is what we can understand very well; but this is neither a rational nor a moral argument for the abolition of slavery. A man finds a loaded pistol presented at his breast, and to save his life gives up his purse; and the slaveholder finds the community pointing the finger of scorn at him, and to save his reputation, which he holds dearer than life, emancipates his slaves; which is the more moral and rational argument of the two? An army, organized and marching upon the South to free the slaves at the point of the bayonet, would, in principle, be an argument to the individual reason and conscience of the slaveholder, equally as forcible, appropriate, and convincing, as an associated multitude pointing the finger of scorn, or shouting denunciation, and threatening the vengeance of heaven.

Nor is it true that our abolitionists contemplate no action on the subject, but the action of truth and moral suasion. They do contemplate political action. They let pass no possible opportunity of bringing the subject of slavery before the state legislatures; and they are constantly at work to get it discussed on the floor of Congress. What, we ask, is all this agitation for? Why is abolitionism organizing a political party in the states and the nation? Why does it want abolition members in our state legislatures? Why does it interrogate candidates for office as to their views of slavery? Is there no political action intended? Give it a majority in Congress and will it not legislate on the subject? It will at once abolish slavery in the District of Columbia, and in the territories. Will it stop there? Who so simple as to believe it? It will usurp, or alter the United States Constitution so as not to need to usurp the power to abolish it in the states. What are paper constitutions in the way of a body of men, women, and children, inflamed, drunken with a great idea, and so much the more drunken because the idea with which they are filled is a holy one—what are paper constitutions in their way, when they have in their hands the actual power to advance? He knows nothing of the power of an enthusiastic multitude, who thinks such feeble barriers would arrest their progress. Their leaders might rush before them, the wise and prudent might beg them to pause; but leaders, and the wise and prudent are as chaff before the wind, and on will the multitude press, sweeping them away, or trampling them under their feet, to the realization of the idea which inspires them. Here is the danger. Let the abolitionists get the majority banded together in or under the control of their affiliated societies, pledged to the immediate emancipation of the slaves, and they will throw into Congress the power to do it; that is, power to regulate the internal institutions of the states; gone then is the independency of the states; and then goes individual freedom; and then all power is in the central government; Greece or Rome is reproduced; the absolutism of the state is established, which merely preludes the absolutism of the emperor. God grant that in the honest and earnest defense of liberty we dig not her grave!

We speak on this subject strongly but we have no fears of being misunderstood. There is not a man or woman living that can accuse us of defending slavery. This whole number of our Review is devoted to the defense of the rights of man, not to the rights of one man, of a few men, but of every man. We can legitimate our own right to freedom, only by arguments which prove also the Negro's right to be free. We have all our life long sympathized with the poor and the oppressed, and we yield to no abolitionist in the amount of the sacrifices we have made, wisely or unwisely, needlessly or not, in the cause of human freedom. It is not today, nor this year, that we have pledged ourselves, for life or for death, to the holy cause of universal liberty. But everything, we say, in its time. First, we must settle the bases of individual freedom, settle the principle that man measures man the world over, and establish our government upon it, and secure the action of the government in accordance with it and then we may proceed to make all details harmonize with it.

To explain ourselves; the work to be done in this country today is to place the government in the hands of the people, not only in principle, but in fact. Hitherto the government, in point of fact, has been in the hands of the businessmen, who have shaped legislation to their especial interests. We are struggling now to get it out of their hands, not to the disadvantage of the businessmen, but to hinder them from having an exclusive control over it. The businessmen form a part of the people, a large part, and a respectable part, and we must not wish to turn the government in any respect against them; but we must seek so to arrange matters, that they shall share only an equal protection with all the other sections of the community. The object is to effect such changes, that there shall henceforth, in all governmental relations and actions, be no classes, but simply the people. This done, we shall have established the principle of universal liberty and opened the door for every man to enter into the possession of entire freedom under the dominion of equal laws. We shall then have all the individual freedom of the savage state with all the order and social harmony of the highest degree of civilization. This is the end to be gained as we have attempted to show in the article which precedes this.

Now, our danger is not from an excess of individuality, but from centralization. The danger to be apprehended is from the strength, not the weakness of the government. Nearly the whole North has a strong tendency to merge the individual in the state. The North is enterprising, fond of undertaking great things, which are to be accomplished only by concentrating the power of masses, to be wielded by a few directing minds. This tendency is good, and springs from noble qualities; nevertheless it may, in its eagerness to reach its end, so centralize power, that the individual from an integer may become a mere fraction of the body politic. It therefore needs a check, a counterbalancing power, at least until the bases of legislation and social action become so fixed, that there shall henceforth be no danger that the state will swallow up the individual.

This check is found in the strong individuality of the South, arising from the individual importance which each man there possesses in consequence of being himself a sort of petty sovereign. The southern planter keeps alive here the very element of individual freedom, represented by the feudal baron in Europe. The South therefore becomes the defender of individual freedom, as the North is the great advocate of social freedom. One represents the individual element, as the other does the social element of human nature. Hence the North demands a strong government, and the South a strong people. The North have been Federalists, the South Democrats. Now if we weaken the southern individuality before the northern centralization be fixed by laws, which leave the individual in possession of all his natural rights, we destroy the equilibrium between the individual and the state, and endanger the freedom of both. This is one reason why we regret the present agitation of the slave question, and why we see danger, not to the Union merely, but to liberty herself in the abolition movements.

This strong individuality of the South is the effect of the institution of slavery. The South without slaves would have had the same tendency to centralization that we have at the North. The cause of it here is the fact that no individual here feels himself of much importance by the side of the state. Individually he can do but little and feels himself small. Hence his strong desire to lean on the state, his uncommon fondness for associations, corporations, partnerships, whatever concentrates power and adds to individual strength. Then again our commercial and manufacturing pursuits also tend to make us desire somewhere the social power, we can call in to supply our individual deficiency in strength, capital, or skill. The southern planter is a sort of prince. Living in the center of his plantation, of his own principality, absolute lord and proprietor of a number of human beings, he feels that he, individually, is a man; that his rights as a man are of too much consequence to be swallowed up in the rights of the state. It is true, he ought to reflect that his Negroes have the same rights by nature, as himself, and so he will one day; but first he must secure his own rights. After he has secured his own rights as a man, and finds them no longer in danger from the northern tendency to centralization, he will perceive that he has, in defending them, been defending those of his Negroes; and then he will take up in earnest the matter of freeing them. To free them before were of no use, because before he has secured his own rights, there can be no security for theirs.

Here is the aid which slavery itself, through the providence of God, is made to contribute to liberty. Good always comes out of evil; and southern statesmen are nearer the truth than we commonly think them, when they say, that "southern slavery is the support of northern liberty." We confess, that as things were, we see no way in which freedom could have been established in this country, without the strong sense of individual freedom which slavery tends to produce in the planter. When the world has become Christianized, we shall support individual freedom on the maxim, that "you are as good as I"; but in an earlier stage of social and individual progress, we must do it by means of this other maxim, "I am as good as you." Now this feeling of personal importance, of egotism, if you please, was in no way, that we can see, to be introduced but by slavery, and without this, our Republic would not have had the checks and balances needed. The time will come, when this will not be needed, and then slavery will cease. Before, it will not.

Another means of saving individual freedom is in the sovereignty of the individual states. Destroy the states as sovereignties and make them only provinces of one consolidated state, and centralization swallows up everything. The individual finds the government so far from him, and his own share in it comparatively so insignificant, that he soon comes to feel himself individually of little or no importance, and when he so feels he ceases from all manly defense of his rights, and loses himself in the mass. Now the South, in consequence of having peculiar state institutions to defend, has been the foremost in defense of state rights, the sovereignty of the states in its plenitude, so far at least as all their internal affairs are concerned. It is because they have had slaves, not to be retained without the supreme control of all state institutions, that they have been so earnest in defense of state sovereignty. There is some analogy between the relation a state holds to the Union, and that held by the individual to the state. The arguments which defend the rights of the individual defend those of the state, and those which defend the rights of the state defend those of the individual. The South may have sometimes carried her doctrine of state rights too far, but her repeated assertion of it has done not a little to save American liberty.

Now, until we have settled the controversy about state rights and individual rights, and obtained the amplest security for both, it is as unwise as it is useless to touch the question of slavery. As yet there is no security given, or capable of being given, that the slave will be a free man even if declared free by the laws. Let this security be obtained before you attempt to emancipate him. He is now, paradoxical as it may seem, aiding in laying the foundation of universal liberty to universal man, and when the superstructure is reared, and the multitude throng its courts, he shall appear in the temple a free and equal worshiper.

Hard undoubtedly is it that liberty should be purchased at the slave's expense, and we confess we have no fondness for the idea; but less injustice is done the slave than we commonly imagine. The Negro on a southern plantation is unquestionably a superior being to the Negro in his native Africa. By being enslaved, he has been elevated, not degraded. Degraded he no doubt is in comparison with his master, but his captivity shall redeem his race. The years of his bondage shall not be so long, his labors, sufferings, and sacrifices in becoming a civilized man shall be far less, than ours have been. So far as we may judge from the past, it is the settled order of God's providence, that man shall be saved only by crucified redeemers. Man is never to receive freedom and civilization as a boon; he can obtain them only by toil and struggle and blood. Why it should be so is one of the mysteries of Providence for which we might perhaps assign some good reasons, but which we do not undertake to solve. The world is full of mysteries, and this is no more dark and perplexing than a thousand others. Time will clear it up.

Tendency of Modern Civilization
April 1838

Very few of our readers, we presume, have ever heard of this new Association,¹ and most of them, on reading its name, will probably be somewhat puzzled to make out who may be its members, or what can be its object. Are its members abolitionists, infidels, fanatics? Or are they philosophers? What propose they to do? Why do they associate in defense of the rights of man, especially in this free country, where the rights of man are acknowledged and secured? Perhaps the following, which they have put forth as their confession of faith, may throw some light on these questions.

"*Principles*. 1st. The *rights of man* are not grants or privileges; they are derived from no compacts; but are founded on the simple fact that man is man. They cannot be alienated by the individual, given nor taken away by civil authority.

"2d. Every man, by virtue of the fact that he is a man, has the right to develop freely, and to perfect all his faculties, his whole nature, as a moral, intellectual, and physical being.

"3d. Every man has a right to freedom of industry, freedom of thought, and freedom of conscience.

"4th. The rights of society can never be in opposition to the rights of the individual. If they could be, right would be able to change its nature, and become wrong, and there would be the foundation of a perpetual war between the individual and society, in which both parties would be, at the same time and in relation to the same proposition, in the right and in the wrong.

"5th. That social state, therefore, which does not respect all and every one of the rights of its members, is by virtue of that fact wrong, and needs to be revolutionized, reformed, or ameliorated.

"6th. Government is the creature of society, and is restricted in its functions to the mission of maintaining, from all encroachments, the rights of the individual and of society.

"Objects. Our objects are to ascertain in detail and to determine with precision what are the rights of man and of society; to ascertain and fix the boundaries of the legitimate province of government; to keep government within its province; and lastly, to labor for such reforms in governments, in the individual, and in society, as will secure to every member of the community the opportunity and the means to be and to do, what he is fitted to be and to do, by the nature and faculties with which he is endowed.

"Means. Our means are simple, but mighty, and such as can work no injustice to governments or to individuals. The causes of all existing abuses are ignorance and selfishness; abuses, therefore, can be removed only by knowledge and love; these are our means. We wish to direct our own attention, and that of the whole community, more directly than it has heretofore been, to the whole subject of the rights of man, and the means of promoting the progress of man, and of society.

"We therefore propose to inquire into the whole subject, and to inform ourselves as to what the rights of man and society really are; also to ascertain how far those rights are acknowledged, secured, or enjoyed in our present social state, and how far custom, prejudice, false notions, governments, or legislation, disregard, abridge, or attempt to disannul them.

"If we can do something by private discussions, by public debates, by lectures, and the publication of well written essays, and select libraries, to diffuse just knowledge among the people on these great subjects, and to kindle up in our own hearts and in the hearts of others a love of virtue, and the genuine sentiments of humanity, we shall at least do something to preserve our rights as far as already obtained, and to obtain them where they are yet denied.

"Let the people once perceive and understand their rights—perceive and understand what is wrong in our present systems of legislation, and defective in our social arrangements, and let them be inspired by a true sense of the worth of man as man, and they will easily and peaceably effect all the governmental and social reforms needed to place every man in the free and full enjoyment of all his faculties.

This to our way of thinking is not a bad confession of faith; and it indicates very good intentions on the part of those who make it. It proves that the members of this new association are not wholly ignorant of the subject with which they concern themselves; that they have lofty aims; that they take broad and comprehensive views; and that they contemplate a most thorough, radical reform, one which will root out nearly all existing evils, and base governments and society itself on the laws of universal, eternal, and unalterable justice. For such a reform, every heart must cry out, and every hand exert itself. The members of this association may never live to realize it; they will in all likelihood die without having been able to witness any perceptible change in the world for the better; but we cannot but deem them deserving high praise for contemplating such a reform, and for undertaking to effect it. Men who have bright and glorious dreams are never to be spoken lightly of. They have rich stuff in their souls, and may always be relied on as true friends to the cause of humanity.

We may also add that this association is composed mainly, if not exclusively, of mechanics and other workingmen; and it is this fact, more than any other, that has induced us to place its name at the head of this article. This is the age of associations. Men nowadays associate for every purpose, great or small, good, bad, or indifferent. The simple fact of the organization of a new association deserves of itself no attention. But we confess we cannot view an association like this with indifference. We feel something of patriotic pride swelling our hearts when we find even our workingmen associating for the study and defense of the rights of man, and putting forth such declarations as the one we have laid before our readers. It is a proof that our free institutions work well, and that their quickening and elevating influences reach even to the lowest ranks of society. Nowhere but in this democratic country of ours could we think of finding an association like the one we are considering. The workingmen must have advanced far, and attained to a good share of well-being, before they could think of their rights, before they could have the leisure, the intelligence, and the means of investigating such great subjects as those set forth in this confession of faith. The fact then of the organization of this association is a proof of the comparatively good condition of the workingmen in this country, that their condition has been improved, and that though it may not yet be as good as it should be, or as it one day will be, yet that it has become tolerable. This fact should endear our free institutions to the friends of mankind, and forbid us ever to despair of popular liberty.

We have been struck, coming as it does from the workingmen, with the catholic spirit that pervades this confession of faith. It breathes peace and good will; it censures nobody, makes war upon no class of society, and manifests hostility to no existing institution. It makes war, if war it makes, upon ignorance and selfishness only; and the weapons of its warfare are those of knowledge and love; powerful weapons indeed, but harmless save against evil and evildoers. These workingmen seem to forget themselves, to sink themselves in common humanity, and to dream of no good for themselves, which is not at the same time a good for universal man. Changes they no doubt contemplate, reforms they may demand, thorough, radical reformers they may wish to be, but not with a view to their own interests alone—not with a view to the interests of a class, sect, or party; but with a view to the interests of mankind. We commend this fact to those of our friends who are apprehending a "war of the poor against the rich," who have feared that the movements of the workingmen would render property insecure, throw the whole community into a universal hubbub, and send us all back to the savage state to go naked, to feed on nuts and the scanty and precarious supplies of fishing and hunting. The workingmen will respect the rights of property, for they have a natural love of justice, and because they have no design in what they are attempting, but that of making justice universally triumphant.

More might be said against the visionary or impracticable character of what these workingmen propose than against its dangerous tendency. It might be said, with some plausibility perhaps that hopes of a reform so vast, so thorough, so radical, of results so desirable and so felicitous as they contemplate, are perfectly idle, and that no sane man, at all acquainted with the world, can indulge them for a moment; that the world is as good, society, here especially, as perfect, as we have any right to expect; and that instead of wasting ourselves in fruitless efforts to make the world better, we ought to do our best to keep it from growing worse. This all may be so. We have a great respect for the practical men, the men of routine, who say so; that is, when they keep in their own sphere; but when they undertake to prophesy, we have no disposition to lend them our ears. We cannot but distrust their capacity to look through the whole future, and tell us exactly what can and what cannot be done. They would themselves do well to bear in mind that he, who undertakes to tell what cannot be done, may be as much out in his reckoning, as he who undertakes to tell what can be done. For ourselves, we rarely tell a man that he is a visionary, that his schemes are impracticable. We do not know everything. We have not been able, as yet, to find out the exact boundary between the possible and the impossible, the practicable and the impracticable, between the man who is verily a visionary, and the one who entertains projects which are rational and may one day be realized. We do not know what may or may not yet be done. For aught we know, man may yet rise above the loftiest and loveliest ideal, which the most rapt dreamer in his most ecstatic moments has ever bodied forth to his dreaming fancy. "The prophet that hath a dream let him tell a dream," for who knows but the dream may turn out to have been from God, and to contain a truth in the diffusion of which all coming ages are interested?

More than all this we would not discourage these dreamers as the world calls them. The man whose mind never strays beyond the actual, never soars into the ideal, and loses itself in that which is not and perhaps will not be realized, is never able to perform any great and glorious deed. The mind moves before the hand; and he who contemplates nothing great or good in his soul, will accomplish nothing great or good in his deeds. It is by communing with the sweet, and holy, and sublime visions which ever and anon flit across the soul, by seizing, seeking to embody, and preventing them from escaping us, that we ever become able to do anything for which the world should bless our memories. He who has a glorious ideal will achieve glorious deeds. He who hopes much will accomplish much. Never should we damp the ardor of hope, or seek to chain to the earth the soul that would rise to heaven. Never should we seek to subdue man's faith in himself or in his race. Faith is the true miracle-worker. To him that believeth, all things are possible. We know not how much injury we have done by clipping the wings of the young eagles, that were, ambitious of taking their lofty flight through the heavens; how much we have dwarfed the intellect and kept back the progress of our race by our sneers at enthusiasm, and our coldwater counsels of experience poured on the ardent hopes, and burning zeal of the young prophets of humanity. Men of the world, who never had any dreams, and old men, who no longer remember the dreams of their youth, should never be suffered to open their lips, or in any way to hint a counsel. They are the Deevs of Ahriman's kingdom, the kingdom of darkness, and should ever be avoided by the children of Ormuzd, the children of the light.

But we are not sure that these workingmen deserve to be accounted visionaries. We confess that we see nothing in the result they would bring about, in the end they are in pursuit of, that even *practical* men, men of routine, men wise for yesterday and not for tomorrow, men with pleasant country seats, who think only of enjoying snug quarters for the rest of life's campaign, need regard as visionary or chimerical. They, who oppose the result, who think they can arrest the workingmen's movements, and prevent this result; they are the visionaries, the real dreamers. This result, this end the workingmen are pursuing, of which they have a lively sentiment, if not a clear perception, is that towards which the whole force of modern civilization is bearing us. These workingmen's movements, which have alarmed some, and which short-sighted politicians have thought to arrest by a sneer or a nickname, by crying out "workie," "locofoco," "agrarian," and other like terms of presumed reproach, are but so many proofs that the great law of modern civilization is still in force, and that its influence is at work in the heart of the millions. The workingmen in these alarming or visionary movements are only, consciously or unconsciously, exerting themselves to fulfill the mission of that order of civilization to which Christianity has given birth. The whole tendency of this civilization is in the direction these workingmen are looking, to the realization of such "reforms as will place every man in the free and full enjoyment of all his faculties."

They who have no faith in the progress of man and society are always very fond of appealing to history, as though history was in their favor; and they are always ready with a pile of individual facts, with which to drive back the reformer or beat out his brains; but happily for humanity, the reformer can read history today as well as they, and it shall go hard but his reading shall turn out to be as correct as theirs. According to his reading, history shows us everywhere progress and is ever with her ten thousand angel voices calling us to a loftier and lovelier future. They who find history against the reformer may perhaps be convicted of having never read history. Descriptions of some famous battles they may have read, some court anecdotes they may have picked up, and the dates of certain events they may have ascertained, but the concealed causes in operation, the invisible forces, the spiritual facts, the laws of the great events which have occurred, and to which the facts usually narrated in history owe their birth, and which are the only things in history it concerns us to know; these it is altogether likely they have not discovered, have not stumbled upon in any of their historic researches. To know history is to know these; and these, with modesty be it said, bear witness to the kindling truth that the human race is progressive, and that society is ever struggling to realize a more and more perfect ideal.

How many different orders of civilization have, each in its turn, ruled the world, we know not. Some think they catch here and there a glimpse of an earlier civilization, which they call the Cyclopean, the "golden age" of the poets; but the earliest civilization, of which we can affirm anything with certainty, is the sacerdotal civilization, as we find it in ancient India, Egypt, and Syria; in its greatest perfection, perhaps, in Judea. The idea of God is the dominant idea of this order of civilization. God reigns, in principle, supreme, though, in fact, his symbol, or representative, the priesthood, possesses all the power. The state and the individual, as we have shown in another place, succumb to the priesthood. Everything, all ideas and all actions, are held to be subordinate and subservient to the worship of God.

To the sacerdotal civilization succeeds the Greek and Roman, or political civilization. The dominant idea of this order of civilization is the state. The state is everything. The priesthood is a function of the state, and religion is regulated by a decree of the senate, or an edict of the emperor. The individual man is not yet born. There is no people. There is the Roman city, but no Roman people, as we understand the term people now.

The mission of this order of civilization was the realization of the majesty of the state. This mission it accomplished. We stand in awe, even today, of the majesty of the Roman state. Wherever Rome set her foot she left the imprint of her majesty. The modern traveler, over what was once her dominion, is struck with a sense of her greatness in every fragment of her antiquity he meets. The language she has left us, reveals in every phrase, in its very construction, in its single words even, her majesty. We can hardly, by imagination the most creative, conceive of the greatness and power of that City of the Tiber, which could make her presence felt, her faintest whisper heard, and obeyed as law, at the same moment, throughout the extremities of Europe, Asia, and Africa. But the majesty, before which we stand awestruck, is always the majesty of the state, never of the people as individuals. The individual is merely a member of the corporation, and aside from his corporate capacity has no recognized existence, no rights, no worth. If he is cared for, it is solely because he is an appendage to the state, a part of the body politic.

This fact becomes apparent, if we merely glance at the conquest of the Roman empire by the barbarians. In the long agony of that struggle, the barbarian encounters no forces but those of the Roman legions. In scarcely an instance does he find a people to resist him. The moment the Roman state is overthrown, nothing is to be found standing. From the general silence of history, we might almost infer that just in proportion as the Roman legions were withdrawn from the provinces, especially from the provinces of Gaul, they became deserts, and that of all the numerous populations which covered them none were left. In most instances of a conquered country, the conquerors do not gain at once a peaceful and undisputed possession. The conquered revolt, rebel, rise against their conquerors, and attempt to throw off their yoke. But nothing of this meets us in the history of the conquest of the Roman empire by the barbarians. When once the regular forces of the empire have been overcome, the conquest is complete. We take our stand in the heart of the Western Empire at the close of the Fifth century; the Franks are seated in Gaul, the Visigoths in Spain, the Vandals in Africa, and the Ostrogoths in Italy, and of that vast empire we see nothing, unless it be a few of its municipal institutions in the city of Rome itself, and some of the larger towns. Wherever the eye extends, nothing is to be seen but barbarians, the church, and slaves. The reason of this must needs be in the fact that under the Roman civilization all authority, all energy was absorbed in the state, and none was left to the people. That civilization created a majestic city but not a majestic people. The populations which lived under it had no inherent vigor, no self-reliance, no resources in themselves. Consequently, when the protection of the city was withdrawn, they had no power to beat back the invader; and when fallen under the barbarian rule, no energy to revolt and to struggle to regain their independence.

Rome called herself a Republic, and boasted of her liberty; but the people had less freedom under her dominion than they now have under the most despotic of Christian princes. Beneath the overshadowing majesty of the government, the dazzling prosperity of the state, there was the most abject servitude, the most inconceivable wretchedness. The masses were degraded below the condition of our southern slaves. Human rights, human well-being, a regard for man simply as man, efforts to raise every man to the true dignity of manhood, were unknown, undreamed of. Now was this to be the definitive state of human society? Could this civilization be the term of human progress? It could not. Something better for man was needed, and must come. The good of humanity required a new and a different order of civilization; one which should substitute the majesty of man for the majesty of the state. This new order of civilization is the natural fruit of the Christian idea of the worth of man as man. Christianity gives to man precisely the place given by the political civilization to the state. But by its great doctrine of the universal brotherhood of humanity, the enfranchisement it demands for one man, it demands for every man.

Modern civilization is the offspring of Christianity. It is the attempt to realize the great idea of the equal worth of every individual man as man. Its mission is the perfect realization of this idea in the new society to which it gives birth. Now the perfect realization of this idea is precisely what these workingmen, of whom we have spoken, are striving after. Will this idea be realized? That is, will modern civilization fulfill its mission? Will it fail, die before its time comes? Did Judaism fail before it had fulfilled its mission? Did Greece and Rome expire before their work was done? Has a nation ever been known to die before realizing the idea on which it was founded? Are there any indications of disease, weakness, decline, decrepitude, in modern civilization? Has it ceased to extend itself, to make conquests? Is there a new order of civilization springing up and threatening to invade its territory? Is it not still vigorous, young, and full of the future? What reason have we, then, to think that it will fail to do its work?

When modern civilization began its career, the individual, we have said, was nothing, the state was everything. The first thing to be done was to break down the state and raise up the individual. But this could be done only by destroying the old order of civilization and of course not without overthrowing the Roman empire which it had created and which was its last word. This could be done only by raising up a new and vigorous society in its bosom, which should contain the germs of the new civilization, and by the influx of a new people, in whom the individual should still live in all his integrity. The first was found in the church which undermined the Roman state from within, and the second was supplied by the barbarians who invaded and conquered it from without.

In the savage state, individuality predominates. There is in that state no society. The elements of society are there, but they are isolated, and for the most part inoperative. Each man is his own center and forms a whole by himself. The city is not yet organized and counts for nothing. The tribe counts for something but it can never absorb the individual. The attachment to the tribe or to its chieftain is personal, not political. The barbarians who supplanted the Roman empire cannot be said to have been pure savages, nevertheless they had not advanced so far as to lose sight of the individual. Personal freedom was still the dominant sentiment. Individual barbarians indeed grouped at unequal distances around a chief; but he was their leader, not their master; and their attachment to him was by no means a political attachment. He was not in their eyes the representative of the majesty of the state, but a man like the rest of them, only perhaps a little taller, or the descendant of a more respected branch of the common family. The barbarians' idea of freedom was always that of personal freedom, freedom of the individual, not the freedom of the state, or body politic. In seating themselves in the Roman territory, they necessarily introduced into that territory this element of individual freedom. This is one of the benefits which has resulted from the overthrow of the Roman empire, and may induce us to regard the destruction of the Roman civilization as a blessing, not as a curse, to humanity. As we come to know more of the designs of Providence, and to see more clearly their wisdom, we shall be less and less disposed to complain of what has been.

If we take our stand again in the Western Empire immediately after the Conquest, immediately after the irruptions of the barbarians have ceased, we shall discover, already at work, all the elements of modern civilization. These elements are, first, the church, depositary of the earlier or sacerdotal civilization, invigorated by the infusion of the Christian idea of the majesty of man; second, royalty, or recollections of imperial Rome, mingled with the barbarian notions of chieftainship; third, republicanism, or recollections of republican Rome which survived in the city of Rome, in some of the Italian cities, and a few towns in southern Gaul; and fourth, feudalism, in germ, which embodied the new element, that of personal freedom.

Each of these elements is good and essential to a perfect state of society. The fundamental idea of the church is that of the supremacy of moral power. Its aim is to substitute, in the government of the world, moral power for brute force. The order of civilization it represents, the sacerdotal, is that which breaks down the savage state, and rescues man from the dominion of brute force. It must necessarily precede the political civilization. Theocracy is older than monarchy, aristocracy, or democracy, as the priesthood is older than the state. The church becomes mischievous only when it becomes exclusive, and governs in the interests of the priesthood, and not according to the law of God; when it resorts to material force to make what it calls moral right prevail. It then becomes a theocracy, and practices a tyranny over man, of all tyrannies the worst; for it strikes not only the body, but the soul also, perverts conscience, and makes man a slave within as well as without.

Royalty, as it exists in modern Europe, is a branch of republicanism. All governments, whatever their form, which represent the majesty of the state and are held to be instituted for the public, are republican. Asiatic monarchies are instituted not for the public, but for the monarch; they therefore are not republics. But the governments of France and England, for instance, are held to be instituted not for the benefit of the monarch, but to take charge of the public affairs for the public good. The real idea which lies at the bottom of republicanism, whether bearing a royal or popular form, is that of the state. The idea of the state is that of the social nature of man. Its mission is to realize the social instincts of mankind, to give order, regularity, harmony, stability, to all social actions and social intercourse. When it becomes exclusive, separated, on the one hand, from morality, and, on the other, from personal freedom, it degenerates into despotism either of the one, the few, or the many, and becomes unjust, cruel, and oppressive.

The fundamental element of feudalism is, as we have said, the element of individuality or personal freedom. It is the recognition of the fact that there are rights of man as well as rights of the priesthood and of the state. But when this element is predominant, not limited by the moral and the social elements of our nature, it breaks all social bonds, destroys everything like social order, and precipitates us into the savage state. When it is not generalized, or when it is coupled with the notion that might creates right, and that he only deserves to be a freeman who is able to assert and maintain his freedom, it establishes an order of things like that which prevailed in Europe from the sixth century to nearly the close of the fourteenth. It gives us then only here and there a man (a baron, for baron means man, a man, or the man, probably from the Latin, *vir*), while the many are his vassals, serfs, bond men, or slaves. An exemplification of this may be seen on any southern slave plantation, and a reminiscence of it in a cotton factory in our own New England.

The exclusive predominance of any one of these elements would have defeated the design of modern civilization. Has any one of these been able to obtain exclusive dominion over modern society?

Each of these elements of modern civilization has made its effort to reign without a rival. The church made the attempt, and appeared to succeed, but it did not. The progress of civilization is not backward. The past never returns. The success of the church would have been the reproduction of the sacerdotal civilization of Egypt, India, Judea, which had yielded to the political civilization of Greece and Rome. It therefore failed. It reached its culminating point under Hildebrand, Gregory VII, and from that time, notwithstanding appearances and pretensions, it steadily declined till Luther appeared to prepare the way for its reconstruction under a more liberal form. Royalty attempted to gain exclusive dominion and under the Frank emperor, Charlemagne, seemed to have reproduced imperial Rome; but feudalism was too strong for it, and Charlemagne was hardly laid in his tomb, before his empire was dissolved. Republicanism, especially in the Italian cities and the large towns in the south of France, made an effort, threatened for a time to reproduce republican Rome on a small scale, and to cover Europe with a multitude of city-republics; but it could not succeed against royalty, feudalism, and the church. Feudalism made its effort also, and nearly plunged the European world into primeval barbarism. It resisted all the tendencies to centralization which manifested themselves under Charlemagne and Gregory VII. It held the burghers in subjection, and yet it enfranchised the slave. Under Louis XI, it was shorn of its power, and it lost itself in the public under Louis XIV. Not one of these elements has been able to succeed in obtaining exclusive dominion, and yet all the ideas they represent have ever been gaining power.

The conquest of England by the Normans hastened in that country the march of civilization, and tended to establish and develop those free institutions, which have for so long a time been the boast of Englishmen. The first effect of the conquest was a large accession of power to the central government, that is, to the monarch. This was necessary in order to keep the Saxons, or native English, in subjection, and to secure to the Norman adventurers the quiet possession of their estates. But this accession of power to the central government led to tyranny on the part of the monarch and for a time threatened the triumph of absolutism. Feudalism took the alarm and calling to its aid a portion of the burghers, principally of the Saxon race, wrested Magna Carta from king John at Runnymede, a sort of compromise between feudalism and royalty. For a time the preponderance might have been on the side of feudalism; but the barons found themselves arrested in their progress by the burghers. They had used the burghers against king John, against royalty, and these uniting with royalty under Henry VII, restrained and all but annihilated them, weakened as they had become by the Wars of the Roses. Royalty threatened again to become absolute under Henry VIII and Elizabeth, but it was resisted under James I and decapitated under his successor. The Republic appeared with the Long Parliament; but inasmuch as sufficient account was not made of personal freedom, it gave way to the Restoration, which in its turn yielded to the Revolution of 1688, a compromise between all the elements of modern civilization, the church, royalty, feudalism, and republicanism.

Thus we see that not one of these elements has succeeded, though all have made the attempt. Each in turn has been defeated. Yet in being defeated it has not been destroyed. Defeat has brought along with it a modification, but an increase rather than a diminution of real power. Royalty, meaning by it either the central government or the representative of the majesty of the state, has been always on the advance. Order has been ever on the increase, and social relations have ever been becoming more determinate and fixed, social action and intercourse freer and more regular. The church, though shorn of some of its material splendors, has lost nothing of its spiritual power. Moral power has been continually gaining on brute force. France was more truly religious in the eighteenth century than it was in the eleventh. Feudalism had lost much of its exclusive dominion, but personal freedom and security, the ideas it represented, were much greater under Louis XIV, or James II, than under Saint Louis, or Henry III. Republicanism had not succeeded in establishing the communal regime; yet in the sixteenth century, we find a PUBLIC, and the burghers sitting in Parliament as one of the three estates of the realm, and exerting an influence on public affairs, almost infinitely greater than they did in the most palmy days of the communes.

Though all the elements of modern civilization existed and were at work as soon as the barbarian conquest had been effected, yet they existed separately and were at work each on its own account. Before modern civilization could achieve its destiny, all these elements were to be brought together and molded into an harmonious whole. They must needs go through a process of fusion. The governing forces, the church, royalty, and republicanism needed to be fused into one uniform power; and the feudal or conquering population, and the conquered or indigenous population, into a uniform population, in which every member should be free and equal to every other member. This was the work to be done. How far has it been accomplished?

One great imperfection in modern society has been the separation of church and state. The separation of church and state is the separation of morality and politics. The church, faithfully or unfaithfully, represents the ideas which belong to the moral order; the state represents those which belong to the social order. The church separated from the state gives us a moral, spiritual code indeed, but one which embraces no social idea, which in no wise regulates the intercourse of man with man, as a social being, or directs him to labor for the melioration or progress of society. The state separated from the church establishes a social order indeed, but a social order that embraces no moral idea, and which is supported by no appeals to conscience, or to a sense of justice inherent in man. It is founded on physical might, and is sustained by the sword, the *posse comitatus*, the dungeon, the scaffold, and the gibbet. The two, not united, but, blended into one, forming a unity rather than a union, give us a government resting for its support on moral power, and a social order founded on justice. The unity of church and state is the great desideratum. Now to this unity, we think, both church and state have been tending. This is what the Puritans had a presentiment of, precisely what Vane, the Fifth Monarchy men, and the Quakers sought to realize in the English Revolution of 1648.

There should be in no country two societies, one spiritual and the other political. During the past, this division has been doubtless the less of two evils; but it always marks an imperfect social state. Civil government should be instituted for the purpose of maintaining social order, and that social order too, which is founded on absolute justice; the means it makes use of to establish and maintain social order, should always be strictly moral, spiritual, holy. Its symbol should not be the sword, but the crosier. If this were the case, civil government would be as holy as the church has ever claimed to be. The church, as a governing or controlling body, would then be superseded, or rather, the state having become the church as well as the state, no separate church would be needed or admissible. Religion we should still have, preachers we should have, meeting houses we should have, but no ecclesiastical corporation. The duty of the preacher would cease to be that of gathering people into an outward, visible church, and become that of infusing into all hearts a love of goodness, and that of directing all minds to the decrees of strict justice, as the laws to be obeyed in all social and individual action. Clergymen might make public prayers, administer the sacraments, and wear a surplice or a black gown; but they would not constitute a separate class of men, organized into a distinct body, whose members must be accounted, *par excellence* men of God. They would be teachers of righteousness, men laboring to promote knowledge, justice, piety. Now this is precisely the condition to which, with us, both church and state are tending. The separation of church and state hardly exists in this country, especially in this Commonwealth, which stands as it should and as it becomes it, in the front rank of the advanced guard of the great army of progress. All the ecclesiastical establishments of this country are breaking up. The Episcopalians gain few converts to the doctrine of the divine right of bishops; the Methodist church has reached its culminating point, and its members, democrats as most of them are, will soon see that their church establishment is an engine which may be directed with but too much success against freedom. As soon as they discover this, they will abandon it, which they may do without abandoning their doctrines or their piety. The Presbyterian church is torn by intestine divisions, and is penetrated in all directions by Congregational notions, and it must ultimately adopt the Congregational form of church government, the only form of church government that can long coexist in harmony with democracy in the state. To the same result England and

France are tending. To no other end can tend the writings of the Abbé de La Mennais and his party.

Not only do we perceive an approximation to the unity of church and state but a sort of blending of royalty and republicanism. The notion that kings own their subjects, are their absolute lords and proprietors, is growing obsolete. Kings are beginning to be regarded as public officers, and royalty is considered, as we have said, the representative of the majesty of the state. The king is not considered now as governing for his own good, but for the public good. He is not above, but under law. The Republic, which may be said to represent the majesty of the people, is also under law. The people may do what they will, but not unless they will that which is lawful, right. All governments are now, at least in the principal states of Christendom, held to be public, to be instituted for the public, and to have it for their mission to make justice prevail. The question between monarchy and its rivals is merely a question of expediency, a question as to what form of government is most likely to secure the prevalence of justice. There is then a sort of fusion of the church, the empire, and the commune, taking place, and they must soon lose their opposition, and become one under the dominion of law—justice.

On the other hand, a similar fusion has been taking place in relation to the different populations of Christendom. At the beginning of the sixth century, all that part of Europe, which had been under the Roman dominion, was covered over by two distinct populations, one noble, and the other ignoble. The barbarians, with a very few exceptions, constituted alone the noble population. The native population, saving that portion of it which belonged to the ecclesiastical society, was ignoble, deemed an inferior and degraded race. It was the conquered population, and to that fact, to a great extent, must be attributed the ideas which the conquerors entertained respecting its inferiority. It was everywhere oppressed. It had no rights, no protection. All employments deemed noble or honorable, except those of the church, were reserved to its masters, the barbarian nobility. It could not meet the barbarian on equal terms. It could approach him only at a humble distance. It was in relation to the conquerors what the ancient Gibeonites were to the ancient Israelites, "hewers of wood and drawers of water." The distance between these two classes, two populations, was not to be passed at once. Not in one day was the slave to become the equal of his master, the serf, to stand up by the side of his lord, and all traces of conquest to be wiped out. Yet the distance between the two populations has been lessened. The two races have been brought together and so intermixed that their separation is henceforth impossible. Not all the noble families in France or in England can trace their descent to the conquerors. The descendants of the conquered have frequently risen to the highest ranks, and those of the conquerors have fallen in many instances to the lowest. The English of today are neither Normans nor Saxons, but a people formed from the union of both. Robert of Glocester says,

> The folk of Normandie
> Among us woneth yet, and shalleth evermore.
> Of Normans beth these high men thath beth in this land,
> And the low men of Saxons.

But this cannot be said now. Some of the "high men" in the land are of Saxon origin and some of the "low men" are of Norman blood. In France, the Franks are not now the exclusively noble. The Franks and the Gallo-Romans have commingled. There is now a French nation, as there is a French language. In this country, the fusion of the two populations is complete. We have no noble, no ignoble race. Saving the Negroes and Indians, not included in the civilized population, we know only one race; and we have adopted in state and in society, as well as in the church, the doctrine that "God hath made of one blood all the nations of men." Here few traces of the conquest are discernible. We recognize no distinction of ranks, no inferiority or superiority of classes. No honest employment unfits any one for any social circle, any office of honor, trust, or emolument. There is not here and there a baron with his army of retainers, bondmen and slaves. All are barons, that is, men. No man is more than man, and no one is less than man. At least this is our theory, though it must be admitted that our practice does not as yet fully conform to it. All Europe is tending to this same result. The distinctions of rank are wearing away; the prejudices of blood are losing their force; the burghers are up with the lords, and, in point of intelligence, influence, and social importance, even beyond them. The people have become the nation; royalty and nobility are their servants, and maintain themselves standing, only on the plea of the public good. The London Quarterly itself is forced to admit that De Tocqueville is right in saying that all Western Europe has been for several hundred years hastening to democratic equality. The progress is assuredly in that direction and no earthly power seems able to arrest it, or even for a moment to divert it from its course.

How has this change been effected? What are the causes which have produced it? Are these causes still in operation? And may we hope that they will be as efficient in accomplishing what remains to be done as they have been in accomplishing what has already been accomplished?

One of the most efficient causes of this change is Christianity. By Christianity, in this connection, we do not mean exclusively the church, but the new life revealed, the philanthropic movement commenced, by Jesus for humanity, and of which we have spoken in a foregoing article. Christianity surrounds every man with a bulwark of sanctity. It declares the unity of the human race, that God has made of one blood all the nations of men, and that all men are equal before him. This declaration cannot remain unfruitful. When it is once received, when the idea of man's worth as man, together with that of man's brotherhood to man, is once entertained, has once become a sincere, an earnest, a religious conviction, it becomes all-powerful for human enfranchisement. To the influence of this idea must be attributed the manumission of the slaves of modern Europe, which, in nearly all cases, has been the voluntary act of their masters, done from religious motives.

The church, properly so called, has done something. It opened its bosom alike to the children of both races. In the house of God, in its services for the sick and dying, and in its solemn funeral rites, the high men and the low men were reduced to a momentary level. They were alike amenable to its discipline; they alike partook of its sacraments, and alike might aspire, so far forth as their blood was concerned, to fill the highest offices in its gift. The perpetual presence of a society that recognized no distinctions of blood, which, so far as itself was concerned, declared all men as men, equal, could not fail to weaken the prejudice of race, and to attack all social inequalities. The bondman was not wholly vile in his own estimation, for he might hope that his son would find his way to the papal chair, and make the proud monarchs of the conquering race doff their diadems before him, and the most powerful of his oppressors court his favor and sue for his benediction. The passage from equality in the spiritual order to equality in the social order was neither long nor difficult, and more than once was it made by the simple-hearted and simple-minded peasants, under the guidance of the lower orders of the priesthood. An instance of this is in the Insurrection of the Peasants, in the time of Richard II of England, led on by Wat Tyler (Walter the Tiler), John Ball, a priest, Jack Straw, Hob Carter, and Tom Miller, all men of low origin.

This Insurrection of the Peasants is generally regarded as a war of the poor against the rich, and much is made of it against every man who comes forward in defense of what are termed the lower classes. If one speaks in favor of equality and bears his testimony against the inequality which obtains, but which ought not to obtain, between members of the same community, forthwith he is a Wat Tyler, or, in allusion to another leader of the peasants at a later day, a Jack Cade. Yet we own we have a sort of fellow feeling with this same Walter the Tiler, who led on his sixty thousand peasants towards London, singing,

> When Adam delved, Eva span
> Where was then the gentleman?

And we are inclined to think that no man somewhat in love with humanity should feel it a reproach to be called a Wat Tyler, or even a Jack Cade. Many a name is now banded about as a term of reproach, which will be seen one day to stand high on the calendar of saints.

These peasants attempted nothing for which they should be censured. Their condition at the time of their insurrection was anything but enviable. They were serfs in person and in goods, and obliged to pay enormous rents for the small piece of land on which they raised the means of supporting themselves and families, and which they could not abandon without the consent of their lord; whose husbandry, gardening, and labor of all kinds he chose to demand, they were obliged to perform gratuitously. The lord could sell them, their houses, their utensils of labor, and their children, born and even unborn. Their condition was worse than that of our Negro slaves; for our slaves are fed and clothed and taken care of in sickness and in old age; but these were obliged to take the same care of themselves that they would have been obliged to do had they been freemen, and at the same time to labor as much for their masters as our slaves do for theirs. Resentment of the evils inflicted on them by the oppression of the noble families, joined to a total forgetfulness of the fact that these noble families were of Norman origin, since they no longer called themselves Normans, but Gentlemen, very naturally conducted them from the injustice they endured to the injustice of servitude itself, independently of its historical origin. In the southern provinces, where the population was numerous, especially in Kent, whose inhabitants preserved a vague tradition of a treaty concluded between them and William the Conqueror, for the maintenance of their ancient franchises, there were strong symptoms of popular agitation near the beginning of the reign of Richard II. Expenses of the court and the gentlemen were great in consequence of the war which was then carried on against France, whither each nobleman went at his own charges, and where he sought to distinguish himself by the magnificence of his arms and equipage. The proprietors of the seigneurs and manors, loaded their farmers and villains with excessive taxes and exactions, alleging, as a pretext for each new demand, the necessity they were under of going to fight the French in France, to prevent them from making a descent on England. But the peasants said to themselves and to one another, "they tax us to aid the knights and country squires to defend their possessions; we are their bondmen; we are their flocks which they fleece; and yet, taking all in all, if England were lost, they would lose altogether more than we."

To such words as these, on their return from the fields, by the way, or in the clubs where they met in the evening, after the labors of the day were ended, succeeded words of far graver import. Some of the orators at these clubs were *priests*, who drew from the *Bible* their arguments against the social order of their epoch. "Good folks," said they, "things cannot and will not go right in England until there be no more villains, nor gentlemen; until all are equal, and the lords be no more masters than we. Why should they be? Why do they hold us in bondage? Have we not all, they and we, sprung from the same parents, Adam and Eve? They are clothed in velvet, and crimson, and fur; they have flesh-meat, and spices, and good wines, and we have only miserable orts to eat and water to drink. They have ease in their beautiful manors, and we have pain and labor, wet and cold in the fields." At such discourses as these, the multitude cried out in tumult, "There must be no more villains; we will be treated as beasts no longer; and if we work for the gentlemen, they SHALL PAY US WAGES!"

Surely this demand of the villains was by no means an extravagant one. It was simply that they should be no longer held in bondage, that they should henceforth be treated as men, not as beasts, and that they should receive wages. They made no war on the rich as such; it entered not into their minds that these estates, held by the descendants of the conquerors, had been unjustly wrested from their fathers; they had no thought of stripping the gentlemen of their property; they merely wished to be accounted freemen, and to be paid for their labor. Was this unjust, unreasonable? Certainly not. The lower classes have never been known to make an unjust demand. They always claim altogether less than their rights, and, we may add, the terror they inspire by their demands is always in consequence of their justice, and not their injustice. The lords and gentlemen have always seemed to hear, in the faint voice of the feeble peasant, the awful voice of God summoning them to judgment. The simple demand of these peasants not to be treated as beasts, and to be paid for their labor, struck all the upper classes of England with consternation. However, the peasants gained nothing. The day of their deliverance had not yet dawned. They were cajoled by a few lying words of the king, their leaders were killed, themselves dispersed, and fifteen hundred of their number put to death by the common hangman. Their movements have no great historical importance, except as showing that they drew their arguments for equality from the Bible; that they legitimated them on the ground of the unity of the human race, that high men and low men have the same parents, even Adam and Eve, and therefore are brethren and equals.

Christianity also did much to effect the change of which we have spoken, by its spirit of tenderness and compassion, by the generous and humane sentiments with which it sought to inspire men one towards another, and by encouraging the practice of the kindly charities of social and private life. It did much by exalting the sentiments; and it elevated the poor by giving them the assurance that though forsaken by men they were yet remembered by God, and though destitute, wronged, downtrodden here, they should be kings and priests hereafter. It did something too by inspiring the ministers of the church with courage to rebuke the king and the feudal lord, and to remind them, that the truest nobility they could aspire to was the practice of the Christian virtues.

Philosophy, or the spirit of inquiry, the desire for general intelligence, which had been kept alive by the church, and which took a new start after the feudal régime had become somewhat fixed, also contributed its share towards effecting the social change we have noted. The desire to philosophize, or to know the reason and nature of things, manifested itself in a striking degree in the twelfth century, and has been manifesting itself more and more strikingly ever since. The first subject to which it applied itself was theology. There was at first no disposition to disprove nor even to question the truth of theology but a craving to establish its truth on rational conviction, and not on positive authority. Abelard attempted to do this, and gave birth to the Scholastic philosophy, a philosophy more ridiculed than understood, and whose influence on the progress of society has been altogether underrated.

To the Scholastic philosophy succeeded the revival of letters, and the study of Grecian antiquity. The study of ancient literature and philosophy enlarged the modern circle of ideas, and introduced a more liberal and just mode of thinking into the affairs of the world. From the study of antiquity and the human mind, men passed to the study of nature, and opened a new career to science. Scientific discoveries followed in rapid succession, and gave a new face to war, commerce, and manufactures, which in their turn reacted upon the social state, and lessened its evils. No small portion of the evils of the lower classes was owing to their ignorance. As soon as they began to think, to find out that they had thinking faculties, and to use them, their condition was ameliorated. The lowborn man by means of intelligence became the equal of the highborn; he became a minister of state, an influential prelate, one of the real nobility of his country. By means of knowledge the two classes were occasionally brought into contact and the plebeian found himself the master of the patrician.

The habit of looking into the reason and nature of things soon disclosed the unreasonableness of the pretensions of the church, the illegitimacy of the authority of the Pope, and brought about the Reformation. It carried more intelligence and order into the administration of government, into legislative enactments, and the interpretation of laws, which produced in return something like social order, and gave something like security to persons and property, facilitated industry, and by that elevated the industrious class.

But the cause, to which, more than to any other, we are indebted for this change, is to be found in the rise, progress, and dominion of the moneyed power, represented and sustained by what we term the business part of the community Much is said against this power at present, and perhaps justly. It has attained its zenith. Businessmen have had their golden age. They have become the sovereigns of the world. Kings, nobilities, hierarchies, legislators, are their servants. The world, it may be, is growing weary of their dominion, and perhaps restless under the weight of their tyranny. A strong party is organizing itself against them; and in this country we are in the midst of a revolution which must overthrow the money-king, and inaugurate humanity. Nevertheless the money-king was once a slave, as vile a slave, as maltreated a slave, as any on whom kings and nobility trampled, and his accession to power marks the enfranchisement of industry. Whether desirous or not of prolonging his reign, we must all admit that his reign *has been* for the best interests of the human race.

Owing to conquest as the proximate, if not as the ultimate cause, the immense majority of mankind at an early day were reduced to a servile condition. Hence the reason why the workingmen, the manual laborers, the creators, in one view of the case, of all the wealth, comforts, and luxuries of a nation, are themselves, always and everywhere, poor, ignorant, degraded, accounted the lower class, an inferior order of being. This is owing to conquest, not, as the advocates of aristocracy ignorantly allege, to the natural inequality with which God creates men. The laboring class has been always the lower class, poor, and ignorant, and menial, because the tribe or nation to which it originally belonged was conquered by another tribe or nation, stripped of its possessions which went to increase the stock of the conquerors, reduced to slavery, and compelled to perform all the labor of the community, and by its labor to augment that stock still more.

Rome was conquered by the barbarians; the wealth of the Roman world, at least the greater part of it, passed into their hands; consequently the indigenous population was left destitute. Destitute of property, they were entirely at the mercy of their barbarian lords. Poor, dependent, enslaved, they of course must be regarded as inferior, and as unworthy as incapable of associating with the conquerors on equal terms. Poor, dependent, enslaved, regarded as inferior, as low, vile, they must needs be deprived of all means of improvement, excluded from what was held to be good society, and debarred from all opportunities of cultivating elegant manners and refined tastes. It needs no argument, therefore, to prove that they must cease to be dependent, that they must acquire some portion of this world's goods and a certain degree of leisure, intelligence, and refinement before they could claim to be of an equal race with those who constituted the upper classes. The laboring or conquered population could rise to a level with the conquerors, and thus regain their lost independence, only by the acquisition of wealth. They must become capitalists, proprietors. The man, who has nothing in this wide world that he can call his own, can hardly exhibit the bearing or the virtues of a man. A man must feel that he has something before he can feel that he is something.

This is not all. The laboring class, so long as they are doomed to perpetual toil, must needs be ignorant and brutish. They cannot take their place with the upper classes of society, until they have become intellectually, and in point of intelligence, their equals. But their equals they cannot become in the lowest depths of poverty. Great wealth is no doubt unfavorable to mental growth; but a certain degree of wealth is needed in order that the mind may have leisure to concern itself with something besides mere animal wants. The laborer must be able to live like a man, before he can think like a man, have a man's intelligence. The distinction between the upper classes and the lower, the conquerors and the conquered, could then be obliterated only by means of a physical amelioration of the lower or laboring class. The interests of this class, then, at first were necessarily identified with the moneyed interest. The first service to be rendered it was to open to it the road to wealth.

Now the road to wealth this depressed, enslaved population was obliged to open to itself, by its own efforts. Nothing was to be hoped from the upper classes. Whatever was obtained from them was to be obtained by main force. The conquerors will hold with all their power the conquests they have made. The conquered must rely on themselves alone. The odds are altogether against them. They are poor and naked, and the earth and nearly all the means of gain are in the hands of their masters. They are placed under almost every conceivable disadvantage. Nevertheless they must work out their own salvation; and by their own energy and perseverance rise from bondmen to freemen, and from slaves to be the sovereigns of the world. Their work is a great one, and ages must elapse before we can perceive that they have made any progress. Yet progress they do make; and after centuries of secret, silent working, ever interrupted, but ever beginning anew, perpetually thwarted, but never despairing, we see that they have made a mighty advance.

The plebeian population, on the establishment of the barbarians, though all equally vile, were not all in precisely the same condition. The agricultural portion was the most unfavorably situated. The land, whether cultivated or not, was all appropriated in the hands of a few, and for the most part locked up in entail. The agricultural laborers could therefore have no hope of becoming proprietors. All they could hope for was to be tenants on such terms as their masters should be pleased to grant. The inhabitants of the towns or cities were somewhat better situated. They were held to be as vile, as menial, and as far removed from freemen as were the villains or agricultural bondmen; but they were mainly tradesmen and artisans, who could manufacture articles for sale, and carry on a species of traffic with the upper classes themselves. The barbarian population, calling itself noble, disdained to be traders or handicraftsmen. Consequently trade and manufactures fell to the indigenous population, and of course to the inhabitants of the towns. Trade and manufacture, though insecure, subjected to innumerable risks, and loaded with vexatious and all but ruinous exactions, nevertheless enriched the traders and the artisans, who became in due time merchants and manufacturers. The mercantile and manufacturing population, as the most favorably situated for the acquisition of wealth, therefore take the lead in the enfranchisement of industry, and are the first of the conquered population to become free and independent.

Trade and manufactures require outlays, and when they are carried on to a great extent, they demand large capitalists. This gives rise to a division in the conquered population itself, a division between capitalists and simple operatives—a division which may one day lead to a war between capital and labor, but which at this epoch could work no ill. The amount of capital in the hands of the industrious class, including the mercantile and manufacturing portion, in comparison with that possessed by the feudal population, was exceedingly small, and it was necessary to concentrate it in as few hands as possible, in order to increase its productiveness and augment its power. It was so small that if equally distributed among the whole population, it would have been lost, at least have had no power to redeem the class. Every trader or manufacturer, who had capital which he invested in commercial or manufacturing enterprises, became a public benefactor because he was increasing the amount of wealth belonging to the industrious class and throwing into its hands the power with which it was one day to conquer equality with the feudal lord.

Trade and manufactures, though they did not distribute wealth equally among all the members of the industrious class, nevertheless augmented the gross amount of its wealth, enriched it as a class. But for them the capital of the world would have remained in the hands of the feudal society, in the hands of the nobility and of the church. In their hands it must have remained virtually unproductive. No addition to its amount would or could have been made. But just in proportion as capital came into the hands of the trader and the manufacturer, it became productive, and the wealth of the world was augmented. Individuals amassed large estates; but not by impoverishing others, as was the case when a nobleman became rich, or richer. The wealth they amassed they had called into existence; not, it is true, with their own hands, but by the profitable employment of the hands of others. In creating this additional amount of wealth, they did a real good, without doing any injury. The operatives they employed, indeed, did not become rich themselves, but they did not become the poorer. Their condition, on the contrary, was much improved. The laborer at wages, though his wages were below what they ought to have been, was in a condition altogether superior to that of a bondman, which he was before he became a workman at wages.

Trade gives a spring to manufactures. It finds out markets and thus creates a demand for them. By creating a demand for them, it aids their growth, calls a greater number of workmen into the factories. This in its turn increases the demand for agricultural products, and with this increased demand for the products of agriculture, agricultural labor rises in importance, and as a necessary consequence the agricultural laborer finds his condition improving. The smaller nobility, proprietors of a portion of the soil, turn their attention to the better cultivation of their lands, and take pains to increase their productiveness because they find a market for their produce or because they wish to obtain a larger supply of the articles furnished them by the merchant and the manufacturer. An additional amount of capital, a portion of that invested in land, is thus added to that employed in the interests of industry.

As the merchant and manufacturer, the tradesman and artisan, increase in wealth, they form a sort of middle class, or a class of commoners. Gradually they give to their children a decent education, and prepare them to compete, successfully in many respects, with the children of the nobility. Intelligence, polished manners, and refined taste are, after a while, associated with the names of some wealthy commoners. Some casual intercourse is commenced between them and the nobility.

A marriage between one of their daughters and one of the sons of the nobility, desirous of replenishing his estate, now and then occurs—and the process of amalgamation begins, never to cease till it becomes complete.

It is only by slow degrees that the money power is instituted, and businessmen obtain an influence in the affairs of the world. Businessmen require a fixed order, security for persons and property. They can do little for themselves or for the cause of industry when they can count with no tolerable certainty on a return for their outlays. Now through long ages of modern Europe, order, security for property or persons, there was little. The banker was not always a nobleman. The capitalist was not always a lord. From the fifth century to the tenth, moneyed men in no sense of the word constituted an aristocracy. No class of the community were more harassed or more exposed than they. Kings, lords, and bishops, harassed, vexed, taxed, despoiled them at their will. Nevertheless they contrived to prosper. Their wealth, power, importance, were ever on the increase. This is seen in the communal movement, in the eleventh, twelfth, and thirteenth centuries, of which we have already spoken. The burghers were then able, in a multitude of cases, to force the kings, lords, and even bishops, to grant them charters of incorporation, securing to them important privileges, and allowing them, within the walls of their town, to live under laws of their own making, and magistrates of their own choosing. Some, we are aware, pretend that these charters were granted to the towns, through the generosity or policy of the kings; on the one hand to aid the people, and on the other to secure their assistance in controlling the feudal lord, of whose power the kings were jealous. But they who attribute the least of the good, which they find the people enjoying, to the generosity or policy of kings, are the worthiest interpreters of history. Kings play a much less conspicuous part in the real history of the world than they do in the narratives of historians. The communal charters, in nearly all cases where they secured any important franchises, were obtained because the commune was powerful enough to conquer them, or rich enough to buy them. That the kings of France and of England as well as some of the great feudal lords and perhaps now and then a bishop did grant charters of incorporations to some old towns, and to some new ones, is very certain; but they did it as a means to obtain money. Whether, therefore, the burghers conquered or purchased their charters of incorporation, the fact of the charters being granted proves their growing importance, their increasing wealth, and their efforts to obtain a fixed order, favorable to trade and manufactures.

The communal movement failed before the end of the fourteenth century, and in the fifteenth century, the towns and boroughs, as a sort of petty republics, have no longer any significance. But the wealth and influence of the burghers or commoners have increased. They constitute now one of the three estates of the States-General. They were first compelled to send their deputies to the Parliament to vote the supplies demanded by the king, that the town or borough might be held to pay it, because voted by its deputy. But this, which was at first a compulsory duty, becomes with the improved condition of the commoners, a valued right, not to be surrendered, and the origin of representative government. The commons remembering that they originally voted supplies, and forgetting that they did it because compelled, and in the interest of the king, not of themselves, come to claim the exclusive right to vote them, and therefore become masters of the government, and from an estate, become the nation.

These, of course, are only loose hints on the influence of the moneyed power in elevating the plebeian class, in creating the commons, and in amalgamating the two populations which occupied the European territory at the commencement of modern history. We should be glad to be more explicit and minute; but we have been enough so for our present purpose. The moneyed power has been one of the great agents by which modern civilization has advanced, and the businessmen have contributed their full share to the progress of popular liberty. By means of trade and manufactures, the majority of the available wealth of Christendom has been thrown into the hands of the commons, and this has given the commons a preponderance in the government of the world. It must be added, too, that trade and manufactures have not robbed the feudal lord of the wealth they have placed in the hands of the commons. They have created it, and by so much augmented the wealth of Christendom, of the world. Having now, at least in England, France, and America, a majority of the wealth on their side, the commons are the real rulers. They have as a class risen from their degradation, broken the yoke of the conqueror, and recovered their independence.

The progress of society has brought up the industrious class as far as it was identified with the moneyed power. But the work of modern civilization is not completed. The feudal lord restrained the absolutism of the monarch; the moneyed power has restrained, supplanted, taken the place of the feudal lord, and made the government of the world pass from the hands of the soldier to those of the banker, and substituted the pen for the sword. But it places that government still in the hands of a class, not in the hands of humanity. It has brought up a much larger class than the old feudal nobility, and a class, too, which has come out from the bosom of the people and can claim no preeminence over them in point of blood or race; but still it leaves the immense majority below the proper estate of man. The distinction between the capitalist and the laborer now manifests itself and becomes an evil. Till the moneyed power had triumphed over the old nobility and lodged the government in the hands of the businessmen, the interests of capital and labor were one and the same. It was necessary to secure the victory to the moneyed power, in order to redeem the people, that population to whom the businessmen belong. That victory is gained; the class is redeemed, as a class; and the work now is to redeem the class *as individuals*, that henceforth the government of the world shall be in the hands of no class, but in those of humanity.

This new work was seriously begun with the American Revolution. The world had, here and there, attempted it before, but without success. It was attempted in England, in the seventeenth century, but the agricultural population were too weak to perform their share of it. The soil, or the greater part of it, was in the hands of the nobility, and its cultivators were too poor and too dependent. The work failed, or rather was suspended, adjourned. This country had been discovered. The land here was unappropriated. Its cultivators became its owners. The agricultural population here became, therefore, independent proprietors, without ceasing to be laborers. Their influence, and a powerful influence too, was therefore capable of being thrown into the scale, not, as in England, against the laborers in towns, cities, and factories, but against the power of any dominant class.

Our Revolution was effected not in favor of men in classes; not in favor of orders or estates; but in favor of man, men as integers. It marks a new epoch in human progress. The influence of capital, or the moneyed power, as the ruling power, had then ceased to be legitimate. Man, not money, was then to be sovereign; and the whole people, not the businessmen merely, were to hold the reins of government. But this was not fully understood at the time. Alexander Hamilton and his party thought matters stood as they ever had done, and that the moneyed power was still the legitimate sovereign. They were doubtless sincere. They had not that order of mind which is first to discern when old watchwords change their meaning. The country, in consequence of the war of the Revolution, was embarrassed with a national debt and the aid of the businessmen was needed to pay it off. A national bank was therefore established, and the money-king suffered to wear the crown yet longer. In 1800, an effort was made to dethrone the money-king, and enthrone the people, and attended with partial, which would have been complete, success, had it not been for the war of 1812. That war plunged us again into debt, and made it necessary, in 1816, to recall the money power. The debt is now paid off the nation owes not a cent; and the great contest has recommenced between capital and labor, or more properly, between man and money—between the moneyed power supported by the businessmen, and the entire people sustained by a majority of the agricultural and mechanical population.

It is not likely that this contest will be immediately ended, yet we cannot doubt the final result. Modern civilization has brought up the nobility against the king, and maintained them; it has brought up the businessmen against the nobility, enfranchised capital and capitalists, and sustained them; it now brings up the laborer, that portion of the plebeian class whose enfranchisement was adjourned, so as not to prejudice the interests of capital; and shall it fail now? It shall not. Humanity, from the depths of her universal being, utters the word, it shall not fail. The struggle may be long, arduous, and perhaps bloody; the oppressed may have to groan yet longer; the friends of humanity may experience more than one defeat; but they will never give over the struggle or despair of ultimate success. They have been too long victorious, and too often have they gained the victory, in darker days than these and with feebler forces than they now have at their command, to despair, or "bate a jot of heart or hope."

All classes, each in turn, have possessed the government; and the time has come for all predominance of class to end; for man, the people to rule. To this end all modern civilization has been tending, and for this it gives valiant battle today. Its forces appear to us as numerous, as well disciplined, as skillfully drawn up in battle array, as ever; and unless God has changed his purposes, and inverted the order of his Providence, it shall come off conqueror; and man be redeemed; and the work for his friends henceforth cease to be the melioration of society, and become that of perfecting the individuals of each successive generation, as they appear in time and pass off into eternity. This done, and the wish of the workingmen is fulfilled; the visions of the prophets are realized; and the prayers of the philanthropist are heard in heaven, and answered on the earth.

Religion and Politics

JULY 1838

A Review of Henry Whiting Warner's *An Inquiry into the Moral and Religious Character of the American Government* (New York: Wiley & Putnam, 1838)

*T*his is a work written with some ability, possibly with a sincere intention, and probably for a good end. Most religious people,—not accustomed to much reflection on the subject it treats,—will think it an admirable book, and be inclined to receive it as a sort of second Gospel. In our judgment it is the production of a man who has very little knowledge of religion in general, and none of Christianity in particular. The author designs to point out the relation which should subsist between Christianity and civil government, and to place certain matters, which have not hitherto been very well understood, in a new and clearer light; but so far as we can come at the results of his Inquiry, he merely makes "confusion worse confounded."

Who the author of this book is we know not;[1] but, be he who he may, we should like to know his name, that we might give him an immortality, which he has not secured to himself by this production. He belongs to the "Blue Ruin" party, both in politics and religion. He is a genuine croaker, though somewhat cunning, and withal, capable of croaking in a tolerable voice, and is less disagreeable than most of his family connections. Our country, to believe him, is assuredly ruined; the altars of religion are all desecrated; pestilential heresies are rife in the land; Socinians and Jews, and even Unbelievers, vote, and are sometimes voted for; and the awful visitations of God's wrath cannot be delayed much longer. One may almost fancy him a second Jonah, lately disgorged from some whale's belly, come to denounce divine judgments upon another Nineveh. The good people of America, it is devoutly hoped, may take warning and repent, ere the "forty days" be run out.

The sum of all his complaints is, he tells us, "that one way or another, that religion, which has given us a name among the states of Christendom, and which many of us deem essential to our future well-being, as a people, is everywhere *politically set at nought*; regarded as an outlaw to the institutions of the country; a feather in the scale of its interests; as useless, if not discreditable in public life; and in reference to the elective sovereignty itself not to be thought of!" Surely this is a grievous complaint. But on what facts does the author rest for its justification? And what kind of political recognition of religion does he demand?

The facts, which justify the complaint, and prove all here set forth, are: 1st. President Jefferson refused to appoint a fast when some of his political opponents wanted one, for the purpose of fasting over some of his political sins, and alleged in his own defense, that he could not find any power delegated to him by the constitution of the United States, authorizing him to interfere with religious doctrines, institutions, discipline, or exercise. 2dly. The refusal on the part of General Jackson to appoint a fast, to keep the cholera, when certain religious people requested him to do it. 3dly. The assertion of a United States Senator, that a reference to the Bible, in the Senate, as authority, was not fortunate, that book not being the statute book of that body. 4thly. The refusal on the part of Congress to stop the Mail from running on Sunday. 5thly. The fact, that the New York Legislature, during its last session, refused to appoint a chaplain. 6thly. The fact, that the Legislature of pious Connecticut debated the question, whether they would not do the same. 7thly. Electors do not inquire whether candidates for office are orthodox or not, and orthodox electors do sometimes vote for anti-orthodox, or heterodox candidates.

These are the facts which justify his complaint, and authorize him to call our government an irreligious one. What would he have as a remedy for evil? What kind of connection between religion and politics does he demand? A union of church and state? No; that is not to be thought of. Have the state become the servant of the church? Most likely; but he does not say so. Have the state decree a body of Divinity, which all must embrace, a ritual all must observe? No. What then? Enact that the Bible is the holy word of God; that no man who does not profess to believe it shall be eligible to any office; that to deny the existence of God, the truth of the doctrine of the Trinity, or the inspiration of the Old and New Testaments, is blasphemy, to be punished as a criminal offense; to prohibit by strong penal enactments all profane swearing, and all Sabbath-breaking, and to appoint fasts whenever the clergy or the church say the occasion demands them.

The author of the book contends that ours is a Christian commonwealth, and therefore infers that all which comes or may come under the denomination of Christian ethics should be legally enforced. He divides Christianity into two parts, *Ecclesiastical Christianity* and the *Ethics* of Christianity. The first belongs exclusively to the church, which is a body distinct from all civil polity, and raised infinitely above the reach of the civil legislature; it asks and will submit to no civil protection or control. The ethics of Christianity are binding on legislatures, and are proper objects of legislation; it is the duty of civil governments to respect them and to cause them to be respected.

That the government of this country is a Christian government, is inferred from the fact, that in no case is it positively declared not to be. The constitution of the United States repudiates some of the abuses of Christianity, but says nothing against Christianity itself. The first settlers of this country were Christians, and in nearly all cases designed to found a Christian commonwealth, and did found one. Nearly all the state constitutions originally recognized Christianity, and the greater part of them do it even now. Christianity is part and parcel of the common law of England, (doubted,) which was brought here by our fathers, and which is still in force. The majority are Christians; and as the majority have an absolute right to rule, it follows that they have a right to form a Christian commonwealth, and to insist upon Christianity as the religion of the government. Moreover, in practice, the government in all its branches, saving the cases of Presidents Jefferson and Jackson, the majority of the committee on Sabbath mails, the New York legislature, in dispensing with a chaplain, has always recognized Christianity, and respected it as the religion of the country.

Ours being a Christian commonwealth, it follows that our government must regard Christian ethics as its own, and that it can have no right to introduce Pagan, Jewish, or Mahometan ethics; and it also follows that none but Christians can really be citizens or members of the commonwealth. Governments are instituted to protect rights, not to create them; and its mission is to protect the rights of all its citizens. For this end the American government was instituted. It was instituted by Christians to nurse and maintain their rights as Christians. Christians did not institute it for Unbelievers, Socinians, and Jews, but for themselves. Its functionaries are then under no obligation to consult the prejudices, beliefs, or pretended consciences of these. These have no rights in a Christian commonwealth; and if they choose to live in one must take up with such franchises as Christians choose to grant them.

This, then, is the amount of freedom secured to us, or designed to be secured to us, by our boasted free institutions. It is freedom to Christians but to none others. The people here comprise not the whole population, but the Christian majority. Christians are the favored class. The rest are out of the pale of citizenship, are denied to have any rights, and are reduced to virtual slavery, liable at any moment to be prosecuted and punished as criminals. This is the doctrine of a professed Christian, and of a pretended friend of liberty! After avowing this doctrine, he has the effrontery to say Christianity is favorable to liberty! So is Christianity favorable to liberty, but not such Christianity, not such liberty as this.

The pretense set up by some religious people, that our government is a Christian government, that our commonwealths are Christian commonwealths, deserves more than a passing notice. Mischief lurks beneath it. If it be sustained, we undergo a revolution and must bid farewell to liberty. The several states or commonwealths, which form the confederacy of the United States, are not Christian commonwealths, in the sense in which our author and those who think with him, contend they are. The design of our fathers, when first landing in this country, was not to found a Christian commonwealth. The idea that brought them here was liberty, still more than it was religion. Their dominant idea was freedom. They wanted, and they aimed to establish, a free commonwealth. They may not have fully possessed their idea, they may not have generalized it to the extent it will bear, but nevertheless they have it from the first moment fermenting in them.

Religion and Politics

The age, in which the colonies were planted, was an age in which all great ideas appeared in a theological envelope. Our fathers wanted liberty. This was their first want. But they had no conception of a liberty worth having, not founded on justice. In this they were right. Liberty is derived from justice. But justice, in their minds, was Christianity, and Christianity was their theology and church polity. Hence the reason why Christianity held the place it did in the commonwealths they founded. Their mistake was a natural one, an inevitable one in their age. It consisted merely in taking their notions of Christian ethics as their measure of natural right, instead of taking, as we do, man's innate sense of natural right, as the proper measure of Christian ethics. If they disfranchised all but Christians, it was not because they sought to found a commonwealth for Christians alone, but because they regarded all who were not Christians, either as having not as yet risen to man's estate, or as having forfeited their rights as men, and fallen into the class of the guilty. They did not know, did not admit, that men were men, and possessed of all the rights of men, though opposed to the Christian faith, and they made that crime, which is not crime; but they did not do this to secure a monopoly to those who professed to be Christians, but to secure a liberty supported on justice, an order of government founded on their highest idea of Right, and maintaining it in the state.

That the real idea of our fathers was liberty, that liberty was the dominant idea of the institutions they founded, is evident from the history of these institutions. The institutions of a nation rarely if ever receive a new idea. The history of the nation is but the history of the practical development of the ideas with which it starts. A theocracy can never grow naturally into a government in which the interests of man are paramount to all others; a monarchy never softens down into an aristocracy, especially not into a democracy. The old nation is destroyed, and a new one takes its place, whenever a change similar to any of these is observed to occur. The natural growth of a nation is the natural unfolding of the ideas with which it begins its career. If theocracy had been the dominant idea of our fathers, if their leading design had been to found Christian commonwealths, then the natural growth of our institutions would have manifested this idea, this design, more and more clearly. But instead of this, the idea of liberty, of the rights of man, is the idea which has been gradually unfolding itself from our institutions. Every advance, every change has tended to bring out this idea.

The tendency from the first has been to prune away whatever conceals the majesty of man or overshadows his rights. Church membership was first made a prerequisite to citizenship, because at first it was thought none others were really men. But this is no longer the case, because we have ascertained that individuals, who are not church members, may be men. Property qualifications for the exercise of the right of suffrage have, in most cases, been abandoned; for it has been ascertained that a man has rights, though he have not property; religious tests have been dispensed with, not because the people have become less religious, but because it has been found that religious tests are inconsistent with the rights of man. In every case of amendment to our state constitutions, the idea of the rights of man has been brought out more clearly, and liberty extended or surrounded with new guarantees. This fact is decisive. It proves that freedom, not religion, is the dominant idea of our institutions. Our commonwealths are free commonwealths, rather than Christian commonwealths. Their genius is liberty, not Christianity, *anthropocratic*, if we may use the term, not theocratic.

Now, should we find in our institutions certain provisions favorable to a theocracy,—which we take it is what is meant by a Christian commonwealth, in the sense the term is used by this author and his friends,—we must regard them as exceptions, anomalies, which are not yet brought under the general rule, not as indications of their real character and design. All these provisions must be interpreted in favor of liberty,—as much in accordance with the genius of our institutions as they will bear. The fact, that the author finds some such provisions in the constitutions and laws of the several states, is not, and should not be regarded by him as proof, that our commonwealths are Christian commonwealths, in his sense of the term; but merely as a proof, that many of our ideas are yet in their theological envelope, and that we have not brought all our constitutional and statutory provisions into perfect keeping with our great, our dominant, idea of liberty.

Assuming then, as we do, that the great idea, the genius, of our government, is that of a government instituted for nourishing and maintaining the rights of man, we deny that a Christian, as such, has any preeminence over any other man. We speak now of Christianity as a positive system of religion, a positive institution. In this sense Christianity is younger than man. Man existed in all his integrity and with all his rights as a man, before it was instituted. His rights as a man are older than his claims as a Christian. They are not derived from Christianity, they are not dependent on Christianity; then their enjoyment and exercise cannot be made to rest, under a government which professes to recognize and is bound to maintain them, on the fact of embracing Christianity. Give Christianity, or take it away, man and his rights remain the same. Governments, then, that are instituted for the purpose ours are, have precisely the same rights to recognize and maintain in the case of him who is not a Christian, as in the case of him who is. If there are any provisions in the constitutions and laws of our several states in opposition to this, they are inconsistencies, incongruities made null and void, in justice, by the genius of our institutions.

It behooves professed Christians to beware how they controvert this position. On what ground will they do it? On what ground will a man pretend that he has a right to be a Christian, if he denies to his brother the right not to be one? The right of any one to be a Christian can be legitimated only by the admission of that more general right of every man to choose his own religion. And, as religion is in all cases a matter of opinion, of belief, the right of a man to choose his own form of religion can be legitimated only by admitting a right still more general, that of the entire liberty of every man to form and express his own opinions. This last right is virtually recognized and secured in those constitutional provisions which guarantee us the freedom of speech and the press. The greater always includes the less. It would be absurd to admit that we have the liberty to propagate by speech or by the press our opinions, whatever they may be, and yet to deny us the right to form our opinions by the free action of our own understandings.

The Christian claims protection under our government, not by virtue of the fact that he is a man, and because it is one of the rights of man to be protected in the peaceable enjoyment of his religious belief. If he withhold this right from another, if he prohibit another from the free enjoyment of his religious belief, then he denies that this right to the enjoyment of one's own religious belief is one of the rights of man. In doing this, he denies his own right as a man to be a Christian, and bases his right to protection in his religious faith on mere accident, on the accident that he lives under a government favorable to his views, or that he has the good fortune to be of the majority. But, if he claim his protection on the ground that he is a man, and ought not to be molested in his belief, then his plea is equally good for every other man, whatever may be that other man's belief.

Lay down the rule that government has a right to protect one belief in preference to another, or to make any exceptions to a man in any case on account of his belief, and where shall we stop? If the state may declare it necessary to believe in a God in order to be a citizen with all the rights and immunities of a citizen, then it may declare what God must be believed in, whether it must be the Hindu God, the Greek and Roman God, the Jewish God, the Mahometan God, the Catholic God, the Calvinistic God, the Materialist's God, or the Spiritualist's God. If it may do this, it may do more. It may declare the Bible to be the word of God; and if this, still more; it may determine the interpretation that may be put upon the Bible; it may decide whether the Trinitarian or the Unitarian commentators shall be the orthodox commentators, whom it is lawful to read. In fine, once begun, there is no stopping place, this side of absolute religious despotism. Is our author in favor of this? O no. The doctrines of religion belong to the church, and the state may not meddle with them. What then? He merely asks that Christians be protected in their religion. What, protected in the enjoyment of their religion, as all men are protected in their opinions? If this be all, he asks nothing unreasonable; but he asks what he already has. This, however, is not all. He asks as a Christian to be protected in his religion, not only so far as concerns his own freedom of professing it, but also in preventing any body from opposing it. He thinks it a grievous wrong that in this country, where the majority are Christians, he must submit to hear the truth and sacredness of that religion, he embraces and reveres, questioned and even ridiculed. He wishes not that any body should be required by law to believe it, but merely that nobody shall be permitted by law to oppose it, and that whoever does oppose it shall not only be without note, but also without civil rights in the commonwealth.

Very well. On what grounds does he make this modest demand? Is what he asks one of the rights of man? Does he claim it on the ground that he is a man, and therefore has a right to profess his faith without being opposed or questioned? If so, his plea is equally available in the case of any one who adopts a different faith. If the atheist may not question his faith in God, then may he not question the atheist's faith in no God. If the disbeliever in the inspiration of the Old and New Testaments may not speak against his belief in that inspiration, what right has he to speak against disbelief in it? If he have a right to demand that the legislature decree it blasphemy to deny the doctrine of the Trinity, the Unitarian has an equal right to demand that it decree it blasphemy to assert it. Will our author do as he would be done by, treat the beliefs and disbeliefs of others as he would have his own treated? Not at all. He wants a preference shown to himself and all of his way of thinking. Very well, we say again. But we beseech him to tell us on what ground he legitimates his right to the preference he demands. Not on the simple ground that he is a man, for all men are equal as men, and he must give what he asks to receive, and this excludes all idea of preference. On what ground then? That his faith is true, and therefore must not be opposed? But they, who oppose him, say his faith is false, and therefore ought in justice to truth and Humanity to be opposed. Why shall the government credit him rather than them?

But our author claims this preference to his faith, because it is the faith of the majority. The majority are Christians; and as the majority have a right to rule, they have a right to enact that their religion shall be respected as the religion of the country, which may not be lawfully denied. But will he admit the soundness of this argument? We ask why the majority have any more right to decree that their religion is the religion of the land, than the minority have to decree the same thing of theirs? We should like to know why a man has any more right to have his religion respected, because he is in the majority, than he would have, if he were in the minority? Are the rights of man matters dependent on the will of the majority? Does one's rights as a man vary as he chances to be in the majority or in the minority? What may be one's rights to-day, then, may not be one's rights tomorrow, for majorities may change.

Our author, we presume, is a Christian as he understands Christianity. There are countries in which Christianity is in a feeble minority. Suppose our author should have his lot cast in one of those countries, would he think that it would be wrong for him to profess his religion there, or that it would be right, if born there, that he should not be permitted the freedom of the commonwealth, because the majority embraced a religion different from his own? Jesus and the Apostles were once a small minority, a little band with the whole world against them. Were they justified in opposing the religious notions of the majority? and were those Roman laws wise and just, which required the early Christians to respect the pagan Gods? Luther and Calvin were in a small minority; they denounced the religion of the majority. Were they right, or were they wrong? The author has arraigned the report of the majority of the committee of Congress on Sunday Mails. As that report was the report of the majority, would our author, had he been on that committee, have deemed himself justified in making a minority report against it? Had he been in Congress at the time, would he have spoken against it, in the minority, as he would have been? Nay, was he not there? and did he not make a speech there against the opinions of the majority of the House? This book reminds us very much of a certain speech made on the occasion by a distinguished Senator from New Jersey, who, for aught we know may be its author. But what right would he have had to say anything against the opinions of the majority? If the majority have a right to prohibit all speech against their opinions, the rule is absolute; and it applies to the majority of a committee, or of Congress, as well as to any other majority. Will the author follow his doctrine to this, its logical result? If not, where will he stop? Why stop there, rather than somewhere else?

We have spoken of the rights of man. Now the rights of man go with man wherever he goes. He does not acquire them by being in the majority, nor does he forfeit them by falling into the minority. The Christian has a right to be protected in his honest belief, and in the peaceable exercise of his religion, worship are individual matters; and so long as they are not made pretexts for injuring the rights of others, the individual has a perfect right to enjoy them. It is the grossest tyranny, either by legislative enactments or by public opinion, to make him suffer for them. If the Christian has the right, as a man, to defend his honest belief, the Deist, the Jew, the Atheist must have the same right. A law making it criminal to disavow faith in God, in the Scriptures, or in the Trinity, is as much an infringement upon the rights of man, as a law making it criminal to profess to believe either one or the other. If one man has as much right to avow atheism as has theism, one must have as much right to speak against theism as the other has against atheism. If the majority today have a right to decree that Christianity is the religion of the country, and to make it criminal to speak against it, it may decree, if it choose, the reverse tomorrow. If the majority have the absolute right to rule, it has the same right to make a law against asserting the existence of a God, that it has against denying his existence. All which our infidels want then to justify them in making strong penal enactments against Christianity, is merely to become the majority. Has our author thought of this?

Christianity itself is decidedly against this author. It recognizes the great brotherhood of men, and teaches that all are equal. It teaches this when it commands us to do unto others as we would have others do unto us. This command can be legitimated only on the ground that man is everywhere equal to man. Man being everywhere equal to man, it follows that whatever it is proper for one man to do by another, it is proper that other should do by him. Men are men, whatever their beliefs. The respect one claims for his belief, he must show to the belief of others. This is the Christian law. Our author as a Christian is bound to obey it. As he would have infidels treat his belief, so let him treat theirs then. If he does this, how can he demand the preference to be shown to his faith by the government, which he has pointed out, and on which he so earnestly insists?

The writer falls into the common mistake in relation to liberty of conscience. He thinks he has a right to enjoy liberty of conscience, and that his conscience, as a Christian, should be respected. Is he not correct, justifiable in this? But he forgets that other men have consciences as well as he, and that government is as much bound to respect their consciences as his. He forgets that to construe one's own liberty of conscience, so as to interfere with another's liberty of conscience, is to misconstrue it.

We hold to liberty of conscience. Conscience we regard as the supreme law, for the individual, in all cases whatsoever. It is more ultimate than the *lex scripta*, that the *lex non scripta*, of paramount authority to all creeds, confessions, rituals, dictates of fashion, public opinion, or decrees of the majority. It is to the individual, the voice of God, which he may not disregard without sin, and which he is bound to follow, though it lead to reproach, poverty, the dungeon, the scaffold, or the cross. But by the very fact, that we recognize the supremacy of the individual conscience, we necessarily restrict the sphere of its supremacy to the individual himself. Conscience cannot be divided against itself. Consequently the persuasion one may have, which would lead him to force or restrain the exercise of conscience in another, can never be conscience. The liberty of conscience in each individual must then be always so construed as to leave an equal liberty in every other individual. They pervert conscience, who make it the plea for exercising a control over others, which they will not suffer others to exercise over them. One's conscience leads him to observe the Sabbath. It is well. Let him obey his conscience. But let him at the same time remember that he must not impose his conscience on another. That other has a conscience of his own, which is his supreme law.

Our author we suppose would, in part, admit this. But he does it on the ground, that unbelievers have no conscience. We shall not dispute this ground. We should prefer to question, whether he who assumes it has a conscience or not. The man who really supposes that unbelievers are destitute of moral feelings and moral judgments, or who supposes them in general less conscientious than Christians, has no right to set himself up as one capable of instructing the commonwealth. If he assert it without seriously believing it, what is his own conscience worth? Unbelievers are to be compassionated because they want that serenity of soul, that inward repose which faith alone can give; but we are never to suppose them necessarily more deficient in the moral qualities of human nature than the rest of mankind. Indeed, in the majority of instances, we presume, the unbeliever is so called, because he has more faith than his neighbors. We shall make little progress in the work of converting unbelievers to Christianity, till we learn that they are men, to be respected and loved as brothers. The arguments which will convince their understandings, or win their hearts, are not those which exclude them from the freedom of the commonwealth, and deny them to be human beings. Christianity is most grievously wronged when we make it the pretext for imposing on others burdens, which we would not submit to have others impose on us. Jesus wept with unbelievers, and died on the cross that they might have faith in man and in God. It was in enduring, not in inflicting, legal penalties, that the early Christians arrested the attention of the world, and prepared the way for its conversion.

"Our fathers," says this author, "had no conception of some of the modern notions of what are called state-rights; and I believe they would have stood amazed at the kind of suggestion now current in the country, that a government, such as they have left us, so respectful of the rights of man, ought yet to be administered with as little avowed deference as possible for those of the Supreme Being." What is meant by the rights of the Supreme Being? Are governments instituted for God, or for man? Is it their especial province to guard the rights of God? Does

God stand in need of human governments, and look to them for protection? God is his own guardian, his own avenger. He asks no aid of man, no human arm to be raised in his defense. But suppose it not so, we would ask, how can we better respect his rights than by protecting those of his children? If we have studied Christianity to any purpose, it teaches us that we serve and honor God by loving and serving his children, our brethren.

Our author contends that we ought to respect Christianity legally, politically, because Christianity is favorable to liberty. If he means by this that our laws should be enacted and administered in accordance with the great principles of justice, meekness, and love, which constitute the essence of Christianity, assuredly we have no controversy with him. We contend earnestly, in season and out of season, for the same. But if he means that Christianity is to be recognized legally, politically, in its character of a positive religion, we do not agree with him. Religion is an individual concernment. It is what there is most intimate and holy in man. Governments have no right to interfere with it. They must put off their shoes when they approach it, and stand in awe before it, as Moses did before the Burning Bush. Its place is in the interior sanctuary of the individual heart, where it should be screened from all human observation, save as it manifests itself through a sweet and gentle, a just and beneficent life.

Christianity, no doubt, forms the moral sense of this community, and therefore should always be consulted by government and its functionaries; but it is Christianity only as the religious name for what we usually term natural morality, or in its broadest sense natural right. In this sense, nearly all men embrace it, and all desire to have it respected. But to conclude from this to legal and political sanctions, either to the dogmas or discipline of Christianity, as a positive system of religion and ethics, though our author does it, is bad logic. He concludes from this, if we understand him, though he says not so in just so many words, that the denial of the existence of God, of the inspiration of the Bible, profane swearing, and Sabbath-breaking, should be deemed offenses against the peace of the community. Here is his error. He will find few atheists or deists, who will question the Gospel morality, or who will differ with him in any rational interpretation of natural justice. The moral worth of men, so far as regards their actions towards one another, is not to be judged of by their faith, or their want of faith, in moral or religious codes. Unbelievers, saving the positive duties of the church, are, in general, as good Christians as Christians themselves. They have as warm a love for man, take as much interest in the progress of man and society, are as honest, as upright, as conscientious, as believers. They are no more immoral, unless conventionalism be called morality, than any other class of the community. The charge of licentiousness brought against them, if understood to mean licentiousness in regard to natural morality, or even the moral precepts of the Gospel, cannot be sustained.

The error of our author, and those who agree with him, is in confounding *natural* and *positive* morality. Natural morality is that which is founded in human nature, and is the same wherever man is; positive morality rests merely on arbitrary authority, and varies with time and place. The former is immutable, save that it is more fully comprehended in proportion as civilization advances; the latter varies with the opinions, fashions, and usages of different ages and countries. The one comes from within, the other from without. The first is developed, the last is imposed. Now the first is the only morality that may be legitimately recognized by government. All legislation in this country has reference to it, and professes to aim at its realization. So far as this morality is concerned, and this is Christian morality,—the Gospel being, as Bishop Butler well remarks, only a republication of the law of nature, all men of whatever sect, party, or religion, agree that it may and should be legally and politically recognized. The dispute is in reference to the positive morality. Positive morality, as our author understands it, acknowledges no man to be moral, who does not admit the existence of God, the inspiration of the Old and New Testaments, and the doctrine of the Trinity; who does not keep the Sabbath holy, refrain from profane swearing, and maintain some form or other of public worship. The several moral qualifications here implied he requires in every candidate for office, and all these are to be enjoined and enforced by law, not under plea of maintaining religion, but that of maintaining morality. He wishes every man, who does any one of the things here prohibited, or neglects any one here enjoined, to be declared by law an offender against the peace of the commonwealth, and punishable as such. And he alleges that he and his friends cannot enjoy their rights of conscience, unless it be so. Now, if he will reflect a moment, that all these injunctions are injunctions of positive, not of natural morality, resting upon an arbitrary authority for their obligation, he must see that they cannot be legally recognized and enforced, without denying all freedom of opinion. Whether they have anything to do with real worth of character or not, is a matter of opinion. They are not felt to be universally obligatory. This man may contend for them, that one may oppose them. I may believe that I ought to be just and merciful, to do no harm, and to, do all the good I can, and I may labor to be true to my faith; yet I may regard all this positive morality as of no binding force, and think that I am at liberty to observe it or not, according to my own convictions. Bring in the government now with its positive law, and it reduces me to slavery. If it may command me to observe the first day of the week as holy time, it may enjoin any religious observance it pleases. If it may forbid me to labor on that day, if it may command me to attend church on that day, it may tell me on what days of the week I shall plough my ground, what days hoe my corn; indeed prescribe to me every act of my life, I am permitted to do, and the time and manner of doing it. The same may be said of all the other particulars specified.

The only safe rule is for government to confine itself to natural morality, and leave positive morality to every one's own conscience. They who believe in the Trinity ought to be protected in the enjoyment and expression of their belief; they who do not believe it, should have full liberty to oppose it. So of all other matters of belief. They who regard the first day of the week as holy should have the right to keep it holy, but not, as they claim to have, the right to force those to keep it holy who do not regard it as holy. They who reverence the Bible should have full liberty to reverence it, but no authority from government to exact reverence from those who do not believe it worthy of reverence. It may hurt the feelings of Christians to hear it spoken against, and so may it hurt the feelings of unbelievers to hear their favorite books spoken against; and if it be blasphemy to hurt the feelings of the one, there is no reason in the world why it should not be blasphemy to hurt the feelings of the other. If the Christian demands a law prohibiting unbelievers from reviling his sacred books, he must submit to a law prohibiting him from reviling the sacred books of unbelievers. He has not always done this. He has said as hard and as malignant things against the Age of Reason, as believers in the Age of Reason have ever said against believers in the Bible.

We are aware that this rule, so far as government is concerned, places men of all opinions on a par, and gives the Christian no legal or political advantage over the infidel. Shall the Christian object to this? Shall the Christian ask for a legal and political advantage over his unbelieving brother? Has he not God and truth on his side, and is not this advantage enough? Has he not also the majority, fashion, public opinion on his side; all the schools and colleges and most of the means of influence in his hands; and does he ask for more? Shall the Christian intimate that he is unwilling to meet the infidel on equal terms? Let him blush then to call himself a Christian. *He* is the infidel who wants faith in Reason, and fears to trust it.

It is often alleged that atheism is incompatible with the stability of government, and the peace and welfare of the community, and may therefore be punished as an offense. We have not the space to enter far into the matter involved in this statement. We hold that no government can have any right to maintain itself by the sacrifice of private right. The powers of government are not made up from the individual rights surrendered to it. The notion that individuals give up a portion of their natural rights to society, in order to secure protection for the remainder, is a false notion. Government is not a contract, a bargain. It rests on Divine Right. The Jus Divinum must be reasserted, if there be any government to be maintained. The magistrate is ordained of God. Define the legitimate powers of government, and those powers are sacred, and are derived from God. But as they are derived from God, they can never be in opposition to individual rights, which are also derived from God. If then we have established the fact, that a man has a natural right to profess atheism, the consequences of professing it, to the government, be they what they may, can never invalidate one's right to profess it. The good of the community may be consulted and ought to be; but only in harmony with the good of each part. The greatest good of the greatest number is not the end to be sought, but the greatest good of the whole. The few may never be sacrificed to secure the safety and well being of they many. No individual, however lowly may be overlooked. No individual can ever be without significance; and whenever the rights of one individual are disregarded, be the end what it may, the rights of every individual and of the whole community are invaded.

But let this pass. Atheism, we deny to be dangerous to communities, and we might quote as high authority for our assertion as that of Lord

Bacon, but that we are not much given to quotations. An atheistical community cannot be found. The history of our race contains the record of no such community. Mankind almost universally regard the atheist with horror. This horror, which we naturally feel at the denial of God, and the declaration of our own orphanage, is a sufficient protection against the spread of atheism. If it were a seducing doctrine, one, to the profession of which there were many and strong temptations, then it might, perhaps, be necessary to consider whether we have the right to suppress it. It has hitherto been rarely if ever professed for its own sake, but because it has been a refuge from oppression. Men oppressed, despoiled of their possessions and their rights, overwhelmed with the weight of tyrannical kings, nobilities, and hierarchies, professing to reign in the name of God, and by divine ordination, have sought relief in atheism, and denied God, that they might shake off a tyranny which had become too grievous to be borne. Give the atheist perfect liberty to profess his atheism, take away from him the conviction that in professing it he is warring against an arrogant authority, and he will himself be disgusted with it, and no longer have any wish to profess it. When men are permitted to see in God a father, they have no disposition to deny him; and when they see belief in him drawing mankind together as brothers, they will love that belief and do their best to acquire it.[2]

Similar remarks may be made in regard to Sabbath-keeping and attendance on public worship. The first question is always, whether the government have a right to enforce them? The Sabbath, it is said, should be kept holy, but they only will keep it holy who believe it to be holy time, law or no law;—and they who believe it to be holy time will keep it holy, although not legally enjoined. They who believe in the propriety of public worship, and who would profit by attendance on it, will attend it, if they can. They who do not believe in its propriety, and have no relish for it, would not worship, though compelled to attend the places of worship. Religious worship, to be acceptable, must be free and sincere. If it be not offered freely, from the spontaneous promptings of the heart, it can have no worth. All laws, having for their object the enforcement of religion, or a respect for its ordinances, are therefore useless in the case of those who are religious, and can only produce hypocrisy in the case of those who are not. And hypocrisy, in our estimation, is a much more heinous sin in the sight of God, than Sabbath-breaking, or neglect of public worship.

We have spoken, as we have, from no indifference to religion or to its ordinances, but from the over-flowings of our zeal for Christian freedom. We would by no means encourage atheism, Sabbath-breaking, non-attendance on public worship, or the habit of elevating to office men deficient in high moral and religious worth. But we are convinced that the best way to secure belief in the existence of God, reverence for religion, its ordinances, and the practice of the Christian virtues, is for Christians to be just, to respect all the rights of man, and to attempt to secure no legal or political advantages to themselves. We would leave religion perfectly free, and rely solely on arguments addressed to the reason and the conscience for its maintenance and prosperity.

The disposition on the part of churchmen to arrogate to themselves rights, they will not concede to others, the practice believers indulge of denouncing unbelievers, treating them with bitterness, scorn, and contempt, of ridiculing their notions and their writings, publishing from the pulpit and the press gross exaggerations of their doctrines, and utter falsehoods about their personal characters, the low and vulgar rank to which they seek to sink them in the social scale, and their unwillingness to respect them for what is just and true in their doctrines and characters, may be set down among the chief causes of existing indifference to religion, and the spreading infidelity, which every true Christian deplores; and till the church become Christianized, and professed Christians imbibe the spirit and follow the example of their Master, it will be of little avail to demand laws against unbelievers and Sabbath-breakers, to speak against infidels, or to labor for their conversion.

The American Democrat

JULY 1838

A Review of J. Fenimore Cooper's *The American Democrat, or Hints on the Social and Civic Relations of the United States of America* (Cooperstown: H. & E. Phinney, 1838)

The creator of *Natty Leatherstocking* and the author of the *Bravo* can hardly write a book that shall be read without interest, or fail to deserve the respectful consideration of his countrymen. He possesses talents of a high order, is not wholly without genius, and has, in the course of his reading and travels, amassed much useful information. He has contributed something to American literature, and gained a name that will not be forgotten for some time to come.

It would be interesting to ourselves, and perhaps to our readers, were we prepared to do it, to enter into the consideration of Mr. Cooper's merits as a writer, into a critical examination of his works, and some speculations as to their probable influence upon the thought and literature of this country. The thing is to be done, and will be done; but is not for us, at present at least, to do it. His earlier novels amused us; his later productions have done something to quicken our thinking powers, and to instruct us.

We have a high regard for Mr. Cooper, for his love of independence, and his willingness to hazard his literary reputation in the cause of the people. We respect him for the fact, that he had the moral courage to approve and defend some of the measures of General Jackson's administration, and those measures, too, the most assailed by that portion of the community on which literary men are thought to be the more immediately dependent, and with which they are the more intimately connected. We respect him for his rebellion against Cant, for his earnest defense of individual freedom, and his manly assertion of every individual's right to form and express his own opinions, without being called to an account, abused, insulted, injured in his person, feelings, or reputation, for so doing. We respect him because he loves his country, and would make her true to the democratic creed she avows, as independent on foreign nations in her thoughts, as she is in her politics. In these particulars at least, he deserves the gratitude of his countrymen, and we trust he will receive it. He is willing to be known as a democrat, and the literary man, not ashamed to be called a democrat, in this democratic country, deserves to be held in more than ordinary consideration.

The work before us is written with ability, in a clear, strong, and manly style, and handles a subject with great freedom and with much justice, on which American citizens,—shame to say,—need to be instructed. Mr. Cooper thinks he sees two tendencies among us, which are alike dangerous to the stability and beneficial working of our free institutions. The upper classes, the affluent, the fashionable, he thinks are somewhat Anti-American in their thoughts, principles, and affections. They do not accept heartily our free institutions, and set themselves seriously at work to develop the practical good they contain. They imbibe too readily the notions as the fashions of foreign countries, especially of England, and sigh to reproduce an order of things, which can never exist, and which ought never to exist on this continent. They magnify the evils of the American system of government and society, and laud beyond measure the excellences of the monarchical or aristocratical institutions of the Old World. "Fifteen years since," he says, "all complaints against our institutions were virtually silenced, whereas now it is rare to hear them praised, except by the mass, or by those who wish to profit by the favors of the mass."

The lower classes, or the mass, he thinks, are governed by an opposite tendency, which is pushing them to a dangerous extreme. Notions that are impracticable, and which, if persevered in, cannot fail to produce disorganization, if not revolution, are getting to be widely prevalent; and there is a multitude who are looking ahead in the idle hope of substituting a fancied perfection for the ills of life. This disorganizing tendency in the mass, he thinks, if not arrested, will check civilization, destroy the arts and refinements of civilized life, and reduce us all to a dead level of barbarism. This book, it may therefore be readily conjectured, is a double battery, charged alike against those who believe too much in the past, and those who believe too much in the future. The author aims to demolish those who have too much democracy and those who have too little. To be democratic over much, is ungentlemanly, and may lead to a kind of leveling not agreeable to those who are ambitious of being distinguished, and to be democratic not enough, is unwise, not to say absolutely foolish.

This is, no doubt, to a certain extent, true, and the author's efforts to recall his countrymen from extremes, and to induce them to maintain the golden mean, are, no doubt, praiseworthy; but that they will be successful is not altogether so certain. Men in masses, as well as in their individual capacity, are logicians, and have an irresistible tendency to push their first principles to their last consequences. They can never be arrested by being pointed to the dangerous extremes into which they are running. Wise, practical observations are useless. The masses go where their principles logically developed require them to go. To arrest them we must change their principles, alter or enlarge their premises. But this is what Mr. Cooper has not done, and what he has not attempted to do. He does not seek for the causes of these opposite tendencies to dangerous extremes, to point out the defects in our first principles, and by changing our logical direction, to change also our practical direction. He does not appear to believe that the practice of a nation is merely its experimenting in verification of its theory, or the mere practical application of its theory. Change the theory, the philosophy of a nation, its ideas, and you change its history. But Mr. Cooper has no faith in theories, no love for the abstract. He affects the character of a wise man, who has seen the world; of a shrewd observer, who is above the speculations of the student, and not at all dependent on closet thinkers. He has seen, and he knows. He is a common sense man, and says, away with your visionary theories, and let us have a little common sense. All this is very well. Common sense is unquestionably a very excellent thing, and Mr. Cooper, no doubt, has it; but if it be *common* sense, we see not why we may not claim it as well as he. We think he ought to pronounce the word with fewer airs, for, if what he calls common sense, really be common sense, it must be common to all men, and he can in no wise claim a monopoly of it.

Again; Mr. Cooper, though he abjures all theories, and has many a biting sarcasm at theorizers in general, is himself a theorizer, and that too of no commendable sort. Does he not theorize, when he lays it down as a general proposition, that common sense is worthy of credit? Does he not theorize, when he declares this notion is practicable and that is not? When he tells us this amount of equality may be attained, and this other amount cannot be? He affects to have analyzed the powers of the human mind, and to have ascertained how much it is wise to aim at, and what it is merely visionary to attempt. And what are his views on these matters, but the theories he has adopted respecting the Desirable and the Undesirable, the Wise and the Foolish, the Attainable and the Unattainable? Has he not speculated in coming to his conclusions? or has he jumped to his conclusions? And is it his theory that all men ought to jump to their conclusions? If so, we say he is a theorizer, whom a wise man may well hesitate to follow. Mr. Cooper does not, we must needs think, prove himself so wise in declaiming against theorizing, which is in fact declaiming against reasoning, reflection, as he fancies; and his common sense, we imagine, may, in many instances, be found to be very uncommon sense, a very peculiar sense, even an idiosyncrasy.

This is not all. The man who is accustomed to analyze the works he reads, and reduce them to their lowest denominations, will, without much difficulty, perceive that Mr. Cooper's common sense rests, in most cases, for its support on the philosophy of Hobbes. We presume he has never read Hobbes, perhaps he has never heard of him, certainly, we presume, is unconscious of ever coinciding with his philosophic theory. But Hobbes's philosophy is, in political matters, the common sense of most Englishmen and Americans; and all Englishmen and Americans, who eschew philosophy and professedly follow common sense, are sure to be Hobbists. Mr. Cooper, we are sorry to say, forms no exception to this remark. For proof of what we allege we refer to his definition of liberty, and to the fact, that he seems to have no faith in abstract justice. Liberty with him is the right to do what one pleases. Perfect liberty, or a state of society, if society it may be called, in which there is no restraint placed on men's natural right, is a state of war, oppression, injustice. Government is instituted for the purpose of maintaining peace and order, by restraining natural liberty. This is Hobbism, and it is the doctrine of the book before us; only Mr. Cooper thinks we may leave men a larger portion of their natural liberty than Hobbes believed could be done with safety.

Now we contend that the design of government is to maintain to every man all his natural liberty. Liberty, according to our definition of it, is freedom to do whatever one has a natural right to do; and one has a natural right to do whatever is not forbidden by natural or absolute justice. Mr. Cooper admits the right of governments to restrain the natural liberty of the citizen, to a certain extent, but we admit no such right. The government that restrains or abridges in any sense, in any degree, the natural liberty, that is the natural rights, of any, the meanest or the guiltiest citizen, is tyrannical and unjust. In checking the tendency to extremes then, which Mr. Cooper deplores and against which he arms himself with so praiseworthy a zeal, we should endeavor to point out the precise limits prescribed by justice. We should deny the justice of all restraints upon natural rights. We should then check at once the tendency to arbitrary government. Mr. Cooper, however, permits restraint to a certain extent. Why not to a greater extent? say his fashionable, affluent, and polite acquaintances. Why to so great an extent? Why not give more liberty yet? say the visionary mass, in pursuit of an ideal perfection never to be realized. What can he answer? Nothing that will satisfy either, because the question is in both cases, not a question of principle, but merely a question of more or less. This book, therefore, we think, will hardly succeed in arresting the tendency to extremes, because it leaves both parties their starting-points, and with their faces in the same direction, and merely beseeches them not to go quite so far as they have hitherto been disposed to go.

But notwithstanding our want of faith in the great influence of this book in accomplishing the object for which it has been sent forth, and notwithstanding our objections to its want of faith in reasoning, and to the Hobbian philosophy which lies at the bottom of the author's common sense, we still welcome the book as a very timely and a very valuable publication. It is full of wise and just observations; it is in most cases characterized by good sense, and its views, on all the great political topics it treats, are in the main just and democratic. It corrects many false notions, separates numerous matters which had become confounded, and gives much useful information, for the want of which our citizens have suffered, and our free institutions been endangered. We have more faith in the masses and more sympathy with them than Mr. Cooper appears to have; and we have altogether a stronger love for progress. He seems to be a little sour, half mad at mankind, and to do little for their cause, because he loves it. He too often confounds the actual with the possible, and mistakes what is for what ought to be. But his book breathes in the main a free and independent spirit, and may be said to be written in the interests of the people. It preaches democracy, not exactly according to our reading, nevertheless it preaches it; and if, as we have heard it contended, as much through spite as through love, we complain not. We are thankful that democracy is preached, though it be through spite, through ill-will to the aristocracy.

The following chapter on an Aristocrat and a Democrat, gives a very good idea of the whole work, at least of the spirit in which it is written.

AN ARISTOCRAT AND A DEMOCRAT

"We live in an age, when the words aristocrat and democrat are much used, without regard to the real significations. An aristocrat is one of a few, who possess the political power of a country; a democrat, one of the many. The words are also properly applied to those who entertain notions favorable to aristocratical, or democratical forms of government. Such persons are not, necessarily, either aristocrats, or democrats in fact, but merely so in opinion. Thus a member of a democratical government may have an aristocratical bias, and *vice versa*.

"To call a man who has the habits and opinions of a gentleman, an aristocrat, from that fact alone, is an abuse of terms, and betrays ignorance of the true principles of government, as well as of the world. It must be an equivocal freedom, under which every one is not the master of his own innocent acts and associations, and he is a sneaking democrat, indeed, who will submit to be dictated to, in those habits over which neither law nor morality assumes a right of control.

"Some men fancy that a democrat can only be one who seeks the level, social, mental, and moral, of the majority, a rule that would at once exclude all men of refinement, education, and taste from the class. These persons are enemies of democracy, as they at once render it impracticable. They are usually great sticklers for their own associations and habits, too, though unable to comprehend any of a nature that are superior. They are, in truth, aristocrats in principle, though assuming a contrary pretension; the ground work of all their feelings and arguments being self. Such is not the intention of liberty, whose aim is to leave every man to be the master of his own acts; denying hereditary honors, it is true, as unjust and unnecessary, but not denying the inevitable consequences of civilization.

"The law of God is the only rule of conduct, in this, as in other matters. Each man should do as he would be done by. Were the question put to the greatest advocate of indiscriminate association, whether he would submit to have his company and habits dictated to him, he would be one of the first to resist the tyranny; for they, who are the most rigid in maintaining their own claims, in such matters, are usually the loudest in decrying those whom they fancy to be better off than themselves. Indeed, it may be taken as a rule in social intercourse, that he who is the most apt to question the pretensions of others, is the most conscious of the doubtful position he himself occupies; thus establishing the very claims he affects to deny, by letting his jealousy of it be seen. Manners, education, and refinement, are positive things, and they bring with them innocent tastes, which are productive of high enjoyments; and it is as unjust to deny their possessors their indulgence, as it would be to insist on the less fortunate's passing the time they would rather devote to athletic amusements, in listening to operas for which they have no relish, sung in a language they do not understand.

"All that democracy means is as equal a participation in rights as is practicable; and to pretend that social equality is a condition of popular institutions, is to assume that the latter are destructive of civilization; for, as nothing is more self-evident than the impossibility of raising all men to the highest standard of tastes and refinement, the alternative would be to reduce the entire community to the lowest. The whole embarrassment on this point exists in the difficulty of making men comprehend qualities they do not themselves possess. We can all perceive the difference between ourselves and our inferiors; but when it comes to a question of the differences between us and our superiors, we fail to appreciate merits of which we have no proper conceptions. In the face of this obvious difficulty, there is the safe and just governing rule, already mentioned, or that of permitting every one to be the undisturbed judge of his own habits and associations, so long as they are innocent, and do not impair the rights of others to be equally judges for themselves. It follows, that social intercourse must regulate itself, independently of institutions, with the exception that the latter, while they withhold no natural, bestow no factitious advantages beyond those which are inseparable from the rights of property, and general civilization.

"In a democracy, men are just as free to aim at the highest attainable places in society, as to obtain the largest fortunes; and it would be clearly unworthy of all noble sentiment to say, that the groveling competition for money shall alone be free, while that, which enlists all the liberal acquirements and elevated sentiments of the race, is denied the democrat. Such an avowal would be at once, a declaration of the inferiority of the system, since nothing but ignorance and vulgarity could be its fruits.

"The democratic gentleman must differ in many essential particulars from the aristocratical gentleman, though in their ordinary habits and tastes they are virtually identical. Their principles vary; and, to a slight degree, their deportment accordingly. The democrat, recognizing the right of all to participate in power, will be more liberal in his general sentiments, a quality of superiority in itself; but, in conceding this much to his fellow man, he will proudly maintain his own independence of vulgar domination, as indispensable to his personal habits. The same principles and manliness that would induce him to depose a royal despot, would induce him to resist a vulgar tyrant.

"There is no more capital, though more common error, than to suppose him an aristocrat who maintains his independence of habits; for democracy asserts the control of the majority, only, in matters of law, and not in matters of custom. The very object of the institution is the utmost practicable personal liberty, and to affirm the contrary would be sacrificing the end to the means.

"An aristocrat, therefore, is merely one who fortifies his exclusive privileges by positive institutions, and a democrat, one who is willing to admit of a free competition, in all things. To say, however, that the last supposes this competition will lead to nothing, is an assumption that means are employed without any reference to an end. He is the purest democrat who best maintains his rights, and no rights can be dearer to a man of cultivation, than exemptions from unseasonable invasions on his time, by the coarseminded and ignorant." — pp. 94–98.

Great men are rarely above taking notice of small things. Mr. Cooper forms no exception to this remark, and small things at his touch become matters of considerable magnitude.

"Some changes of the language are to be regretted, as they lead to false inferences, and society is always a loser by mistaking names for things. Life is a fact, and it is seldom any good arises from a misapprehension of the real circumstances under which we exist. The word 'gentleman' has a positive and limited signification. It means one elevated above the mass of society by his birth, manners, attainments, character, and social condition. As no civilized society can exist without these social differences, nothing is gained by denying the use of the term. If blackguards were to be *called* 'gentlemen,' and 'gentlemen,' 'blackguards,' the difference between them would be as obvious as it is today.

"The word 'gentleman,' is derived from the French gentilhomme, which originally signified one of noble birth. This was at a time when the characteristics of the condition were never found beyond a caste. As society advanced, ordinary men attained the qualifications of nobility, without that of birth, and the meaning of the word was extended. It is now possible to be a gentleman without birth, though, even in America, where such distinctions are purely conditional, they who have birth, except in extraordinary instances, are classed with gentlemen. To call a laborer, one who has neither education, manners, accomplishments, tastes, associations, nor any one of the ordinary requisites, a gentleman, is just as absurd as to call one who is thus qualified, a fellow. The word must have some especial signification or it would be synonymous with man. One may have gentlemen feelings, principles, and appearance, without possessing the liberal attainments that distinguish the gentleman. Least of all does money make a gentleman, though, as it becomes a means of obtaining the other requisites, it is usual to give it a place in the claims of the class. Men may be, and often are, very rich, without having the smallest title to be deemed gentlemen. A man may be a distinguished gentleman, and not possess as much money as his own foot man.

"This word, however, is sometimes used instead of the old terms, 'sirs,' 'my masters,' &c., &c., as in addressing bodies of men. Thus we say 'gentlemen,' in addressing a public meeting, in complaisance and as, by possibility, some gentlemen may be present. This is a license that may be tolerated, though he who should insist that all present were, as individuals, gentlemen, would hardly escape ridicule.

"What has just been said of the word gentleman is equally true with that of lady. The standard of these two classes rises as society becomes more civilized and refined; the man who might pass for a gentleman in one nation, or community, not being able to maintain the same position in another.

"The inefficiency of the effort to subvert things by names, is shown in the fact that, in all civilized communities, there is a class of men, who silently and quietly recognize each other, as gentlemen; who associate together freely and without reserve, and who admit each other's claims without scruple or distrust. This class may be limited by prejudice and arbitrary enactments, as in Europe, or it may have no other rule than those of taste, sentiment, and the silent laws of usage, as in America.

"The same observations may be made of relation to the words master and servant. He who employs laborers, with the right to command is a master, and he who lets himself work, with an obligation to obey, a servant. Thus there are house, or domestic servants, farm servants, shop servants, and various other servants; the term master being in all these cases the correlative.

"In consequence of the domestic servants of America having once been negro-slaves, a prejudice has arisen among the laboring classes of the whites, who not only dislike the term servant, but have also rejected that of master. So far has this prejudice gone, that in lieu of the latter, they have resorted to the use of the word *boss*, which has precisely the same meaning in Dutch! How far a subterfuge of this nature is worthy of a manly and common sense people will admit of question.

"A similar objection may be made to the use of the word 'help,' which is not only an innovation on a just and established term, but which does not properly convey the meaning intended. They who aid their masters in the toil may be deemed 'helps,' but they who perform all the labor do not assist, or help to do the thing, but they do it themselves. A man does not usually hire his cook to *help* him cook his dinner, but to cook it herself. Nothing is therefore gained, while something is lost in simplicity and clearness by the substitution of new and imperfect terms, for the long established words of the language. In all cases in which the people of America have retained the *things* of their ancestors, they should not be ashamed to keep the *names*." — pp. 120–122.

It is devoutly to be hoped that all this, and much more like it in the volume before us, will be duly regarded by our democratic friends. It is very important that our democrats should be taught good manners, and probably no man amongst us is better qualified to be their teacher than Mr. Cooper. He has resided long abroad, travelled much, seen much, observed much, and is himself, we presume, *au fait* in all that appertains to good manners. We hope he will meet with success, proportioned to the zeal and diligence with which he takes himself to his task. An unmannerly democracy must always be distasteful and even revolting to a *gentleman*. In sober earnest, he who improves the manners of a nation, does much for its morals. Let there be care, however, that the improvement attempted be something more than the transplanting of the conventionalisms of one country to another. "The wise are polite the world over; fools are polite only at home," says, very truly, the Citizen of the World. True politeness is made up of good sense and good nature, and no man, who has good sense and good nature, can ever be wanting in the manners of the gentleman, in the only worthy sense of the term, though he may be wanting in the conventionalisms of different countries, or of a particular clique or coterie. Really good manners always have their foundation in human nature, and must always take their hue from the age and circumstances of the individual, and the institutions of the country. The manners most appropriate to an aristocracy, or to a monarchy, can never be the most appropriate to a democracy. But we beg pardon of Mr. Cooper for trespassing on his peculiar province.

Mr. Cooper thinks the application of the terms *gentleman* and *lady*, to footmen and cooks, is very unbecoming, and ought not to be tolerated. We are sorry not to sympathize with him in this, as fully as he may desire. We applaud his motives, but we confess that we look with pleasure on the fact, that footmen and cooks are rising to the dignity of gentlemen and ladies; and it is also an article in our creed that all who are born at all are well-born. Every human being, in our belief, is of noble, ay, of royal birth, and may stand up and claim to be a king, and demand regal honors. This is the foundation stone of our democracy, and he, who has yet to learn that no human being is or can be ignoble, is in our judgment a sorry democrat.

We confess that as concerns this leveling tendency, we are unable to sympathize with the fears Mr. Cooper seems to indulge. We see no disposition among our countrymen to bring all down to a dead level of ignorance and barbarism. They, against whom the charge of desiring to do this is sometimes brought, are in no sense obnoxious to it. The workingmen, agrarians, locofocos, Jacobins, or by whatever name they may be designated by themselves or by their enemies, have made certain movements which have created some alarm, and made some say that they are for arresting civilization, and for plunging us into primitive ignorance and barbarism; but these same dreaded levelers have been the first in this country to advocate equal, universal education. They demand reforms, radical reforms, it is true; but they expect them almost solely from an improved system of education. They propose to raise the standard of education, to breathe into education a free and living spirit, and to extend it equally to all, to every child born in the land, whether rich or poor, male or female. Is this to show a love for ignorance and barbarism? Is this a kind of leveling that should alarm a wise man, a Christian, and a democrat?

Distinctions there are in society, and distinctions there always will be; but distinction implies diversity, not necessarily inequality. The footman is diverse from the cook, but not necessarily inferior or superior to the cook. There is a difference between Mr. Cooper's gentleman and his footman, yet the two may be equal in moral worth, in knowledge, in wealth, and social position. Nevertheless admitting inequalities, they may be real, not factitious. Now all the war which has been carried on against the inequalities which do obtain in society, has had for its object, not the suppression of those inequalities which are founded in nature, or which rest on merit, but those which have no real foundation but an ignorant and barbarous public opinion, or an ignorant and barbarous state of society. Factitious inequalities, not natural, not moral inequalities, are the ones that the Radicals are striving to destroy. Beyond these they have no thought of going. There is in every man, in Jacobins as well as in conservatives, a natural instinct which leads him to bow down to superior worth. The great man can never be lost in the crowd. He who is really and intrinsically superior to the common mass will always be permitted to tower above them. Carlyle is tight in his remarks on hero-worship. It is the natural and earliest religion of mankind, and it remains and will remain, though all other religions be out grown, their altars broken down, and their temples moldered to dust. No man, who is conscious that the royal blood flows in his veins, that the royal heart beats under his ribs, need fear that the honors of royalty will not be decreed him. Let a man be a king, and as a king shall he be owned, reverenced, and obeyed. Human nature is rich in loyalty, and will pour out her blood like water in honor of even a semblance of a king. Let the wise man be ashamed then to tremble at a supposed tendency to wipe out all distinctions, and to confound the great with the little.

One tendency we do discover, and that is to strip off disguises and compel people to pass for what they are. There is a growing disgust at all make-believe, at all shamming, and a demand for reality. Therefore is there danger that some men may not always succeed in bearing the characters they once contrived to obtain. The men rather short by nature, but who have hitherto been accounted tall, because they were standing on stilts, may hereafter be taken at their true altitude, and laughed at into the bargain, for the pains they have taken to add a cubit to their stature. Mr. Cooper has nothing to apprehend from such a leveling tendency as this, nor has any other man who is conscious of true worth, and who is willing to be estimated at his real value. Others may fear,—let them.

Mr. Cooper's remarks "On the Public" are to the point, and deserve to be read and pondered well. We should be glad to extract them, but have not the room.

We must bring our remarks to a close, and we do it by throwing out a few suggestions for the consideration of American Democrats. The democracy of the last century was materialism applied to politics; it sought equality by lopping off the heads of kings and priests, and its natural tendency was to universal anarchy. We do not complain of it on this account. Kings and priests, when they have lost the true kingly and priestly nature, have no more right to wear their heads than they have to wear crowns and mitres. But democracy has changed its character. The democrat of today is not destructive, but constructive; he does not lop off the heads of kings and priests, but he seeks to arrive at equality by making every man a king and a priest. He is a leveler, but he levels upward not downward. He is not affected by the fact that some are higher than others, but by the fact that some are lower than others. He grieves over the fact that human nature is wronged, that its inborn nobility is not brought out, that the mass of men are not true men, but something less than men; and he sets himself seriously at work to remove all obstacles to the full development of the true man, and to call forth the might which has for so many ages slumbered in the peasant's arm. He holds up the standard of the True Man, and labors to bring all men up to it. He therefore is eminently religious, eminently christian, eminently philosophic. He avails himself of all the means and influences, of all the arts, sciences, literature, everything, by which the universal soul of Humanity may be quickened, thought awakened, moral power increased, and the majesty of man made to appear. Be assured then that the democrat of today is no barbarian. He is a man, a free man, a Christian man, who believes in the powers and capacities of all men to be men, in the full significance of the term, and who labors to make them so, or to induce them to make themselves so.

Again, in a more restricted sphere, the American democrat is one who is jealous of power, and always interprets all doubtful questions so as to increase the power of the people, rather than of the government. In this, his first duty is to watch that the Federal Government do not swallow up the State governments. Power has a perpetual tendency to extend itself. The functionaries of government, whether executive, legislative, or judicial, almost inevitably so exercise their functions as to enlarge the sphere of government. There is a tendency in the Federal Government, from its central character, to engross as much of the public business of the country as possible. The first danger to our liberty is to be apprehended from this quarter. Cooks may be called ladies, and footmen gentlemen, and still our liberty be tolerably secure; but when the Federal Government has succeeded in getting under its control, directly or indirectly, nearly all the internal affairs of the States, and is able to make its acts, like the frogs of Egypt, reach to our domestic hearths, and to come up into our sleeping chambers and kneading troughs, we may be assured that the first barriers to a consolidated despotism have been leaped. This was well nigh done. The friends of freedom have made an effort to arrest the dangerous tendency; but whether with success or not time must determine. The universal tendency through out Christendom to centralization, a tendency accelerated a hundred fold by the "thousand and one" voluntary associations of the day, is somewhat alarming, and should teach our democrats, that this is no time to sleep at their posts, or to expect a victory without a long and obstinate struggle. They must be awake, always prepared for the battle, well armed, and stout of heart.

Lastly, the American Democrat must be on his guard against the tendency of the State governments to enlarge the dominion of the state at the expense of that of the individual. There are two antagonist tendencies at work; one to individual freedom, a tendency we traced in our April number, in our remarks on modern civilization; the other, a tendency to centralization, to the merging of the individual in the state, in the mass. This last is the only dangerous tendency in this country. The philosopher cannot fail to perceive that we have much more to apprehend from our reverence for law than from our disregard of it. Mobs, bad as they are, are not half so threatening to liberty, to the true working of our institutions, as the prosecution of a man for advocating an unpopular doctrine, or as is the prevalence of that modern doctrine of "vested rights," a doctrine, which, if admitted and practiced upon, may in time cover all the property of the State with charters, and lock it up forever in close corporations. We are called upon as democrats by every consideration that can touch our sensibility, arouse our patriotism, or our love of humanity, to contend manfully for individual rights, and resist at the threshold every encroachment of power. We must frown upon every legislative enactment, upon every judicial decision, that restricts the sphere of individual freedom, and especially upon all those huge associations which cover the land, though called moral, religious, benevolent, which tend to swallow up the individual, and are a device of the devil, by which the same control under a free government may be exerted over individual opinion and action, that is exerted over them by despotisms and hierarchies. We must throw around each individual a bulwark of sanctity, and not permit society to break through it, though it were to do the individual an unspeakable good. God leaves man his freedom, and does not control it, though man in abusing it brings damnation to his soul. Let the Divine government be a model of ours. We may not control a man's natural liberty even for the man's good. So long as the individual trespasses upon none of the rights of others, or throws no obstacle in the way of their free and full exercise, government, law, public opinion even, must leave him free to take his own course. In order to secure this end we must breathe a freer spirit into our schools, place men at the head of our colleges and higher seminaries of learning who sympathize with our democratic institutions, demand, will, create, and sustain a truly democratic literature.

Abolition Proceedings

OCTOBER 1838

A Review of S. B. Treadwell's *American Liberties and American Slavery, Morally and Politically Illustrated* (New York: John S. Taylor, 1838)

Mr. Treadwell has attempted in this book to settle definitively the whole question, as to the right of the abolitionists to labor for the emancipation of the slaves. He takes up and professes to answer some forty popular objections to the proceedings of the abolitionists. He has done the thing admirably, no doubt, and to the entire satisfaction of his friends. But we are sorry to find that he has mistaken entirely the real question at issue, and paid not the least attention to what we regard as the really weighty objections which may be urged against abolition proceedings.

Mr. Treadwell proceeds through his whole book, at least so far as we have read it, on the ground that the real question at issue is, Have the Northern abolitionists a right to *discuss* the abstract question of slavery? Now this is a great mistake, and this way of putting the question is altogether unpardonable. We have a right, as men and as citizens of an independent State, to discuss any question and all questions which concern any portion of the human race, and to discuss them freely and unreservedly. There is no limitation to this right, except as to the manner of exercising it. In discussing any question whatever, we are bound to show that respect for the opinions and characters of others, we exact from others for our own. Nobody objects to the mere discussion of slavery; and anybody may advocate, in the freest and ablest manner he can, the inalienable right of every man, whether black or white, to be a freeman.

We insist on this point. The abolitionists make no small outcry about the right of free discussion; they represent themselves as the champions of free discussion; and they take unwearied pains to make it believed that the whole cause of free discussion is involved in the Abolition question. Nothing is or can be more disingenuous than this. Abolitionists are in no sense whatever, either in principle or in practice, the champions of free discussion. Their conceptions of free discussion, so far as we can gather them from their publications, are exceedingly narrow and crude. In their estimation free discussion is to denounce slavery and slaveholders; and opposition to free discussion, is the free expression of one's honest convictions against abolition proceedings. A man who supports them defends the rights of the mind; he who opposes them attacks the rights of the mind. Now this sort of free discussion is altogether too one-sided to suit our taste. It is very much like our pilgrim fathers' respect for the freedom of conscience. Our pilgrim fathers loved freedom of conscience so much, that they took it into their own especial keeping, and spurned the idea of sharing its custody with others.

Moreover, the abolitionists do not, properly speaking, discuss the subject of slavery. Nay, it is not their object to discuss it. Their object is not to enlighten the community on the subject, but to agitate it. Discussion is a calm exercise of the reasoning powers, not the ebullition of passion, nor the ravings of a maddened zeal. To discuss an important question we need not the aid of women and children, but of wise and sober men, men of strong intellects and well-informed minds. Discussion is also best carried on in one's closet, at least where one can keep cool; not in a crowd, where people of all ages and both sexes are brought together, and by the strong appeals of impassioned orators thrown into a state of excitement bordering upon insanity. When men have made up their minds, when the epoch for deliberation has gone by, and that for action has come; when their object is less to convince than it is to rouse, to quicken, to inflame; then proceedings like those of the abolitionists are very appropriate, and it is only then that they are ever adopted. It is perfect folly therefore for the abolitionists to talk about discussion. Any man, with his eyes half open, may see clearly that all this is mere pretense. Action, not discussion, is what they demand. Deeds, not words, are what they contemplate. To agitate the whole community, to inflame all hearts, to collect the whole population into one vast body, and to roll it down on the South to force the planters to emancipate their slaves, this is what they are striving to do. It is the *abolition* of slavery, not its *discussion*, they band together for, and it is idle for them to pretend to the contrary.

If any proof of this were wanted, it might be found in their treatment of every man who adopts conclusions different from their own. Do they reason with him? Not they. They denounce him. They rush upon him with the fury of cannibals, and, as far as it depends on them, destroy his character, and make it impossible for him to hold up his head in the community. Do they answer the arguments urged against them? They? Mr. Garrison, we have it on good authority, stated in a public meeting in this city, that the arguments adduced against the abolitionists had never been answered, and he did not wish to have them answered. Discussion do you call this? Discussion! They know better than to stop to discuss the matter. We are right, say they. God and man are with us. We have a holy cause. Woe, woe, to whomsoever opposes us; mark him, friends of freedom; mark him, friends of the slave; he is a robber, a man-stealer, a murderer, and it requires "a pencil dipped in the midnight blackness of hell" to paint in appropriate colors the foulness of his heart. This is discussion, is it? The rights of free discussion are invaded, are they, because opposition to this method of treating our brethren is sometimes shown?

Abolitionists are merely discussing the question of slavery, are they? What mean then these thousands of Petitions to Congress, with their seven hundred thousand signers, a large portion of whom are women and children? What kind of arguments are these? What new light do they throw on the question of slavery? What understanding do they convince? What conscience do they persuade? They are merely discussing the subject of slavery, are they? What mean then these political movements they are preparing, these interrogatories they are addressing to candidates for office? Take the following from their official publications.

> "The candidates presented to your choice will, of course, be nominated either by the whigs or democrats. The most

prominent individual of the whig party, and probably their next candidate for the presidency, is a slave-holder, president of that stupendous imposture, the Colonization Society, author of the fatal Missouri 'compromise,' and of the slavish resolutions against the abolitionists, lately passed by the Senate of the United states. On the other hand, the leader of the democratic party, 'the northern president with southern principles,' has deeply insulted this nation, by avowing his determination to veto any bill for the abolition of slavery in the District of Columbia, which may be passed by a majority of the people, in opposition to the wishes of the slave States.

"No consistent abolitionist can vote for either of those individuals. It does not however follow, that he cannot vote for candidates for State offices, or for Congress, who may be their friends and supporters. If the candidate before you be honest, capable, and true to your principles, we think you may fairly vote for him, without considering too curiously, whether his success might not have an indirect bearing on the interests of Mr. Clay, or Mr. Van Buren. It is a golden maxim, 'Do the duty that lies nearest thee.' Vote for each man by himself, and on his own merits. If you attempt to make your rule more complicated, so as to include distant contingencies and consequences, it will be found perplexing and impracticable.

"The independent course in politics, which we have recommended, supposes great prudence, disinterestedness, energy of purpose, and self-control, in those who are to adopt it. May you justify our confidence in you. Do your duty. Come out, in your strength, to the polls. Refuse to support any public man who trims, or equivocates, or conceals his opinions. Beware of half-way abolitionists; and of men, who are abolitionists but once a year. Prove that you do not require the machinery of party discipline, to vote strictly according to your professed principles. Do this, and you will rapidly acquire a deserved influence. 'Such a party,' as Mr. Webster justly said, in speaking of the abolitionists, 'will assuredly cause itself to be respected.' *Within the next two years, the friends of freedom might hold the balance of power in every free State in the Union; and no man could ascend the presidential seat against their will."*

So say the Board of Managers of the Massachusetts Anti-Slavery Society in their Address to Abolitionists, an address, by the way, the least exceptionable and the best written of any abolition document we have seen. But does this look like *discussing* the subject of slavery? Take also the following from the "Human Rights," published by the American Anti-Slavery Society.

> "*There is but one remedy.* Men must be sent to Congress, made of sterner stuff—men who, like Senator Morris of Ohio, are not ashamed to advocate the *rights* of their constituents. Dough-faces have had their day. Let us keep them at home,— their proper vocation is to head our Northern pro-slavery squadrons, armed with brick-bats and stale eggs. State offices too, and County and Town offices must be filled with men who will at least show as much zeal for the great objects which the 'Union' was intended to secure, as for the 'Union' itself,—men who will not esteem it their duty to choke discussion and encourage mobs to please the slaveholders. We need not debate this point. Every man's conscience will show him his duty.
>
> "What we beg is, that duty may be done *in season*. Don't wait till candidates are before the people, and the elections are at the door, and the lines of party are drawn—and its wire work all fixed. Let your voice be heard at once. Let your determination be known, not to support any man who will not unequivocally pledge himself to *free discussion, free petition, and abolition where Congress has the power.* Let the political parties have this to reflect on before they select their candidates. No candidate ought to expect the vote of an abolitionist, who is not prepared to answer the following questions in the affirmative.
>
> "1. Are you in favor of abolishing slavery in the District of Columbia—for the honor and welfare of the nation?

"2. Are you in favor of so regulating commerce among the several states, that human beings shall not be made subjects of such trade?

"3. Are you opposed to the annexation of Texas to this Union, under any circumstances, so long as slaves are held therein?

"4. Are you in favor of acknowledging the independence of Haiti, and of establishing commercial relations with that nation on the same terms with the most favored nations?

"But they *will* expect votes unless abolitionists bestir themselves in time. Crafty politicians always calculate on humanity's *'dying away.'* By our 'fathers' ashes' let them be disappointed henceforth and forever. Let the abolitionists meet in their societies, resolve on energetic and up-to-the-mark political action, and *publish* their resolution in the *county* as well as the abolition papers. Such demonstrations, in good time, will not be without their effect. Above all things, let the action when begun, like the good cause itself, *'die away'* bigger and bigger."

The abolitionists are merely *discussing* the subject of slavery, are they? What have the respective merits of candidates for office, State or Federal, to do with the merits of slavery? What has the recognition of the independence of Haiti to do with the merits of slavery? If abolitionists are merely discussing slavery, we ask, what they have to do, *as abolitionists*, with questions like those here introduced? But we need dwell no longer upon this point. Abolitionists may say and believe what they will, but it is perfectly idle for them to dream of convincing any intelligent observer, that they are merely discussing the question of slavery. As we have said, their object is to abolish it, not to discuss it, and their means for abolishing it are not calm and rational discussion, but agitation, the agitation of the community, inflaming its passions, and directing, by means of the ballot box, the force they thus collect to bear directly on Southern institutions.

We say again, then, that Mr. Treadwell has not stated the real question at issue, and his book is therefore worthless. The real question at issue is, Have the citizens of the non-slaveholding States the right to set on foot a series of measures—no matter what measures—intentionally and avowedly for the purpose of emancipating the slaves? This is the question. Have we the right to commence a series of operations for the accomplishment of an object, and to prosecute them with strict and sole reference to the accomplishment of an object, over which we have no rightful jurisdiction?

Why is it that the abolitionists shrink from this question? Why is it that,—so far as our knowledge extends,—they have never in a single instance met this question, or even alluded to it? Shall we say, because they are conscious that they cannot meet it, without being forced to acknowledge that they are wrong in their proceedings, and ought forthwith to disband their associations?

Doubtless somebody must have the jurisdiction of the slave question. Who is it? Who has the legal right to abolish slavery? The States in which it exists, and the sole right to do it, says the constitution of the American Anti-Slavery Society. If this be so, it is certain that the abolitionists, as citizens of non-slaveholding States, have not the right to abolish slavery. In laboring to abolish it then, they are laboring to do that which they have no legal right to do, even according to their own official confession. They then, so far as they labor to abolish it, are acting against law, are transgressors of the law, and obnoxious to its penalties. There is no gainsaying this.

This being so, on what ground will the abolitionists justify their proceedings? Will they take their stand above law, appeal from law to their individual conceptions of right, to the paramount law of Humanity—of God? We presume so. We believe this is their appeal, this the ground on which they attempt to legitimate their proceedings. Be it so. In taking this ground they set the law at defiance, and are either a mob or a band of insurrectionists. In taking this ground they justify all the lawless violence against which they have so vehemently declaimed. If one class of the community may set the laws at defiance, why may not another? If the abolitionists may set at nought the international law, which gives the slaveholding States the exclusive jurisdiction of the slave question, why may not other citizens say they have a right by mob-law to prevent them, if they can, from doing it? It were not difficult to convict the abolitionists of preaching the very doctrines the mobocrats attempt to reduce to practice. They ought not therefore to think it strange, that they have been in but too many instances the victims of lawless violence. When a portion of the community take it into their heads that they are wiser than the law, and commence the performance of acts in contravention of law, they ought to be aware that they open the door to every species of lawless violence, unchain the tiger, and must be answerable for the consequences.

Nevertheless we cheerfully admit, that, in saying the abolitionists appeal from law as it is to what they consider it ought to be, to the paramount law of Humanity, we do not necessarily condemn them, nor even cast a shadow of a reproach upon them. There may be cases in which men shall be justified in doing this; nay, when it shall be their duty to do this. But this cannot be done without rebellion. They who do it declare the bonds of society broken, and society itself reduced to its original elements. It cannot be done in accordance with any existing social order; it therefore can be justified only in such cases as do justify rebellion, revolution. Revolutions are sometimes justifiable, and we as a nation hold to the sacred right of insurrection. If the abolitionists take the ground we suppose they do, they are in fact insurrectionists, they are revolutionists. This is their character. Now in order to justify themselves they must make out a clear case, that the present circumstances of our Republic are such as to warrant a revolution.

No doubt Justice, the paramount law of Humanity, demands the abolition of slavery. But of whom does it demand it? And on what conditions does it demand it? Does Humanity command us to abolish it in contravention of law? Is Humanity, all things considered, more interested in declaring the negroes free, than in maintaining those laws which the abolitionists violate in laboring to bring about the declaration? We say *declaring* the slaves free, and we do so designedly; for this is as far as the efforts of the abolitionists, if successful, can go. They cannot make the slaves free. The slave is never converted into a freeman by a stroke of the pen. Freedom cannot be conferred; it must be conquered. The slave must grow into freedom and be able to maintain his freedom, or he is a slave still, whatever he may be called. If then the abolitionists cannot make out clearly and beyond the possibility of cavil, that Humanity is more interested in declaring the slaves free than she is in maintaining the laws, the citizens of non-slaveholding States must violate, before they can cause them to be declared free, they cannot make out a case that justifies revolution, nor a case that justifies their proceedings even admitting their own premises.

Slavery ought to be abolished, says the abolitionist, and what ought to be done it is right to do. It is right then to abolish slavery. This is enough for me. Ask me not to stop and consider what may be found in statute laws and paper constitutions. The tyrant's foot is on the neck of my brother; don't tell me to stop and ask whether, all things considered, it be my duty to run to his rescue. It may not be expedient to do it. But what of that? Let me alone. I will hurl the tyrant to the dust, and deliver my brother. We understand this feeling very well, and by dwelling upon it could work ourselves up, as we often have done, into a glorious passion, and become quite heroic. Still we believe harm seldom comes from stopping to consider.

We eschew expediency as a rule of action as heartily as do our friends the abolitionists. We are not among those who sneer at abstract right, and say we are not to regard it in practical life. Abstract right, as we view it, is absolute right, which is simply right, neither more nor less. Now we hold that every one is bound to consult the right and the right only, and having found it, to do it, let who or what will oppose. But we believe it is, before acting, very proper to determine what is right, not only in a general case, but in the particular case in which it is proposed to act. In determining what is right in any given case, it is necessary to take into consideration all the circumstances and bearings of that case. Right, it is true, never varies, but the action varies according to the circumstances under which it is performed. An action with certain general characteristics, performed under certain circumstances, shall be right, but performed under other circumstances shall be wrong; because in the latter case it is in fact a different action from what it is in the former. A given action viewed in one of its relations may be right, yet viewed in all its relations it shall be improper to be done. It is therefore always necessary, in order to determine whether a particular action should be done or not, to survey it in all its relations, and to examine as far as we can all its bearings. The consequences of the action are by no means to be overlooked. True, the consequences of an action do not *constitute* its moral character, but they are necessary to be consulted in order to *ascertain* its moral character. The idea of right is unquestionably intuitive, of transcendental origin; but its proper application to practical life is a matter of experience, to be determined by the understanding.

Admit then that slavery is wrong, that it is right to abolish it, it does by no means follow that the citizens of non-slaveholding States have the right to abolish it; nor that the abolition proceedings are commanded by that law of right, to which the abolitionists so confidently appeal. A fellow citizen has wronged us. It is right that we should have redress; but it is right that we should seek redress only in conformity to the law of the land. We shall be held justifiable in morals, no more than in law, if we undertake to obtain redress ourselves, without reference to the legal method of obtaining it. The abolitionist must do more than prove that slavery is wrong, that it ought to be abolished, and that it is right to abolish it; he must prove first, that *he* has a right to abolish it, and secondly, that he has a right to abolish it in the way he proposes to do,— two things we hope he will forthwith undertake to prove, but which we fear he will be able to prove not without difficulty.

We go as strongly for liberty as the abolitionist. We protest with the whole energy of our moral being against the right of any man to hold his brother man in slavery. To the slaveholder, boasting the beauties of the slave system, its happy effects, and the sweet ties it creates between the master and slave, we have no answer, but "Do unto others as you would they should do unto you." When we find the master willing to become, and desirous of becoming a slave, then, and not till then, will we listen to his defense of slavery. Man is born with the right to be free. Liberty is his inalienable right, and there is nothing in heaven or on earth to justify one man in depriving another of his rights. We can see, we think we do see, how God overrules slavery for good, and makes it serve to restrain or destroy other evils, which might perhaps lead to consequences still worse than those of Negro slavery itself; but this is in our judgment of the matter no excuse, no palliation of the guilt of those, by whose agency slavery was introduced and is perpetuated. On this point we have no controversy with the abolitionist. We sympathize with slavery no more than he does; and we are as far as he would be from appearing as the defender or the apologist of the slaveholder. Slavery is wholly indefensible; it ought to be abolished; it must be abolished; it will be abolished. But does it belong to us, who are citizens of non-slaveholding States, to abolish it? This is the first question we want answered.

To emancipate the slaves, viewed in itself, might be a praiseworthy deed. It were, if it could be done, a good work. But it is not therefore necessarily true that it is a work for us to perform. It is not only necessary to prove the work a good one, but that it is *our* work, before we have proved that we have a right to undertake it. Every man has, in the general allotment of Providence, his special work. Every community its special mission; and it is each man's duty to ascertain and perform his own work, each community's duty to ascertain and fulfill its own mission. Evil always results from the attempt of any one man to be that for which God and nature have not designed him, and consequently evil must always proceed from the attempt of any one to perform the task assigned another.

The emancipation of the slaves, we say, is not our work. Slavery may be a sin,—but it is not ours; and there is no occasion for us to assume the responsibility of other people's sins. We have sins enough of our own, and more than we can answer for; we have more work to perform for freedom here, within the limits of our own territory, than we can perform in many centuries, even should we direct to its performance our exclusive attention and all our energies. Slavery, it may be, is a stain, a disgrace upon the community that tolerates it; but if so, it is not a stain nor a disgrace on non-slaveholding communities. We are not disgraced because Constantinople is a slaveholding city, nor are we because Charleston is a slaveholding city. The States that hold slaves are alone responsible for the institution. If, as they pretend, it be a good and praiseworthy institution, theirs be the glory of maintaining it; if it be, as the abolitionists regard it, a disgraceful, a wicked institution, theirs be the sin and disgrace of perpetuating it. They are of age, and are responsible for their own deeds.

The abolitionist considers that it is our duty to labor for the emancipation of the slaves, because our nation is a slaveholding nation, and is therefore disgraced in the eyes of foreigners. To foreigners, who reproach us with slavery, all we have to say is, when you have done as much to elevate labor and the laboring classes, as we have, we will hear you; till then hold your peace. To the abolitionists we deny the fact in toto, that we are a slaveholding nation. We are made one nation by the constitution of the United States, and are one nation no further than that declares us to be so. Now in the sense in which these United States are one people we do not hold slaves. Slavery is not recognized by the constitution; that is, it in no sense whatever exists by virtue of the constitution. It is not established by the laws of the Union, nor is it protected by those laws. In our capacity of one people, in the sense in which we are one nation, we have no cognizance of the subject of slavery. We deny therefore that our republic is a slaveholding republic. We deny that it tolerates slavery, and request the abolitionists not to be too ready to assume a reproach to which they are not obnoxious.

But some of the members of the Confederacy hold slaves. Granted. So does Brazil, so does Turkey, so do a great many nations. But the members of the Confederacy that hold slaves, do it not by virtue of constitutional grants, not by virtue of powers conferred on them by their sister States, but by virtue of their State sovereignty, which they did not surrender into the hands of the Union, and which they still retain in all its plenitude, at least so far as this question is concerned. They stand then in regard to this question, as we have shown on a former occasion, precisely as independent nations, and we of course are no more responsible for their deeds, or affected in our national character by their misdeeds, than by those of any independent or foreign community whatever. Let us talk no more then about a slaveholding republic. We are not a slaveholding republic.

We must again point out to our abolitionists, that the Federal Republic is limited to a very few specific purposes. The States, for their mutual convenience, for the general welfare and common defense of the whole, formed themselves into a Federal league or Union. In the constitution is specified the extent to which the States, as free, independent, sovereign nations, consented to merge their State character and sovereignty into one nation. To the extent there specified, we regard the people of the several States as one people, and no further. To the extent there specified, and for the purposes there specified, a citizen of Massachusetts is also a citizen of the United States, and has the same right to concern himself, according to the mode there pointed out, with the affairs of South Carolina that he has with the affairs of Massachusetts. But beyond this extent he has no more right to concern himself with the affairs of any State but the one of which he is specially a citizen, than he has with the affairs of France or China. Our duty, as citizens of the United States, is to observe in good faith the stipulations into which we have entered with our sister States; and so long as the slaveholding States perform towards us all the engagements they have made to us, we have, as citizens of the United States, no fault to find with them.

Now have the slaveholding States ever entered into an engagement to emancipate their slaves? Is it in the bond? When they came into the Union, did they stipulate to abolish slavery? Not at all. They retained that matter in their own hands. What right have we then to insist upon their doing it now? In what capacity do we call upon the Southerner to free his slaves? In our capacity as citizens of the United States? But in that capacity we have no right to meddle with the matter, because slavery is not one of the matters which come under the jurisdiction of the United States. The people of the United States have no legal cognizance of it. In our capacity as citizens of Massachusetts then? But as citizens of Massachusetts, we hold no other relation with the slaveholder in South Carolina, than we do with the slaveholder in Constantinople. In what capacity then? In our capacity as men and as Christians?

We are far from denying that, as men and Christians, we have no concern with the slave question. As a man, as a Christian, I have a right to concern myself with whatever affects my brother man wherever he is. But has this concern no limitation? Limitation or not, it is no greater in the case of Southern slavery, than in the case of slavery anywhere else. Our right and our duty to labor for the emancipation of Southern slaves, rest on our general right and duty to labor for the abolition of slavery wherever it exists. Now, before the abolitionist can make out that it is my right and my duty to make any special efforts to effect the emancipation of the slaves in the Southern States, he must show that it is my right and my duty to make special efforts for the abolition of slavery everywhere. Nay, more than this, he must prove that it is my right and my duty to make special efforts for the correction of all abuses of all countries, to abolish every bad or wrong institution of every nation, to remove all national sins of all nations. Can he do this? He can do it only by doing another thing which is yet more difficult. He must prove that every man has the right and the duty to concern himself with the whole conduct, the entire life, of every other man, and that every man has the right and the duty to see that every other man forsakes his sins and does his duty.

It is the duty of Massachusetts to educate all her children; but is it the duty of South Carolina to undertake to compel her to do it? It is the duty of the citizens of this State to abolish the barbarous law that treats poverty as a crime; but is it the duty of the citizens of Georgia to compel us to do it, or to do it for us? The Autocrat of the Russias ought to restore Poland to her national independence; but is it our duty to do it for him, or to undertake to force him to do it? England ought to abolish the laws of primogeniture and entail, monarchy, and the hereditary peerage; but is it our duty to make special efforts to induce her to do it? Is that abolition her work, or is it ours? Universal freedom should be established throughout the earth; is it therefore our duty to become propagandists, and band our whole community together into associations for carrying on a war with all nations who have not adopted a republican form of government?

Freedom requires us to recognize in each individual certain rights, and rights which we may no more invade to do the individual good, than to do him harm. He must have a certain degree of liberty. That liberty he may abuse; but so long as he does not attack our liberty, we cannot, without sapping all liberty in its very foundation, interfere with him. So of communities. They stand in relation to one another as individuals. So long as any given community respects the rights of all other communities, no other community has any right to interfere with its conduct. Its external relations are just, and its internal affairs, so far as other communities are concerned, it has a right to regulate in its own way. To deny this is to deny its independence, is to strike at its liberty; and to attempt to interfere with its internal policy, is to declare war upon it, and must, if it be a spirited community and able to fight for its independence, lead to bloodshed and incalculable sufferings. Peace among the nations of the earth is to be maintained only by each nation's attending to its own concerns, leaving all other nations to regulate their internal policy in their own way. This principle is even more imperative in the case of the States which compose this Republic, than in that of nations generally. Our relations are so multiplied, are so intimate, and our intercourse is so frequent and various, that, without the most punctilious respect for the reserved rights of each, perpetual embroilment must result, and our union instead of harmony be a source of perpetual discord. We say therefore, inasmuch as slavery is an institution over which the slaveholding States have the exclusive jurisdiction, inasmuch as we, as citizens of the United States and of non-slaveholding States, have no concern with it, we are not called upon, whatever may be our opinion of it as an institution, to labor specially for its abolition. We are not called upon to abolish it.

But even admitting we were called upon to abolish it, or to labor for the abolition of slavery wherever it exists, we should still deny that the abolition proceedings are justifiable. They are contrary to the genius of our institutions; they make war upon the relations, which it was intended by our Federal system should subsist between the States which compose the Union, and are therefore, as we have said, revolutionary in their character and tendency.

We do not say that to abolish slavery is contrary to the genius of our institutions. The genius of our institutions is liberty, and unquestionably is repugnant to every species of slavery. If the institutions subsist, they must in their gradual unfolding sweep away slavery, and every vestige of man's tyranny over man. But according to our Federal system, all the internal affairs of the several States are to be managed by the States themselves. When, therefore, the citizens of one State disregard this system, and labor to control the internal affairs of another State, in the manner we have shown the abolitionists do, they are acting in opposition to the American system of government. The citizens of slaveholding States might, if they chose, adopt all the measures our abolitionists do, without being liable to this charge, and perhaps they ought in justice to labor even more zealously than do the abolitionists for the abolition of slavery. The error of the abolitionists consists in concluding from the duty of the citizens of the slave-holding States to their own,—of concluding from the fact that it is right for South Carolina, for instance, to labor to emancipate the slaves, it is therefore right for citizens of Massachusetts to do the same. The wrong is not in the end sought, but in the persons who seek it, and the means by which they seek it.

The abolitionists are wrong as to their point of departure. They begin, consciously or unconsciously, by assuming that the people of the United States are one people, not in the restricted sense in which they are so declared by the constitution, but in all senses, to the fullest extent, as much so as the people of France or England. They regard themselves not as citizens of Massachusetts or of New York, but as citizens of the United States. The division of the territory into separate States, they regard as merely for administrative purposes, or for the convenience of transacting governmental business. They see not and understand not that the division into separate States, is a division, in point of fact and in theory especially, into distinct communities, separate nations, afterwards to be united by a league or compact; but a division altogether analogous to the division of a State for municipal purposes into counties, townships, and parishes. In giving the legal form to any public measure, they indeed recognize the boundaries of the States in like manner as they do the boundaries of a county, a township, or a parish; but in all else, in preparing the measure, in urging its adoption, in the combination and direction of influences which shall lead to or compel its adoption, they know no geographical boundaries, no civil or political divisions. Here is the source of their error. They begin by denying the sovereignty of the States, and consequently the Federal Republic created by the constitution, and by asserting the system of consolidation, another and altogether different system,—a system by which we become one vast centralized republic, adopting the division into States only as a convenient regulation for facilitating the administration of the affairs of government.

We say not that the abolitionists are in general aware of this, or that they would knowingly and intentionally do all this. They are probably aware of nothing but a morbid craving after excitement, and the determination, cost what it may, to abolish slavery. But we do say that the doctrine of consolidation, which we have stated, is that which lies at the bottom of their proceedings, and which has influenced them, and led them to adopt the proceedings they have. Had they been in the habit of contemplating the American political system in its true character, had they been in the habit of seeing in the division into States something more than a municipal regulation, than an affair of internal police, had they been accustomed to see in each State a distinct, independent, and sovereign community, in all matters, except the very few specified in the constitution of the United States, they had never taken those peculiar views of their own relations with the slaveholding communities, which have led them to adopt the measures of which we complain. Anti-slavery men they might have been, but abolitionists they could not have been.

We would acquit the abolitionists also of all wish to change fundamentally the character of our institutions. They are not, at least the honest part of them, politicians; but very simple-minded men and women who crave excitement, and seek it in abolition meetings, and in getting up abolition societies and petitions, instead of seeking it in ball-rooms, theaters, or places of fashionable amusement or dissipation. Politics, properly speaking, they abominate, because politics would require them to think, and they wish only to feel. Doubtless some of them are moved by generous sympathies, and a real regard for the well-being of the Negro; but the principal moving cause of their proceedings, after the craving for excitement, and perhaps notoriety, is the feeling that slavery is a national disgrace. Now this feeling, as we have shown, proceeds from a misconception of the real character of our institutions. This feeling can be justified only on the supposition that we are a consolidated republic. Its existence is therefore a proof that, whatever be the conscious motives in the main of the abolitionists, their proceedings strike against our Federal system.

Well, what if they do? replies the abolitionist. If Federalism, or the doctrine of State sovereignty, which you say is the American system of politics, prohibits us from laboring to free the slave, then down with it. Any system of government, any political relations, which prevent me from laboring to break the yoke of the oppressor and to set the captive free, is a wicked system, and ought to be destroyed. God disowns it, Christ disowns it, and man ought to disown it. If consolidation, if centralization be the order that enables us to free the slave, then give us consolidation, give us centralization. It is the true doctrine. It enables one to plead for the slave. The slave is crushed under his master's foot; the slave is dying; I see nothing but the slave; I hear nothing but the slave's cries for deliverance. Away with your paper barriers, away with your idle prating about State rights; clear the way. Let me run to the slave. Anything that frees the slave is right, is owned by God.

We express here the sentiment and use very nearly the language of the abolitionists. They have no respect for government as such. They indeed are fast adopting the ultra-radical doctrine that all government is founded in usurpation, and is an evil which all true Christians must labor to abolish. They have, at least some of them, nominated Jesus Christ to be president of the United States; as much as to say, in the only practical sense to be given the nomination, that there shall be no president of the United States but an idea, and an idea without any visible embodiment; which is merely contending in other words that there shall be no visible government, no political institutions whatever. They have fixed their minds on a given object, and finding that the political institutions of the country, and the laws of the land are against them, they deny the legitimacy of all laws and of all political institutions. Let them carry their doctrines out, and it is easy to see that a most radical revolution in the institutions of the country must be the result.

Now, we ask, has a revolution become necessary? Is it no longer possible to labor for the progress of Humanity in this country, without changing entirely the character of our political institutions? Must we change our Federal system, destroy the existing relations between the States and the Union and between the States? Nay, must we destroy all outward, visible government, abolish all laws, and leave the community in the state in which the Jews were, when there "was no king in Israel, and every man did that which was right in his own eyes"? We put these questions in soberness, and with a deep feeling of their magnitude. The abolition ranks are full of insane dreamers, and fuller yet of men and women ready to undertake to realize any dream however insane, and at any expense. We ask therefore these questions with solemnity, and with fearful forebodings for our country. We rarely fear; we rarely tremble at the prospect of evil to come. The habitual state of our own mind is that of serene trust in the future; and if in this respect we are thought to have a fault, it is in being too sanguine, in hoping too much. But we confess, the proceedings of the abolitionists, coupled with their vague speculations, and their crude notions, do fill us with lively alarm, and make us apprehend danger to our beloved country. We beg, in the name of God and of man, the abolitionists to pause, and if they love liberty, ask themselves what liberty has, in the long run, to gain by overthrowing the system of government we have established, by effecting a revolution in the very foundation of our Federal system?

For ourselves, we have accepted with our whole heart the political system adopted by our fathers. We regard that system as the most brilliant achievement of Humanity, a system in which centers all past progress, and which combines the last results of all past civilization. It is the latest birth of time. Humanity has been laboring with it since that morning when the Sons of God shouted with joy over the birth of a new world, and we will not willingly see it strangled in its cradle. We take the American political system as our starting-point, as our primitive data, and we repulse whatever is repugnant to it, and accept, demand whatever is essential to its preservation. We take our stand on the Idea of our institutions, and labor with all our soul to realize and develop it. As a lover of our race, as the devoted friend of liberty, of the progress of mankind, we feel that we must, in this country, be conservative, not radical. If we demand the elevation of labor and the laboring classes, we do it only in accordance with our institutions and for the purpose of preserving them by removing all discrepancy between their spirit and the social habits and condition of the people on whom they are to act, and to whose keeping they are entrusted. We demand reform only for the purpose of preserving American institutions in their real character; and we can tolerate no changes, no innovations, no alleged improvements not introduced in strict accordance with the relations which do subsist between the States and the Union and between the States themselves. Here is our political creed. More power in the Federal government than was given it by the Convention which framed the constitution would be dangerous to the States, and with less power the Federal government would not be able to subsist. We take it then as it is. The fact that any given measure is necessary to preserve it as it is, is a sufficient reason for adopting that measure; the fact that a given measure is opposed to it as it is, and has a tendency to increase or diminish its power, is a sufficient reason for rejecting that measure.

The constitution then is our touchstone for trying all measures. Not indeed because we have any superstitious reverence for written constitutions, or any overweening attachment to things as they are; but because we have satisfied ourselves by long, patient, and somewhat extensive inquiry, that the preservation of the constitution is strictly identified with the highest interests of our race. Its destruction were, so far as human foresight can go, an irreparable loss. We would preserve it then, not because it is a constitution, not because we are averse to changes, nor because we have a dread of revolutions, but because the safety and progress of liberty demand its preservation.

But can efforts in behalf of liberty be repugnant to the spirit of a constitution established avowedly in the interests of liberty? The abolitionists are in pursuit of liberty; liberty is their great idea; liberty is the soul of their movements; liberty is to be the end of their exertions; how then can their proceedings be dangerous to liberty? Very simply. In their character of efforts merely in behalf of liberty, of course they are neither unconstitutional nor dangerous; but they may have another character than that; beside being efforts in behalf of liberty they may be efforts which strike against international law. The abolitionist would free the slave. So far so good. But he would free the slave by forgetting that slavery is an institution under the sole control of a State of which he is not a citizen. Here comes the danger to liberty. Here is a blow struck at the rights of communities, and as dangerous to liberty as a blow struck at the rights of individuals. He would free the slaves by combining the non-slaveholding States against the slaveholding States, by collecting in the non-slaveholding States a force sufficient to control the internal policy of the slaveholding States. Let him do this, and where is the independence of the States? Let him do this, and one part of the Union has the complete control of the other; and when this is done, is not our Federal system destroyed? It is possible then to pursue liberty in such a manner that the pursuit shall be in open violation of free institutions; and this is, as we allege, the case with the abolitionists.

But we can pursue the subject no farther at present. We are sorry to be compelled to separate ourselves from the abolitionists. There is something exceedingly unpleasant in being, even in appearance, opposed to the advocates of freedom. We have ever been with the movement party; our own position, the much we have suffered from things as they are, the wounds yet rankling in our heart, together with our own love of excitement, of new things, to say nothing of certain dreams we indulge concerning a golden age that is to be, strongly dispose us to join with the abolitionists, and to rush on in the career they open up to a bold and energetic spirit. There is something too in the very idea of freeing two or three millions of slaves, which, in these mechanical and money-getting times, is quite refreshing and capable of dazzling many an imagination. It addresses itself to some of the strongest propensities of our nature, and gives us apparently an opportunity to indulge a taste for the adventurous and the chivalric. There is something almost intoxicating in the idea of going forth as a bold knight in the cause of Humanity, to plead for the wronged and the outraged, to speak for the dumb, and to do valiant battle for the weak and the defenseless. Much that is noble, that is generous, that is godlike, naturally combines itself with such an idea, and enters into the motives of him who goes forth at its bidding. It may be that we have felt something of all this. But self-denial, even in the indulgence of what we call noble impulses, or rather the subordination of our impulses to the clearest and soberest convictions of our understandings, is one of the first laws of morality.

So long as we regarded the abolitionists as merely contending for the right to discuss the subject of slavery, we were with them; we spoke in their behalf, and were willing to be reckoned of their number. Later developments on their side, and a closer examination of the bearings of their movements on the political institutions of this country, into which we have entered, have convinced us that the cause of free discussion is not now, if it ever was, at all involved in their proceedings; that the cause of liberty even, is by no means in their hands; and therefore that we ought to separate from them, and to state clearly and boldly, the reasons which we think should induce all lovers of our common country to combine to stay their progress. It may be too late. We fear it is. The ball has been set in motion. It increases in momentum and velocity with every revolution, and the result we pretend not to be able to foresee. Already is it hazardous to one's reputation in this part of the Union to oppose them; already is it nearly impossible for any political party to succeed unless it can secure their suffrages. They have become a power. It is in vain to deny it. They are not likely to become weaker very soon. We have not, therefore, dared to keep our convictions in regard to them to ourselves. In opposing them, we have had to show as much moral courage as they profess to have shown in opposing slavery. We have not, therefore, spoken from considerations we need be ashamed to avow. We may have spoken in vain. But we have said our word, feebly we own, but in sincerity; and we leave the result to God. We see danger ahead. We tremble for the fate of our republic; there are mighty influences at work against it; the money power is seeking to bind its free spirit with chains of gold, and mistaken philanthropy is fast rending it in twain; associations, sectarian and moral espionage are fast swallowing up individual freedom, and making the individual man but a mere appendage to a huge social machine, with neither mind nor will of his own; but we do not, we will not, despair of the republic. We hope with trembling, nevertheless we hope. The destinies of individuals or of nations are not left to blind chance. There is a providence that rules them, and we will trust that in due time the clouds that lower over us shall break and disperse, and the glorious sun of freedom and Humanity shine forth in all his noonday splendors. We cannot go back to the night and gloom of the past; the irresistible law of progress does and will bear us onward; and this republic shall yet prove itself the medium through which the human race shall rise to the knowledge and enjoyment of the inalienable rights of Man.

In conclusion, we would merely add, that in our judgment the first duty of the friends of freedom, of democracy, of progress, is to secure the political institutions established by our fathers. Nothing can come but in its time and its place. There is a method to be followed in taking up and discussing the great questions which concern mankind, or the progress of society. Errors always come from the fact that we take them up in a false order. Our inquiry should be, What is the question for today? Having ascertained the problem for today, we should bend our whole attention to its solution. The answer to the question of today, will of itself lead to the solution of the problem which shall come up tomorrow. The question for today is the currency question,—not the most interesting question in itself surely, nor a question of the first magnitude; but it is the first in the order of time. It must be disposed of before we can proceed systematically to the disposition of any other. What will be the question for tomorrow, we ask not. Sufficient for the day is the evil thereof. It will doubtless be a question of magnitude. Great questions are hereafter to be ever expected. Humanity approaches manhood, grows serious, and refuses to trifle. As it regards the slave question, we leave it to those whom it more immediately concerns. If our republic outlive the dangers to which it is now exposed, the gradual unfolding of its spirit will abolish slavery; and we believe slavery will be sooner abolished, that is, the negro race sooner elevated to the rank of freemen, by leaving the whole matter to time, to the secret but sure workings of Christian democracy, than by any violent or special efforts of abolitionists, even if successful in declaring slavery abolished. Leave the whole matter to the slave-holding States, and in proportion as the negro advances internally, the legislature will spread over him the shield of the law, and imperceptibly but surely shall he grow into a freeman, if a freeman he can become.

If we would serve him and hasten that day, we shall best do it, not by direct efforts in his behalf, but by a steady development and realization of democratic freedom within the bosom of the non-slaveholding States. Let us correct the evils at our own doors, elevate the free white laborer, and prove by our own practice, and by the state of our own society, that the doctrine of equal rights is not a visionary dream. O we have much to do here at home. The beggar full of sores lies at our own gate. In our own dark streets, blind courts, narrow lanes, damp cellars, unventilated garrets, are human beings more degraded, and suffering keener anguish, and appealing with a more touching pathos to our compassion, and demanding in more imperative tones our succor, than is the case with the most wretched of Southern slaves. O here are objects enough for our humanity. We walk not through the streets of a single Northern city without a bleeding heart. Wash the faces of those children, Abolitionists, which meet you in our cities encrusted with filth, clothe their shivering limbs, let in light upon their darkened minds, and warm their young hearts, before it is too late, with the hope of being one day virtuous men and women. Instead of poring over the horrors of slavery, read your police reports, and see your own society as it is. You have work enough for all your philanthropy north of Mason and Dixon's line. Do this work, do it effectually, and you shall aid the cause of oppressed Humanity everywhere, and the slave a thousand times more than by your direct efforts for his emancipation.

Specimens of Foreign Literature

OCTOBER 1838

A Review of George Ripley's *Philosophical Miscellanies, translated from the French of Cousin, Jouffroy, and Benjamin Constant* (Boston: Hilliard, Gray, & Co., 1838; 2 vols.)

These two volumes are the first of a series of translations, Mr. Ripley proposes to bring out, from time to time, under the general title of Specimens of Foreign Standard Literature. The works he proposes to translate, or to cause to be translated, are the works in highest repute in France and Germany, the best works of the ablest scholars and most distinguished authors of the two nations in the departments of Philosophy, Theology, History, and General Literature. He will be assisted in this undertaking by some of our first scholars and most eminent literary men, and will, if he realizes his plan, give us not only specimens of foreign standard literature, but also specimens of correct and elegant translation.

Mr. Ripley's undertaking is a noble one, and one in which our whole country is deeply interested. The importance of reproducing in our own language the standard literature of other nations cannot easily be overrated. Every nation has its peculiar idea, its special manner of viewing things in general, and gives a prominence, a development to some one element of universal truth, which is given by no other nation.

The literature of one nation has therefore always something peculiar to itself; something of value, which can be found in the literature of no other. The study of the literatures of different nations will necessarily tend, therefore, to liberalize our minds, to enlarge our ideas, and augment our sum of truth. Very few among us have the leisure or the opportunity to make ourselves sufficiently acquainted with foreign languages, to be able to relish the works of foreigners save in translations. It is always on translations that the great mass of the people must depend for all the direct benefit they are to receive from the labors and researchers of foreign scholars; and it is the direct benefit of the great mass of the people, that the American scholar is bound always to consult.

If translations are to be made at all, they ought to be well made, and to be of the best works, the standard works of the languages from which they are made. We have many translations from the French and German, but in a majority of cases, perhaps, we may say of works that were hardly worth the translating. This may be said especially in reference to the German. The American public study Germany not in the mature productions of her ripest scholars. Second and third rate authors, and second and third rate performances, at best, are those most generally translated. This is a grievous wrong to Germany, for it compels us to judge her for altogether less than she is; it is also a grievous wrong to ourselves, for it deprives us of a good we might receive, and which we need. Translations too are in general miserably executed, by persons who are in no sense whatever qualified to be translators. This perhaps is more especially the case in England than in this country. They are made too often by literary hacks, who must make them or starve, and who have adequate knowledge of either the foreign language or their own, and not the faintest conception of the thought they undertake to reproduce. In consequence of want of taste and judgment in selecting the works to be translated, and of proper qualifications on the part of translators, translations in general, unless of purely scientific works, serve little other end than to encumber our book-shelves, corrupt the language, and overload it with foreign idioms and barbarous words and phrases. Both these evils are sought to be avoided by Mr. Ripley's plan, and will be, if his plan be realized, as we doubt not it must. His plan ensures us a French or German classic reproduced in English, and constituting ever after an English classic, whereby the intellectual and literary treasures within the reach of the mere English student will be greatly augmented, the language itself enriched and perfected, the national taste refined and purified, and the national character elevated.

We are also much in want of the works Mr. Ripley proposes to reproduce. We have much to learn in the departments of Philosophy, Theology, and History, from the literatures of France and Germany. We are comparatively a young people. We have had a savage world to subdue, primitive forests to clear away, material interests to provide for. Our hands have necessarily and rightly been employed, and our thoughts busy, in procuring the means of subsistence and in preparing the theater of our future glory; and we have not had the leisure to pore over the records of the past, to push our inquiries into surrounding nature, to sit down and patiently watch the fleeting phenomena which rapidly pass and repass over the field of consciousness, or to engage with spirit and ardor in high and extensive literary pursuits. It is not our fault, then, if we are in some respects behind the cultivated nations of the Old World. We shall not be behind them long. There is a literature in the American soul, waiting but a favorable moment to burst forth, before which the most admired literatures of the Old World will shrink into insignificance, and be forgotten. This nation is destined to excel in every department of human activity. It now takes the lead in commercial and industrial activity; it will take the lead in the sciences and the arts. From us is, one day, light to radiate, as from the central sun, to illumine the moral and intellectual universe. To us shall come, from all lands, the statesman, the philosopher, the artist, to gain instruction and inspiration, as from the God-appointed prophets of Humanity. We need not blush, then, to avail ourselves for the moment of foreign resources. The capital we borrow from abroad we shall profitably invest, and be able to repay, and with usury too.

This is not all. We are now the literary vassals of England, and continue to do homage to the mother country. Our literature is tame and servile, wanting in freshness, freedom, and originality. We write as Englishmen, not as Americans. We are afraid to think our own thoughts, to speak our own words, or to give utterance to the rich and gushing sentiments of our own hearts. And so must it be so long as we rely on England's literature as exclusively as we have hitherto done. Not indeed so much because that literature is not a good one. English literature, so long as it boasts a Shakespeare and a Milton, cannot suffer in comparison with the literature of any other nation. For ourselves we reverence it, and would on no account speak lightly of it. But it cramps our national genius, and exercises a tyrannical sway over the American mind. We cannot become independent and original, till we have in some degree weakened its empire. This will be best done by the study of the fresher, and in some respects superior literatures of continental Europe. We must bring in France and Germany to combat or neutralize England, so that our national spirit may gain the freedom to manifest itself.

Moreover, excellent as is the English literature, it is not exactly the literature for young republicans. England is the most aristocratic country in the world. Its literature is, with some noble exceptions, aristocratic. It is deficient in true reverence for man as man, wholly unconscious of the fact that man is everywhere equal to man. It is full of reverence for that mass of incongruities, the British Constitution, which contains more of the character of the institutions of the Middle Age, than any other constitution or form of government to be found in Europe. It bristles from beginning to end with Dukes and Duchesses, Lords and Ladies, and overflows with servility to the great, and with contempt, or what is worse, condescension for the little. The constant and exclusive study of a literature like this cannot fail to be deeply prejudicial to republican simplicity of thought and taste, to create a sort of disgust for republican manners and institutions, and to make us sigh to reproduce, on American soil, the aristocratic manners and institutions of England. Things seen at a distance are always more enchanting than when seen close by. Did we live in England we should spurn her institutions; but seeing them only at a distance and through the idealizing medium of poetry and works of fiction, they appear unto us beautiful and exceedingly desirable. We think it would be a fine thing to be Dukes and Duchesses, Lords and Ladies, to wear titles, ribbons, stars, and coronets, and to be elevated above the vulgar herd. We grow aweary of our democratic institutions, submit to them with an ill grace, and do what in us lies to hinder their free and beneficial working. It does not occur to us that those of us, who sign to reproduce English institutions, might, were the thing done, possibly be at the foot instead of the summit of the new social hierarchy; nor do we reflect that a nobility is elevated to its height only by making the immense majority of the people serve as its pedestal. It may be pleasant to be one of the nobility, to stand with one's head far above one's fellows; but it is not very pleasant to be the pedestal on which another stands. We wish no brother man to appear tall because his feet stand on our head; and rather than be obliged to run the risk of having some vain, fat, ignorant, proud, titled mortal stand on our head, we choose to forego the pleasure of standing on another man's head.

The corrupting tendency of English literature in this respect, on our young men and young women too, is easy to be seen, and threatens to be disastrous. Patriotism dies out; and our own government, in proportion to its fidelity to American principles, becomes the object of the severest censure, the most uncompromising hostility, or the most withering ridicule. Our own writers cannot arrest the tendency; because of considerable portion of them, formed by the study of English literature, are themselves carried away by it; and because the remainder are too few in number, and their voices, though clear and strong, are lost in the universal din of English voices, which we are continually importing. In other words, English works reprinted and circulated here are so much more numerous, and owing to the fact that they can be furnished much cheaper, are so much more extensively circulated than the works of native authors, that they overpower them, and almost wholly counteract their influence.

Now in this situation nothing can be more suitable or more succoring for us, than large importations of French and German literature. France and Germany are monarchical, it is true, but not aristocratic. Monarchy has been, in Europe in general, popular rather than aristocratic in its tendency. The people have in most countries less to dread from the monarch than from the noble. Monarchy raises one man indeed above, far above the people, but in doing this, it lessens or neutralizes to some extent the distinctions which obtain below it. The writings of French or even German scholars breathe altogether more of a democratic spirit than do those of the English. Those of the French are altogether more democratic than the writings of American scholars themselves. Then again, we have in this country not much to fear from the monarchical tendency. There is nothing monarchical in the genius or temper of the American people. We remember yet the struggles our fathers had with the king, and that we are the descendants of those who dethroned Mary Stuart, and brought Charles Stuart to the scaffold. Then we have no powerful families as yet that could make interest for a throne, no individual influential enough, universally popular enough, or far enough elevated above his brethren to be thought of in connection with a crown. We have too long been accustomed to govern ourselves, too large a portion of our citizens have taken a direct share in the affairs of government, and may always hope to take a direct share in them, to think of abandoning them to any one man. We can arrive at monarchy in this country only through aristocracy. We do not apprehend that this will ever be the case. The aristocratic tendency is the only tendency we have to apprehend serious danger from; but even this tendency will, we trust, be arrested before it shall have done any lasting injury to our institutions. The study of French and German literature will arrest this tendency. It will break the dominion of England; and, without excluding English literature, will furnish us new elements, and a broader and more democratic basis for our own.

We are also anxious that French and German literature should be cultivated among us, because it will correct in some measure the faults of our own democracy. One extreme always begets another. The tendency on the one hand to adore England, and approach English manners and institutions, begets on the other hand a tendency to a rabid radicalism, from which danger may be apprehended, but from which good is not to be looked for. If the wealthy, the cultivated, and literary, as is and has been too much the case, approach England, the democracy of the country becomes to a great degree deprived of the helps of refinement, cultivation, literature, and the conservative element which always goes with them. True democracy has always a conservative element, and is no less wedded to order than to liberty. It unites the two; and is always normal in its proceedings. It is broad enough to take in all Humanity, and free enough to allow all the elements of human nature to develop themselves fully and harmoniously. Now in English literature this is never the case. The element of order and its adherents are separated from the element of liberty and its adherents. The exclusive study of that literature has to a considerable extent produced the same result here. Hence our democracy becomes in some measure partial, exclusive, and able to enlist on its side only at best a small majority of the nation. This is a serious evil, and it is that from which we have more to dread than from anything else whatever. Democracy so long as it is broad and comprehensive, so long as it is true to itself, and to all elements of human nature, is invincible, and able to go forth "conquering and to conquer."

Now in the master-pieces of French and German literature we shall find the two great elements, of which we have spoken, always united and working in harmony. There is nothing rash, nothing violent, destructive. Progress, the perfectibility of man and society is admitted and contended for, at the same time peaceable and orderly means by which to effect it are pointed out. The tree has its natural growth, and by natural growth attains its height. It is not made higher by being plucked up by the roots, and held up by artificial means. Erudition, science, philosophy, religion, art, refinement, are all combined with the spirit of progress, and made subservient to the elevation of the people. The cultivation of French and German literature must have a similar effect here, and thus is what we want, and what, if Mr. Ripley's plan succeeds, we shall have.

This too is the country in which the noble ideas of man and society, which French and German scholars strike out in their speculations, are to be first applied to practice, realized in institutions. There the scholar may study; there the philosopher may investigate man; there the politician may explore the city, and ascertain how the state should be organized; and there they all may deposit the result of their speculations, their researchers, their inspirations in books; but, alas, in books only; for to them is wanting the theater on which to act them out, the practical world in which to realize them. They have old institutions to combat; old prejudices to overcome; old castles and old churches to clear away; an old people to re-youth, before they can proceed to embody their ideas, or to reduce them to practice. More than all this, they want freedom to do it. Authority is against them, and armed soldiery are ready to repulse them. But here is a virgin soil, an open field, a new people, full of the future, with unbounded faith in ideas, and the most ample freedom. Here, if any where on earth, may the philosopher experiment on human nature, and demonstrate what man has it in him to be when and where he has the freedom and the means to be himself. Let Germany then explore the mines, and bring out the ore, let France smell it, extract the pure metal, determine its weight and fineness, and we will work it up into vessels of ornament or utility, apply it to the practical purposes of life.

In passing from the proposed series of translations and the importance of the undertaking to the volumes before us, we would remark that, viewed simply as translations, they must possess in the estimation of every scholar a high worth. We doubt whether better specimens of translation are to be found in the language,—better specimens certainly *we* have never met. Familiar as we are with the originals, we read these translations with pleasure. They do not seem to be translations. They have all the freedom and freshness of original compositions. Yet they are faithful and literal even, altogether more so than translations in general. They are true reproductions, and could have been made only by a man who comprehended their subject-matter hardly less thoroughly than did their original authors. Mr. Ripley deserves high praise for the example he has set to all future translators. He has not only reproduced his authors, but he has done it in pure classic English, in which the most fastidious critic will be troubled to find a single idiom, word, or phrase at which to take offense. In doing this he has done much. He has proved that translations may be made without corrupting the language. He has also rendered an important service, in these volumes, to the philosophical student, by doing much to fix our philosophical language, and to free it from that vagueness and uncertainty, which have heretofore so grievously afflicted all who have attempted to write or read on philosophical subjects.

The several pieces which make up these volumes are selected with great judgment and taste. They are, of their shorter productions, the most important productions of their authors, and are superior to any thing else of the kind that we know of in any language. They are so selected and arranged as to form, with the Introductory and Critical Notices by the translator, very nearly a continuous whole, and to constitute something like a regular treatise on the object, method, and history of philosophy, the philosophy of history, morals, and religion, and the destiny of man and society. The Notices are in part original, and in part selected or translated. They are of great value, and were other proof wanting, would prove the translator an acute critic, an accomplished scholar, an able philosopher, and a true and warm-hearted friend of his race.

As to the general merits of the authors of these Miscellanies, we refer our readers to the introductory notices by the translator. They are three authors, who are an honor to France, and to mankind. Benjamin Constant was long known throughout Europe as an ardent lover of liberty, as the devoted advocate of constitutional government, and as a distinguished literary and political writer. His great work, *De la Religion considree dans sa Source, ses Formes, et ses Developpements*, exhibits much erudition, philosophic insight, and religious and philanthropic sentiment. We are glad to find that it is to be included in Mr. Ripley's series. It is just the work needed in the present state of religious doubt, indifference, and fanaticism in this country, and its study would do much to reconcile Faith and Reason, and to restore us to a pure, rational, and living faith in Christianity. Jouffroy is a profound psychologist, a clear and eloquent writer, and one of the ablest and safest moral philosophers, it has ever been our good fortune to meet. He was a pupil of Cousin, is a professor of philosophy in the Faculty of Letters at Paris, and one of the principal disciples of the New French School. Cousin is well known as the chief of the New French Philosophy, and he is unquestionably, if not the first, one of the first philosophers of the age.

The subject-matter of these volumes is worthy of the most serious attention. The time has gone by in this country, when it could be accounted a mark of good taste or of superior wisdom to sneer at metaphysical studies. The public mind has been awakened, and mental and moral science is henceforth one of our most cherished studies. Men have outgrown tradition, and they begin to find themselves unable to legitimate their beliefs. They begin to be troubled with the problem of human destiny. They ask themselves, enigma of human existence; what man knows, and wherefore he can know that he knows. They find themselves forced by the state of their spiritual affairs to give an account to themselves of themselves, of their knowledge and their belief, their hopes, fears, and doubts. They are compelled therefore to philosophize. And they must continue to philosophize, for the problem once raised, it will not down till it is solved. Every work therefore that treats on this problem which torments the soul, every work which proposes to aid us to meet this inward questioning, of which we have become conscious, and which we indulge more and more every day, must be hailed with joy, and sought after with avidity. We have lost the early faith of childhood, we have arraigned the catechism, and we must now wear out a life of painful doubt, or attain to a rational conviction.

These Miscellanies will aid us. They state with great clearness and distinctness the principal problems which have tormented the soul in all ages; and if they do not solve them, they at least give us the law of their solution. If they do not give us a philosophy which is perfectly satisfactory, which exhausts human nature, they do give us the true method of philosophizing, of legitimating scientifically the universal beliefs of mankind. More appropriate to the present state of the public mind they could not be. The scholar will read them with delight; the divine, the moralist, the statesman will find them invaluable in directing them in the discharge of their several functions, and in solving the theological, moral, and political doubts they everywhere meet, and which seem almost to paralyze the spiritual powers of man. They are full of masculine thought. They breathe a liberal tone, assert with earnestness and power the rights and the worth of man, as man, and show a profound reverence for truth, beauty, goodness,—God. They are just the volumes for us young Americans, to quicken within us a sense of the dignity and reach of our mission, to kindle our faith in ourselves and in Providence, and to enable us to elaborate the glorious future which awaits mankind.

Democracy and Reform

OCTOBER 1839

A Commentary on Robert Townsend's *An Inquiry into the Cause of Social Evil; with its Remedy* (New York: 1839); Samuel Osgood's *An Oration, delivered on the 4th of July, 1839, before the Citizens of Nashua* (Nashua: Allen Beard, 1939); Seth Thomas's *An Address, delivered before the Democratic Citizens of Plymouth County, July 4, 1839* (Boston: Beals & Greene, 1839); and John P. Tarbell's *An Oration, delivered before the Democratic Citizens of the North part of Middlesex County, July 4, 1839* (Lowell: Abijah Watson, 1839)

The first pamphlet on our list is a tract, issued by a society for social reform in the city of New York, of which society we know nothing, and have no wish to know anything. We do not see any call for social reform societies. There are already so many associations for religious, social, and philanthropic objects, that we can rarely find an individual with a sense of individual independence, and responsibility. The pamphlet, however, is respectable. We know nothing personally of its author, Mr. Townsend, but his Address speaks well for his talent, acquirements, and philanthropic feelings. His views strike us as being in general just and well-timed.

The second pamphlet enumerated is from the pen of a young clergyman of great promise, and is written, for the most part, with rare beauty and power. It clearly defines and ably sustains the democratic principle. It, however, shuns all allusion to what may be considered democratic measures, and democratic men. Mr. Osgood, as a clergyman, may think that he is not required to take a very decided party stand, but he seems to recommend on principle all wise and good men to keep as much aloof from party as possible. He appears to adopt for his motto, "principles, —not measures, nor men."

The third pamphlet is from a plain, self-made democrat, who makes no pretensions to literary culture. But his Address is written with great clearness and force, and is an eloquent and able vindication of the principles and measures of the democratic party. Mr. Thomas possesses a strong mind, is a sound logician, and is fitted to be a popular political writer.

Mr. Tarbell's Oration is also a defense of the democratic principles and measures. It is sound in its doctrine, and in some passages genuinely eloquent. Mr. Tarbell is a young man, who somewhat distinguished himself last winter, as a member of our General Court. As a writer he wants practice. His Oration smacks too much of the strained, the affected style, for which Fourth of July Orations have been but too remarkable. He will do much more honor to himself by cherishing a severer taste, and adopting a simpler style of oratory. Homer, we have heard it said, was not less remarkable for simplicity, than for sublimity. Our American writers are too apt to get on stilts, which makes them appear rather awkward. The truly great man goes calmly to his work, is always self-possessed, always unaffected, and able to breathe an air of repose, of quiet dignity over all his productions.

All these pamphlets show that their authors belong to the movement party, and that they are looking forward with the eye of hope to great and important changes in man's social condition; and what has pleased us even more than this is the fact, that, whatever meliorations of society they may anticipate or struggle for, they evidently expect them from the more perfect application of Christian principles to man's social and political relations. They all apparently cherish the conviction, that democracy is nothing but the political application of Christianity; and not one of them seems to dream of hitching the car of reform, on to that of infidelity. This to us is a cheering fact, a proof that our social reformers are beginning to take juster views of religion, and that the friends of religion are beginning to feel more deeply, that their faith requires them to labor for man's earthly well-being.

Some ten or twelve years ago, there were indications, that the cause of social reform in this country would be connected with that of disbelief in the Gospel. The attention of the American people was first seriously called to the defects of all existing social organizations, and to the importance and duty of laboring for social progress, by Robert Owen, his son Robert Dale Owen, Miss Frances Wright, and others, whose shallow philosophy was represented in the "Free Enquirer," and the "Lectures on Knowledge." The Owens and Miss Wright produced a profound sensation; they quickened many a young heart, and recalled enthusiasm to many an old man, who had fondly dreamed that his labors for this world were over. They were the immediate occasion of the workingmen's movements, which took place in various parts of the country, cheering some and alarming others; and they have contributed not a little to that general examination into the actual state of American society, which has been for some time going on amongst us. This is the good side of their influence. But unhappily, these generous and philanthropic foreigners had no just appreciation of the Gospel, and assigned no place to religion in the new order of things they sought to bring about. They considered religion, even in its purity, a vulgar superstition, they looked upon it as favoring priestcraft and tyranny, and as hostile to all exertions for the improvement of society. They wished to brush it out of the way, recall men from the contemplation of another world, compel them to limit their hopes and affections to the narrow compass of this life, so that their attention should not be distracted from their earthly dwelling, and so that they might be left free to labor for its embellishment. The world, said they, lies waste, society is infested with noxious weeds, overgrown with thistles and brambles, because men have neglected this world for another. They must, therefore, leave the world after death, cease to be amused with dreams of paradise, or alarmed by dreams of Tophet, and think only of making the earth the abode of peace, love, and happiness.

This was their doctrine, and there was apparently some danger, that it would spread further than the safety of the commonwealth would permit. The Owens and Miss Wright did not oppose religion on its own account. They disdained to concern themselves with so vulgar a subject. It became worthy of their opposition, only inasmuch as it appeared to them to be an impediment to the social progress they were desirous of realizing. But, there were others amongst us, who were opposed to what they called religion, on its own account. They were infidels, rather than social reformers. They believed in disbelief, and had a creed to propagate. Such were the late leader of the Free Enquirers in this city, and his more prominent friends. These men saw the strong democratic tendency of the American people, and fancied, that if they could bring about a union between infidelity and radical democracy, they should be able, by means of the popularity of the democracy, to make infidelity triumph. Here was a deep-laid scheme; and there were many things, which seemed to favor its success. Most of the champions of the people in the old world, had. been, and were at war with religious establishments; the French democrats, with La Fayette at their head, were claimed to a man to be infidels. In our own country, the father of American democracy, Thomas Jefferson, was looked upon as an unbeliever; Washington's orthodoxy was said to be questionable; the elder Adams was at best a heretic, and Franklin, in early life, an infidel, and there was no proof that he had ever changed his opinions. Add to this, the clergy,—especially the clergy of New England, and of the more influential sects,—were pretty generally found on the side against the democracy. They had opposed Jefferson, they had opposed Madison and the War, and were at best indifferent to the subject of social progress. From these facts, it was not worse logic than often obtains to infer, on the one hand, that, to be thorough-going democrats, we must be infidels; and on the other hand, to be thorough-going Christians, we must uphold social abuses.

But happily the dark cloud has passed, or is now passing away. The reformers are now pretty generally coming to the conclusion, that infidelity is a mere negative force, and can effect no solid, enduring reform; and that Christianity, originally taught by a carpenter's son, and, under the Providence of God, propagated by fishermen and tent-makers, declaring all men equal in the sight of God, and, therefore, equal to one another, so far from tending to uphold social abuses, commands us, with all the authority of God, to labor for the elevation of the masses, and permits us to hope for heaven only on the ground, that we have fed the hungry, given drink to the thirsty, clothed the naked, visited the sick, and unloosed the captive. Christianity is the very creed of the reformer;

its spirit is the spirit of reform itself; and the unbelievers who are laboring for a reform, are unconsciously obeying it.

We consider this a great gain. It is a result, that we have been many years laboring, apparently almost alone, to bring about, and we can but rejoice, that in this direction our labors are no longer needed. By understanding that the social reformer, the friend of the "largest liberty," may also be the truest and most pious Christian, we do away with an antagonism, which has heretofore been injurious to both religion and social progress. We effect by this a union, from which we may look for the noblest offspring. We bring the whole force of the religious sentiment, the strongest sentiment in our nature, and the source, or the ally of all our generous and disinterested affections,—we bring the whole force of this sentiment, and the whole authority of the church, to strengthen the reformer; while we bring the whole force of our love of freedom, our desire to perfect social institutions, of the whole democratic movement of the age, to the aid of religion and the church. It is, in fact, a sort of realization of the atonement, a bringing together, if we may so speak, of God and man. It unites the instinct of a Deity with the instinct of Humanity, and gives us the God-man, in whom is redemption from all sin.

The reconciliation between Christians and reformers is now virtually effected. Religion is taking a social direction, and reform is becoming spiritual. On the side of progress, and especially social progress, we see the most advanced philosophy of the age, and the noblest creations of literature. Philosophy, literature, art, religion, all with us, are enlisting in the service of the democracy. This is well. It is encouraging to the true philanthropist. But, there is a still further reconciliation, which we wish to see brought about. We wish to see the union consummated between the reformers and the democratic party, so called. We contend, and it is the purpose of this article to prove, that it is the interest and the duty of the friends of progress, in whatever direction, to unite cordially with the democratic party, so called, and to give it all the support in their power. The ends they have in view, so far as they are practicable, will be obtained by so doing, and they can obtain them by no other method.

It is not pretended by anybody, that all who are contending for the progress of Humanity act with the democratic party. There is among us a large number of educated and intelligent men, who have outgrown the old-fashioned Federalism, in which they were reared. These men now take broad and generous views of human nature; they have protested against old forms, against conventionalisms and factitious distinctions, which make enemies of brethren; they have seen the necessity, and believe in the practicability of great social meliorations; but they cannot bring themselves to cooperate with the democratic party. They have been accustomed, from their earliest life, to look upon it as made up of a disorderly rabble, led on by unprincipled demagogues, and they cannot stoop to enter its ranks. They like the democratic principles, claim to be thorough-going democrats themselves, and would be much hurt, should we deny them the democratic name; they even like, and some of them profess to approve, the more prominent and leading measures of the democratic party; but then the democratic men, the men, what pure-minded, philanthropic, enlightened, disinterested Christian and patriot can associate with them? A difficult question no doubt to answer. But, we apprehend, a little more intimate acquaintance with the democratic men, would soften this repugnance somewhat. Furthermore, with the most profound respect for these men, we must suggest, that their democratic progress has not been quite so great as they fancy. The democratic party embraces the majority of the people of the United States. To complain of the party as these men do, is but saying, that the majority of the people of the United States are unworthy to be the party associates of a man of respectability. This is not very complimentary, and we suspect they who say so still retain a considerable portion of the leaven of the Pharisees, of which they would do well to get rid as soon as possible. And lastly, if the democratic party is composed of such a worthless rabble, there is but so much the greater necessity that these good and wise men should enter its ranks, so that it may have some virtue whereof to boast. If all good men keep aloof from the party, is it possible that it should be composed entirely of good men and true?

We are aware, that we have many excellent men among us, who entertain a most lively repugnance to party, and party action. We ourselves, without claiming either matchless wisdom or immaculate virtue, have all our life long declaimed against party. But a little practical acquaintance with the affairs of the world, and some reflection on the laws which control the action of society, have finally convinced us, that whatever be our aversion to party, parties are inevitable, and will be till all men become perfect, or until a uniformity of opinion is brought about by means of absolute despotism. Doubtless, no man should seek, party for party's sake; but who so would take a part with his fellow-men in the management of what concerns the public good, must act with a party, unless he fancies himself capable of constituting, in himself alone, a party strong enough to cope with all existing parties.

Parties are not arbitrary creations. They are called forth and sustained by higher laws than any of human enactment. They are inseparable from the imperfect development of humanity, and will ever be a source of complaint to those, who think more of the end to be gained, than of the power which is created in struggling to gain an end. It was the will of Providence to make man an imperfect being, to give him his point of departure in weakness and ignorance. As an indemnity for this, he gave him the capacity for illimitable progress. Parties grow, on the one hand, out of this imperfection, and on the other, out of the unfolding of this capacity. Society, in its various institutions, is but the reflex of human nature. Contemplated at any given epoch, it merely marks the point to which the progress of Humanity has attained. It must, therefore, at any given epoch, fall just as far short of perfection, as human nature at that epoch rails short of its complete development. A portion of every community will be more alive to this imperfection than the rest, and also more confident in the power of human nature to advance. These will constitute a movement party, or party of the future; the rest of the community, either satisfied with things as they are, or destitute of faith in man's power of progress, will constitute the stationary or stand-still party. In some epochs, in some countries, the first of these parties will be in a feeble minority; in others, it will be in a majority, as it is at present in this country. The first of these parties with us is called the democratic party, the other is denominated the whig party. These two parties have existed among us from the first settlement of our country; and analogous parties may be found in every country that possesses freedom enough to allow of any mental activity. We must accept them, or abandon our freedom.

The democratic party is, no doubt, an imperfect embodiment of the great idea of progress. Nobody pretends, that it is faultless. It would be saying not a little for the American people, to say, that the majority of them constitute a party, which has not a single fault. It would also be virtually saying, that we have no further progress to make, that we have realized the idea of our institutions, finished our work, and have nothing before us, but to die. The democratic party, doubtless, partakes of all the faults of the country, and shares in all the imperfections which belong to our stage in the general progress of Humanity; but it represents what is most advanced in our condition. Its virtues are always the living virtues of the times, and its intelligence, that which reaches farthest into the future, and which is to be for the longest time to come the dominant intelligence. The virtues of its enemies will be always the virtues which were most in repute yesterday, and its intelligence that which was novel, and truly admirable in our fathers.

But our friends, with whom we are at this moment engaged, doubt much of this, and tell us, that, although they do not like to be enrolled in the stand-still party, or, if you please, the party of yesterday, they cannot consent to join the democratic party. It is too coarse, too vulgar. It wants refinement, elevation, high moral aims, and disinterested affections. Let us have, say they, a third party, composed of virtuous and enlightened men, who will labor for the public good, without any reference to their own interest. This is very fine. Who would not like to be a member of such a party? But on what principle shall we call forth such a party? What shall be its watch-word, its rallying cry? You can call forth a third party only when there is some great and pressing interest, which the two existing parties neglect. Is there such an interest in this country? If so, what is it? If this interest relates to progress, then it is an interest for the democratic party to take up, and if that party has not yet taken it up, what should be the inference, but that the country is not yet prepared to act upon it? If it be an interest opposed to progress, there is already your stand-still party, your whig party, to espouse it. If the question concern merely its discussion, it can be discussed in the bosom of that existing party, whose general principles embrace it, and it will not cost more time or trouble to bring that party, as a party, to act on it, than it will to raise up a new party, sufficiently large to act on it with effect.

Moreover, we wish to be informed whence we are to obtain all these excellent men, who are to make up our third party. If the third party be but a minority, it will not be able to accomplish much. If the two parties now existing are so corrupt as to render a third necessary, whence can we obtain good men enough to constitute a party, which shall embrace a majority of the people of the United States? We are speaking to reformers, who, of course, wish their third party to be a party of progress. Its recruits, then, must be taken front the democratic party, as the members of the whig party are not in favor of progress. So, if your third party rise to a majority, it will be little else than the present democratic party under a new name. Will a change of name change its character? Judging from what we know of our whig friends, who have had considerable experience in this matter of changing names, we should infer not.

A few years ago there was organized amongst us what was called the workingmen's party. We know something of that party, for we were among its earliest friends and supporters, and have made some sacrifices for it. So far as it raised up certain questions for discussion, and so far as it called the attention of our countrymen more immediately to the interests and rights of labor, it was not without its results. But, where is the party now? Has it failed because its leaders betrayed it, because the American people have reprobated its doctrines, or because there was not virtue and intelligence enough in the laboring classes to sustain it? Not at all. No party is, or ever can be betrayed by its leaders, if it have a living principle for its basis. When a Benedict Arnold undertakes to betray the cause of American liberty, he merely betrays himself, and obtains everlasting infamy. Your Washingtons always arrive in time to prevent the threatened mischief, and to disconcert all the plans of the traitor. The cause of American liberty goes on, conquering and to conquer, for it contains in itself the seminal principle of victory. Nor have the American people reprobated the doctrines put forth by the workingmen. So far as these doctrines were applicable to our present stage of development, they have been accepted, and do now constitute an integral portion of the democratic creed, as we may learn from the nickname, loco foco, given to the democracy by their enemies. Nor have the workingmen failed for the want of sufficient virtue and intelligence to sustain a party. They yield to no portion of our population in either. It is no rare thing to find an ordinary mechanic able to refute Mr. Webster's "Great Speech" on the currency question. The true cause of failure should be sought in the fact, that there was no general and permanent demand for such a party. The population, which could be enlisted in such a party, were not numerous enough to make it sufficiently powerful to accomplish anything. Its doctrines, so far as they were true and immediately practicable, were parallel with those of the democratic party. The few social abuses which gave rise to the party were of a local nature, and were scarcely felt out of our cities and large towns. Few, therefore, could be drawn into the party, except journeyman mechanics, and, in fact, but a small portion of these. But, could all these have been enlisted, they would have constituted but a feeble minority, compared with the whole population of the country. The great body of the agricultural population was not to be enlisted. These constituted the main portion of the democratic party, so called. They were democrats, but democrats in the sense in which the party itself was democratic. They had not outgrown their party, and could not outgrow it; for being, as it were, the party itself, that must needs advance just in proportion as they advanced. The agricultural population, therefore, could see no necessity of separating from the democratic party for the purpose of uniting with the journeymen mechanics of the towns. If they approved the measures contended for by the mechanics, they could support them without leaving their party, or deserting the principles, which constituted its basis. Here is the true cause of the failure of the workingmen's party, as a party. Similar causes will always be found to check the growth of every third party which comes up. Its doctrines and measures must needs be, in this country, parallel with those of one or the other of the two existing parties, with which they will very soon become coincident. The workingmen are now an integral portion of the democratic party, if they did but know it, and a separate party organization is out of the question.

The Reformers, then, whether we mean the workingmen, or the other class of whom we have spoken, must see, it strikes us, the utter inutility and impracticability of attempting to raise up a third party. A third party is not wanted. Nothing can be gained by means of such a party, which cannot be gained just as well without it. And, moreover, it is utterly impossible to raise up such a party, that shall last for any length of time, or be powerful enough to effect anything. The proper course is for both of these classes to join and support one or the other of the two existing parties.

We are addressing ourselves to reformers, to men, who profess to believe in progress, and to be desirous of laboring in the holy cause of social melioration. Can they hesitate, which party to join, when the alternative is to join one or the other of the two existing parties? We have no disposition to speak disparagingly of the whig party. In that party are many men whom we are proud to reckon among our personal friends. We freely acknowledge, that it embodies much talent, and not a little private worth. But every party, if it be worth considering, has a set of principles, which it must develop, and which it is compelled, by the laws of Providence, to push to their last consequences. These principles are stronger than individuals. They carry away individuals, in spite of themselves. There is an invincible logic, which conquers the stubbornest will. He, who refuses to go where the principles of his party lead, is inevitably left by the way, and he, who steps before his party to arrest its onward career, is swept away by a resistless current, or trampled in the dust by a thousand feet. To judge a party, you need not to inquire what are the private virtues of the individuals which compose it, but, what are the principles on which it is founded, the idea around which it rallies, and which it is its mission to realize. This idea, nakedly presented, may be repudiated by a large portion of the party, few of the party may comprehend it, or will its realization; nevertheless, they must all obey it, and nearly all will ultimately adopt its last consequences.

The idea of the whig party in this country is of yesterday, not of today, far less of tomorrow. The party is the anti-progress party. Its doctrines were doctrines of progress once, but they are not now. They were proper, once, to be supported, and were the doctrines of the movement party. In the progress of Humanity, there was a period, when it was necessary to bring up the interests of what may be termed commercial capital, against landed capital, which was almost exclusively possessed by an hereditary and titled nobility. Then the whig party was the party of progress; and where it is still necessary to break down an aristocracy founded on the rights of birth and the sword, and monopolizing the greater part of the soil, the whig party is even now the party of progress, because its principles are the proper antagonist of the principles of such an aristocracy. Hence, in England, in 1688, and subsequently, the true friends of progress sided with the whigs, because the whigs were against the old hereditary, landed aristocracy of the kingdom. They supported the Bank, the Funds, the Merchants, and the East India Company. But their doctrines were tolerable only for a time, only so long as it was necessary to humble the landed or military aristocracy.

Now this state of timings has never existed with us, and never can exist here. The English nobleman, or rather the old feudal baron is represented in this country, it is true, but he is represented by the American farmer, whose estate is so cut up and parceled out among his brother barons, that he no longer possesses any undue preponderance in the commonwealth. The capital invested in the soil has with us not even its legitimate share of influence. The commercial capital, the capital employed in business operations, is the preponderating power. To give it additional weight, is, therefore, to war against the true interests of Humanity. The party, which labors to do this, is not, and cannot be, in this country, the party of progress. But the leading idea of the whig party is the preponderance of commercial capital. As the old English whigs supported the Bank of England, so they support the Bank of the United States; as the old English whigs supported the merchants, corporations, funding systems, so our American whigs support the same. The American whigs possess the larger portion of the commercial capital of the country, and they contend, that, therefore, they ought to control the government of the country. They ask, with the celebrated Addison, in his "Whig-Examiner," is there anything more reasonable, than that they, who have all the riches of the nation in their possession, or that they, who have already engrossed all our riches, should have the management of our public treasure, and the direction of our fleets and armies? This question might be very proper, if our work were to put down an aristocracy founded on birth and the sword, like the old feudal aristocracy; but it indicates the worst possible system, here, where our work is to raise up Man, and give him the preeminence over Money.

The whig party also is a foreign party, and anti-American in its principles. Its policy and movements are necessarily controlled, not by a regard to true American interests, but by a regard to the interests of the "credit system," which the party is wedded to, of which the Bank of England is the common center, and whose ramifications extend to all parts of the globe. By commerce and manufactures, by their various business operations, which are carried on mainly by means of credits, they are intimately connected with this system, and virtually enslaved by it. We should be asking more than our knowledge of the weakness of human nature warrants, were we to ask them, in case of collision between this "credit system" and their country, to be faithful to the latter. Where a man's treasure is, there will be his heart also. Their treasure is in the "credit system," the principal seat of which is not in this country; consequently their hearts are abroad, rather than at home. So long as the "credit system" is controlled by foreign nations, or in other words, so long as our country is not the first commercial nation of the world, support of the system must be incompatible with patriotism. England is, at present, the ruling commercial nation; she controls the credit system, so far as it can be controlled; and consequently controls all who are dependent on it. In case of collision between this country and Great Britain, during the existence of the "credit system," we must always look to see all true whigs sustaining Great Britain, as its grand supporter, although her "cannon should be battering down the walls of our Capitol,"—resolving, that it is unbecoming a moral and religious people to rejoice at American victories over her armies, and singing Te Deums, whenever her mercenaries succeed in suppressing the democratic movements of the Old World. We must expect them to do this, for the system they have espoused will compel them to do it; and they will do it spontaneously, religiously, with the feeling, that in so doing they are honoring God, and serving man. Whiggism with us is, therefore, incompatible with patriotism. The whig virtually expatriates himself, or rather, forswearing the land of his birth, adopts the "credit system" as his country, makes it his home, in it erects his altar, and places his household gods. When that system coincides with American principles, he is an American; when they do not, he is an Englishman, a Frenchman, a Chinaman, or one of that nation, with whose interests, for the time being, they chance to be coincident.

Mr. Biddle, who is not altogether destitute of patriotic feelings, had, we apprehend, a glimpse of this fact, and hence his efforts to transfer time seat of the credit system from London to Philadelphia. He probably dreamed of making the American merchants, through the Bank of the United States, all that English merchants now are through the Bank of England. This was a lofty ambition, only a single remove from the sublime. All that was wanting for its complete success was, that this country should stand first in the scale of commercial nations, a rank it unfortunately does not hold, and will not, for some considerable time to come. So long as this country is only a second or third-rate commercial nation, it cannot be the principal seat of the "credit system." So long as it retains its present position in relation to Great Britain, a Bank of the United States can only be a branch of the Bank of England. The Bank of England, as the great center of the credit system of the world, can, at any moment it chooses, ruin the credit of American merchants, and crush our whole banking system, as past experience fully demonstrates.

By the intimate connection, which has heretofore existed between the fiscal concerns of our government, and the general business of banking, we have, government and all, been virtually under the control of Great Britain. Hence, the reason why, whenever we have demanded justice of Great Britain, we have uniformly armed our business men against our own government. The war, which we have been carrying on against the banking system for the last ten years, has been really a war for national independence, and General Jackson, in warring against the Bank, was fighting in the same cause in which he fought at New Orleans, and against the same enemy. It was therefore that the people, by an unerring instinct, selected him, the hero of New Orleans, to be their chief in the new campaigns, of which they had a forefeeling.

The whig party is also the anti-Christian party. We mean not by this, that all whigs reject Christianity, but that whiggism embraces certain principles, which the party are developing, and which they will, if they meet with no counteracting force from without, push to their last results; and that these principles do necessarily involve the rejection of our holy religion, and can end in nothing short of infidelity and universal skepticism. This is ascertained from the whig doctrines on the origin and nature of government, on the origin of ideas, and on the grounds of faith.

The Christian doctrine is, that government is of divine origin, and rests for its legitimacy on the authority of God. This, we take it, is the meaning of that famous passage of St. Paul, "the powers that be are ordained of God." The apostle, we apprehend, was not so much intent on asserting the divine appointment of the then or any actually ruling magistrates, as on asserting the divine institution of government itself, as the foundation of the virtue of loyalty, which he was enforcing. According to Christianity, man is bound to obey no authority, but that of God; consequently, he can owe allegiance to no earthly government, unless it be of divine ordination. Either, then, give up the duty of obedience, and consequently, all government, or assert that government is of divine origin. It is oppression, it is rank tyranny, to compel me to obey my fellow-man. To this as a Christian I will not submit, for I have but one master, and he is in heaven. Consequently all governments resting on human authority are illegitimate, are usurpations; their acts are not, and cannot be, laws; and, therefore, they can never have the right to demand, much less to coerce, obedience.

On this ground, which, if we rightly comprehend it, is that of the most perfect freedom, the whole Christian Church has ever taken its stand. The Catholic Church has always taught the princes, that they have no right to reign in their own name, but that they must reign as the servants, the deputies of God. Bossuet thundered in the ears of the "Grand Monarque" himself, that kings reign only by the authority which they receive from God, and are as much bound to obey God, as the meanest of their subjects. King James, in his Remonstrance for the Right of Kings, is merely defending the divine right of civil government against the exclusive claims of the Pope in favor of the Church. He would merely show, that kings receive their crowns from as high and as sacred a source as the bishops do their mitres. The great idea which was in the minds of the advocates of the divine right of kings, and of passive obedience, which fill so much space in the history of England during the seventeenth century and the first part of the eighteenth, was that mere human authority is not obligatory on man, that allegiance to a king is due only on the ground, that he is the representative of the will of God. They dared not declare the king's will the law, and teach men, that they were bound to obey it. The king was to be obeyed only as the Lieutenant of the Almighty; consequently God only was in reality acknowledged as the sovereign. This, at the moment, was supposed to favor the doctrine of absolutism, and to clothe the tyrant with divine authority. In this sense it was urged. It was, no doubt, urged against subjects, in favor of kings; but who sees not, that it may be urged with equal force against kings, in favor of the people. Government is of divine appointment; and because it is of divine appointment, you are bound to obey it; therefore, obey the king. Stop there, if you please. We admit your premises, but deny your conclusion. We believe government is a divine ordinance, and that we are bound to obey God; but prove to us, that the king is God's Lieutenant, that God speaks through him, for this is not quite so clear to us. But be this as it may, that civil government is of divine origin, and is, for this reason, and this reason alone, obligatory, endowed with the right to exact obedience, is the great idea, which lies at the bottom of the doctrines of the divine right of kings, and passive obedience, and of their apparent antipodes, the Fifth Monarchy men in England, Samuel Gorton, Roger Williams, and others, in our early colonial days, and the Non-Resistants and No-Government men of our own times. This doctrine, however it may have been perverted to the purposes of tyranny, or anarchy, is in fact the only solid and enduring ground, on which government can be established, for it is the only ground, on which the legitimacy of government can be maintained, and disloyalty made a crime *in foro conscientiae*. It is also the only ground, on which freedom can be safely rested; for freedom consists, not in the absence of restraint, but in being subjected to no restraint but the will of God.

Let no one start at the doctrine we here put forth. We all feel, that the word of God is our supreme law. This word is truth, is justice, is love, whatever we conceive of the highest. How it has been or may be uttered, we do not now inquire. Whether it has pealed in thunders from heaven upon the ears of startled Humanity, and been caught up and recorded in a book, or whether it has sounded out in that voice, which comes to us from all nature, declaring its wondrous beauty and harmony, and revealing the law by which it is governed, or whether it has been whispered to the soul in its moments of quiet, in the still small voice of conscience; or whether it has been, as we believe, uttered in all these ways, is foreign to our present purpose. God is the Creator of the Universe, he is its sovereign, and his word, whether speaking through hierarchies, monarchies, aristocracies, democracies, inspired prophets, or the reason with which we are endowed, is our supreme law, and obedience to this, and this alone, is freedom. No man feels, that he is oppressed, because he is bound to conform to truth, to obey justice, to be holy; and to conform to truth, to obey justice, to be holy, is precisely what is meant, if we understand ourselves, by obedience to the will of God.

Now whiggism denies the divine origin of government. It gives it a human origin, and founds it on contract, a bargain, wherein it is stipulated by the magistrates, of the first party, that they will rule, govern, command the people, and by the people, of the second party, that they will consent to be ruled, governed, and commanded by the aforesaid magistrates of the first party. The idea of a contract, whatever may be its terms, evidently assigns to government a human origin, and admits no authority above that of man. Government demands loyalty, but loyalty is due only to that which is above us. How, then, can we be loyal towards a government, which is the work of our own hands, and which originates in a bargain, which we ourselves have made?

This doctrine of the mere human origin of government was introduced into England by Hobbes, if we remember aright, and it was taken up and enlarged upon by John Locke, the apostle and philosopher of whiggism. Hobbes regarded man merely as susceptible of pain and pleasure, and assigned him no other rule of morality than that of seeking the last and avoiding the first. He talks of a state of nature, prior to the institution of civil society, in which all men are equal; and which, in consequence of this equality among men, is a state of war. The design of civil society is to put an end to this war, and maintain a state of peace. As war is the greatest of evils, so peace is the greatest of blessings, and cannot be purchased at too high a price. Mankind become convinced of this, and institute civil government, and surrender to it all their natural rights, clothe it with absolute power, that it may preserve them thenceforth in a state of peace. Locke's idea is similar. He contends, with Hobbes, for a state of nature, regards it as a state of war, and supposes, that men, by a voluntary and deliberate act, instituted civil government. In instituting this government, he supposes the people gave up a certain portion of their rights to government, that they might enjoy the rest in peace and safety. He is less liberal to government than Hobbes, for he does not allow the surrender of *all* our rights, only in fact as many as are necessary to clothe the government with the requisite power to fulfill its functions. But government, according to him, has no authority, but what is derived from the terms of the original bargain. Its rights are merely the rights of individuals, voluntarily surrendered to it. This makes it of mere human authority. Obedience to government, then, is obedience to a human power. According to this theory, I am obliged to obey man, which is slavery, instead of God, as Christianity teaches, which is freedom.

But in their doctrine on the origin of ideas, the whig party are still further removed from Christianity. Christianity requires a belief in a supersensual world, a world of reality, which lies back of the world of merely sensible forms and logical deductions. By the senses, we look out upon the material world; but if we have no eye by which we can look in upon the world of reason, and take cognizance of God and Duty, Christianity has for us no certain ground of evidence, and its truth is in no way perceptible. The world, it professes to reveal, it does not reveal, because there is nothing in us, which can perceive it. The Christian, talking to us of his spiritual world, is as one talking of colors to a man born blind.

Now, what is the whig doctrine on the origin of ideas? Hobbes and Locke are here again our authority. They are the politicians of the whigs, and their politics grow out of their metaphysics. Hobbes assigns man two faculties, force and cognition. The cognitive faculty is merely sensation; for he admits no source of knowledge but the senses. Hence his nominalism, his denial of the reality of all abstract ideas. General, universal, eternal, infinite, are in his philosophy mere words, which serve to abridge discourse, but which name no realities. Locke's doctrine is but a modification of the same. Locke allows two sources of knowledge, sensation and reflection. From sensation we derive all our primary ideas, on which reflection subsequently acts. Through the senses we receive notices of the external world merely. Reflection adds to these notices simply a knowledge of the mind's own operations. According to Locke, therefore, we can take cognizance of no existences, but those of the external world, and ourselves. We can, then, have no knowledge of the world Christianity professes to reveal. That world is neither ourselves, nor the external world. Nor can it be a deduction of logic from either. Logic can deduce from the data furnished it, only what those data contain. External nature and ourselves are evidently both finite. They, then, neither of them, nor both of them, contain the infinite. Then the infinite cannot be deduced from them. Then, for us, the infinite does not exist. Then Christianity, as a professed revelation of the infinite, can receive no faith from us.

This is the inevitable result, if we start with Hobbes and Locke. Hobbes was aware of this, and scarcely disguises it. Locke, who was a man of some religious feeling, and never disposed to push matters to extremes, does not appear to have perceived it. He was a religious man, and professed faith in Christianity; but he pared his faith down to the smallest point compatible with any faith at all. He disrobed our religion of all its mysteries; and in endeavoring to show it *reasonable*, endeavored to make it, as he had government, a mere human authority; for in his philosophy reason is human, not the word of God, "which was in the beginning, which was with God, and which was God." He admitted another life, but asserted that we can have no proof of it, but an outward revelation, authenticated by miracles addressed to the senses; and, though he did not assert the materiality of the soul, he thought it not unreasonable to suppose, that God might confer on matter the power of thinking. Virtue with him was an empty name; pleasure the supreme good; and in his "Private Thoughts," he declares, that the end, a man should always have in view, is the promotion of his own happiness.

The consequences of this doctrine of Locke have been none of the best. On this point, Shaftesbury, his friend and pupil, and also, under other relations, an eminent whig, is good authority. "Although I honor infinitely," he says, "the other writings of Locke, whom I knew, and for whose sincere faith in Christianity I can answer, I am, nevertheless, forced to confess, that he took the same route that Hobbes did, and that he has been followed by Tindal, and other free thinkers of our times. It was Locke himself who struck the fatal blow, for the known character of Hobbes, and his slavish principles, by discrediting his philosophy, deprived it of its poison. But Locke struck the very basis of the edifice, *banished all order and all virtue from the world, placed out of nature ideas* which are intimately blended with those of the Divinity itself, and asserted that they had no foundation in the human mind." In England, we know Locke has produced Tindal, Toland, Collins, Chubbs, Morgan, Mandeville, Woolston, Hume, Hartley, Dodwell, Darwin, Priestley, Belsham; in France, Voltaire, Condillac, Diderot, Helvetius, D'Holbach, Volney, and many others of nearly equal notoriety; and in this country, Norton and Palfrey. Some of these, it is true, have professed, and no doubt entertained, a sort of faith in Christianity, and several of them, by virtue of one of those sublime inconsistencies, which do so much honor to human nature, have been generous defenders of liberty; but they have all denied us all intuition of a spiritual world, and most of them have questioned, or denied all existences, but such as fall under the senses. According to them all, we can have no certain knowledge of the truth of Christianity. Of what we are not certain we must doubt. Consequently, we must always doubt the truth of Christianity. We find this conclusion expressed in still stronger terms by an eminent ex-professor in the Theological School of Cambridge University, a firm adherent of Locke's philosophy, and as good authority as can be desired on its actual tendency. Mr. Norton, the gentleman of whom we speak, says, in his late publication, entitled "The Latest Form of Infidelity," "To the demand for certainty, let it come from whom it may, I answer, that I know of no absolute certainty, beyond the limit of momentary consciousness, a certainty that vanishes the instant it exists, and is lost in the regions of metaphysical doubt . . . There can be no intuition, no direct perception of the truth of Christianity." This is strong language, plain and unequivocal; and it exhibits, we must needs think, not merely the "latest," but also a very old "form of Infidelity." There can be no direct perception of the truth of Christianity. There can, it seems, be no certainty, but that of momentary consciousness. Mr. Norton has not had even a momentary consciousness of the fact of the Divine Mission of Jesus; and if he could have had such a consciousness at any period of his life, it would have "vanished the instant it existed, and been lost in the regions of metaphysical doubt." But we have, and can have, no absolute certainty. Then all inquiry, concerning the evidence of any subject, resolves itself into a balancing of probabilities. Nay, how can we be sure, that this or that is probable, if there be no certainty for us? If we say there can be no absolute certainty, we must accept universal skepticism, and go so far as even to

"Doubt, if it doubt itself be doubting."

This anti-Christian character of the party in question will show itself, perhaps, still more clearly, if we advert to its doctrine on the grounds of Faith. The Christian doctrine on the grounds of religious faith is, that man, unassisted by the inspiration of the Almighty, is incapable of discovering the objects of religious faith; but, with the assistance of Divine inspiration, which, to a certain extent, is vouchsafed to all men, he is able to perceive and know the objects, the spiritual realities of that world which Christianity professes to reveal. The soul has an eye, which looks in upon that world, by means of which it sees and knows it, as certainly as it knows the sensations produced in it by means of the objects of sense. The Church implies this in its doctrine of experimental religion. It teaches us, that, in experimental religion, we see and know the truth of Christianity. We do not merely believe the simple fact, that there is a spiritual world, but we become acquainted with it, know it, even better than we know the world of sense. Ask the true Christian, if Christianity be true, and he answers, it is true, and he knows it is true, because he *feels* it is true. Hence it is, that we are exhorted in Scripture, not merely to believe there is a God, but to make ourselves acquainted with him, and be at peace, and are assured, that it is life eternal to know the only true God, and Jesus Christ, whom he hath sent. When the soul perceives the truths of religion, it knows them, and at once recognizes them as truths. It asks not for arguments to prove them. It has the witness within itself. There is a divinity within, that receives the message which God sends, responds to it, and vouches for its truth.

This we regard as the Christian doctrine, and it is, in substance, what has been the prevailing doctrine of the Church, from its birth, down to our own times.

But the party we are speaking of adopting Locke's philosophy, which denies that the human mind can take cognizance of any existences but those of the outward world and itself, necessarily denies, that we can take any cognizance of the objects of religious faith. Those objects we cannot be acquainted with; they cannot even by Omnipotence be revealed to us, because we are endowed with no capacity to perceive them. Divine revelation does not make them known to us; it merely assures us, that off in a world, of which w know nothing, such objects do really exist. The fact of their existence we cannot judge of, and we must take it solely on the authority of him who reports it. The credibility of the reporter becomes, therefore, the question. If he be worthy of credit, then we may believe that the spiritual world is a reality; if he be not worthy of credit, then we have no evidence of the existence of a world transcending the world of the senses and that of our own minds. By what means can the credibility of the reporter be established? By miracles, addressed to the senses. The Divine authority of him, whom God commissioned to speak to us in his name, Mr. Norton assures us, can be attested only by miraculous displays of his power. Miracles, if they occurred every day, would cease to be miracles, as we learn from the erudite Dr. Palfrey. Consequently, they can occur only at distant intervals. The great mass of mankind cannot, therefore, be eye-witnesses of miracles, and must depend on the record, which may be made of them. They can have no evidence of their actual occurrence, but the evidence of history, written or unwritten. But, of the truth of the history, as things go, they cannot judge. The generality of men must, then, rely on the testimony of the few scholars, who have leisure and means to investigate the proofs of its genuineness and authenticity. The fact of the occurrence of the miracles, by which we establish the authority of the reporter, whose authority must, in turn, establish the fact, that off in the vast unknown, there is a spiritual world, in which we should believe,—but whether it really exists, or not., we can never know,—must be taken by the generality, on the authority of a few learned men. According to Mr. Norton, in his "Latest Form of Infidelity," already quoted, the condition of faith in Christianity, for the great mass of mankind, is "trust in the capacity and honesty of others." We must rely on the knowledge of others, which reliance *"may be called belief on trust, or belief on authority."*

This, it will be seen at once, leaves Christianity, for the great mass of mankind, a very doubtful matter; for who will assure us, that these privileged few, this learned caste, are not themselves deceived, or at least deceivers? May not these scholars have an interest in deceiving us? Do they not derive rank, consideration, and wealth, from inducing us to believe what they tell us? And do they not, by inducing us to believe them, really become our masters? Let the people once entertain a suspicion of this sort, and you will need an inquisition, dungeons, fire, and sword, to maintain even a decent outward regard to religion. On the other hand, this doctrine of belief on authority, if once admitted, strikes at the root of all free faith in God, all voluntary obedience to his command; perpetuates the worst features of Catholicism, establishes a sacerdotal caste, and plunges the human race into the gloomiest and most debasing of all servitudes. It is essentially a skeptical doctrine, and strikes at the root of all faith. They, who support it, fear that the human mind, if left to its own free and honest action, would reject all religion, and they, therefore, seek to keep up religion by means of coercion. It is this doctrine, which has done and is doing so much mischief to the Church. The worst of all heresies is that, which strikes out from the human soul the capacity to see and know God.

But we cannot pursue this train of remark further. What we have thus far said, applies not, we readily own, to all the individuals who belong to the whig party. We have described the party, not according to the actual characters of its members, but according to the principle, which lies at the bottom of its reasoning, and its measures. We have seized the ultimate doctrine of the party, and pointed out the results, to which it must inevitably come, in the development of its idea, providing it meets, as we have said, with no counteracting force from without. Viewed as the opposite of the democratic party, in the light of its own peculiar, fundamental principle, it is the anti-progress party, the anti-American party, and the anti-Christian party. Its complete triumph would be fatal to the progress of the race, to the development of American institutions, and to the continuance of the Christian religion. This fact shows at once, that so long as there is an overruling Providence, there can be no ground to apprehend its success. It will always fail. Yesterday never returns. When yesterday becomes today, or today tomorrow, the whigs will come into power throughout the United States, but not till then. The friends of progress, of reform, men whose faces are on the front side of their heads, and whose hearts are in the future, and whose souls leap up to meet the good that is to be, we are sure cannot, for one moment, dream of uniting their fortunes with those of the whigs. Nothing remains for them, then, but to unite with the democratic party, so called, and through that labor to carry the race forward to its destiny.

The democratic party is the American party. That party is the American party, which gathers round the idea, which it is the mission of American institutions to realize. The idea, which lies at the bottom of our institutions, is the supremacy of Man. Here is to be established and developed not the sovereignty of the sacerdocy, not the sovereignty of the city or state, not the sovereignty of the king, not the sovereignty of the noble few, the high born, not that of the rich, nor yet that of estates, or corporations, but the sovereignty of Man. Here man is not made for the state, but the state is instituted for man. The order of civilization, which it is ours to develop, is an order of civilization, in which things are subordinate, and subservient to humanity. Humanity, in all its integrity, is in every individual man. Then every individual man is to be raised to empire, so they shall be, in the the language of Scripture, "kings and priests." This is the American idea. This idea in the political world is translated by universal suffrage, that is, the equal right of every man to his voice in the choice of political agents, and through them, in the laws, which shall be enacted, or governmental measures, which shall be adopted. Now, is not the democratic party the acknowledged universal suffrage party? From the first, it has regarded suffrage as a right belonging to every man, by virtue of his human nature, and it has contended, that the people, taken individually, have not only the right, but, taken collectively, will exercise it judiciously, ultimately in accordance with the public good, and universal reason. The whig party waives the question of right, contends that the people are not sufficiently enlightened to be *entrusted* with universal suffrage, and that we ought to educate them before we allow them the *privilege* of voting.

The democratic party is also the patriotic party. It is the party jealous of national honor. The whig party, composed in the main of business men, whose idea is property, not man, are insensible to national honor, when its maintenance requires the sacrifice of the facilities of trade or commerce. In their estimation, the national honor is well enough, when they are making large profits, and is endangered only when their chances of gain seem to be diminished. Hence it is, that every measure taken to maintain the honor of the nation, or to enhance its real prosperity, has been taken by the democratic party, amidst the most violent, and all but treasonable hostility of the whigs. The democracy purchased Louisiana, and thus secured to trade the Mississippi, to agriculture an immense territory of unrivalled fertility, and to free institutions many millions of supporters. The democracy declared and sustained the war against Great Britain, in which we vindicated our national honor, and asserted the freedom of the seas. And during its continuance, the whig party were plotting treason with the enemy, refusing all support to the government of their country, and cutting off, as far as they could, its supplies. It was the democracy also, that compelled France, much against the will of the opposition, to do us tardy justice for its spoliations of our commerce.

The democratic party is the party of liberty. This is involved in the fact, that it is the American party. The idea of this country is, we have said, the supremacy of Man. This supremacy is attained only by the broadest freedom. The American idea, under another aspect, then, is that of liberty. The truly American party always rallies around the quickening idea of liberty. No man can have the hardihood to pretend, that liberty is the idea, the whigs are struggling to bring out. The whig party is not particularly anxious to sustain or extend liberty, even according to its own account. Its sole objects, taken as its own witness, are the preservation of the Union of the States, and the support of the credit system. In this, it is true to itself. It is the business party of the country, and it is, and must be true to its idea. The Union of the States was, and is desirable, almost solely on account of the interests of trade and commerce. It facilitates trade between the different States, and gives us an imposing aspect, which favors our foreign commerce. Take away the aid, which the Union of the States gives to trade and commerce, and the whigs would estimate its value somewhat below par. Their cry about the preservation of the Union, does not, then, proceed from their anxiety to maintain freedom, but to preserve certain advantages to trade. It is in relation to its bearing on business operations, that they wish to sustain the credit system. So that their dominant idea, according to their own showing, is the preservation or increase of facilities for business operations, they pursue business, of course, for the purpose of accumulating property. So in the last analysis the dominant idea of the whigs is not MAN, but PROPERTY; and the contest between them and the democracy was rightly declared by Mr. Benton to be a contest between MAN and MONEY.

As the whig party is the party seeking to give predominance not to the idea of freedom, but to the idea of property, the protection of which Locke declares to be the end of government, it follows, that the democratic party is the party of freedom, or else we have no such party in this country. Its history proves that it is. In all controversies, it takes the side of liberty. In the convention which framed the Federal Constitution, it opposed centralism, and defended State rights. In the conventions which have framed our State constitutions, it has always favored those clauses, which leave the most liberty to the people, and best protect the rights of the individual. In the great struggle between the aristocratic and democratic elements of European society, which broke out in the French Revolution, and which has been continued, with various success, even to our own times, it has always sympathized with the people, and rejoiced in their successes. Its sympathies were with France, so long as France represented the democracy; while the whigs, or Federalists, sympathized with England, as the representative of the aristocracy. In the late unsuccessful struggle of the Canadians for independence, the democratic party has been true to its idea of liberty. It has given them its sympathies and its prayers, and trusts yet to see the Canadas a free and independent nation. The day of emancipation yet lingers, but it will come, and we shall have a great and noble people for our Northern neighbor.

The democratic party has always been faithful to freedom of mind and conscience, the basis of all freedom. It has always opposed everything even approaching a religious establishment, and contended, that man's intercourse with his Maker should be free and voluntary. It has opposed all test laws, and uniformly frowned upon every effort to molest a man for his opinions. It inserted in the Federal Constitution the amendments, which forbid Congress to establish a religion, or to pass any law prohibiting freedom of speech, or of the press. It opposed the elder Adams and his party, because, in their Alien and Sedition Laws, they proved themselves the enemies of free thought, and free utterance; and it raised Thomas Jefferson to the Presidential chair, because he was the unflinching friend of freedom of mind. It has always said, with

Milton, "Let truth and falsehood grapple. Who ever knew truth put to the worse in free and open encounter? Her confuting is the best and surest suppressing."

The democratic party is the Christian party. Christianity is a revelation of God's mercy to man. It is always on the side of freedom and Humanity. It addresses man as endowed with the capacity to judge of himself what is or is not right. Democracy is based on the fact, that man does really possess this capacity. Christianity, by addressing itself to all men, necessarily recognizes this capacity in every man; democracy, by defending universal suffrage, does the same. Christianity values man for his simple Humanity, not for his trappings, the accidents of birth, wealth, or position; so does democracy. Christianity, aside from its design to fit the individual for communion with the blest after death, seeks to introduce a new order of things on the earth to exalt the humble, abash the proud, to establish the reign of justice, and enable every man to "sit under his own vine and fig-tree, with none to molest or make afraid"; and who knows not that this is the aim and tendency of the democratic party?

Christianity recognizes God as the only rightful sovereign, and regards all government not founded by him, as usurpation. Man is bound to obey God, and God only. Therefore, it commands us to call no man master on earth, for one is our master in heaven. Translated into the language of politics, this teaches us, that government is legitimate, and laws are obligatory only as they represent the will of God, that is, the decrees of eternal and immutable Justice. Is not this the doctrine of the democratic party? Jefferson, a good authority on this point, says, "the will of the majority must govern, but in order to govern rightfully, it must be just." The orations and addresses named at the head of this article, as well as several others now lying before us, delivered by democrats on the last Anniversary of our Independence, with one accord, assert the supremacy of Justice; and the whole party adopts the definition of democracy, given in a Lecture by the Historian of the United States; "Democracy is Eternal Justice ruling through the People."[1] Justice is the political name of God. The reign of Justice is the reign of God; and in defining democracy to be Eternal Justice ruling through the people, we identify the doctrine of the democratic party with the doctrine of the New Testament, namely, that government is of Divine ordination, and in all legitimate governments God is king.

The idea of justice, in all its length and breadth, is undoubtedly in every man; but it exists in the individual mixed up with much, which belongs to the individual, rather than to the race. The individual, therefore, cannot be a safe interpreter of justice. For the voice of Eternal Justice he may mistake the voice of his own passions or interests. We must, therefore, listen to the voice of the race. The race can agree only in that which is universal, invariable, and eternal, only in justice and truth. Hence, the unanimous assent of the race is justly regarded as the highest evidence of truth. In order, then, to make as near an approach as possible to the decrees of Eternal Justice, we must place the government, not in the hands of one man, not in the hands of a few men, nor in the hands of a class, corporation, or estate, but in the hands of the whole people, whose voice will always be our best representative of the voice of the race, and whose decisions are the nearest approximation a nation can make to the decisions of Justice itself. Rightly, then, is Democracy defined Eternal Justice ruling through the People. Rightly, too, is the democratic party termed the Christian party, since it, like Christianity, acknowledges God alone as the rightful sovereign, and labors incessantly to wrest the government from the hands of individuals, classes, castes, estates, corporations, and to place it in the hands of the whole people, in their character of simple human beings, so that justice may reign on the earth.

The democratic party is the party of progress. This is involved in what has already been said. A party gathers round an idea, or principle, which is its life, its soul. That idea it can never abandon, and live; nor can it ever receive a new idea, without losing its identity. If left to itself, it will unfold, exhaust its idea; and having done this, it dies. Thus, English whiggism, having exhausted its original idea, having found its euthanasia, in the Reform Bill, has gone the way of all the earth, and is suffered to lie in state still, merely because neither Tories nor Radicals are prepared to assume the responsibility of heirs, and give it burial. The whigs in this country are demonstrating the same law. The idea, around which they gather, is offensive to a majority of the American people. This the more discerning of our whig friends perceive, and, therefore, they would fain change the doctrines of the party. They have even tried to make it pass for the democratic party. Vain efforts! They may change its name, receive into its ranks many, who once thought themselves republicans, and submit to be led on by men, who once enjoyed the confidence of the democracy; but nothing can change its character; its identity remains; and your Lincolns, Seldens, Duanes, Verplancks, Tallmages, and Riveses, who generously undertake to give it a democratic aspect, can change nothing in its principles or direction, but are themselves swept away by its resistless current,

"To that bourne, whence no traveler returns."

The idea of the whig party is one, which cannot, in this country, rise to empire, because it is not broad enough to comprehend the work which God has given us to do. Always, therefore, will it be in the minority, or if not absolutely in the minority, so torn by intestine divisions, and so destitute of "available" leaders, that it must uniformly fail of success.

The democratic party is governed by the same law. It can receive no new idea, and it must share the fortunes of the idea with which it originally started. But there is a difference between the two parties. The whig party gathered around an idea, which is of a limited and transient nature; the democratic party rallied round an idea, which is universal, immutable, and eternal. The whig seized upon one of the accidents of Humanity, the democrat upon Humanity itself. The democrat planted himself in the center of the vast globe of Humanity, the whig placed himself on the circumference, where he hangs as a foreign substance, and from which he must be thrown the moment the globe revolves. The great idea of the democratic party is, as we have shown, under one aspect, the supremacy of man over his accidents, under another aspect, the reign of Eternal Justice. The two aspects are, in fact, one and the same. The mission of the democratic party is to unfold the great idea of Justice, and reduce it to practice in all man's social and political relations. It stands, therefore, not as the representative of a fraction of the race, but of the race itself; and, therefore, like the race, it is immortal. This great idea of justice the party is destined to realize. From this work it cannot withdraw itself, even if it would. Its leaders may be false to it, and seek to betray it; but it leaves them by the way, and with or without new leaders, continues its march. No matter how high a rank a man may have held in its estimation, the moment he proves false to the mission of the party, he is left, though leaving him be like plucking out a right eye, or cutting off a right hand. Nothing from within can betray it or divert it from its onward course. Many of the most active members of the whig party were once in its ranks, but it has not missed them. It is never in want of a man competent to lead on its forces, nor of an "available" candidate for its suffrages. A panic may now and then occur, and produce a momentary confusion, but it instantly recovers itself, re-establishes order, and takes up its line of march, ready to grapple with any force it may meet.

Now as the party, according to the general laws of party, must go on unfolding its idea, and as that idea is universal and all-comprehensive, we say truly, that it is the party of progress. Justice is its idea, and this idea it must unfold, and this idea in its unfolding must reach all the reforms the friends of progress can desire. Progress is simply the better and fuller application of Justice to our social and political relations. All the progress, which in the very nature of things now can be, must come from the unfolding of the idea which constitutes the life and soul of the democratic party. Then as friends of progress you should support that party, and contribute what you can to help it onward in the development and application of its general principles.

Are you contending for universal education? What principle will establish a true system of universal education, but that which declares the supremacy of Man over Money, and recognizes Man in all his integrity in every individual man? Are you the advocate of the rights of woman? How will you succeed but by appealing to the great principle of the democracy, that Right is paramount to Might? Are you a non-resistant, a peace-man? What means have you to compass your ends, but by aiding the democracy to introduce the rule of Justice into all public affairs? Are you an advocate for the working-man, anxious to secure to honest industry its due reward, and to the laborer his true social position? You must do it by means of that party which struggles to raise up universal Humanity, to abolish all Privilege, and to place the government in the hands of MAN, instead of MONEY. Are you an abolitionist, and would you free the slave? What party puts forth general principles, which in their gradual unfolding must break every unjust bond, and set every captive free? The day of emancipation is not yet. It were useless to emancipate the slave today, because we should be merely changing the form not the substance of his slavery. But the democratic party puts forth principles, which must in the end abolish slavery, and do it too at the very day, the very hour, when it can be done with advantage to the cause of freedom, of justice. Slavery is doomed; man will not always tyrannize over man. There are causes at work, which will free the slave, and free him too with the consent and to the joy of his master. Let these causes work on, and do not murmur because their full effects are not realized today. God doubtless could have made the world in one day, but we are told that he chose to employ six days in creating it. The seed is not sown, and the corn harvested the same day. Be sure that you have principles in operation that will effect your work, and you may retain your composure. The democratic party embraces the idea of universal freedom to universal man, and it will realize this idea, just as fast as we can urge onward the general progress of Humanity, and no faster.

We have now given some of the reasons why reformers should sustain the democratic party. That party embraces the general principles of liberty, of progress, which include within them, as the oak is included in the acorn, all possible reforms. It represents today, in this Western world, entire Humanity, and as such has a right to demand the hearty cooperation of every true friend of his race. We see many and essential reforms, for which we have labored, and still labor, which it has not yet taken up; but we see that, following its principles, obeying the high laws to which in God's providence it is subjected, it must and will take them up in due time, and in due order. Today it is engaged in rescuing the government from the grasp of associated wealth, which it will do by adopting the Independent Treasury Bill, and causing the revenues of the country to be collected and disbursed in gold and silver. When it has effected this, it will proceed to reform the banking system as it exists in the States. In what way it will reform the system, as time moment for acting has not yet come, it is not wholly agreed. Whether it will do it, by abolishing all banks and returning to an exclusively metallic currency, as is the wish of some, or by instituting a system of free banking, as is the wish of a still greater number, or by devising a new scheme based upon a combination of the elements of free banking with what may be termed government banking, as we ourselves should propose, it is at this moment impossible to determine; but be it as it may, the party will dispose of the question in that way which shall best advance the cause of individual freedom and national prosperity. This question disposed of, the party will proceed to reform the judiciary, and to revise our criminal code. Then it will proceed to other reforms which perhaps have not yet been dreamed of save by a few visionaries, who would gain nothing but a smile of compassion were they to tell their dreams. Where it will stop we know not; for we are not able to set bounds to the spirit of improvement, or to say where the progress of the race is to be arrested. We speak not as the seer, but as the philosopher, who, from the causes he sees in operation, and which he understands, infers the effects which must inevitably follow, unless God changes the order of his providence. The reforms which the party effects in legislation, the principles which it infuses into public institutions, will gradually pass into social life, form our manners, our morals, and determine our social relations and intercourse.

Sinking now the editor, and speaking in my own name, I may say, here is my view of the democratic party, and here are my reasons for enrolling myself among its members. I have formed this view not hastily, nor without considerable reflection; I have adopted it only as I have been compelled by my general principles of politics, religion, and philosophy. I have never been a partisan. I have, it is true, always been a democrat. I sucked in democracy with my mother's milk; I imbibed a feeling and a love of independence, as I roamed a child over the Green Hills, or clambered up the scarped rocks, or plunged in the dark forests of my early home. I could not have been a Green Mountain Boy, bred in a mountain home, in what may one day be regarded as the Switzerland of America, without cherishing a free spirit, and becoming the friend of the "largest liberty." I have always been found on the side of freedom in its widest signification. To my love of it I have given years of intense study, sacrificed ease, sometimes reputation, pecuniary independence, and professional success. But, except on rare occasions, I have never acted with the democratic party so called. I have had many prejudices against it, and against its prominent members. I have thought it too intent on office, on maintaining itself as a party, and too indifferent to the progress and application of free principles. It may readily be believed, then, that I have not given in my adhesion, so unequivocally, without having been compelled by, what have seemed to me, cogent reasons. These reasons are given to some extent in this article. They are to me weighty and sufficient. They may be carped at, they may be denied; but I must give up all the confidence I have hitherto placed in religion or philosophy, before I can believe they can be successfully refuted. I am therefore compelled, not merely to declare myself a democrat, but a democrat, if you will, in a party sense. I take my stand with the democratic party. Its fortunes, whatever they may be, I am content to share.

If I can in any way aid it onward, and assist it in carrying out its principles, my ambition and my conscience will be satisfied. I say this in no partisan spirit, but in obedience to those broad principles of freedom, to which, with or without success, my life has thus far been devoted. I do this because I am required to do it by my love of freedom and of man, because through this party, and this party only, can be carried out into all the relations of life those great principles of justice, on which the institutions of this country are based. Through this party it is possible to reach Humanity; with it is bound up the cause of freedom in this country, on this continent, and throughout the world.

Observations and Hints on Education

April 1840

*E*ducation is the great problem of the age. The education of the people is held to be the first condition of the stability of free social institutions; the only efficient means of social progress. Especially is the necessity of popular education in democratic communities insisted on. So imperative is this necessity considered, that the want of education is even sometimes held as a sufficient cause of social, political, and personal disfranchisement. To this principle our most democratic of all democracies presents a sublime example of devotion; retaining one sixth of its whole population in hereditary, perpetual slavery, for the want of this indispensable, to them impossible, prerequisite for freedom so that a man here is not always a man, "endowed by his Creator with certain natural, essential, and inalienable rights." Obviously, then, it is a fundamental maxim, that democratic institutions, as they are the result of, can be made permanent only where a certain degree of intelligence exists in the whole mass of the people. This was once thought to be the especial mission, the peculiar glory of republican governments; the necessity of knowledge widely diffused, for their own preservation. It was also supposed to be an equal and inevitable necessity of arbitrary governments, that their subjects should be kept in profound ignorance; not merely of the rights, relations, and destiny of man and society; but ignorance of letters and of all knowledge, not required for the fit discharge of their servile duties and occupations. Ignorance was regarded as both the mother of devotion, and the best security for the unresisting acquiescence of the masses in the domination of the privileged few. Ignorance and slavery were held to be correlative and synonymous.

But this century witnesses the phenomenon of absolute governments laboring for the education of their subjects, with a zeal and earnestness not yet felt in this community of nations, which professes to rely specially for its continuance upon the popular intelligence. The king of Prussia seems to have exploded completely the old doctrine of the necessary connection between ignorance and servitude. He has made education the handmaid of despotism. Under his auspices, it prevents, instead of promoting social progress; instead of being the herald of freedom, it is the prime minister of an authority, which allows hardly a figment of political liberty. The House of Hapsburg is repeating the experiment without fear; even in its subjugated Italian Dominions, in the scenes and amid the slumbering but unextinguished memories of old Roman freedom, kindling the lamp of knowledge, in order to impress more deeply and surely the sternest maxims of royalty. Even Nicholas is said to be introducing normal schools into his dominions. The experiments, which his brethren of Austria and Prussia have so successfully carried out, have demonstrated to him, that the A, B, C, by itself, has no spell of intrinsic power to break the chain on the shoulder of the serf. Liberty, it thus appears, is not a necessary concomitant or consequence of any extant system of education; since Prussia, with liberal and enlarged provisions for the instruction of the whole people, remains in the passive apathy of despotism, and is as stern an opposer of every movement towards popular freedom, under the rule of the third Frederic, as she was under that of the first or the second. Do we not find this seeming paradox corroborated by some recent developments of our American experiment? Within a few years, such things as mobs, usurping the functions of law, trampling upon natural rights guaranteed by constitutions, have been events of not unfrequent occurrence. It has been boasted by the parties and vindicators of these anarchical tribunals, that they were honorably distinguished from European, monarchical mobs, that they were not assemblies of the vulgar and ignorant; but that they were composed of gentlemen, respectable men, men of refinement and education; and they have even been placed in honor side by side with the men of the Boston revolutionary tea-party.[1] If we were not called upon to reverence them as patriots, a sort of qualified admiration seems to have been expected for them as respectable incendiaries, gentlemanly ruffians, educated assassins, the "*Dii minores gentium.*" The schoolmaster, then, may be abroad over the whole land, and the people may be, according to the common forms of expression, an educated people, without communicating, or acquiring the first elements of liberty, or catching a glimpse of the true destiny of man and society.

Nevertheless, without paradox, the schoolmaster must be abroad, or the notion of liberty is a dream and delusion. Neither self-regulated freedom, nor even liberty under law, can exist without him. None but an educated can be a permanently free people. The question is not of the importance of education; but what is education? that which is the support and safeguard of personal and political freedom? And who is the schoolmaster? I am not about to answer these questions. The subject is too wide and profound to be treated in a brief periodical essay. I shall only put down some desultory thoughts, not claiming them as the most important, or as suggesting a reply to the questions. If I should deal more in negatives than affirmatives, declare what is not education, who is not the schoolmaster, rather than state a system, and describe qualifications; it will readily occur to every one, that it is easier to innovate than to reform, to destroy than to build up. The dullest engineer, with cannon and match, can batter down stone and mortar; but it requires a genius of quite another sort to build a Parthenon, or a St. Peter's. Perhaps, even that, which to the common sight is deformity, may be a grace in the eye of the true seer; what to me seems discord, to the ear of the authentic hearer may be notes of the universal harmony.

It may be true, that every degree of knowledge, however small, does to its extent exercise a beneficial influence upon society; that, other things being equal, even one, who has only learned to read and write, is more likely to be a peaceable citizen, regardful of the laws and of public order, than one who is entirely ignorant of letters. The records of public prisons and penitentiaries have been thought to go far towards proving this position. But reasoning from such premises is extremely doubtful. There is no obvious, or easily traced connection between the A, B, C, and moral conduct; and it is possible in any case to ascertain but a small part of the influences, which have made any individual a subject of the penal justice of society. It is, therefore, unwise and dangerous to draw general inferences from particular habits or deficiencies, between which and the offenses for which punishment is inflicted no very direct relation is perceived. Invariable coincidence would hardly be sufficient to establish the relation of cause and effect in such cases; even if a much higher standard of education were supposed than is implied in the popular systems. But the coincidence is not universal. Two remarkable exceptions are before me. In the Coldbath Field's Prison, near London, there were, in 1834, 967 prisoners. The chaplain of the prison ascertained and reported to the Middlesex magistrates, that 104 of these were uneducated, of whom 48 had been imprisoned before; while 863 were educated, 217 of whom were undergoing a second imprisonment. Neither the amount nor the mode of education is stated.

The second exception is presented in the return of 326 prisoners in the Glasgow Bridewell, from June 1834 to June 1835. Of these only 52 could neither read nor write, 143 could read only, and 131 could read and write. These are exceptions to the general current of reported observation on this subject. It is confidently inferred from numerous criminal statistics, that much the largest portion of criminals are uneducated; and that the proportion constantly decreases according to the degree of education. But admitting this proposition in its largest extent, some important particulars are to be considered, before any authentic practical inference can be drawn from it. The greater part of criminal statistics is furnished by those countries where the horizontal division of society exists; that is, where the community is composed of two classes, between which there is no social sympathy, and few common interests; the one, and the least numerous, hereditary proprietors of the land, tracing through endless genealogies, titles, which they deem almost divine, and possessing nearly a monopoly of the political power. The other, and vastly most numerous class, is regarded as an inferior order of being, born for servitude, to be hewers of wood and drawers of water. A division of society, in short, where *man* is unknown and unrecognized; but were man is degraded, on one side of the line into a king or a lord with hereditary honors, traced through robbers, courtesans, and "scoundrels ever since the flood;" and on the other into a peasant, villain, serf, vassal, or whatever other name of contumely may be used to cover up and smother Humanity. This class is poor and oppressed, and poverty and oppression beget resistance, and occasion acts which the laws call crime. If we examine, for example, the condition of the masses in Ireland, or in England, there will be no necessity for inquiring into the comparative degrees of ignorance and knowledge, to account for the number of legal offenses. The true lesson to be learned from these phenomena is reverence, trust; reverence for man, trust in his instincts; admiration that in a social condition, which presents scarcely anything but temptations, nay, where the first law of nature, self-preservation, operates as almost a necessity for violence and plunder; man is yet so steadfast to his higher nature, so much observant of the universal law of order. The wonder is not that he is so often a criminal; but that he is not much oftener and a much greater criminal.

Another circumstance is to be noted in this connection. By far the greater part of the offenses, which fill the records of criminal justice, are offenses against property. The general right of property is not one of the clearest of the natural rights, any farther, certainly, than it is a personal acquisition, gained by one's own labor. As a subject of transmission and inheritance, the natural right is somewhat questionable. Some writers, who cannot be suspected of a disposition to rob man of any portion of his original garniture of rights, maintain that property is altogether a conventional arrangement, to which no one has a right absolutely independent. However this may be, it is certain that offenses against property are not the grossest violations of natural justice, and very rarely indicate the deepest moral depravity. Compared with injuries to some other natural rights, it seems to be true, practically as well as poetically, that "who steals my purse steals trash."

Whatever may be the foundation of the *right* of property, the conventional *laws* of property in most European countries, and to a less extent in our own, are in the highest degree artificial, arbitrary and absurd. In those countries the object of the laws is to perpetuate the horizontal division; and as a necessary consequence, a large proportion of crime consists of violations of these arbitrary enactments, of laws for the preservation of game, oppressive revenue and excise laws, police regulations, and the like. Offenses against such laws, or against any merely arbitrary law, do nowhere denote a very deep depravation of the universal moral instincts of man. Analyzed, they amount to little more, even if we give the law the best condition, that of being the act of the majority, than a disregard of the public opinion, of which the statute is the exponent. In a society horizontally divided, in which the mass below the line are oppressed, poor, and ignorant, and their poverty and ignorance are the consequences of their social condition, established and maintained by law; violations of such laws are, as nearly as possible, mere venial trespasses, if indeed they are not obedience to higher laws of nature. Obedience to one universal and invincible law they certainly denote, *the law of hunger.*

The offenses of the poor and ignorant class are public, notorious, observed, and recorded in their beginnings. Consider, on the other hand, the crimes of the higher educated class; the cheateries of trade, the quackeries of professions, the frivolity and heartlessness of fashionable life, the contempt for the masses, the immeasurable sacrifices and miseries of war, the oppressions and frauds of legislation, the slavery and ignorance of the people, the private and social luxury, licentiousness, and debauchery: not crimes against the statute, or if so, hard to define, hard to detect, difficult to prove; not all open to the world's gaze; not filling the calendars of penal justice; but crimes against the laws of nature, written in the institutions of the universal reason; visible only in their effects upon the manners and moral sentiment of the community; visible not until the pollutions they engender have broken out upon the surface of society in ulcers and putrefying sores. This picture must be placed by the side of that; the vices of the higher classes contrasted with those of the ignorant lower, and the temptations and tendencies of their respective conditions compared; before any invariable and unquestionable rule of relation can be established between knowledge and ignorance, virtue and vice. Nay, is it not the consummation of all crime, that the educated, who have the control of social institutions, should place one human being in a position, where ignorance is almost a necessity? " 'Tis not because of his toils that I lament for the poor. We must all toil, or steal, (however we name our stealing,) which is worse. No faithful workman finds his task a pastime. The poor is hungry and athirst, but for him also there is food and drink; he is heavy-laden and weary, but for him also the heavens send sleep, and of the deepest. In his smoky cribs, a clear dewy heaven of rest environs him, and fitful glitterings of cloud-skirted dreams. But what I do mourn over is that the lamp of his soul should go out; that no ray of heavenly, or even earthly knowledge, should visit him, but only in the haggard darkness, like two specters, fear and indignation. Alas, while his body stands so broad and brawny, must his soul lie blinded, dwarfish, stupefied, almost annihilated. Was this, too, a birth of God; bestowed of heaven, but on earth never to be unfolded? That there should one man die ignorant, who had capacity for knowledge, this I call a tragedy, were it to happen twenty times in a minute."[2]

A convict in one of the state prisons, so says one of those very witty gentlemen, who enlighten and reform their age through the periodical press, traced his downfall to the original sin of subscribing for a newspaper, and neglecting to pay for it. This pleasant piece of editorial humor is quite as rational an account of the matter, as that which refers differences of character and conduct to the letters of the alphabet. The learning of those cabalistic signs, so full of mystery and perplexity to the child, is made the basis of education, as commonly understood and conducted; and education is reckoned completed by the attainment of the power to read and write, the use, dextrous or otherwise, of the mechanical rules of numbers, a smattering of geography, and some few other elements. But the letters of the alphabet are not knowledge, but only symbols of sounds. Their only use is to enable men to receive the thoughts of others, and communicate their own, in the absence of oral intercourse. Reading and writing are not ends, but means; "means, by which ignorance may converse with wisdom." The A, B, C are the first things learned, after the faculty of speech has been completely acquired. For the highest ends of education, might they not be postponed to a much later period of life? Might they not be more beneficially reserved for some of the higher parts of the superstructure, or even for the ornaments and capitals?

Induction is the foundation of all practical knowledge, and the habit of observation, which it requires, is, like all other habits, most easily acquired in early life. If not formed then, it cannot be in after life, but by constant watchfulness and painful discipline; the process of self-culture, meanwhile, is at a stand, or but tardily progressive. Argue as we may concerning different systems of instruction, no system is of much value, which does not aim at making education a self-discipline, at making every man, in truth, a self-taught man. The chief value of books is to assist, not to supersede, the process of self-culture. Great is the theory of self-taught men, and full of wisdom. Little are they indebted to Faust's wondrous art; they derived their knowledge from that universal revelation of knowledge in man and nature, of which books only copy and often misquote the language. And have they not been, in all ages, the mighty of the earth, the seers and prophets of mankind? "Not out of those, on whom systems of education have exhausted their culture, comes the helpful giant to destroy the old, or build the new; but out of unhandselled savage nature, out of terrible Druids and Berserkirs, come at last Alfred and Shakespeare."

The child, the infant, is constantly making observations; the whole of his studious play is a process of Induction. Instead of fostering this habit, do not the practiced systems of education tend directly to prevent its formation, to crush the awakening energies of the intellect, to connect learning with the most disagreeable and painful associations? At the time when the young spirit is full of the opening slush of life, gushing over with uncontrollable activity, impatient of restraints, impatient of rest, as long as its bodily organs hold out, ravished with the mysterious beauties and glories of the new universe, into which it has just emerged, longing to go out and inquire of everything concerning its whence and why; instead of following out these indications of nature, these clear revelations of instinct, systems of education take him wholly away from nature and her inspiring loveliness and grandeur, and confine him for nearly half of his waking existence between six dull walls, to hard and wearisome wooden seats, chaining his free limbs; where he is not permitted without rebuke even to glance out into the bright world, which half-revealed invites him forth through the windows of his prison; there impelled for six interminable hours, each moment a pang, to fix his eyes and pore over mysterious, uncouth figures, which contain no revelation for him, of whose present, or ultimate use he in vain labors to form a conception; and all this under the guard and watch of a stranger, whom men call pedagogue (child driver), schoolmaster, who works for wages in odd seasons, when he cannot get them in any other occupation, and who "knows thus much of the human soul, that it has a faculty called memory, and can be acted on through the muscular integuments by application of birch rods." Give the child a set of pothooks and the range of the kitchen at home, and in most cases he will work out for himself more elements of knowledge in a day, than he can, with grief and indignation, compass in half the term of his scholastic inflictions. And that no accompaniment of discomfort may be wanting,—the schoolhouse, in the dusty highway, every pleasant association carefully excluded from its precincts; in many cases a thing which a family, retaining a decent self-respect, would feel it shame to occupy! Are not all the substance and environments of systematic education calculated to quench instead of keeping alive the excited curiosity, the thirst for knowledge? Is it strange that education comes so miserably short of its high pretensions?

Why do we not here, as elsewhere, found our systems upon induction? Why, instead of counteracting, do we not follow and assist the instinctive developments of the young mind? That is ever active, ever seeking knowledge by observation. From the moment the child begins to crawl, he lays hold of everything, feels, tastes everything, and from everything gets knowledge, is teaching himself, learning the nature and properties of substance, acquiring ideas of extension, solidity, and the other mysteries of matter. He pulls his miniature go-cart to pieces, and his nurse, in her ignorance, bewails his precocious propensities for destruction. Miscall not that mischief, though it cost you money. He is trying to solve high problems in philosophy, inquiring what his go-cart was made of, how it was put together, comparing it with other forms and cohesions; nay, if you knew it, he is learning the rudiments of a mechanical trade. In his nursery he is constantly laying up materials for many high processes of thought; not indeed unaided by books. Books are now his delight, because they present to him several new problems in mechanics and natural philosophy, and also enable him to demonstrate his own force in pulling them to pieces. It may be announced as a general, if not a universal, proposition, that he learns more from books at this time, than in any subsequent equal period of his life. He masters their material riches. Is it not an evil, more or less, that any untoward associations should ever make them aught to him but large depositories of intellectual treasures?

When he throws off his leading-strings, having acquired the power of walking erect, he continues with new activity his unwearying process of observation, comparison, generalization. The nursery, the house, are all too narrow for his swelling curiosity. He rejoices, with the instinct of his own freedom, to go forth into the free air, to mingle his glad voice with the music of the birds, to float with the clouds, to ride upon the wings of the wind, to revel among the flowers, to listen to the thousand melodies, audible or inaudible to the senses, which rise and swell around him, harmoniously mingled, from the air, the earth, and the waters. Call him not idle. He is not idle. No one is ever idle, until the unnatural restraints of unnatural systems of education have destroyed the freshness, and broken up the delightful and harmonious associations of his first intercourse with nature. He is now the pupil of nature, in her wide schoolhouse of diverse and ever changeful beauty. Did we but know it, and how to use it, he is now, if he shall never be again, the ardent and successful student, daily adding knowledge to knowledge, and laying up rich materials of wisdom. The flower he plucks, and as we name it, *idly* throws away, is a text book, from which he learns lessons, that "the whining schoolboy, creeping like a snail unwillingly to school," will probably forget, but will not be likely to learn. He studies the first written book, of which all printed books are only translations, more or less tolerably, some execrably done, but none conveying the full spirit, truth, and beauty of the original.

Let him stay in this school yet a little longer. Follow, assist the direction of nature, but do not thwart her. Give him a teacher, if you will, to help him to observe, and aid him in his interpreting. Indeed some such interpreter, or seeing teacher, not a pedagogue, would seem to be necessary. But do not quench his spirit in its time by immuring him between walls (of brick or wood and mortar), and compel him to turn from the living, God-written page, to the dark, dead, perplexing hieroglyphics, (nay double hieroglyphics; for are not most words, to the child as to many men, as much hieroglyphic mysteries, as the literal symbols which compose them?) from which as yet he can only and reluctantly draw small rills of nourishment for his infinite curiosity. Let him acquire many of the first truths of nature, the elements of which books are made; let him have some conception of the proper use of letters and words, of the functions of books, and a strong yearning to enter the wide domains of thought of which books are the portals; in short let him learn to be an authentic and judging reader, before he learns to read; lest he bow his mind to authority, and fail to be a man, "man thinking." Said he not truth, who wrote, "I had better never read a book, than to be warped by its instruction clean out of my own orbit, and made a satellite instead of a system?"

The only use of letters being to make us acquainted with books, in pursuance of the spirit of the first step, the substance of education is laid in books, so far as education is a system. If the first steps do not create an unconquerable distaste or disgust, the child learns to consider books as almost the only sources of knowledge. Hence a reverence is acquired for books, merely as books, paralyzing to the energies of the intellect, and not to be removed in after life, but with serious, painful, and long continued discipline. Hence the whole process of education is mere instruction, authoritative teaching, dogmatical. It does not draw out the powers of one's own mind; the true purpose of education, as its etymology indicates. The memory is almost the only mental faculty called into active exercise, while the higher powers of induction, comparison, reasoning, abstraction are almost inert, or but partially developed, never attaining their full maturity, except in rarely fortunate circumstances, or in minds of superior native energy. "The intelligent soul is not roused to free and vigorous activity." Hence there is so little of self-reliance, so much of servile dependence on the thoughts of others, the reverence for the past, the slow and contentious progress of improvement, the acquiesence in authority, the seeing and hearing with the organs of others, the using of other men's heads instead of our own.

This dogmatical character pervades the whole course of instruction. The child believes what is told him on the authority of the teacher, the master, or the book, without being taught to inquire into the validity of the authority; whether the professed revelation made to him is authentic, a fact or a fable. The mind is nearly passive during the process. If the teacher or the book be authentic, it is better so to learn, than to be ignorant. But he is not able to judge whether they be or not. A true book, true teaching, as I have said, are but transcripts of the facts of nature, more or less legibly written, according to the clearness of the vision of the seer. Of the greater part of those facts every person may acquire a competent knowledge, by the proper use of those instruments, which are furnished to all; namely his five or six physical senses, and his intuitions. Books and teachers do not originate, create, but only declare; and nothing which is not, for the most part, accessible without their aid. For were not all the things contained in books known, or to be known, before they were recorded in books? Were they not in the universe, not hidden but only invisible, until the eye of some seer was opened upon them? Every eye, that chooses, may be a seer. To make all eyes such is the mission of education.

This dogmatical teaching conveys no knowledge, nothing beyond belief. Of all the things that may be poured into the mind, the truth of little is known until it is verified by the use of one's own faculties. The child is taught (for a modicum of astronomy is included in the prevalent systems of education; if only so much as is supposed to be a necessary preliminary for the study of geography) that the earth is round, it revolves round the sun, and certain problems concerning the stars. How knows he this? He believes it because Copernicus, Galileo, and certain other astronomers are reported to have ascertained it. Nay not on information so authentic as this; but for the most part on the authority of teachers without eyes, as well as himself. Why may not he hold these magnificent truths with the certainty of sight, instead of dreamy assent? Why not be himself a Copernicus? What hinders that he should trace the paths of the planets in their plain, though invisible orbits; that he should correct for himself the first error of his senses, and demonstrate by his own faculties, that the sun and the gorgeous heavens are not satellites of this our earth, performing around it their daily revolutions? He has all the instruments that Pythagoras had, who first gave the true solution of the celestial phenomena. He has all that Copernicus had, who in modern times rediscovered it. He needs no telescope, except that curious miraculous pair of telescopes, which the Creator has placed in his forehead. The old Greek, and the modern Prussian stargazers had no other. The successor of Copernicus, the Father of modern astronomy, was no better provided. Kepler's instrument for celestial observation was nothing more than a wooden right-angled triangle, with sides of 6, 8, and 10 feet, suspended by the right angle, from which a line and plummet was hung. In one of the sides about the right angle, were struck several small quills, through which he observed the stars. This was Kepler's telescope, the rude instrument with which he discovered and demonstrated the laws of the planetary motions. "Three pieces of wood set in a triangle," says a German writer, "were the magic instruments, wherewith Kepler drew from the muse Urania secrets unknown to all antiquity, and on which the whole of modern astronomy rests." Cannot our scholar make a Kepler telescope? Let every one be, according to the intellect that is given him, a Kepler. Let the first lesson inculcated be to see with his own eyes, to reason with his own judgment. Let him discover all that he can discover, and demonstrate all that is by him demonstrable. Are not the objects to be examined all around him, and within him, accessible to the lowest intellect as to the highest? Is not the book of nature written in the universal language, vernacular to all men, intelligible to all, who will learn to read it? That language let him read first of all; and if, with his best endeavors, he cannot unravel all the puzzles of the earth and sky, it will be time enough to go to commentators, his text books and teachers, and learn as much as he is able to understand.

Having touched upon astronomy for the purpose of illustrating my thought, I may mention an error of instruction of some importance, inculcated in the elementary books of the schools, and also in the higher literature, for children of a larger growth. From the contemplation of the grandeur and vastness of the celestial phenomena, devout men are accustomed to inculcate the sentiment of the extreme littleness of man. Even from exhibitions of great power in the natural elements, or from the sublime and majestic scenes of the earth, as boundless prospects from high mountains, wild Alpine solitudes, stupendous precipices, foaming cataracts, the moral still is man's insignificance, insignificant certainly, contrasting himself with the Creator of these wonders. Considering man in this relation, such sentiments are a just expression of devotion. Man is in no danger of exalting too high his conceptions of God. Infinitely below his perfections are the highest conceptions of the loftiest cherub. But there is an exaggerated and unbecoming humility in thus belittling man before mere material forms, abstracted from their origin and author, be they the sublimest or most terrible. They are the creations of the Almighty; but is not man above them all, a more mysterious and glorious creation? Is not he, the true man, he whom we may justly call a man, God-like and immortal? Has he not a capacity to comprehend, be it imperfectly, these wonders; to question the stars, and be answered, concerning their author and their laws; to look beyond the visible concave of the heavens, and see system upon system of worlds, about center upon center of systems, revolving their endless circles about the universal center of immensity? Is not this vast capacity a proof that he is greater than they? Why should his spirit bow itself, or stand in awe before them? They are symbols of the Infinite, "the time-vesture of the Eternal, the time-woven garments by which God is seen." And so is everything. Not a blade of grass but is full of the mystery of the Divinity. The sun and stars, the precipice and the cataract, are no more.

Men have stood under Niagara, and professed, with a true heart, or an ostentatious humbleness, to feel an utter prostration, an overwhelming sense of the littleness of man. Fools, or weak! Why there more than in the verdant landscape, in the field or the forest? What is Niagara, but a mass of unconscious matter, impelled by the law to which it is subjected, tumbling some one hundred and sixty feet down a precipice, as it needs must, and can no otherwise do? By the judicious application of certain mechanical contrivances, you can compel it to turn grindstones, or spinning jennies, or serve other economical purposes of this moneymaking world. Nay, as a sartorial artist once said, or is said to have said, in a fine glow of professional enthusiasm, "Is it not a capital place to sponge a coat?" Nay farther, is it inconceivable that the silent attrition of its own waters (indeed it is believed to have receded several miles from its primeval locality), or even the labors of man, moved by some great impulse to undertake a stupendous experiment, may reduce its channel to a long and gradual slope, or a succession of low cascades? Where then is Niagara, with its appalling roar, and terrible magnificence?

If some seers have reported their impressions truly, the sentiment of littleness in these cases is a violation of man's instincts. Looking down from the top of a very high precipice, nothing but empty space before it, some men have said that they felt an almost irresistible inclination to leap off into the void.[3] Immensity is there almost visible. Is not the feeling described the outswelling of the soul's instinct of the infinite? Man's mind is in a condition unfavorable to its full, perfect, and harmonious development, when he feels himself insignificant and belittles himself before mere magnitude, space, or time; when he transfers to the material symbols, in any measure, the homage they were intended to claim for the infinite, which they shadow forth. Material magnitudes, be they ever so vast, are all changeable, perishable, subject in some degree to the control of man. He can dissolve their masses, break up their combinations, reorganize them in new forms. He knows that "the great globe itself shall fade away." Is it thus with man? Is not he immortal? Has he not a soul, which, though the minutest particle of matter may destroy its outward visible symbol (the body), myriads of Niagaras, the avalanche of a universe of matter, cannot annihilate, cannot touch?

And what to him are time and space? Is he not greater than either, than both? Does he not, in a sense, fill all space; a greater portion than all matter? Is he not with all the stars; rolls there an orb in the remotest region of space, of which he cannot firm a conception; and is his conception not a real spiritual presence? Nay, beyond all material creation, if to it there be a beyond, does not his thought reach, and discern there the universal Presence? And time; is he not spiritually in all time; is not the past and future present with him? Before time was, is he not there, when the spirit of God first moved upon the face of the watery chaos? Is he not with Adam in his innocence, and in his transgression? Is he not in every successive period of time, in every epoch of history? Is he not at the final consummation of earth's affairs, when the elements shall melt with fervent heat; beyond the end of time, is he not present amid the solemn realities, the compensations and retributions of eternity? And they, the loved departed, whom day and night we see, and, not in dreams, commune with, in the scenes we loved together, and in other spheres; is it but a vision, and not a reality, spiritual, the only realities in the universe? "Is the past annihilated, or only past? Is the future now existent, or only future? Those mystic faculties of thine, memory and hope, already answer; already through those mystic avenues, thou, the earth-blinded, summonest both the past and the future, and communest with them, though as yet darkly, and with mute beckonings. The curtains of yesterday roll down; the curtains of tomorrow roll up; but yesterday and tomorrow both *are*. Pierce through the time-element, glance into the eternal. Believe what thou findest written in the sanctuaries of man's soul, even as all thinkers, in all ages, have devoutly read it there; that time and space are not God, but curtains of God; that with God as it is a universal *Here*, so it is an everlasting *Now*."

Man's body, and his bodily actions, his garments, his "time-vesture," are all that belong to earth. Man himself is not a child of time and space. For he has conceptions of the infinite, fainter or more vivid, but for ever approximating to it; and the universe is in his mind. Is not this mysterious power, this multipresence of his spirit, a testimony that he is Godlike? Let him stand in awe before the mystery of his own soul; but refuse, not in pride, but with true reverence, to bow before aught save the Incomprehensible One, who alone is infinite, who is infinity. Man's thought should be that of Kepler, "Father of the world! what moved thus to exalt a poor, weak creature of earth so high, that he stands in light a far-ruling king, almost a God, for he thinks thy thoughts after thee?"

Education should be practical, it is said; its proper function is to train up youth into practical men; and practical men are the only useful men in society. In one sense, unquestionably true; in another sense, unquestionably false. All scripture is given by inspiration. All knowledge is essentially practical, calculated to enable man to accomplish the purpose of man's being; and all knowledge is worthless, which is not made to polarize around the central law of his being. In this sense the proposition is unimpeachable, that education should be practical. But what is meant by *practicalness*; who is the practical man? Is it he who judges of what may be done, from what has been done, and deems every theory a chimera, every project impossible, for which he does not remember a precedent; who refers everything to the maxims and usages of the past? Such a man may lie very skilful in the traditionary routine of his particular occupation, industrious and devoted to it; may be conversant with established forms of ordinary business; know the marketable value of most kinds of property, and be willing to accept such innovations upon old customs, as it has been demonstrated will yield a tangible per cent. But the idea of social progress is not in his conceptions. Is this the end of practical education? Is it not a vast waste of the resources of society, to expend its thought and treasure in devising and maintaining elaborate systems, for accomplishing only this? An end, too, that would come as certainly, in the natural course of things, without the costly apparatus, that is wasted upon it?

On the contrary, can any system of education be truly practical, which has not reference to man in his whole capacity, obligations, and destiny, as something more than a money-getting animal; which does not aim to draw out into free activity the whole faculties of his mind? And is not he the only practical man, who has formed himself under such a system of culture; who has taken in the widest range of investigation and discovered most of the laws of nature and of the human mind; who has attained the clearest insight into the relations of things, and established his principles of judgment and conduct, upon the widest observation of facts, material and spiritual? He has no dread of innovation, reform, whether in the applications of labor, or the institutions of society; because he has seen and knows that progress, improvement, is the constant obligation of man's being, individually and socially. He is not satisfied with the present, of his own mind, or of social institutions; but looks forward, striving with patient hope, to a gleaming future, when "that which is perfect shall come, and that which is in part shall be done away." He is conscious that he knows but the minutest portion of the universe and its laws, and is not rash to pronounce anything impossible, however incredible it may appear, and contrary to all former experience. He does not attempt to fix the limits of the possible or the credible; much less to limit them by the actual. Therefore new discoveries in science and art, the announcement of an unheard of law of nature, a new application of elemental force, transcending all that is known, he does not reject with contemptuous scepticism; but hailed them as new revelations of the inexhaustible mysteries of the universe. He has faith in man; because he knows him by a wide and profound study of his nature, capacities, and destiny; in his strength as well as his weakness, his spiritual grandeur as well as his physical littleness, his infinitude as well as his feebleness; because he knows that his destiny is endless progress; and that, though the individual beset by untoward environments, may falter and turn back, and may even, in self-inflicted blindness or insanity, cast down and trample under his feet his spiritual crown; yet the race is ever going forward, the period ever drawing towards its consummation, when even this time-and-space-enveloped world, the finite shall be to every man a symbol of the infinite. This man the world calls a philosopher, a theorist, a visionary, a dreamer; and pronounces him unfit to be entrusted with the practical operations of social life. Had not Teufelsdröch a true insight into things, when deserted and given up by his patrons as "a man of genius," he said, "as if the higher did not presuppose the lower; as if he, who can fly into heaven, could not also walk post, if he were resolved on't;" and queerly enough concludes, "The world is an old woman, and mistakes any gilt farthing for a gold coin; whereby being often cheated, she will thenceforth trust nothing but the common copper."

To the so called practical man, whom for distinctness and brevity let me call *the* practical man, the golden age is in the past. The reign of Saturn, if it is not placed in hoariest antiquity, comes no nearer his own era than the times of his father. He is a laudatory of the old times, and deplores the changes which have taken place since he was a boy. He is an inveterate conservative, and repudiates all innovations upon establishments. He walks backward through the world, fixing his mournful gaze upon the vanishing glories of the past; and, as "the eyes of a man are not in his hindhead," blind to the kindling splendors of the future behind him, until, as sweeping by, they too become mingled with the past. "Philosophers, we grant, are attached to theories; but really what are called practical men are the greatest theorists in the world; the difference is, that the philosopher's theory is a general view derived from a large induction of authenticated facts; the practical man's theory is a partial view based on the maxims of his nurse or his grandmother, on some unmeaning phrase of sounding words devised and perpetuated by faction, or at best on the induction of his own narrow judgment and limited experience. The false doctrines of some philosophers have produced a certain amount of mischief; but it is as a drop of water to the whole Atlantic, compared with the vast mass of evil perpetuated by the legislation of those, who call themselves emphatically "practical men."

Man's knowledge consists in the truth of the ideas, facts, in his mind; his power in their number and just connection. Ideas are infinite; their relations various, but regular. The philosopher, as contrasted with the practical man, is by the terms of the comparison supposed to have acquired a great number of ideas, and must, therefore, be in a more favorable position for observing their relations and discrepancies. The observation of these relations, and the application of them to the various objects of business of man's being, is the end of knowledge; is knowledge reduced to practice; practical knowledge. Every idea in the infinite chain of thought has its appropriate place, and it is important to ascertain its true place and connections. This, the links we have before us, we shall be more likely to discover. The practical man has, confessedly, fewer than the philosopher, and consequently will be more liable to mistake the true position of each, and to establish false connections between them. This is even worse than absolute ignorance, for "in order to acquire true knowledge, the wholly ignorant man has only to learn; the partially ignorant (he who has established wrong connections) has both to unlearn and to learn, and to unlearn is the most difficult task that can be imposed on the human mind."

There is still another difference, which has been glanced at. The philosopher "stands in the middle, looking before and after." The practical man, too, stands in the middle, but he looks only one way. His maxims are drawn from the past, or at the widest from the narrow segment immediately before him. To him "the thing that has been will be, and there is no new thing under the sun." Coming events cast their shadows before them in vain. He cannot see them, for his eyes are turned in an opposite direction. To the philosopher whatever there is of darkness is behind his path; and that is illuminated by the advancing and increasing brightness of the glowing future. To the practical man, the darkness is before his path; what light he has decreasing as the past recedes and is lost in the shoreless inane.

In proportion to the paucity of ideas will be the tenacity with which they are maintained. Be it supposed, for illustration, that an individual has two ideas. We must needs allow him two, for no man can act with only one, any better than he can walk on one leg; nay, not so well, for he cannot even hop upon it. The whole strength of his conviction will be concentrated upon these two, simply because they are his whole stock. By the laws of the mind, order, arrangement, must exist among its thoughts; if the association is not natural, the mind will force it; for here, as everywhere, "order is heaven's first law." If the two ideas are both true, it may be well. But if they lie both false; or if one be true, and the other false; or if, both being true, they are widely separated, and have no natural connection, except through a chain of intermediate ideas; or even, both being true and contiguous, if they are brought together in erroneous juxtaposition; the practical results of their combination must be mischievous. But he can have no doubt of his ideas, or inferences; for they stand alone in his intellectual firmament, where there is nothing else to disturb the entireness and intensity of his faith. He will deem he has a clear view of the universe, because his two ideas are all of the universe which is visible to him. Hence he is intolerant of opinions opposed to his own, not being able to conceive that what fills his mind with so clear a conviction, should not produce the same in that of others; that even in a mind no better furnished than his own, occupied by the same two ideas, the ideas may have a different arrangement amid relation; nor that the same evidence may produce a quite different effect upon different minds, according to the medium through which it is presented, and the number and nature of the objects with which it may be composed.

They were the practical men, who persecuted Jesus, because he taught the spiritual worship of the Father, and rebuked the narrow exclusiveness of the traditional faith resting upon "our fathers worshipped in this mountain." They were the practical men of their age, who plunged Galileo in a dungeon, for demonstrating a system of the universe, opposed to the common sense of the age, and which contravened the canons of the Church. They are the practical men, who, in all ages, have stoned the prophets, established inquisitions, punished heresy as crime, enacted penal statutes against opinion, extended legislation over the whole business of society, into even man's bosom, making his tastes, habits, private responsibilities, subjects of statute enactments.

The practical man has no faith in man; little in individual men, excepting himself and his sect; because he is ignorant of human nature, or his partial knowledge is derived from his individual nature, or the limited social sphere in which he moves. Hence he deems the notion of man's indefinite progress a chimera. Man, according to his theory, is a thing to be governed, and the great social problem is to ascertain how little of free agency he may be safely entrusted with. His only idea of man free, without statute law, is that of a ferocious, rabid beast, left without restraint to glut his appetite for carnage. The possibility of individual self-government is not dreamed of in his philosophy. In all states he is the High Church and Tory partisan, and dreads innovation more than the continuance of the most flagrant abuses. Whatever his professed creed may be, he practically believes and acts upon the theological paradox of total depravity, that men are born under the wrath and curse of God, prone to evil and that continually; because he knows something of the vices of mankind, and deems that knowledge of human nature. Man has no absolute rights; none independent of society; none, which he may not be required to surrender to "that incarnation of despotism, that most unintelligible of all abstractions," the public good. Is it the just and highest function of education, as the handmaid of free institutions, as conferring the power of self-government, to produce only such results as these; to convert men into social machines?

Be education practical; and the more practical any system is, the more perfect it is. This it can never be, unless it has reference to man in his whole nature and destiny; unless it aims at something higher than to fit men for the routine of pretty occupations, for the handicrafts and mechanical business of society; unless it contemplates for man a nobler destiny than that so strikingly depicted by a living American writer. "Man thus metamorphosed, is a thing, many things. The planter is a man sent into the fields to gather food, and is seldom cheered with the idea of the true dignity of his mission. He sees his bushel and his cart, and sinks into a farmer, instead of *man on a farm*. The tradesman scarce gives an ideal value to his work, but is ridden by the routine of his craft, and his soul is subject to dollars. The priest becomes a form; the attorney a statute book; the mechanic a machine; the sailor a rope of a ship."

Considering education more directly with reference to popular institutions, at the first view a remarkable anomaly is presented. Our nation professes to rely for its permanence upon the general understanding, by the people, of their rights, and of the nature and value of freedom. Yet here there is not, that I am aware of, in any system of education practiced among us, any direct provision for teaching the elementary principles of freedom. Wiser than we are the absolutisms of the old world, who are careful, along with the manuals of philosophy and science, to send into their schools catechisms of political duty, inculcating political subjection. They, as well as we, rely upon the intelligence of the people. But where shall we find, in our institutions for education, the text book of man's natural rights, or scarcely even a recognition of them? In our Colleges and Universities? Nay, they are wedded to ancient routine, occupied in teaching " dead vocables," and systems of philosophy, that have become obsolete. Social progress has swept by them, and left them back in the dark ages. Not from them comes the guiding light, and the helpful arm.

In the popular literature? The popular literature is, for the most part, an aristocrat; and, excepting some sounding generalities concerning popular sovereignty, and the majesty of the people (not, however, perceiving man as an individual) uttered in deference to certain antiquated constitutional abstractions of liberty and equal rights; it has hardly a conception of man, except as a mass. There are exceptions; but these scarcely come into the category of *popular* literature. Few are the bards, nor highly praised, who strike the lyre for simple, unranked man; and he is deemed but little better than a fanatic, a "rabid radical," who would pluck the veil of abstraction from acknowledged first truths, and make them practical and universal.

Shall we go down among the elements; to the dust-begrimmed, wayside temples of popular education? There, out of doors and the eye of the birch-sceptered monarchs of those dingy halls of science, there is abundance of practical teaching on the subject. But within, alas, the Peter Parleys and Robin Carvers, with their nutshell compendiums of science, and royal roads to knowledge, monopolize all space, and gibber, to little purpose, about beasts, and fishes, and birds, and other miscellaneous elements.

Or shall we seek the development of our theory of equal rights, where indeed, if anywhere, it should be found, in the commentaries of the *practical* men, written out in the statute book? Worse and worse. The practical men have acted on a theory of their own, through which our grand national theory, scarce with faintest glimmerings, is visible.

They recognize man only in the aggregate, and not in the individual; as a many-headed subject of statute regulation; or as a sort of complex machine, not finished, of which it is the province of the legislator to apply certain needful wheels and gauges, checks and balances. Natural rights are here metamorphosed into corporation charters; universal rights are superseded by grants of exclusive privileges; statute prosecutions for the expression of unpopular opinion, stand in the place of the individual right of thought and speech; property becomes of more worth than man; and instead of general laws, extending over every one equal protection, thus give a special legislation. Not there shall we find our text book, or an authentic commentary thereon.

If we seek for the illustrations of our fundamental principles in their results upon the general character and spirit of society, shall we find there the theory of natural rights planted and flourishing in the strong foundations of public opinion? Nay, here least of all. Here, too, individual man is scarcely known, and only as an undistinguishable element of a mass. He does not stand out prominently as a separate integral existence; but, from being a unit, has almost vanished into an infinitesimal fraction. Public opinion, or gigantic associations usurping its attributes, are swallowing up the individual in their huge vortices. All the force there is in man is in his social accidents and connections; he is not strong by himself, but only by his party. Society has become a machine, or combination of machines. Moral force is losing its power, and giving place to mechanism. By societies of every type and object, by party mechanism, by statutes, which, never more than one form of the expression of public opinion, are now only results of social and party mechanisms; the individual is in danger of becoming nothing, of sinking into oblivion, and leaving time and space to that aggregate irresponsibility, *the public.* And more; he is in danger of losing the power of independent volition, of forsaking a vice, or practicing a virtue, without putting himself into the leading-strings of association. Associations assume and control his personal responsibilities, until it will be happy for him if he do not cease to be conscious that he has any. We shall, therefore, seek in vain in society for the illustrations which we are in search of; but we shall discover something of the modes, "by which the same control under a free government, may be exerted over individual opinion and action, that is exerted over them by despotisms and hierarchies."

But man was not made to be a machine, a fraction; to lose his separate existence, and be incorporated in a mass; nor to suffer his free volitions to be overwhelmed by his social sympathies. It is the mission of education to rescue him from this individual annihilation; to develop the great central law and attribute of his being; that man, each man by himself, in reference to all other men, is essentially and inalienably free, and the brother and equal of every man. This great first truth must be roused from its almost dead sleep in constitutions and popular declamation, and brought out again, with new annunciations, into the high-ways and bye-ways of society; into the humble roadside schoolhouse, and into the halls where high science has her throne. Instead of being a parchment formula, let it be made a living, all-pervading energy; presiding in the assemblies of legislation; and giving an irresistible, but tranquil and legitimate power to public opinion. From this central principle let all social doctrines radiate; by this primary law be all social maxims and usages tried. It will then be perceived that society, or government, as embodying and representing the material force of society, is but the creature of man's individual freedom, and not the controller. In its ultimate analysis, society is an association for mutual protection; the security of each individual in the possession and exercise of his natural, absolute rights. Within the limits of those rights, society has no authority of government over him; and if she exercise any, she is guilty of tyranny; the laws, she enacts to limit or restrain them, are repugnant to the higher law of man's nature and of no validity. This freedom, these rights, are a wall of sanctity around each individual, which society should not dare to scale, which cannot be broken over without unspeakable injury to society itself. On the recognition of these principles, the stability, even the existence, of free communities depend. I can form no conception of a freedom in society, of which the freedom of individual man is not the primary element; of man as man, with rights not derived from society, prior to society, beyond the control of all other men, beyond the reach of government, laws, or public opinion. It is no impeachment of the validity of these rights, that the individual may and does abuse them. The power to abuse them is a necessary element of liberty. "God leaves man in his freedom, and does not control it, though man, in abusing it, brings damnation to his soul." The legitimate exercise of freedom can never work harm to others, or to society. There can be no collision between the clear rights of one individual, and those of another, any more than in the use of the all-pervading elements; for the rights are identical and universal. "So long as one does not trespass upon the rights of others, nor place obstacles in the way of their full and free exercise, society has no authority to interfere with his course."

These principles are in the highest degree practical; for in man's freedom lies his power of full and perfect development. They should be made the starting-point, and fixed as landmarks along the whole course of practical education. They should cheer the schoolboy's wearisome discipline with hope and confidence. To man they should be a universal presence, filling him with the fullness of strength, courage, and indomitable energy for all the "sublime possibilities" of his being.

The Laboring Classes

JULY 1840

A Review of Thomas Carlyle's *Chartism* (Boston: C. C. Little & James Brown, 1840)

*T*homas Carlyle unquestionably ranks among the ablest writers of the day. His acquaintance with literature seems to be almost universal, and there is apparently no art or science with which he is not familiar. He possesses an unrivalled mastery over the resources of the English tongue, a remarkably keen insight into the mysteries of human nature, and a large share of genuine poetic feeling. His works are characterized by freshness and power, as well as by strangeness and singularity, and must be read with interest, even when they cannot be with approbation.

The little work, named at the head of this article, is a fair sample of his peculiar excellences, and also of his peculiar defects. As a work intended to excite attention and lead the mind to an investigation of a great subject, it possesses no ordinary value; but as a work intended to throw light on a difficult question, and to afford some positive directions to the statesman and the philanthropist, it is not worth much. Carlyle, like his imitators in this country, though he declaims against the destructives, possesses in no sense a constructive genius. He is good as a demolisher, but pitiable enough as a builder. No man sees more clearly that the present is defective and unworthy to be retained; he is a brave and successful warrior against it, whether reference be had to its literature, its politics, its philosophy, or its religion; but when the question comes up concerning what ought to be, what should take the place of what is, we regret to say he affords us no essential aid, scarcely a useful hint. He has fine spiritual instincts, has outgrown materialism, loathes skepticism, sees clearly the absolute necessity of faith in both God and man, and insists upon it with due sincerity and earnestness; but with feelings very nearly akin to despair. He does not appear to have found as yet a faith for himself, and his writings have almost invariably a skeptical tendency. He has doubtless a sort of faith in God, or an overwhelming Necessity, but we cannot perceive that he has any faith in man or in man's efforts. Society is wrong, but he mocks at our sincerest and best directed efforts to right it. It cannot subsist as it is; that is clear: but what shall be done to make it what it ought to be, that he saith not. Of all writers we are acquainted with, he is the least satisfactory. He is dissatisfied with everything himself, and he leaves his readers dissatisfied with everything. Hopeless himself, he makes them also hopeless, especially if they have strong social tendencies, and are hungering and thirsting to work out the regeneration of their race.

Mr. Carlyle's admirers, we presume, will demur to this criticism. We have heard some of them speak of him as a sort of soul-quickener, and profess to derive from his writings fresh life and courage. We know not how this may be. It may be that they derive advantage from him on the homoeopathic principle, and that he cures their diseases by exaggerating them; but for ourselves we must say that we have found him anything but a skilful physician. He disheartens and enfeebles us; and while he emancipates us from the errors of tradition, he leaves us without strength or courage to engage in the inquiry after truth. We rise from his writings with the weariness and exhaustion one does from the embraces of the witch Mara. It is but slowly that our blood begins to circulate again, and it is long before we recover the use of our powers. Whether his writings produce this effect on others or not, we are unable to say; but this effect they do produce on us. We almost dread to encounter them.

Mr. Carlyle would seem to have great sympathy with man. He certainly is not wanting in the sentiment of humanity; nor is he deceived by external position, or dazzled by factitious glare. He can see worth in the socially low as well as in the socially high; in the artisan as well as the noble. This is something, but no great merit in one who can read the

New Testament. Still it is something, and we are glad to meet it. But after all, he has no true reverence for Humanity. He may offer incense to a Goethe, a Jean Paul, a Mirabeau, a Danton, a Napoleon, but he nevertheless looks down upon his fellows, and sneers at the mass. He looks down upon man as one of his admirers has said, "as if man were a mouse." But we do not wish to look upon man in that light. We would look upon him as a brother, an equal, entitled to our love and sympathy. We would feel ourselves neither above him nor below him, but standing up by his side, with our feet on the same level with his. We would also love and respect the commonplace mass, not merely heroes and sages, prophets and priests.

We are moreover no warm admirers of Carlyle's style of writing. We acknowledge his command over the resources of our language, and we enjoy the freshness, and occasional strength, beauty, and felicity of his style and expression, but he does not satisfy us. He wants clearness and precision, and that too when writing on topics where clearness and precision are all but indispensable. We have no patience with his mistiness, vagueness, and singularity. If a man must needs write and publish his thoughts to the world, let him do it in as clear and as intelligible language as possible. We are not aware of any subject worth writing on at all, that is already so plain that it needs to be rendered obscure. Carlyle can write well if he chooses; no man better. He is not necessarily misty, vague, nor fantastic. The antic tricks he has been latterly playing do not spring from the constitution of his mind, and we must say do by no means become him. We are disposed ourselves to assume considerable latitude in both thought and expression; but we believe every scholar should aim to keep within the general current of his language. Every language receives certain laws from the genius of the people who use it, and it is no mark of wisdom to transgress them; nor is genuine literary excellence to be attained but by obeying them. An Englishman, if he would profit Englishmen, must write English, not French nor German. If he wishes his writings to become an integral part of the literature of his language, he must keep within the steady current of what has ever been regarded as classical English style, and deny himself the momentary éclat he might gain by affection and singularity.

We can, however, pardon Carlyle altogether more easily than we can his American imitators. Notwithstanding his manner of writing, when continued for any considerable length, becomes monotonous and wearisome, as in his *History of the French Revolution,* a work which, with all its brilliant wit, inimitable humor, deep pathos, and graphic skill, can scarcely be read without yawning, yet in his case it is redeemed by rare beauties, and marks a mind of the highest order, and of vast attainments. But in the hands of his American imitators, it becomes puerile and disgusting; and what is worthy of note is, that it is adopted and most servilely followed by the men among us who are loudest in their boasts of originality, and the most intolerant to its absence. But enough of this. For our consolation, the race of imitators is feeble and short-lived.

The object of the little work before us, is one of the weightiest which can engage the attention of the statesman or the philanthropist. It is indeed, here, discussed only in relation to the working classes of England, but it in reality involves the condition of the working classes throughout the world, a great subject, and one never yet worthily treated. Chartism, properly speaking, is no local or temporary phenomenon. Its germ may be found in every nation in Christendom; indeed wherever man has approximated a state of civilization, wherever there is inequality in social condition, and in the distribution of the products of industry. And where does not this inequality obtain? Where is the spot on earth, in which the actual producer of wealth is not one of the lower class, shut out from what are looked upon as the main advantages of the social state?

Mr. Carlyle, though he gives us few facts, yet shows us that the condition of the workingmen in England is deplorable, and every day growing worse. It has already become intolerable, and hence the outbreak of the Chartists. Chartism is the protest of the working classes against the injustice of the present social organization of the British community, and a loud demand for a new organization which shall respect the rights and well-being of the laborer.

The movements of the Chartists have excited considerable alarm in the higher classes of English society, and some hope in the friends of Humanity among ourselves. We do not feel competent to speak with any decision on the extent or importance of these movements. If our voice could reach the Chartists we would bid them be bold and determined; we would bid them persevere even unto death; for their cause is that of justice, and in fighting for it they will be fighting the battles of God and man. But we look for no important results from their movements. We have little faith in a John Bull mob. It will bluster, and swagger, and threaten much; but give it plenty of porter and roast-beef, and it will sink back to its kennel, as quiet and as harmless as a lamb. The lower classes in England have made many a move since the days of Wat Tyler for the betterment of their condition, but we cannot perceive that they have ever effected much. They are doubtless nearer the day of their emancipation, than they were, but their actual condition is scarcely superior to what it was in the days of Richard the Second.

There is no country in Europe, in which the condition of the laboring classes seems to us so hopeless as in that of England. This is not owing to the fact, that the aristocracy is less enlightened, more powerful, or more oppressive in England than elsewhere. The English laborer does not find his worst enemy in the nobility, but in the middling class. The middle class is much more numerous and powerful in England than in any other European country, and is of a higher character. It has always been powerful; for by means of the Norman Conquest it received large accessions from the old Saxon nobility. The Conquest established a new aristocracy, and degraded the old to the condition of Commoners. The superiority of the English Commons is, we suppose, chiefly owing to this fact.

The middle class is always a firm champion of equality, when it concerns humbling a class above it; but it is its inveterate foe, when it concerns elevating a class below it. Manfully have the British Commoners struggled against the old feudal aristocracy, and so successfully that they now constitute the dominant power in the state. To their struggles against the throne and the nobility is the English nation indebted for the liberty it so loudly boasts, and which, during the last half of the last century, so enraptured the friends of Humanity throughout Europe.

But this class has done nothing for the laboring population, the real *proletarii*. It has humbled the aristocracy; it has raised itself to dominion, and it is now conservative, conservative in fact, whether it call itself Whig or Radical. From its near relation to the workingmen, its kindred pursuits with them, it is altogether more hostile to them than the nobility ever were or ever can be. This was seen in the conduct of England towards the French Revolution. So long as that Revolution was in the hands of the middle class, and threatened merely to humble monarchy and nobility, the English nation applauded it; but as soon as it descended to the mass of the people, and promised to elevate the laboring classes, so soon as the starving workingman began to flatter himself that there was to be a Revolution for him too as well as for his employer, the English nation armed itself and poured out its blood and treasure to suppress it. Everybody knows that Great Britain, boasting of her freedom and of her love of freedom, was the life and soul of the opposition to the French Revolution; and on her head almost alone should fall the curses of Humanity for the sad failure of that glorious uprising of the people in behalf of their imprescriptible, and inalienable rights. Yet it was not the English monarchy, nor the English nobility, that was alone in fault. Monarchy and nobility would have been powerless, had they not had with them the great body of the English Commoners. England fought in the ranks, nay, at the head of the allies, not for monarchy, not for nobility, nor yet for religion; but for trade and manufacturers, for her middle class, against the rights and well-being of the workingman; and her strength and efficiency consisted in the strength and efficiency of this class.

Now this middle class, which was strong enough to defeat nearly all the practical benefit of the French Revolution, is the natural enemy of the Chartists. It will unite with the monarchy and nobility against them; and spare neither blood nor treasure to defeat them. Our despair for the poor Chartists arises from the number and power of the middle class. We dread for them neither monarchy nor nobility. Nor should they. Their only real enemy is in the employer. In all countries is it the same. The only enemy of the laborer is your employer, whether appearing in the shape of the master mechanic, or in the owner of a factory. A Duke of Wellington is much more likely to vindicate the rights of labor than an Abbot Lawrence, although the latter may be a very kindhearted man, and liberal citizen, as we always find Blackwood's Magazine more true to the interests of the poor, than we do the Edinburgh Review, or even the London and Westminster.

Mr. Carlyle, contrary to his wont, in the pamphlet we have named, commends two projects for the relief of the workingmen, which he finds others have suggested, universal education, and general emigration. Universal education we shall not be thought likely to depreciate; but we confess that we are unable to see in it that sovereign remedy for the evils of the social state as it is, which some of our friends do, or say they do. We have little faith in the power of education to elevate a people compelled to labor from twelve to sixteen hours a day, and to experience no mean portion of the time a paucity of even the necessaries of life, let alone its comforts. Give your starving boy a breakfast before you send him to school, and your tattered beggar a cloak before you attempt his moral and intellectual elevation. A swarm of naked and starving urchins crowded into a schoolroom will make little proficiency in the "Humanities." Indeed, it seems to us most bitter mockery for the well-dressed and well-fed to send the schoolmaster and priest to the wretched hovels of squalid poverty, a mockery at which devils may laugh, but over which angels must weep. Educate the working classes of England; and what then? Will they require less food and less clothing when educated than they do now? Will they be more contented or more happy in their condition? For God's sake beware how you kindle within them the intellectual spark, and make them aware that they too are men, with powers of thought and feeling which ally them by the bonds of brotherhood to their betters. If you will doom them to the external condition of brutes, do in common charity keep their minds and hearts brutish. Render them as insensible as possible, that they may feel the less acutely their degradation, and see the less clearly the monstrous injustice which is done them.

General emigration can at best afford only a temporary relief, for the colony will soon become an empire, and reproduce all the injustice and wretchedness of the mother country. Nor is general emigration necessary. England, if she would be just, could support a larger population than she now numbers. The evil is not from over population, but from the unequal repartition of the fruits of industry. She suffers from over production, and from over production, because her workmen produce not for themselves but for their employers. What then is this remedy? As it concerns England, we shall leave the English statesman to answer. Be it what it may, it will not be obtained without war and bloodshed. It will be found only at the end of one of the longest and severest struggles the human race has ever been engaged in only by that most dreaded of all wars, the war of the poor against the rich, a war which, however long it may be delayed, will come, and come with all its horrors. The day of vengeance is sure; for the world after all is under the domain of a Just Providence.

No one can observe the signs of the times with much care, without perceiving that a crisis as to the relation of wealth and labor is approaching. It is useless to shut our eyes to the fact, and like the ostrich fancy ourselves secure because we have so concealed our heads that we see not the danger. We or our children will have to meet this crisis. The old war between the King and the Barons is well nigh ended, and so is that between the Barons and the Merchants and the Manufacturers, landed capital and commercial capital. The business man has become the peer of my Lord. And now commences the new struggle between the operative and his employer, between wealth and labor. Every day does this struggle extend further and wax stronger and fiercer; what or when the end will be God only knows.

In this coming contest there is a deeper question at issue than is commonly imagined; a question which is but remotely touched in your controversies about United States Banks and Sub-Treasuries, chartered Banking and free Banking, free trade and corporations, although these controversies may be paving the way for it to come up. We have discovered no presentiment of it in any king's or queen's speech, nor in any president's message. It is embraced in no popular political creed of the day, whether christened Whig or Tory, *Justemilieu* or Democratic. No popular senator, or deputy, or peer seems to have any glimpse of it; but it is working in the hearts of the million, is struggling to shape itself, and one day it will be uttered, and in thunder tones. Well will it be for him, who, on that day, shall be found ready to answer it.

What we would ask is, throughout the Christian world, the actual condition of the laboring classes, viewed simply and exclusively in their capacity of laborers? They constitute at least a moiety of the human race. We exclude the nobility, we exclude also the middle class, and include only actual laborers, who are laborers and not proprietors, owners of none of the funds of production, neither houses, ships, nor lands, nor implements of labor, being therefore solely dependent on their hands. We have no means of ascertaining their precise proportion to the whole number of the race; but we think we may estimate them at one half. In any contest they will be as two to one, because the large class of proprietors who are not employers, but laborers on their own lands or in their own shops will make common cause with them.

Now we will not so belie our acquaintance with political economy, as to allege that these alone perform all that is necessary to the production of wealth. We are not ignorant of the fact, that the merchant, who is literally the common carrier and exchange dealer, performs a useful service, and is therefore entitled to a portion of the proceeds of labor.

But make all necessary deductions on his account, and then ask what portion of the remainder is retained, either in kind or in its equivalent, in the hands of the original producer, the workingman? All over the world this fact stares us in the face, the workingman is poor and depressed, while a large portion of the non-workingmen, in the sense we now use the term, are wealthy. It may be laid down as a general rule, with but few exceptions, that men are rewarded in an inverse ratio to the amount of actual service they perform. Under every government on earth the largest salaries are annexed to those offices, which demand of their incumbents the least amount of actual labor either mental or manual. And this is in perfect harmony with the whole system of repartition of the fruits of industry, which obtains in every department of society. Now here is the system which prevails, and here is its result. The whole class of simple laborers are poor, and in general unable to procure anything beyond the bare necessities of life.

In regard to labor two systems obtain; one that of slave labor, the other that of free labor. Of the two, the first is, in our judgment, except so far as the feelings are concerned, decidedly the least oppressive. If the slave has never been a free man, we think, as a general rule, his sufferings are less than those of the free laborer at wages. As to actual freedom one has just about as much as the other. The laborer at wages has all the disadvantages of freedom and none of its blessings, while the slave, if denied the blessings, is freed from the disadvantages. We are no advocates of slavery, we are as heartily opposed to it as any modern abolitionist can be; but we say frankly that, if there must always be a laboring population distinct from proprietors and employers, we regard the slave system as decidedly preferable to the system at wages. It is no pleasant thing to go days without food, to lie idle for weeks, seeking work and finding none, to rise in the morning with a wife and children you love, and know not where to procure them a breakfast, and to see constantly before you no brighter prospect than the almshouse. Yet these are no unfrequent incidents in the lives of our laboring population. Even in seasons of general prosperity, when there was only the ordinary cry of "hard times," we have seen hundreds of people in a no very populous village, in a wealthy portion of our common country, suffering for the want of the necessaries of life, willing to work, and yet finding no work to do. Many and many is the application of a poor man for work, merely for his food, we have seen rejected. These things are little thought of, for the applicants are poor; they fill no conspicuous place in society, and they have no biographers. But their wrongs are chronicled in heaven. It is said there is no want in this country. There may be less than in some other countries. But death by actual starvation in this country is, we apprehend, no uncommon occurrence. The sufferings of a quiet, unassuming but useful class of females in our cities, in general sempstresses, too proud to beg or to apply to the almshouse, are not easily told. They are industrious; they do all that they can find to do; but yet the little there is for them to do and the miserable pittance they receive for it, is hardly sufficient to keep soul and body together. And yet there is a man who employs them to make shirts, trousers, &c., and grows rich on their labors. He is one of our respectable citizens, perhaps is praised in the newspapers for his liberal donations to some charitable institution. He passes among us as a pattern of morality, and is honored as a worthy Christian. And why should he not be, since our *Christian* community is made up of such as he, and since our clergy would not dare question his piety, lest they should incur the reproach of infidelity, and lose their standing, and their salaries? Nay, since our clergy are raised up, educated, fashioned, and sustained by such as he? Not a few of our churches rest on Mammon for their foundation. The basement is a trader's shop.

We pass through our manufacturing villages, most of them appear neat and flourishing. The operatives are well dressed, and we are told, well paid. They are said to be healthy, contented, and happy. This is the fair side of the picture; the side exhibited to distinguished visitors. There is a dark side, moral as well as physical. Of the common operatives, few, if any, by their wages, acquire a competence. A few of what Carlyle terms not inaptly the *body-servants* are well paid, and now and then an agent or an overseer rides in his coach. But the great mass wear out their health, spirits, and morals, without becoming one whit better off than when they commenced labor. The bills of morality in these factory villages are not striking, we admit, for the poor girls when they can toil no longer go home to die. The average life, working life we mean, of the girls that come to Lowell, for instance, from Maine, New Hampshire, and Vermont, we have been assured, is only about three years. What becomes of them then? Few of them ever marry; fewer still ever return to their native places with reputations unimpaired. "She has worked in a Factory," is almost enough to damn to infamy the most worthy and virtuous girl. We know no sadder sight on earth than one of our factory villages presents, when the bell at break of day, or at the hour of breakfast, or dinner, calls out its hundreds or thousands of operatives. We stand and look at these hard working men and women hurrying in all directions, and ask ourselves, where go the proceeds of their labors? The man who employs them, and for whom they are toiling as so many slaves, is one of our city nabobs, reveling in luxury; or he is a member of our legislature, enacting laws to put money in his own pocket; or he is a member of Congress, contending for a high Tariff to tax the poor for the benefit of the rich; or in these times he is shedding crocodile tears over the deplorable condition of the poor laborer, while he docks his wages, twenty-five per cent; building miniature log cabins, shouting Harrison and "hard cider." And this man too would fain pass for a Christian and a republican. He shouts for liberty, stickles for equality, and is horrified at a Southern planter who keeps slaves.

One thing is certain; that of the amount actually produced by the operative, he retains a less proportion than it costs the master to feed, clothe, and lodge his slave. Wages is a cunning device of the devil, for the benefit of tender consciences, who would retain all the advantages of the slave system, without the expense, trouble, and odium of being slaveholders.

Messrs. Thome and Kimball, in their account of emancipation in the West Indies, establish the fact that the employer may have the same amount of labor done, twenty-five per cent cheaper than the master. What does this fact prove, if not that wages is a more successful method of taxing labor than slavery? We really believe our Northern system of labor is more oppressive, and even more mischievous to morals, than the Southern. We, however, war against both. We have no toleration for either system. We should see the slave a man, be a free man, not a mere operative at wages. This he would not be were he now emancipated. Could the abolitionists effect all they propose, they would do the slave no service. Should emancipation work as well as they say, still it would do the slave no good. He would be a slave still, although with the title and cares of a freeman. If then we had no constitutional objections to abolitionism, we could not, for the reason here implied, be abolitionists.

The slave system, however, in name and form, is gradually disappearing from Christendom. It will not subsist much longer. But its place is taken by the system of labor at wages, and this system, we hold, is no improvement upon the one it supplants. Nevertheless the system of wages will triumph. It is the system which in name sounds honester than slavery, and in substance is more profitable to the master. It yields the wages of iniquity, without its opprobrium. It will therefore supplant slavery, and be sustained for a time.

Now, what is the prospect of those who fall under the operation of this system? We ask, is there a reasonable chance that any considerable portion of the present generation of laborers, shall ever become owners of a sufficient portion of the funds of production, to be able to sustain themselves by laboring on their own capital, that is, as independent laborers? We need not ask this question, for everybody knows there is not. Well, is the condition of a laborer at wages the best that the great mass of the working people ought to be able to aspire to? Is it a condition, nay can it be made a condition, with which a man should be satisfied; in which he should be contented to live and die?

In our own country this condition has existed under its most favorable aspects, and has been made as good as it can be. It has reached all the excellence of which it is susceptible. It is now not improving but growing worse. The actual condition of the workingman today, viewed in all its bearings, is not so good as it was fifty years ago. If we have not been altogether misinformed, fifty years ago, health and industrious habits, constituted no mean stock in trade, and with them almost any man might aspire to competence and independence. But it is so no longer. The wilderness has receded, and already the new lands are beyond the reach of the mere laborer, and the employer has him at his mercy. If the present relation subsist, we see nothing better for him in reserve than what he now possesses, but something altogether worse.

We are not ignorant of the fact that men born poor become wealthy, and that men born to wealth become numbers of the poor; but this fact does not necessarily diminish the numbers of the poor, nor augment the numbers of the rich. The relative numbers of the two classes remain, or may remain, the same. But be this as it may; one fact is certain, no man born poor has ever, by his wages, as a simple operative, risen to the class of the wealthy. Rich he may have become, but it has not been by his own manual labor. He has in some way contrived to tax for his benefit the labor of others. He may have accumulated a few dollars which he has placed at usury, or invested in trade; or he may, as a master workman, obtain a premium on his journeymen; or he may have from a clerk passed to a partner, or from a workman to an overseer. The simple market wages for ordinary labor, has never been adequate to raise him from poverty to wealth. The fact is decisive of the whole controversy, and proves that the system of wages must be supplanted by some other system, or else one half of the human race must forever be the virtual slaves of the other.

Now the great work for this age and the coming, is to raise up the laborer, and to realize in our own social arrangements and in the actual condition of all men, that equality between man and man, which God has established between the rights of one and those of another. In other words, our business is to emancipate the proletaries, as the past has emancipated the slaves. This is our work. There must be no class of our fellow men doomed to toil through life as mere workmen at wages. If wages are tolerated it must be, in the case of the individual operative, only under such conditions that by the time he is of a proper age to settle in life, he shall have accumulated enough to be an independent laborer on his own capital, on his own farm or in his own shop. Here is our work. How is it to be done?

Reformers in general answer this question, or what they deem its equivalent, in a manner which we cannot but regard as very unsatisfactory. They would have all men wise, good, and happy; but in order to make them so, they tell us that we want not external changes, but internal; and therefore instead of declaiming against society and seeking to disturb existing social arrangements, we should confine ourselves to the individual reason and conscience; seek merely to lead the individual to repentance, and to reformation of life; make the individual a practical, a truly religious man, and all evils will either disappear, or be sanctified to the spiritual growth of the soul.

This is doubtless a capital theory, and has the advantage that kings, hierarchies, nobilities, in a work, all who fatten on the toil and blood of their fellows, will feel no difficulty in supporting it. Nicholas of Russia, the Grand Turk, his Holiness the Pope, will hold us their especial friends for advocating a theory, which secures them the odor of sanctity even while they are sustaining by their anathemas or their armed legions, a system of things of which the great mass are and must be the victims. If you will only allow me to keep thousands toiling for my pleasure or my profit, I will even aid you in your pious efforts to convert their souls. I am not cruel; I do not wish either to cause, or to see suffering; I am therefore exposed to encourage your labors for the souls of the workingman, providing you will secure to me the products of his bodily toil. So far as the salvation of his soul will not interfere with my income, I shod it worthy of being sought; and if a few thousand dollars will aid you, Mr. Priest, in reconciling him to God, and making fair weather for him hereafter, they are at your service. I shall not want him to work for me in the world to come, and I can indemnify myself for what your salary costs me, by paying him less wages. A capital theory this, which one may advocate without incurring the reproach of a disorganizer, a Jacobin, a leveler, and without losing the friendship of the rankest aristocrat in the land.

This theory, however, is exposed to one slight objection, that of being condemned by something like six thousand years' experience. For six thousand years its beauty has been extolled, its praises sung, and its blessings sought, under every advantage which learning, fashion, wealth, and power can secure; and yet under its practical operations, we are assured, that mankind, though totally depraved at first, have been growing worse and worse ever since.

For our part, we yield to none in our reverence for science and religion; but we confess that we look not for the regeneration of the race from priests and pedagogues. They have had a fair trial. They cannot construct the temple of God. They cannot conceive its plan, and they know not how to build. They daub with untempered mortar, and the walls they erect tumble down if so much as a fox attempt to go up thereon. In a word they always league with the people's masters, and seek to reform without disturbing the social arrangements which render reform necessary. They would change the consequents without changing the antecedents, secure the men the rewards of holiness, while they continue their allegiance to the devil. We have no faith in priests and pedagogues. They merely cry peace, peace, and that too when there is no peace, and can be none.

We admit the importance of what Dr. Channing in his lectures on the subject we are treating recommends as "self-culture." Self-culture is a good thing, but it cannot abolish inequality, nor restore men to their rights. As a means of quickening moral and intellectual energy, exalting the sentiments, and preparing the laborer to contend manfully for his rights, we admit its importance, and insist as strenuously as any one on making it as universal as possible; but as constituting in itself a remedy for the vices of the social state, we have no faith in it. As a means it is well, as the end it is nothing.

The truth is, the evil we have pointed out is not merely individual in its character. It is not, in the case of any single individual, of any one man's procuring, nor can the efforts of any one man, directed solely to his own moral and religious perfection, do aught to remove it. What is purely individual in its nature, efforts of individuals to perfect themselves, may remove. But the evil we speak of is inherent in all our social arrangements, and cannot be cured without a radical change of those arrangements. Could we convert all men to Christianity in both theory and practice, as held by the most enlightened sect of Christians among us, the evils of the social state would remain untouched. Continue our present system of trade, and all its present evil consequences will follow, whether it be carried on by your best men or your worst. Put your best men, your wisest, most moral, and most religious men, at the head of your paper money banks, and the evils of the present banking system will remain scarcely diminished. The only way to get rid of its evils is to change the system, not its managers. The evils of slavery do not result from the personal characters of slave masters. They are inseparable from the system, let who will be masters. Make all your rich men good Christians, and you have lessened not the evils of existing inequality in wealth. The mischievous effects of this inequality do not result from the personal characters of either rich or poor, but from itself, and they will continue, just so long as there are rich men and poor men in the same community. You must abolish the system or accept its consequences. No man can serve both God and Mammon. If you will serve the devil, you must look to the devil for your wages; we know no other way.

Let us not be misinterpreted. We deny not the power of Christianity. Should all men become good Christians, we deny not that all social evils would be cured. But we deny in the outset that a man, who seeks merely to save his own soul, merely to perfect his own individual nature, can be a good Christian. The Christian forgets himself, buckles on his armor, and goes forth to war against principalities and powers, and against spiritual wickedness in high places. No man can be a Christian who does not begin his career by making war on the mischievous social arrangements from which his brethren suffer. He who thinks he can be a Christian and save his soul, without seeking their radical change, has no reason to applaud himself for his proficiency in Christian science, nor for his progress towards the kingdom of God. Understand Christianity, and we will admit, that should all men become good Christians, there would be nothing to complain of. But one might as well undertake to dip the ocean dry with a clamshell, as to undertake to cure the evils of the social state by converting men to the Christianity of the Church.

The evil we have pointed out, we have said, is not of individual creation, and it is not to be removed by individual effort, saving so far as individual effort induces the combined effort of the mass. But whence has this evil originated? How comes it that all over the world the working classes are depressed, are the low and vulgar, and virtually the slaves of the nonworking classes? This is an inquiry which has not yet received the attention it deserves. It is not enough to answer, that it has originated entirely in the inferiority by nature of the working classes; that they have less skill and foresight, and are less able than the upper classes, to provide for themselves, or less susceptible of the highest moral and intellectual cultivation. Nor is it sufficient for our purpose to be told, that Providence has decreed that some shall be poor and wretched, ignorant and vulgar; and that others shall be rich and vicious, learned and polite, oppressive and miserable. We do not choose to charge this matter to the will of God. "The foolishness of man perverteth his way, and his heart fretteth against the Lord." God has made of one blood all the nations of men to dwell on all the face of the earth, and to dwell there as brothers, as members of one and the same family; and although he has made them with a diversity of powers, it would perhaps, after all, be a bold assertion to say that he has made them with an inequality of powers. There is nothing in the actual difference of the powers of individuals, which accounts for the striking inequalities we everywhere discover in their condition. The child of the plebeian, if placed early in the proper circumstances, grows up not less beautiful, active, intelligent, and refined, than the child of the patrician; and the child of the patrician may become as coarse, as brutish as the child of any slave. So far as observation on the original capacities of individuals goes, nothing is discovered to throw much light on social inequalities.

The cause of the inequality, we speak of, must be sought in history, and be regarded as having its root in Providence, or in human nature, only in that sense in which all historical facts have their origin in these. We may perhaps trace it in the first instance to conquest, but not to conquest as the ultimate cause. The Romans in conquering Italy no doubt reduced many to the condition of slaves, but they also found the great mass of the laboring population already slaves. There is everywhere a class distinct from the reigning class, bearing the same relation to it, that the Gibbeonites did to the Jews. They are principally *Colons*, the cultivators for foreign masters, of a soil of which they seemed to have been disposed. Who has dispossessed them? Who has reduced them to this present condition, a condition which under the Roman dominion is perhaps even ameliorated? Who were this race? Whence came they? They appear to be distinct from the reigning race, as were the Helotae from the Doric-Spartan. Were they the aborigines of the territory? Had they once been free? By what concurrence of events have they been reduced to their present condition? By a prior conquest? But mere conquest does not so reduce a population. It may make slaves of the prisoners taken in actual combat, and reduce the whole to tributaries, but it leaves the mass of the population free, except in its political relations. Were they originally savages, subjugated by a civilized tribe? Savages may be exterminated, but they never, so far as we can ascertain, become to any considerable extent "the hewers of wood and drawers of water" to their conquerors. For our part we are disposed to seek the cause of the inequality of conditions of which we speak, in religion, and to charge it to the priesthood. And we are confirmed in this, by what appears to be the instinctive tendency of every, or almost every, social reformer. Men's instincts, in a matter of this kind, are worthier of reliance than their reasonings. Rarely do we find in any age or country, a man feeling himself commissioned to labor for a social reform, who does not feel that he must begin it by making war upon the priesthood. This was the case with the old Hebrew reformers, who are to us the prophets of God; with Jesus, the Apostles, and the early Fathers of the Church; with the French democrats of the last century; and is the case with the Young Germans, and the Socialists, as they call themselves in England, at the present moment. Indeed it is felt at once that no reform can be effected without resisting the priests and emancipating the people from their power.

Historical research, we apprehend, will be found to justify this instinct, and to authorize the eternal hostility of the reformer, the advocate of social progress, to the priesthood. How is it, we ask, that man comes out of the savage state? In the savage state, properly so called, there is no inequality of the kind of which we speak. The individual system obtains there. Each man is his own center, and is a whole in himself. There is no community, there are no members of society; for society is not. This individuality, which, if combined with the highest possible moral and intellectual cultivation would be the perfection of man's earthly condition, must be broken down before the human race can enter into the path of civilization, or commence its career of progress. But it cannot be broken down by material force. It resists by its own nature the combination of individuals necessary to subdue it. It can be successfully attacked only by a spiritual power, and subjugated only by the representatives of that power, that is to say, the priests.

Man is naturally a religious being, and disposed to stand in awe of invisible powers. This makes, undoubtedly, under certain relations, his glory; but when coupled with his ignorance, it becomes the chief source of his degradation and misery. He feels within the workings of a mysterious nature, and is conscious that hidden and superior powers are at work all around him, and perpetually influencing his destiny; now wafting him onward with a prosperous gale, or now resisting his course, driving him back, defeating his plans, blasting his hopes, and wounding his heart. What are his relations to these hidden, mysterious, and yet all-influencing forces? Can their anger be appeased? Can their favor be secured? Thus he asks himself. Unable to answer, he goes to the more aged and experienced of his tribe, and asks them the same questions. They answer as best they can. What is done by one is done by another, and what is done once is done again. The necessity of instruction, which each one feels in consequence of his own feebleness and inexperience, renders the recurrence to those best capable of giving it, or supposed to be the best capable of giving it, frequent and uniform. Hence the priest. He who is consulted prepares himself to answer, and therefore devotes himself to the study of man's relations to these invisible powers, and the nature of these invisible powers themselves. Hence religion becomes a special object of study, and the study of it a profession. Individuals whom a thunderstorm, and earthquake, an eruption of a volcano, an eclipse of the sun or moon, any unusual appearance in the heavens or earth, has frightened, or whom some unforeseen disaster has afflicted, go to the wise-man for explanation, to know what it means, or what they shall do in order to appease the offended powers. When reassured they naturally feel grateful to this wise-man; they load him with honors, and in the access of their gratitude raise him far above the common level, and spare him the common burdens of life. Once thus distinguished, he becomes an object of envy. His condition is looked upon as superior to that of the mass. Hence a multitude aspire to possess themselves of it. When once the class has become somewhat numerous, it labors to secure to itself the distinction it has received, its honors and its emoluments, and to increase them. Hence the establishment of priesthoods or sacerdotal corporations, such as the Egyptian, the Braminical, the Ethiopian, the Jewish, the Scandinavian, the Druidical, the Mexican, and Peruvian.

The germ of these sacerdotal corporations is found in the savage state, and exists there in that formidable personage called a *jongleur*, juggler, or conjurer. But as the tribe or people advances, the juggler becomes a priest and the member of a corporation. These sacerdotal corporations are variously organized, but everywhere organized for the purpose, as that arch rebel, Thomas Paine, says, "of monopolizing power and profit." The effort is unceasing to elevate them as far above the people as possible, to enable them to exert the greatest possible control over the people, and to derive the greatest possible profit from the people.

Now if we glance over the history of the world, we shall find, that at the epoch of coming out of the savage state, these corporations are universally instituted. We find them among every people; and among every people, at this epoch, they are the dominant power, ruling with an iron despotism. The real idea at the bottom of these institutions, is the control of individual freedom by moral laws, the assertion of the supremacy of moral power over physical force, a great truth, and one which can never be too strenuously insisted on; but a truth which at this epoch can only enslave the mass of the people to its professed representatives, the priests. Through awe of the gods, through fear of divine displeasure, and dread of the unforeseen chastisements that displeasure may inflict, and by pretending, honestly or not, to possess the secret of averting it, and of rendering the gods propitious, the priests are able to reduce the people to the most wretched subjection, and to keep them there; at least for a time.

But these institutions must naturally be jealous of power, and ambitious of confining it to as few hands as possible. If the sacerdotal corporations were thrown open to all the world, all the world would rush into them, and then there would be no advantage in being a priest. Hence the number who may be priests must be limited. Hence again a distinction of clean and unclean is introduced. Men can be admitted into these corporations only as they descend from the priestly race. As in India, no man can aspire to the priesthood unless of Braminical descent, and among the Jews unless he be of the tribe of Levi. The priestly race was the ruling race; it dealt with science, it held communion with the Gods, and therefore was the purer race. The races excluded from the priesthood were not only regarded as inferior, but as unclean. The Gibeonite to a Jew was both an inferior and an impure. The operation of the principles involved in these considerations, has, in our judgment, begun and effected the slavery of the great mass of the people. It has introduced distinctions of blood or race, founded privileged orders, and secured the rewards of industry to the few, while it has reduced the mass to the most degrading and hopeless bondage.

Now the great mass enslaved by the sacerdotal corporations, are not emancipated by the victories which follow by the warrior caste, even when those victories are said to be in behalf of freedom. The military order succeeds the priestly; but in establishing, as it does in Greece and Rome, the supremacy of the state over the church, it leaves the great mass in the bondage in which it finds them. The Normans conquer England, but they scarcely touch the condition of the old Saxon bondmen. The Polish serf lost his freedom before began the Russian dominion, and he would have recovered none of it, had Poland regained, in her late struggle, her former political independence. The subjection of a nation is in general merely depriving one class of its population of its exclusive right to enslave the people; and the recovery of political independence, is little else than the recovery of this right. The Germans call their rising against Napoleon a rising for liberty, and so it was, liberty for German princes and German nobles; but the German people were more free under Napoleon's supremacy than they are now, or will be very soon. Conquest may undoubtedly increase the number of slaves; but in general it merely adds to the number and power of the middle class. It institutes a new nobility, and degrades the old to the rank of commoners. This is its general effect. We cannot therefore ascribe to conquest, as we did in the former number of this journal, the condition in which the working classes are universally found. They have been reduced to their condition by the priest, not by the military chieftain.

Mankind came out of the savage state by means of the priests. Priests are the first civilizers of the race. For the wild freedom of the savage, they substitute the iron despotism of the theocrat. This is the first step in civilization, in man's career of progress. It is not strange then that some should prefer the savage state to the civilized. Who would not rather roam the forest with a free step and unshackled limb, though exposed to hunger, cold, and nakedness, than crouch an abject slave beneath the whip of a master? As yet civilization has done little but break and subdue man's natural love of freedom; but tame his wild and eagle spirit. In what a world does man even now find himself, when he first awakes and feels some of the workings of his manly nature? He is in a cold, damp, dark dungeon, and loaded all over with chains, with the iron entering into his very soul. He cannot make one single free movement. The priest holds his conscience, fashion controls his tastes, and society with her forces invades the very sanctuary of his heart, and takes command of his love, that which is purest and best in his nature, which alone gives reality to his existence, and from which proceeds the only ray which pierces the gloom of his prison-house. Even that he cannot enjoy in peace and quietness, not scarcely at all. He is wounded on every side, in every part of his being, in every relation in life, in every idea of his mind, in every sentiment of his heart. O, it is a sad world, a sad world to the young soul just awakening to its diviner instincts! A sad world to him who is not gifted with the only blessing which seems compatible with life as it is absolute insensibility. But no matter. A wise man never murmurs. He never kicks against the pricks. What is it, and there is an end of it; what can be may be, and we will do what we can to make life what it ought to be. Though man's first step in civilization is slavery, his last step shall be freedom. The free soul can never be wholly subdued; the ethereal fire in man's nature may be smothered, but it cannot be extinguished. Down, down deep in the center of his heart it burns inextinguishable and forever, glowing intenser with the accumulating heat of centuries; and one day the whole mass of Humanity shall become ignited, and be full of fire within and all over, as a live coal; and then slavery, and whatever is foreign to the soul itself, shall be consumed.

But, having traced the inequality we complain of to its origin, we proceed to ask again what is the remedy? The remedy is first to be sought in the destruction of the priest. We are not mere destructives. We delight not in pulling down; but the bad must be removed before the good can be introduced. Conviction and repentance precede regeneration. Moreover we are Christians, and it is only by following out the Christian law, and the example of the early Christians, that we can hope to effect anything. Christianity is the sublimest protest against the priesthood ever uttered, and a protest uttered by both God and man; for he who uttered it was God-Man. In the person of Jesus both God and Man protest against the priesthood. What was the mission of Jesus but a solemn summons of every priesthood on earth to judgment, and of the human race to freedom? He discomfited the learned doctors, and with whips of small cords drove the priests, degenerated into mere money changers, from the temple of God. He instituted himself no priesthood, no form of religious worship. He recognized no priest but a holy life, and commanded the construction of no temple but that of the pure heart. He preached no formal religion, enjoined no creed, set apart no day for religious worship. He preached fraternal love, peace on earth, and good will to men. He came to the soul enslaved, "cabined, cribbed, confined," to the poor child of mortality, bound hand and foot, unable to move, and said in the tones of a God, "Be free; be enlarged; be there room for thee to grow, expand, and overflow with the love thou wast made to overflow with."

In the name of Jesus we admit there has been a priesthood instituted and considering how the world went, a priesthood could not but be instituted; but the religion of Jesus repudiates it. It recognizes no mediator between God and man but him who dies on the cross to redeem man; no propitiation for sin but a pure love, which rises in a living flame to all that is beautiful and good, and spreads out in light and warmth for all the chilled and benighted sons of morality. In calling every man to be a priest, it virtually condemns every possible priesthood, and in recognizing the religion of the new covenant, the religion written on the heart, of a law put within the soul, it abolishes all formal worship.

The priest is universally a tyrant, universally the enslaver of his brethren, and therefore it is Christianity that condemns him. It could not prevent the reestablishment of a hierarchy, but it prepared for its ultimate destruction, by denying the inequality of blood, by representing all men as equal before God, and by insisting on the celibacy of the clergy. The best feature of the Church was in its denial to the clergy of the right to marry. By this it prevented the new hierarchy from becoming hereditary, as were the old sacerdotal corporations of India and Judea.

We object not to religious instruction; we object not to the gathering together of the people on one day in seven, to sing and pray, and listen to a discourse from a religious teacher; but we object to everything like an outward, visible church; to everything that in the remotest degree partakes of the priest. A priest is one who stands as a sort of mediator between God and man; but we have one mediator, Jesus Christ, who gave himself a ransom for all, and that is enough. It may be supposed that we, Protestants, have no priests; but for ourselves we know no fundamental difference between a Catholic priest and a Protestant clergyman, as we know no difference of any magnitude, in relation to the principles on which they are based, between a Protestant church and the Catholic church. Both are based on the principle of authority; both deny in fact, however it may be in manner, the authority of reasons and war against freedom of mind; both substitute dead works for true righteousness, a vain show for the reality of piety, and are sustained as the means of reconciling us to God without requiring us to become godlike. Both therefore ought to go by the board.

We may offend in what we say, but we cannot help that. We insist upon it, that the complete and final destruction of the priestly order, in every practical sense of the word priest, is the first step to be taken towards elevating the laboring classes. Priests are, in their capacity of priests, necessarily enemies to freedom and equality. All reasoning demonstrates this, and all history proves it. There must be no class of men set apart and authorized, either by law or fashion, to speak to us in the name of God, or to be the interpreters of the word of God. The word of God never drops from the priest's lips. He who redeemed man did not spring from the priestly class, for it is evident that our Lord sprang out of Juda, of which tribe Moses spoke nothing concerning the priesthood. Who in fact were the authors of the Bible, the book which Christendom professes to receive as the word of God? The priests? Nay, they were the inveterate foes of the priests. No man ever berated the priests more soundly than did Jeremiah and Ezekiel. And who were they who heard Jesus the most gladly? The priests? The chief priests were at the head of those who demanded his crucifixion. In every age the priests, the authorized teachers of religion, are the first to oppose the true prophet of God, and to condemn his prophecies as blasphemies. They are always a let and a hindrance to the spread of truth. Why then retain them? Why not abolish the priestly office? Why continue to sustain what the whole history of man condemns as the greatest of all obstacles to intellectual and social progress?

We say again, we have no objection to teachers of religion, as such; but let us have no class of men whose profession it is to minister at the altar. Let us leave this matter to Providence. When God raises up a prophet, let that prophet prophesy as God gives him utterance. Let every man speak out of his own full heart, as he is moved by the Holy Ghost, but let us have none to prophesy for hire, to make preaching a profession, a means of gaining a livelihood. Whoever has a word pressing upon his heart for utterance, let him utter it, in the stable, the marketplace, the street, in the grove, under the open canopy of heaven, in the lowly cottage, or the lordly hall. No matter who or what he is, whether a graduate of a college, a shepherd from the hill sides, or a rustic from the plough. If he feels himself called to go forth in the name of God, he will speak words of truth and power, for which Humanity shall fare the better. But none of your hireling priests, your "dumb dogs" that will not bark. What are the priests of Christendom as they now are? Miserable panders to the prejudices of the age, loud in condemning sins nobody is guilty of, but silent as the grave when it concerns the crying sin of the times; bold as bold can be when there is no danger, but miserable cowards when it is necessary to speak out for God and outraged Humanity. As a body they never preach a truth till there is none whom it will indict. Never do they as a body venture to condemn sin in the concrete, and make each sinner feel "thou art the man." When the prophets of God have risen up and proclaimed the word of God, and, after persecution and death, led the people to acknowledge it to be the word of God, then your driveling priest comes forward, and owns it to be a truth, and cries, "cursed of God and man is he who believes it not." But enough. The imbecility of an organized priesthood, of a hireling clergy, for all good, and its power only to demoralize the people and misdirect their energies, is beginning to be seen, and will one day be acknowledged. Men are beginning to speak out on this subject, and the day of reckoning is approaching. The people are rising up and asking of these priests whom they have fed, clothed, honored, and followed. What have ye done for the poor and friendless, to destroy oppression, and establish the kingdom of God on earth? A fearful question for you, O ye priests, which we leave you to answer as best ye may.

The next step in this work of evaluating the working classes will be to resuscitate the Christianity of Christ. The Christianity of the Church has done its work. We have had enough of that Christianity. It is powerless for good, but by no means powerless for evil. It now unmans us and hinders the growth of God's kingdom. The moral energy which is awakened it misdirects, and makes its deluded disciples believe that they have done their duty to God when they have joined the church, offered a prayer, sung a psalm, and contributed of their means to send out a missionary to preach unintelligible dogmas to the poor heathen, who, God knows, have unintelligible dogmas enough already, and more than enough. All this must be abandoned, and Christianity, as it came from Christ, be taken up, and preached, and preached in simplicity and in power.

According to the Christianity of Christ no man can enter the kingdom of God, who does not labor with all zeal and diligence to establish the kingdom of God on the earth; who does not labor to bring down the high, and bring up the low; to break the fetters of the bound and set the captive free; to destroy all oppression, establish the reign of justice, which is the reign of equality, between man and man; to introduce new heavens and a new earth, wherein dwelleth righteousness, wherein all shall be as brothers, loving one another, and no one possessing what another lacketh. No man can be a Christian who does not labor to reform society, to mold it according to the will of God and the nature of man; so that free scope shall be given to every man to unfold himself in all beauty and power, and to grow up into the stature of a perfect man in Christ Jesus. No man can be a Christian who does not refrain from all practices by which the rich grow richer and the poor poorer, and who does not do all in his power to elevate the laboring classes, so that each man shall not be doomed to toil while another enjoys the fruits; so that each man shall be free and independent, sitting under "his own vine and fig-tree with none to molest or to make afraid." We grant the power of Christianity in working out the reform we demand; we agree that one of the most efficient means of elevating the workingmen is to Christianize the community. But you must Christianize it. It is the Gospel of Jesus you must preach, and not the Gospel of the priests. Preach the Gospel of Jesus, and that will turn every man's attention to the crying evil we have designated, and will arm every Christian with power to effect those changes in social arrangements, which shall secure to all men the equality of position and condition, which it is already acknowledged they possess in relation to their rights. But let it be the genuine Gospel that you preach, and not that pseudo-gospel, which lulls the conscience asleep, and permits men to feel that they may be servants of God while they are slaves to the world, the flesh, and the devil; and while they ride roughshod over the hearts of their prostrate brethren, suffering from iniquitous laws, from mischievous social arrangements, and pining away for the want of the refinements and even the necessaries of life.

We speak strongly and pointedly on this subject, because we are desirous of arresting attention. We would draw the public attention to the striking contrast which actually exists between the Christianity of Christ, and the Christianity of the Church. That moral and intellectual energy which exists in our country, indeed throughout Christendom, and which would, if rightly directed, transform this wilderness world into a blooming paradise of God, is now by the pseudo-gospel, which is preached, rendered wholly inefficient, by being wasted on that which, even if effected, would leave all the crying evils of the times untouched. Under the influence of the Church, our efforts are not directed to the reorganization of society, to the introduction of equality between man and man, to the removal of the corruptions of the rich, and the wretchedness of the poor. We think only of saving our own soul, as if a man must not put himself so out of the case, as to be willing to be damned before he can be saved. Paul was willing to be accursed from Christ, to save his brethren from the vengeance which hung over them. But nevertheless we think only of saving our own soul; or if perchance our benevolence is awakened, and we think it desirable to labor for the salvation of others, it is merely to save them from imaginary sins and the tortures of an imaginary hell. The redemption of the world is understood to mean simply the restoration of mankind to the favor of God in the world to come. Their redemption from the evils of inequality of factitious distinctions, and iniquitous social institutions, counts for nothing in the eyes of the Church. And this is its condemnation.

We cannot proceed a single step, with the least safety, in the great work of elevating the laboring classes, without the exaltation of sentiment, the generous sympathy and the moral courage which Christianity alone is fitted to produce or quicken. But it is lamentable to see how, by means of the mistakes of the Church, the moral courage, the generous sympathy, the exaltation of sentiment, Christianity does actually produce or quicken, is perverted, and made efficient only in producing evil, or hindering the growth of good. Here is wherefore it is necessary on the one hand to condemn in the most pointed terms the Christianity of the Church, and to bring out on the other hand in all its clearness brilliancy, and glory the Christianity of Christ.

Having, by breaking down the power of the priesthood and the Christianity of the priests, obtained an open field and freedom for our operations, and by preaching the true Gospel of Jesus, directed all minds to the great social reform needed, and quickened in all souls the moral power to live for it or to die for it; our next resort must be to government, to legislative enactments. Government is instituted to be the agent of society, or more properly the organ through which society effects its will. Society has never to petition government; government is its servant, and subject to its commands.

Now the evils of which we have complained are of a social nature. That is, they have their root in the constitution of society as it is, and they have attained to their present growth by means of social influences, the action of government, of laws, and of systems and institutions upheld in society, and of which individuals are the slaves. This being the case, it is evident that they are to be removed only by the action of society, that is, by government, for the action of society is government.

But what shall government do? Its first doing must be an *un*doing. There has been thus far quite too much government, as well as government of the wrong kind. The first act of government we want, is a still further limitation of itself. It must begin by circumscribing within narrower limits its powers. And then it must proceed to repeal all laws which bear against the laboring classes, and then to enact such laws as are necessary to enable them to maintain their equality. We have no faith in those systems of elevating the working classes, which propose to elevate them without calling in the aid of the government. We must have government, and legislation expressly directed to this end.

But again what legislation do we want so far as this country is concerned? We want first the legislation which shall free the government, whether State or Federal, from the control of the Banks. The Banks represent the interest of the employer, and therefore of necessity interests adverse to those of the employed; that is, they represent the interests of the business community in opposition to the laboring community. So long as the government remains under the control of the Banks, so long it must be in the hands of the natural enemies of the laboring classes, and may be made, nay, will be made, an instrument of depressing them yet lower. It is obvious then that, if our object be the elevation of the laboring classes, we must destroy the power of the Banks over the government, and place the government in the hands of the laboring classes themselves, or in the hands of those, if such there be, who have an identify of interest with them. But this cannot be done so long as the Banks exist. Such is the subtle influence of credit, and such the power of capital, that a banking system like ours, if sustained, necessarily and inevitably becomes the real and efficient government of the country. We have been struggling for ten years in this country against the power of the banks, struggling to free merely the Federal government from their grasp, but with humiliating success. At this moment, the contest is almost doubtful, not indeed in our mind, but in the minds of a no small portion of our countrymen. The partisans of the Banks count on certain victory. The Banks discount freely to build "log cabins," to purchase "hard cider," and to defray the expense of manufacturing enthusiasm for a cause which is at war with the interests of the people. That they will succeed, we do not for one moment believe; but that they could maintain the struggle so long, and be as strong as they now are, at the end of ten years' constant hostility, proves but all too well the power of the Banks, and their fatal influence on the political action of the community. The present character, standing, and resources of the Bank party, prove to a demonstration that the Banks must be destroyed, or the laborer not elevated. Uncompromising hostility to the whole banking system should therefore be the motto of every working man, and of every friend of Humanity. The system must be destroyed. On this point there must be no misgiving, no subterfuge, no palliation. The system is at war with the rights and interest of labor, and it must go. Every friend of the system must be marked as an enemy to his race, to his country, and especially to the laborer. No matter who he is, in what party he is found, or what name he bears, he is, in our judgment, no true democrat, as he can be no true Christian.

Following the destruction of the Banks, must come that of all monopolies, of all PRIVILEGE. There are many of these. We cannot specify them all; we therefore select only one, the greatest of them all, the privilege which some have of being born rich while others are born poor. It will be seen at once that we allude to the hereditary descent of property, an anomaly in our American system, which must be removed, or the system itself will be destroyed. We cannot now go into a discussion of this subject, but we promise to resume it at our earliest opportunity. We only say now, that as we have abolished hereditary monarchy and hereditary nobility, we must complete the work by abolishing hereditary property.[1] A man shall have all he honestly acquires, so long as he himself belongs to the world in which he acquires it. But his power over his property must cease with his life, and his property must then become the property of the state, to be disposed of by some equitable law for the use of the generation which takes his place. Here is the principle without any of its details, and this is the grand legislative measure to which we look forward. We see no means of elevating the laboring classes which can be effectual without this. And is this a measure to be easily carried? Not at all. It will cost infinitely more than it cost to abolish either hereditary monarchy or hereditary nobility. It is a great measure, and a startling [one]. The rich, the business community, will never voluntarily consent to it, and we think we know too much of human nature to believe that it will ever be effected peaceably. It will be effected only by the strong arm of physical force. It will come, if it ever come at all, only at the conclusion of war, the like of which the world as yet has never witnessed, and from which, however inevitable it may seem to the eye of philosophy, the heart of Humanity recoils with horror.

We are not ready for this measure yet. There is much previous work to be done, and we should be the last to bring it before the legislature. The time, however, has come for its free and full discussion. It must be canvassed in the public mind, and society prepared for acting on it. No doubt they who broach it, and especially they who support it, will experience a due share of contumely and abuse. They will be regarded by the part of the community they oppose, or may be thought to oppose, as "graceless varlets," against whom every man of substance should set his face. But this is not, after all, a thing to disturb a wise man, nor to deter a true man from telling his whole thought. He who is worthy of the name of man, speaks what he honestly believes the interests of his race demand, and seldom disquiets himself about what may be the consequences to himself. Men have, for what they believed the cause of God of man, endured the dungeon, the scaffold, the stake, the cross, and they can do it again, if need be. This subject must be freely, boldly, and fully discussed, whatever may be the fate of those who discuss it.

Progress Our Law—A Discourse

October 1840

"Brethren, I count not myself to have apprehended: but this one thing I do, forgetting those things which are behind, and reaching forth unto those things which are before, I press toward the mark for the prize of the high calling of God in Christ Jesus."

—Philippians 3:13–14

*P*aul, notwithstanding his great natural endowments, his acquired abilities, and his special illumination as an apostle of Jesus, was always remarkable for his modesty, and his honest conviction that there was more truth than he had seen, and higher eminences of moral and religious worth, than he had yet attained to. He did not look upon himself as having apprehended, much less as having comprehended, all things; or as having risen "to the stature of a perfect man in Christ Jesus." He felt his own deficiencies; that there was still something for him to learn, and virtues for him to acquire; and instead of being contented with merely surveying the ground over which he had passed, or contemplating the achievements which he had already made, he looked forward, and was eager to press onward to new truths, and upward to higher spiritual worth. He looked upon himself as a progressive being, as a being of growth, and he was desirous of fulfilling his destiny.

This, which was true of himself, he recommended to the consideration of his followers; and he exhorted them not to be contented to remain as they were, but to press toward the mark of their high calling of God in Christ Jesus. And if Paul was still below that mark, we may well believe that they were; that if progress was necessary in his case, it was altogether more necessary in theirs.

It is possible also, that the same thing may be said of us today. Perhaps we can say, or that we ought to say, of ourselves, with even more truth than he could, "we count not ourselves to have apprehended": and we should therefore feel ourselves admonished, that this "one thing should we do, forgetting those things which are behind, and reaching forth unto those which are before, we should press toward the mark for the prize of the high calling of God in Christ Jesus." We are yet but in the twilight of truth. We have seen only at a feeble distance around us, and within the circle of our vision, we have seen nothing clearly, distinctly. There is a universe of the Unknown before us, into which we have not penetrated; and as much as we may think ourselves to have apprehended, dark and perplexing problems are hourly coming up, which we feel that we are unable to solve. The mind is still tormented with doubts, and we seem to ourselves to know nothing unless we can know more. In a moral sense, we feel still more our deficiency. We fall perpetually in our performances below the ideal excellence we contemplate in the visions of our souls. Morally speaking, we are in the low valley, and our prospect is bounded by hills, that rise on every side, and seem to lose themselves in the clouds. We feel the need of progress, and that we are comparatively worthless, unless we can rise higher.

Whether, therefore, we take the remark and the example of Paul, or what we are conscience of in ourselves, we are irresistibly led to the idea of progress. We are told that we are not all that we should be, and made to believe that we are not all that we may be. We may rise yet higher, become wiser and better; and our duty is to aim at this. It is our duty then to aim at, to seek progress.

View Christianity in whatever light we may, we cannot fail to perceive that its great demand is progress. It addresses itself to man as a weak and helpless infant; and it offers to take him by the hand and lead him forth into the strengthening air to behold the beauties which bloom around him, and up to the rainbow glories that dazzle him from afar in the distant heavens. It comes as a kind, instructing angel, to develop the germs of truth and excellence deposited by the Creator in the soul; and with its gentle and encouraging voice it is forever urging us forward to a loveliness and worth which lie before us. It bids us be ever strengthening our limbs by exercise for greater activity, and purging our vision to take in a broader, a more beautiful, and a more varied landscape of truth and holiness. It permits us never to sit down with the feeling, that the race is run, that the victory is won, and that there are no more worlds to conquer. As soon as one conquest is made, it shows us another that we must make; as soon as we have risen to one eminence, scaled one height, it shows us another, rising and frowning above us. Ever in the prospect,

"Hills peep o'er hills, and Alps on Alps arise."

This truth is plainly taught in my text, and it is corroborated by what every true Christian is conscious of in his own experience. There is for us no stopping place; no period when we may retire from our work, and feel that for the rest of life we may take our repose. Repose, in the sense of absence of exertion, is not for man. The student of nature never finds it. Penetrate as far as he may into the secrets of the world around him, he sees that there is an infinite depth for him yet to sound; and he feels the same need of experimenting, when his head is whitened over with the frosts of fourscore winters, as when he first, in life's gay morning, commenced his career of scientific discovery. A Newton, a Laplace, went down to the grave, feeling their work was but merely begun. The student of Humanity has the same experience. The philosopher finds no resting place, no end to his work. The poet goes forth on the wings of his imagination, through the heavens and over the earth, and always stretching out in the distance, he beholds fields of unexplored beauty, over which he would sail, on which he would feast his ravished soul, and with which he would touch his lyre and immortalize his song. The Unknown is ever before us; the Unattained ever rises above us; and we must be ever nerving our souls to the one, and purging our vision to the other. "Onward and upward" is the only motto a Christian man may adopt; "onward and upward," the only hope of repose that the soul may ever indulge.

There may at first sight seem to be something sad and discouraging in this view. The soul, wearied and worn with the struggles and perplexities it meets, with the length and tediousness of its way, sighs for the end of its journey, when it may, as it were, lie down and be at rest.

The soldier, covered over with scars and grown old in a thousand battles, prays that the wars may one day be over, that peace may return, and he find his way back to repose his weary and stiffened limbs, and recruit his exhausted spirits, in the home of his childhood, amid the innocent scenes and objects, in which he so delighted before he went forth on his career of battle and glory. We grow tired of exertion, and wish to sit down and be at peace. We would not be always on the road, and eat ever our meals, and sleep only at an inn. We would unbend ourselves in our own homes, by our own firesides, and feel that our journeyings are over and we may repose in peace. We would see the end of our work, and feel that our last struggle has been made, our last battle has been fought, and that the sweet strains of the peaceful flocks, and the shepherd's pipe, have forever succeeded to the martial clangor of the trumpet and drum, and the neighing of the warhorse.

And yet these are but momentary feelings. They are but passing clouds over the face of the noonday sun, and do but render the heavens more beautiful. We indulge them at times; and they come unbid-den when we have been baffled in some enterprise, when we have lost the day in some encounter with sin and Satan; when we are smarting under the wounds received in some recent battle, or suffering the reaction of a day's over exertion. But in general we love this law of progress, and regard it as one of the chief glories, one of the brightest signatures, of our divine nature. We prefer action to rest. The old soldier, who had sighed for peace and the quiet of his early home, shall no sooner hear the earpiercing fife and martial drum, than his head is erect, his step measured, and his heart is in the thickest and hottest of the fray. The stormbeaten sailor, in the tempest at sea, when riding on his mountain billows, when his ship heaves and breaks against the swelling surge, may wish himself on land, and feel that, if once his feet touch the shore, he will tempt the dangers of the deep never again. And yet soon shall he be weary of his landsman's life, and the very memory of that storm at sea, its thrill, its agony, its terror, shall make him more anxious to go forth again upon his loved ocean.

Man may exist in what is called a state of repose, but he lives only in action. Life is action, and our lives are longer or shorter not according to the number of our years, but the more or less intensity with which we have acted. There is no difference between absolute rest, inactivity, and death. The more active we are, the further we are removed from death, the fuller we are of life, the more truly do we live. We weary of inaction much sooner than we do of exertion; and the idle, we all feel, are the most wretched of the sons of wretchedness. There is then in fact nothing sad or discouraging in the doctrine of eternal progress. On the contrary it is encouraging. We are assured by it, that we shall never be obliged to weep, that we have no more worlds to conquer; that we can never be any wiser or better than we are now. It opens to us a glorious career, along which lies a track of heavenly radiance. It opens to us a prospect of boundless extent, and gives us the hope that, when we have feasted our souls on it as long as we would, another, and another still, of richer and more varied beauty, shall be opened before us. It gives us assurance that these dark and perplexing problems, we are now studying day and night to solve, shall one day become plain to our understandings, although new problems may come up to engage our minds afterwards; that this universe of darkness, on the borders of which we stand, shall be ever recoiling from our searching glance, and the objects, it conceals from our sight, shall be perpetually opening to our view in the dewy freshness and rosy light of the morning. I am then not only satisfied, that I am created to be a progressive being, and to be forever a workingman, forever employed; but I am grateful that I am so made, and rejoice that I have a work before me, which will require all my exertions for eternity. In this fact I read the pledge not of an eternal existence, but of an immortal life.

We may, then, lay it down, that we are ever to regard ourselves as not having apprehended, to feel ourselves below the mark, and that it is our duty to be ever pressing onward and upward. We may also lay it down, that the fact, that we may ever be apprehending, but never completely apprehend, be ever nearing perfection, but never becoming wholly perfect, discouraging as it may at first seem, is after all one of our chief glories, and shows the wisdom and goodness of God in our creation. The law of progress is a law we should willingly accept, for which we should be thankful, and which we should seek to obey.

With what I have thus far said, I presume, all reflecting people will agree. On the fact that man is a progressive being, rests the legitimacy of all the measures adopted by individuals or society for moral, intellectual, and religious improvement. It is on this fact, that we vindicate the utility of Schools and Colleges, and especially the institutions of Religion. Why do you employ schoolmasters and professors, if man be not born with the capacity for progress? If people are wise and as good as they can become, what need of churches, what need of preaching? These all certainly contemplate progress, at least a moral and religious progress.

The doctrine of progress is admitted by every body, too, in relation not only to individuals, but to society and social institutions. If not, why do we choose every year an army of legislators, and make some three or four hundred new laws in each State in the Union? Do not people support legislators, and the propose legislation, for the purpose of perfecting our social institutions, of obviating some evil, or of supplying some defect? Why, then, is the social Reformer, the man who demands progress in the State, looked upon as a disturber of the peace, and called hard names, and marked as a man to be avoided? He merely acts on the principle recognized by the Gospel, enjoined by Paul, taught by the experience and nature of man, and admitted by every body.

Progress in the case of an individual all readily admit to be possible and desirable. John may become altogether a wiser and a better man. He may know more of himself than he now does; more of the world in which he lives; may become more amiable and obliging in his intercourse with his fellowmen; obtain a purer heart, more elevated moral affections; and live in a closer communion with God. And may not Peter also, and James, and Andrew? Yes. It is admitted all these may, and that it is lawful to labor for their progress. And where is the individual that may not become a wiser and better, a really greater being? Where is the man, for whose progress it is not lawful to labor? No where? Then all men may become wiser and better, greater men; it is lawful then to labor for the progress of all men; that is, to labor to set the race forward in wisdom and goodness. Why then must he who labors to do this, and has faith that it can be done, be called by some odious epithet; a disorganizer, a Jacobin, or a visionary? Why may he not be considered a very sober, and a very serious man, with a clear mind and a good heart?

Here is a wrong we do to the men, who show themselves in earnest to aid the progress of Humanity. These men, whom we often condemn and usually neglect, are after all doing only what we all allege it is their duty to do. They have no other sin than that of being true to principle. It may be said, that what they call progress would not be progress, and that what they propose as the means of accelerating progress, would have a deteriorating tendency. All this is very possible, and may no doubt be said with truth of many popular declaimers. But those, of whom this may be said with any degree of justice, are generally followed by crowds. They have a multitude with them, and are indebted to their passionate zeal, and to the specialty of their projects, rather than to their sober sense and enlightened minds, for their success. But even these will always be found to have hit upon some good principle, to have embodied some useful, though perhaps not a very far-reaching truth. The Reformers, however, most seriously condemned, the most wrongfully accused, and called the hardest names, and whose plans are deemed the most visionary, are your men of sober minds, of calm judgment, accustomed to observe and to reflect, and who have brought to the matters on which they speak their ripest thoughts and holiest feelings. They may indeed be wrong; but are they more likely to be in the wrong than those who condemn or ridicule them? Which have thought the most on these subjects, and are the best informed respecting them? When a man, who has some sense of what it is to be a man, comes before the public with a new doctrine, or a new measure, he takes himself to know something of the matter, and he feels that a careless hearer, who has given it no serious attention; perhaps has never heard of it before, ought to have too much modesty to pronounce it at once false or chimerical. We are, unconsciously, every day crucifying our redeemers. Of the men now living, the names of none will go down to posterity, as true men, but of those few, whom the great mass of us regard as teaching "damnable heresies," or as outraging the moral sense of their epoch. We, who have called the bold theological reformer an enemy of the Church, and the warmhearted pleader for the progress of man and society a disturber of the peace, or an idle dreamer, shall be forgotten, our names unregistered, and our generation remembered not, when he shall stand out as one of the few who have redeemed humanity, and done honor to human nature. Let us beware how we pass a verdict against the men of ideas, the men of progress; for posterity, God himself, will reverse it.

Not only is it lawful to contemplate the progress of all the individuals of this generation, but it is also lawful to contemplate the progress of one generation upon another. The human race does not come to maturity in one generation. It has the same law of progress, as a race, that you and I have as individuals. One generation accumulates a stock of wisdom and virtue, which serves as an outfit, a setting out, for its successor. Each new generation, in relation to its predecessor, starts on a vantage ground. It has its point of departure farther on, and higher up;

because it enjoys, in addition to its own peculiar resources, all the accumulations of all who have gone before it. The progress we make, we make not for ourselves alone. This generation is linked with all coming generations. This opens to us a glorious prospect, and makes it delightful to take on the prospect, and makes it delightful to take on the wings of faith frequent excursions into the Future. These excursions I have found not only pleasant, but profitable. Oppressed with the selfishness I find in my own heart and around me, overcome by the thousand ills I see Humanity enduring, I find it necessary, in order to raise my drooping spirits, recover my faith in man, and nerve myself to his service, to look forward to what the human race will one day become; and I return from these excursions renewed in my feelings and strengthened in my soul. I am strengthened for the battle, and can take myself to the combats with my age, and to the endurance of the neglect which I know awaits me, with cheerfulness and courage. For the joy set before, one may cheerfully endure the cross.

If one generation may advance on its predecessor, if the human race be always on the march towards perfection, then must it be ever receding from the past, outgrowing old institutions, and becoming too wise for old doctrines. It is not only wrong, but it is in vain to attempt to chain us back to the creeds framed in by-gone ages, and insist upon our adhering old usages. We might just as well insist upon it, that the man shall wear the garments of the child. We cannot, if we would, cramp the mind and heart, and keep them forever of the size of the infant's, as the Chinese do the feet of their women. Mind has an expansive force, that will break the strongest bands and ligaments that the wit of man can devise. Creeds cannot confine it forever. Though you clasp it in bands of steel, it will snap them, and break through even those which shall be made of gold. It has a portion of the Divinity from whom it emanates, and it will not be fettered. Free it will be, and free it should be.

Would we but lay this truth to our hearts, we should disdain to contend for old dogmas, and blush to censure all opinion because it is new. They, who now hold on to old creeds, and insist that we shall believe just what our fathers believed, and tread only the road our father's trod, probably are not aware of their consummate folly, nor indeed of their high-handed treason against man. They call themselves wise and prudent; they believe themselves to be doing God's service; but would they reflect a moment, they would see that they are running against time, and contending against Omnipotence. Can they make the grown up man return to the baubles, the whistle and rattle, that pleased his childhood? Would they reverse the law of God's providence and arrest the march of improvement? And are they so ignorant as to think that they can do it? What Luther and Calvin taught, I respect as their belief; but must I be compelled to see but with Luther's or Calvin's eyes, and to think but Luther's or Calvin's thoughts? Am not I also a man? Have not I also eyes? Have I not also a reasonable and a reasoning soul? But why am I a man, why have I eyes, why have I a soul, if I may only reproduce Luther or Calvin? As well might I not be; for in such a case I should be only a duplicate of that of which one specimen is enough for all honest purposes. Why then am I to be arraigned because I choose to be true to my nature, to see with my own eyes, and think my own thoughts?

The past did its duty. It did what it could. It embodied in creeds and catechisms its conceptions of truth. Let us take what truth we can find in its symbols, and add to it whatever additional truth the untrammeled action of our own minds and hearts can discover. It is our duty to aim at progress in our ideas, as well as in our moral affections, and as much our duty to aim at progress in our religious ideas as in any other order of ideas. Let us beware how we entertain the notion that we have already ascertained all truth. Paul's example should ever be before us; "Brethren, I count not myself to have apprehended: but this one thing I do, forgetting those things which are behind, I press toward the mark for the prize of the high calling of God in Christ Jesus." Let us beware, too, how we condemn the man who comes forward to arraign old dogmas, and to call the people to the search after new ones. He is but doing his duty; he is laboring for God and man; and it is our duty to sustain him. On this score men have much to answer for. They cannot tell how many warm hearts they have broken, how many generous spirits they have sent down with sorrow to an untimely grave!

Moreover, if we may count on the progress of the race, if it be lawful to labor for the improvement of individuals and society, and for progress in our religious ideas, we must not think that we can hinder the utterance of new ideas on government and social order in general. If progress be a law of our race, as it unquestionably is, we must accept it in everything, and not only tolerate it, but labor for it everywhere. As a friend of progress, I ask more than toleration. I do not stand up before my age, and ask it merely to permit me to bring out my ideas on man and society, on God and religion. I demand cooperation, that the public not only tolerate me in doing this, but that it aid me in doing it. I ask it not to embrace my ideas, but I do ask it to listen to them, and set itself at work in earnest to augment the sum of truth in our possession. It has no right to turn a deaf ear to the voice that calls it to take another step forward. We have no doubt, in matters of government and social arrangements, advanced far on our predecessors; but we have no reason to believe, that we have attained to perfection in these matters more than we have in others. There are truths in relation to government and society, that we have not yet learned, and we should be laboring to discover them. Let us turn no cold looks, cast no contemptuous sneers on the young prophets of Humanity, who come forth to prophesy unto us in the name of the Lord. They deserve honor at our hands, and should receive it. Let us hear their prophecies, and pay them all due respect, though they convict us of not having had as much truth as we fancied we had, and enjoin changes which it may cost us some painful sacrifices to introduce.

In a word, let us bear in mind, that in all things we come short; that in all things we are imperfect; and that as true Christians we must be ever exerting ourselves to near perfection. We are placed here for progress, the progress of the individual, and the progress of the race; for progress in our moral feelings, progress in ideas, and progress in institutions. Always must we forget the things which are behind, and reach forth to the things which are before, and press onward to the discovery of new truth, and upward to purer and serener regions of moral worth.

Conversations with a Radical—By a Conservative
January–April 1841

January

My attention was arrested one day, during a short residence in a Western city, by a crowd collected before the principal hotel. Wedging my way into the crowd, I soon discovered that the object of attention was a coarsely clad fellow, holding forth to the multitude from the very top of his lungs. He appeared to be speaking under strong excitement. He gesticulated rapidly and with violence. His tones were harsh and bitter; his looks were wild and haggard; and his whole figure and manner indicated a madman, or a person uttering himself on a subject, which absorbed the whole energy of his soul.

"Ye make us beasts of burden;" were the first words I could make out. "Ye call yourselves the higher orders, because ye can task the labors of the poor and wretched. Ye are the higher orders, are ye, because ye wear fine clothes, have long purses, live in splendid palaces, and recline on soft couches; because ye have large estates, well cultivated fields, rich harvests, groaning granaries, and crowded storehouses? By whose labor are ye what ye call yourselves? By your own? 'Tis false. 'Tis by the labor of those ye call the lower class, on whose rights, feelings, and interests ye trample every moment, and for whom ye care less than ye care for your oxen or your horses. Ye strut and swell with a boasted superiority, do ye? Know ye not that ye purchase it by the tears of the widow, the wrongs of the orphan, and the blood of those ye should have loved as ye love yourselves?

"The higher orders, are ye? Ay, for ye make men carry you on their shoulders; ay, for ye ride on the backs of those of your fellow beings who have too much honesty, or too much simplicity, to be riders themselves. And now, forsooth, ye raise a terrible lute and cry because we, whom ye have ridden for ages, show ourselves a little restive and unwilling to stand ready bitted and saddled, for you to vault upon our backs, and plunge your rowels deep into our flanks. Order is in danger, is it, because the horse learns his strength and turns upon his rider? Society is to be dissolved, is it, because your oppression is to end? Vain are your threats; vain are your pictures of mobocracy and anarchy; ye shall be unhorsed. We have sworn it in the depths of our souls, on the altars of our country, in the presence of our God. We will carry you no longer. Use your own limbs. Ye may as well go on foot as we. Go build your own houses, cultivate your own fields, make your own tools, man your own ships, work your own engines. Ye may as well do it for yourselves, as that we should be poor and ignorant in order to do it for you. No longer will we toil, and sweat, and suffer, that ye may enjoy, or be corrupted by wealth and luxury. The higher orders, are ye? Puling babes, miserable victims of your own avarice or extravagance, worshippers of fashion, men forsworn, who study only to profit by the labors of others! The higher orders, are ye? Go then and form a nation of higher orders, a nation apart by yourselves, and see how long ye will maintain your elevation."

As he uttered these last words in a tone, which one must have heard, in order to form any conception of its provokingness, a stone, sent from no unskillful hand, struck him on the side of the head, and knocked him senseless to the ground. "Good!" shouted the multitude, and dispersed to their several places of business. Though provoked by the fellow's radical nonsense, and uncalled-for declamation, I ran to ascertain the effects of the blow, and to see whether any assistance was possible or needed. I found him stunted, but not seriously injured. It is no easy matter to kill an enthusiast. His body is so completely under the control of the spirit, and so saturated with it, that it becomes itself all but spiritual and impassible. I had him conducted to my lodgings, where all needed assistance was rendered him. In a few hours he was perfectly recovered, except a slight contusion on his head, from which, however, he assured me he suffered no pain.

I have not a spice of radicalism in my nature. It is true, I was a poor boy, and that for some years I had a hard struggle; but now, all my habits, my interests, and, I may add, my convictions, are with the Conservatives. I do not feel it my duty to set up for a Reformer, to be wiser than all who went before me, than most of my contemporaries. I am not yet capable of so much arrogance. I am content to follow on in "the path my forefathers trod." I have aimed to check whatever tendencies I may possibly have had towards enthusiasm, and I am in general as cold and as immovable as the granite hills of my own New England. Yet this ranting street orator affected me, and made me wish to examine him at my leisure. He struck me as a riddle, but also as a riddle worth the reading. Perhaps there is something in lofty enthusiasm, in the power of self-sacrifice, in a disposition, that goes straight to its object, regardless of difficulties, or dangers, or death, however mistimed or misplaced, which cannot be witnessed with indifference; something perhaps to warm the coldest hearts, and agitate minds the best disciplined. No philosopher seems able to offer a more convincing argument for his system than to die for it. Samson destroyed more of his enemies by his death, than by his life; and the early Christians conquered the world by dying for it.

There was another reason why I wished to examine this fellow, who was the incarnation of Radicalism. Radicalism was rife in my native city. It was threatening everything with destruction. Insubordination was becoming universal. Strikes and combinations, and trades' unions, were paving the way for a return to the savage state. Property was becoming insecure, and there was no foreseeing what the sovereign mob might not, one day, take it into its head to do. Perhaps it would even go so far as to propose a division of property, and to distribute among the idle and vicious the fruits of the labors of the industrious and the virtuous. I wished to make myself thoroughly acquainted with the character, designs, resources, and expectations of Radicalism. This fellow, whom chance had thrown in my way, might instruct me. I therefore urged him to spend a few days with me, which he readily consented to do, as he was one of those who go about doing *good* when they have no where to lay their heads. During his stay with me, we ran over a great variety of topics, some of which we discussed with a little closeness and depth, and others we merely touched upon. The principal results of our intercourse and discussions, are contained in the following Conversations, which were written down immediately after, and as nearly as they occurred, as possible. If I have not in all cases refuted his mischievous notions, it must be borne in mind, that my chief object was not to show my own argumentative powers,—which those who know me will admit to be not contemptible,—nor to vindicate my own doctrines; but to draw out the Radical, and made myself, if possible, acquainted with his inmost soul. My friends, I am sure, will agree with me, that his notions in general need no refutation. I soon perceived that his conversion to rationality was hopeless, and I ceased to attempt it. Whatever I said was intended to give him an opportunity to express his opinions.

One by reading these Conversations will hardly form an adequate conception of the Radical as he really appeared. Sometimes, his manner was courteous, his tones were bland, and he showed clearly that he had seen good society; at other times, his voice was harsh, and his whole manner coarse and revolting. There were times when the proudest and firmest must have quailed beneath the withering scorn of his look, and the biting sarcasm of his tones; times there were too, when he seemed inspired, and you felt that you were in the presence of a God-ordained prophet. He was a mystery. Whether hate, envy, spleen, or love, high undying philanthropy governed him, I could never satisfy myself; and the only conclusion to which I have been able to arrive is, that he was intended for a great man, but disappointment, misfortune, struggles with the world, and perhaps ill health, had affected his brain, and that at the time I saw him, he was in need of a strait jacket. Perhaps, however, I am mistaken. Let those who peruse the following Conversations judge for themselves. Let them determine whether he should be reverenced as a prophet, dreaded as a devil incarnate, or confined as a madman.

Conversation I

C. That was a saucy fellow who threw that stone at your head; had he killed you, as I was afraid he had, I should have deemed it a disgrace to my country.

R. If my blood could redeem my brethren, and restore them to their long lost, and long forgotten rights, freely would I pour it out like water.

C. You use strong language, but I see nothing to warrant it. This is the land of freedom, of equal rights, where man is man and nothing more. We open the road to merit alone; and if some obtain richer prizes than others, it is because they are more deserving. Really, Sir, I see no cause of excitement or even complaint.

R. You are pleasant.

C. Not at all. I never treat with lightness that which is a matter of gravity with another. But I cannot avoid believing him, who complains in this blessed country, a grumbler by nature, or else out of his wits. We are all substantially equal.

R. Equal! pray, Sir, where have you lived?

C. With my countrymen, who have at times reposed some little confidence in me, and whom I have endeavored to serve according to the measure of my ability.

R. You are in easy circumstances?

C. I am not what is called poor.

R. You have leisure to ride about and see the country, to view the beauties and wonders of nature, the miracles of art and science, to cultivate your taste and enrich your mind with ancient and modern lore?

C. Through the goodness of God, who has prospered me, I have something of this.

R. And your friends and associates are among the fashionable and polite, the educated and refined, persons belonging to the upper classes, with leisure like yourself, taste, habits, and pursuits similar to your own?

C. I rarely choose my friends from the vicious and vulgar.

R. You can take your choice of schools and teachers, give your children the best education afforded by the country, and a vantage ground on commencing their active career in life?

C. I am thankful that I can.

R. And these advantages are worth something in your estimation?

C. I certainly prize them very highly.

R. How large a proportion of our whole population, do you suppose, possess the same or similar advantages?

C. Probably not more than one in a hundred.

R. Yet we are all substantially equal!

C. Not precisely equal, I admit; but we are as nearly so as is possible or desirable.

R. I know not that. I know not where the possible ends, or the impossible begins. A greater degree of equality *you* indeed may not desire; but what will say the ninety and nine who are not so favored as you are?

C. There are indeed always some malignant spirits to envy the prosperous, and to declaim against the virtue which is above them. Such may desire a greater degree of equality, as the rascal with the halter round his neck, may desire the abolition of capital punishment.

R. The ninety and nine, whom God, according to your reckoning, has not seen fit to favor as much as he has you, will no doubt feel obliged to you for likening them to the rascal with a halter round his neck, declaiming against hanging. You, who are at the top of society, are very apt to think that your opinions and your wishes are the only ones worth regarding; and you think that you have a perfect right to sneer at the views and wishes of those who are at its base. But the time has gone by when you could sneer with impunity. From time out of mind we have looked up to you as oracles; we have received your decisions as those of a god. When you told us, that it was necessary that some should be rich and reverenced, and that others should be poor, miserable, despised, and trampled on, we believed you, and submitted to our hard fate. It did not occur to us, that the advice you gave us was the advice of the rider to his horse. But now we understand you. We know the value of your opinions. When you tell us no more equality is desirable, we immediately ask ourselves, whether you ride or are ridden; whether you are those who reap all the benefits of society, or those who bear all its burdens. It is pleasant to ride, but hardly so to be ridden. It is very pleasant to reap the benefits, but not quite so pleasant to submit to the labor of producing them for others.

C. But who can better judge of the value of the social system as it is, than they who are the most enlightened, and whose elevated position enables them to see it as a whole, and to mark all its workings?

R. The master would no doubt tell his slave, who should question the justice or utility of slavery, that his position was too low to see its beauties. It is only the master, who stands on the slave's shoulders, that can see the excellency of slavery. So, only you, who are at the topmost round of the social ladder, are raised high enough to see the beauty and excellence of the present order of things. But, if we are not high enough to see its beauty and excellence, we are low enough to feel its weight, and to suffer from its injustice; and we know not why we should bear this oppressive weight, and endure this injustice, merely that you alone may be elevated, and be freed from all burdens, and have nothing to do but to praise the system of things from which you alone profit. We are the many; our interests are as sacred in our eyes as yours are in yours; we desire a greater degree of equality, and as we are as ninety and nine to one, we can hardly be persuaded that what is desirable to us, is upon the whole undesirable.

C. You labor under a grevious mistake. It is for the benefit of the low that some should be above them. Those who are up, help raise those who are down.

R. Admirable way indeed to raise a man, that of planting your feet on his shoulders! Be so good as to step off of our shoulders, and we will get up of ourselves.

C. The upper classes do not stand on the shoulders of the lower. This is all fancy on your part.

R. On what then do they stand? What keeps them up? Where there are several strata, one lying above another, I have always supposed the one above rested for its support on the one below.

C. In physics you may be right, but in moral science things are different. The upper classes rest on their own merit.

R. Very modest! Not content with depriving us of the fruits of our labors, you would monopolize all the merit in God's universe! Moderate your pretensions. Merit, moral merit, is confined to no stratum of society; but may be found in all, and as often in the lowest as in the highest; in the hovel as in the palace; clad in rags as in embroidery. But enough of this. Even you, notwithstanding your social position, I trust, retain some of the feelings of the man, and even you, I believe, if you would take an impartial survey of society as it is, would admit, that more equality than now obtains, is desirable.

C. I have seen society; I think I know what it is.

R. You have seen it from a lofty position, and at a distance; come now and view it nearer by, and from a lower position. Down here, in these valleys, are many things which you may not have seen, or which you may have forgotten, or not considered. Go with me along our public works, our unfinished railroads and canals, and observe attentively this mass of abject beings whose labor constructs them. The contractors, who grow rich by working them as the teamster works his horses or his oxen, no doubt delights in their abjectness, for were they less abject, or were there fewer of them, he would be obliged to treat them better and pay them more wages, and perhaps be unable to hire them at all. Mark them, Sir, kicked and knocked about by those petty tyrants, called overseers, and tell me if you see no distance between them and the nabob corporator, which it would be desirable to lessen?

C. You speak of foreigners. The old World annually disgorges upon us her thousands and tens of thousands of vagabonds. I wish it could be prevented.

R. These vagabonds, as you call them, are human beings; and human beings, wherever born, and whatever color of their fate or their skin, are to me not foreigners, but fellow citizens and brethren. But leave them; they are mostly Irish, and we are yet hardly able to reckon the Irish within the pale of Humanity. Go into your factories—you may be a factory owner for aught I know—go into your factories and mark those pale-visaged girls chained to the spindle or the loom, growing "part and parcel" of the machinery on which they tend, and the bare mention of whom would make the wives and daughters of the factory owners turn up their noses, and tell me if you desire greater degree of equality than now exists between those pale-visaged girls, and the up-nose-turning wives and daughters of the factory owners? Or go into your cities, into the back streets, dark lanes and blind courts, the damp cellars and unventilated garrets, crowded with human beings incrusted with filth and wallowing in the mire; and then go and view the mansions of the rich, fronting our broad, clean, and airy streets or open public squares; and tell me honestly if you see no more inequality than you deem desirable?

C. That there are some degraded and suffering beings among us, I do not mean to deny; but their own vice and folly, ignorance or crime, make them so. Nobody need be poor and miserable in this country.

R. Nor in any other. I thank you for the admission. If none need be poor and miserable, what mean you when you say a greater degree of equality is impossible? I had hoped to find you too clear-headed to fall into a contradiction so common. You tell me—as almost every man tells me—that a greater degree of equality is neither possible nor desirable; when I point you to instances which you cannot see without having all the better part of your nature cry out for more equality,—instances of poverty which it is shocking to behold and painful to remember,—you relieve yourself by saying, this poverty, though not desirable, is unnecessary; it originates in the ignorance or depravity of the poor. That you may not feel any qualms of conscience for living in luxury while others are suffering for the necessaries of life, you assert that they suffer through their own fault, and that they need not be so poor. But in asserting this, you admit the possibility of producing a greater degree of equality. According to your own account, poverty then, is not necessary. Then it may be removed; then a greater degree of equality is possible.

C. I mean a greater degree of equality is impracticable. We might indeed divide all the property of the community equally among all its members; but three days would not elapse before some one would dispose of his share to another, and the old inequality would soon be reproduced, and in an aggravated form.

R. Admit this; it only shows that the method, you mention, is not the right method for introducing equality.

C. But, Sir, there have always been the poor, and there always will be, and the sooner we come to this conclusion the better.

R. If it comes to prophesying, I may as well prophesy as you; I have as good a right to prophesy good as you have to prophesy evil. Poverty, you say, will never be cured; it requires not a little prophetic power to be able to look far enough into futurity to be certain of that.

C. "The poor ye have always with you," said Jesus, and Moses assures us they "shall never cease out of the land." Whatever you may say of my prophetic power, I hope you will not call in question that of Moses and Jesus. God has in the depths of his own wisdom ordained poverty. I consider poverty an appointment, an express and beneficent appointment of God.

R. Then go and give away what you have, and be poor.

C. It is my duty to take care of what God has entrusted to my keeping.

R. And so thought, I presume, the young man who came to Jesus to inquire what he should do to inherit eternal life. It is easy for you to say that poverty is a beneficent appointment of God; for in one sense it is beneficent to *you*; you could not be rich if others were not poor. It is their poverty that makes your wealth. You can have wealth and leisure, because there are many poor to labor for you. But is poverty a beneficent appointment to the *poor*? Do you believe it! Why then have you ransacked heaven and earth, fire and water, sea and land to become rich? Do you believe it! Why then do you submit to the self-denial of being rich, and to the care of your huge estate? Do you believe it! Go then and take the place of him who is kicked from good society, because he wears a thread-bare coat and a sun-burnt face, who is made the common drudge, who must bear all the burdens of society, minister to the wants of the rich, and be despised and trampled on for it; go place yourself by the side of that poor mother weeping over her naked, freezing, starving children, and enduring the agony of a thousand deaths, as she sees them drop piecemeal into the grave; and then talk of poverty as a beneficent appointment of God!

C. You are warm. Poverty is a blessed means to prepare its subjects for another world.

R. What then, shall become of the rich? Do you believe this? How then do you hope to prepare yourself for another world? Shame on your base hypocrisy! Poverty a blessed means to prepare its subjects for another world! Did you not but now charge the poverty of the poor to their indolence, their vice, and their crime? Are indolence, vice, and crime the true preparations for heaven? Is he, whose every thought is racked to devise means to support the human animal, passing under the best discipline to prepare him for Heaven? Away with such nonsense. It has already done injury enough to religion. You and your allies, the priests, have so effectually charged the sufferings we endure upon God, that they have succeeded in filling the land with Atheism. Has the poor man complained of poverty; happy is the poor man, for though poor and miserable here, he is sure of heaven hereafter, it is replied; and the priest pockets his tithe, and the tyrant sits secure on his throne.

Conversation II

C. You have evidently received a superior education, and yet I find you the very incarnation of Radicalism. This to me is a mystery.

R. Why so? Is there any necessary incongruity between a good education, and a sincere devotion to the interests of mankind, an unquenchable thirst to promote the well-being of the poor and the neglected?

C. Perhaps not. But I have not been accustomed to look for Radicals among the educated.

R. Nor anybody else that knows anything. Still, education has no higher or holier vocation than that of fitting its subjects to be stern, uncompromising, and indefatigable Reformers. But the educated among us belong to the more favored classes, and the more favored classes are always opposed to Reform, or—if it suit you better—to Innovation. A part of the educated owe their superior education to the fact, that they belong by birth to the more favored classes; and the rest are placed in the category of the more favored classes by the fact, that they are educated. In either case, whether educated because their fathers were rich, or whether poor boys who have contrived to get an education, they then belong to the aristocracy. And why should the aristocracy be Reformers? What have they to allege against society as it is, since they have it altogether their own way; since it is altogether in their interest? A man like yourself has few inducements to be a Reformer; you can hope to gain nothing by a Reform. Bred to regard only yourself, inured by the habits of your life, and the circumstances in which you have been placed, to a selfishness all but diabolical, tolerating no upshootings of the soul for the happiness of your fellow-beings, incapable of looking for, or tasting pleasure in doing them good, what can made you engage in the grand and glorious work of social regeneration? The man who blacks your boots and brushes your coat might engage in the work of Reform, and the poor woman stewing over your kitchen fire preparing you a luxurious dinner, or a late supper, from the ill effects of which you will never recover, may be a Radical. But not you;—you have nothing to gain. You have drawn the highest prize; you have won the stake, and why hazard another game? You may lose, but you have nothing to hope from further winnings. You are now at the top of the social ladder. A change may place you at its foot. This is the case with nearly all the educated—or if it be not the case with all, each one trusts that it will be in a few days—and can you then wonder that so few of them are Radicals? It is not because they are too wise, but because they have too great a stake in the existing order.

Nor is this all. Our young men, who receive a superior education, are not educated to regard the well-being of Humanity, to be Reformers, the champions and servants of the people; but they are educated to get their living out of the people. None of our colleges or higher seminaries imbue our young men with an unquenchable zeal for human improvement, kindle up in their hearts a burning desire to set mankind forward, a disinterested love which weds itself to the cause of Humanity, and pursues it through good report and through evil report, and never in the darkest hours relaxes its exertions. They train up our sons to manage the people skillfully, and to ride them gracefully and securely. Our professors are mere riding masters, giving lessons in the noble art of horsemanship. No man can be a Professor unless he be an aristocrat or a conservative.

C. Why not?

R. Because our colleges and higher seminaries are founded by the wealthy, and are under the control of those whom the present order of things most favors, and because these will choose no man to be a professor, unless he be one in whom they can confide. They can confide in no man who is in favor of any social changes, innovations, or improvements. They are men of the present, whom the present most favors, and they must naturally distrust all who do not in return favor the present. Moreover, to be chosen a professor a man must be a popular man. But the men, who are devoted to the highest and most enduring interests of mankind, are never popular. He who has the misfortune to think in advance of his contemporaries, and to desire a good for mankind beyond that already attained, is necessarily unpopular. If he venture to translate his thoughts into words, and his hopes into actions, he will be branded a Jacobin, an agrarian, a leveler, an anarchist, or at best, a visionary, who, though he may mean well, is to be pitied, not trusted. Men who have faith in the future, whose mental vision sweeps broader than the vulgar horizon, whose souls burn to raise up the low, to break the fetters of the slave, to open the prison doors to them that are bound, to preach glad tidings to the poor, hope to the desponding, consolation to the sorrowing, and life to the dead, must always count on being discarded by their own age and country. They cannot be misinterpreted. They cannot but pass for what they are not, and would abhor to be. And how is it possible, that such men should be chosen to superintend the education of our children?

To be popular one must be a man of the present, uphold things as they are, never disturb the world with new views, but merely echo the sentiments he finds in vogue. He who can echo these the loudest, and with the greatest distinctness, is sure to be the most popular. Such men never trouble their age; they disturb no one's prejudices, excite no alarm, produce no commotion. Such men always look for in colleges, and therefore never look to colleges for Reformers, for new ideas, or for encouragement to labor in the cause of mankind. New ideas are placed in the world by those whom the world knows not, or whom it disowns if it knows them. Reforms come from the obscure and the unheeded; from a peasant and his fishermen followers, not from the popular and the honored. The weak things of this world are chosen to confound the mighty, and foolish things to bring to naught the wisdom of the wise.

C. You do not appear to hold popular men in very high esteem.

R. Not I. That is, if you mean by popular men those whom everybody praises, whose name is in everybody's mouth, and whom their own age holds up as worthy of all imitation. I for one, claim no affinity with such men, and stay as short a time in their presence as possible. I am not of their parish. I cannot hurrah with the multitude, when they pass by, or deign to make a speech. God knows I do not envy, but pity them. Poor creatures! It is their fate to live and die without ever having felt the throe of a single idea, and without the consolation of having contributed aught to the movement of the race. With the present, pass away the popular men after whom the multitude now run; and as yesterday is swallowed up in today, so will they be lost in the generation to come, and be remembered no more forever. The future will preserve of the men now living only those who have had some forecast of that which is to come, and shooting by their own generation, have dared live, and labor, and suffer, for posterity.

C. You talk strangely for a Radical. I have always supposed a Radical a mere compound of envy and malignity.

R. And may you live long enough to repent of your error. What is there in this world to envy! I have seen all that it has to offer; I have tasted of all that, which the many pursue as their chief good. I know what it is to be honored, and eulogized, to be rich and courted, to have my name in the gazette, and made the theme of the orator and the bard. It is all vanity. Wealth, fame, pleasure, pomp, place, power,—they are mere shadows. I look with pity on him who sighs after them, and with unaffected sorrow on him whom they encumber. Poor things! bask in your little hour of sunshine; make the most of its warmth, for an eternal winter of neglect and forgetfulness awaits you. Could I envy, it should be none but a Socrates drinking his hemlock, a Paul brought before Nero, a Vane at his prayers on the scaffold. I know not but I might envy the martyr burning at the stake, for religion, for country, for justice, for unswerving devotion to truth, duty, God, man; but I can conceive of nothing else in this world to envy. But enough of this.

To return to education. Our colleges and higher seminaries are not only instituted by, but for, the more favored classes. These classes—and you attest it—are always, taken collectively, conservative. They seek no social progress. They think, if we can keep things from growing worse, we shall do well to be satisfied. They therefore steadily oppose all radical changes in the social system. Details may be modified, but the groundwork must not be touched. The rough fetters of the slave, which eat into his flesh, may be polished or converted into fetters of gold; but they must not be broken. This or that poor widow may be relieved, and the great body of the poor may have the priest come and tell them, that if they will be quiet and patient here, never seeking to unhorse their riders, they shall go to heaven hereafter; but the poor, as a body, must not be elevated, and above all, must one beware how he proposes the complete and entire removal of poverty. These classes allow us to plead with all our might for the poor as individuals, for they are charitable and humane, but they forbid us under severe penalties to adopt effectual measures for the removal of the evils under which they labor. They permit us to give alms, but not to remove the necessity of almsgiving. They would mitigate the pain, for they do not delight to inflict suffering, they would mollify, but never heal the wound. This being the character of the more favored classes touching the point in question, and their character presented in its best light, is it reasonable to ask them to commit the education of their children to the care of men, who have full faith in the practicability of removing all social evils, and who would do their best to communicate that faith to their pupils? I need not ask you, if you would choose a man of my opinions to be the educator of your children; for I know you would not. You would not send your children to a college of which I could be president. My radicalism alone, without any other consideration, would prevent you from doing it. The same principle, which in this case governs you, would govern the whole of your class. I know you all. You have no wish to have your children educated to be Reformers, because you have no faith in nor desire for Reform yourselves. You have the instinct of self-preservation. You are not likely to be suicides; and yet it were suicidal for you to encourage Reformers; for they would reform the abuses by which you are made the more favored class. Reform would deprive you of all your exclusive privileges. You would be obliged to black your own boots, sweep your own chimneys, and in all cases perform your own drudgery. Not willingly will you consent to this. You do not choose to be your own servants, and you will not be, so long as you can find others who will be servants to you; and not till you consent to be your own servants, will you consent to sustain professors who aim to prepare your children for the work of perfecting the social organization. As things now are, professors, who desire to perfect the social organization, must leave their professorships, or withhold their own convictions. If they choose to retain their chairs, they must consent to support the existing order of things; lecture in favor of order, not liberty; against anarchy, not against tyranny; and labor to send out every year an army of young conservatives, prepared to put down all tendencies to philanthropic enthusiasm, to crush every effort of the people to meliorate their condition and to perfect society; not an army of reformers, trained to their work, and able to bring science, and literature, and taste, and genius, and religion to their aid, and prepared to die, if need be, in obtaining for the human race an advanced position. No; they must wither the holiest affections, and chill the noblest aspirations of the young heart, and send it out dead and cold.

The same influence corrupts our literature and renders it hostile to democracy. Few things are more to be deplored by a true American, that what passes for American literature. It is tame and servile, so servile that it might excite the derision of an Asiatic despot. Scarcely a writer among us dares utter an original thought, or breathe a noble aspiration. No writers have a more sovereign dread of Radicalism, than American writers. With what contempt must those Europeans, who are enlightened, and who understand that America stands pledged to what you call Radicalism, turn over the leaves of our popular Reviews and Magazines! And how discouraging indeed, must it be to the friends of Humanity in other countries, the noble spirits who plead with ignorance, combat prejudice, and struggle with the tyrant, to listen in vain for a cheering and strengthening word from America, the boasted land of the free! That word they hear not. Let not the Reformers in other lands look to us for sympathy. Our sympathies are not with the friends of truth, freedom, justice. Our writers are the faint echos of the hired defenders of priests, kings, and nobility. The world is cursed with few periodicals,—so far as they have any character,—more strictly antiradical and purely conservative than the New-York and North American Reviews. Even Blackwood and the London Quarterly are less so. The New-York Review is rescued from contempt, because it has courage enough to avow its real character; but the North American hardly ever dares say, good Lord or good devil, though it has a manifest longing to say good devil, having, I presume, a presentiment that it must fall into his hands at last.[1] We sometimes complain that the old world does not respect us. Let us cease to complain, and study to deserve respect, by being true to our principles. No object is more contemptible than a democratic people apologizing for their democracy, and trying all possible methods to resemble those who are cursed with monarchies. *America will never be respected till she is worthy of respect, and never will she be worthy of respect, till she shall be true to herself, and dare avow and defend the doctrine of equality on which her institutions are founded.* She must have a Literature in harmony with the rights of man; and her writers, must draw from the minds that have been formed in schools of equality, and from hearts that are large enough to embrace the whole family of man, and keep them warm. Man and man only must be able to kindle their enthusiasm, and inspire their strains. They must rise above all factitious distinctions, be able to pierce beneath every garb, to discover the Incarnate God though clad in rags. They must dare speak out from full minds and hearts, their free thoughts, and give them to us with all the freshness and vigor with which they come to themselves; and to send out their feelings as warm as they gush up in their own hearts, if they would make her respectable in the eyes of those whose respect is worth having.

This is not the case now, and the reason why it is not, is obvious. Aside from the newspaper press, at present our only hope, all our literature is designed for the wealthy and educated, for the American aristocracy. I have told you the character of this aristocracy. It has no stars, no coronets; but it has the exclusive spirit which pervades all aristocracies, less of liberality than the aristocracies of the old world, because its tenure is less secure, and because each member of it knows that it is possible he may tomorrow be at the lowest depth of the people. They who write for this aristocracy, must write to suit its views and prejudices. Most of our books, our Quarterlies, and our

Monthlies, are designed for this portion of the community, and hence their conservative character. Let one of our Quarterlies admit an article which goes for the many instead of the few, and the few who are its supporters will at once stop their subscriptions. Without subscriptions the periodical cannot be continued, and subscriptions it cannot have unless it appeal to the exclusive interests of those who are expected to patronize it. Publishers have then their option, either to appeal to that exclusive interest, or to stop publishing.

A book written in the interests of Humanity, full of rich thoughts and noble sentiments, expressed in a style of classic elegance and purity, and with a power almost superhuman, will find few purchasers beyond the ranks of the workingmen, and even the workingmen, prone to take their cue from their supposed betters, will not venture to approve it. In this way nearly all the advantages of a free press are lost. Some of the best minds among us are silent, because they can find no medium through which they can utter their thoughts. A mind conscious of great wealth, of high and generous aims, noble and kindling thoughts, will not consent to pare itself down to a saleable size in the book stall. It must be allowed to speak out, and speak out freely in its own way, and its own burning words, or it will not speak at all. How much is lost by the miserable censorship, which a sickly public opinion establishes over the American press, for which our whole nation "must fare the worse," God only knows. And how many of the noblest and most gifted of our contemporaries lock up their thoughts in their own bosoms, and die because they cannot utter themselves, is a secret which will be known at the day of judgment. Our press is muzzled, because no book can be published unless it find a publisher, and if it contain an Idea, a publisher it will hardly find; because the bookseller will be afraid that the Idea will render it unpopular, and therefore unsaleable.

The pulpit is gagged in the same way. Clergymen are in some instances from the conservative class, in all cases their education, habits, and associations, tend to identify them with the aristocracy. They thus catch the aristocratic tone of thought and feeling. Restricted in their own studies principally to their professions, they depend on the better educated and wealthier members of their congregations, for their views of political economy and the social state, and consequently must adopt, even with the best intentions, conservative notions. This is not, however, true of all. Some of them see the truth; but then how mighty are the temptations with which they are surrounded to conceal it! The clergyman depends on the aristocracy for friends and supporters; to receive the friendship and support of the aristocracy he must enter into their views, and support their interests. If he does not please the aristocracy of his parish, he may be dismissed supperless to bed; or sent out into the world, with a wife and children depending on him for support, and he not a penny in pocket, or in reputation with which to support them. To preach the Gospel in these times, and in this country,—that is, to preach it as it should be preached,—one should have the spirit of martyrdom, he prepared to live alone in the world, to be looked upon with distrust wherever he goes, to be called, a visionary, or a fanatic, to be familiar with poverty, to be harassed in body and in mind, to die of disappointment and grief, and leave behind a helpless widow and friendless orphans. If he would avoid this, he must temporize, form an alliance between Christ and Belial, God and Mammon, and beware how he touches a new idea. New ideas will render him unpopular. If unpopular, he cannot collect an audience; if he cannot collect an audience, he can have no salary; and if no salary, he must cease to preach, or starve. They who hold the purse, therefore, virtually write his sermons. In a vast majority of cases the clergyman is but a speaking machine, from which the aristocracy grind out just such discourses as best please them.

These views, Sir, which doubtless are very pleasing and encouraging to you conservatives, are very saddening to me. My heart is oppressed and filled with grief. O, my countrymen,—and yet why complain? No man, who does not uphold the present, though he have a heart that would take in the whole family of man, and a mind, that with a prophet's ken, sees the future and what it demands, can obtain a hearing from his contemporaries. His own generation know him not; they neither see nor hear him. They know not how much rich thought, how much disinterested love, what power to do and dare anything and everything for human regeneration, there may be in that heart, into which they look not, and which they will not suffer to be laid open to them. When the man of new views, the reformer, is dead, men will build him a tomb, or garnish his sepulcher; but so long as he lives they leave him to be stoned. Yet let me not "bate a jot of heart or hope," but bear on my way. Mankind, thou canst be saved only by crucified redeemers. Ay, it is so. The Cross is the true symbol of regeneration. He, who will go forth to defend the right, to plead for the poor and the neglected, the oppressed and the enslaved, must take up his cross and follow Jesus. He, who condemns the present, and he, who demands reform, does condemn it, must be himself condemned in return. The present attacks those by whom it is attacked. They are wolves in sheep's clothing, they, the pretended reformers, who find wind and tide in their favor, and whose bark is wafted gently forward by the breath of popular applause. The future is elaborated in the present; but its elaborators must work in dark laboratories, silent retreats, or subterranean caverns, unseen, unknown, unvisited, uncheered, unaided. It cannot be otherwise. Christ must needs suffer. They are of the future, and the future must be their reward. Their views, their ideas, their wishes, their hopes are dark mysteries to their contemporaries. They are the prophets of a new age. The world is not worthy of them. There is no world for them. They must be the builders as well as the heralds of their own world. And while they seem to those around them but the mere pullers-down of the world, in which they appear, but to which they belong not, how can they excite any other shout than that of "crucify them, crucify them." And yet the cross is sometimes all but too heavy to be borne, and the firmest and stoutest faint beneath its weight. O, it is bitter to be cursed with thoughts beyond your age, to see truths invisible to all eyes but your own, to be compelled to utter prophecies you know will not be credited, to be alone in the thronged city, a stranger in the home of your childhood, and amid faces familiar to you from your youth up. O, this is a solitude in which a man agonizes, sweats as it were great drops of blood! Mankind, thou little knowest what it costs to save thee from thyself. No matter. Thou deservest to have martyrs, for thou art the child of God. But why talk I in this strain? You understand me not. I talk mysticism, fanaticism, or barbarism to your comprehension.

C. You are right now. All this stuff about what the Reformer suffers is all foolishness to me.

R. And so, Sir, must be all great truths, and pure philanthropy, and lofty enthusiasm, to you and to such as you. When you have felt a desire for human happiness, for the progress of mankind, so strong that you could not sleep; when you have given years of intense study to the means of doing good, and sacrificed wealth, ease, reputation, friends, and found yourself alone, considered by one a madman, and by another an imp of hell, and found that after all your exertions, no man understands you, no bosom responds with sympathy to the holy love struggling in your own, and that you must after all die, without having finished your work; then you may sneer at the Reformer, and call what he says foolishness; till then be silent, lest you be found blaspheming God.

Conversation III

C. There is no ground for the distinction of which you speak. We are all workingmen. The lawyer, the physician, the clergyman, the merchant, the statesman, the philosopher works as hard, perhaps harder, than your ploughman, your ditcher, your carpenter, shoemaker, or blacksmith.

R. Admitted; but the difference is this, one class works to produce, the other class works to secure for itself the proceeds of the other's producing. The community is divided into two classes; one class, which I denominate the workingmen, are producers, the other class are accumulators, of wealth. The first class create wealth, the second transfer it to their own pockets.

C. But there is one thing you Radicals seem always to overlook. You either cannot or will not regard the aid which the producers receive from the skill, science, enterprise, and capital of those you call the accumulators. Your producers would be in a sad box, if they were deprived of the capital of the accumulators, and of their science to direct their mere brute labor. The labor of those heads, which to you seem idle, is doing more than all the labor of the hands of your producers, to facilitate the work of production.

R. But production for whom? These accumulators with their capital and their head-work, I know, multiply productions far exceeding in amount anything we could do by our mere handwork; but who secure the profits? You, and all the economists with whom I am acquainted, seem to take it for granted, that the well-being of the producer is always in exact proportion to the amount of production; and they would be right, if every man produced for himself; but as things now are they are most sadly mistaken. The accumulators study to employ their science and capital in that manner which will give them the greatest profit; that is, so that they may derive the greatest possible amount of production from the labors of the producers. The advantages, to which you allude, then, of increased production, are advantages almost exclusively to the accumulators.

C. In point of fact, you are greatly out in your reckoning. The expense of manufacturing a yard of calico bears no comparison with what it was fifty years ago. A similar change has taken place in the expense of producing almost all the articles consumed by the common laborer; and do you mean to tell me the laborer has gained nothing by this cheapness of production, and this low price he has to pay for whatever he consumes? The laboring classes are in a condition almost immeasurably above that in which they were at the epoch of our Revolution. To be assured of this, you need but compare the price of labor with that of bread stuffs then, and the price of labor with that of bread stuffs now. You may also be convinced of this by observing the houses, dress, and style of living of laborers now, which in many respects are superior to what those of the rich were then.

R. This mode of judging is fallacious. That there has been a general increase of wealth throughout the civilized world for the last forty or fifty years, nobody is fool enough to deny. Man's empire over Nature, during this period, has been greatly extended and consolidated; the powers of production of all kinds, as well as productions themselves, have been so multiplied as to baffle efforts at calculation. The laboring classes most certainly account many things necessaries of life now, which they then accounted its luxuries. But they are not the less poor. Poverty and wealth are merely relative terms. The only true method of judging of this matter is to ascertain whether the position of the producer, relatively to that of the accumulator, be higher or lower, than it was at the epoch of the Revolution, before the marvelous powers of machinery, of science, and capital had been made to bear on production, as they have been since. Grant that a yard of calico may be purchased now at an eighth of what it cost fifty years ago; what is gained, if in order to maintain the same relative social position, the blacksmith's wife must put seven yards more into her gown, or have eight gowns to that one then? You know, Sir, if you know anything about it, that, notwithstanding the general advance of wealth and the vast multiplication of the necessaries and conveniences of life, it is altogether more difficult for the common laborer to maintain the same social position now, than it was fifty years ago. The general style of living has more than kept pace with the increase of wealth. The mechanic, it may be, receives two and even three times as much, nominally, for his labor now as he did then, and is required to pay two or three times less for what he purchases; but then he must have as much more as this difference implies in order to be a man of the same consequence that he was. The blacksmith's wife must have a carpet now, where a nicely sanded floor was enough then; and a French calico instead of a homemade, copperas-dyed, tow-and-linen gown, which was her pride then. Then she could spin and weave, and with butternut bark, dye her husband a coat from the wool he received for blacksmithing; but now she can only do some fine needlework, and he can wear only broadcloth; both of which things demand corresponding changes in the style of living.

C. And I should suppose that with your great affection for blacksmiths, and especially for blacksmiths' wives, you would rejoice that it is so.

R. No. My friends, the blacksmith and his wife, the shoemaker and his wife, the housewright, and the wheelright and their wives, are all poorer than they were. Their houses may look better outwardly, but they are not so comfortable inside. They have more compared with what they then had, but less compared with what is now the general style of living. The sanded floor, the copperas gown, the checked apron, the butternut coat, and the tow shirt, frock, and trousers, were good enough for them then, for they were as good as their neighbor's had. Some little vanity or uneasiness might now and then be occasioned by the quality, the skill of the housewife in making, in dying, or in fitting, but it amounted to very little. Each family manufactured for itself, and felt itself independent; and the feeling of independence, that we have within ourselves the means of providing for our own wants, is worth more than all the carpets, French calicoes, French silk, satin, lace, and the like things in the world. Those were happy times. Labor was no disgrace, for all labored; and homespun was no badge of inferiority, for all wore it. I remember how delighted I used to be when I was a boy, at evening, to seat myself on the dye-tub, which stood in the corner, and hear the maid, who was doing our spinning, accompany the music of her wheel with such old songs as "Jemmy and Nancy," and "The Cruelties of Barbara Allen." I have heard some famous singers in my day; but no songs have ever charmed me like those old songs sung by our neighbor's daughter who did our spinning. What though she had but one calico gown for Sunday; what though that was often turned and altered to look unfaded and to be within hailing distance of the fashion; and what though she worked for forty cents a week, and had no gilt album or souvenir lying in her boudoir? She had health and cheerfulness, bloom on her cheek, an elastic bound in her step, heartiness in her laugh, witchery in her smile, and—was as good as any of us. It was no disgrace that "she went out to work." No young spark made any account of that. At all gatherings and merrymakings, her head was as high as any one's, and her chance for a worthy and respectable companion was as good as hers who never worked in or out of her father's house. Nobody complained of bad servants. The daughters of the best families would go and help the poorest, if they could be spared from home. Thus was it in one of thy mountain towns, my native State, in my young days. Then the hearts of thy children were as fresh as the verdure of thy mountains, and their spirits as free as the winds that sweep over them. I have seen many countries; I have visited lands most renowned in song or story; I have lived in cities, consorted with the great, and wedged my way into the charmed circles of the fashionable; but give me back the mountain home of my childhood, and let me hear again the wheel, and our neighbor's eldest daughter accompany the music of her spinning with the old songs of "Jemmy and Nancy," and "The Cruelties of Barbara Allen." In that home I was made a freeman. I drew in a love of equality with the milk from my mother's breast. There I learned to look on man, to see the man and not his clothes; and for this I bless thee, my native State. Fame gives thee credit for no great men, but I know thou hast a great people, and my old Geography yet reads, and I hope not in vain, "Vermont is an independent State."

Forgive me, Sir, for this allusion to my native State, and to the home of my childhood. That home is changed now. The same blue sky bends over it, the same golden sun sheds its beams upon it; but old faces have gone, old manners have given way. The summer's stock of cloth no longer lies bleaching on the grass plat before the door; my sister is not there with her waterpot; and the sound of the waterfall, and the spinningmaid's song, has succeeded the endless clack of the cotton mill.

C. You are a strange Radical. I knew not before that Radicals ever thought of the Past save to condemn it. I have always supposed that they had eyes only for the Future.

R. That is, you have supposed we were only half-men. This is a mistake. For my part, I love the ancient and the time-hallowed. I delight to stand on spots renowned in story; amid the fragments of earlier worlds, to conjure up the dread Spirit of the mighty Past, and question him concerning those who were, but are not. I never had even a cane that I carried for a long time, a knife which had done me good service, that I could lose without a pang. But I have learned to sacrifice the Poetical to the Useful. I love the old oak which yet stands by the home of my childhood, under whose shade I have so often played when life was full, and by which I whispered the tale of my earliest and truest love; but I would cut it down sooner than I would see my children freeze, or want fuel to cook their food.

C. Then you would not really destroy our factories, demolish all our laborsaving machinery, and go back to the hand-cards, the hand-loom, the spinning-wheel, and the songs of Jemmy and Nancy and the Cruelties of Barbara Allen!

R. Not I. I would never go back. If I sometimes give a tear to the Past, it is never to evoke it from its tomb. No. Let it rest in peace. The Past which is revived is never the Past which lives in our memories. It is only the ideal Past which lives in our memories. It is only the ideal Past that is venerable. These old songs would not please me now. The bloom is no longer on the maiden's cheek who bounded at her wheel, and gone is the mischief from her eye, and the witchery from her smile. We have lost the religion of our youth. The fairies no longer keep holiday on the green knoll in the pasture, or pinch the milkmaid because she stints our supper. But I do not regret it. All changes in the end are proved to be steps forward in the march of

Humanity. Yet the step we have taken during the last fifty years is shorter than we pretend. We have changed the mode of production; for our neighbor's daughter, who used to do my mother's spinning and weaving, who nursed her in her confinement, and who was one of us, good as the best in the neighborhood, we have now the pale and sickly factory girl, who must up at the ringing of a bell, eat and sleep at the ringing of a bell, obey the whistle of a petty overseer, never leave her jail limits without permission and whose average working life is only about four years. The one was our equal, whom the sons of our best farmers were willing and often glad to marry, and the other can get her a husband among the factory population perhaps—but rarely elsewhere. She is only a *factory* girl, and you know what that means. And surely here is some loss,—a loss of health, cheerfulness, freedom, and social position; and what is gained to balance this loss? At best two dollars a week instead of forty cents, and which two dollars does less to satisfy her wants, than the forty cents did to satisfy the wants of the one who did our spinning. The difference between these two girls is the difference between the working classes of our country fifty years ago and now.

Yet, improvements have been effected, important inventions have been made and labor-saving machinery introduced which abridges labor many thousand fold. As soon as the producers can so arrange matters as to produce for themselves, they will reap the full advantage of this labor-saving machinery, and of the increased capital of the country. At present they receive no direct profit from either. The accumulators reap the profits. This discloses the true aim of the Radical. His aim is not to produce equality in property, nor in anything else, but to make every man a proprietor, so that the producer and the accumulator shall always be united in the same person. To this point, I would have governments direct their attention; all the friends of the people should keep it in view, and all Legislative and educational measures should tend to it.

C. You have now stated your object clearly. I must think of it. And tomorrow I hope you will get the better of your sentimentalism, so far at least as not to talk nonsense.

Conversation IV

C. Your plan is more plausible than sound, and appears much better in theory than it will appear in practice. Division of labor is essential to the very existence of society. But your plan requires every man to do everything for himself.

R. Not at all. The shoemaker may stick to his last, and the blacksmith may work at his forge. All the division in labor how recognized, may continue under the regulation, that every man works for himself, as well as under our present arrangement. The only division of labor to which I object, is that which assigns the head-work to one part of the community, and the handwork to another. Since man is both soul and body, I would have no division of bodywork and soul-work. Both should be as inseparable as soul and body. In the present slate of things all the soul-work devolves on a distinct class of the community, and they are treated as though they were all soul; all the body-work falls to another class, and they are treated as though they were all body. But this is unnatural and unjust. The body-workers have souls as well as the soul-workers. They who do our handwork are of the same order of being with those who do our head-work.

C. That is true. But still, it is a very great advantage to the handworkers, to have the aid of the head-workers. This you Radicals seem to overlook. You complain bitterly, that those who work with their heads are rewarded for their labor. You are not willing to give any share of the fruits of handwork to him, who by his inventions has given to your hands a hundred fold their natural strength. Brute labor is all that you seem to regard as worthy of compensation. The philosopher, the naturalist, the mechanician, the painter, the poet, the sculptor, the musician, soul-workers as they are, must not be paid for their labors, though without their labors, life would be hardly worth possessing.

R. Stop there, if you please. You mistake us greatly. We would have all these soul-workers paid. But soul-work always pays itself. If these soul-workers could have wherewithal to provide for the body, while they were at work with the soul, it would be all that they would demand. No man, who pursued his profession for the sake of money, was ever yet a great philosopher, or a great artist. My rule is, that soul must pay for soul, and body for body. I object to an exchange of the products of the one for those of the other. At present, necessity may demand the unholy barter; but when society becomes what it should be, it will be discounted.

C. How then are these soul-workers, as you call them, to live? Are we to have no men of science, no philosophers, no artists?

R. Millions to one in comparison with what we now have, I hope; but you seem very slow of apprehension. I would have every man labor for himself on his own capital, and then every man would have the time to produce all that is needed for the body; and also as much as can be devoted with any degree of advantage to moral, intellectual, and aesthetical pursuits.

C. Are you sure of that?

R. Some nice calculators have ascertained that if all men would labor, each three hours a day, they would produce all the material goods which they would need, or which could be enjoyed by the body. Now any physiologist will tell you, that three hours' labor a day is no more than is needed for the health of the body; and any man, who has any acquaintance with mental pursuits, will assure you that six hours a day are as much as any man can profitably devote to them. He, who labors three hours a day and studies six, will make much greater progress, than he who studies nine and labors none at all. This would leave every man fifteen hours a day for refreshment, social intercourse, and sleep. Under such an arrangement, you see, every man would be able to devote all the time necessary to head-work,—to science, philosophy, poetry, music, painting, or sculpture. There would then be no need of a separate class for these pursuits, to be paid out of the handwork of the rest.

C. I suppose then you would not pay the clergy, physicians, lawyers, nor public officers?

R. No. They would need no pay. Each one would give three hours a day to labor as a matter of exercise, for health and that would produce him all he would need for his body. His other labors being mental, would be recompensed by a mental reward. Besides, in this case, clergymen would not be needed; every man would know the Lord for himself, and be his own priest. Physicians would hardly be needed for temperance and proper exercise would maintain almost uninterrupted health. Lawyers would not be in much request; for roguery would then hardly exist, and public officers would have but little employment.

C. Upon my word, you are a beautiful dreamer! And how do you expect to realize this dream?

R. As I have told you, by having every man do his own hand-work and head-work.

C. And you suppose the workingmen, mere brute laborers, can become intellectual beings, philosophers, learned men, artists.

R. Why not? Are not we of the same order of being with those who think themselves above us? We care not with what contempt they look upon us, nor how contemptuously they sneer at our hopes for the future; we know that our bosoms burn, amid our eyes sparkle with a fire as pure and as eternal as that which they bid us worship in their idol temples. Of the dust of the earth we indeed are, and downtrodden to the dust too we long have been; but we are also the offspring of God, and upward to our Father and our native heaven we may rise.

C. You have, for six thousand years, given brave proofs of your celestial origin! One would think that in so long a series of ages your inward fire might have been kindled into a blaze.

R. *Full many a gem of purest ray serene*
The dark, unfathomed caves of ocean bear;
Full many a flower is born to blush unseen,
And waste its sweetness on the desert air.

And beware, Sir, how you add insult to injury. You put out our eyes and reproach us for our blindness; make us blind and then tell us we shall tumble into the ditch, unless we have somebody to lead us. In our mother's arms the fire of intellect is smothered, and you and your caste keep watch by us ready to dash on your pail-fulls of cold water whenever a symptom of its revival is discovered. Now that we have been kept in ignorance, deprived of the means of developing our powers, and obliged to conceal the God laboring in our breasts under the veil of idiocy, you have the effrontery to mock us because we are not philosophers, and to tell us that we must work hard to pay you for your great condescension in thinking for us; and you might add, for condescending to be happy for us. Base hypocrites! We understand you. We will not trust you to do our thinking; for we are suspicious, that your thinking is much more to your profit than to ours. Your thinking for us amounts to little else than how to make us work to the best advantage, while you shall pocket the proceeds. You are fond of extolling the importance of head-work; but, as we have learned, that you may contrive to get your living without working at all. For you do not think as much, nor do you turn out to be such profound thinkers, as you pretend. Most of the discoveries of which you boast, and inventions and improvements in the arts of production, from which you derive so much profit, are the result of *our* thinking; and nearly all the individuals, who have saved your body from putrefaction, have been supplied from our ranks. We comprehend you; and hereafter will endeavor to do our own thinking and if we think not so much to your interest as you have done, we may think perhaps more to our own, which will be still better.

C. In most of your remarks you labor under a mistake. You seem to believe that there is a class in this country hostile to the workingmen, seeking to circumvent them, and to keep them from rising. All this is mere fancy. I can speak for myself, and I think for all of those whom you brand as aristocrats, that nothing would give them or me more sincere pleasure than to see the workingmen all in comfortable circumstances. We have no pleasure in poverty, no delight in seeing, and certainly none in causing human suffering. You do us great injustice, and you do a serious injury to the workingmen themselves. You stir up their jealousies, excite their hostility against those you call the accumulators, and throw the whole community into a state of intestine war. Now this is no way to bring about a reform. The rich are necessary to the poor, and the poor are necessary to the rich, and as the friend of either class, you should seek to make both live together as brothers.

R. The lamb is necessary to the wolf; for without the lamb the wolf might want a dinner; and the wolf is necessary to the lamb, for without the wolf the lamb might fail to be eaten. "Therefore," says the benevolent wolf to the lamb, "do not be hostile to us, nor excite your brother lambs against us; for you see we wolves and you lambs are mutually necessary to each other. We are as dependent on you for something to eat, as you are on us to be eaten." "But I don't want to be eaten," exclaims the lamb in great trepidation. "Not want to be eaten!" replies the wolf. "Now that's odd. You and I are very far from thinking alike, and I must needs consider you very unreasonable, and radical in your mode of thinking."

C. Do you mean to call the rich wolves?

R. Apply my comparison as you please. All I mean is that the reasoning of the wolf appears to me as conclusive and every whit as just as yours.

C. I anticipated nothing of this from you, who evidently have had the means of knowing better. Some ignorant workingman might have been pardoned for talking so, but you, whoever or whatever you are, have seen too much of the rich to believe any such thing as you assert. You must have some base and sinister purpose in supporting the workingmen. You have some personal pique to gratify, and I no longer believe you honest but mistaken, as I did at first.

R. As you please. I profess to have no control over your opinions. You are not the first man whom the truth has offended, and will not be the last. But be cool. Now I know the rich; I know the accumulators of wealth in this country and in most others, and it is because I know them that I speak as I do.

C. If you continue to talk thus, I must break off the conversation, and relieve myself of your company.

R. As it suits your pleasure. I neither court nor avoid any man. But listen a moment. Now I have not the most distant suspicion that there is a class among us that wishes to keep down the workingmen, or that wills their poverty. The rich have no disposition to injure the poor. They are not hostile to the poor. The wolf does not by any means dislike the lamb, or wish to injure it. He only wants a dinner, and lamb is his most agreeable food. He loves lamb most affectionately.

C. No more of that, Sir.

R. Well, well, Sir, I see you do not like the comparison; you probably are afraid of the consequences. The wolf—

C. I tell you I will hear no more of that.

R. Very well, Sir. I only wanted to say that, the wolf might be afraid, if the lambs should once know that they were necessary to the wolf only for the purpose of furnishing him dinners, and that he was necessary to the wolf only for the purpose of eating them, that they might, as they probably have no great desire to be eaten, combine against him, and thus leave him to feed on something else; but as it is disagreeable to you, I won't say it. And besides the wolf must be very foolish to apprehend any danger from a combination among the lambs. What could they do against the wolf? By combining they would only give him an opportunity to make his dinner on the fattest instead of the leanest. But seriously, Sir, your talk about the necessity of the rich to the poor is all a humbug, and fully justifies my comparison. The poor are necessary to the rich, I admit; but that the rich are necessary to the poor, I deny; and you know they are not, as you testify by your dread of my saying so. It is out of no love to the poor, no tender regard for their welfare, that you wish to have it understood that the rich are necessary to them.

C. You seem to think that we are a set of selfish wretches, who detest the poor and do all we can to make them miserable.

R. No, I do not. I acquit you of all hostility to the poor. I am even willing to admit that you have a certain affection for them, and would do your best to preserve and multiply them.

C. Come, cease your pleasantry, and speak seriously.

R. I am serious, and speak with all the truthfulness I can command. The wolf certainly has no disposition to destroy the race of lambs. Nor do I blame the wolf for making his dinner of lamb. It is his nature to do it. Nor do I blame the accumulator for transferring the profits of the workingman's labor into his own pockets. It is his nature to do it. He could not be an accumulator if he did not. What I complain of is that there are wolves, or accumulators of wealth, separate from the producers of wealth. In sober earnest, you can assign but two reasons why the rich are necessary to the poor; one reason is that they may be the *instructors of the poor*, and the other that *they may give them employment*. Have you any other reasons to allege?

C. Those are enough.

R. But we have disposed of these already, by contending that the poor should do their own thinking, and also work for themselves. There is no good reason in the world to be assigned, why one class of the community should be dependent on another for its instructors. The whole community may and should be equally educated, and every man may and should work for himself. So long as the wealth of the community is in the hands of only a certain number of individuals; or, in other words, so long as the community is divided into two classes, one of which owns the funds, and the other of which must perform the labor of production, the poor are undoubtedly dependent on the rich for employment; and since without employment, the poor must beg, steal, or starve, the rich may be said to be necessary to them. But this is the precise evil I complain of in the present social arrangement of wealth and labor. Let each man become an independent proprietor, and then the rich would not be necessary to the poor, in order to give them employment, for each man could employ himself on his own capital, and instead of working for another he could work for himself.

C. Every man does work for himself now. I do not know what you mean by this senseless clatter about every man's working for himself on his own capital. Every man does so work now. One man's capital is his farm, his workshop, or his store and goods, another's his ability to labor, the strength and activity of his limbs. In the great copartnership of society each man invests his capital, whatever it be, and receives his share of the gains. Some invest more than others, and therefore receive and ought to receive a proportionally larger share. You and I too form a copartnership when I employ you as a common laborer to plough, plant, hoe, or reap for me. You are not indeed an equal partner. Your investment is less than mine. You invest merely your bodily strength and activity, while I invest house, barn, outhouses, land, oxen, horses, sheep, and hogs, together with my own labor, bodily or mental. Now as my investment is more than yours, I ought to receive a larger portion of the gains. Your share is called your wages, and when you consider that in copartnerships of this kind, I have all the vexation and labor of superintending the joint concern, that I have to pay all the incidental expenses, run all the risk, and be responsible for all the debts, and to you also for your share, I think that you must admit that your wages amount to your full proportion. Certain it is, that many an employer would do well to exchange places with those he employs. They in fact often run away with all the gains, and seldom suffer when the concern is a losing one.

This matter of wages, about which workingmen have so much to say, is, after all, a thing beyond human control. A stern and unyielding necessity governs it. There is a natural ratio established between wages and the price of articles demanded for consumption, which no power on earth can alter. If wages rise, articles of consumption rise in the same proportion; if wages fall, then articles of consumption fall. Let the workingmen double their wages, and what they gain on the one hand they will find they lose on the other. They will have to pay double for everything they consume. When masons, and carpenters, and house-joiners rise in their wages, house-rent will rise; when house-rent rises real estate will rise in value, land will bear a higher price, and of course the productions of the soil. Flour must rise; the baker then will ask more for his loaf or make it lighter; and when the shoemaker must pay more for his bread, he will charge more for his shoes, and so it will be with all the trades. This shows in a clear light the fallacy of Strikes, Trades' Unions, and all combinations of workingmen for higher wages, which are seldom successful; and when they are, amount to nothing. In the transition from one price to another, the trade which gets the start of the rest may gain something, but as soon as one trade rises, all the rest will rise, and then things are as they were before. When a day's work will buy a bushel of wheat, and only a bushel, it makes no difference whether you call the price of a day's work sixpence or five dollars.

Ignorance of this fact does great harm. Mechanics in our cities become uneasy, they spend a portion of their earnings in the grog-shops, in oyster-cellars, in houses of prostitution, or in theaters, and finding what remains too little for their necessary expenses, they cry out for more wages, put the business part of the community to great inconvenience, often embarrassing them seriously, and subjecting themselves to loss of time and of money, when even were they to succeed nothing would be gained. No, Sir; these things must be left to take care of themselves. The partner who has the smaller investment must not expect to share equally with him who has the larger, much less to possess himself, as the workingmen seem to desire, of all the profits of the firm. Let the workingmen limit their desires to what is their due, and they will have justice done them; but if they can be satisfied only by having their share, and that which belongs to the other members of the firm into the bargain, then I must for one resist them, and if I fail, society will fail to exist.

Sir, let me beseech you to bear this in mind. A laboring man's capital is his bodily strength and activity, a kind of capital which is essential to the copartnership, but which is only an item and a small item in the immense amount invested. What that is entitled to out of the general gains let him have. He works on his own capital and has what he produces; with that let him be satisfied. Nobody wishes to wrong him. Tell him so, use your eloquence to persuade him to be virtuous, economical, to avoid haunts of dissipation, to keep clear of the theater and bawdy-houses, and you will do him a real service and deserve well of the whole community. Then you would prove yourself the workingman's true friend. I beseech you to do so, and forbear to say or do aught to stir up the laboring classes against the rich. Your present language makes me believe you a dangerous man. I beseech you to use a different language hereafter.

April

Conversation V

R. That was an ingenious argument with which you closed our conversation yesterday.

C. It must have shaken your theory a little.

R. Perhaps so. And yet it was not quite satisfactory. Every man, of course, should draw according to his investment; but since all men are born equal, will you be so good as to inform me how it happens, that one man, on commencing in life, is able to make a larger investment than another?

C. All men may perhaps be born with equal rights, but they are born with very unequal capacities.

R. And one's superior natural capacity consists in his having houses and lands, shops and tools, sheep and cattle, ships and merchandise to invest, while another has only his bodily activity?

C. I do not comprehend you.

R. You claimed in our conversation yesterday, the right to a larger proportion of the income of the copartnership existing between you and your hired man, on the ground that your investment was greater than his. I ask, how you were able to make this greater investment, and you virtually answer, that it is owing to the fact, that you were born with a capacity superior to his. Does this superior capacity of yours consist in the possession of more capital than he has?

C. My capacity is purely personal, and has no relation to my external possessions. But having this superior natural capacity, I have been able to accumulate more than he, and am therefore able now to make larger investments than he can.

R. You assume then, that the differences one sees in wealth among men, are all owing to the differences the Creator establishes in their natural capacities?

C. Certainly.

R. And since the Diety must have willed these different capacities, or he would not have suffered them, and since inequality in wealth follows as a necessary consequence of inequality of capacity, you infer that it is the will of Providence that some should be rich, and others poor?

C. Precisely. And therefore I contend that in seeking to bring about equality as to men's possessions, you are warring against God.

R. Some men I believe inherit wealth. These inherit, I suppose, because they are born with a superior natural capacity. The son of a rich man, then, has always a larger natural capacity than the son of a poor man?

C. I do not say that. Most of our rich men were poor men's sons.

R. And yet you tell me that all the differences, which exist among men in regard to wealth, are the necessary result of their different capacities. If you are right in this, it follows as a matter of course, that the children of the rich, who become rich by inheritance, inherit not because they are the children of the rich, but because they are born with superior natural capacities.

C. I claim no natural superiority of capacity for the children of the rich over the children of the poor.

R. Then I suppose you will modify your statement a little, and admit that those differences, which are introduced by the principle of inheritance, are exceptions to your general rule, and are not in fact the result of unequal capacities?

C. Very well.

R. I am aware that the differences introduced by the principle of inheritance are not all the differences or inequalities which do exist in regard to wealth; but still they form directly or indirectly no small portion of them. Now will you tell me on what principle you legitimate the right of inheritance?

C. What! Would you deprive me of my right to leave what little I may have saved from my hard earnings to my children? What! Would you rob my children of their right to inherit the estate of their father?

R. Nobody, my dear Sir, has any wish to deprive you or your children of any right which nature or nature's God may have given you or them. I am not among those who would do evil that good may come, or who would seek good at the sacrifice of right. Be just though the heavens fall!, is my motto. Prove that what you call your right, is your right, and I certainly will respect it.

C. Have I not a right to do as I will with mine own?

R. No, Sir; you have no right to use your property to injure your neighbor, your country, or your fellow-men anywhere; you have no right to use it for the production of a smaller good, when it is in your power to use it for the production of a larger. You are bound to be good, and to do good, and not only to be good a little, but in the highest degree possible; not only to do a little good, but the greatest amount of good possible. You see, Sir, that what you call yours, is by no means yours. You are in relation to all you call yours, but God's steward, and are bound in morals and in religion to use it as he commands, that is to say, in obedience to the commands of justice and love; and society has the right to force you to use it so. So it does not necessarily follow that you have the right to leave your estate to your children.

C. But my children have a right to inherit my estate. This is a right universally acknowledged, and sanctioned by the practice of every age and nation.

R. A right universally *denied* and sanctioned by the practice of no age or nation. The right of the father to disinherit, so far as my information extends, unless the Code de Napoleon furnish an exception, is universally admitted; and the right to disinherit negates the right to inherit.

C. But the hereditary transmission of property is a wise and judicious disposition of it.

R. Are you sure of that?

C. What is more natural or reasonable than that I should leave my property to my children whom I have loved, and whose welfare is dear to me? Or what is more natural or reasonable, than that my children should remain where they were born, amid the scenes of their earliest recollection, and enjoy what they had themselves assisted in accumulating? The hope of leaving something to our children stimulates our exertions, and the desire to labor for the welfare of our children purifies our affections, and makes us greater, wiser, and better. It is this which keeps society together. Take away the need of laboring for the welfare of our children, and their dependence on us for their support, and the family home is broken, isolation is introduced, and the very elements of society annihilated. Sir, the wildest and wickedest scheme devisable is that of the abolition of hereditary property.

R. I have not proposed to abolish it; I have merely asked you to show the justice of those inequalities in our social condition, which are produced by the hereditary transmission of property. But let this pass. I am not so confident as you seem to be, that the hereditary transmission of property is an advantage even to the children of the rich; nor am I by any means satisfied, that that portion of industry which is stimulated by the wish to leave my estate to my children is at all desirable. I have heard rich men say, that they considered it a very great misfortune for children to inherit a large property, and my own observation tends to prove that they are right. They who inherit property are rarely valuable members of the community. Moreover, children who are brought up in the expectation of wealth, of inheriting a fortune, rarely acquire moral and virtuous habits. They may have a blandness and grace of manners, fine taste in dress and equipage; but they have rarely the feelings of moral, accountable beings, who are placed here not for their own pleasure, but to be good and to do good; not unfrequently are they corrupted by indulgence, by their excesses, while still in early youth, and I have sometimes thought, that the rich father or mother might envy the poor widow the feelings with which she contemplated her naked, houseless, homeless, fatherless boy. These palaces of the rich, had they tongues, could tell us tales. These rich dresses, that we envy, conceal much.

Nor can I believe it desirable that a man should labor for the purpose of leaving a fortune to his children. While he is amassing the estate, in nine cases out of ten, his children are acquiring the habits which least of all fit them to use it. There was an old acquaintance of mine, Jack Turnpenny. Jack was a poor boy, brought up to the trade of a hatter, and worked some three or four years at hatmaking after he was of age. But he had no inclination to go through life as a mere mechanic. He felt that he was made to be a rich man, and that to be a rich man he must go into trade. He shut up therefore his shop, disposed of his tools, paid up his debts, and found himself at the age of twenty-five, in possession of just twenty-five dollars in money. With this capital he commenced business; after a few years, he was able with a friend to establish himself in one of our Atlantic cities, and also a mercantile house in one of the Canadas. The world seemed to favor Jack; he grew rich with great rapidity, and became a large importer from England, a wholesale dealer, a president of a bank, an alderman, an extensive manufacturer and woolgrower, and a heavy land-speculator. Thus was he when I first formed his acquaintance, some dozen years ago. He was a leading man in public affairs, a man of high standing, generally courted, and envied, and often pointed out as an instance of the extreme facility with which in our country a poor man may become rich. Jack heard me one day preaching my radicalism, and having, above all, known my father and been much indebted to him for his early start in the world, invited me to his house, and finally told me his story. He was now about sixty-five years of age, had been twice married, and had ten children, five by his first wife and five by his second. His eldest son, Frank, was a boy of bright promise, born with a high order of intellect, but his early education was neglected; his father was too busy to attend to it; and he fell early into dissipated habits; and though his father was liberal, his means were inadequate to his expenses. To help himself he broke into the strong box of an uncle, and escaped the penitentiary only because both father and uncle were rich and influential, and disposed to hush the matter up. The second son was established in business with a capital of forty thousand dollars in this very city where we now are. This capital he soon sunk twice over. His father recalled him, and obtained a situation for him in South America; but all to no purpose. He keeps him now at home, and regular by prohibiting all persons from trusting him, and by refusing him a single cent of money which he may himself control. His third child was a daughter, a sweet lovely girl, but she was married to a man she could neither love nor esteem, and with whom she would not live. His next two children were, one of them like the two eldest, a drunkard, and the other, having taken it into his head to be a preacher was externally decent. The rest were still young, but promising to follow in the footsteps of their seniors. "O," said he to me one day, "O, I have been a fool. If I had labored to train up my children in the way they should go, instead of laboring to leave them an establishment, I had not been desolate now in my old age, not compelled to go down in sorrow to my grave. I have ruined my children, damned them for time and for eternity. O, I have been a fool, a fool." Poor Jack, poor man, most wretched father, thou was but a type of what most of us are or would be. Thy story is less tragic than many that might be told. My heart clung to him, for he was miserable. He has gone to his long home now. His estate descended to his children, who have scattered it to the four winds, and who are, as you might expect, themselves, now little better than mere vagabonds. You, I presume, are a father; would you such a fate for your children?

C. Touch not that chord, I pray you. I *am* a father, and I too have a profligate son, but I hope to be able to reclaim him yet.

R. God forgive me, Sir; you too have grieved. Then there is brotherhood between us. May you be able to reclaim your son. But suppose you do, the end is not yet. There are few families in this country which retain wealth for many generations.

C. That I regard as one of the best features of our system, and proves that we can never have a large, overgrown, and overshadowing aristocracy. What one generation amasses the next disperses, so that the grandchildren of the rich man are generally the poor, while the grandchildren of the poor have their turn, and are the rich.

R. O, Sir, I begin to lose the respect for you that I felt a moment ago. Can your love descend no lower than your children? Have you no affection for your grandchildren? And is it not as great an evil for them to be left destitute, as for your children, their parents, to be so left? O, my brother, you are shortsighted and heartless. These poor grandchildren must not only endure their poverty, but their poverty must be deepened by knowing that their parents were once wealthy. It is not the least of our evils in poverty, to feel that we are poor and wretched, through the vices, the folly, the extravagance of our fathers. I am one of those grandchildren. My mother's father was a man of great wealth, and so was my father's father. My mother had eight sisters, and if I may judge from what they were in my early youth, they were women of rare beauty and accomplishments. The eldest married young, a worthy mechanic, and was disowned by her family, but being left a widow in about a year, was received into favor again. She married some two years after, an only son of a wealthy merchant. The son, expecting his father's property, made no exertions of his own, but lived for some twenty years in virtual poverty, when his father died, and bequeathed his whole estate to a stranger. Thus he was at the age of forty-five, with a wife and six children, with habits of idleness, unfitted for any kind of business, and not worth a groat. He could not endure it, and disappeared, and we have never heard of him since, now some twenty-five years. Her second sister married a foreigner, who professed to be a gentleman, who had great expectations, which were never realized. She was a beautiful woman, and possessed of an uncommon intellect. She has been a maniac for this twenty years, and he died a sot a few years since. My mother was the third daughter, possessed of wit, beauty, and feeling. Hers was accounted a happy marriage. But she was left a widow at the age of twenty-six, with five children, of which I, the youngest, was but a few months old. My father had become bankrupt, and the portion which was our due from our maternal grandfather's estate was seized by an uncle, who, under the character of executor, suffered none of it ever to come to us. A maiden aunt, a sister of my father, left me a small property, which enabled me to acquire a little education, and for a time to assume a decent rank in society. But that I have long since expended in my efforts at reform. Another of my mother's sisters, the youngest, I visited a few years since. She too had married the only son of a rich man; but I found her with a family of seven children, living in a miserable hut, with only one room not more than twelve feet square, in most splendid wretchedness. Her husband was doing nothing, would do nothing but wait for his father to die. The history of the rest is of a piece with what I have given. Of the nearly fourscore grandchildren of my mother's mother, now living, and whose history I know, not one is in the least benefited by the wealth to which their parents were born heirs. This, Sir, is merely a brief sketch of my own family. If you were to tax your memory, perhaps you might tell me as much.

C. I have no wish to make you my confidant. But is there not another class of grandchildren that have come up, whose story would be the opposite of yours?

R. Perhaps so; but what comfort is that to me and my cousins? Property shifts hands, I own; and there are constantly individuals rising and individuals going down; but alas, to go up is not happiness, and to go down is misery. This shifting of individuals, which seems to you so blessed a thing, serves but to augment the sum of the general misery. Every time that property is forced from the hands of one into those of another, there is untold suffering. We suffer if it is taken from us; and if we are those who take it, we suffer, if we are human, at the misery we occasion. No, do not talk to me of this system of compensations, which you conservatives applaud so much. Regarded as final, it but aggravates the wretchedness of the community. On this point I must read you an article which I find in one of the papers you handed me this morning. The first part of it bears on a point we discussed yesterday; the last part on the point now under consideration. It places the arguments you would use in a strong light.

Rich and Poor[2]

"'Never was an error more pernicious than that of supposing that any separation could be practicable between the interests of the rich and the working classes. However selfish may be the disposition of the wealthy, they cannot benefit themselves without serving the laborer. Let the rich proprietor improve his land; let him build houses or ships; he must employ the poor; and while it is thus certain that the rich cannot serve themselves without serving the laborer, it is evident that whenever the rich are injured, the laborer must suffer. If the laboring classes are desirous of having the prosperity of the country restored, they must sanction all measures tending to reinstate our commercial credit, without which the wealthy will be impoverished, and the needy be rendered still more necessitous.'"

—PROF. HARE

"'One of the features which society has presented within the last few years, the most fearful in its aspect, and destined if unremoved to be most disastrous in its issue, is its contentions and animosities, its divisions into parties, where the dividing line has reference not to policy or principle, but condition, where the poor are arrayed against the rich, the mechanic against the merchant, the laborer with his hands against the laborer with his head. In a community like ours, where arbitrary distinctions are not admitted, where the *fluctuations of families is a necessary law of the system, where the poor of today are the rich of tomorrow, the laborer of today the capitalist of tomorrow, where few can go back more than a generation without coming to an ancestry, poor in wealth, however rich and honorable in virtue, and could they look forward as far, would see perhaps a posterity poor in both these respects,* it seems strange that, in such a community, such a division should have ever been suggested or cherished.'"

— *Christian Examiner* for July, 1837.

"These two paragraphs, one from a Professor of Chemistry, we believe, in Philadelphia, the other from a grave Divine in our goodly city of Boston, may be taken by our readers as a demi-official statement of the views of the aristocracy concerning the points of social science therein touched upon. The truth of these views may not at first sight be perceptible to all readers; we must, therefore, be allowed to occupy some little space in elucidating and verifying them.

"The doctrine set forth in these paragraphs is, that the interests of the working classes and those of the rich are one and the same. This must be evident to all who are capable of seeing things as they are. We may show this by taking the instance of the horse and his rider. The interest of the rider is undoubtedly to ride. It is not for the interest of the horse, however, to be ridden, you may think; but you think so only because you are shortsighted, and see only the surface of things. The interest of the horse is a stable and provender. The stable and provender are in the possession of the rider, and the horse can obtain them only by yielding his mouth to the bit, and his back to the saddle, and by consenting to be ridden. If it be the interest of the horse to obtain a stable and provender, as it unquestionably is, then it is the interest of the horse to be ridden; and as it is the interest of the rider to ride, it follows irresistibly, that the interest of the horse and that of the rider are one and the same.

"Now the interest of the working classes is to obtain what corresponds to stables and provender for horses. But these stables and provender are in the *possession of the rich*, and can be obtained only by working *for* the rich. If, then, it be the interest of the working classes to have stables and provender, as it unquestionably is, then it is the interest of the working classes to work for the rich. The interest of the rich is of course to have the working classes work for them; consequently it is as clear as any demonstration in Euclid, that the interests of the rich and those of the working classes are identical.

"Now is disclosed the wonderful insight into the workings and nature of things—of horses and laboring men—possessed by this scientific Professor and this grave Divine. The one must have carried into the study of political economy the searching analysis which belongs to his favorite science, and the other must have availed himself of the up-gushing, and spontaneous wisdom so peculiarly characteristic of Divines, in order to combine the universe into one sublime synthesis, in which all variety is swallowed up in unity, and all differences of things, all diversity between the horse and the rider, the jackass and his driver, cease to be perceptible. It is wonderful!

"'Society,' says the *Examiner* in continuation, 'is to be surveyed as a whole, and the parts are to be judged by their relation to the whole.' If society have a top, unless it be the bottomless pit we read of, it must have a bottom; if it have a right side it must have a left side; rich men, it must have poor men; the high, it must have the low; riders, then the ridden. How absurd for the bottom to claim to be the top, the left side to be the right side, the poor to be the rich, the low to be the high, the ridden to be riders, (the horse would look well riding the man) one part to be another! Here, Jack, carry me over that mudhole, so that I need not wet my feet or soil my finely polished boots. What, won't you? Do you say it is not for your interest to carry me on your back through the mud? Nonsense. You are merely a part of a beautiful and sublime whole. You can have no interest contrary to, or separate from, any other part. I am also a part of this same beautiful and sublime whole, and it is my interest that you take me on your back and carry me safely over this mudhole, so that I shall not wet my feet or soil my finely polished boots. It being settled that this is for my interest, it follows as a matter of course that it is for yours. So no more words, but take me on your shoulders instantly, for I am in a hurry, and am beginning to grow cold. This reasoning must of course convince Jack unless he be a very dunce, as it must be admitted is the case with many people.

"Some plain folks might ask, how happens it that the rich own all the stables and provender in the world? and what's the need of their owning them all, so that the working classes can have none without laboring for the rich? But it is obvious that these questions are very impertinent; and besides, they may be answered, that if the rich had not all the stables and provender in the world, they would not be the rich, which is a manifest contradiction in terms. Should some ask, what need then of having rich men at all? let them be answered in turn, if there were no rich men, who would employ the working classes and give them stables and provender for their labor?

"If anybody should be so stupid as to allege that it is for the interest of the working classes to get as much stabling and provender for their labor as possible, and that it is for the interest of the rich to give as little its possible, and therefore infer that the interests of the two classes are necessarily hostile; they may be answered, that we have already proved that the interests of the two classes are one and the same, and the Professor thinks to maintain the contrary is the most pernicious error which can be entertained, and the Divine thinks nothing is more to be deprecated than such an error, and that the evils which flow from it are the greatest calamity that can befall a nation.

"Should some perverse minds still persist and maintain that the existence of the two classes, one rich and the other poor, is itself inconsistent with justice and republican institutions, that so long as the classes coexist in the same community they will be mutually hostile, and that instead of useless efforts to reconcile them we should do away with them, abolish the distinctions of class altogether, and thus have neither rich nor poor, the Divine is ready with his reply, the 'order of Providence makes great distinctions in individual condition.' The order of Providence makes the distinctions of rich and poor, and whoever would do away with these distinctions, wars against God. This reply must be satisfactory.

"If, however, there should be here and there a downright infidel, not having the fear of the clergy before his eyes, to arraign the justice of the Providence which ordains these distinctions, and which some are foolish enough to deplore, the sagacious Divine with a marvelous foresight, meets them with his 'System of Compensations'—a sublime system which, if he could make good his claims to it as originator, would secure him an immortality on earth hardly less desirable than that which awaits him in the world to come. This system may be illustrated in this way: Jack strikes Sam, Sam compensates himself by striking Dick; Dick by striking Jonathan, and Jonathan by kicking Obadiah, and thus on through the whole list of Christian names. It is a system which bears some resemblance to the old play in which every one is required to strike his next neighbor. It is possible, though we have no proof of the fact, that the Divine in question, may have been familiar with this play in his earlier life, and that he has taken the hint for his system from his reminiscences of it. Perhaps he may have taken a hint or two from his college recollections. Freshmen are usually (we are told, for thank God, by good fortune we escaped going to college) kicked about by the classes above them very much as they please; but in a year the Freshman enters a higher class and can then kick those below him, in like manner as he had been kicked before.

"This is a beautiful and consoling system. The kickee of today may be the kickor of tomorrow. My children are poor and slighted by my neighbor Longpurse's children; but my parental affection may be perfectly satisfied by the prospect there is that my grandchildren will treat his grandchildren as his children now treat mine. My father was rich and I am poor; but this same Mr. Longpurse's father was poor and he is rich; so I ought to be consoled for my poverty, and to count it a great blessing to live in a community where 'the fluctuations of families is a necessary law of the system, where the poor of today may be the rich of tomorrow, where few can go back a generation without coming to an ancestry, poor in wealth, however rich and honorable in virtue, and could they look forward as far would see perhaps a posterity poor in both these respects.' What blessed things these same 'fluctuations in families' must be! They are almost equal to the principle of 'Rotation in Office.'

"We hope our readers will make themselves familiar with this doctrine of 'Compensations.' We assure them it is thought very favorably of by quite a number of the Boston clergy, and Boston aristocracy. We are inclined to the opinion that it is the reigning doctrine of the city; if so, it is orthodox of course. It probably will require some learned dogmatist and scriptural interpreters to make it square with the great doctrine of love which lies at the foundation of Christianity; but Christianity is rather old fashioned and somewhat *passe* in our Metropolis. The doctrine of Compensations bids fair, therefore, to be in vogue for sometime to come. They who are the kickors are well satisfied with it, and as the kickees are hoping every day to get into the class of kickors, they will not contend very strenuously against it. It would be hard to rise to a kickor and then have nobody to kick."

> But to leave this part of the subject; I suppose you will admit, that our aim as parents should be the real good of our children. You and I both have children that we love, and that we would leave in the best possible condition when we are called from this world to another. You are rich. But are you sure that you will be able to leave your children rich? Or if you leave them rich, are you sure that they will continue so for any length of time? Or if they continue rich, are you sure that they will not abuse their riches, and prove themselves a curse to their generation? All these are questions which must pass through your mind. How do you answer them?

> C. I have not the surety you speak of. Man can be certain of nothing that is future. But I trust Providence, and hope for the best.

> R. Trust in your wealth, you should say. He who trusts in Providence, fears not to do right lest evil come to him or his. But can you conceive of no greater surety which it is possible to have than that you now have? To be brought up with the expectation of wealth, and not to receive it, is a serious evil; to have had wealth, and to lose it, is also an evil of no small magnitude. Now to both of these evils, your children or their children, as the world goes, are exposed. Would it not be better that wealth, instead of descending as now, and causing this vast amount of evil, which we can but deplore, it should descend by such a law that all, on starting in life, would receive an equal portion, and none more nor less than an equal portion? Then none would be brought up to expect greater wealth than they would receive; consequently no expectations would be disappointed. None would fare worse than the rest; consequently your children would fare as well as the best, and what more have you a right to ask for them? None would be rich; none would be poor; none would have enough to live without moderate labor, and none would have so little as to be obliged to live but to labor, as is now the case with the immense majority of our race. It would seem that under such a state of things, a man

might be down in the grave without a fear for the children he leaves behind.

C. So you would introduce a dead level! what do you suppose would keep society in motion under such a state of things as you imagine?

R. Hunger, if you can conceive no higher, holier motive. Men will be obliged to labor or starve and they will be willing to labor, for labor will be honorable, since all will labor; and pleasant, since it will be only what is needed for exercise.

C. Well, dream away, but for my part, I think your millennium would be but a "dull dunce."

R. You differ in opinion, I perceive, from the wise Agur, whose prayer we learned when we were children: "Give me neither poverty nor riches; feed me with food convenient for me; lest I be full and deny thee, and say, who is the Lord? Or lest I be poor, and steal, and take the name of my God in vain?"[3]

C. If you could abolish hereditary property, do you suppose that would cure all the ills of society?

R. By no means. It would, however, pave the way for curing many of them, and the greater part of those which now weigh the heaviest upon us.

Conversation VI

R. Bating the inequality in property traceable to the principle of inheritance, the inequalities we meet are fairly deducible, you think, from our unequal capacities?

C. Yes.

R. You told me the other day that you drew more than your hired man because you had made a larger investment that you had invested houses and lands, shops and tools, &c., while he had invested only his bodily activity.

C. True.

R. And did you inherit these funds of production, as we may call them, which you have invested?

C. No. I was a poor boy, and have nothing now but what I have worked hard for.

R. Then on commencing in life, your investment of capital was no greater than your hired man's?

C. No.

R. Then originally you were entitled to no larger a proportion of the gains of the social firm than he?

C. Well.

R. How comes it, then, if every member of society receives in exact proportion to his investment, as you allege, that you, beginning on a par with your hired man, are now able to invest so much more than he?

C. I have answered your question by suggesting the primitive inequality of man's capacities.

R. I am then to infer that you claim a natural capacity superior to that of your hired man?

C. Well.

R. And it is owing to this superior capacity of yours, that you are now richer than he? that you are wealthy and he is poor?

C. Well, go on.

R. And have you really *produced* so much more than he? or have you merely used your superior capacity in the *accumulation* of wealth?

C. In the accumulation of wealth unquestionably.

R. Do you suppose that you were ever able to produce by your own labor more than your hired man?

C. Probably not. At any kind of labor, he has always been able to do as good a day's work as I.

R. Then in point of fact, you probably have performed during your life no more productive labor than he? If then he had received all that he produced, and you had received no more than you produced, you would have been no richer than he?

C. Go on.

R. This being so, to what end has served your superior capacity? Has it served any other and than to enable you to pocket the proceeds of other's producing?

C. But you forget that I have furnished the capital on which they have labored, and my share has been no more than capital ought to draw.

R. But, my dear Sir, I have been for sometime trying to ascertain how you came, in the first instance, by this capital to invest. You began poor you tell me; when and whence did you, who at first were entitled to no more than your hired man, obtain the capital on which you could set him at work? In point of fact, did you ever begin to prosper, to do well, that is, to make money, till you began to obtain a premium on the labors of others?

C. Probably not.

R. The whole question comes then to this; your hired man has had merely the capacity to produce, and he remains poor; you have had what is called a business talent, that is, the capacity to transfer to your own pockets the proceeds of other's producing, and are rich.

C. Do you mean to insinuate that a man cannot become rich without robbing the laborer?

R. I mean to say, Sir, that no man can become rich by trade, when he could not by an equal amount of labor in the work of production, without robbing productive labor of its just reward. If the trader, starting with the same amount of capital with the ordinary laborer, can become rich, while the laborer working equally as intense, and for as long a time, must remain poor, productive labor does not receive what it is entitled to; for a man should receive no higher wages for making a bargain, or measuring tape, than the laborer for hoeing corn. But I am not disposed to continue this discussion today.

C. Why not?

R. Because were I to do it, I should say some harsh things, and disturb your digestion.

C. Well, and what then?

R. A disturbed digestion impairs the sweetness of one's temper, and renders him very disagreeable.

C. Have you a good digestion?

R. For the most part.

C. Other things than indigestion impairs the sweetness of one's temper, and renders him very disagreeable.

R. Not many, if any. I have known many a man praised for every virtue under heaven, who would have been counted a very devil, if anything had occurred to disturb his digestion.

C. Would you make a man's character depend on the state of his bowels?

R. I have just listened to a course of Graham Lectures, and I have resolved never to make up my opinion of a man's moral worth, till I have ascertained how he digests. Dive into the secrets of a man's digestion, if you would know the secret of his character. What noble schemes of philanthropy, what strong devotion, and what sweet temperedness shall not a fit of indigestion destroy! Wry actions as well as wry faces proceed from the gripes. You shall rise in the morning, break the heart of your wife, box the ears of your favorite boy, scold your most faithful servant, and wish your cook to the devil, and yet you shall be the best and kindest of husbands, the most indulgent of fathers, the most considerate of masters, and the easiest satisfied with the cook. Whence the contradiction? You supped on tripe or turtle-soup, and did not digest well. Your Alexanders, Caesars, Napoleons, Byrons, Dantons, are men of bad digestion, and the world is indebted to the irritation caused by their indigestion, for their famous exploits, whether good or ill, grand or pitiable. On the other hand your Shakespeares, Miltons, Goethes, Wordsworths, are men of a most excellent digestion.

C. And yourself? Shall I not place you among the indigesters?

R. That would be hardly just. And yet time was when my digestion was bad enough. Many is the time that I have been set down as an ill bred, snappish, passionate, ever-to-be-avoided fellow, simply because my bowels were not in a right state; and I can say with truth, that I have never in my life done aught to be ashamed of, save when my digestion had been disturbed. When I commenced my career, my health was poor, my stomach was out of order, and the gastric juice was not secreted; I was then melancholy by fits, sometimes a little crazy, but generally short and crusty; I was most of the time mad, mad with myself and mad with the world.

C. And have not got over your mad fit yet?

R. Surely I have not had much to cure me. The world has treated me but scurvily, and of the people in it few are entitled to my gratitude. Still, I am not what I was. My digestion is better. The world is less dark, and I find now and then a sunny spot, and the clouds which obscure my heavens are less dense, and here and there break away, and show a little blue sky beyond. O, Sir, it is most wretched to travel over this fair creation in company with the horrors of indigestion. My coat is coarse and threadbare, and my purse is empty, but it was not always so with me, and that it is so now, I am not ashamed. Humanity is perhaps the richer for my poverty. In my younger days I was a traveler; but a traveler, suffering from a bad state of the bowels. I found nothing to please. In this country the climate was too hot or too dry, in that it was too wet or too cold; in some countries the roads, the coaches, the horses, the drivers, the taverns, the cooking; in others the language, the manners, the soil, the flocks, and herds, the mountains and valleys, the forests and pasture lands, the thunder and the lightening, displeased me. Everywhere I found cause to complain, for everywhere taken for an Englishman, a circumstance which has since led me to imagine that all English travelers have a most miserable digestion.

C. But I can hardly believe that your digestion has much improved.

R. Yes it has. I look forth on Nature with other eyes. This is a glorious world. Everywhere does my heart leap to behold the beauty which surrounds me. The flowers delight me, and I turn aside my foot that I may not bruise the humblest that springs up spontaneously in my path. The birds soothe me with their wild notes, and hours do I lie in the shade listening to their gladsome song. I love Nature, for all begins, ends, and is informed with Love.

C. You forget this when you talk of the rich, and represent them as riding or eating the poor.

R. No; I do not. I love all animate and inanimate creation. All has a lesson and a charm. But I have a mission. I am called to espouse the cause of the laboring classes. I have studied their condition in this and other countries. My life is devoted to their service; for them I will live, and if need be die. My head is gray with my efforts in their behalf. I have grown old, though yet hardly a middle aged man, in seeking to elevate their condition. No matter; I devote myself to their interests without wrath or bitterness. It is not that I hate, or envy, or despise the more favored classes, that I proclaim myself the champion of the less favored; but because with the workingman is today the cause of Humanity. Humanity goes forward; through centuries it makes its way, overcomes one difficulty, surmounts one obstacle after another, gains one position and then another, and onward forever will it march towards its union with God. At other times its friends may have been called upon to contend for other specific objects. Humanity once required the Greeks to beat back the Persians at Marathon and Salamis, Alexander to overrun Asia, and mingle Western with Eastern civilization; at another, that the Socratic philosophy should be kept alive, that Judaism should be destroyed, Christianity installed, Rome overthrown, and the Barbarians of the North brought into the civilized family; at another, that Luther should defy the Pope, and philosophers vindicate the sovereignty of Reason, that kings should be decapitated, and nobility reduced to the rank of commoners; but now Humanity cries out for the elevation of the hand-workers, and that the *exploitation* of man by man shall cease. If then I speak for the hand-worker, it is because that he today is Humanity. His triumph is the triumph of the race. What Humanity will demand of her servants and friends tomorrow I know not. I only know what she demands today. I hear her voice, which is to me the voice of God, and

I dare not hesitate. I must speak. I am full of words, and I must utter myself. But if I speak hot, scalding words, words which go to the quick, it is because none other can do justice to myself, or to the work I am sent to perform. Grant that my words are exciting, that I provoke divisions, and set man against man, lead to a fierce, bloody, and protracted war, they proceed from love, they are full of love, and shall end in love, in love universal and perennial. But I speak in riddles to your understanding. You cannot comprehend me. To you I am a mass of contradictions which you cannot reconcile, a labyrinth of which you have not the thread, a riddle whose word is not given you. No matter. I cannot explain myself to you. A blind man cannot be made to comprehend colors. Men, good easy men of the world, are not they who can comprehend him of lofty purpose, solemn thought, and kindling enthusiasm, who feels himself called by an eternal voice to the achievement of a grand, a glorious mission. Ever must he be to them a contradiction and a puzzle.

C. Not at all. All the difficulty is removed by supposing the state of his digestion varies.

R. Right. That solves the mystery. Hence learn why I contend so earnestly for the improvement of the external condition of the laboring classes.

C. That you may support your digestion on something better, more substantial than cold potatoes and Graham bread, I suppose.

R. No. But because the state of a man's mind and heart depends very much on his digestion, and his digestion is intimately connected with his social position.

C. I am not prepared to admit that.

R. Say, then, merely that in this mode of being, the body, whether it be the whole body, the bowels, stomach, or brain, exerts a powerful influence over the mind. This everybody knows to be true. We also know that our external condition, and of course the kind of influence it must exert over the inner man. What I mean is, that physical circumstances do have an important influence in making up our character.

C. It is the man that makes the circumstances, and not the circumstances that make the man. The man who has any inborn nobleness of soul will rise superior to his external condition; he will make everything bend to the irresistible energy of his will. Besides, virtue consists in struggling with difficulties, and in rising superior to them, not in having them cleared from our path.

R. All this I understand. I shrink not from the struggle. I may have struggled as hard as most men. Do what we can and there will be the combat, and I admit that it is well that we all be inured to the camp. I have no hope of realizing in all its fairy features either the poet's dream of the golden age, or the saint's vision of paradise. Do the best we can, make all the improvements in our power, and earth will still bear a rugged aspect, a stern, forbidding brow; this world will always be a scene of trial, where the lesson to bear will never come amiss. But this is no reason why we should not remove as many obstacles as we can. There will always be difficulties enough, and nobody need fear that the time will come when there will be too little suffering. I have no fears of making the world so happy, so free from difficulties, that there will be no room for virtue. And besides, your definition of virtue, is only a definition of what is virtue under certain relations. Virtue consists in overcoming difficulties, only when difficulties exist. It is virtue to relieve suffering, but only when there is suffering. We must not suppose virtue becomes impossible when suffering ceases, for then what should we do in heaven? The saints would have no virtue. Virtue consists in the love and realization of goodness. The form in which it is to realize it necessarily varies with time and space, with circumstances. Virtue never changes its nature, but it varies its aspects and dress.

C. I understand nothing of all this.

R. I am sorry for that, but let it pass. We are here for improvement, for progress. We are here to be and to do good, and it is our duty to modify, change, or remove altogether, those external circumstances which prevent us from being or doing good, which continually lead us into temptation and abandon us to evil. Now, the inequality in men's external condition, in their social position, is the most fruitful source—I do not say of suffering, but of evil, vice, sin, depravity, which is known. There are few things of which we complain that have not their origin in this same inequality.

C. That it holds out many temptations I admit, but moral force, religious principle, would prevent its doing any harm.

R. To talk to a man suffering all the horrors of indigestion, of moral force, of religious principle, were talking to the insane man, of reason. This inequality throws men into a state in which you cannot bring religious principle or moral force to bear upon them. Religious principle, moral force, must be in the man before it can govern him or aid him. You must cast out the devil before you can form Christ within. Christ and the devil will not cohabit together. You have tried the experiment. You have preached religion and morality for ages, exhorted to virtue by a million of tongues trained to all the arts of persuasion, and what have you achieved? According to your own reckoning, though mankind were totally depraved at first, they have been growing worse ever since. What is the use of preaching religion and morality to the rich voluptuary, sunk in his sensual pleasures, when he is but doing that which everybody desires to do, and would do if he could?

C. I hope you do not mean to treat religion and morality with disrespect, especially religion, for without that society could not exist.

R. Have no fears on that score.—Would to God that you and your caste treated religion and morality with one half the respect I do. If ye would but practice them, instead of extolling their utility in keeping the lower orders in submission, I should be thankful. But man has a body as well as a soul, and though the soul is the most important, the bodily wants are first developed and should be first provided for. Give the beggar a supper before you preach him a sermon or read him a moral lecture, and a cloak before you lead him to church, if you wish to influence him. Take away the luxury of the rich, make them feel that they are no better, no more favored than the rest of the community, if you wish their real prayers to be different from his who stood and thanked God that he was not as other men.

C. You approach agrarianism now.

R. What then? Do you fancy that I am to be deterred from speaking the truth through fear of a bad name? There is no charm in names now to exorcise the spirit you dread. Men there are now who pass from words to things;—men there are too, who are not afraid to look Truth herself in the face, and to utter in a clear, distinct, and firm voice, her most startling words. Better beware of applying nicknames;—they sometimes become battle-cries. The wood on which you crucify the Reformer becomes the sign in which his successors shall conquer.

But, I am no agrarian, in the sense in which you use the term. Yet I am, as you well know, opposed to the present unequal distribution of wealth. Its consequences are most disastrous. It puffs up the rich with pride and the lust of the flesh, makes them false, hypocritical, atheistical; and it fills the poor with a sense of wrong, with envy, discontent, and useless longings; and I war against it, and will war against it, single-handed if I must, to the death, if need be. Sir, I am a follower of him, whose express mission it was to bring down the high, and bring up the low,—to level the mountain and fill up the valley, to make the crooked straight and the rough smooth and even.

C. What! Have you the audacity to pretend that Jesus preached such leveling doctrines as you do?

R. Ay, have I. Jesus was a sublime Leveler. Ay, I repeat it, Jesus was a sublime, a God-commissioned Leveler, and this is wherefore the common people heard him gladly, and the chief priests, the scribes, the Pharisees, the aristocracy of his age and nation, crucified him between two thieves. Why do you turn pale? Did you fancy that you had Jesus on your side? Were you dreaming of entertaining him in your gorgeous palace, feasting him on your sumptuous diet, and lodging him on your bed of down? Poor man! The young child was not found in Herod's palace, nor in the mansions of the rich, but wrapped in swaddling clothes and lying in a manger; and the Son of Man, when on earth, hath not where to lay his head. I see you are moved. Not to such as you is assurance given of being lodged at last by angels in Abraham's bosom; but of taking up your final abode in hell, with not one drop of water to cool your parched tongue. "Son, remember,"—these are the words thou must hear, "that thou in thy lifetime receivedst thy good things, likewise Lazarus evil things; but now he is comforted and thou art tormented." Ay, rage, if you will, but there is no alternative. You must either forsake Jesus, whose name you have assumed merely to take away your reproach, or submit to his doctrine, and become the bold and unflinching advocate of equality.

C. I shall advocate no such disorganizing, demoralizing, and leveling doctrines, as these you are putting forth.

R. Then take your place with the rich man in hell! You will not? No; nor would the young man, who came to Jesus to learn what he should do to inherit eternal life; *for he had large possessions.* You are too rich to be a follower of Jesus.

C. You wrong me. I aim to follow him, and I desire nothing more than to obey his commands.

R. Then go and sell what you have, give it to the poor, and follow him. What! Do you hesitate? *You* a Christian? Why, you have large possessions.

C. This is nonsense.

R. And did Jesus speak nonsense, when he said, "How hardly shall they that have riches be saved? Verily I say unto you, it is easier for a camel to go through the eye of a needle, than for a rich man to enter the kingdom of heaven?"

C. Surely you do not understand that passage literally?

R. Ay, it comes a little too close, does it? We must call in the priest to explain it away, must we? False hypocrite, a moment ago you were chiding me for my supposed want of respect for religion, and were pluming yourself on your orthodoxy; but who is the Christian now? Who now asks that God's word may be explained away, so that it may not rebuke his ungodly practice? There is the written word, the word uttered by him who was the Way, the Truth, and the Life, and whom you *profess* to take as your master. Do you believe him? Do you obey him? No; you know you do not. But you acknowledge him for your master, you own yourself accountable to him; go then and settle your disobedience with him as best you may.

C. But, I ask again, do you understand the passage you have quoted literally?

R. I am not wise enough, Sir, to revise the language of the Holy Ghost; nor am I base enough to be willing to use any portion of the ingenuity I may possess, in smoothing away the reproof his language necessarily brings to those who worship mammon and not God, and who prefer earth to heaven, or if heaven, solely for the gold which lines its pavements. You have priests enough, trained to the work of adapting the words of God to the peculiar state of your conscience, who, in honeyed tones, can sooth it, and with right reverend unction, allay remorse, and make the respectable sinner dream that God will think twice before he damns a man of his rank and standing. I, Sir, am no hireling preacher; I receive no fat salary for preaching so as not to disturb your slumbers in your softly cushioned pew. Nor is it my vocation so to preach. You are a rich man. You have become rich by the labors of others, by trade, by buying cheap and selling dear, that is, by cheating at both ends of the bargain; and Jesus tells you it is easier for a camel to go through the eye of a needle, than for a rich man to enter into the kingdom of heaven, and I leave you to draw your own inferences.

C. But can no rich man go to heaven?

R. Not if Jesus speaks truth.

C. Still, I cannot believe that Jesus meant precisely what you infer he did.

R. I understand him to assert that it was impossible for a rich man to have that spirit of self-denial, self-sacrifice, without which he could not be his follower, or engage with him, in effecting that new order of things, which he came to introduce and establish on the earth, and which is called the kingdom or reign of God. And I assert, today, that it is easier for a camel to go through the eye of a needle, than it is for a rich man to engage with me, in my efforts to establish the reign of justice and equality. In these efforts I have not the rich for my coadjutors. They have large possessions, and turn away sorrowful.

C. Your digestion, I fear, is somewhat impaired today. You are a illiberal, and altogether too censorious.

R. You rich men may call us laboring men, the rabble, the vulgar, the many-headed monster, the swinish multitude, the scum of offscourings of creation, and nobody cries out against your want of charity or good taste; but let one of us call you by your right names, tell you in plain, forcible words what you are, and forthwith your Christian feelings are outraged, we are thought to be exceedingly uncharitable, venomous, and—impolite. But I tell you, ye rich men, that while I scorn to feel the least bitterness towards you, as I would towards the worm at my feet, I regard you as worshippers of mammon, as servants of the devil, of whom a wise man will expect nothing, and over whom the good man must weep with bleeding heart.

C. Come, do not grow sentimental, my good fellow.

R. My good fellow! Who gave you the right to *fellow* me? Am not I a man, as well as you? And am I less a man because my coat is coarser, and my hand harder? My good fellow! So you dare speak to me, because I advocate opinions not in good repute in the gay saloons of the rich and fashionable. But were I rich and popular, you would stand in awe of me, and feel that you were unworthy to unloose the latchet of my shoes.

C. Forgive me. I meant no offense.

R. *Meant* no offense! That is the greatest offense of all. Had you *felt* the respect I am entitled to, you could not inadvertently have said aught improper. The offense is not in your words, but in the feelings which prompt such words, or suffer you to use them.

C. Say no more. It is foolish for you to be angry at my thoughtlessness.

R. *Angry at you?* Poor worm of the dust, do not flatter yourself that you can provoke me to anger. I can be angry only at him who is my superior, or at least my equal, and my equal you are not.

C. At least not in your aristocratic feelings.

R. Sir, I own that if by aristocratic feelings you understand a strong sense of one's own individuality, personal rights and independence, I have them in no small abundance, and should despise myself if I had not. I am as proud perhaps in my poverty, as you are in your wealth.

Of pride I complain not. Be proud, if you will, but be proud of what you *are*, and not of what you *have*. But if you *are* nothing to be proud of, do not fancy that such as I will respect your pride for what you *have*. I can look with as much contempt on you, as you can on me, and at the curl of my lip you shall feel as much as I at yours. Mine, Sir, in my estimation is not by any means the lower rank. I have not yet sunk so low as to esteem a little paltry pelf, which the moth may destroy, or the thief break through and steal, above true courage, nobleness of purpose, rectitude of heart, and the power to live, and suffer, and die for God and man. But all this is aside the mark.

You think rich men may be good men. I would I could think so too. I am willing to believe that few of them know what they are about, or are conscious of the iniquity of the system they uphold. Nor am I disposed to regard them in intention, touching the motives of their conduct, as at all worse than the rest of the community. There are few among us who would not be rich if they could, and by the very means adopted by those who do become rich. Yet, Sir, I hold that the possession of great wealth, the condition of the majority of mankind being what it is, is incompatible with Christianity.

Look over the world, Sir, behold the great mass of mankind, poor and ignorant, all directly or indirectly, laboring for a few capitalists. Their laborers, in the case of each one of them, are far more intense and continued for a far longer time than the labors of the rich, and yet obtain they but the minimum of human subsistence, and not always that. They dwell in darkness, and sit in the region and shadow of death. Is their enlightenment and moral and physical elevation a prime motive with you? Are you thinking of doing them good when you are compassing sea and land to grow rich?

Look too at these millions of young immortals daily coming into the world, and coming into the world too to run the same hopeless career of their parents. These young beings are born with noble natures, with capacities for all the eloquence of feeling, the sublimities of thought, and the majesty of virtue,—of binding themselves by the sweet ties of love to their kind, and by gratitude and reverence to their Maker. Yet on them no star of science ever rises; no day of hope ever dawns; the infinity of their nature lies shrouded in night, and they grow up with low thoughts, base feelings, and groveling propensities; with no eyes for the beauty which everywhere blooms around them, no ears for the sweet music which eternally rings out from all nature, and no heart for the bounty which is strewed on either hand, even to profusion. To them, nature and nature's God, this rich and glorious universe, on which I could gaze eternally and find fresh delight, must lie forever colorless and obscure—a mere vacancy. For them there is on earth nothing but to delve to live, and live but to delve. O, my brother! Can you behold them born and dying, and ask for them nothing better? Was it for such a fate God created and sent them hither?

C. I should be very glad to see those children decently educated, and fitted for usefulness and happiness.

R. On you and such as you we depend for the means of educating them, and putting them in the way of attaining their glorious destiny. You have all the wealth of the world, and what do you do for these young immortals? What sacrifice do you make for them? Of what comfort, nay of what luxury you desire for yourself or family, have you ever deprived yourself, that you might benefit them?

You call yourself a Christian, and deem me censorious, uncharitable, venomous, when I tell you that you are no Christian. Now, Christianity is easy to come at. It commands us to love one another as Jesus loved us. We are to love the poorest, the meanest, the vilest of God's offspring, well enough, if need be, to die on the cross for them, as Jesus did for us. You are no Christian unless you love these laboring masses, these ignorant and wretched children, born to no inheritance but toil, ignorance, misery; unless you feel a craving for their welfare that will enable you, though rich, to become poor for their sakes, and though held in honor to become of no repute, that you may breathe hope into their chilled hearts, and strength into their stiffened limbs, and life into their souls so long dead. You must feel a longing for their moral, physical, and intellectual elevation, that you shall live but for them, and find your meat and drink only in securing their redemption. Is this the case with you? Is it your constant study, how you may benefit them; your constant, burning desire to dissipate the night that hangs over them, and usher them into the glorious liberty of the sons of God? Why do I mock? You know that you have felt nothing of all this. You can live in luxury, tread on the rich carpets of Turkey, tinge the light of your halls by the purple silks of

India, and feast your palates on the dainties culled from every clime, while at your next door, the poor mother, pale and emaciated, sits watching over her starving boy. You a Christian! You spending your thousands for your own gratification, steeped in selfishness, caring for the poor and needy only to use them for your own advantage, *you*, a Christian! *You* hope for heaven! God Almighty, why then didst thou make a hell, and threaten the sinner with eternal vengeance: If there be a being on earth infinitely removed from Christ, it is he who in this world of wailing and woe, listens to no calls but those of avarice; in this world of suffering, degraded Humanity, is intent only on growing rich; in this world of poverty and dependence, studies the condition of the poor and dependent only for the purpose of making them the instruments of increasing his own wealth and importance. And such are our rich men. Were you to find yourselves in the possession of wealth, if you had the spirit of Christ in you, how long would you continue rich? He, though rich, for our sakes became poor, and though entitled to reverence as a god, for our sakes made himself of no reputation. If you had his spirit, you would soon impoverish yourselves that you might enrich Humanity, and make yourselves of no reputation, that you might rise up the poor and needy. But you do not this. The rich never can do it and continue to be rich. The rich have not then the spirit of Christ. If they have not the spirit of Christ, then are they none of his; and if none of his, on what can they rest their hopes of acceptance with God?

I pass over now the means by which men become rich; I say nothing of the widows they despoil and the orphans they rob; I say nothing of the sweat and toil, the hunger and nakedness of the poor slave that toils to feed their avarice; I say nothing of the wrongs of the poor sailor, who braves the tempests of man's passions, to bring you the rich stuffs out of which you coin your wealth; I pass over all this, and confine myself solely to the use you make of your wealth, when once it is accumulated. I charge you with using it for yourselves, when you should use it for Humanity. I charge you with selfishness. You amass wealth to gratify yourselves; you hold it to feed your own vanity; you spend it for your own pleasure; you have no love of your race; no deep, burning desire to redeem man. You are cold and heartless; as polished it may be, and as impenetrable as marble. You worship the Respectabilities. You may build the tombs of the prophets, and garnish the sepulchers of the righteous, but you leave the Son of Man, who comes to redeem his race, not the stone whereon to lay his head. You contemn the just and seek to impede the progress of the righteous; the man who loves his race you count your enemy, and the prophet of God a child of Satan. You take the name of Jesus on your lips, you build him costly houses, you pay liberally his professed ministers, you dress his altars in purple and scarlet, and with gold and silver, but your heart's incense you withhold. God is not in all your thoughts; your faces never look upward to heaven; your eyes are cast down to the earth, and your souls have become of the earth earthy. Man of wealth, worm of the dust, who fanciest thou art somebody, and deemest thou hast a right to look down as from heaven upon the poor and needy, the toil-worn and the weary, speed on thy way. Speed on thy way; trust in thy shining dust, in thy respectability and high standing, and commanding influence over thy brother clay; pass on unheedingly by the houseless and friendless, or cast them a penny to make their wretchedness more palpable; but know that for all this God shall bring thee to judgment. Ere thou art aware thy career shall be cut short, and thou shalt be ushered into the presence of thy Judge. There, poor and naked, must thou stand in the full blaze of eternity, and be seen and judged as thou art. There thy wealth will stand thee in no stead; there will be none to applaud thee for thy sins, because the sins of a rich man, a man of property and standing; there thou wilt receive the contempt thou deservest for having lived for thyself alone, the derision thou meritest for having fancied that *thou* wast the center of the universe, and that all things should conspire for *thy* good. Go. I can endure thy presence no longer.

Conversation VII

C. Are you aware of what you do, when you charge the vices of individual character to the inequalities of our social condition?

R. I charge to society what you probably charge to the individual. The depravities of individual character originate in the depravities of the social state much oftener than in the perversity of the individual will. I therefore seek to reform society as one of the means of reforming individuals.

C. You place the cart before the horse. You should seek to reform individuals as the means of reforming society.

R. That is, take the end in order to obtain the means. Society is not ultimate. Its improvement is never to be regarded as an ultimate good. The proper object, and the only proper object, of pursuit, is the perfection, or the perfecting, of human nature, in each and every individual. The perfection of society is useless after this perfection is once attained. Your notion, although a common one, is unsound. Society was made for man, not man for society. Man is paramount to society. Society is subordinate and subservient, or should be subservient, to man. It has no value aside from the aid it gives man in developing and perfecting his nature. That social state in which every individual has free and full scope for the harmonious development and play of all his faculties, is a perfect social state. The present social state is imperfect because it does not give this free and full scope, and just so far and no farther than it does not give it.

C. But it is sheer folly to talk of a perfect state of society without perfect individuals.

R. And not the less so, to talk of perfect individuals in an imperfect social state. An imperfect state of society, can turn you out only imperfect characters.

C. Not so. Man is not dependent for his virtue on the state of society in which he lives. He can attain his growth under all circumstances, and prove himself worthy of himself, in spite of circumstances. The truly great and good man grows but the more luxuriantly, the more adverse his circumstances. All that which the world most dreads and pronounces the greatest of evils, he bends under him, molds to his purposes, or converts into the means of enlarging his greatness or his goodness. No, Sir; virtue comes from within, not from without; and place it in what light you will, it is but the victory of the Inward over the Outward.

R. All this is very fine, very eloquent, and would be very true, if men only were good and great; but of what avail is it to him who is neither one nor the other? The question is not, what one in whom human nature is already largely and harmoniously developed may do; but how it is to be developed in all its energy and glory in those in whom it is now underdeveloped, or but imperfectly developed. Give me the self-control, the energy of will, the moral force, of your man who masters all outward circumstances, and I too will bend all nature beneath me, and compel it to minister to my virtue; but in case I have not this self-control, this energy of will, and this moral force, how am I to get them? Here is the point which you wise men of the church and the world overlook. Certain it is, that a large proportion of mankind are deficient in this moral power, and yet you address them all as if they already had it. Their vice consists in their not having it; and yet you tell them to make use of it as the means of curing their vice!

C. You do not state the case correctly. All have it.

R. If all have it, all do not exercise it; if it be in them it is undeveloped. How shall it be developed?

C. Nothing tends more to develop it than these very evils of which you complain. God permits this to be a world of evil as well as of good, that the evil may be the means of calling forth our moral force and enlarging the sum of our virtue.

R. Theory is worthless when unsupported by experience. In some cases the sufferings of this world unquestionably improve the character of the sufferers; but not in all. In a large majority of cases they have a most deteriorating influence. Poverty, sickness, grief, misfortune, suffering of whatever name of nature, usually hardens the heart, blunts the sensibility, sours the temper, and makes the subject of it harsh, peevish, morose, and selfish.

C. It is people's own fault if it do have that effect. They do not make the right use of the afflictions which God sends them.

R. But does that remove the difficulty? Grant that it is their own fault, the question is varied, not answered. How shall we cure them of that fault? The insane man, were he only so considerate as to exercise his reason, would at once be rid of his insanity; but, unhappily, the inability to exercise his reason is his insanity. No doubt men would get along very well, were they only to make a right use of evil; but their inability to make a right use of evil is the greatest evil of all. How will you enable them to make a right use of evil?

C. They can do it if they will.

R. But suppose they do not will, how will you make them will? But is it quite certain, that if they do will, they will be able to perform? There are some limitations to this omnipotent will of ours, about which some folks take it into their heads to talk so much. A fit of indigestion, a mistake of your tailor in the cut of your coat, a blow on your head by an angry fellow, shall suddenly bring to nought one of the finest omnipotent wills imaginable. You may will, but a stronger arm than yours may hold you back from the performance. The drunkard, sober today, resolves, with the whole energy of his soul, that he will never drink again; but he shall find the first gay fellow who invites him to a social glass able to upset his omnipotent will. You may throw away your tobacco-box, and swear in the very depth of your being that you will never taste the nauseous weed again, but two hours shall not elapse before you buy another and roll the sweet morsel in your mouth, say your omnipotent will what it may to the contrary. Alas, we are feeble omnipotents, when a little indigestion, a glass of toddy, or a chew of tobacco can make us forswear ourselves, change our firmest resolutions, and do precisely what we willed not to do! We are free to will; we may will as we please; but to do, to perform—that is quite another affair. There is a stern Necessity which, while it leaves To Will unfettered, binds To Do in a chain of adamant. We are bound, and struggle as we may, we cannot break our chains. We would do good, but evil is present with us; and the good that we would, we do not, and the evil that we would not, that we do. We have all felt the struggle between the freedom of the will and the necessity which controls our actions. Everywhere do we meet resistance; on every side are we hemmed in, and every moment, though rising to heaven in our wills, are we dragged down to hell in our deeds.

C. Where now is what you have said of man's greatness, his godlike nature and tendency? You seem to have a most wonderful facility in contradicting yourself.

R. So you may think; but the contradiction you remark exists not in my words, but in human nature. Man is at once great and small, wise and foolish, strong and feeble, a spirit and a clod of earth, a god and a devil. If you fix your eye on one side of him, you are struck with his weakness, his nothingness; if on the other, you are equally struck with his greatness, his sublime faculties and godlike tendencies.

What I have just said of his weakness is true, too true, as our daily experience proves; but it is not the only truth, by no means the whole truth. Under certain relations the human will has great energy, and seems all-conquering and unconquerable. Yet the power, we then ascribe to the will, is more properly the power of Faith, which brings the will into harmony with the primordial laws of the universe, and strengthens it by all the forces of Nature. "If ye had faith as a grain of mustard seed," said Jesus, "ye could say unto this mountain, be removed and planted in yonder sea, and it should obey you." I am far from being able to prescribe the limits of full, undoubting, unwavering faith. Faith is thaumaturgic in its nature, always a miracle-worker, and if we could only undertake with a calm and full confidence of success, I have little doubt but the meanest of us might work greater miracles than any recorded in history. "If ye believe," says Jesus, "ye shall do greater works than these."

There is something in the power of faith, which my philosophy has not yet fathomed. By it one's eyes are often opened, and he seems to penetrate the profoundest mysteries of the universe even to the essence of the Godhead. We mark it in all our undertakings. Whatever we attempt, nothing doubting, we are almost sure to accomplish. Let me desire as a public speaker to produce a certain effect, and let me have full confidence that I shall succeed, and I am sure not to fail. Let me utter a sentence with my whole soul absorbed in it, confident that it is going right to the hearts of my hearers, and it goes there, and they are electrified. Whenever I am conscious in what I am saying of this calm, undoubting faith, I am sure of my audience. I no sooner open my lips than I have them at my command, and I can do with them as I please till I cease speaking. More than this; when I have felt this faith in what I was about to utter, I have felt even before uttering it, its effect upon the assembly, and my whole frame has been sensible of something approaching an electric shock, and that they and I were connected by a sort of magnetic chain. In conversing with a friend too, in whom I have full faith, and to whom therefore I can speak with entire confidence, I have felt the same. Our souls seem to be melted into one, to move by one will, and each is strengthened and exalted by the combined power of both. Then we rise into the upper regions of truth, far above the unaided flight of either. Heaven opens to us, and we behold the hidden things of God. Something the same is felt when one goes forth in love with nature, and yields to her gentle and hallowing influence. We inhale power with her fragrant odors, and become conscious of loftier thought, of nobler feelings, and we form holier resolutions. Our very eyes glow with a brighter flame, our countenances assume a heavenlier hue, our frame becomes instinct with life and energy, and our step free and firm.

C. Nonsense! What seems to you so wonderful and mysterious, is nothing but the power of sympathy and imagination.

R. Will you be so good, Sir, as to explain to me what this power of sympathy is, and this power of imagination? Let us not fancy that we have removed our ignorance by giving it a name. I know that this power, is under one of its aspects called love, under another sympathy, under another imagination, under still another faith; but what it is in itself I know not. Be it, however, what it will, it is daemonic, supernatural, an element in human nature, of which men in all ages have caught some glimpses, but of which we have as yet had only glimpses. I do not pretend to understand it. I stand in awe of it both when manifested in myself and in others. I regard it as the link which connects man with his Creator, and in it we may yet perhaps discover the secret of his redemption.

The history of our race bristles with prodigies. These prodigies were once accounted miracles, and supposed to be wrought by the finger of the Divinity; now, an unbelieving age treats them as impostures, cheats, fabrications, proving nothing but people's love of the marvelous, and the ease with which they may be gulled. I believe them for the most part real. I believe that there are times when man has a power over the elements, and may make the spirits obey him.

Who knows but the time will come, when the law by which this power operates will be discovered, and this power, which has been hitherto irregular and transient, will become common and regular in its influence; and therefore bear the marks of a fixed law of nature?

But, this power, be it what it may, is by no means identical with the human will, nor is it, in my belief, strictly speaking a property of human nature. It is an overshadowing, an allpervading Power, most likely identical with the Power that creates and sustains the universe. We avail ourselves of it, not because it is ours, but by placing ourselves in harmony with it, or so that it flows as a mighty current through us.

Now, although I by no means comprehend this power, I find in its reality the principle of all my efforts at reform. By its light I proceed, and by its aid I hope to be able to set the human race forward towards a higher and a more glorious destiny.

Man is a complex being, the junction of two forces. He is both active and passive; he acts and is acted upon. His power to act is what I term the will. This, the proper human power, is unquestionably a reality, and must be exerted; but it is not alone sufficient. As a mere individual relying on my own strength alone, I am a feeble creature, and my strivings come to nothing. I will nobly, but perform pitiably. My will, that is, my own activity, must be brought into harmony with the activity of the universe, so that what in me are the active and the passive, free will and necessity, may conspire to the same end. When you would erect a mill, for instance, you so erect it as to bring the forces of nature to bear upon and drive your machinery. In all handiwork our study is to do the same.[4] So in all our moral workings, our aim should be to place ourselves in such attitudes that the moral forces of the universe shall work for us. "I can of mine own self do nothing; but through Christ, strengthening me, I can do all things," is the testimony of an inspired apostle to the doctrine I would establish. When once by love, sympathy, faith, I have placed myself in harmony with the law of the universe, that is, the will of God, my will is reinforced by the will of Omnipotence. Then nature, man, God works in me, for me, and I can do all things. The elements then are mine; the winds are my messengers, and flames of fire my ministers; for it is no longer I, but God himself that works.

This must explain to you the contradiction you have pointed out. Man acting alone, as a mere individual, is weak and pitiable; in harmony with his race, with nature, with God, is the sublime and godlike being I have called upon you to love and reverence.

Understand now the first principle of all real reform. You must study to place yourself in harmony with the law of the universe, and to avail yourself of the moral forces everywhere at work in it. The law of your race, the law of nature is a transcript of the will of your Creator. Whenever you overlook the factitious distinctions of men, and place yourself in harmony with the law of Humanity, you are in harmony with God, and act with his might to reinforce yours.

Reformers are weak and inefficient, because they go forth in their own strength, because they act from their own individuality, without regard to the will of God as manifested in the fundamental law of human nature. They have then for their aid nothing but their own individuality, which is the essence of weakness. You can do nothing for man in opposition to the law of Humanity. Write if you will a book; bestow upon it all the labor, the strength of intellect, and power of genius you can, and it shall be counted a small affair, unless it meet, in some degree, the sympathies of the race, embody some of the views and wishes of mankind. It is purely idiosyncratic in its character. It may be read for the purpose of ascertaining your idiosyncracies, but for nothing else. It will exert no influence; it will not fasten itself on the public mind, and become an integral part of it. You alone produce it; it is your book. The human race does not assist at its birth, and will not contribute to its growth. No man, who stands alone, repels his race, and acts in opposition to them, can be a great man or do great things, however great he may be as an individual. A great man is one whom everybody conspires to make. If you cannot enlist the cooperation of your race, make yourself the focus in which are concentrated all their thoughts, wishes, sympathies, hopes, and fears, you had better give up the idea of being a great man. You cannot be a great man in spite of your race. You can do nothing unless you can secure the aid of your fellow beings. What could have been in Washington, or *who* could have been a Washington, without the cooperation of his race? Or a Napoleon, had he not succeeded in securing the cooperation of the party in favor of New Institutions? So long as Napoleon could secure that cooperation he was invincible.

He lived and acted in concert with Humanity, and was the center and outlet of the general will. As soon as he lost that and sought merely an individual, a selfish good, what was he? The battle of Waterloo may answer. When Humanity cooperated with him, we called him a great man; he appeared able to do whatever he willed; he overran Europe in mere pastime, took an empire with the ease with which one takes his dinner, made and unmade kings with less trouble than one shifts his dress. But the power he wielded was not his, but Humanity's. Would you learn the power of the individual Napoleon, the energy of his will as a simple individual, go see him on his Rock in the Ocean, quarrelling with his jailor about the quality of his wine. All men, as individuals, are pitiable creatures, the good and great no less than the bad and little. You can be nothing unless you can avail yourself of the cooperation of Humanity.

To bring us or to enable us to come into this harmony, there are two forces of which we must avail ourselves. The first is our individual will, or voluntary striving, the other the influence of society, understanding the word society, in its largest sense, together with its institutions of whatever name or nature. This is the influence on man from without. The voluntary strivings must be of two kinds, or have two different directions. In the first place we must strive to get the command of ourselves, and to bring all our wishes, purposes, feelings, passions, into harmony with the law we are to obey. This is what is enjoined upon us by the clergy, and moral reformers generally, as contradistinguished from social reformers. In this we may do something, but not much, as the history of six thousand years abundantly proves, and as our own experience of the weakness of our wills but too clearly demonstrates. The other direction of our voluntary strivings must be towards society, to the molding of the institutions which act upon us. This is the direction taken by the social reformers proper. But I, who am never satisfied with anything exclusive, contend for both, and would always combine the moral reformers with the social. As a moral reformer, I must study to harmonize my own moral nature; as a social reformer, I must aim to make all the influences, which come from without, push us towards the destiny we could accomplish.

If we look at the world as it is, we shall find that the social influences, which act upon us, have a corrupting tendency. Society, as now organized, tends to develop the lower propensities of our nature, and to unfit us for obeying the higher law of Humanity; stimulates from the first the passions to which we cannot yield without moral degradation. All, or nearly all social tendencies, of which we are now the victims, serve to stimulate the three passions of love, ambition, avarice. To enjoy love, in its lowest sense, to become distinguished and famous, to obtain large possessions, are what we are impelled to by the books we read, the examples we see, and the influences to which we are subjected. These are so early developed in us, that if we have any largeness of nature, we are never able in after life fully to control them. If we are weak beings by nature, possessing the faculties common to our nature only in the mediocre degree, we may pass along without running into any excess, or experiencing any great difficulty in maintaining what is called self-control. But if we have rich natures, the various tendencies which belong to our nature, in their highest degree, if we are born nature's noblemen, with the strength and energy of faculties to distinguish ourselves from the common level, we either waste our lives and suffer the tortures of hell in seeking to restrain our passions, or we run into guilty excesses, and create the impression, that a great man is almost necessarily a great sinner.

In fact all the influences upon us from without are deleterious, and deprive us of moral strength, just in proportion as they stimulate our passions. Temptations are soon thick around us. We are beset on either hand by enemies to our virtue. We are weak and in want of help. This help society does not give. She multiplies these temptations, reinforces our enemies, then leaves us to the combat, and punishes if we do not conquer. She smooths the road to hell, and makes that to virtue steep and rugged.

> "facilis descensus averni:
> Noctes atque dies patet atri janua Ditis:
> Sed revocare gradum, superasque evadere ad auras,
> Hoc opus, hic labor est."

Nearly all the instruction we receive tends to give the world, the flesh, and the devil dominion over us. In our infancy we are hushed by falsehood, or quieted by baubles; in youth our brains are drilled out by the priest and pedagogue; and in manhood dried up by intercourse with the world. From earliest childhood we are accustomed to see things valued in an inverse ratio to their real worth, place, wealth, or fashion control the many, and to find regarded as the nobility of the race not those who labor honestly and efficiently for mankind, but those who have been most successful in love, avarice, or ambition. A poor man who gets tipsy is brought up before your city police and fined or sent to the house of correction; a rich man may get drunk in his own house and be carried to his bed he knows not when or how, and yet be counted a gentleman. He who kills but one man is a murderer; he who can kill or cause thousands to be killed is a hero; and everything else in society is of the same stamp. Is virtue possible,—I mean virtue beyond the virtue of intention,—is virtue possible in such a state of society? He who would be strictly honest, unless he have some capital in advance, must beg or starve. Men live by cheating,—grow rich by cheating,—high-minded, honorable men, by cheating. A man, by way of commerce, may rob, make poor, a thousand widows and orphans in some uncivilized island of the ocean and yet be one of our first and most respectable citizens. And if, out of his superabounding wealth, he give a few hundreds to some benevolent society, as old sinners formerly made donations to the Church, he shall be praised in all the public prints, and held up as one whom every young man should study to imitate. He who by some strange mischance finds himself encumbered with a conscience somewhat tender, and disposed to inquire into the rectitude of his doings, is counted a mere simpleton by the business world. Go into a bank, a broker's office, a factory, or into any of your legislative halls or courts of justice, if you would ascertain what are one's chances of being virtuous in society as it is. Or go into the charmed circles of Fashion, or into one of your popular churches, if you would learn the temptations to sin, which society furnishes and will furnish as long as it remains in its present half-civilized state. Fashion makes people afraid to act themselves and enjoy themselves in their own way, lest their fashionable acquaintances *cut* them; and the church makes them afraid to think freely and utter themselves honestly, lest they be turned out of the synagogue, and sent to hell before their time.

C. Come, come, man, you are growing crazy.

R. Would to God I were crazy. Would to God the evils I see were only the visions of my own disordered fancy. Would to God that all I have uttered were but the ravings of the madman. But I fear, Sir, that I am but too sane. I fear that it will be found that what I say is but too true. I shall not be believed now. I know my fate. I know I am doomed to utter prophecies that will not be believed. Yet I must speak. I must lay down my burden, however bitterly I may weep to foresee that it will be disregarded. No matter. I speak not in wrath; I blame not individuals; I know human weakness; I know what men have to combat, and my heart bleeds for them. If, as I glance at their conduct, I sometimes find my mind growing dark and perplexed, and a curse rises in the bitterness of my soul to my lips, I check myself, and lay the blame to systems and not to individuals. Individuals are our brothers; they are made as you and I are; they would do good; the basest of them kindles up at sight of the disinterested and the heroic; the most abandoned love virtue, and long to return to their Father's house and hold communion with the wise and good; but alas, the temptations to sin are too strong; a false standard of worth, a wrongly organized society, mischievous social influences hurry them onward and downward to hell. O, Sir, I would not censure a single human being as an individual. I know not what struggles may have torn the bosom of that poor brother they are dragging to prison, on whom that iron door is soon to be closed and those bolts are to be drawn. I know not how those whom society brands as felons, may have struggled to be good and great, and till I do, I dare not condemn them. The hardened villain, as he was called, who, a few days since was choked to death by law, may have started in life with a noble ambition, with warm and generous sympathies, looking forward to be one of the greatest and best of the human race. Had his heart been responded to by society, had he found the influence needed to bring out in full glory and omnipotence the infant god within him, who can tell what he might not have been? Who can tell the efforts he had made, the good resolutions he had formed, and the anguish he had suffered, the fire which had burned within him, the hell which had consumed him! O, if the hearts of those, we must condemn, were laid open to our inspection, could we but see their workings, examine their scars, and judge of their conflicts with sin and the devil, and know how a word, a thoughtless word, a discouraging look, a temptation thrown in their way by that very society which condemns, hangs, or imprisons them, has proved their ruin, overpowered them, sunk them, as the feather too much broke the camel's back, my life on it, we should find infinitely more to commiserate and forgive, than to condemn and punish.

And yet, Sir, do not fancy that I am a whit more charitable than I was yesterday. I admit men are weak rather than wicked, and the depravities of their character I am too disposed to charge to the depravities of the social state, rather than to the perversity of their wills; nevertheless they are not wholly blameless. Man is not wholly a passive being. He can act as well as be acted upon. If circumstances act upon him, up to a certain extent, he can act upon them, and so modify them that their reaction upon him shall be salutary. I blame individuals, not because they cannot, by a mere effort of volition, make themselves highminded and virtuous beings; but because they do not exert the moral power given them to mold society, so that it may be in harmony with the higher laws of man's nature. I blame you, Sir, as a rich man, that instead of making the social influences to which you are exposed favorable to the growth of moral excellence, you have been intent merely on amassing an estate. I blame the learned and the gifted, because they devote their learning and gifts, not to the improvement of man's social condition, but to their own aggrandizement. I blame politicians and statesmen for their selfishness and neglect of the true end of government, the elevation of man.

C. And what would you have these men you blame attempt for the elevation of man, as you term it?

R. Much. But I am fatigued now, and you must wait for my answer till I am disposed to give it.

Social Evils and Their Remedy II

JULY 1841

We have never pretended, and we do not now pretend, to be able to point out any specific remedy for social evils, or to show how a series of causes may be put in operation, which shall prevent their recurrence.

In the greater part of what we have written in the pages of this Journal, as well as elsewhere, on the subject of social evils, our main purpose has been to bring the subject itself distinctly before the minds of those among us, who give tone to thought and direction to affairs, and to engage them in its serious and earnest consideration. The remedy itself we have expected only as the result of time, and the general activity of the public mind directed to its discovery.

But the subject has finally begun to arrest the attention of the community. Throughout the whole length and breadth of the land, men's minds are busy with it. The problem has come up, and will not down till its solution, at least to a partial extent, is found. We may, then, now desist from our efforts to provoke discussion, and proceed to discuss. The audience is assembled, and a calm, dispassionate, philosophical discussion will now be listened to with eagerness and respect.

Though we confess, in the outset, that we have no specific remedy for social evils to bring forward, yet we feel competent to indicate the method the inquirer must take in order to find one, and the law by which it is to be applied. And this we proceed now to do so as briefly and as clearly as we can.

The end the Reformer contemplates, and seeks to gain, is the production of harmony, the realization of order in the bosom of the individual, between the various elements and tendencies of his nature, and in the bosom of society, between its several members, and between its members and itself.

The power which we have for accomplishing this end is our activity, or free-agency. This power may or may not be adequate, but it is all that we have, and we can go no further than it can carry us.

But we may make of our activity a twofold application, and realize the end sought, directly, by efforts to control the appetites and passions; and indirectly, through institutions, by efforts to make them bear on our passivity, and, so far as we are passive beings, aid in molding us into the sort of beings we should be.

Moral and religious teachers rely chiefly on the first application of free-agency. They proceed on the ground, that direct efforts of free-will in the interior of man are adequate to the realization of order, let external institutions and influences be what they may. They have proceeded on this ground for six thousand years, and with results, which ought ere this to have convinced them that they were guilty of some mistake. In our appetites and passions, from which all disturbing forces proceed, there is at work an activity, which, strictly speaking, is not our activity, and which ours can at best control only to a limited extent. "Evil communications corrupt good manners." Institutions, moral, religious, social, civil, and political, have an almost irresistible influence in determining our characters. Within certain limits they are absolute, and mold us in spite of ourselves. Instead, then, of exhorting men to be what they ought to be, or wasting ourselves in fruitless efforts to make them what they ought to be, in spite of these institutions, against the resistance they offer, we should modify, alter, or reconstruct them, so that they shall aid in the production and maintenance of the individual character desired. We cannot carry the river over the mountain, for the law of gravitation is against us; but we can tunnel the mountain, and then the same law of gravitation which before was against us, will operate in our favor, and cause the river to flow in the direction we wish it to flow.

In plain words, the doctrine we would lay down is this: Individual character is the result of the combined action of free-will and necessity, and is to be made what it should be mainly by the efforts of free-will not to overcame necessity, but to avail itself of necessity; as in constructing a mill we avail ourselves of the law of gravitation to drive our machinery. The problem to be solved, then, is, how to modify institutions, whose action on us is that of necessity, so that they shall always aid the growth of individual virtue and happiness.

This problem can never be completely solved. The harmony, the order we are in pursuit of, may be approximated, but we are far from believing that it can ever be fully attained. There is a necessary antagonism in human nature itself, which must forever balk and baffle our wisest and most strenuous efforts to realize perfect peace and harmony in either the bosom of the individual, or in that of society. Man is in his nature a limited, that is, an incomplete, an imperfect being. He has in him elements of growth, of progress, but not of perfection. He can, then, never become, in the strict sense of the word, a perfect being. If he could, he could become God. Society has its root in human nature, can never surpass the capabilities of that nature. These capabilities reach to progress, but not to perfection; consequently, while we may hope for a continued progress of society towards perfection, we must, forever despair of its attaining to perfection.

Man has a twofold nature. One set of instincts and faculties, which center in himself, and another set, whose center is out of himself. By the first set, he is an individual, is affected by what immediately concerns himself, and induced to look out for himself, to assert and maintain his own personal rights, interests, and dignity. By the second, he is rendered social, capable of binding himself by love and duty to others, and of becoming self-denying, disinterested, and heroic. Between these two sets of instincts and faculties, there is, and there must be, in the very nature of things, antagonism; consequently, the struggle, the combat, the victory, the defeat. This antagonism will reproduce itself in society, and render the struggle there as permanent and as fierce as it is in the bosom of the individual.

Both of these sets of instincts and faculties, or elements of our being, are in their nature indestructible and essential to man. The individual element, the abuse of which is selfishness, is not less essential to man than the social, disinterested, or heroic. It is the element of liberty and of progress. If destroyed, or denied its legitimate scope, the individual is no longer regarded; his well-being is neglected; all individuality expires; society becomes supreme, and exerts the most absolute and galling sway over all her members. On the other hand, if we destroy or neglect the social element, the disinterested, the heroic, we have no social bond, no union, no cooperation, no mutual assistance, no protection for even individuality itself. For all individuality being exclusive, infinitely repellent to every other individuality, each would seek its own gratification at the expense of another; one would prey upon another, the stronger would oppress the weaker, and we should have but one unvarying scene of wrongs and outrages, tyranny and slavery, anarchy, confusion, and war.

Every scheme of reform which overlooks or neglects either of these elements, as well as every scheme which proposes a perfection beyond the capabilities of human nature, must prove abortive, and be merely a monument to the want of practical wisdom in its author.

This fact Reformers are prone to overlook. For ourselves, we have never yet seen a scheme proposed for either individual or social reform, that did not either neglect one or the other of these elements, or contemplate a perfection, to which neither human nature nor human society can attain.

Mr. Fourier has given us an example of a scheme of this latter sort. His scheme, as ably and faithfully developed in Mr. Brisbane's interesting and valuable volume on the Social Destiny of Man, is ingenious and striking, and at first view attractive, and even plausible. He recognizes the antagonism which actually obtains in both the individual and society, and proposes to get rid of it by harmonizing the passions. His scheme may, therefore, be called a scheme of *passional* harmonies, to be produced not by denying, destroying, or subduing the passions, but by affording to each its legitimate gratification. This would, no doubt, succeed, were man only a perfect being, or capable of becoming perfect. Were he so made, that all his passions could be gratified, and so that he would always be satisfied when the passions had attained their special gratification, a scheme of passional harmony might be contemplated with some degree of practical wisdom, as well as with enthusiastic hope; but man, from the very fact, that he is and always must be imperfect, incomplete, is incapable of having all his passions harmonized. He is a musical instrument, that can neither be put nor kept in perfect tune. He was made for progress. Progress consists in overcoming disharmony; and unless it is one day to cease, implies that disharmony can never be entirely overcome.

Moreover, each passion seeks its own special gratification, and can rarely obtain it without thwarting another. It is impossible, for instance, to harmonize benevolence and the love of accumulation; for one finds its gratification in giving away, the other in acquiring and hoarding. Nature, again, is no economist. She secures her ends by an excessive expenditure of means. The end she proposes to secure by any given passion is always good and sacred, but in order to secure it, she lavishes the passion in excess. Take the passion of love, given to secure the continuance of the species. Wherever this passion exists in sufficient strength and activity to ensure the end for which it was given, it exists in a degree which would push us beyond that end. It demands more than the other elements of our being, without self-denial, can yield it. Restrain it, and it rebels, and makes a disturbance; let it go unrestrained, it becomes morbidly active, destroys the equilibrium of the passions, and both the moral and physical well-being of the individual. And what we say of this passion, we may say of all the passions.

Nor is this all. There is no passion satisfied by possession. Each has a tendency to enlarge its desires in proportion as it obtains. On wishes, wishes grow, and one demand is no sooner complied with, than another and a larger is made. The harmony of all the passions is, therefore, out of the question.

The harmony of the passions, so far as attainable, is to be obtained not by gratifying the desires of each, but by denying to each its special gratification, whenever its special gratification would lead to disorder, either in the bosom of the individual or in that of society; that is, by following the Christian rule, deny thyself, which we shall find but poorly substituted by Mr. Fourier's rule, please thyself. In fact, the pleasure of self-denial often exceeds that of indulgence. But in all self-denial there is antagonism.

Mr. Owen's community scheme is an example of a different sort. It has some good points. It recognizes the influence of institutions, of "circumstances," in forming our characters, and for this it deserves commendation; but it overlooks several essential elements or wants of human nature. In denying the innateness and indestructibleness of the religious element of man, Mr. Owen proves himself a careless psychologist, and a superficial philosopher. This element is essential to man, and is one of the stronger elements of his being. No scheme of society is practicable, that neglects it, and none were desirable, even if practicable. It must have a prominent place in every plan of social reorganization intended to be acceptable to the race, or permanent and beneficial.

Mr. Owen also neglects activity, free-agency, and, therefore, strictly speaking, man himself. In his scheme, man is the mere creature of circumstances. He has, then, in himself, no active power. He cannot create or modify his Creator. What, then, can he do by way of reform? By denying free-agency, Mr. Owen denies the very instrument with which he must work, and without which it would be absurd to call upon man to be a reformer. Man is active as well as passive, and can act on and mold circumstances as well as they him.

In contending for a community system, Mr. Owen depresses, if he does not wholly destroy, individuality. He seizes on the social or communal element of our nature. This is, unquestionably, the element of union, order, justice, peace; but, when taken exclusively, it makes the community everything, the individual nothing; establishes the absolute authority of the community, which cannot fail to degenerate into practical tyranny, under which both liberty and progress become impossible.

The right of property is denied, too, by his scheme of a community of goods. A community of goods cannot coexist with property; for all property is individual, exclusive. The tenure by which property is held in some countries, and the mode of its transmission and reappropriation in all, may need some important modifications; but the right to property itself is one of our primitive rights, and is, therefore, sacred and divine. Properly speaking, man never feels himself man, till he has something to which he can point and say, "that is mine; touch it not, save as I give thee leave." It is idle to war against this right, for it is indestructible in the human soul; it is wrong to do it, because we should respect all the rights of man, and because its recognition and security have been and ever must be a powerful agent in advancing civilization.

Mr. Owen, also, in our judgment, errs, by denying the necessity of marriage laws. The actual laws on marriage, in most countries, may, doubtless, need some ameliorations, but the continuance of the marriage relation cannot be left to the discretion of the parties interested, with safety either to society or the parties themselves. Marriage is not a mere private agreement, nor civil contract even, but also a sacrament, and should, therefore, be placed under safeguard of both religion and law. The passion usually most active leading to marriage is good and holy, as are all the passions; but reason and morality are not sufficient to keep it within bounds. All the passions have a tendency to grow tired of what is familiar, and to crave, what is novel. Make the continuance of the marriage relation a mere matter of caprice, as it would be, if all laws on the subject were abrogated, and it would not be seldom that we should find a man divorcing the wife of yesterday to take another that strikes his fancy today, who will be equally distasteful tomorrow, and must in her turn give way to another.

Doubtless there are evils, to which married life is now subject, that it were desirable to remedy. Marriage is not always that solace and relief to man's estate it should be. We have ourselves, on a former occasion,[1] entered our indignant protest against the unhallowed restraint which society exercises over the indulgence of the affections. But the evils complained of are the result of causes which operate before the marriage law takes effect, and are deeply seated in the artificiality of the present social organization,—in its family pride, its factitious distinctions of blood and fortunes, which interrupt the natural course of young affection, and but too often make marriage a mere legalized prostitution, a mere contrivance for uniting families and estates, or for acquiring a fortune. Abolish your factitious distinctions, do away with your gross inequalities of fortune, educate and refine all your children, make honest industry honorable, and so profitable, that a young couple may always feel that they will be able to secure a comfortable living by their own labor, and that too *without losing caste*, and the evils now complained of will in a great measure cease to exist.

Mr. Owen, paradoxical as it may seem, relies too much on reason and morality. But these are feeble barriers against passion in its vehemence. We have these now, and law to boot, and yet passion laughs us in the face, not seldom bids us defiance, and goes unwhipt of justice. They may do for those who are naturally frigid, and or those who are "too old to sin," but to rely on them alone for the, great mass of mankind, were to open the door to unbridled lust, and its whole desolating train. We should do all in our power so to reorganize society that it shall minister no unnatural stimulus to the passions, but we should also stand ready with law in our hands, to whip them back whenever they undertake to leap their bounds.

This leads us to the conclusion, that they who contemplate reforming society without the aid of government, or introducing a state of society in which government will be superfluous, are also far remote from true practical reformers. This class of reformers are becoming somewhat numerous in our own community. They are a class for whom we have great respect, and among whom we reckon some of our warmest personal friends. They admit the present existence of the antagonism of which we speak, but they think that by a judicious system of moral, intellectual, religious, and physical culture they can overcome it.

But have they reflected on what condition and at what cost they must overcome it, if they overcome it at all? They have a lively sense of individual rights, and they regard government not only as superfluous, but as an unjust restraint upon individual freedom. Now individual freedom and well-being are promoted only by what are called the selfish instincts, or rather those which lead the individual to assert and maintain his own rights and dignity. We have seen already the result to which we must come, if we take our point of departure in exclusive individuality. Exclusive individuality destroys all individuality, because one individuality cannot tolerate another. You must then control individuality by bringing up the social element. But in order to control it, or rather as some friends propose, subdue it, you must give supremacy to the social element. You must weaken the sense of individuality, and strengthen the sense of society. Now if this be done so far as to get rid of all antagonism, it is done only by the entire suppression of individuality. This would be, if successful, so to enfeeble, to emasculate man, that he would be utterly incapable of fulfilling the functions of his being. He would no longer seek to provide for himself, to prolong his own existence, or even to contribute to the continuance of the species.

To this extent the suppression of individuality is impossible. The element will survive all efforts to destroy it, and exert itself legitimately or illegitimately. The practical effect, therefore, of the effort to destroy it and dispense with civil government, would be to reestablish a theocracy, the worst and weightiest of all tyranny. The success of our no-government friends, on either hand, would be their defeat. Seeking freedom, they would find slavery; scope for individual, activity, they would find themselves without power to act; progress, they would obtain immobility; relief from the burdens of civil government, they would be pressed to the earth by the overwhelming weight of the hierarchy.

These reformers proceed on the ground, that what they term the lower nature of man is too active. They regard, whether aware of it or not, the selfish instincts as immoral; and they place morality in the exclusive exercise of the social, the disinterested, the heroic. These are the higher nature, those the lower. The lower should submit to the higher; and government is now necessary only because the lower are *unduly* active. Government, has, therefore, its necessity in human wickedness, and of course must become unnecessary just in proportion as men become upright and moral. This is the view taken of human nature by all theocrats, and is the view on which are founded the claims of supremacy set up by the church. This view, taken exclusively, depresses the body, the state, all material interests, and exalts the soul, the church, and spiritual interests generally. It generates mysticism, asceticism, contempt of the world; builds monasteries, nunneries, and establishes the unlimited authority of the priests. The evils of its dominance may be seen through all past history, and in all countries still subjected to a theocratic government.

For ourselves, we protest against this exclusive spiritualism. The soul is no more holy than the body; and morality attaches necessarily no more to the exercise of what is called the higher nature, than to what is called the lower nature. We may be as moral in the exercise of the functions of the body as in the exercise of the functions of the soul, in yielding to the selfish instincts as in yielding to the disinterested. Morality is predicable only of the *motive* with which we act; it matters not whether the *mobile* to act be furnished by one set of instincts or another. The selfish instincts, as they are called, are neither effects nor evidences of the Fall, but are as primitive in man and are as necessary to make up the glory and excellence of his character, as the disinterested and heroic. They should not be cursed, nor should there be any effort to get rid of them. According to Christianity the antithesis between body and soul, insisted upon by the old religions, is done away, and now we should write "Holiness to the Lord," on everything. Man's whole nature rightly exercised, is alike holy.

The selfish instincts, within their legitimate sphere, are as worthy to be obeyed as the disinterested and benevolent; and it is necessary for the well-being of both the individual and the race, that they be always the strongest and most active. The good of the whole is best provided for by making each individual the special guardian of his own.

But if these instincts be the strongest and the most active, the others will be too weak to control them, and to prevent one individuality from occasionally encroaching on the equal individuality of another. This encroaching neither the individual nor the race can tolerate. Both morality and utility demand its suppression. Hence the necessity of society for perfecting the individual,—society, which may be defined the union of all for the protection of each.

Man has primitive and indestructible wants which crave society and lead to it; he has also instincts essential, as we have shown, to his very existence, and to that of the race, which must be stronger and more active than those, that demand the supervision and control of society. These too are permanent and indestructible, and consequently create a permanent demand for social supervision and control.

But social supervision and control is government; consequently government has an eternal necessity in the permanent and essential nature of man. Society is needed to maintain, in all its entireness, the equal individuality of each and every of her members; and government is the force needed to enable her to do this, and to enable the aggrieved party to compel her to do it, in case she neglects or refuses to do it.

Now as the great work for the social reformer is to provide for the maintenance to each and every individual to his entire individuality, and as this can be done only by society, and by society through government, so far from being an obstacle to reform, a superfluous machine which we should throw aside, is in fact the great and indispensable agent of reform. They, then, who are warring against government, are warring against themselves, throwing away the arms without which their defeat is certain. Instead of advocating their no-government schemes, they should plunge into the science of politics, acquaint themselves with practical statesmanship, and turn the purity of their hearts, the intelligence of their minds, and the enthusiasm of their souls to the work of making government what it ought to be.

We have arrived now at two important conclusions. 1. Man is to be perfected in society; and 2. Society is to be perfected, that is, enabled or compelled to discharge its office in perfecting the individual, by the agency of government.

It follows also from what we have said, that the office of society, so far as concerns our present inquiry, is to maintain for each individual member his entire individuality. This implies the maintenance not only of one individuality against another, but also of the individual against society itself.

The maintenance of each member of society in his entire individuality, is what is commonly meant by maintaining equal rights. But the phrase equal rights does not necessarily cover the whole ground. Rights may be equal without being entire. Society may maintain equal rights, that is, the same number of rights to each of her members, and yet to no one all his rights. She may maintain all the rights of one individual in relation to another, and yet deny to all their rights in relation to herself. We prefer, therefore, the statement we have adopted, which means, for us, all the rights with which the individual is endowed by his Creator, whether they relate to other individuals or to society.

In contending, that it is the office of society to maintain each and every individual in his entire individuality, we of course reject the old doctrine, that the rights of society are made up of the rights surrendered by individuals. Men on coming into civil society do not surrender a portion of their rights for the sake of enjoying the remainder, man comes in, if the expression *comes in* be allowed, for the purpose of having all and every of his rights protected, even to the minutest and apparently the most insignificant. Every member of society, that is, every citizen,—and every one who is properly a man should be a citizen, has the right to demand the protection here implied, and society fails in her duty, whenever she fails from any cause whatever to afford it.

The rights of the individual may be invaded in two ways. 1. By the encroachment of one individual upon another. 2. By the encroachment of society herself. The practical political problem then is, how to organize civil society, or how to constitute the government, so as to afford an effective guarantee to all against this double invasion. Government, to meet the exigencies of the case, must be an instrument in the hands of society for protecting one individual against another, and in the hands of individuals for protecting themselves against the encroachments of society. It must then be a contrivance for governing society as well as individuals.

A contrivance of this sort it is not easy to find. It presents the only really difficult problem in political science. Some have thought they found it in monarchy, some in aristocracy, some in democracy, and others in various combinations of these, or in what they have termed mixed governments. In this country the popular solution of the problem is the democratic. We fancy that we find in democracy the form of government needed, and that if we so arrange matters, that the will of the people can always make itself felt and obeyed, all rights are sure to be protected, and the interests and well-being of all secured.

But democracy, as popularly taught, affords the citizen no protection against society. By democracy, as a form of government, is understood generally that form of government in which the people, taken as the state or body politic, are supreme, and may, if not morally, at least in point of fact, do whatever they please. The state is then absolute, and you have an unlimited government, just as much as you would have, were your government an unlimited monarchy. Minorities and individuals have nothing but the wisdom and justice of the majority on which to rely. They are at the mercy of the sovereign, and have no resource if he choose to play the tyrant. Here is no true liberty, no effective safeguard for individual freedom, no power in the hands of the party whose rights may be invaded, except the good pleasure of the invader, with which to obtain redress.

We speak here of democracy in its absolute sense, and solely as a form of government. Democracy, when understood to mean the end that government should seek, to wit, the maintenance of each individual in the free and full possession of all his natural rights as a man, is unquestionably the creed of every true American, and as one of our distinguished scholars has well said, "practical Christianity;" for in this sense it realizes in our social and political relations the end enjoined by the fundamental principles of the Christian religion. But the growing tendency of our countrymen is to understand by democracy a form of government in which the majority, the absolute numerical majority, may rule unrestrained. The government of this country is regarded as resting solely on the will of the majority. In the words of the late President of the United States, "a breath of the majority has made and can unmake" it. Hence we hear of the "democracy of numbers," and are told on high authority that the "democracy of numbers" is the only intelligible democracy. Then the majority is always the democracy; the party in the majority is always the true democratic party, and the principle and measures of the majority are always democratic principles and measures. Majorities are perpetually shifting. The minority of yesterday is the majority of today, and of course what was anti-democratic yesterday is democratic today, and will be anti-democratic again tomorrow.

There is among us a strong tendency to sweep away every institution, every organic form, whether in the executive, judicial, or legislative branches of the government, which may have heretofore interposed an obstacle to the free and full expression of the irresponsible will of the majority. Every amendment proposed or adopted of any of our civil constitutions has a direct tendency to throw additional power into the hands of the party, which chances to be in the majority, and to remove some safeguard from the minority. The whole spirit of the American people, not of one party only, is to sweep away all barriers to the establishment of absolute democracy, which shall cause the government in its administration to feel and respond to every wave of public opinion, or popular caprice. This is easily accounted for, and is by no means an unnatural tendency; but it is perhaps time to inquire whither it is likely to lead, and whether it is likely to increase the security we demand for individual rights?

We are aware that there is growing up among us a feeling, that majorities can do no wrong, but we have not yet satisfied ourselves that this feeling has any warrant in theory or experience. Majorities, for aught we can see, are as liable to err as minorities. The truly wise and just man not seldom finds himself obliged to desert the majority, nay to stand alone with his single breast against an opposing world. Not seldom is he jeered and scoffed by the multitude, his name a by-word and a reproach.

Our democrats, however, contend that the interests of the majority are in point of fact identical with the interests of the minority, and therefore if the majority can actually be free to promote their own, they will of necessity promote the interests of the whole. All that is necessary, then, is universal education, which shall enable all to see and comprehend their rights and interests, and the measures necessary to secure them; and universal suffrage, by which every man shall have a voice in determining the action of the government. This is plausible, but nevertheless unsatisfactory to those who look at things as they are.

Admit for the present, that the will of the majority, freely expressed, and rendered effective, will secure to every individual the free and full enjoyment of all his natural rights, still universal suffrage coupled even with universal education of the most approved pattern, will by no means secure the free and effective expression of the actual will of the majority. The actual majority of our countrymen are the laboring men. But universal suffrage secures not the expression of their views, convictions, and wishes. They almost uniformly vote against themselves, not through ignorance, but what is to them a moral necessity. They must have employment, or they and theirs must beg, steal, or starve. This employment they feel that they can obtain only by voting with the small minority on whom they are dependent for it. They dare not vote independently, lest they lose their employment; and consequently they are in elections little else but the servile tools of their employers. This fact is notorious, and it is no uncommon thing for a working man to shift his politics with his employer. Political leaders usually count, as so many votes for their party, the number of voters in the employ of their friends. The friends of the workingmen see and lament this, and seek, vainly, to get rid of the evil by means of the secret ballot.

But waiving this, there is another obstacle, if possible still greater. We suppose that all democratic communities will divide themselves into parties, especially if under the régime of pure, unmixed, unlimited democracy, and usually into two parties of nearly equal strength. There are permanent causes for this division in the antagonism of which we have already spoken. Whatever measure is carried, must then be carried by means of a party. If your party be not in the ascendency, you cannot carry your measure. Your first study must then be to secure the ascendency of your party. This can be done only by means of union and concert among all its members; and union and concert can be obtained only by establishing and respecting what are termed party usages. These usages will require you to support the measures and candidates of your party.

But these measures and candidates are rarely determined on by the spontaneous voice of the whole party. They are determined on by the few more active partisans, usually designated party leaders. These cut and dry the policy of the party. The party may not approve this policy, but it must adopt it, or endanger its success, and give ascendency to the opposing party; which will generally be regarded as the greater evil of the two. A majority of the more active members of the party, therefore, adopt what their leaders propose, pass resolutions in its favor, and rally the whole party to its support. The party, we will suppose, succeeds, elects its men and carries its measures. Are these measures really carried by the majority of the whole people? Are they in truth expressions of the actual will of the majority? Not at all. They are in truth only the expressions of the will or the policy of the active minority of the party, which is itself but a lean majority of the whole people. If the actual opinion of those who in both parties are really opposed to them could be collected, you would not unfrequently have an overwhelming majority against them. In point of fact, what we call the decision of the majority in this country, is rarely anything more than the decision of the active or adroit minority which controls the party, that for the time being chances to be in the ascendant. Universal suffrage then, coupled with universal education, cannot secure even the expression of the will of the majority, to say nothing of giving us assurance that the will of the majority shall always be just and right.

Nor is this all. Government, as soon as it goes into operation, divides the community into two classes, and creates an inequality, and an opposition of interests between the few and the many. It collects its taxes from the whole people indeed, but it pays them out to the few. These few consequently receive more from the government than they pay to it; and the many consequently lay more than they receive from it. The interest of the many is to pay as little as possible, and of the few to make them pay as much as possible. The few are, by their position and their relation to the government, constituted a plunder party, and they are induced by all the force of selfishness, which always increases by what it feeds upon, to make the government an instrument for plundering the people to the greatest possible extent. These few have the command of the government, for they are the small minority governing the ruling party. Now against these plunderers, these wielders of the whole organized power of the community, what are single individuals, however independent in their suffrages, or however moral and enlightened in their aims? They are as the reed before the blast. They may be trampled on with impunity.

It may be said that they may denounce the party in power, raise the cry of "retrenchment and reform," and bring up and bring in a new party. Be it so. The chiefs of the new party as soon as in power will constitute a new plunder party, more greedy than the last, because they have for some time been keeping Lent. They will find "retrenchment and reform" difficult. The business of the country is increasing, new settlements are springing up, population is enlarging, interests and relations are multiplying, and demanding a larger number of public officers and additional expenditures. Every new party coming into power among us comes in on the cry of "retrenchment and reform;" but alas! each new one proves itself more burdensome than the last.

The security we demand for individuality, therefore, is not to be found in universal suffrage and universal education, good and indispensable as both unquestionably are. No unlimited form of government will answer our purpose; because every unlimited form of government establishes the absolute rule of society, and therefore deprives the individual of all guarantee for his individuality,—placing him entirely at the mercy of an arbitrary will, and as much so when it is the will of the many, as when it is the will of the one or the few.

The individual, however enlightened and moral, we have seen is too weak to withstand the cupidity of the plunder party, which the party of the government always is, and always will be. He alone cannot protect his rights, or compel society to do it. In order to protect him you must league him with a part or a portion of the community, which shall make common cause with him, and have the power to arrest the action of government the moment it invades or threatens to invade his rights.

The framers of our institutions have not altogether overlooked this. They have sought to protect minorities and individuals, by the separation of the functions of government, into three departments, each in the main independent of the other; by dividing the legislative branch into two houses; and by the adoption of written constitutions defining the powers of each department, and of the whole government. They have had a horror of all absolute governments, and have sought to limit the government they established. They were wiser than we commonly present them, and many of the checks and balances they introduced, which we are warring against, are of no small use in protecting minorities and individuals in their rights. They sought, in one word, to establish a CONSTITUTIONAL government, a government of limited powers, containing in itself a power of arresting its own action whenever disposed to transcend its legitimate bounds.

This idea is fundamental and just. Constitutional government is the only government under which there can be any real liberty, any effective safeguard for the rights, the individuality of the citizen; and it will be a sad day for us, when in obedience to monarchical, aristocratical, or democratical tendencies, we are led to abandon constitutional forms of government for an absolute government.

Our countrymen are in general strongly attached to constitutional forms of government, and have no intention of weakening or abandoning them, but they do not, as it appears to us, always fully comprehend the precise nature of constitutional government. It is generally admitted that the constitution prescribes the mode and the limits within which the several departments of the government shall act; but it is not always perceived that the constitution is in fact only so much waste paper, if it proceed from the same power which performs the ordinary functions of government and legislation. The ordinary power of government and legislation, in a government like ours, is the will or assent of the majority. Now if this same majority make the constitution, or may unmake it at will, the constitution can at best impose only a temporary check on its will. It is as absolute as if there were no constitution at all. Does the constitution emanate from the simple numerical majority of the people? Then it is nothing but a self-imposed restraint, a charter granted by the sovereign, but revocable at will. Have the majority an absolute right, or the absolute power, of interpreting the constitution, of determining the meaning of its provisions? Then the constitution is nothing but what the majority choose to make it, and consequently we are just as much under the absolute majority, as we should be in case we had no constitution. Nor will it alter the case if a special umpire for deciding on the constitutionality of questions be instituted, if that umpire be appointed by the majority, or be so constituted as naturally to express the sense of the majority.

It is essential to constitutional government, that the constitution be made by a different power from the one which acts in ordinary legislation, and that it rest for its support on a power which can effectively maintain it, in case the government proper manifests a disposition to transcend its limits. The people assembled in convention differs in no respect from the people assembled in the halls of legislation, as to the actual power which is at work. If the delegates chosen to the convention represent the numerical majority of the people, what do they represent but the very majority represented by the members of the legislature, in case that legislature be based solely on population? We want in fact in the state two powers, which shall serve to restrain each the other. One of these powers should make the constitution, the other should operate within the limits of that constitution in the performance of the ordinary functions of government. The constitution is then a real check on ordinary government and legislation, the real sovereign of the country, of which government in its restricted sense is merely the agent or minister.

This constitution-making power we have not in all cases provided for. In our own Commonwealth, the same power, with a slight restriction, that makes the laws, can alter the constitution. The constitution with us is only what the will of the majority makes it, or suffers it to be. It is in fact then no restriction on the power of the majority. It is only the restriction the majority imposes on itself during its pleasure.

But how are we to obtain a constitution-making power different from the power of the majority? We must do it, if we may borrow the words of a distinguished American statesman,[2] "by means of some contrivance for collecting the sense of the community through its parts." By the concurrence of the several parts we form the constitution, which must be the enumeration and limit of the powers to be exercised by the simple numerical majority.

A contrivance of this sort would give us a double majority; the simple, absolute, numerical majority of the whole community, and the concurring majorities of the several parts. The concurring majorities of the parts would be the sense of a much larger portion of the community than is represented by the numerical majority, and would also embody the sense of parts, which might have interests and wishes different from those of the numerical majority. So long as this sense could be effectively expressed, no part could be injured, and the numerical majority would be obliged to confine its action to those matters and interests which were common to the whole. The concurring majorities, or the sense of the community as collected through its parts, should make the constitution. The numerical majority should operate only within the limits of the constitution.

Take, as an illustration of this, the constitution of the United States. This constitution was not formed by nor does it rest on the will of the majority of the people of the United States, as contended by the late President in his Inaugural Address; but was formed and can be altered only by the concurring majorities of the several States. It embodies the sense of the American community as collected through its parts, without reference to absolute numbers. The sense of Rhode Island, as an independent part, counts as much in forming or amending the constitution as the sense of New York. The majority of the whole people can therefore legitimately exert no more power than will be concurred in by the several parts, or to speak strictly no power that one fourth of the parts withhold. The constitution is therefore an example of what we term concurring majorities, or majorities of the several parts. The lawmaking power of Congress, on the other hand, is an example of the absolute or numerical majority, and being limited by the constitution, is restricted, restrained in its exercise by the concurring majorities.

A contrivance analogous or equivalent to this, is needed in the several States. But here it is less easy to introduce it, because interests and localities are more homogeneous, and it is more difficult to organize the community into distinct parts. To introduce some distinction of the kind, some contrivance for taking, in addition to the sense of the absolute majority, the sense of the natural divisions of the community, is and should be the aim of every true statesman. Universal suffrage collects, after a sort, it is true, the sense of the parts; but these parts are simple individuals, and the simple individual is too weak, as we have shown, to constitute a sufficient barrier to the invasion of the numerical majority, or rather the plundering minority that controls it. How it shall be introduced we do not now undertake to point out. The contrivance must vary with localities and the peculiar habits, tastes, customs, and pursuits of the community. The same contrivance will not answer for every community. Nor can it anywhere be arbitrarily introduced. It must ever be merely a modification or development of what already exists. In Rome it was obtained by the establishment of the Tribunitial power. In England it is obtained by means of Three Estates, each having a negative on the others; in France they have attempted it by the same means, but have unfortunately given the balance of power to the king. In this State we formerly sought it, by basing one House on valuation, and by representing townships rather than population in the other. Vermont, which is the most truly democratic in her legislation, composes her legislature entirely of delegates from townships or corporations. Each township is a distinct part, and is represented in the government, without any reference to the number of its inhabitants. The small township has the same representation with the large. This is a wise regulation, and Vermont is much indebted to it for the liberal character of her legislation, and the free and independent spirit of her inhabitants. She is never subjected to the sway of the absolute majority, but even in her ordinary legislation collects the sense of her community through its parts. The particular manner of organizing the State, so as always to have the concurrence of the parts as a check upon the absolute numerical majority, must he left to the particular State, to be determined according to its already existing natural or artificial divisions. In some States it may be done by regarding territorial divisions, in others, perhaps, by making valuation instead of population the basis; in some by taking the concurring majorities only in forming the constitution, and in others by representing these in one House and the numerical majority in the other. The precise manner of getting at it is the question for the practical statesmen of the community it concerns. All we can add is, that without some contrivance of the sort, a wise administration of government, and its beneficial working will be a matter of accident, never to be counted on with any degree of certainty.

In passing, we may remark, as it concerns our own Commonwealth, the tendency has been in an opposite direction. Our Senate was formerly based on valuation; we have now based it on population; our House of Representatives was formerly based on corporations, (townships); but we are every year approaching nearer and nearer to population, and have already come so near, that Boston and three or four other large towns control the whole legislature. This tendency has been looked upon as democratic. Perhaps it were well to inquire, if it has rendered legislation more favorable to the rights of individuals, and afforded additional protection to minorities. Many things are thought to be democratic, against which a wise statesman will set his face. It is not democracy we want, but good government, a government which secures to each individual, by effective guaranties, the free and full enjoyment of all his natural rights. These guaranties, which are the substance, may be lost, while we are in pursuit of abstractions, and theoretic unity, which are often but mere shadows. All good government is founded in compromise, and is more or less complicated. To simplify it is nothing else but to render it absolute. If we simplify so as to render all consistent with the popular idea of democracy, we only bring individuals and minorities under the absolute sway of the majority. If we simplify in favor of aristocracy, it is to subject the many to the absolute supremacy of the few. If in favor of monarchy, it is to reduce all under the dominion of one. We must take care not to simplify till we simplify away all our rights, all that government is instituted to protect.

The right organization of the government, that is, such an organization of the commonwealth, of civil society, that the parts may always have a sort of suspensive veto on the whole, when its action becomes oppressive to any part, or goes beyond its constitutional limits, we hold to be the first object to be aimed at by the reformer as well as by the statesman. The first thing is to get a good government. This is the greatest of all earthly blessing to any people. Till this be obtained, there is no security for individual freedom, and consequently none for individual or social progress. The germs, or rather the outlines of a good government, each State in our confederacy has already adopted. Some modifications in accordance with various localities, ways of thinking, and pursuits, will give good governments, so far as concerns their organic forms, to all. This done, it will not be difficult to secure their wise and faithful administration, to make them in fact as well as in name, agents for protecting each individual in the free and full enjoyment of his entire individuality.

We have in this paper endeavored to give a practical direction to our remarks. We have heretofore speculated not a little, and presented the subject of social reform on its ideal side, which was not amiss. For the ideal has its place, and an important one too, more important than our countrymen usually give it. But the practical also has its place; and when we come to the matter of acting, the question is never, what is in the number of future possibilities, but what is possible now, men and things being as they are, and what they are? We must come down from the ideal to answer this question, and forego our ecstasies. We must take sober views, and be after all somewhat moderate in our demands.

We have also given the direction we have to our remarks, with the hope of drawing attention more directly to the importance and precise nature of constitutional government. Our countrymen are all attached to constitutional government, and so far very well; but they seem to us to be far from comprehending the real nature of constitutional government in general, and their own in particular. We would, if we could, provoke the discussion of constitutional questions. The popular textbooks and interpretations of our existing constitutions are unworthy a people engrossed in political matters as we are. In this part of the country constitutional law is hardly recognized. We have been engaged in the discussion of merely local or temporary questions, or in attempting to define abstract democracy. We complain not of this, but we think it is time to sink our political attorneyism, and even our political metaphysics, in wise, liberal, and philosophical statesmanship.

In conclusion, we would say, that in appealing so directly as we do to government, and making it almost the sole agent through which we are to remedy social evils, we by no means forget religion, morality, or individual intelligence. No man can rate them higher than we do. We hold them absolutely indispensable. But they must not be imprisoned in the bosom of the individual. They must be brought out of the interior of man, and made to disclose the true end of all social institutions, and to contribute to their adoption. We would always write as the Christian and the moralist, as well as the statesman. But we would use Christianity and morality in organizing the state and shaping its measures, not less than in our private exhortations to individuals. The end disclosed by true religion, the one enjoined by morality, and that sought by the state, are one and the same; to wit, the freedom and progress in virtue and happiness of every individual. Unless the state maintain freedom for the individual, religion and morality can do little besides solace him in his sufferings, and strengthen him for his trials. This is no doubt a high office, and never to be thought lightly of; but the intelligence, purity, and loftiness of soul, religion and morality are fitted to quicken, should be directed to the establishment of such institutions, and the enactments of such laws, as shall always favor truth, justice, freedom, order, and well-being.

Notes

Editor's Introduction

1. Octavius Brooks Frothingham, *Transcendentalism in New England: A History* (Philadelphia: University of Pennsylvania Press, 1959; first published in 1876 by G. P. Putnam, New York), 128–29.
2. See my brief points in "The Strange Ride of Orestes Brownson" (*Weekly Standard*, June 12, 2000). I elaborate fully in *In Search of the American Spirit: The Political Thought of Orestes Brownson* (Carbondale, IL: Southern Illinois University Press, 1992).
3. Eric Voegelin, *The New Science of Politics* (Chicago: University of Chicago Press, 1952).
4. Jean Jacques Rousseau, *Discourse on the Origin of Inequality*, in *Jean-Jacques Rousseau: The Basic Political Writings*, ed. Donald A. Cress (Indianapolis: Hackett Publishing Co., 1987), 46.
5. Ibid., 59.
6. Frothingham, *Transcendentalism in New England*, 46.
7. Immanuel Kant, "What is Enlightenment?" in *Foundations of the Metaphysics of Morals*, ed. Lewis White Beck (Indianapolis: Bobbs-Merrill, 1959), 86–90. Pierre Hassner has noted the Rousseuistic and "rights of man" influence on Kant's moral and political thought in "Immanuel Kant," in *History of Political Philosophy*, 2nd ed., ed. Leo Strauss and Joseph Cropsey (Chicago: University of Chicago Press, 1981), 554–93.

8. Frothingham notes the appreciable Kantian influence upon Fichte (*Transcendentalism in New England*, 28–31).

9. Ibid., 33.

10. Johann Fichte, "The Destination of Man," as quoted in Frothingham, *Transcendentalism in New England*, 37.

11. Voegelin, "The Political Religions," in *Collected Works 5: Modernity Without Restraint* (Baton Rouge: Louisiana State University Press, 2000), 61.

12. Ibid. See also Voegelin's *New Science*, 113; the section on Schelling in volume 25 of the *Collected Works* (1990), 224, and the essay "The Eclipse of Reality" in volume 28 of the *Collected Works* (1990), 144.

13. Talmon, *Political Messianism: The Romantic Phase* (New York: Praeger, 1960): 186–90.

14. Rousseau, *The Social Contract*, in Cress, 163.

15. Rousseau, *The Social Contract*, 163, 148.

16. Ibid., 203.

17. Emerson, "Politics," in Joel Porte, ed. *Ralph Waldo Emerson: Essays and Lectures* (New York: Library of America, 1983), 561.

18. Brownson, "Observations and Hints on Education," herein p. 396.

19. "An Essay on the Progress of Truth," November 24, 1827, herein p. 4.

20. Brownson, "Observations and Hints on Education," herein p. 397.

21. Brownson, "Progress of Society," herein on p. 128. In this essay, Brownson's remarks represent a sympathetic summary of a similarly-minded author; as he says, "we are happy to agree entirely with [his] general theory."

22. Brownson, "Democracy" (January 1838), herein p. 203.

23. Brownson, "Progress of Society," herein on p. 141.

24. Rousseau, *The Social Contract*, 155.

25. Brownson, "Progress of Society," herein on p. 125.

26. Ibid., 138.

27. Ibid., 146.

28. Brownson, "Democracy" (January 1838), herein p. 235.

29. Ibid. In a surprising retreat from this position, Brownson professed his commitment the following year to the democratic party as the "the Christian party.... It is always on the side of freedom and Humanity" ("Democracy and Reform;" herein p. 235).

30. See, for instance, Brownson's argument in the essays "Church and State" (May 1829; herein p. 57) and "Religion and Politics" (July 1838; herein p. 287).

31. "An Essay on the Progress of Truth," November 17, 1827, herein p. 3.

An Essay on the Progress of Truth (November 1827–March 1828)

1. When I attribute the doctrine of election and reprobation to John Calvin I would not be understood as asserting that the sentiment originated with him, for I believe it was held by Luther in a light not less abhorrent; but as we know the sentiment now only as a part of the antiquated system of the Genevan Reformer it may receive his name.

New Views of Christianity, Society, and the Church (1836)

1. I use these terms, spiritualism and materialism, to designate two social, rather than two philosophical systems. They designate two orders, which, from time out of mind, have been called *spiritual* and *temporal* or carnal, *holy* and *profane*, *heavenly* and *worldly*, etc.

2. Brownson is referring here to Dr. William Ellery Channing. In the 1883 edition of *New Views* (in *The Works of Orestes A. Brownson* IV [Detroit: Thorndike Nourse]), editor Henry F. Brownson says in this context that Channing "was regarded by the Unitarians as their most prominent and genuine representative, at the time *New Views* was written" (p. 45).—Ed.

Tendency of Modern Civilization (April 1838)

1. Reference here is to the Boston Association of Friends to the Rights of Man, particularly their broadside document produced at the meeting of January 4, 1838.—Ed.

Religion and Politics (July 1838)

1. It is unclear why Brownson is unaware of the author here. If the title and publisher indicated in the original *Boston Quarterly Review* are accurate, the author is indeed Warner.—Ed.

2. It may also be remarked, that society depends not on religion for its subsistence, but on the social instincts of human nature. Man lives in society, not because he has a religion, but because he is man, and is created with a social nature. The instinct of society is a primitive, not a secondary instinct. It is not a result of a belief in God, nor of any other belief. Men have not reasoned

themselves into society; they have not said to themselves, Let us create society. They have always lived in society. Society is as old as man himself. God, in giving us social instincts, social affections, and cravings, which society alone can satisfy, has amply provided for its subsistence. If men would believe more in God, and understand a little more of human nature, and rely less on their positive creeds, they would have fewer fears of the disastrous effects of the propagation of error. He, who really believes in God, believes that the Power which controls all worlds and events is mightier than any false opinion. They who think a little heterodoxy can bring the world to an end, or essentially alter its course, who fear that it can dissolve society, and prevent men from uniting with one another, be they called what they may, or profess they what faith they will, are the genuine infidels, the real atheists, against whom the friends of religion should be most on their guard, and against whom, if against any, laws of blasphemy should be enacted and enforced.

Democracy and Reform (October 1839)

1. Brownson is referring here to the eminent nineteenth-century American historian George Bancroft.—Ed.

Observations and Hints on Education (April 1840)

1. See Att. Gen. Austin's speech at Faneuil Hall.
2. Carlyle.
3. I believe Walter Scott felt and describes this sensation, as he stood upon one of the high banks of the Orkneys or Shetland. I have seen it alluded to by others.

The Laboring Classes (July 1840)

1. I am aware that I broach in this place a delicate subject, though I by no means advance a novel doctrine. In justice to those friends with whom I am in the habit of thinking and acting on most subjects, as well as to the political party with which I am publicly connected, I feel bound to say, that my doctrine, on the hereditary descent of property, is put forth by myself alone, and on my own responsibility. There are to my knowledge, none of my friends who entertain the doctrine, and who would not, had I consulted them, have labored to

convince me of its unsoundness. Whatever then may be the measure of condemnation the community in its wisdom may judge it proper to mete out for its promulgation, that condemnation should fall on my head alone. I hold not myself responsible for others' opinions, and I wish not others to be held responsible for mine.

I cannot be supposed to be ignorant of the startling nature of the proposition I have made, nor can I, if I regard myself of the least note in the commonwealth, expect to be able to put forth such propositions, and go scathless. Because I advance singular doctrines, it is not necessary to suppose that I am ignorant of public opinion, or that I need to be informed as to the manner in which my doctrines are likely to be received. I have made the proposition, which I have, deliberately, with what I regard a tolerably clear view of its essential bearings, and after having mediated it, and been satisfied of its soundness, for many years. I make it then with my eyes open, if the reader please, "with malice prepense." I am then entitled to no favor, and I ask as I expect none. But I am not quite so unfortunate as to be wholly without friends in this world. There are those to whom I am linked by the closest ties of affection, and whose approbation and encouragement, I have found an ample reward for all the labors I could perform. Their reputations are the least censured for the fact, that one whom they have honored with their friendship, and in a journal which, in its general character, they have not hesitated to commend, has seen proper to put forth a doctrine, which, to say the least, for long years to come must be condemned almost unanimously.

Conversations with a Radical—
By a Conservative (January–April 1841)

1. This abuse of the North American Review is very unchristian. We can bear witness that this Review never intentionally offends God, man, or the devil, and therefore should not be so abused.—EDITOR [O. A. Brownson].
2. Boston Reformer, July 21, 1837. O. A. Brownson, Editor.
3. Proverbs 30:8, 9.
4. See this finely illustrated in its bearing on Art, in a late number of the Dial, in a paper entitled "Thoughts on Art,"—a paper which some of our wise newspaper critics have attempted to ridicule for its absurdity, but which is quite creditable to its distinguished author.

Social Evils and Their Remedy (July 1841)

1. See *Quarterly Review*, Vol. III. No. xi. Article "Laboring Classes."
2. John C. Calhoun.

Index

A

Aaron, xv, 26
Abelard, Peter, 276
abolitionism, 237–54; free discussion, right of and, 321–26, 340–41; institutions and, 335–39, 341–42; justification of, 321–43; law and, 328; liberty and, 339–40; South and, 240, 241. *See also* slavery
Abraham, 17, 19
absolutism, 206, 221
Adams, John, 379
Addison, Joseph, 366
Address, delivered before the Democratic Citizens of Plymouth Count, July 4, 1839, An (Thomas), 355, 356
Aeschylus, 174
Africa, 32
Age of Reason, 301
agrarianism, 507–8
Alien and Sedition Laws, 379
America. *See* United States
American Anti-Slavery Society, 325, 326
American Democrat, or Hints on the Social and Civic Relations of the United States of America, The (Cooper), 305–20
American Democrats, 318–21
American Liberties and American Slavery, morally and politically illustrated (Treadwell), 321
American literature, 466–68
American Renaissance, ix
American Revolution, 102, 135, 283–84
Anti-Federalists, 204
antiquity: moral progress and, 7–8; Protestantism and, 164–65, 170–71; religion and state and, 166; rights of man and, 221–22
Apollo, 174
Apostles, 24
Arabia, 32

Arianism, 162

Aristides, 32

aristocracy: clergy and, 468–69; democracy vs., 310–16; popular sovereignty and, 207, 220; social progress and, 134–36; sovereignty and, 214; wealth and, 135–36

Arnold, Benedict, 363

Asia, 155

Asiatic Society, 174

assocation: laboring classes and, 257–58; modern civilization and, 257

atheism, 169, 296, 302–3

atonement: Christianity and, 156, 157, 158, 159; indications of, 187–93; materialism and, 193–94; new doctrine of, 193–97

Augustine, St., 193–94

Baal, 8

Bacchus, 18

Bacon, Francis, 105, 127, 168, 169, 303

Ball, John, 273

Bank of England, 366, 367

Bank of the United States, 366, 367, 418

Baptists, 79–80

Bazard, Saint-Amand, 101

Beecher, Lyman, xv

Belsham, Mr., 174

benevolence, code of, 29, 128–30

Berkeley, George, 168

Beton, Mr., 379

Bible, 167; authority of, 20; faith and, 42; God, goodness of and, 36; priests and, 24; religion vs. philosophy and, 46

Biddle, John, 367

Bossuet, Jacques Bénigne, 369

Boston Quarterly Review, xiv

Boston Tea Party, 388

Brahe, Tychi, 65

Brahmins, 67, 239

Brazil, 332

Brisbane, Mr., 532

Brownson, Orestes: Catholicism, conversion to of, ix; changes of heart of, x; conservatism of, xvi; criticism of, x; literary temperament of, x; modernity and, xi–xii; political philosophy of, x–xi, xvii

Bruno, 98

Bull, John, 415

Butler, Bishop, 300

Byron, Lord, 174

C

Cade, Jack, 273

Calvin, John, 295–96, 449

Calvinism, xv, 29, 64, 183–84

Carlyle, Thomas, 317; criticism of, 411–12; man, sympathy with of, 412–13; style of writing of, 413–14

Carter, Hob, 273

Carver, Robin, 407

Catholicism, ix, 376; Calvinism and, 183; church of the future and, xv; government, divine origin of and, 369; laboring classes and, 258; Protestantism vs., 169–70, 174–75; spiritualism and, 183 centralization, 252, 319–20, 337

Channing, William E., 237

Charlemagne, 102, 266

Charles Stuart, 242, 349

chartism, 414–15

Chartism (Carlyle), 411

Christian Examiner, xiv, 494

Christianity: atonement and, 156, 157, 158, 159, 179–80; Calvinism and, 183–84; church and, 158–62; democracy and, 356, 380–81; ecclesiastical, 289; equality and, 112, 117–19; ethics of, 289–91; faith and, 41–42, 374–76; history of, 8–12; introduction of, 23; of Jesus Christ, 23, 149, 153–58, 434–37; Judaism vs., 130; justice and, 291, 380–81; laboring classes and, 434–37; liberty and, 290–91, 299, 304; love and, 132, 143, 146, 156, 497; materialism and, 155, 156; modern civilization and, 263, 272–75; modernity and, xvi; morality and, 134–35, 138–47, 299; moral progress and, 8–12; politics and, ix; progress and, 441–43; religion and politics and, 296–99; rights of man and, 223; Saint-Simon, Claude Henri, and, 109–10; science and, 27; sects of, 180–87; slavery and, 238–40; social evils and, 95–96; social progress and, 125, 129–32, 138–47, 358–59, 425–26; society and, ix; spiritualism and, 155–56, 158–59, 161; Unitarianism and, 186–87; Universalism and, 184–86; wealth, possession of, and, 508–15; Whig Party and, 368–76. *See also* church; religion

Christian party in politics, 40, 79–81, 82–84

Christian sects, 180–87; association and, 190–91; human nature and, 180–83; materialism and, 183, 185; spiritualism and, 183, 185

Chubbs, Mr., 373

church: authority of, 160, 161, 167, 168; Catholicism and, xv; causes of, 187–93; Christianity and, 158–62; of the future, xv–xvi; infallibility of, 160; materialism and, 162–65; modern civilization and, 264, 265, 266, 267; power of, 160–61; Protestantism and, xv; reason and, 167–68; spiritualism in, 171–75; state and, 57–84, 89–92, 161, 268–71; supremacy of, 160, 217, 265, 537. *See also* Christianity; religion

Church of England, 29–30

church of the future, xv–xvi

Cicero, 174

Clay, Henry, 324

clergy: aristocracy and, 468–69; authority of, 69–71; celibacy and, 161–62; church-state relations and, 64–78; equality and, 86; infidelity, opposition to and, 73–76; marriage and, 432; message of, 70–71; "national costume" of, 76–77; power and, 64–68, 68–69; as privilieged class, 64

Collins, Mr., 373

Colonization Society, 324

Columbus, Christopher, 98
Compensation, System of, 496–99
Comte, Auguste, xvi
Condillac, Etienne Bonnot de, 169, 373
Confederacy, 332
Congregationalists, 80, 269
conscience, liberty of, 322; moral progress and, 3–4; moral progress of and, 2; priesthood and, 2; Protestantism and, 168; religion and politics and, 297–98
Constant, Benjamin, 150, 352–53
Constantine, 61
Constantinople, 165, 331
Constitution, U. S., 379; Bill of Rights of, 226–27; Democratic party and, 204; majority and, 545–46; religion and, 288, 379; slavery and, 241, 242, 246, 250, 331, 339; Union and, 240
constitutionalism, American: decentralism of, xvi; form of, xvi; human nature and, xvi; liberty and, 544; philosophic underpinnings of, xvi; progress and, xvi; separation of powers and, 544–46
"Conversations" (Brownson), xvi
Convert, The (Brownson), x
Cooper, James Fenimore, 305–20; American literature, contribution to of, 305; common sense and, 307–8; influence of, 305; as writer, 305
Copernicus, Nicolas, 398
Correspondent, The, 53–56
Cousin, Victor, 189, 353

crime, education and, 390–93
Crusades, 15

d'Alembert, Jean, 104
Danton, Georges, 413
Dark Ages, 162, 174
Darwin, Charles, 373
David, 61
decentralism, xvi
Declaration of Independence: equality and, 111–13; slavery and, 237
Deism, 10, 53, 55, 60
De la Religion considèrèe dans sa Source, ses Formes et ses Dèveloppments (Constant), 150, 352–53
democracy, 203–25; American literature and, 466–68; ancient, 222–23; aristocracy vs., 310–16; centralization and, 319–20; Christianity and, 356, 380–81; conservative element of, 350; in England, 225; equality and, 230, 318; in France, 225–26, 379; humanity and, 229; human nature and, 221; liberty and, 220–23; majority and, xiv, 207–11, 228–29, 540–49; materialism and, 318; meaning of, 203–5, 311–12; morality, Christian and, xiv; of numbers, 540; party, 205; philosophical, 205–6; popular sovereignty and, 227–28; popular sovereigny and, 206–21; privilege and, 230–33, 383; reform and, xiv; rights of man and, 221–25, 229–30; social progress and, 355–86; society and, 540; state sovereignty and, 219;

states' rights and, 226–28; in United States, 226–29; universal suffrage and, 223

"Democracy" (Brownson), xiv

Democratic party: as American party, 377, 378; Christianity and, 380–81; democracy, meaning of and, 204–5; justice and, 382–83; liberty and, 378–80; majority and, 360; patriotism and, 377–78; progress and, 381–86; social reform and, 359–62, 361–64, 377–86

Descartes, Rene, 105, 168

D'Holbach, Paul Henri Thiry, 373

Dial, xiv

Diderot, Denis, 373

divine right of kings, 66

Dodwell, Mr., 373

Dwight, Timothy, xv

E

East India Company, 173, 188

eclecticism, 187, 189, 191, 205

Edinburgh Review, 416

education, 387–410; crime and, 390–93; dogmatical character of, 397–99; equality and, 121–23, 409; government and, xiii; induction and, 393–97; infinite, conceptions of and, 399–401; laboring classes and, 416–17; liberty and, 388–89, 409–10; popular institutions and, 406–7; practicality of, 401–8; progress and, 445–46; purpose of, 397, 409; radicalism and, 453, 461–68; reform and, xiv; religion and, 96–97; republican, 121–23;

"self-taught man", ideal of and, xiii–xiv; social evils and, 96–99; social progress and, 387–88, 461–68; society and, 389–90; universal, 383, 541

Edward, King, 229

Edwards, Jonathan, 29

Egypt, 97, 175, 261, 266

Egyptians, 18, 26, 213

Elizabeth I, Queen, 267

Ely, Ezra Stiles, 40, 59–60, 78–84'

Emerson, Ralph Waldo, xiii

Enfantin, Barthélemy Prosper, 101

England: Christianity in, 74; democracy in, 225; French Revolution and, 415–16; literature in, 347–50; Norman Conquest of, 267

English Revolution of 1688, 267, 268

enlightenment: morality and, xiv; moral progress and, 5–6; reason and, xiv; science and, 5; spiritual renewal through, xii–xiii, xiv–xv

Epicurus, 54

Episcopalians, 80, 269

equality, 85–88; Christianity and, 112, 117–19; clergy and, 86; Declaration of Independence and, 111–13; democracy and, 230, 318; education and, 121–23, 409; God and, 6; government and, 119–20; of human family, 3; human nature and, 426–27; inheritance, principle of and, 487–93; laboring class and, 88; law and, 86–87, 114–15; middle class and, 415; moral progress and, 3; natural differences and, 85–86; priesthood and, 428–

34; privilege and, 232; radicalism and, 455–61; religion and, 86; slavery and, 115, 457; social progress and, 133–36; wealth and, 142
Essay on the Moral Constitution and History of Man, An, 125
Euclid, 495
Euripides, 174
Europe: Christianity in, 10; Holy Alliance of, 6; romanticism in, xv; socialism in, x
evil: origin of, 125; progress, doctrine of and, 197–200

F

faith: Bible and, 42; Christianity and, 41–42, 374–76; God, pleasing and, 42–43; morality and, 9; philosophy vs., 40, 43; radicalism and, 519–20; reason and, 353; religion and, 40–43
family, 3, 5
Federalism, 337, 360
Federalists, 252, 379
feudalism, 265–66, 267–68
Fichte, Johann, xii, xiii
Follen, Dr., 150
foreign literature, 345–54
Founding Fathers, 338; religion and politics and, 290, 291, 298; separation of powers and, 544; states' rights and, 298
Fourier, Mr., 532, 533
France, 6, 101, 171, 225; democracy in, 225–26, 379
Franklin, Benjamin, 76, 98, 102, 357
Frederic III, 388
freedom. *See* liberty
freedom of inquiry, 49–50
Free Enquirer, 53–56, 257–58
free enquirers, 53–56
free inquriy, 49–50
French literature, 348, 349–51
French Revolution, xiii, 28, 102–3, 105–6, 172–73, 379; England and, 415–16; Protestantism and, 171, 175
Frothingham, Octavius Brooks, x
Fulton, Robert, 98

G

Galileo Galilei, 65, 98, 398, 405
Gall, Mr., 174
Garrison, William Lloyd, 323
Genesis, 19
gentlemen, aristocratic vs. democratic, 312–16
German literature, 348, 349–51
Germany, xiii, 167, 168, 174
Geschlossene Handelsstaat, xiii
Gnosticism, 159, 162; neo-, xvi
God: as angry, 42; character of, 26; denial of, 302–3; equality and, 6; goodness of, 36–37, 52; justice of, 139; moral character of, 20–22, 23; Providence of, 21; reason and, 171; sovereignty of, 170, 217, 219, 380; suffering and, 35–36; unity of, 139; universal benevolence of, 29
Goethe, Johann Wolfgang, 413
Good, Dr., 54
Gorton, Samuel, 369
Gospel, 10; morality of, 129, 134–35, 138–47; originality of, 140; pecu-

liarity of, 129; social progress and, 138; as workingman's religion, 93

Gospel Advocate, xv, 53

government: atheism and, 302–3; culture and, xiii; divine origin of, 368–70; education and, xiii; equality and, 119–20; laboring classes and, 437–39; liberty and, 309; moral progress and, 3; property and, 379; rights, security of and, 3; rights of man and, 290, 292–93; social progress and, 136–38; social reform and, 536–40, 540–50; society and, 538

Greece, 32, 97, 117, 155, 266; church in, 10; literature of, 163; priests of, 8

Gregory VII, 266

H

Haiti, 326

Hamilton, Alexander, 284

happiness: human nature and, 35; ignorance and, 37

Harry, King, 229

Hegel, Georg Wilhelm Friedrich, 189

Helvetius, 373

Henry III, King, 268

Henry VII, King, 267

Henry VIII, King, 166–67, 267

Herder, Mr., 191

hereditary total depravity, 184

hero-worship, 317–18

high modernity, xi

Hildebrand, 163, 217, 266

history: progressivist ideology of, xv; of religion, 16–27

History of the French Revolution (Carlyle), 414

Hobbes, Thomas, 308–9, 370–72, 373

Homer, 19, 174

Hopkins, Samuel, 29

Horace, 174

Houston, George, 55

humanism, Renaissance, xi

humanity: democracy and, 229; morality and, 4; popular sovereignty and, 215, 218; religion of, xvi; universal brotherhood of, 263

human nature: American constitutionalism and, xvi; Christian sects and, 180–83; democracy and, 221; dignity of, 2; equality and, 426–27; free will and, 521, 530–31; happiness and, 35; individual aspect of, 531–33; inherent depravity of, 129, 159, 170, 515–16; limits of, xvi; morality and, xii; moral progress and, 2; possibilities of, xvi; religion and, 4, 151; rights of man and, 229–30; social aspect of, 531–33; social progress and, 132, 132–33; social reform and, 531–33, 537; society and, 361, 531; suffering and, 35–38; theocracy and, 537. *See also* man

"Human Rights", 325

Hume, David, 168, 373

Huss, 98

I

idealism, 168, 189

ignorance: happiness and, 37; reason and, 49; suffering and, 37

Immaculate Conception, 159

independence, mental, 2, 3–4, 14, 16, 40

Independent Treasury Bill, 384

India, 32, 173, 175, 261, 266, 430

individualism, xii–xiii; Renaissance and, xii

individuality: feudalism and, 265–66; social reform and, 536, 538; society and, 538–39

inequality: capacities of men and, 499–503; evils of, 87–88; social progress and, 506–7

Infidels, 15

inheritance, principle of, 487–93

Inquiry into the Cause of Social Evil; with its Remedy, An (Townsend), 355

Inquiry into the Moral and Religious Character of the American Government, An (Warner), 287

institutions: abolitionism and, 335–39, 341–42; education and popular, 406–7; freedom of, 38–40; moral progress and, 2, 4, 5–8, 6–8, 15

Insureection of the Peasants, 273–75

international law, slavery and, 248–49

Introduction aux Travaux Scientifiques du XIX Siècle, 105

Isaiah, 1, 22

Israelites, 213

J

Jackson, Andrew, 288, 289, 306, 368

Jacobi, Mr., 189

Jacobins, 317

James, King, 369

James II, King, 268

Jefferson, Thomas, 76, 204, 288, 289, 357, 379, 380

Jennings, R. L., 54–55

Jerome, 98

Jesus Christ, 8; Christianity of, 23, 149, 153–58; Christian morality and, 138–47; Divine Mission of, 374; as God-Man, 157, 159, 181, 184, 193, 432, 433; Gospel of, 10; as Leveler, 508–9; as mediator, 156, 158; morality and, 44; religion and, 8; Second Coming of, 179–80; social reform and, 100; suffering of, 470

Jews, 67

John, King, 229, 267

John, St., 93, 156–57

Johnson, Col., 77

Jones, Sir William, 173–74

Joseph the Second of Germany, 136

Joshua, 21

Jouffroy, Theodore Simon, 353

Judaism, 130, 139, 263

Judea, 266

Juno, 19

Jupiter, 18, 19, 174

justice: Christianity and, 291, 380–81; democratic party and, 382–83; earthly reign of divine, xvi; of God, 139; liberty and, 291; religion and, 4; slavery and, 328; sovereignty of, 211–12, 219

K

Kant, Immanuel, xii–xiii, 306

Kepler, Johannes, 398, 401

Kimball, Mr., 421
Knox, John, 60

L

laboring classes, 411–39; assocation and, 257–58; Catholicism and, 258; chartism and, 414–15; Christianity of Christ and, 434–37; Compensation, System of and, 496–99; condition of, 414; disorganizing tendency of, 306–7; division of labor and, 477–80; education, universal and, 416–17; equality and, 88; general emigration and, 416, 417; government and, 437–39; hostility to, 480–84; inequality and priesthood and, 428–34; interests of rich and, 493–96; middle class vs., 415–16; moneyed power and, 277; privilege and, 438; production of wealth and, 471–76; property, hereditary descent of and, 438–39; property rights and, 258; slave vs. free labor and, 419–21; social reform and, 423–28; as visionaries, 259–60; wages and price and, 484–85; wealth and labor, relation of and, 417–23

"Laboring Classes" (Brownson), xvi
laboring classes's party, 363–64
La Fayette, Marquis de, 244, 357
La Mennais, Abbé de, 270
Laplace, Pierre Simon, 443
"The Latest Form of Infidelity" (Norton), 373
"Latest Form of Infidelity" (Norton), 375

law: abolitionism and, 328; equality and, 86–87, 114–15; marriage and, 534–35; religion and, 195
Lectures on Knowledge, 357
Leo X, Pope, 163
L'Exposition de la doctrine de Saint-Simon, 101
liberty: abolitionism and, 339–40; Christianity and, 290–91, 299, 304; of conscience, 2; constitutional government and, 544; democracy and, 220–23; democratic party and, 378–80; education and, 388–89, 409–10; government and, 309; of institutions, 38–40; justice and, 291; majority and, xiv; moral progress and, 14, 16; natural, 309; perfect, 308; popular sovereignty and, 215; privilege and, 231; religion and politics and, 290–92; slavery and, 251–52, 328, 334; United States and, 57; universal, 251–52, 334; Whig Party and, 379
literature: American, 466–68; English, 347–50; foreign, 345–54; of Transcendentalism, xiv–xv; for young republicans, 348
Locke, John, 169, 370–72, 375, 379
London Quarterly, 467
Louis, Saint, 268
Louis XI, King, 217, 266
Louis XIV, King, 206, 226, 266, 268
love: Christianity and, 132, 156–57, 497; morality and, 129, 143, 146
Luther, Martin, 164, 167, 170, 266, 295–96, 449, 504

M

Madison, James, 76, 357
Magna Carta, 225, 229, 267
Mahometans, 239
majority: democracy and, xiv, 207–11, 228–29, 540–49; Democratic party and, 360; liberty and, xiv; popular sovereignty and, 207–11; religion and politics and, 295–97; rights of man and, 296–97; separation of powers and, 545–46; will of, 540–44
Mammoth Bible Society, 84
man: inequality in capacities of, 499–503; perfectibility of, xii; perfection of, 538; philosophy and, 168; physical circumstances and character of, 505–6; religious element of, 533–34; unequal capacities of, 486–87. *See also* human nature
Mandeville, Geoffrey de, 373
Manicheans, 162
marriage, 162, 432, 534–35
Martineau, Miss, 207
Marxism, xiii
Mary, Mother of God, 159
Mary Stuart, 349
Massachusetts Anti-Slavery Society, 324–25
materialism, 53, 55, 178, 179, 189; atonement and, 193–94; Christianity and, 155, 156; Christian sects and, 183, 185; democracy and, 318; philosophical, 168–69; philosophy and, 168–69, 174; Protestantism and, 162–65, 166, 167–71; reason and, 167–68, 168–69, 169–70

Matthew, St., 23
Maximus, 166
"Memoirs" (Saint-Simon), 102
mental independence, 2, 3–4, 14, 16, 40
Methodists, 30, 79–80, 269
Mexico, 32
Micah, 22
Middle Ages, 169, 174, 183
Miller, Tom, 273
Milton, John, 110, 348, 380
Minerva, 174
Mirabeau, Honoré Gabriel Riqueti, 413
Missouri Compromise, 324
modern civilization: assocation and, 257; Christianity and, 263, 272–75; church and, 264, 265, 266, 267; feudalism and, 265, 265–66, 267; moneyed power and, 276–84; Norman Conquest and, 267; philosophy and, 275–76; republicanism and, 264–65, 267, 268, 270; rights of man and, 255–57; royalty and, 264, 265, 266, 267, 270–72; state and, 263–64; tendencies of, 255–85
modernity: Brownson, Orestes and, xi–xii; Christianity and, xvi; church-state relations and, 268–71; high, xi; rationalism and, xi; religion and, xi; symbols of, xii; Transcendentalism and, xii
monarchy: hereditary, 216–18; legitimacy and, 216–18; popular sovereignty and, 216–18; sovereignty and, 213–14

monkism, 60

monotheism, 19

Montezuma, 32

Montgomery, Mr., 59

morality, 537; Christianity and, 134–35, 138–47, 299; democracy and, xiv; enlightenment and, xiv; faith and, 9; of Gospel, 129, 134–35, 138–47; humanity and, 4; human nature and, xii; Jesus Christ and, 44; love and, 129; natural, 299–301; positive, 300–301; social reform and, xiv

moral progress, 1–33; antiquity, example of and, 7–8; Christianity and, 8–12; conscience, liberty of and, 2, 3–4; education and, 6; enlightenment and, 5–6; equality and, 3; government and, 3; human nature and, 2; institutions, ecclesiastical and, 6–8; institutions and, 2, 4, 5–8, 15; liberty and, 14, 16; mental independence and, 2, 3–4, 14, 16; obstacles to, 1–12; priesthood and, 7–8; priests and, 14–15; reason and, 4, 12–14; religion and, 4, 5, 16–27. *See also* progress; social progress

Morgan, Mr., 373

Morris, Gouvernor, 325

Moses, 139, 299; system of religion of, 19–25

Mussulmans, 67

mysticism, 17, 162, 168, 172

N

Napoleon, 104, 173, 213, 413, 430, 488, 522–23

national bank, 284

National Tract Society of New York, 70–71

Neptune, 19

Nero, 464

Nettleton, Asahel, xv

New Christianity (Saint-Simon), 107

New Science of Politics (Voegelin), xi

New Testament, 157, 289, 294, 300, 381, 413

Newton, Isaac, 105, 443

New Views of Society, Christianity, and the Church (Brownson), xv–xvi

Nicholas, Czar, 388

Nicholas of Russia, 423

nominalism, 372

Norman Conquest, 267, 415, 430

Norton, Mr., 373–74, 375

Nouveau Christianisme, 191

O

Old Testament, 139, 289, 294, 300

"On the Public" (Cooper), 318

Optimus Maximus, 19

Oration, delivered before the Democratic Citizens of the North part of Middlesex County, An (Tarbell), 355, 356

Oration, delivered on the 4th of July, 1839, before the Citizens of Nashua, An (Osgood), 355–56

Orientals, 8, 10, 127, 174

Original Sin, 159

Osgood, Samuel, 355–56

Osis, 18
Owen, Robert, 357
Owen, Robert Dale, 54–55, 137, 357, 533–35

𝒫

Pagans, 67
Paine, Thomas, 429
Palfrey, Mr., 373, 375
Parley, Peter, 407
patriotism, 224, 367, 377–78
Patton, Mr., 242
Paul, St., 368, 441–42, 464
Pelagianism, 163, 170
Pelagius, 163
people: Christian movement of, 187–88, 189–91; democracy and, 204. *See also* popular sovereignty
Persia, 175
Philosophical Miscellanies, translated from the French of Cousin, Jouffroy, and Bemjamin Constant (Ripley), 345
philosophy: Alexandrian school of, 187, 188, 189; faith vs., 40, 43; man and, 168; materialism and, 168–69, 174; modern civilization and, 275–76; religion vs., 44–47, 51; science and, 27–28; social progress and, 275–76; spiritualism and, 168
phrenology, 174
Plato, 32, 127, 139, 174
Pluto, 19
politics: Christian party in, 40, 79–81, 82–84; Christian view of, ix; religion and, 287–304
Pope, Alexander, 36

popular sovereignty: aristocracy and, 207, 220; democracy and, 206–21, 227–28; humanity and, 215, 218; legitimacy and, 215–16; liberty and, 215; majority and, 207–11; monarchy and, 216–18; progress and, 215
Potosi, 32
poverty: science and, 85–86; virtue and, 163
Presbyterianism, Presbyterians, 269; church-state relations and, 58, 60–63, 78, 79–80, 91
Priestley, Joseph, 174, 373
priests, priesthood: Bible and, 24; conscience, liberty of and, 2; equality and, 428–34; moral progress and, 7–8, 14–15; religion, history of and, 26–27; religion and education and, 428–29; state and, 8
"Private Thoughts" (Locke), 372
privilege: democracy and, 230–33, 383; equality and, 232; laboring classes and, 438; liberty and, 231
progress, 441–50; American constitutionalism and, xvi; Christianity and, 441–43; democratic party and, 381–86; disharmony, overcoming and, 532–33; education and, 445–46; evil, origin of and, 197–200; human nature and, 444–45; individual, 125–28; of moral reform, 1–33; popular sovereignty and, 215; Saint-Simon, Claude Henri, and, 109. *See also* moral progress; social progress
progressivism, humanitarian, xvi–xvii

property: community of goods and, 534; government and, 379; hereditary descent of, 438–39; laboring classes and, 258; radicalism and, 453; rights of man and, 391; Whig Party and, 379

Protestantism, 162–65, 172; Catholicism vs., 169–70, 174–75; church, supremacy of and, 217; church of the future and, xv; classical antiquity and, 164–65, 170–71; conscience, liberty of and, 168; French Revolution and, 171, 175; industry and, 170–71; materialism and, 162–65, 166, 167–71; New England, x; religion and state and, 166–68; religious character of, 169; spiritualism and, 171–75; Unitarianism and, 186

Protestant Reformation, xi, xii, 164, 276

Providence: of God, 21; social progress and, 125

Psalms, 22

Puritanism, xv, 268

Q

Quakers, 268

radical, conversations with a, 451–527

radicalism: danger of, 453; education and, 453, 461–68; equality and, 455–61; faith and, 519–20; poverty and, 459–61; property and, 453; savage state and, 453; slavery and, 457

rationalism, 162, 174, 193–94; modernity and, xi; secular, xi

reason: authority of, 167–68, 170; church and, 167–68; enlightenment and, xiv; faith and, 353; God and, 171; ignorance and, 49; materialism and, 167–68, 168–69, 169–70; moral progress and, 4, 12–14; religion and, 8–12, 12–14, 43–44

reform: democracy and, xiv; education and, xiv

Reign of Terror, 173

religion: of antiquity, 16–19; Church of England and, 29–30; church-state relations and, 81–84; Constitution, U. S. and, 288, 379; education and, 96–97; equality and, 86; externals of, 21–22; faith and, 40–43; free inquiriy and, 49–52; history of, 16–27; of humanity, xvi; human nature and, 4, 151; Jesus Christ and, 8; justice and, 4; law and, 195; missionary scheme and, 31–32, 91; modernity and, xi; monotheism and, 19; moral progress and, 4, 5; Mosaic system of, 19–25; necessity of, 54; philosophy vs., 44–47, 51; politics and, 287–304; reason and, 8–12, 12–14, 43–44; religious institutions vs., 151–52; rights of man and, 290–97; science and, 26–28; scriptural authority and, 23–24; social reform and, 356–58; state and, 166–68; virtue and, 46. *See also* Christianity; church

Religion and Church (Follen), 150

Renaissance: American, ix; humanism and, xi; individualism and, xii; social transformation and, xii
republicanism, 264–65, 267–68, 270
Republican Party, 204
Restoration, 267
revivalism, xv
Richard, II, 274
Richard II, King, 273, 415
rights of man: antiquity and, 221–22; Christianity and, 223; democracy and, 221–25, 229–30; government and, 290, 292–93; government and security of, 3; human nature and, 229–30; majority and, 296–97; modern civilization and, 255–57; religion and politics and, 290–97; slavery and, 251
Ripley, George, 345
romanticism, xv
Rome, 8, 10, 155, 163, 266, 277
Rousseau, Jean-Jacques, xii, xiii, xiv, xv
Rouvroy, Claude Henri de, 101
royalty, modern civilization and, 264, 265, 266, 267, 270–72

S

sacerdotal corporations, 429–31
Saint-Simon, Claude Henri, xvi, 101–10, 134, 143
Sartre, Jean-Paul, 413
Saul, 61
savage state, 264, 429–31, 453
Schelling, Friedrich von, 189
Schlegels, 174
Schleiermacher, Friedrich, 150, 191
Scholasticism, 276

science: anarchy of, 106; Christianity and, 27; enlightenment and, 5; philosophy and, 27–28; poverty and, 85–86; religion and, 26–28; Saint-Simon, Claude Henri, and, 104–7
Second Coming, 179
Second Great Awakening, xv
sectarianism, 63–64
separation of powers, 544–46
Sermon on the Mount, 140
Shaftesbury, Mr., 373
Shakespeare, William, 348
skepticism, 53, 168, 368
slavery, 177, 194–95, 231, 237–54; centralization and, 337; Christianity and, 238–40; Confederacy and, 332; Constitution, U. S. and, 241, 242, 246, 250, 331, 339; Declaration of Independence and, 237; equality and, 115, 457; freedom and, 328; international law and, 248–49; justice and, 328; liberty and, 251–52, 334; radicalism and, 457; religion, Mosaic system of and, 22–23; rights of man and, 251; as social institution, 239–40; state sovereignty and, 240–47, 253–54, 332, 334–35, 337; states' rights and, 240–41. *See also* abolitionism
Slavery (Channing), 237
social evils: cause of, 141–43; Christianity and, 95–96; education and, 96–99; remedy for, 93–100, 529–50. *See also* social progress
Social Evils and their Remedy (Taylor), 93–100

socialism, x

social progress: aristocracy and, 134–36; benevolence, code of and, 128–30; Christianity and, 125, 129–32, 138–47; divine revelation and, 128–29; duty and, 506; education and, 387–88; equality and, 133–36; Gospel and, 138; government and, 136–38; human nature and, 132, 132–33; individual vs., 125–28, 129, 136–37, 515–22; inequality and, 506–7; moneyed power and, 282–83; natural order of, 125–28; philosophy and, 275–76; Providence and, 125. *See also* moral progress; progress

social reform: Christianity and, 358–59, 425–26; democracy and, 355–86; Democratic party and, 359–64, 377–86; education and, 461–68; government and, 536–40, 540–50; human nature and, 531–33, 537; individuality and, 522–23, 536, 538; Jesus Christ and, 100; laboring classes and, 423–28; religion and, 356–58; Transcendentalism and, xiv–xv; Whiggism, Whig Party and, 361, 362; Whiggism and, 364–78

society: Christian view of, ix; corrupting tendency in, 523–27; democracy and, 540; education and, 389–90; government and, 538; human nature and, 361, 531; individuality and, 538–39. *See also* social progress; social reform

Society for Christian Union and Progress, The, 150

Socinianism, 80

Socrates, x, 98, 139, 166, 209, 222, 464

South: abolitionism and, 240, 241; individuality of, 252; slavery and, 237

sovereignty: aristocracy and, 214; of God, 170, 217, 219, 380; of justice, 211–12, 219; monarchy and, 213–14; theocracy and, 214. *See also* popular sovereignty

spiritualism, 178, 537; authority and, 167–68; Catholicism and, 183; Christianity and, 155–56, 158–59, 161; Christian sects and, 183, 185; classical literature and, 165–66; mysticism and, 172; philosophy and, 168; reaction of, 171–75; revival of, 171–75, 176

state: church, 268–71; church and, 57–84, 89–92, 161; Marxism and, xiii; modern civilization and, 263–64; priesthood and, 8; religion and, 166–68; savage, 264, 429–31, 453

state sovereignty: democracy and, 219; slavery and, 240–47, 253–54, 332, 334–35, 337

states' rights: abandonment of, xvi; democracy and, 226–28; Founding Fathers and, 298; slavery and, 240–41

Straw, Jack, 273

suffering: cause of, 35–38; God and, 35–36; human nature and, 35–38; ignorance and, 37; of Jesus Christ, 470

Syria, 261

System of Compensation, 496–99

T

Tarbell, John P., 355, 356
Taylor, Charles B., 93–100
Teufelsdröch, Diogenes, 403
Texas, 245, 326
theism, 296
theocracy, 8, 214, 219, 265, 291, 292, 537
Thomas, Seth, 355, 356
Thome, Mr., 421
Thrity Tyrants, 209
Tindal, Mr., 373
Tocqueville, Alexis de, 271–72
Toland, John, 373
Tories, 381
Townsend, Robert, 355
Transcendentalism, ix, x; American, xiii; literature of, xiv–xv; modernity and, xii; Rousseau, Jean-Jacques and, xii; social transformation and, xiv–xv
Transcendentalism in New England: A History (Frothingham), x
Treadwell, S. B., 321
Turkey, 332
Turnpenny, Jack, 489–91
Tycho Brahe, 65
Tyler, Wat, 273

U

Ueber die Religion: Reden an die Gebildenten unter ihren Verächtern (Schleiermacher), 150
Union, 240
Unitarianism, x, 150, 174, 186, 295
United States: democracy in, 226–29; religion and politics in, 287–304; Second Great Awakening in, xv; social perfection of, xvi
universal benevolence, 29
Universalism, x, 64, 184–86
universal reconciliation, doctrine of, 184–85, 186
universal suffrage, 223
utilitarianism, 175

V

Van Buren, Martin, 209, 324
Virgil, 174
virtue: poverty and, 163; religion and, 46
Voegelin, Eric, xi, xiii, xvi
Volney, Mr., 373
Voltaire, 373
voluntary association movement, xv

W

Walter the Tiler, 273
Warner, Henry Whiting, 287
Washington, George, 102, 357
Wayland, Francis, xv
wealth: aristocracy and, 135–36; equality and, 142; labor and, 417–23; laboring classes and interests of, 493–96; natural capacity and, 486–87; unequal distribution of, 508
Webster, Daniel, 324–25, 363
Western Messenger, xiv
Whig Examiner, 366
Whiggism, Whig Party: anti-Americanism of, 366–68; as anti-Christian, 368–76; as foreign party, 366–68; government, origin of and,

368–71; liberty and, 379; origin of ideas, doctrine of and, 368–71; property and, 379; social reform and, 361, 362, 364-378
William, King, 229
Williams, Roger, 369
William the Conqueror, 274

Woolston, Mr., 373
Wordsworth, William, 174
Wright, Frances, 54–55, 357–58

Z

zetesis, x
Zoroaster, 67